# Action and Adventure Cinema

Action has established itself as one of the leading genres of contemporary Hollywood cinema, generating extensive critical debate in the process. This exciting collection addresses action and adventure from the silent era to the present day, exploring diverse questions of aesthetics, industry and ideology.

Contributors consider how action might best be defined, how it has developed historically, and how it works formally. The critical reception and standing of action and adventure cinema is considered in relation to questions of national culture, violence and the 'art' of cinema.

Themes explored include genre and definitions; early action, sensation and melodrama; authorship; national and transnational action-adventure traditions; action aesthetics; spectacle and narrative; stars and bodies; class; gender, and race and ethnicity. Individual chapters discuss action cinema from early melodrama and serials such as *The Hazards of Helen* through classic films of the 1960s including *Bullitt*, *The Wild Bunch* and *The Dirty Dozen* up to contemporary blockbusters *Die Hard*, *Lara Croft: Tomb Raider* and *Crouching Tiger, Hidden Dragon*. The book considers the action genre outside Hollywood, in Greece, Italy and Japan, and also views action and adventure cinema through the work of individual directors including D.W. Griffith, Akira Kurosawa, Sam Peckinpah and Kathryn Bigelow.

Essays by: Richard Abel, Jennifer M. Bean, Mary Beltrán, Dimitris Eleftheriotis, Martin Flanagan, Martin Fradley, Barry Keith Grant, Michael Hammond, Christine Holmlund, Leon Hunt, Mark Jancovich, Susan Jeffords, Peter Krämer, Steve Neale, Marc O'Day, Lydia Papadimitriou, Stephen Prince, Tico Romao, Ben Singer, Yvonne Tasker, Linda Ruth Williams, Rachel Williams, Tony Williams, Aylish Wood.

**Yvonne Tasker** teaches Film and Television Studies at the University of East Anglia, UK. She is the author of *Working Girls: Gender and Sexuality in Popular Cinema* (Routledge, 1998) and *Spectacular Bodies: Gender, Genre and the Action Cinema* (Routledge, 1993).

# Action and Adventure Cinema

Edited by

## Yvonne Tasker

Routledge
Taylor & Francis Group

LONDON AND NEW YORK

First published 2004
by Routledge
2 Park Square, Milton Park, Abingdon, Oxon OX14 4RN

Simultaneously published in the USA and Canada
by Routledge
270 Madison Avenue, New York, NY 10016

*Routledge is an imprint of the Taylor and Francis Group*

Typeset in Perpetua and Bell Gothic by
Florence Production Ltd, Stoodleigh, Devon
Printed and bound in Great Britain by
TJ International Ltd, Padstow, Cornwall

*British Library Cataloguing in Publication Data*
A catalogue record for this book is available from the British Library

*Library of Congress Cataloging in Publication Data*
    Action and adventure cinema/edited by Yvonne Tasker.
        p. cm.
    Includes bibliographical references.
    1. Adventure films – History and criticsim.  I. Tasker, Yvonne, 1964–
PN1995.9.A3A28 2004
791.43′655 – dc22                                    2004001612

ISBN 0–415–23506–5 (hbk)
ISBN 0–415–23507–3 (pbk)

# Contents

List of illustrations                                                    viii
Notes on contributors                                                    ix
Acknowledgements                                                         xiv

Yvonne Tasker
INTRODUCTION: ACTION AND ADVENTURE CINEMA                                 1

## PART I
## History, criticism and style                                         15

1  Jennifer M. Bean
   'TRAUMA THRILLS': NOTES ON EARLY ACTION CINEMA                        17

2  Richard Abel
   THE 'CULTURE WAR' OF SENSATIONAL MELODRAMA, 1910–14                   31

3  Ben Singer
   'CHILD OF COMMERCE! BASTARD OF ART!':
   EARLY FILM MELODRAMA                                                  52

4  Steve Neale
   ACTION-ADVENTURE AS HOLLYWOOD GENRE                                   71

5  Mark Jancovich
   DWIGHT MACDONALD AND THE HISTORICAL EPIC                              84

## PART II
## Theorising action aesthetics                                        101

6   Martin Flanagan
    'GET READY FOR RUSH HOUR': THE CHRONOTOPE IN ACTION      103

7   Aylish Wood
    THE COLLAPSE OF REALITY AND ILLUSION IN *THE MATRIX*      119

8   Tico Romao
    GUNS AND GAS: INVESTIGATING THE 1970S CAR CHASE
    FILM                                                             130

9   Michael Hammond
    *SAVING PRIVATE RYAN*'S 'SPECIAL AFFECT'                  153

## PART III
## Gender, stars, bodies                                               167

10  Linda Ruth Williams
    READY FOR ACTION: *G.I. JANE*, DEMI MOORE'S BODY AND
    THE FEMALE COMBAT MOVIE                                          169

11  Mary Beltrán
    MÁS MACHA: THE NEW LATINA ACTION HERO                     186

12  Marc O'Day
    BEAUTY IN MOTION: GENDER, SPECTACLE AND ACTION BABE
    CINEMA                                                           201

13  Susan Jeffords
    *BREAKDOWN*: WHITE MASCULINITY, CLASS, AND US ACTION-
    ADVENTURE FILMS                                                  219

14  Martin Fradley
    MAXIMUS MELODRAMATICUS: MASCULINITY, MASOCHISM
    AND WHITE MALE PARANOIA IN CONTEMPORARY
    HOLLYWOOD CINEMA                                                 235

15  Yvonne Tasker
    THE FAMILY IN ACTION                                        252

## PART IV
## Nation, ethnicity and stardom

267

16   Leon Hunt
     THE HONG KONG/HOLLYWOOD CONNECTION: STARDOM AND
     SPECTACLE IN TRANSNATIONAL ACTION CINEMA                         269

17   Christine Holmlund
     EUROPEANS IN ACTION!                                             284

18   Lydia Papadimitriou
     GREEK WAR FILM AS MELODRAMA: WOMEN, FEMALE STARS,
     AND THE NATION AS VICTIM                                         297

19   Dimitris Eleftheriotis
     SPAGHETTI WESTERN, GENRE CRITICISM AND NATIONAL
     CINEMA: RE-DEFINING THE FRAME OF REFERENCE                       309

## PART V
## Action, authorship and industry

329

20   Stephen Prince
     GENRE AND VIOLENCE IN THE WORK OF KUROSAWA AND
     PECKINPAH                                                        331

21   Tony Williams
     *THE DIRTY DOZEN*: THE CONTRADICTORY NATURE OF SCREEN
     VIOLENCE                                                         345

22   Peter Krämer
     'IT'S AIMED AT KIDS – THE KID IN EVERYBODY': GEORGE
     LUCAS, *STAR WARS* AND CHILDREN'S ENTERTAINMENT                  358

23   Barry Keith Grant
     MAN'S FAVOURITE SPORT?: THE ACTION FILMS OF KATHRYN
     BIGELOW                                                          371

24   Rachel Williams
     'THEY CALL ME "ACTION WOMAN"': THE MARKETING OF
     MIMI LEDER AS A NEW CONCEPT IN THE HIGH CONCEPT
     'ACTION' FILM                                                    385

     *Index*                                                          398

# Illustrations

| | | |
|---|---|---|
| 2.1 | Poster for Pathé-Frères, *Nuit de Noël* (*Christmas Eve Tragedy*) | 34 |
| 2.2 | New York Motion Picture, *War on the Plains* | 38 |
| 2.3 | 'The Auto Cracksman Loots – Sometimes Slays – and Is Off Like a Flash', *New York Tribune* | 40 |
| 2.4 | Gaumont ad., *Moving Picture World* | 41 |
| 2.5 | Colonial Theatre ad., *Cleveland Leader* | 43 |
| 2.6 | Selig ad., *Moving Picture World* | 45 |
| 8.1 | Stage mounted action: rear screen projection in *Bonnie and Clyde* | 133 |
| 8.2–8.4 | Camera set up and the reinforcement of character placement in *Bullitt* | 135 |
| 8.5 | Steve McQueen as stunt driver in *Bullitt* | 136 |
| 8.6–8.7 | Facial recognition and character placement in *Bullitt* | 137 |
| 8.8 | Narration and suspense: concealment of vehicle in *The Seven-Ups* | 144 |
| 8.9 | Narration and suspense: narrational perspective in *The Seven-Ups* | 145 |
| 8.10 | The slow motion insert and the spectacularization of the stunt in *Smokey and the Bandit* | 147 |
| 8.11 | Facial expression and character centered functions of POV shots in *The French Connection* | 148 |
| 11.1 | Ice Cube and Jennifer Lopez in *Anaconda* | 191 |
| 11.2 | Michelle Rodriguez and Jaime Tirelli in *Girlfight* | 194 |
| 12.1 | Angelina Jolie as Lara Croft in *Lara Croft: Tomb Raider* | 213 |
| 19.1 | The opening shot of *Ringo and His Golden Pistol* | 315 |
| 19.2–19.3 | Shots from the opening sequence of *Ringo and His Golden Pistol* | 316–19 |
| 19.4 | Shots from the opening sequence of *Django the Bastard* | 322–3 |

# Notes on contributors

Richard Abel is Robert Altman Collegiate Professor of Film Studies in the Film and Video Studies Program at the University of Michigan. His essays have appeared in dozens of journals and been translated into French, German, Italian, Spanish and Dutch. His books include: *French Cinema: The First Wave, 1915–1929* (Princeton University Press, 1984); *French Film Theory and Criticism, 1907–1939: A History/Anthology*, in two volumes (Princeton University Press, 1988); *The Ciné Goes to Town: French Cinema, 1896–1914* (University of California Press, 1994); *Silent Film* (Rutgers University Press, 1996); and *The Red Rooster Scare: Making Cinema American, 1900–1910* (University of California Press, 1999). Recently, with Rick Altman, he edited *The Sounds of Early Cinema* (Indiana University Press, 2001); currently, he is editing the *Encyclopedia of Early Cinema* (forthcoming from Routledge) and completing *The 'Imagined Community' of US Cinema, 1910–1914* (forthcoming from the University of California Press). His next project is a study of the 'courtship and marriage' of two ephemeral discourses in the US: newspapers and moving pictures, 1910–15.

Jennifer M. Bean is Assistant Professor of Cinema Studies and Comparative Literature at the University of Washington–Seattle. She is co-editor of *A Feminist Reader in Early Cinema* (Duke University Press, 2002), and of a special issue of *Camera Obscura* on 'Early Women Stars'. She is currently completing a book titled *Bodies at Play: Gender, Genre, and the Cinema of Modernity* (Duke University Press).

Mary Beltrán is Assistant Professor of Communication Arts and Chicana/o Studies at the University of Wisconsin–Madison. She is currently working on a book-length project, *Bronze Seduction*, on the marketing, aesthetics, and racial politics of Latina stars in Hollywood and American popular culture since the silent film era. She has also written and presented on such topics as Latino/a and mixed-race representation in action cinema, ethnicity in entertainment television, ethnic media advocacy, and beauty and body ideals in US popular culture.

**Dimitris Eleftheriotis** is Senior Lecturer in Film and Television Studies and Director of the Centre for Screen Studies at the University of Glasgow. His publications include the forthcoming *Asian Cinemas: A Guide and Reader* (Edinburgh University Press, 2005) and *Popular Cinemas of Europe: Studies of Texts, Contexts and Frameworks* (Continuum International, 2001). He is a regular contributor to *Screen* and a member of the Editorial Advisory Board of the journal.

**Martin Flanagan** is Course Leader and Senior Lecturer in Film Studies at Bolton Institute. He is preparing a study into the cinematic application of the theories of Mikhail Bakhtin, and has published articles on the science-fiction genre, cultural specificity in the films of Robert Rodriguez, and authorship in the cinema of Terrence Malick. He is also currently researching the animated films of Pixar.

**Martin Fradley** is Lecturer in the Department of English and Film Studies at the University of Aberdeen. He has previously contributed to Yvonne Tasker (ed.), *Fifty Contemporary Filmmakers* (Routledge, 2002) and Alastair Phillips and Ginette Vincendeau (eds), *Journeys of Desire: European Stars in Hollywood* (British Film Institute, forthcoming).

**Barry Keith Grant** is Professor of Film Studies and Popular Culture and Director of the Graduate Program in Popular Culture at Brock University in Ontario, Canada. He is the author of *Voyages of Discovery: The Cinema of Frederick Wiseman* (University of Illinois Press, 1992), co-author of *The Film Studies Dictionary* (Arnold, 2001) and editor of several widely used anthologies, including *Film Genre Reader* (University of Texas Press, 1986), *The Dread of Difference: Gender and the Horror Film* (University of Texas Press, 1996), and (with Jeannette Sloniowski) *Documenting the Documentary: Close Readings of Documentary Film and Video* (Wayne State University Press, 1998). Grant is also editor of the Film and Television series for Wayne State University Press and the Genres in American Cinema series for Cambridge University Press. His most recent books are *John Ford's Stagecoach* (Cambridge University Press, 2003) and *Fritz Lang Interviews* (University Press of Mississippi, 2003).

**Michael Hammond** lectures in Film Studies at the University of Southampton. He has just completed a book-length study of cinema culture in Britain during the Great War.

**Christine Holmlund** is Professor of Cinema Studies, Women's Studies and French at the University of Tennessee. With Justin Wyatt, she is editing an anthology entitled *Contemporary American Independent Film: From the Margins to the Mainstream* (Routledge, 2004) and working on a book on action films for Cambridge University Press. She has written a study of bigger budget Hollywood films, *Impossible Bodies: Femininity and Masculinity at the Movies* (Routledge, 2002), and also co-edited, with Cynthia Fuchs, *Between the Sheets, In the Streets:*

*Queer, Lesbian, Gay Documentary* (University of Minnesota Press, 1997). Individual essays on feminist theory and North American, European, and Latin American film and video have appeared in several anthologies and journals.

**Leon Hunt** is Senior Lecturer in Film and TV Studies at Brunel University. He is the author of *British Low Culture from Safari Suits to Sexploitation* (Routledge, 1998) and *Kung Fu Cult Masters: from Bruce Lee to Crouching Tiger* (Wallflower Press, 2003).

**Mark Jancovich** is Professor of Film and Television Studies at the University of East Anglia. He is the author of several books, including *Rational Fears: American Horror in the 1950s* (Manchester University Press, 1996) and, with Lucy Faire and Sarah Stubbings, *The Place of the Audience: Cultural Geographies of Film Consumption* (BFI, 2003). He is also the editor of several collections including: with Joanne Hollows, *Approaches to Popular Film* (Manchester University Press, 1995); with Joanne Hollows and Peter Hutchings, *The Film Studies Reader* (Arnold, 2000); and, with James Lyons, *Quality Popular Television: Cult TV, the Industry and Fans* (BFI, 2003). He is also a founder member of *Scope: An Online Journal of Film Studies*; and series editor, with Eric Schaefer, of the Manchester University Press book series, *Inside Popular Film*.

**Susan Jeffords** is Professor of Women's Studies and English Studies at the University of Washington, where she is currently serving as Dean of Social Sciences. She is the author of *The Remasculinization of America: Gender and the Vietnam War* (Indiana University Press, 1989) and *Hard Bodies: Hollywood Masculinity in the Reagan Era* (Rutgers University Press, 1994), and is currently at work on a book exploring narratives about terrorism.

**Peter Krämer** teaches film studies at the University of East Anglia. He has published essays on American film and media history, and on the relationship between Hollywood and Europe, in *Screen, The Velvet Light Trap, Theatre History Studies,* the *Historical Journal of Film, Radio and Television, History Today, Film Studies, Scope* and numerous edited collections. He is co-editor of *Screen Acting* (Routledge, 1999) and *The Silent Cinema Reader* (Routledge, 2003). He also co-authored a children's book entitled *American Film: An A-Z Guide* (Franklin Watts, 2003).

**Steve Neale** is Chair of Film Studies at Exeter University. He is the author of *Genre and Hollywood* (Routledge, 2000), editor of *Genre and Contemporary Hollywood* (BFI, 2002), co-author of *Popular Film and Television Comedy* (Routledge, 1990) and co-editor of *Contemporary Hollywood Cinema* (Routledge, 1998). He has recently contributed to Julian Stringer (ed.), *Movie Blockbusters* (Routledge, 2003).

**Marc O'Day** is Associate Dean of Humanities at Suffolk College, Ipswich, an associate college of the University of East Anglia. He has published on fiction, film and television, including essays on Angela Carter, David Lynch, David Cronenberg, *The Avengers* and postmodernism and television.

**Lydia Papadimitriou** is Senior Lecturer in Screen Studies at Liverpool John Moores University. Her main area of research is Greek cinema. She has published articles in the *Journal of Modern Greek Studies, Screen* and edited collections. Her book *The Greek Film Musical (1955–75): Genre and Identity* is forthcoming (Flicks Books, 2004). She is currently working on the monograph *Borders and Journeys: The Cinema of Theo Angelopoulos* (Wallflower Press, forthcoming).

**Stephen Prince**, Professor of Communication at Virginia Tech, is the author or editor of numerous books, the latest of which are *Classical Film Violence: Designing and Regulating Brutality in Hollywood Cinema* (Rutgers University Press, 2003) and *Movies and Meaning: An Introduction to Film*, third edition (Allyn and Bacon, 2004).

**Tico Romao** is Senior Lecturer in Film Studies at the University of Gloucestershire. His article 'Engines of Transformation: An Analytical History of the 1970s Car Chase Cycle' (2004) is in the inaugural issue of *The New Review of Film and Television Studies*.

**Ben Singer** is Associate Professor of Film in the Department of Communication Arts at the University of Wisconsin–Madison. He is the author of *Melodrama and Modernity: Early Sensational Cinema and its Contexts* (Columbia University Press, 2001) and editor of a volume on early spectatorship theory entitled *Alexander Bakshy: Modernism and the Space of Spectatorship* (Indiana University Press, forthcoming).

**Yvonne Tasker** teaches film studies at the University of East Anglia. She is the author of *Spectacular Bodies: Gender, Genre and the Action Cinema* (Routledge, 1993) and *Working Girls: Gender and Sexuality in Popular Cinema* (Routledge, 1998).

**Linda Ruth Williams** is Senior Lecturer in Film Studies at the University of Southampton. She has published on contemporary British and American cinema, feminism and censorship, and is a regular writer for the British Film Institute journal *Sight and Sound*. Her most recent publications are *The Erotic Thriller in Contemporary Cinema* (Edinburgh University Press, forthcoming 2004) and, co-edited with Michael Hammond, *American Cinema Since 1960* (Pearson Education, forthcoming). She is currently writing the BFI Modern Classics volume on Terry Gilliam's *Brazil*.

**Rachel Williams** took her PhD from the University of Nottingham. Her research explores the work and public profile of women filmmakers in contemporary Hollywood.

**Tony Williams** is Professor and Area Head of Film Studies in the Department of English at Southern Illinois University Carbondale. He has recently completed a manuscript on the films of Robert Aldrich and has written books on the film versions of Jack London novels, the American family horror film, Larry Cohen, wartime and post-war British cinema, and the films of George Romero. He has also co-edited a filmography of Vietnam War films and recently co-edited a collection of essays on international horror films. Other interests include Hong Kong cinema. He is also a frequent contributor to *Asian Cult Cinema* and *Psychotronic*.

**Aylish Wood** is Lecturer in Film Studies at the University of Kent. She is the author of *Technoscience in Contemporary American Cinema* (Manchester University Press, 2002).

# Acknowledgements

The development of *Action and Adventure Cinema* has been a lengthy process and there are several people I would like to thank for helping to ensure its final completion. First and foremost amongst these are the contributors who have been consistently good-spirited and patient, bearing with delays and supporting the project throughout. I'm also grateful to the editorial team at Routledge, particularly Rebecca Barden but also Lesley Riddle. Over the last few years I've talked about action and adventure with more people than I can recall or credit in this space. However, particular thanks are due, as ever, to Rachel Hall and to Marc and Judy O'Day for sharing many nights at the movies. Finally, I'd like to dedicate this collection to Amy and Henry: though it might have been finished faster without them, speed isn't everything.

Some of the chapters have previously been published, and are reprinted with the permission of the copyright holders:

Peter Krämer 'It's Aimed at Kids – the Kid in Everybody': George Lucas, *Star Wars* and Children's Entertainment (Chapter 22), originally published in *Scope: An On-line Journal of Film Studies* (www.nottingham.ac.uk/film/journal/#articles), December 2001. Reprinted with the permission of the author (revised from the original).

Steve Neale 'Action-adventure as Hollywood Genre' (Chapter 4), originally published in *Genre and Hollywood*, London: Routledge, 2000, pp. 52–65. Reprinted with the permission of the author and publisher.

Ben Singer 'Child of Commerce! Bastard of Art! Early Film Melodrama' (Chapter 3), originally published in *Melodrama and Modernity: Early Sensational Cinema and Its Contexts*, New York: Columbia University Press, 2001, pp. 189–220. Reprinted with the permission of the author and publisher (abridged version).

Rachel Williams 'They Call Me "Action Woman"': The Marketing of Mimi Leder as a New Concept in the High Concept 'Action' Film (Chapter 24), originally published as '"It's Like Painting Toys Blue and Pink" (Martha Coolidge, 1996): Marketing and the Female-Directed Hollywood Film' *Scope: An On-line Journal of Film Studies* (www.nottingham.ac.uk/film/journal/#articles), December 2000. Reprinted with the permission of the author (revised from the original).

# YVONNE TASKER

## INTRODUCTION
## Action and adventure cinema

ACTION HAS EMERGED AS A PRE-EMINENT commercial genre of the New Hollywood cinema, exemplifying and extending what Thomas Schatz has termed the blockbuster logic of recent cinema production.[1] Critics and journalists have on occasion looked to the under-performance of movies like *Last Action Hero* (1994) or *Godzilla* (1998) – and conversely to the success of small-scale, lower-budget and/or 'independent' films – as marking the death of what Larry Gross has so resonantly dubbed the 'Big Loud Action Movie'.[2] Yet action genres and adventure narratives continue to form a lively component of popular US cinema. Moreover, recent years have seen scholarly interest in action cinema develop significantly. The continued presence of action-adventure as a genre within contemporary cinema culture and the dynamism of the scholarship that explores it form the dual context within which this collection of essays has taken shape.

The book is divided into five sections, exploring an overlapping series of concerns to do with the historical, aesthetic, generic, institutional and political significance of action and adventure cinema. Some contributors deal with the broadly ideological questions of meaning and identity that dominated writing on action during the early 1990s and which continues to produce fascinating work on areas including stardom, gender, class, race and ethnicity. Others explore action and adventure within specific historical and national contexts, in relation to its formal qualities, debates about value, developments within the film industry or in terms of authorship. Collectively the essays presented here emphasise not only the richness of this form of filmmaking but its diversity and longevity. Indeed, although this book is concerned with the historical development of, and patterns of critical engagement with what I will, for the moment, term a genre, a factor of perhaps equal significance is the gradual change discernible in the cultural and critical status of action and adventure movies. As José Arroyo notes, contemporary action cinema has attracted little in the way of prestige, associated as it is with the emergence of the blockbuster and high concept movie making.[3] Deemed noisy and brash, judged empty at best and politically reactionary at worst, action films have consistently failed to meet the markers of aesthetic and cultural value typically applied within contemporary film culture. James M. Welsh, for instance, introduces an essay on action in the 1990s thus: 'They are usually big and often brainless and they are extraordinarily popular.'[4] As Welsh implies, there is a relationship between the popularity of action films and their low status: they exemplify the exaggerated economics of mainstream film production, 'mass culture at its most crudely capitalistic', as Arroyo puts it.[5] Action and adventure narratives have long been embroiled in the kind of debates about value that these terms suggest. In Chapter 2, Richard Abel explores the extent to which taste, and particularly class, informed the emergence, within the discourse of trade papers at least, of a good (US) and a bad (French) sensational cinema in the period 1910–14. In the material reproduced here from his *Melodrama and Modernity*, Ben Singer considers the sensational character, lowbrow antecedents and mass appeal of early serial melodrama. Not only the characteristics of the sensational film serials described by Singer, but the guarded, even hostile reception they received, will be familiar to contemporary action audiences.

Despite the sense in which popular cinema is and has long been a spectacular, indeed sensational tradition, it is nonetheless the case that contemporary film culture tends to value narrative over spectacle: to take an example, the *Sight and Sound* review of *Star Wars Episode I The Phantom Menace* (1999), a film which critic Andrew O'Hehir judges, perhaps rightly, as lacking in narrative coherence. O'Hehir notes that 'the film's extended sojourn on Tatooine mostly serves to set up Anakin's pod race, which may thrill younger viewers who haven't grown tired of Lucas' careening point-of-view shots, but doesn't really advance the story'. Whilst it is certainly true to say that these sequences fail to tell us 'anything about Anakin's childhood [that] we couldn't grasp quickly in a brief flashback'[6] it is also the case that the scenes are extended, pleasurable and serve to establish an adventurous quest-narrative around the character of Anakin. Like *Star Wars* some twenty years before,[7] it would seem that *The Phantom Menace* is being judged here against a classical model of Hollywood narrative, one ruled by principles of economy rather than what has come to be referred to (with all the puritan disdain mixed with guilty pleasure that the term conveys) as 'excess'. As Arroyo writes of *Mission Impossible* (1996), 'just because the plot is simple doesn't mean the movie is – or that it doesn't offer complex pleasures'.[8] Arroyo takes issue here with an assumption that the narrative simplicity of what he terms action/spectacle cinema bears a direct relationship to its thematic or visual complexity. On a different but related point, Richard Dyer notes the accelerated aesthetic of a film like *Speed* (1994) – 'This is the movie as rollercoaster: all action and next to no plot' – but also observes that audiences nonetheless typically expect to experience the exhilaration of cinema within a narrative context: 'We generally want the exhilaration and rush embedded in a fiction. Such fictions situate the thrills. They refer us to the world.'[9]

The implication here is that however spectacular action and adventure movies have been or might become, narrative remains a central, indeed crucial, element (as do both stars and characters). Moreover, the supposed obviousness of the action movie is founded on what is a deceptive simplicity.

It is not my project to argue that action-adventure is more complex or ambiguous than it is actually is. However, I am not alone in arguing that the spectacle of action cinema – whether it is to do with the violence of combat, the thrill of the chase, spectacular landscapes or simply the pace of editing – has if not a narrative, then a thematic significance that is too often overlooked. Certainly the adventure narrative allows a staging of spectacular action sequences, but spectacle is not necessarily best understood as devoid of narrative content. As in melodrama, narrative themes and concerns can be developed as much through visual and aural spectacle (and indeed other aspects of the screen image) as through characterisation or dialogue. We might even argue that such visual elements are more, rather than less cinematic. In the process this may remind us of something important about popular cinema: its meaning and its pleasures are unlikely to be accessed simply through narrative exegesis.

## Genre and mode: defining and historicising action and adventure

If, despite its longevity, action has come to stand metonymically for the post-classical Hollywood blockbuster in much contemporary criticism, one strategy for thinking about action and/as genre involves positioning it precisely within an historical perspective, emphasising not so much its difference from but continuities with earlier patterns of filmmaking. For Steve Neale, understanding the genre depends in part on contextualising (historicising) it. As he notes, although the label has become associated with a particular kind of filmmaking that achieved box-office success in the 1980s and after, 'films in the action-adventure tradition have been a staple of Hollywood's output since the 1910s'.[10] Indeed both Singer and Jennifer Bean's contributions to this book emphasise the importance of sensational melodrama in the development of early film and the significant impact that early action had as a demonstration of the thrilling possibilities of cinema.

Although Arroyo rightly notes the 'problems of applying traditional concepts of genre to contemporary action/spectacle',[11] the terms 'action' and 'adventure' never referred to secure generic objects. For Neale, our approach to genre needs to recognise not only the context provided by film history but the fact that 'many Hollywood films – and many Hollywood genres – are hybrid and multi-generic'.[12] Researching this cinematic form I have found myself relying on not one but several terms or formulations, each with rather different nuances: 'action', 'adventure' and 'action-adventure' of course, but also 'action-thriller', 'action-fantasy' or 'action genres' for instance. This last acknowledges the diverse, and clearly generic, traditions from which our contemporary idea of action cinema is assembled. For Welsh one of the problems with attempting to constitute action as a genre is precisely that 'action films often interface with other genres'[13] (he cites disaster, science-fiction, espionage, caper and crime films).

Most contemporary or post-classical action films are indeed more or less hybrids, drawing on and combining generic plots, settings and character types from sources including science-fiction, the western, horror, the epic, war films, crime cinema and thrillers, disaster movies, swordplay and martial arts, even comedy. Contemporary US action also explicitly registers influences from diverse sources including European and Asian cinemas, American independent cinema, television and comic books. For the purposes of argument, contemporary action can be roughly divided into three broad generic groupings: crime and urban action; fantasy, e.g. science-fiction or horror; and war or military movies (though there are plenty of films that cross these boundaries – or elude them altogether). As much as anything these groupings relate to different settings for action, although in turn they also suggest the different thematic and narrative concerns that may be at issue. Movies of crime or urban action, for instance, are more likely to explicitly address questions of racial identity and ethnic conflict within the US. Fantasy settings, whether utopian or otherwise may lend themselves more easily to an experimentation with established social hierarchies (the play with gender in the *Alien* films is an obvious and well-known example). In Chapter 11, Mary Beltrán elaborates this point in relation to the deployment of the Latina action heroine in future/fantasy settings. While cinematic espionage is often both fantastic and transnational in character (the Bond cycle, *Mission Impossible* or *Nikita* (1990), for instance), the heroics and explosive spectacle of the war film typically have a more complex relationship to history, nation and spectatorship. All three categories invite differing perspectives on key components of action cinema such as the articulation of identity through discourses of gender, race, class and nation, the heroic body and violence.

In trying to make generic sense of contemporary action some critics have looked to analogies with other genres, musicals and melodrama in particular. Discussing *Mission Impossible* Arroyo suggests that the set-piece spectacle sequences are 'woven through the film like songs and dances . . . in an old-fashioned musical: it isn't so much that they don't tell us anything about the characters, but that their function as spectacle exceeds their function as narrative'.[14] Marc O'Day also evokes the genre, writing of action in terms of the 'rarely achieved sublime spectacle of the human body in motion comparable to musical numbers at their best'.[15] Music is of course central to meaning production in the action cinema.[16] I have already touched on the origins of action in sensational melodrama. In this context it makes perfect sense for critics to draw comparisons between the two forms. Moreover, like action, melodrama is characterised by the displacement of meaning onto *mise-en-scène*. And to the extent that action is a mode, it is clearly a melodramatic one.

An interest in action as melodrama(tic) has resulted in part from historical research into the sensational melodrama of silent cinema. In a rather different move, some have argued that post-classical action has been melodramatised through the incorporation of central female protagonists and/or a concern with familial themes. Lydia Papadimitriou's essay on Greek war film as melodrama employs and comments on both strategies, while Martin Fradley's discussion of *Gladiator* (2000) emphasises the relationship between the film's melodramatic strategies and its presentation of a recuperative gendered narrative of nation. Frequently we find critical debates concerning gendered genre (the idea that action is somehow 'male' or 'masculine' against melodrama's 'female or 'feminine' status) mapped onto or confused with a rather different history of female participation in the spaces of cinematic action. As the work of writers such as Singer has shown, the appearance of action heroines in popular cinema is far from new: indeed it was bound up with an early twentieth century articulation of modernity. And while classical Hollywood by no means embraced the action heroine – she is the exception rather than the rule in a relatively small number of films including *Anne of the Indies* (1951) and *Sons of the Musketeers* (1952) – her high-profile appearance in high-concept action blockbusters since the early 1990s has clear precedents. The links between action and melodrama in popular theatre and early cinema if anything underline the limits of understanding melodrama as a synonym for the 'woman's picture' or as an exclusively female preserve. In turn, whilst it might be tempting to employ the gendered associations of melodrama in contemporary parlance to question the construction of action as a male genre, it may be more useful to consider what the analogy tells us about action's characteristic mode of organising and presenting story events and the worlds in which they take place.

Analogies between action, melodrama and the musical are nonetheless productive. At the very least, they remind us that these films *are* typically melodramatic and that they are punctuated by lavish and spectacular action sequences in the manner of the musical. They thus work to underline the important role played by the specific way in which action and adventure films tell stories. Yet as their frequent use would seem to suggest we seem best able to get a handle on action when it is considered in relation to genres or types of filmmaking from which it is in other ways quite distinct. The musical and the melodrama of classical Hollywood are no less ideologically problematic than action and adventure, but they *are* less violent. In this context, we can speculate that the analogy in part serves to implicitly point to (and indeed valorise) the 'innocent' pleasures of action cinema – that is, its spectacular (cinematic) character.

Arroyo suggests that contemporary writings have collectively produced an idea of action/spectacle as 'a type of cinema that cannot quite constitute a mode but which exceeds the boundaries of a genre'.[17] Thus, when critics talk about what constitutes action they focus as much on *how* the story is told as the type of story, setting or other generic elements. The specific qualities of action are, it seems, to do with pace, excitement, exhilaration: a visceral, even sensual, evocation of movement and violence. In this vein, Welsh posits a distinction between 'pure action and action-adventure' that is predicated on the relative complexity of plot and an implicit opposition between spectacle and narrative. Thus in the former, 'spectacular special effects' function as the 'major selling point' whilst in the latter, we see 'more flamboyant and colourful characters, malignant villainy, dastardly deeds and larger-than-life characters who will ultimately save the day'[18] (qualities which are, of course, associated with melodrama). What Welsh seems to be balancing here is the relative importance accorded not only to special effects but also to the action sequence.

## Narrative and spectacle

In a spectacular shoot-out towards the end of *XXX* (2002), Xander Cage (Vin Diesel) seizes a heat-seeking missile launcher from a hesitant Euro-cop, quipping: 'Dude! Stop thinking Prague Police and start thinking Play Station: BLOW SHIT UP!!'. Here is the action movie as dumb-fun spectacle, showcasing the pleasures of humorous destruction and star performance (Vin Diesel as an anarchic extreme sports Bondian hero improbably press-ganged into the CIA). Cage's actions lead to the explosive demise of a singularly unpleasant villain (the missile detects him because he smokes) and a lengthy chase sequence by road and across water that narrowly averts apocalyptic germ warfare. It is no accident that judgements about the aesthetic worth of action as a genre have centred so firmly on the perceived balance of plot and complex characterisation on the one hand, spectacular visual display on the other. Such an opposition goes to the heart of the problems involved in defining and theorising action cinema. Whether explicitly or implicitly, a distinction frequently drawn in reviews and critical writings relating to action-adventure is that between spectacle and narrative. Post-classical action is undeniably a spectacular, star and effects led cinema. Yet it is undoubtedly also the case that action-adventure traditions within the classical and silent Hollywood cinema were both spectacular and star-focused. One need only think of Errol Flynn in *The Adventures of Robin Hood* (1938): with its lavish technicolor spectacle and swordplay, the film teamed up Flynn with co-star Olivia De Havilland and director Michael Curtiz following the success of their previous collaborations on *Captain Blood* (1935) and *The Charge of the Light Brigade* (1936).[19] Equally, the extravagant sets of spectacular Douglas Fairbanks vehicles such as *Robin Hood* (1922) and *The Thief of Bagdad* (1924) marked the productions out as special and distinctive.[20]

Nevertheless, critics repeatedly single out for comment the exaggeration or stylisation, the sheer *excess* of spectacle as the defining feature of contemporary action. High-profile action and adventure movies do indeed provide a testing ground for visual innovations and special effects: this is perhaps the generic terrain on which the impact of CGI is most evident (essays in this collection by Leon Hunt, Marc O'Day and Aylish Wood all touch on this question). But it is the technology that is new, rather than the impulse behind it: the development and use of stop-motion in adventure films from *The Lost World* (1925) with its dinosaurs to *Jason and the Argonauts* (1963) with its skeleton sword-fight underlines this. For some, the narrative of contemporary action is all but subsumed within the spectacular staging of action sequences employing star bodies, special effects, artful editing and percussive music. This is an idea of blockbuster Hollywood cinema as, if not post-narrative, then barely concerned with the narrative dimension, a process that action genres have seemingly come to exemplify more than any other in recent years.[21] It is this that underpins Welsh's notion of 'pure action' and it is in this sense that spectacle defines action and adventure generically.

In thinking about action as a spectacular rather than a narrative cinema, critics have increasingly drawn comparisons between contemporary action movies and the silent cinemas which pioneered key cinematic elements such as the chase sequence. In this context it is interesting to note the influence of what seems in many ways to be a passing remark made by Tom Gunning: 'Clearly in some sense recent spectacle cinema has reaffirmed its roots in stimulus and carnival rides, in what might be called the Spielberg-Lucas-Coppola cinema of effects.'[22] Here Gunning alludes to what would have been at the time of writing relatively recent blockbuster adventures (the essay was originally published in 1986) such as *Star Wars* (1977), *Jaws* (1975) and *Raiders of the Lost Ark* (1981).[23] These films are also of course key texts of the emerging New Hollywood.

Gunning's comments on a new cinema of effects are made in the context of his own observations on narrative and spectacle in examples of the epic (*Ben-Hur*, 1924) and the early western in the shape of *The Great Train Robbery* (1903) a film that he describes as pointing 'in both directions, towards an assault on the spectator (the spectacularly enlarged outlaw unloading his pistol in our faces), and towards a linear narrative continuity'.[24] In relation to action and adventure it is the relationship between the two that concerns us. Or, as Mark Jancovich puts it in relation to the epic, since moments of spectacle are often moments of action, the question is 'not really about how one thinks about the relationship between spectacle and narrative but how the third term of action relates to these two terms, and threatens the clear distinction between them'.[25]

One obvious way to explore this relationship is to focus on the different nuances of the terms action and adventure. At its simplest we can postulate that action suggests a sort of filmmaking (in effect, technique) and a specific set of pleasures, whilst adventure relates to a kind of story. Action presents the story events of adventure in a particular (thrilling) way. We have certain formal expectations of an action sequence and, by extension, an action film. These expectations include elements such as chase sequences, combat of various kinds, a distinctive (typically fragmented) orchestration of space, an accelerated sense of time (a feeling of speed, of modernity perhaps) and pace (in editing or camerawork for instance), visual and aural spectacle and special effects.

Adventure bears much more explicit *narrative* expectations: we will follow the protagonist or protagonists on a journey or quest into the unknown territories of adventure space. Thus the narrative thrust of adventure provides a stage for action. It is also useful to draw a distinction between action which is explicitly staged in adventure space and that which seems to result from the location in which the protagonists find themselves from the outset – as in the urban crime narrative. On the one hand there is the active search for adventure (often imperialist in character) implied by shifting, typically exotic locations: the South America of *The Lost*

*World* or the opening of *The Thief of Bagdad* which discovers Douglas Fairbanks seeming to slumber in 'Bagdad, dream city of the ancient East'; the experimental island that provides the setting for *Jurassic Park* (1993) or the Brazilian jungle of *Anaconda* (1997). On the other hand there are protagonists who do not have to travel to seek out adventure as in *Set It Off* (1996). The film's urban setting (in Los Angeles) and focus on four working-class African-American women – in however fantastical a crime spree scenario – led to the film being discussed in terms of social realism as well as action/spectacle.

In his 1993 study of historical adventure, Brian Taves attempts to draw a distinction between adventure and action on the one hand, fantasy on the other. Though his aim is to bring a specificity to adventure, a term I am using here in a broader sense, his comments on action are worth citing since they emphasise so precisely cinematic qualities, a transgeneric way of telling a story rather than specific story elements:

> The usual definitions of *adventure* stress elements of the unusual, over-coming obstacles with narrow escapes, and vanquishing villains. In this sense, *adventure* becomes linked with *action*, a word attached to any film with a greater emphasis on action than emotion. Indeed, action is a more appropriate word than adventure to describe the *style of storytelling* that runs through many genres, a male-oriented approach dependent on phys-ical movement, violence, and suspense, with often perfunctory motivation and romance. Action tends to shift sentiment, character, dialogue, and family to the background[26] (emphasis added).

Whilst I have reservations about these comments, not least the restatement of an implicit opposition between style and meaning, Taves' emphasis on action as a *way* of telling a story across different genres suggests that it may indeed be understood most productively as a mode and certainly as multi-generic.

## Gender in action

We might note that Gunning invokes Laura Mulvey's proposition of a dialectic between narrative and spectacle, rather than offering an account in which the devel-opment of the former somehow displaces the latter. Gunning's reference to Mulvey, as much as Taves' characterisation of action as a 'male-oriented approach', serves to remind us of the important part played by issues of gender, and the feminist film criticism and theory that seeks to explore such issues, in the analysis of action and adventure cinema. It is with a project of unpacking the ideological significance of action – particularly, but not only with respect to gender – that much of the recent critical work devoted to the genre has been concerned. Whilst contemporary action is regularly dismissed as simplistic or reactionary, the films continue to fascinate and to stimulate discussion. The articulation of gender, particularly as expressed through star images and performance, has been central to critical debate. Indeed for many the functioning of action as a site of gender trouble is one of the factors that makes it so compelling.

Feminist critics have in particular been attracted to iconic images of strong women: the genre's action heroines. Debate abounds as to whether figures such as Ripley in the four *Alien* films (1979, 1986, 1992, 1997), Sarah Connor in *Terminator* (1984) and *Terminator 2: Judgement Day* (1991) or Demi Moore in *G.I. Jane* (1997), for instance, are new women or simply masculine/masculinised travesties. Whilst debate over the meaning of muscle has raged, mainstream American cinema has advanced a modified version of the action heroine as evidenced in movies including *The Mummy* (1999), *Charlie's Angels* (2000), *The Mummy Returns* (2001), *Lara Croft: Tomb Raider* (2001) and *Die Another Day* (2002). The post-feminist character of the action heroines showcased in such movies – physically strong, independent though often emotionally vulnerable, typically glamorous and even overtly sexy – represents an extension of the tradition of feisty heroines I commented on in *Spectacular Bodies* and is aptly designated in this collection by Marc O'Day as an emergent 'action babe cinema'. That *Terminator 3: Rise of the Machines* (2003) showcases its most high-profile female action figure in the form of the latest and most advanced cyborg enemy played (or perhaps embodied) by former model Kristanna Loken accords quite precisely with the terms of O'Day's analysis. As indeed does Demi Moore's latest re-invention as fallen angel Madison Lee in *Charlie's Angels: Full Throttle* (2003).

Despite the strength of scholarly interest in action heroines (whether contemporary or historical), it remains commonplace to critically designate action as a male or masculine genre. Mark Gallagher puts it at its baldest when he asserts: 'The action film has historically been a "male" genre, dealing with stories of male heroism, produced by male filmmakers for principally male audiences.'[27] Given an assumption that action is a masculine arena, it is not perhaps surprising that the genre has been a key site for the development of ideas to do with men, masculinity and the cinema. Much discussion centres on ways of making sense of the seemingly contradictory location of the star-hero as both narrative agent and object of spectacle. For Taves, as we have seen, action involves the relegation of emotion to the periphery. Yet, even while acknowledging the centrality of male figures in the genre, criticism has underlined precisely the emotions on display in the post-classical action film. In this collection Martin Fradley emphasises the sentiment of recent action epic *Gladiator*, pointing to its melodramatic rendering of the latest 'crisis' of white masculinity, whilst Michael Hammond excavates the therapeutic endeavour structuring Spielberg's *Saving Private Ryan*.

The articulation of race and ethnicity in the action cinema has also received attention, though this is by no means as sustained as work on gender. Of course the two discourses are not entirely unrelated and are indeed often bound up together.[28] Exploring the emergence of Latina action heroines through a discussion of stars Jennifer Lopez and Michelle Rodriguez, for instance, Mary Beltrán points to the deployment of stereotypical assumptions about Latina toughness and sexuality in these images. Although action and adventure is a generic space that has, in at least some of its variants, involved a high level of visibility for Black and Asian performers, the terms in which they are incorporated rarely escape the limitations of stereotypes (even though the assumptions on which such stereotypes are built might be cautiously played with at times).

These limitations have had further ramifications in relation to critical work in the field. Reviewing recent writings on masculinity and action it is clear that white stars Sylvester Stallone and Arnold Schwarzenegger (both linked either ethnically or nationally to Europe) remain reference points in critical debates, although neither commands the box-office as they did in the 1980s and to some extent the early 1990s. By comparison, there is relatively little work exploring the star personas of African-American performers – including Will Smith, Wesley Snipes and Laurence Fishburne – who have consistently featured in action and adventure roles (Smith in high-profile movies including *Independence Day* (1996), *Men in Black* (1997), *Bad Boys* (1995) and *Enemy of the State* (1998); Snipes iconically in *Blade* (1998) and *Blade 2* (2002) as well as a series of cop roles in films including *Rising Sun* (1993), *Murder at 1600* (1997) and as action hero in *Passenger 57* (1992) and *Drop Zone* (1994); Fishburne in *Deep Cover* (1992), *Event Horizon* (1997) and as the pontificating Morpheus in *The Matrix* (1999) and *The Matrix: Reloaded* (2003)).

Although the neglect of these figures can doubtless be attributed partly to the fact that writing on action has tended to be restricted to a fairly small number of films and stars, the limited terms in which Black stars are incorporated into Hollywood cinema is surely also at issue. Ed Guerrero has described the containment strategies of the bi-racial buddy movie that found such box-office success in the 1980s, analysing Eddie Murphy's comedy/action roles (notably *48 Hours* (1982) and *Beverly Hills Cop* (1984)). Whilst valuing Murphy's talents as a performer, Guerrero's analysis of these films – and indeed Murphy's roles within them – is damning. Moreover, his comments on the relative lack of commercial success greeting those Murphy vehicles that placed the star in either 'Third World or Black environments' or 'supported him with non-White or Black casts'[29] could be applied to many of the action and adventure roles with which contemporary stars such as Smith, Snipes and Fishburne have been associated. Conversely, interest in a film like *Set it Off* relates not only to its rare status as a tough showcase for Black female performers, but its unproblematic location within a contemporary Black context. More typically action, like comedy, has functioned as a genre of containment in Guerrero's terms – one that showcases Black performers but allows only limited room for manoeuvre.[30]

## Authorship, Hollywood and international action

Though action cinema is typically discussed almost exclusively in relation to Hollywood, it is clearly an international, even transnational business. Despite films such as Luc Besson's *Nikita, The Fifth Element* (1997) and *Jeanne D'Arc* (1999)[31] or the German hit *Lola Rennt / Run Lola Run* (1998), there is a tendency to see the deployment of action genres in Europe at least (not so the Hong Kong industry these days) as an aping of Hollywood, a misconception tackled here by Dimitris Eleftheriotis in his discussion of the Italian western. Even within Hollywood, action is associated with émigré performers and filmmakers of whom directors including Jan de Bont, Paul Verhoeven, James Cameron, Roland Emmerich, Renny Harlin, Ridley Scott and John Woo are only some of the most visible. Many other personnel have migrated to Hollywood as Hunt discusses specifically in relation to the Hong Kong industry. Neither this, nor the trade in stars that both Leon Hunt and Christine Holmlund discuss, is new. Just as it is important to recognise the diversity of personnel working in Hollywood (even while we analyse the tendency to erase visible difference from the screen) work in this area needs to recognise the importance of action and adventure within other national traditions. Indeed, the study of many popular genres – horror for instance – is only enhanced by such an approach. Lydia Papadimitriou's analysis of Greek war films, one of several essays in this collection to focus on the war movie, uncovers the national and cultural specificity resulting from particular star images, the history portrayed (Greece's campaigns overseas combined with her experience of occupation) and the historical context of the film's production.

For Welsh the big-budget action film emerges from an industry that privileges the producer rather than the director: 'Action-adventure pictures are about money, investing huge budgets in order to realise huge returns if the product is successful. The producer is the gambler whose job it is to hedge the bets.'[32] As a commercial phenomenon, the study of action cinema opens up various aspects of the contemporary scene. However, it is interesting in this context to note the emergence of interest in what we might term action auteurs. Authorship remains one of the key ways in which popular cinema is valorised. And while mainstream movies are typically discussed in ideological terms or in relation to their social significance, the adoption of an authorship framework in relation to certain filmmakers signals the increasing legitimacy of action. As action films have received an increasing level of critical interest, the reputations of filmmakers who make forays into, or work almost exclusively within the genre have developed correspondingly: Kathryn Bigelow's relatively small body of films has established her as a strong visual stylist, while James Cameron is known both for the ability to handle large-scale spectacles and his fondness for familial themes. In the early 1990s Quentin Tarantino's stylish and award-winning crime capers and the command of action sequences by filmmakers including Robert Rodriguez (*El Mariarchi* (1992), *Desperado* (1995), *Spy Kids* (2001)) and Steven Soderbergh (*Out of Sight* (1998), *Ocean's Eleven* (2001)) have attracted interest. Enthusiastic western responses to *The Killer* (1989) and *Hard-Boiled* (1992) brought Hong Kong filmmaker John Woo to Hollywood, while Ang Lee's artful *Crouching Tiger, Hidden Dragon* (2000) attracted interest from western audiences not typically enchanted by the action film. Little is new however: acclaim for these directors from action fans, critics and festival audiences can be seen to follow in the wake of those already canonical filmmakers who worked with genres including the western, crime or swordplay film, figures such as Sam Fuller, Howard Hawks, Akira Kurosawa and Sam Peckinpah.

If contemporary cultural criticism continues to value the novelistic over the spectacular, and even to regard the two as distinct, it is nonetheless the case that recent years have seen a developing interest in action cinema with the production of some intriguing critical work in the area. Within film studies, and to some extent beyond the discipline, action and adventure cinema has become at the least a legitimate, if not yet perhaps a reputable, field of study. Action and adventure cinema is a compelling cinematic phenomenon with a long and diverse history. Raising both political and aesthetic questions, it repays close analysis as the essays in this volume attest.

## Notes

1   Thomas Schatz 'The New Hollywood', in Jim Collins, Hilary Radner and Ava Preacher Collins (eds) *Film Theory Goes to the Movies*, London: Routledge, 1993, pp. 8–36.
2   Larry Gross 'Big and Loud', in José Arroyo (ed.) *Action/Spectacle Cinema*, London: BFI, [1995] 2000, pp. 3–9.
3   Arroyo (ed.) *Action/Spectacle Cinema*, pp. viii–xi.
4   James M. Welsh 'Action Films: The Serious, the Ironic, the Postmodern', in Wheeler Winston Dixon (ed.) *Film Genre 2000: New Critical Essays*, Albany: State University of New York Press, 2000, p. 161.
5   Arroyo (ed.) *Action/Spectacle Cinema*, p. ix.
6   Andrew O'Hehir 'Review of *Star Wars Episode I: The Phantom Menace*', in Arroyo (ed.) *Action/Spectacle Cinema*, p. 263.
7   *Halliwell's* cites a 1982 review from the *New Yorker* as follows: 'The loudness, the smash and grab editing and the relentless pacing drive every idea from your head, and even if you've been entertained you may feel cheated of some dimension – a sense of wonder perhaps.' John Walker (ed.) *Halliwell's Film and Video Guide 2000*, London: Harper Collins, 1999, p. 782.
8   'Mission: Sublime', in Arroyo (ed.) *Action/Spectacle Cinema*, p. 23.
9   Dyer in Arroyo (ed.) *Action/Spectacle Cinema* pp. 17, 18.
10  Steve Neale *Genre and Hollywood*, London: Routledge, p. 55 (and in this collection p. 74).
11  Arroyo (ed.) *Action/Spectacle Cinema*, p. viii.
12  Neale *Genre and Hollywood*, p. 51.
13  Welsh 'Action Films', in Dixon (ed.) *Film Genre 2000*, p. 170.
14  Arroyo (ed.) *Action/Spectacle Cinema*, pp. 23–4.
15  Marc O'Day, this collection, p. 212.
16  See Pauline MacRory 'Excusing the Violence of Hollywood Women: Music in *Nikita* and *Point of No Return*', *Screen*, 40: 1, Spring 1999, pp. 51–65.
17  Arroyo (ed.) *Action/Spectacle Cinema*, p. iii.
18  Welsh 'Action Films', in Dixon (ed.) *Film Genre 2000*, p. 161.
19  See Tino Balio *Grand Design: Hollywood as a Modern Business Enterprise 1930–1939*, Berkeley: University of California Press, 1995, pp. 203–5; Ina Rae Hark 'The Visual Politics of *The Adventures of Robin Hood*', *Journal of Popular Film*, 5: 1, 1976, pp. 3–17.
20  Julian Stringer cites a contemporary critic on another Fairbanks spectacular, *The Black Pirate* (1926) as 'an example of the "so-called super-film"'. Stringer (ed.) *Movie Blockbusters*, London: Routledge, 2003, p. 4.

21 For a useful interrogation of such assumptions see Geoff King 'Spectacle, Narrative and the Spectacular Hollywood Blockbuster', in Stringer (ed.) *Movie Blockbusters*, pp. 114–27.

22 Tom Gunning 'The Cinema of Attractions: Early Film, Its Spectator and the Avant-Garde', in Thomas Elsaesser (ed.) *Early Cinema: Space, Frame, Narrative*, London: BFI, 1990, p. 61.

23 Coppola's *Apocalypse Now* (1979) offers a ride of a rather different kind.

24 Gunning 'The Cinema of Attractions: Early Film, Its Spectator and the Avant-Garde', in Elsaesser (ed.) *Early Cinema: Space, Frame, Narrative*, p. 61.

25 This collection, p. 85.

26 Brian Taves *The Romance of Adventure: The Genre of Historical Adventure Movies*, Jackson: University Press of Mississippi, 1993, pp. 4–5.

27 Mark Gallagher 'I Married Rambo: Spectacle and Melodrama in the Hollywood Action Film', in Christopher Sharrett (ed.) *Mythologies of Violence in Postmodern Media*, Detroit: Wayne State University Press, 1999, p. 199.

28 My *Spectacular Bodies* (Yvonne Tasker *Spectacular Bodies: Gender, Genre and Action Cinema*, London: Routledge, 1993), Fred Pfeil's *White Guys: Studies in Postmodern Domination and Difference*, London: Verso, 1995, and Sharon Willis's *High Contrast: Race and Gender in Contemporary Hollywood Film*, Durham: Duke University Press, 1997, analyse Hollywood cinema's deployment of race and gendered discourses in action and other genres.

29 Ed Guerrero 'The Black Image in Protective Custody: Hollywood's Biracial Buddy Films of the Eighties', in Manthia Diawara (ed.) *Black American Cinema*, London: Routledge, 1993, p. 241.

30 The continued use of Black comic sidekick characters as in *Charlie's Angels: Full Throttle* or supporting figures in White male suffering as in *Gladiator* is pertinent in this context. After the 2001 attacks on the US and the Iraq war (not that it could be said to be over at the time of writing) the Hollywood action cinema's strategy of displacing internal racial and ethnic tensions onto external enemies – often Arabic, but also European and Asian – looks even more firmly entrenched.

31 Besson's role as writer and producer of French action-comedy hits *Taxi* (Gérard Pirès, 1998) and *Taxi 2* (Gerard Krawczyk, 2000) indicates his continuing contribution to a popular national cinema.

32 Welsh 'Action Films', in Dixon (ed.) *Film Genre 2000*, p. 165.

PART I

# History, criticism and style

## JENNIFER M. BEAN

## 'TRAUMA THRILLS'
## Notes on early action cinema

THE MOST NOTABLE CHARACTERISTIC of the action cinema is its dynamic tempo: rapid editing at once articulates and accelerates the breathtaking pace of the stunting human body. It is also true that the body takes primacy over voice in the genre, that the action film 'speaks' through visual spectacle, that spectacle, in fact, takes precedence over narrative meaning. The humorous pith verging on bald contempt with which these 'mindless spectacles' are so often received reinforce what we already presume to know: action cinema is bad cinema; its aesthetics (if we can use that word) are rude, its pleasures suspicious. Such hubris turns on a serious critical impasse, at once subordinating the body to the mind and reinforcing their structure as binary opposites. The time has come for us to engage the sheer corporeal effects of film action, to reflect on the genre's propensity for placing the spectator in the balance, for putting the body at risk.

Such a project cannot be conceived outside of the action cinema's historical locus, its overlap with a modernity in which the accelerated motion of transportation technologies and that of optical devices linked together to create fundamental perceptual and psychic changes in human subjects. The wounding effects of modernity's tempo are well known. Pummeled by too much, too fast, the modern subject succumbed to an array of pathologies – nervous tics, psychic blockage, alienation, fatigue – collectively understood in terms of shock and trauma. Yet familiar 'traumatocentric' accounts of modernity, to borrow from Jeffrey Schnapp, miss the era's key aesthetic premise, which is to say, 'trauma thrills'.[1] The conjoining of a medical term with a form of entertainment is more than rhetorical play. Its employment underscores the fact that representations, visual or otherwise, have direct consequences for the body. It also suggests that cultural distress regarding the subject's instability in the late nineteenth and early twentieth centuries provided the historical conditions for the emergence of a distinctively modern aesthetic mode, one that theorists such as Walter Benjamin understood as pre-eminently cinematic. In recent years of course we have assimilated cinema's historic affair with speed, shock, and irrational mechanistic power under the rubric of a pre-narrative 'cinema of attractions'.[2] Yet we have for too long overlooked the fact that the aesthetic privileging of sensational movement, aggressive energy, and unsettling form – in short, a trauma that thrills – over character psychology and meaningful content, was (and is) inextricably hinged to complex narrative techniques through which they found their most sustained expression.

In what follows, I isolate the Kalem company's blockbuster railway series, *The Hazards of Helen* (1914–17), as a particularly compelling instance of American cinema's action aesthetic. Initially released on November 14, 1914, and focusing on what one reviewer described as the 'strenuous existence' of a young female telegrapher, the series promised situations that would compel its eponymous heroine 'to leap off high railroad spans into swiftly running rivers, and even to become involved in railroad smash-ups'.[3] Later press releases offered more precise descriptions of action scenarios, as when Helen 'pursues a train by automobile and then leaps to the car where a struggle with an escaped convict ensues'; or when she 'slides down a construction-camp chute in a small carrier and shoots across the top of a speeding freight train'.[4] Vaunted as sheer sensationalism, the Helen films were wildly successful, their appeal officially proclaimed in December, 1915, when Kalem celebrated 'Helen's' one-year anniversary and announced that 'due to exhibitors' demands' the series would be 'continued indefinitely'.[5] In 1916 one writer for the *New York Dramatic Mirror* gaily predicted that the 'far famed series . . . would run on forever'.[6] To be more precise, it was on February 18, 1917 that *The Hazards of Helen* reached the end of its epic run. Tallying a remarkable 119 episodes in toto, the series garnered applause among domestic audiences of diverse constituencies, while playing a significant role in extending the reach of US markets abroad, especially the relatively new markets opening in the Far East and South America.

Before proceeding to discuss the textual dynamics at work in the series, my use of the label 'action' for classifying an early narrative film cycle demands some clarification. Billed as a 'thrilling railway drama', Kalem's series arguably belongs more properly to the array of Cowboy and Indian pictures, detective, mystery, jungle, and espionage films that, as Richard Abel recounts in this volume, were categorically assimilated by the trade press as 'sensational' or 'thriller melodramas'.[7] Yet a critical uneasiness is felt when we comply with the vagaries of such a category, a gesture that sacrifices the variables of iconicity, characterization, and narrative structure in favor of a perspective oriented solely to thrilling affect. Nor need we travel far to find that exclamatory adjective – thriller-sensation! – run amok in the period, its marketing value as capacious for newspaper dailies as for amusement parks, for stage productions as for film. Of course as Ben Singer has eloquently demonstrated, the relationships among these modern forms of expression are critical. He also demonstrates that part of the burden we shoulder in recovering cinema's generic past is the need to impose finer categorical distinctions than the purview of trade discourse immediately allows. Isolating the variables of form (seriality) and character (active female protagonist), Singer claims categorical integrity for a group of films in which the violent aggression associated with sensational thrills is infiltrated by a discourse on female emancipation, giving way to a peculiar but distinctive version of the 'woman's film'. This he calls the 'serial-queen melodrama', films in which fantasies of 'female power' take precedence, the representations of which Singer links to a 'pervasive and codified discourse on the New Woman'.[8] Moreover, by situating early serials within an intertextual matrix of related forms of popular entertainment (stage melodrama, dime novels, suffragette discourse, fashion advertisements, newspaper stories, etc.), Singer emphasizes the industry's strategy of tapping into an already existing, and rapidly expanding, female readership.

Insofar as Helen's gamble on the railway permits a stunning array of spectacular stunts, the series would seem the 'serial-queen melodrama's' perfect illustration, as feminist historians Miriam Hansen, Lynn Kirby, Eileen Bowser, and Shelley Stamp have recently declared it to be.[9] I, too, have few doubts that *The Hazards of Helen* – as with the array of mystery, patriotic, and jungle-adventure-style films listed in Singer's taxonomy – appealed to the notoriously high numbers of female filmgoers emerging in the 1910s.[10] But I also believe that these films' horizon of reception stretched across a vast cross-market, even transnational, public, and that their appeal hinged on a cinematic register that sensationalized, agitated, and unsettled the very ground of meaning on which distinctions between male and female, and beyond that the logic of subjectivity more broadly, traditionally depends. It is this narrative whimsy that Singer's 'sociological analysis' cannot accommodate, but which his thinking on *The Hazards of Helen* bumps up against. Noting the frequency, intensity, and salience of Helen's 'dare-devil' antics, he speculates thus:

> Helen . . . may have less to do with an earnest stake in a progressive ideology of female emancipation than with the utter novelty and curiosity value of a spectacle based on the 'category mistake' of a woman taking death-defying physical risks, getting filthy, brawling with crooks in muddy riverbanks – in short, of a woman acting like a man.[11]

If the aggressive iteration of physical risk justifies Helen's exclusion from the 'serial queen melodrama', then it is precisely this excess that grants the series special status in what I refer to as early action cinema.

I begin with the premise that risky maneuvers by definition imply a non-normative domain, the category *of* mistake. Another way of saying this is to note that risk 'carries uncertainty with it, an uncertainty intrinsic to it' as Kathleen Woodward claims; or to state, following Mary Russo, that risk 'belongs properly to the discourse of probability and "error"'.[12] These descriptions get at the excesses of risk, its propensity to gamble with cultural scripts, to mock stability in any form. These terms also hint at risk's antagonistic relation to an ethos of rationalization with which bourgeois-patriarchal (industrialist) culture sought to regulate a 'norm', to eliminate differential flux and contingency of all sorts. It is the early action film's 'reflexive' relation to the modernity of which it is both symptom and part that interests me here, and for two reasons, neither separable from the other. To begin, taking seriously the function and appeal of an action narrative means that accounts of American cinema's form and style, its premises and organizing principles, must be rethought. It also means rethinking the heuristics of our critical practice, and the formulations we at once critique and reproduce between the aesthetic pleasures afforded by mass-media and the machinations of ideology.

Our pursuit of these goals can begin with a provisional account of the series' narrative system more broadly, noting in particular its proclivity for technological caprice. Set exclusively on the railway, *The Hazards of Helen* showcases a modern-industrial universe on the brink not of progress, but of catastrophe: skewed tracks, broken safety lines, dangling wires, spontaneous explosions, and, especially, failed breaks assemble a recognizable iconography. We could readily accumulate examples from elsewhere in the period, among them the whirring, circling, imploding vehicles that dictate the hilarious indirection of Keystone's slapstick shorts, or the flattened tires, jerry-rigged airplanes, and warped steering mechanisms that punctuate the action of serialized crime thrillers like *The Exploits of Elaine* (1915) and *The Iron Claw* (1916) among others. Unique to *The Hazards of Helen*, however, is a plot structure that systematically depends on industrialism's malfunctioning, calibrated to explore the 'hazardous' effects of technological failure.

Each of the 119 episodes reiterates a simple, basic scenario: Helen arrives at the station (or is on her way to work); a situation arises that threatens the railway line (alternately in the guise of bandits, human error, or mechanical breakdown); Helen learns of the dangerous situation (her position as telegrapher, and occasionally her proximity to the accident, enables her to receive knowledge instantly); and she leaves her office to 'race to the rescue' (typically by leaping onto the car of a speeding train, airplane, or automobile). Although each film ends when Helen restores the railway to its proper working order, suggesting a tight fit between formal (narrative) and thematic (industrial) equilibrium, what we in fact have is a radically unbalanced plot, warped in the middle, blasted out of proportion. One of the more axiomatic sequences involves an extended chase scene, as in *The Open Track* in which an incrementally rapid cutting pattern that volatizes Helen's successive leaps from horseback to motorbike to automobile to train constitutes almost the entirety of the drama. Similarly, in the latter half of *The Wrong Train Order*, Helen finds herself 'alone on a runaway train', and the narrative sequencing follows her 'breath-taking ride' through 'open switches, an open drawbridge, and an oncoming train on the same track'.[13] The length and incredible pace of these sequences privilege action as the series' organizing principle, action pitched to a degree that movement becomes sensate, visible. The aggressively repetitive posture of the plot warrants comment as well, for it indicates the degree to which these films displace the narrative hermeneutic – the what does it mean? – onto the *how*, onto the velocities and vicissitudes of the moving image. Indeed the runaway engine which provides the series' most emblematic icon may also be seen as the *mise-en-abîme* of its narrative system.

If to what we are saying of narrative structure more broadly we add a consideration of plotting effects, we find a dramaturgy motivated by industrialism's deep instability, its potential to backfire, to generate a world of blind chance in which time is not standardized but relativized – reduced to a series of instants that explode the system's meaning-making economy. Consider, for instance, *The Wrong Train Order*, the 58th episode of the series, which opens as Helen, returning from a vacation, arrives at an unnamed station and boards a train that will take her to her office at Lone Point. A long shot framing the front of the engine as it pulls away is interrupted by a cut to the interior of a telegrapher's station, where a clutter of desks and seated men suggest a central office location. An intertitle declares there has been 'A Delay', and the camera takes us to the side of the track where Helen's express train has stopped. The express shortly resumes its trip, and the camera cuts to the interior of a smaller station where a telegrapher receives a message that he pens, offered to the viewer as a close-up insert: '#13 Eng. #3023 runs ten minutes late. Hoynes to Hunter.' The camera holds momentarily, then, panning slightly to the right, discloses another memo, identical to the first but for a single, significant twist: '#13 Eng. #3023 runs twenty minutes late. Hoynes to Hunter.' The situation could not be more legible: the telegrapher has received updated information on the schedule of the express, which he dutifully records. Insofar as mechanical breakdown provides the initial, motivating cause for the episode's opening actions, however, its salience registers only in relation to another accident, this one involving automobiles. The camera cuts to a city street where a woman and a young boy step off the curb just as a car careens around the corner. Catastrophe in the grander sense is narrowly avoided – there are no mutilated bodies here – but the woman faints, the driver stops to help her, and the boy races off to the nearby train station to alert his father, who happens to be the telegrapher: 'Mama's been hurt!' Immediately registering alarm, and obviously distracted with concern for his wife's well-being, the telegrapher relays the information from the first memo to the engineer waiting to depart, signals for a replacement telegrapher, grabs his son's hand, and races for home. It is not until he nears the outer road of the station that the telegrapher pauses; a dissolve to the previous image of two memos juxtaposed one to the other visualizes that which he is, finally, remembering. Skidding back into the office he alerts his cohort to his disastrous mistake, and together they 'work the wires' in a desperate bid to convey the information that will 'stop the express'. The film's opening sequence thus ends with a telling intertitle: the compensatory action is 'Too Late'.

This scene of vertiginous, overlapping uncertainty takes us to the core of the action film's premise and design. Gone is the accuracy implied by the time-table with its carefully inked calculations. Gone also is the logic of system's management theories which reduce the individual worker to the proverbial cog in the wheel, stripped of his or her individuation. Here editing techniques renounce the insularity of work space from domestic and interpersonal space: the family drama, itself connected to the wild caprice of modern machinery, infiltrates the railway station, distracting the telegrapher and motivating the narrative that follows (as the title foretells, he leaves the 'wrong train order'). But the implication of the scene for industrial dreams of perfect calibration stretches well beyond the messy interference of a worker's personhood. It also illumines the abrasive irony underlying the rationale imperative to systems of mass production and control more broadly. Let me clarify. If, on one hand, systems management theories promised greater cultural power (productivity) by breaking down tasks to isolable functions that together contribute to a larger whole, then it is also true that the system's contrived organicism is contingent on the precise functioning of its atomized parts. In other words, the flip-side of the familiar claim that industrialism made machines out of men is the overt aggrandizement of each mechanized element's singular import. Whether a human worker or the machinery of which he/she is putatively coeval, malfunctioning ignites a chain reaction with disastrous consequences for the mass, the system, the vast public network of which each element is, now, an integrated part.

The treacherous instability inherent to modernity's lust for precision and maximum power surfaces in these films in the form of accident: the railway system's nemesis and the action narrative's motor force. But we must use words like 'nemesis' cautiously, since accident by definition is indiscriminate, which is precisely the point. In other words, if accident is bad, that is, if its effects are dangerous, then 'bad' by no means signifies a state of being, whether a psychological condi-tion or a moral position. An objection may likely be raised here, insofar as the scene we are discussing from *The Wrong Train Order* implies, at first glance, a lesson of moral import, an implicit reprimand to the worker that distraction of any sort simply will not do. Of significance, however, is that the cacophony of disorder mounting in these opening scenes is amplified by yet another accident, disconnected from the previous incidents in terms of cause but decidedly linked in terms of effect. Editing techniques, again, demonstrate the multiplicity of things that concurrently break down. While the male telegrapher rushes out of the station with his son, just before he remembers his 'mistake', another mistake occurs: the camera cuts to a close view of the express train's cab, emphasizing the smoke billowing behind the engine. A second shot cuts to a longer side-view of the train which rushes by the camera, offering a clear position from which to see the engineer and his assistant leap from the smoking cab and hurtle to the side of the track. Hence, when the telegrapher rushes back to the station and 'wires ahead to stop the Express', the compensatory gesture is meaningless. It is 'too late', that is, not simply because the telegrapher left the 'wrong train order', but also because the express is running 'wild', as an intertitle exclaims: 'Without a Guiding Hand at the Throttle.' Entirely unmanned, so to speak, the system's functioning has collapsed, both inside the station and on the tracks.

I should hasten to add that plenty of villains appear in these films, motivated by greed, sometimes revenge: the usual suspects. But even when malicious motives pre-cipitate the crisis of a respective episode and set the narrative sequence in motion, that crisis is invariably staged as a spectacle of technology out of control. The limit case of this shift in register surfaces in those episodes that abandon entirely charac-ters of nefarious intention and even more quickly, to indulge the vernacular, 'cut to the chase'. In *The Race for Life* a pair of malfunctioning brakes prompt Helen's race after the 'runaway engine'. In *The Death Siding* a 'premature blast' in a mining camp 'blows the brakeman off the deck' of a lumber car, causing the freight train to 'run wild'. In *The Death Swing* a 'newly invented safety stop for trains seems certain of success when the locomotive is sent running wild down the tracks'.[14] It is telling in this regard that one writer for *The Moving Picture World* pronounced *A Daring Chance* 'refreshingly lacking' in 'deeply villainous themes'. The 'high pitch' of excitement emerges, rather, when a 'little boy, through a series of circumstances, is left alone on a racing gasoline-driven handcar. He is traveling to certain death through collision with a stalled train, when Helen is notified of the little fellow's plight.'[15] Notwithstanding the reviewer's interest in that 'series of circumstances' which evidently replaces villainy as the motivating cause of thrilling instability, we must not miss a seemingly inconspicuous but related detail: the racing handcar is headed for 'a stalled train'.

As these accumulating examples suggest, the Helen films generate a narrative domain steeped not in the lexicon of personal or ethical dilemmas but much more precisely in a force field of shock and trauma, terms that bear a particularly significant relationship to the entangled histories of modern subjectivity and modern technology, including that of the cinema. As Wolfgang Schivelbusch reveals in his study of the nineteenth century railroad, the recognition that anxiety, fright, and fear of the railway accident could reverberate through the body as a whole and manifest physical symptoms led to the first diagnosis of traumatic neurosis, to the phenomenal growth of nerve study centers across the Western world, and ultimately to the theory of hysteria formulated by Freud and Breuer at the end of the century.[16] In her study of the train as cinema's 'mechanical double', Lynn Kirby shows how a fin de siècle cinema mimics technology's destabilizing effects, providing an experience of hysteria as viewing pleasure: a 'technological seduction fantasy – a culturally based fantasy of desiring displacement, movement, trauma, even destruction'.[17] Read in relation to such films as *Uncle Josh at the Moving Picture Show* (1902), or *The Photographer's Mishap* (1901), both of which display male figures succumbing to hysterical fits in response, respectively, to watching a projected image of a moving train, or while attempting to capture a moving image of the train, the fantasy of which Kirby speaks 'undoes' (shocks or hystericizes) codes of sexual difference. Her work thus extends Tom Gunning's rich theorization of an aesthetics of 'attraction' and 'astonishment' in the earliest cinema to the disorientation of social and subjective forms of identity.

My interest in the study of hysteria, or shock, or astonishment as a key aesthetic effect of early film form, however, emerges from my dissatisfaction with the way that both traditional and revisionist historians have told the story of cinema's turn to a predominantly narrative form. Although it is debated as to when, precisely, the transition to a narrative cinema takes place, it is roughly understood to be ensconced by 1906–7 and linked in conspicuous ways to the construction of a temporal economy. The linearity associated with the chase film in these years stresses the orientation towards temporal flow, but it is the interrelation of different spaces and times provided by parallel editing that provides early cinema with its most basic narrative armature. As Gunning puts it, 'parallel editing typifies, without exhausting, the systematic nature that cinematic narration begins to display around 1908'.[18] This periodizing date is hardly accidental, linked as it is to the inauguration of D. W. Griffith's six-year experiment with race-to-the-rescue films at Biograph, and to the elaboration of a narrative paradigm that has come to mark a crucial and irreducible transition whereby 'the thrills of the cinema of attractions were transmuted into family dramas, and the ballyhoo of the fairground was refined into the suspenseful resolutions of parallel editing'.[19] This constellation of terms is remarkably telling. Here the coalition of a particular genre ('family dramas'), with a formal property of narrative ('resolution'), forged through a cinematic technique ('parallel editing'), emphasizes the interrelated properties of a mechanism that manages to reassert traditional social codes, especially those associated with the bourgeois family milieu and the heterosexual couple, by systematizing both time and space: bodies are put in their 'proper' place; their actions wedded to, and resolved in, time.

This dictum is perhaps most familiar to us from Raymond Bellour's celebrated structural analysis of Griffith's *The Lonedale Operator* (1911). Exemplary as the first 'railway' variation on the domestic-based paradigm that Griffith relentlessly rehearsed at Biograph, *The Lonedale Operator* is reminiscent of *The Hazards of Helen* insofar as it tells the story of a crisis on the railway and prominently figures a young female telegrapher (Blanche Sweet). But here the crisis is prompted by a pair of bandits who invade the telegrapher's isolated station, intent on stealing money locked in the safe, and danger emanates from the threat posed to the telegrapher's body. At the moment she becomes aware of the danger, Sweet frantically telegraphs for help: her message inaugurates an editing pattern that alternates between the bandits breaking into the station, Sweet's attempt to defend herself by tricking them into believing the wrench she holds in her hand is a gun, and her boyfriend/ engineer racing to the rescue. Of particular interest to Bellour are the ways in which this film generates what he terms 'textual volume' – a system of repetitive echoes that structure and unite the narrative level (with its emphasis on sexual difference and the formation of the couple) and the formal level (different patterns of symmetry and asymmetry in the composition of the frame, in figure movement and visual rhymes). Alternation thus emerges as the cinematic armature that weaves together a series of thematic and diegetic contrasts around the basic opposition of the couple he/she, and makes the formation of the heterosexual couple the film's raison d'être and final, meaningful, goal: meaningful, that is, precisely because the end takes us back to the beginning, back to the origin of the drama, to the time before the separation of the couple, the union of which appeared – for a time – to be lost.[20]

The 'repetition-resolution' effect that Bellour extrapolates from this early film defines, he argues elsewhere, the logic of American cinema's classical narrative 'machine' more broadly, one that operates in accordance with the psychical apparatus that Freud described in *Beyond the Pleasure Principle*. Prompted by the phenomena of shell-shocked soldiers, Freud argues that the repetition of traumatic experiences in the soldier's dreams serves to retrospectively master the flood of stimuli by developing an anxiety which earlier was lacking (and hence allowed the break in the stimulus shield in the first place), a psychical process Freud links to the game his grandson played immediately following the mother's departure. While throwing a cotton-string with a reel attached to it out of his crib and then pulling it back in, the child made sounds that Freud interpreted as 'fort' (there it goes) and 'da' (here it is). The psychical significance of the game emerges from a repre- sentational process that replays the loss of that first object – the mother – in a manner that allows the child a sense of mastery over loss.[21] As Tom Gunning aptly notes, although Freud's interest in the 'technical and historical aspects [of psychic trauma] are ultimately superficial', the anxiety of technological breakdown, of being 'cut off' that Gunning reads in relation to Griffith's early rescue films, suggest an important overlap between what we have understood as inherent psychical drives and the 'way technology structures modern life'.[22] Through repeated scenarios of separation, threat, and rescue, Griffith mobilizes an alliance between technology and narrative that brings things back together, injecting time with desire and restoring the promise of continuity and control. Noting in particular the engineer's purposeful race back to the station in *The Lonedale Operator*, Kirby claims that:

> the train in Griffith became an agent and an object made to serve human agents . . . In a sense, one could argue that he tamed the train by recoding it for narrative purposes; his engineer-driven trains are a far cry from the out-of-control thrill train of early films.[23]

For Gunning it is the telegraph in this film, like the telephone in Griffith's earlier *The Lonely Villa* (1909), that gets coded for narrative purposes, 'naturaliz[ing] film's power to move through space and time'.[24] Ultimately what technology naturalizes in these films, as Mary Ann Doane elaborates, is the 'confirmation and reconfirmation of heterosexuality, which in turn lends its "intelligibility" to the cinematic desire to overcome distance, separation, the inevitability of absence'.[25]

To conceptualize narrative cinema as collaborating in this way with desire to 'overcome' the anxieties provoked by technologically induced uncertainty (including cinema's immediate past), however, does not rule out the possibility of cinema inventing an alternative response to the anxieties of the era. In the early action film, as we have seen, editing galvanizes the vision of a world in which things repeatedly, relentlessly break down, dismantling the efficacy of the system that insisted on their conjunction in the first place. Rather than revising the system, the Helen films offer the fantasy of a revised human body, one built to withstand the velocity of speed. This ontological drama is dramatically displayed in the axiomatic chase sequence that concludes most every episode of *The Hazards of Helen* (and remains virtually indispensable to contemporary incarnations of the genre as well). Consider, for instance, this typical review of the series' inaugural five episodes for readers of *Pictures and Picturegoers*:

> In 'Helen's Sacrifice' she rode a horse over a fifty-foot cliff, and leapt from the saddle onto the footplate of a fast speeding locomotive. In 'The Girl at the Throttle' she averted a terrible railroad disaster by driving an engine at sixty miles an hour. In 'The Stolen Engine' she leapt from the footplate of one engine onto the cab of another travelling in the same direction on a parallel track. In 'The Black Diamond Express' she made an exciting dash through the clouds in a monster biplane. In 'The Escape on the Limited' she drove a steam railcar at breakneck speed.[26]

Here the rhythmic repetition of a central referent – 'she' – reifies Helen as the series' irrefutable protagonist. What remains questionable is what we mean when we talk about things like character, or subject, or protagonist. The description of this 'she' is almost entirely devoid of individuation in the traditional sense. Helen never *is*, she only *does* – 'she rode'; 'she averted'; 'she leapt'; 'she drove'. Positioned as fully consistent with 'engines' and 'railcars' and 'monster biplanes', Helen is less a proper subject than what we might call a mechanical character, which is another way of saying this character is flat, lacking traditional forms of psychological depth, absorption, and contemplation. In other words, rather than naturalizing technology, technology here denaturalizes the human body, rendering it surprisingly unfamiliar, its movements astonishing. That this body is specifically a 'she' indicates the degree to which the action film intensifies the upheavals associated at the turn of the century with both technological trauma and emerging instabilities of changing gender identity.

Although likening one of the most dynamic female characters from the silent era to a mechanical object may seem a perverse critical move, it has the advantage of revealing a narrative system necessarily divorced from a psychological framework and, hence, from the fantasies of mastery, perfectibility, and homogeneity such models presuppose. We can explore this hypothesis by considering *The Leap from the Water Tower*, the 9th episode of the series, which articulates a conjunction between the two terms – 'character', 'machine' – with remarkable precision in the eight shots that comprise its opening sequence. The film opens with an intertitle, introducing 'The Largest Locomotive in the World', followed by a medium long shot of its referent. The second shot of the film offers no introduction proper, abruptly cutting to a group of three men standing near the tracks. Two of the men, wearing neatly identical hats, stand in symmetrical positions on either side of the screen. Slouching between them the third figure, visually coded as 'different' by his bare head and dirty overalls, gesticulates wildly, the histrionics suggesting a barely constrained anger. A second intertitle intervenes with a descriptive bit of business, declaring that 'the trainmaster goes over the road', and a medium close shot frames a stately gray-haired gentleman walking along the tracks, studying a clipboard. The remaining five shots follow summarily, beginning with an intertitle introducing 'Helen, the girl telegrapher', followed, in rapid succession, by an alternating pattern that cuts between Helen arriving at the station and the train departing down the line.

As an expository scene this sequence of shots intrigues. The mounting tension enacted between the three men in shot two motivates the sequence of story-events to come: shortly the disgruntled worker will start another fight, will be fired by the trainmaster, and will retaliate by dismantling the brakes on 'The Largest Locomotive in the World'. To the extent that this second shot forms the locus of the story's 'action', however, the camera paradoxically occupies a noticeably stationary position. Rather than mobilizing the film frame as a way of directing the viewer's look at the three men, the physical bodies of the actors function as a framing device. Likewise the trainmaster – whose walk along the tracks in the third shot suggests the proximity of his narrative space with that of the three male workers, and whose figure is preceded with an expository intertitle – is solely *described* vis-à-vis his position with regards to the railway corporation and his narrative activity rather than *identified* or named. In contrast, it is impossible to ignore the camera's diligence in conferring the principle of movement on those two figures introduced as characters per se, namely 'Helen, the girl telegrapher' and 'The Largest Locomotive in the World'. The dynamic conjunction of this pairing begins with the set of mirrored introductory intertitles (each followed with an establishing shot of the respective figure) and culminates in a series of orchestrated 'echoes' and 'visual rhymes' produced across shots four through eight. Shots four, six and eight chart Helen's arrival at the station; shots one, five and seven chart the train's departure down the line. The corresponding movements (though in divergent directions) are quite noticeably matched: in shot four Helen enters the visual field and moves across the frame from right to left; in shot five the train enters the visual field and moves across the frame from left to right. Shots six and seven, each held for similar duration, emphasize through symmetry what is seemingly dissimilar. A long shot centering the train as it moves slowly through the valley corresponds with a medium shot centering Helen's figure as she dismounts from her horse to start her day.

It should be clear by now that all 119 episodes of *The Hazards of Helen* do not uniformly confirm the diegetic arrangement of this opening sequence. I have lingered on this reading, however, because it vividly stresses narrative cinema's capacity for rerouting the motivation and psychology associated with character into sheer spectacle, a technological display. Moreover, it is the intensification of this spectacle, the movement associated with both Helen and the train (rather than the elaboration and alleviation of the villain's crimes), towards which the film relentlessly drives. That it does so through a systematic application of parallel editing cues us to a narrative logic that both mimes and subverts the 'systematicity at the heart of high classicism' which Bellour extrapolated from *The Lonedale Operator*. Speaking of the girl telegrapher and her engineer/boyfriend who walk together to the station in the opening of that film, Bellour writes: 'The diegetic couple, scarcely formed, only separates obviously to meet again, to strengthen its image by the test of a dramatised separation whose internal form is alternation.'[27] *The Leap from the Water Tower* follows, in rudimentary fashion, this logic of alternation, dramatizing a separation of its inaugural terms 'girl' and 'train' only in order to forcefully restore them. Alternating between the train hurtling through the valley and Helen racing on horseback to the side of the track, the editing pattern crescendos to sensational velocity, pausing momentarily when Helen dismounts, lunges toward the water tower and, as the title has foretold, leaps atop the speeding train.

Far from a homeostatic model that 'aims at . . . the regulated order of the spectacle', this narrative machine is calibrated for spectacular excess,[28] relocating the signification of force and power to the performative rather than hermeneutic elements of the film. Seen in this light we may understand why Sergei Eisenstein drew from sensation films like *The Hazards of Helen* when formulating the famous principle of attractions underlying his experiments with shock-like montage techniques. Indeed, as Yuri Tsivian has argued in an illuminating essay, it is possible to see the emergence of a Soviet avant-garde cinema in the 1920s more broadly as a response to the pervasive influence of American series and serial films from the

1910s. Tsivian quotes Viktor Shklovsky, whose 1919 essay 'On Cinema', admonished his comrades: 'stop wasting film on psychological rummaging and all those arty prose poems clearly alien to the constitution of cinema.'[29] Opposed to the general perception that 'nineteenth century novels served as natural prototypes for films', Shklovsky demurred the value of plot and other 'literary devices' as central properties of the film 'material', arguing that 'plot in film is only necessary to motivate the *tryuk* [trick, stunt, acrobatic feat]'. Emphatically, however, this primary unit or material of the cinema is not simply the *tryuk* or physical performance alone, but rather a 'certain method of filming it'.[30] Put simply, at the hinge where cinematic movement links formally to the moving body, the image assumes a dynamic, uncertain volatility, attaining what Shklovsky privileged as the pre-eminent goal of art: the capacity to make things strange (*ostraniene*), and thus to cut a reflexive path through the viewer's habituated responses to the everyday.

Whether or not we want to agree with Shklovsky that early action films like *The Hazards of Helen* manifest cinema's primary raison d'être, it should be clear that the genre's structure and design offer us something different. It offers, that is, a plot designed to flaunt difference, to defamiliarize the familiar, to unsettle (rather than restore) the viewer's equilibrium. What is important for film historical discourse is our capacity to grasp the multiple narrative forms through which American cinema registered and reflected the technological culture of which it was both symptom and part. Only then may we move beyond psychoanalytic (much less cognitive) models of subjectivity and viewing pleasure to account for the body's 'mindless' pleasures in our assessments of twentieth century media culture. That such a project involves a reformulation of our relation to time, a desire for something other than a lost past, is illuminated by modern theorists such as Martin Heidegger and Walter Benjamin for whom the 'lostness' of the ever-evasive *present*, the inability to inhabit 'the moment', conditioned the sense of alienation underlying daily life in the modern metropolis. It also meant that cognitive or rational ideals must be subordinated to alternative models built on bodily sensation, wherein the present might not be recognized but, importantly, experienced. For Heidegger, in Leo Charney's neat summation, the 'present's lostness could be partly redeemed by valorizing the sensual, bodily, prerational responses that retain the prerogative to occupy a present moment'.[31] To experience the moment's intensity – to experience it as a bodily reverberation rather than a cognitive process – was, in Benjamin's terms, an experience of shock. Or, one might say, the experience of a trauma that thrills.

## Notes

1  See Jeffrey T. Schnapp 'Crash (Speed as Engine of Individuation)', *Modernism/Modernity*, 6: 1, 1999, p. 3.

2  'Attractions' is a term Tom Gunning, in conjunction with André Gaudreault, famously borrowed from Sergei Eisenstein to rethink a fin de siècle aesthetic in which spectacle prevails over story-telling, movement over meaning, and astonishment over absorption. Gunning's rich theorization of an early cinema that flaunted its mechanical prowess, effecting an aesthetic on a par with the indeterminacy associated with technological modernity, has influenced my thinking in this essay. I thank him as well for ongoing conversations

that continue to illuminate my work on this material. On the cinema of attractions, see in particular 'Now You See It, Now You Don't: The Temporality of the Cinema of Attractions', *The Velvet Light Trap*, 32, Fall 1993, pp. 3–11; and 'The Whole Town's Gawking: Early Cinema and the Visual Experience of Modernity', *The Yale Journal of Criticism*, 7: 2, 1994, pp. 189–201.

3   *New York Dramatic Mirror*, 24, September 2, 1914. Hereafter *NYDM*.

4   Description of 'Crossed Wires' in '"Helen" Has A Birthday: Kalem's Hazardous Heroine Starts Second Year of Her Charmed Life This Month', *NYDM*, December 4, 1915, p. 34; Review for 'The Gate of Death', *The Moving Picture World*, November 11, 1916, p. 843. Hereafter *MPW*.

5   '"Helen" Has A Birthday', ibid.

6   *NYDM*, October 14, 1916, p. 30.

7   Abel's essay describes pre-1914 'sensational' cinema, and the role American sensation films played in early 'culture wars'.

8   See Ben Singer *Melodrama and Modernity: Early Sensational Cinema and Its Contexts*, New York: Columbia University Press, 2001, p. 224.

9   See Miriam Hansen *Babel and Babylon: Spectatorship in American Silent Film*, Cambridge, MA: Harvard University Press, 1991, pp. 119–20; Lynn Kirby *Parallel Tracks: The Railroad and Silent Cinema*, Durham: Duke University Press, 1997, pp. 110–16; Eileen Bowser *The Transformation of Cinema: 1907–1915*, New York: Charles Scribner's Sons, 1990, p. 187; Shelley Stamp *Movie-Struck Girls: Women and Motion Picture Culture After The Nickelodeon*, Princeton, NJ: Princeton University Press, 2000, pp. 139–40.

10   As Kathy Peiss has noted, following the rise of the nickelodeon, 'women's attendance [at the movies] soared; women comprised 40 percent of the working-class movie audience in 1910'. See Peiss *Cheap Amusements: Working Women and Leisure in Turn-of-the-Century New York*, Philadelphia: Temple University Press, 1986, p. 148.

11   Singer *Melodrama and Modernity*, p. 253.

12   See Kathleen Woodward 'Statistical Panic', *Differences: A Journal of Feminist Cultural Studies*, 11: 2, Summer 1999, p. 187 and Mary Russo *The Female Grotesque: Risk, Excess, and Modernity*, New York: Routledge, 1995, p. 11.

13   'Review of *The Wrong Train Order*', *NYDM*, December 4, 1915, p. 34.

14   On *The Race for Life* see 'Helen Receives a Present', *MPW*, February 26, 1916, p. 1288; 'The Death Siding', *MPW*, February 17, 1917, p. 1074; 'The Death Swing', *MPW*, October 14, 1916, p. 290.

15   *MPW*, October 21, 1916, p. 379.

16   Wolfgang Schivelbusch *The Railway Journey: The Industrialization of Time and Space in the 19th Century*, Berkeley: University of California Press, 1986, chapters 9 and 10.

17   Kirby *Parallel Tracks*, p. 68.

18   Tom Gunning 'Heard Over the Phone: The Lonely Villa and the de Lorde Tradition of the Terrors of Technology' in Annette Kuhn and Jackie Stacey (eds) *Screen Histories: A Screen Reader*, Oxford: Oxford University Press, 1998, pp. 218–19.

19   Tom Gunning *D. W. Griffith and the Origins of American Narrative Film*, Urbana and Chicago: University of Illinois Press, 1991, p. 90.

20   Raymond Bellour 'To Alternate/To Narrate' in Thomas Elsaesser (ed.) *Early Cinema: Space, Frame, Narrative*, London: British Film Institute, 1990, pp. 360–74.

21   Sigmund Freud *Beyond the Pleasure Principle*, trans. and ed. by James Strachey, New York: W. W. Norton and Company, 1961, especially pp. 10–17.

22   Gunning 'Heard Over the Phone', pp. 219, 227.

23   Kirby *Parallel Tracks*, p. 108.

24   Gunning 'Heard Over the Phone', p. 219.

25   Mary Ann Doane *The Emergence of Cinematic Time: Modernity, Contingency, The Archive*, Cambridge, MA: Harvard University Press, 2002, p. 196.

26   *Pictures and Picturegoers*, December 1915.

27   Bellour 'To Alternate/To Narrate', pp. 360, 373–4.

28  The quoted material is borrowed from Raymond Bellour 'Cine-Repetitions', *Screen*, 20: 2, Summer 1979, quoted in Constance Penley *The Future of an Illusion: Film, Feminism, Psychoanalysis*, Minneapolis: University of Minnesota Press, 1989, p. 71.

29  Yuri Tsivian 'Between the Old and the New: Soviet Film Culture in 1918–1924', *Griffithiana*, 55/56, 1996, p. 41.

30  Viktor Shklovsky *Literatura i kinematograph*, 1923, quoted in Tsivian, 'Between the Old and the New', p. 43.

31  See Leo Charney 'In a Moment: Film and the Philosophy of Modernity' in Leo Charney and Vanessa R. Schwartz (eds) *Cinema and the Invention of Modern Life*, Berkeley: University of California Press, 1995, p. 281.

## Chapter 2

## RICHARD ABEL

# THE 'CULTURE WAR' OF SENSATIONAL MELODRAMA, 1910–14

> The foreign manufacturers have been taught their lesson. More and more care is being shown in preparing films for the American market. . . . They are eliminating objectionable scenes, and through their American agents, who strive to give clear, decisive criticisms of the films sent here, the European producers get closer to the American ideal.[1]

**T**HE WORDS ARE HERBERT BLACHÉ'S, from a prominently displayed interview in the *New York Dramatic Mirror* in February 1913, and his position as vice-president of the Gaumont Company – specifically, its American representative – made it easy to assume that he 'should know something about the American market for foreign films'. Nearly a century later, this kind of claim persists as a familiar trope in histories of early American cinema, most recently in Eileen Bowser's admirable *The Transformation of Cinema, 1907–1915*, where one can find this sentence: 'Pathé Frères and other foreign producers were quick to observe American tastes and morals, and as the American market was the biggest . . . the films sent here would be those that they knew to be acceptable'.[2] Strictly speaking, this was true of the early 1910s, if by 'acceptable' one means acceptance by the National Board of Censorship. Yet once one follows the discursive traces of how foreign films, especially French films, circulated and were received during this period, the claim becomes more difficult to substantiate. Indeed, Blaché himself might have found his words a bit embarrassing just six months later, when Gaumont began to release its famous *Fantomas* series on the US market – to a far from welcome response.

Within the context of 'American tastes and morals', the principal object of concern during the early 1910s was what the trade press labeled *thriller melodramas* or *sensational melodramas*. In a survey of film releases during the month of July 1910, for instance, the *Mirror* classified 52 out of a total of 241 titles as 'thriller melodramas', with Cowboy and Indian subjects making up nearly half of them.[3] These melodramas were unusually popular, particularly with what the trade press often described as the 'ordinary moving picture audience', 'average crowd', or 'public' – all terms that served to mask the 'masses' of young working-class and white-collar workers who so often frequented the picture shows.[4] While generally 'not elevating in taste and . . . worthless as examples of art', the *Mirror* argued in early 1912, such thrillers still could be produced in such a way as to 'appeal to all classes' as a 'perfectly legitimate type of drama'.[5] The class division not so artfully elided in this trade press discourse, however, also had a corollary, more fractious component: a perceived difference between American and 'foreign' values and tastes. For both the *Mirror* and *Moving Picture World* assumed a 'European public . . . not yet educated up to the American standard', a public to which French producers in particular catered with the worst 'melodrama thrillers' – full of criminal activity, excessive violence, and morbidity.[6] As exports on the US market, these French crime thrillers seemed a serious moral and social threat to the work of 'uplifting' and 'Americanizing' the masses (many of them recent immigrants); and throughout the period, their 'otherness' provoked a kind of 'culture war' waged in the trade press and newspapers.[7] In short, that culture war served to codify what would be acceptable, even legitimate, and distinctly 'American' about the popular forms of sensational melodrama in moving pictures – and what was not.

As Ben Singer has demonstrated so persuasively, sensational melodrama already would have been familiar in a variety of forms to many movie-goers in the early 1910s.[8] Some might have recalled the fast-paced action, one dangerous situation after another, and frequent violence in the dime novels or story papers of the 1870s and 1880s – from western and detective series to workingman and workingwoman tales.[9] Most, however, would have had firsthand experience of the 'blood-and-thunder sensationalism' that so marked popular 10–20–30 stage melodramas in the 1890s and 1900s.[10] Although the chiefly contemporary stories of great peril presented in these plays retained the basic elements of earlier melodrama – 'moral opposition, pathos, extreme emotion, and structural incoherence' – their 'crucial attraction' now, Singer argues, was 'graphic action and intense spectacles of danger', particularly as worked out in 'sensation scenes' that exploited the latest innovations in stagecraft technology.[11] Lincoln J. Carter's *The Eye Witness* offers just one of many examples:

> A daring leap by a huge automobile over a partially opened jack-knife bridge spanning the Chicago River; then a girl is rescued from the lake in which the hero is seen to dive after her and cut away the weights fastened to her by the villain in his dastardly attempt to murder her; as a hair-raising finish, a great cyclone scene in which houses are wrecked, trees uprooted and the villain finally killed by a shaft of lightning.[12]

In 1907–8, however, these stage melodramas began to suffer what would turn into a precipitous decline as their audience of working-class and white-collar amusement-seekers suddenly abandoned them en masse for the moving picture shows, where they could howl, scream, and marvel at even more 'credible', more spectacular 'sensation scenes' – and at far less expense.[13]

If sensational melodrama already was a popular American cultural form, with a certain class affiliation, long before its prominence in moving pictures, the 'problem' of foreign, particularly French sensationalism also was not without precedent. During the heyday of the dime novel, for instance, publishers reprinted European fiction as often as they printed 'original' American work because costs were lower even if texts had to be translated. French *fait divers* fiction made up an unusually large portion of that translated material, according to ongoing research by Carol Armbruster at the Library of Congress, and its alleged immorality and morbidity often was cited in testimony by librarians at US Congress hearings in the late 1880s.[14] The result of those hearings was a copyright law that banned such piracy, not only to support American writers but to protect American readers from 'unhealthy' foreign influences. A similar 'problem' arose twenty years later, as I myself have argued, when French Pathé-Frères films became the predominant fare of the nickelodeons from 1905 to 1908.[15] Here, the newly emergent trade press, along with certain national magazines, engaged in a loosely coordinated culture war to control what was again seen as undue French influence. An early *Variety* review, for instance, condemned Pathé's *Christmas Eve Tragedy* (see Figure 2.1) – which ended with a horse, cart, and driver thrown off a cliff into the sea – as no less unfit for children than the 'interior view of a slaughterhouse' and so reprehensible as to justify censorship.[16] The film was a prime example of the French *grand guignol* melodrama that the trade press increasingly described as 'inappropriately sensational'. American 'ethical melodrama', it was argued, was very different because, even though filled with equally sensational attractions, it concluded with a 'bright, happy denouement'.[17] In that it drew on all that was considered risqué, deviant, and morally suspect in French culture, therefore, French sensational melodrama had to be curbed and for much the same reasons as before: to support American manufacturers as well as to protect American audiences.

Given this recent history, the culture war that erupted in the early 1910s at first may seem surprising. After all, the Motion Picture Patents Company (MPPC), founded in late 1908, had set weekly limits on the number of imported reels of French films; and the National Board of Censorship, instituted in early 1909, was forcing manufacturers, both French and American, to cut or make other changes in their films and even withdraw some from circulation.[18] Pathé had seemed to capitulate to the American market in 1910, by constructing an East Coast studio to produce its own American films, 'with American actors and scenarios', and by reducing its weekly releases from France.[19] Later that same year, the company also won accolades for arranging a special score of Verdi's music to accompany its stencil-color adaptation of *Il Trovatore*.[20] Moreover, according to a *World* editorial, in June 1910, Gaumont films now rivaled those of Biograph in 'pictorial quality' – the 'chiaroscuro . . . always true to nature and well-balanced'.[21] Yet a residual animosity toward the 'otherness' of French culture persisted, always ready to be tapped. When, in early 1910, the National Board of Censorship passed Pathé's 'ghastly' Russian tale, *Ouchard the Merchant*, for instance, *Variety* harshly criticized

*Figure 2.1* Poster for Pathé-Frères, *Nuit de Noël (Christmas Eve Tragedy)*, 1908

the Board for having the gall to unleash such 'bestialities' on the public.[22] In a crusade against moving pictures the following fall, the *New York World* repeatedly invoked the stereotypes of bad taste and immorality associated with the French, attacking a bull fight film erroneously attributed to Pathé and once again lambasting *Christmas Eve Tragedy*, which it failed to recognize as a two-year old 'junk film'.[23] None of these attacks amounted to more than scattered potshots, however, so what exactly provoked the outcry that for the next few years would increasingly target French 'melodrama thrillers'?

From late 1910 through late 1911, the trade press was preoccupied with riding herd on American rather than French sensational melodramas – especially what the *World* saw as a virtual stampede of 'stupid Indian and Cowboy subjects'.[24] In February, for instance, *Nickelodeon* claimed that 'the Western photoplay [had] outrun its course of usefulness and [was] slated for an early demise'.[25] In campaigning against 'the fla-grant abuse' of 'crime posters', the *World* consistently cited those for 'blood-curdling buffalo, Indians, and cowboy' films.[26] When westerns continued to multiply, *Moving Picture News* later that year cited the great number of letters from movie-goers who were 'utterly sick and tired . . . of Wild West pictures', and prodded independent companies such as the New York Motion Picture Company (NYMP), with its Bison brand, to either stop making them or turn them into 'elevating, uplifting stor[ies]'.[27] The *World* took up the attack once more, grousing that the 'perfect riot of these "Wild West" things' had 'gone far enough' – and the *Mirror* soon echoed the petu-lant complaint.[28] No one, of course, failed to recognize that 'average audiences'

everywhere found westerns enormously appealing, prompting a passel of companies
– Selig, Essanay, Kalem, NYMP, Champion, American (Flying A), and even Pathé
– to invest heavily in their making.[29] Despite its reservations, the *News* had to admit
that 'they abound[ed] in the life, snap, and vigor that mean so much to M. P. audiences'.[30] The problem with westerns, and other thriller melodramas, rarely involved
excessive violence or immorality; rather, the stories were too conventional, the
characters too stereotypical, and the spectacle of action too repetitive. The prescription was a transformation of American sensational melodramas into something
more than the 'ordinary', something capable of attracting a mass audience rather than
just the masses. Evidence of that began to appear not only in westerns but in Civil
War films and jungle or wild animal pictures by late 1911.

Staking a claim as the 'indisputable originators of Cowboy Films',[31] Essanay
offered one example of that transformation in its weekly series of westerns, directed
by and starring G. M. Anderson. Promoted as the 'most photographed man' in the
business, Anderson became known as 'Bullets' in northeastern Ohio, where several
newspapers testified to his status as an early movie personality or star with special
stories in the fall of 1911.[32] In fact, in the steel-producing centers of Canton and
Youngstown, 'Bullets' Anderson, who usually played a 'good badman' – an outlaw
with enough conscience to finally turn away from crime and lead an honorable life
– was a regular favorite with working-class audiences on Sunday movie programs.
This redemptive character also often had the benefit of strong stories, as in *Broncho
Billy's Christmas Dinner*, which, according to the *Mirror*'s unusually warm review,
featured a 'thrilling ride on a stage coach' as well as impressive acting 'in the quieter
moments'.[33] Biograph offered another striking example in *The Battle*: the *Mirror*
described its 'displays of large and realistic battle scenes' that made the spectator
feel like an eye witness to history as the 'most spectacular' in Civil War films –
then just coming into vogue on the fiftieth anniversary of that devastating conflict.[34]
More than a month after its release, in one of its first Sunday pages devoted to
moving pictures, the *Cleveland Leader* still recommended *The Battle* as an 'exceptional' film, 'so much better than even the manufacturers claimed', particularly for
its 'elaborate battle scenes'.[35] Finally, Selig offered a third example in what it then
considered the 'climax' of a popular animal picture series, *Lost in the Jungle*.[36] As
one testament to its appeal, *Lost in the Jungle* was the only film held over for extra
screenings in Canton that fall.[37] Whereas the *World* reveled in the film's thrilling
situations, in which Kathlyn Williams was threatened by leopards and rescued by
an elephant, the *Mirror*, with its eye on potential middle-class audiences, stressed
the undeniably powerful effect of the film's 'jungle atmosphere and . . . dangers'
that held 'the spectator breathless at times'.[38]

None of these sensational melodramas ran more than the standard length of
one reel, but they shared the screen that fall and winter with a number of multiple-
reel films – from Kalem's *Colleen Bawn* or Selig's *Two Orphans* (both adaptations of
familiar stage melodramas) to Milano's *Dante's Inferno* – all of which began to establish the 'special feature' as a successful, regularly released and exhibited format.[39]
Interestingly, several French films were among them, and at least two are especially pertinent. Pathé's *In the Grip of Alcohol*, a two-reel reworking of temperance

stage melodramas, in which an entire family is destroyed by a father's drunkenness, received conflicting critical response. The *Mirror* found it 'one of the most powerful picture sermons ever', and the *Cleveland Leader* echoed that high praise at the beginning of the film's month-long run in that city.[40] Although admitting the force of its 'terrible lesson', however, the *World* believed that its story was so 'sordid, disagreeable' as to overwhelm audiences with a 'feeling of disgust'.[41] Surprisingly, there was no such concern over the effect of Éclair's three-reel *Zigomar*, which, in a series of sensation scenes, recounted the exploits of a master criminal who, often in the disguise of a modern capitalist entrepreneur – 'clever, reckless, and thoroughly immoral in his lust for lucre' – continually eluded capture.[42] Critics everywhere hailed the film as 'a masterpiece of sensationalism', a 'notable film' that masterfully '[held] the mirror up to modern life'.[43] Prominent ads for *Zigomar* ran for more than a month in the *Cleveland Leader*, and the film itself was said to 'pack' no less than three downtown theaters on consecutive Sundays in December and January, before circulating through other theaters and then returning three months later for a three-day run at a new legitimate theater in the suburbs.[44] In Youngstown, the film played on consecutive Sundays at not one but two theaters – one of which, the Rex, was owned in part by the Warner brothers.[45]

How does one account for *Zigomar*'s critical and commercial success, for its acceptance as 'appropriately' sensational? After all, Zigomar was not only the leader of a gang for whom murder simply could be the means to an elaborate robbery but a sexual predator as well, and he was responsible for a number of sensation scenes that masked his repeated escapes from the Paris police: a spectacular fire at the Moulin Rose music hall and an explosion that destroyed his subterranean headquarters in the deserted, ironically named Saint Magloire cathedral.[46] Moreover, the catalogue of 'inappropriate' French behavior or 'bad taste' so often invoked by American writers certainly was in vogue at the time – as a weekly column in the *Chicago Daily News* attests, describing at length 'an average French tragedy' in moving pictures.[47] It is possible that Éclair deleted certain scenes or shots from the film and reworked some intertitles for the US market, yet not all that much must have been cut or changed for it was released, as in France, in three reels. The sheer novelty of the 'special feature', especially one whose subject probably was unfamiliar to American audiences – and to many reviewers, for the fictional series on which the film was based had not been translated – must have contributed to *Zigomar*'s success. An added attraction must have been the film's craft in using the new 'feature' format, making it a model for how filmmakers could develop an intensely exciting narrative over several thousand feet of film. All this must have outweighed any hesitations or doubts felt by a critic such as W. Stephen Bush, who usually detested sensational melodramas, for he cited *Zigomar* as a prime example of the 'quality' that had to be maintained in the continued production of 'long films'.[48] That attitude toward French sensational features would not endure, however, and the reemergence of a 'French threat' can be traced not only in the reception of later French films (and news events) but in that of 'improved' American sensational melodrama features.

In late 1911, NYMP offered a perfect example of the western's transformation with the announcement that it was abandoning the 'regular style of Indian and cowboy pictures' in its Bison films and hiring Thomas Ince to make 'nothing but sensational, spectacular Western subjects, with enormous casts' drawn from the riders, horses, and stock of the famous Miller Brothers 101 Ranch Wild West.[49] These would be two-reel 101-Bison 'features', the earliest to be produced and released regularly on a weekly or bi-weekly basis. According to the company's ads, the first, *War on the Plains* (see Figure 2.2), marked a 'new era in western pictures', and the *World* compared it favorably to the latest historical spectacular from Italy, Ambrosio's *The Golden Wedding*.[50] Others such as *The Indian Massacre*, *The Crisis*, and *The Post Telegrapher* also received glowing reviews; and the *Mirror*, which earlier had denigrated Bison westerns, was especially enthusiastic about *Blazing the Trail*, extolling the 'magnitude of [its] backgrounds' and 'management of . . . exceedingly large number of players' that gave 'an air of reality' to an otherwise familiar narrative of white settlers threatened while crossing the plains.[51] That these spectacular westerns could 'appeal to all classes', and especially the middle class, is clear from the promotional ads and stories that can be found in cities from Cleveland to Des Moines (Iowa).[52] Despite lawsuits, in the summer of 1912, that pitted NYMP against Universal for use of the 101-Bison brand, Ince's productions continued to enjoy unusual critical and commercial success.[53] That fall, for instance, the long-delayed, three-reel *Custer's Last Fight* was promoted in Cleveland on a par with Famous Players' *Queen Elizabeth*.[54] Within months, the company's westerns were being released under the Kay-Bee brand and celebrated even more widely than before. The *Cleveland Leader*, for instance, praised Kay-Bee for 'producing historic subjects . . . worthy of exhibition in any school in the country' and insisted that there was 'no more popular film . . . than [a] Kay-Bee western war picture' such as *The Invaders* or *The Law of the West*.[55]

Similar 'improvements' were noted in other sensational features, from Civil War films to jungle pictures. Before its break-up with Universal, NYMP began adding two-reel 'war pictures' to its growing catalogue of spectacular westerns; and, once they went into release through either the Kay-Bee or Broncho brand, the trade press gave these titles – from *Blood Will Tell* to *The Pride of the South* – an equally warm welcome.[56] At the same time, Universal directed its Bison 101 production unit to make a series of feature 'war pictures' that could compete with those of its former partner/rival. After a special presentation for exhibitors in Columbus, Ohio, in January 1913, for instance, *Sheridan's Ride* was lauded not only as 'the greatest war picture' but the epitome of the 'three salient elements' necessary 'for motion pictures of an educational nature unexpurgated by suggestion, free from crime and clean in text and character': 'intellectual production, veracity, and modified sensationalism'.[57] Yet even this film was topped the following summer by Ince's 'masterpiece', *The Battle of Gettysburg*, whose five reels the *Mirror* described as 'vivid in the extreme and . . . extraordinarily exciting', 'a wonderful visualization of the greatest battle in American history'.[58] Not only was the release of this mammoth production timed for the Independence Day holiday of July 4, but it often played a single theater for more than a week in many cities and also enjoyed

*Figure 2.2* New York Motion Picture, *War on the Plains* (March 1912, Production photo)

return engagements later that summer or fall.[59] Selig continued to exploit the 'novelty and realism' of its popular series of jungle pictures with two-reel features directed by Colin Campbell, from the 'spellbinder' *Kings of the Forest* to *Alone in the Jungle*, the latter of which, in the *World*'s words, 'surpasse[d] all its predecessors in thrilling encounters'.[60] *Kings of the Forest* circulated in Cleveland theaters for at least a month and received a special notice in the *Leader*; and the film's child actor, Lillian Wade, made a stage appearance after each screening at Clune's Main Street Theater in Los Angeles, softening its sensationalism even further with a sentimental touch in one of the earliest such promotional schemes.[61]

In some ways the French themselves sought to 'modify' their own sensational melodramas and minimize any 'threat' they posed on the US market. Both Gaumont and Pathé, for instance, emulated and profited from the vogue for Selig's jungle pictures. Throughout 1912, Gaumont released a series of 'lion pictures' that, in the specific case of *The Lion's Revenge*, won the *Mirror*'s admiration: 'Sensational as it may seem, the circumstance has been treated with much dignity, that both impresses and arouses one's credulance by its plausibility and truth . . . .'[62] As one sign of this series' appeal, the *World* described the 'widely-heralded, sensational, intensely exciting two-reel hand-colored feature entitled *In the Land of the Lion*' as a 'spine tingler' that could not 'be beaten', and the Columbia Theater in Cedar Rapids (Iowa) rebooked the film 'by special request' – and even advised parents to 'bring the children'.[63] Pathé's *The Grotto of Torture* – in which a Hindu priest punishes a 'native' woman who has married an 'English lover' by having her child seized by a 'vicious leopard' and then luring her to a secret grotto from which both have to be rescued – also enjoyed some renown in Cleveland: first screened as a 'special feature' in November at a legitimate theater, the Knickerbocker, it played at other major theaters throughout the following month.[64] Moreover, as long as the sensational was integral to stories 'of a distant era' (even if tragic) – as was the case with American westerns and Civil War films – French features could be not only accepted but lauded. Gaumont's *The Margrave's Daughter*, for instance, won exceptional praise in the trade press: in the *World*, Bush declared the film a 'cinematographic masterpiece' in its 'selection and photographing' of French 'picturesque valleys . . . hills . . . rivers, and ancient castles' and in the 'absolute perfection of detail . . . in the last four or five scenes'.[65] *The Prison on the Cliff* also gained this grudging respect from the *Mirror*: 'The Gaumont Company has again taken a rather sensational situation and idea, and developed it into a most gripping and thoroughly convincing whole.'[66]

Throughout 1912, however, the attitude toward French sensational melodramas began to change, especially toward the crime thriller features with their contemporary stories of 'excessive violence' and 'morbidity'. Although it hardly can be taken as the crucial cause of that shift, one particular news event did serve as a warning signal. In April and May 1912, the capture of the infamous Bonnot gang that had terrorized Paris and other nearby cities received unusual attention in US newspapers.[67] In fact, the *Cleveland Leader* filled the first two pages of its 'Cosmopolitan Section' one Sunday with an extended account of the 'Tiger Bandit' and his gang, written by Maurice Le Blanc, author of *Arsene Lupin*.[68] Previously, such criminals had been depicted as American as often as 'foreign' – as in the full-page 'Auto Cracksman' story published in the *New York Sunday Tribune*, in September 1911 (see Figure 2.3).[69] Thereafter, however, they tended to become fixed as 'foreign' – and typically French. The initial fascination with such a powerful figure, as in *Zigomar* – including its acceptance by moral reformers and the trade press – may have derived from its novelty, in an early 'feature' film, as well as its 'exoticism'. After the Bonnot gang's capture and execution, however, that fascination was tempered as the sensational criminal – especially one who eluded capture and retribution – became a kind of 'foreign' other that definitely could not be assimilated as 'American'.

Towards the end of 1912, the trade press began to express a heightened anxiety over 'the sensational situations' so characteristic of French crime thrillers. In November, Bush voiced his growing unease at the 'influx of foreign "features" . . . dealing with crime'; two months later, that unease had turned to alarm.[70] Among those features, Gaumont thrillers such as *In the Grip of the Vampire*, *When Thieves Fall Out*, and *The White Glove Band* attracted increasing disfavor – in contrast to another 'foreign import', Great Northern's *Gar-El-Hama*, which not only enlisted sympathy for its daring criminal at the outset but imprisoned him in the end.[71] Even the company's jungle pictures, according to the *Mirror*, were being 'overdone': *In the Claws of the Leopard*, for instance, was simply 'a series of villainous machinations leading up to the introduction of an animal'.[72] Not long after Blaché announced

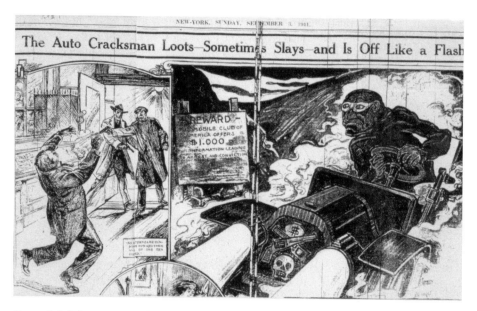

*Figure 2.3* 'The Auto Cracksman Loots – Sometimes Slays – and Is Off Like a Flash',
*New York Tribune* (November 3, 1911)

that 'foreign manufacturers have been taught their lesson', another of the *World*'s
influential writers, Louis Reeves Harrison, felt compelled to renew the attack on
all those who continued to indulge in what he called 'rotten realism': the 'fascinating criminal', he claimed, was 'a thing of the past'.[73] In parallel with this criticism,
the circulation of French crime thrillers also began to suffer. *Zigomar II*, for instance,
showed up initially in the small city of Cedar Rapids rather than Cleveland, and its
appearances in some cities were delayed by four to six months.[74] In Cleveland,
along with Éclair's *The Auto Bandits of Paris*, the film also played primarily at theaters
catering to working-class audiences, including one in the city's black ghetto.[75]
In other words, French crime thrillers now were being linked not to the mass audience promoted by the trade press but to the less desirable masses. Their appearance
in other nearby steel-producing cities provided further evidence. In Youngstown,
a downtown theater played one Éclair or Gaumont crime thriller after another,
including *In the Grip of the Vampire* and *The White Glove Band*, each Sunday, January
through March 1913.[76] In Canton, *The Auto Bandits of Paris*, *The White Glove Band*,
and others did not show up until the following summer, and then only at the
Airdome, a temporary open-air theater.[77]

    The nadir point in the reception of French crime thrillers probably came with
the release of Gaumont's *Fantomas* series, and the (at best) lukewarm response it
received sharply contrasted with that of several American sensational melodramas.
In order to downplay the criminal and sensational in advertising the first *Fantomas*
film, *Under the Shadow of the Guillotine*, in July, Gaumont described it as part of a
'Cracksman vs. Detective Series' (see Figure 2.4), which toned down the violence

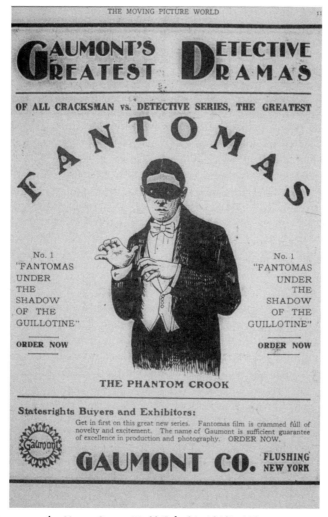

*Figure 2.4* Gaumont ad., *Moving Picture World* (July 31, 1913), 119

of Fantomas's crimes and depicted him as an elegant black-masked gentleman.[78] Yet reviews were not enthusiastic. The *Mirror* found it merely of 'medium interest'[79] and then refused to review the other four films in the series; the *World* gave brief, mildly positive reviews to the first two films[80] and then described the third, *The Mysterious Fingerprint*, as having little appeal except for what Frank Woods called 'the least cultivated persons'[81] of the outmoded nickelodeons:

> . . . where pictures with a decided punch are wanted, where startling and terrible sensations presented with logic enough to make them connect up . . . in a seemingly organized whole are desired, this third instalment of 'Fantomas' will be welcome, will even stir enthusiasm.[82]

The films' circulation seems to have mirrored this trajectory of condescension. Although the first two films in the series played at a major downtown theater in Canton, in October and December, respectively, each was featured just one night in the middle of the week.[83] In Youngstown, *Fantomas II* similarly appeared for just one Sunday in December.[84] In Cleveland, only *Fantomas I* registered (in very fine print) for two nights at a downtown theater; after that, hardly any French crime thrillers were even mentioned in the *Leader*.[85] By July 1914, Gaumont's ad. for the fifth (and last) film was pathetically tiny and placed in the back pages of *Moving Picture News*,[86] eerily marking both the devalued status of *Fantomas* on the US market and the vanishing point of French crime thrillers as a whole.

Compare the phantom presence of *Fantomas* with what continues to be seen as the most controversial American feature of late 1913, Universal's *Traffic in Souls*. The *World* admitted that its subject, the 'white slave' trade, would 'arouse bitter antagonism' from those committed to 'battling with the evil . . . in the old-time secret way'.[87] Yet its reviewer argued that the film showed 'practically nothing of the lure of underworld life', upheld 'the forces of law and order' throughout its six reels, and sustained the suspense of its dramatic story with 'unusual power'. The *Mirror* concurred: the film 'succeeded admirably in handling a subject of morbid interest and difficult situations with nothing that would pander to the evil senses and everything that tends to bring out the finer feeling of the spectator'.[88] As Shelley Stamp has shown, *Traffic in Souls* was unusually popular in New York.[89] But it also scored a hit in other cities such as Cleveland, where it was booked for two weeks at a legitimate theater just before Christmas and the *Leader*, well aware of its New York success, ran a story about how 'Cleveland Loves "Traffic in Souls"' (see Figure 2.5).[90] Most recent analyses have focused rightly on the context of 'white slavery' hysteria surrounding the film, its relation to other white slave productions (on stage and screen), and its narrative construction and ideological contradictions.[91] Yet another context is just as valuable for highlighting its difference from French crime thrillers: the development of the detective film as an 'appropriate' variant of sensational melodrama. The *World* seemed implicitly aware of that in noting that the story centered on a woman's attempt, aided by her 'policeman-sweetheart', not only to rescue her younger sister but to gather evidence, using her father's dictograph invention, against the ring of traffickers. Detective films had grown increasingly numerous during the year, from Kalem's *The Exposure of the Land Swindlers*, starring the famous 'Detective William J. Burns', to Universal's popular King the Detective series named after its star, King Baggot.[92] And they provided the framework for reviewers to praise imports such as Itala's *Tigris* and Gaumont's *The Rajah's Casket* – because the latter's hero was a detective rather than a criminal gang – and for Gaumont's failed attempt to sell *Fantomas* as a detective film.[93]

Compare it also with Selig's *The Adventures of Kathlyn* (see Figure 2.6) whose initial episodes quickly provoked a craze for such 'serial queen' variants of the sensational melodrama.[94] Unlike the *Fantomas* series, whose titles were released at irregular intervals over the course of nearly a year, the thirteen two-reel episodes of the Kathlyn series appeared at regular bi-weekly intervals. Moreover, a full-page

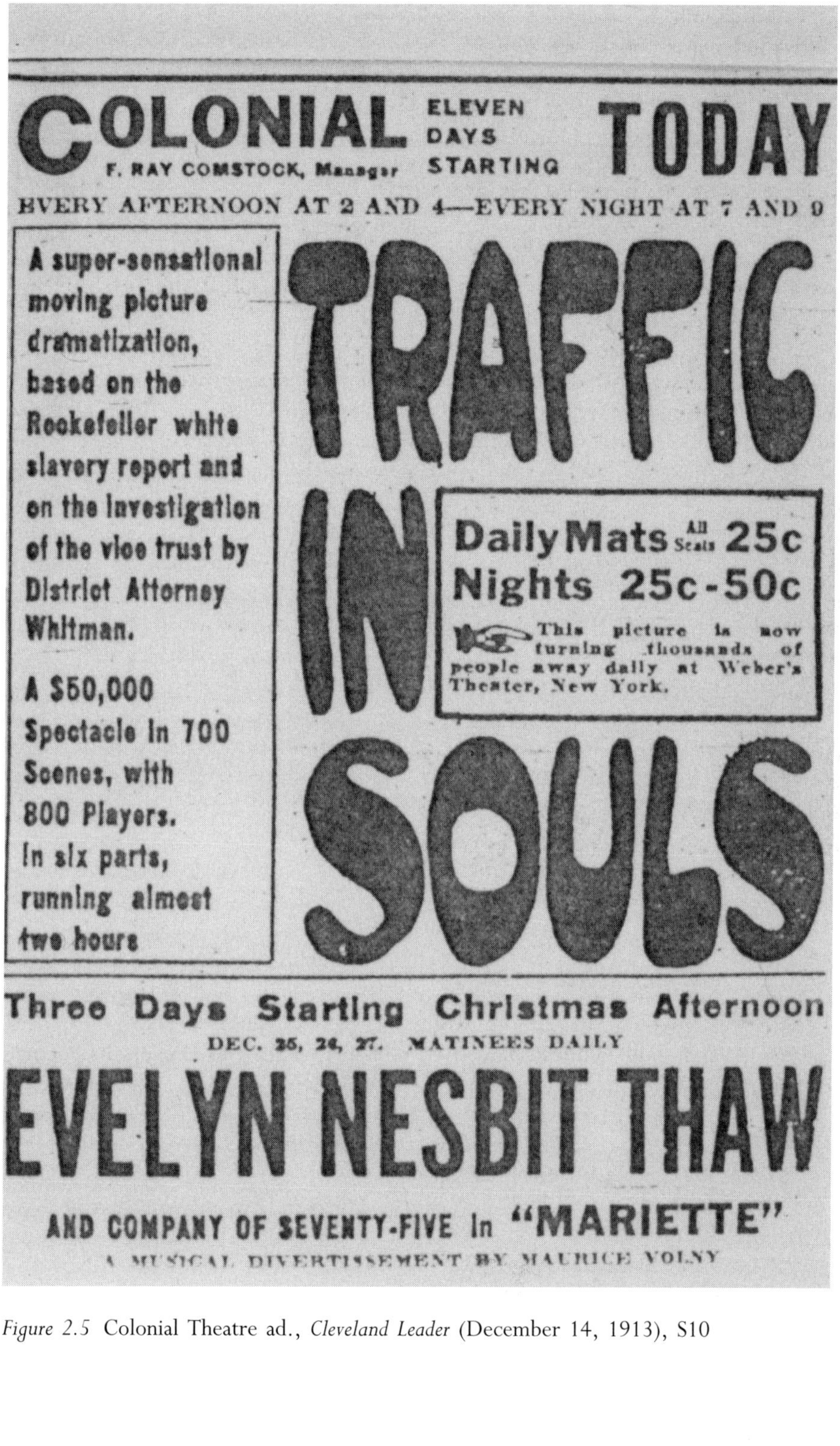

*Figure 2.5* Colonial Theatre ad., *Cleveland Leader* (December 14, 1913), S10

'installment of [the] serial story' was printed in major newspapers of selected cities each Sunday prior to the showing of a new episode.[95] The detective film offered one precedent for such serials, as Bowser suggests,[96] but another more pertinent to the Kathlyn series was the jungle pictures in which Selig specialized. For here again, according to the trade press and newspapers, Kathlyn Williams was 'continuously beset by dangers and seemingly insurmountable odds', at the hands of 'the savage denizens [both animal and human] of Jungle Land'.[97] This time, however, 'the domain of perilous adventure and thrilling photodramatic narrative' was India, stripped of colonial traces and suffused with an 'atmosphere of Orientalism' that reminded the *World* of the 'mysticism' of the 'Arabian Nights'.[98] Although less taken with these films than the *World*, the *Mirror* agreed that Williams's screen 'personality' was 'the true attraction', 'the mainspring of the action and of interest', whether threatened with death or engineering her own escapes from danger.[99] That Kathlyn, again unlike Fantomas, successfully appealed to the new mass audience and not merely the masses Barbara Wilinsky has demonstrated in her fine analysis of the co-production strategies involving Selig and the *Chicago Tribune*.[100] Whereas Selig had a core audience assumed to be working class and white collar, the *Tribune* had a 'largely white, native-born, middle-class readership'.[101] Placing 'teaser advertisements for *Kathlyn*' on the newspaper's 'women's' page, making the story installments part of its Sunday 'Special Features' section (in color), and jointly planting stories on the film's success – with headlines such as 'Crowds Besiege Kathlyn Shows' – Wilinsky argues, allowed the *Tribune* and Selig to 'blend their class-based audiences to attract men and women from all classes'.[102]

'Melodrama of the best sort is always uplifting; right triumphs and evil is either frustrated or gains its just reward.'[103] During the culture war of the early 1910s, this deceptively simple definition served as a mantra with which to separate the 'goats' of the French 'melodrama thriller' from the 'sheep' of the American sensational melodrama. Exceptions to the rules were rare, and historically situated, as in the case of *Zigomar* or Éclair's *Protea* in late 1913: as if responding to implicit directives from the trade press, that film featured a government spy, not a criminal, and a woman no less, who, much like her American counterparts, was more than proficient at disguises and daring escapes in enemy territory. The *Mirror*'s respectful praise gave substance to *Protea*'s popularity: 'it teems with action, yet the excitement is of a healthy sort that does not repel.'[104] *Fantomas* by contrast, proved to be a kind of limit case for what American reviewers – and audiences, apparently – found unacceptable, morally threatening, and even repellent in French 'melodrama thrillers', yet its reception was hardly unusual. Indeed, the polarities of 'appropriateness' in this culture war over sensational melodrama were symptomatic of what was fast becoming an inflated sense of American moral and social superiority in relation to the rest of the world, including the 'old world' of Europe. That superiority not only served to justify certain kinds of moving pictures as a 'social force' for both the masses and the new mass audience but proved a usefully deceptive mask for the imperialistic ventures in which the US was currently engaged. And that would support the US film industry's 'invasion' of Europe and

*Figure 2.6* Selig ad., *Moving Picture World* (January 24, 1914), 426

other countries, just then getting underway, and ultimately sell US cultural imperialism as a 'global good'. For, as the export manager for the Nicolas Power Company bragged, in early 1914: 'There [was] an enormous demand for films of sensational subjects such as war dramas, wild West, jungle stories, good detective and other stories with strong emotional interest'.[105] Appropriately 'modified', the action and behavior in American sensational melodramas, it would seem, made action of a different sort most appropriate elsewhere.

## Notes

For reasons of space, the following acronyms are used for frequently cited period journals and newspapers: CN (Canton News), CL (Cleveland Leader), CRR (Cedar Rapids Republican), DMN (Des Moines News), MPN (Motion Picture News), MPW (Moving Picture World), NYDM (New York Dramatic Mirror), and YV (Youngstown Vindicator).

1   'Foreign Films in the American Market', NYDM, February 12, 1913, p. 29.
2   Eileen Bowser The Transformation of Cinema, 1907–1915, New York: Charles Scribner's Sons, 1990, p. 50.
3   'Pictures Need No Censoring', NYDM, August 13, 1910, p. 25.
4   These phrases come from W. Stephen Bush 'Problems in Pictures', MPW, December 16, 1911, p. 877, and C. H. Claudy 'Modern Melodrama', MPW, January 13, 1912, p. 112.
5   '"Spectator's" Comments', NYDM, December 6, 1911, p. 28, and January 10, 1912, p. 28.
6   'The Dangers of the Foreign Market', MPW, December 16, 1911, pp. 877–8, and '"Spectator's" Comments', NYDM, January 10, 1912, p. 28.
7   For this essay I have relied on an ongoing research project focused on newspaper coverage of moving pictures in the US in the early 1910s. Briefly, I have chosen to look at selected papers in three regions of the country that, although relatively unexplored, were crucial to the emergence of nickelodeons and moving picture theaters and also were marked by different immigrant populations as well as somewhat different socio-economic constituencies. The regions include northeastern Ohio, the upper Midwest from St. Louis through Iowa to Minneapolis, and eastern Massachusetts (my work on the latter remains preliminary). For a fuller account of that research, see Richard Abel 'A Marriage of Ephemeral Discourses: Newspapers and Moving Pictures', Cinéma et cie, 1, Fall 2001, pp. 59–83.
8   Ben Singer Melodrama and Modernity: Early Sensational Cinema and Its Contexts, New York: Columbia University Press, 2001.
9   Astute studies of the dime novel can be found in Michael Denning Mechanic Accents: Dime Novels and Working-Class Culture in America, 2nd edition, London: Verso, 1998, and Bill Brown 'Reading the West: Cultural and Historical Background', in Bill Brown (ed.) Reading the West: An Anthology of Dime Westerns, Boston: Bedford Books, 1997, pp. 1–40.
10  The term '10–20–30 melodrama' came from the price of seating in the theaters that catered to this kind of popular drama. It prospered on a national scale by the late 1890s, according to Singer, as theater circuits and syndicates combined to finance, book, and promote 'the mass production of large scale touring companics'. Ben Singer 'Ten-Twenty-Thirty Melodrama', in Singer Melodrama and Modernity, pp. 149–88.
11  See especially Singer Modernity and Melodrama, pp. 150–1.
12  'Stage Notes: "The Eye Witness"', Brooklyn Daily Eagle, February 24, 1907, 4: 2, quoted in Singer Melodrama and Modernity, pp. 151–2.
13  Singer charts this shift in trade press discourse in Melodrama and Modernity, pp. 163–7.
14  Carol Armbruster 'French Pulp Fiction in Turn-of-the-Century America', Panel on France and America: Exchanges and Rivalries in the Modern Era, Society of French Historical Studies Conference, University of North Carolina, March 10, 2001.

15    Richard Abel *The Red Rooster Scare: Making Cinema American, 1900–1910*, Berkeley: University of California Press, 1999.

16    'Moving Picture News and Reviews', *Variety*, April 18, 1908, p. 13. See also Lucy France Pierce, 'The Nickelodeon', *World Today*, October 1908; reprinted in Gerald Mast (ed.) *The Movies in Our Midst: Documents in the Cultural History of Film in America*, Chicago: University of Chicago Press, 1982, p. 56.

17    'The Melodrama', *NYDM*, June 1, 1907, p. 14; and 'Public Taste in Pictures as Viewed by M. E. Feckles', *Show World*, September 7, 1907, p. 9. Carl Laemmle summed up this difference quite succinctly: 'Let's cater more to the happy side of life. There's enough of the seamy side without exposing it to further view.' 'Moving Picture Industry Great', *Show World*, June 29, 1907, p. 29.

18    Abel *The Red Rooster Scare*, pp. 91–4, 101.

19    Abel *The Red Rooster Scare*, pp. 138–9.

20    'Music and Picture', *MPW*, December 31, 1910, pp. 1518–19.

21    'The Qualitative Picture', *MPW*, June 25, 1910, pp. 1089–90.

22    'Variety's Own Picture Reviews', *Variety*, March 5, 1910, p. 13. *Variety*'s attack also was explicitly anti-Semitic because *Ouchard*'s characters were clearly Jewish.

23    '"World" Crusade a Fizzle', *NYDM*, October 5, 1910, p. 29.

24    'The Indian and Cowboy (By One Who Does Not Like Them)', *MPW*, December 1910, p. 1399. See also an article reprinted from the *Los Angeles Times* as 'The Press and the Picture', *MPW*, December 3, 1910, p. 1290. The only contemporary crime thrillers that regularly drew protests were those produced by Reliance – 'The "Police Gazette" on the Screen', *MPW*, January 7, 1911, p. 31, and 'Sensational Pictures', *MPW*, June 10, 1911, p. 1305.

25    'The Passing of the Western Subject', *Nickelodeon*, February 18, 1911, pp. 181–2.

26    'The Flagrant Abuse of Posters', *MPW*, February 11, 1911, p. 309; and 'The Crime Poster Again', *MPW*, April 15, 1911, p. 814. Likewise, Louis Reeves Harrison used an imaginary western scenario to mock the 'underdone' structure of the sensational melodrama in 'Melodrama', *MPW*, May 13, 1911, pp. 1058–9.

27    'Wild West Pictures', *MPN*, November 18, 1911, p. 6. Even more letters agreeing with this article were cited in 'Wild West Pictures', *MPN*, November 25, 1911, p. 7.

28    'Facts and Comments', *MPW*, December 2, 1911, p. 700; and '"Spectator's" Comments', *NYDM*, February 7, 1912, p. 28. 'Protests against the volume of 'Wild West' films' even got noticed in the newspapers – 'In the Moving Picture World', *Chicago Sunday Tribune*, December 24, 1911, 2.2: 3.

29    Selig and Essanay, for instance, were releasing one or more westerns a week by 1911; Bison, Champion, and American each were releasing two.

30    'Film Charts', *MPN*, April 29, 1911, p. 21.

31    Essanay ad., in *MPW*, October 21, 1911, p. 226.

32    'Today's Entertainments', *YV*, October 15, 1911, p. 14, and 'This Man's Photo Seen Every Day by 300,000', *CN*, November 5, 1911, p. 15. The trade press did not mention that Essanay was sending Anderson's photo to exhibitors for advertising purposes until November – 'The "Most Photographed Man"', *Motography*, November 1911, p. 245; 'The Most Photographed Man', *NYDM*, November 22, 1911, p. 26; and '"Live" Advertising For Exhibitors', *MPW*, December 2, 1911, p. 714.

33    'Reviews of Licensed Films', *NYDM*, January 3, 1912, p. 30.

34    'Reviews of Licensed Films', *NYDM*, November 15, 1911, p. 28.

35    'Films Worth Seeing', *CL*, December 24, 1911, B7.

36    Selig advertised *Lost in the Jungle* for at least a month before its release in late October – see, for instance, the Selig ad., *NYDM*, September 27, 1911, p. 30.

37    'Great Picture Held Over at the Orpheum', *CN*, November 26, 1911, p. 16, and the Orpheum ad., *CN*, November 26, 1911, p. 17.

38   'Lost in the Jungle (Selig)', MPW, October 14, 1911, p. 109, and 'Reviews of Licensed Films', NYDM, November 1, 1911, pp. 30–1. For previous Selig animal pictures, see 'A Remarkable Film', MPW, May 20, 1911, p. 1115; and '"Captain Kate": The Third of Selig's Great African Series', MPW, July 8, 1911, pp. 1569–70.

39   Monopol ad. for Dante's Inferno, NYDM, August 23, 1911, p. 22; 'A Great Triumph', MPW, August 26, 1911, p. 530; 'Washington', NYDM, September 6, 1911, p. 24; 'Reviews of Notable Films', MPW, September 23, 1911, pp. 869–70, and September 30, 1911, pp. 954, 956; and 'Great Success of Colleen Bawn', NYDM, November 1, 1911, p. 27. For a thorough overview of the introduction of American two- and three-reel films, especially in terms of production and distribution, and from the standpoint of the trade press, see Bowser The Transformation of Cinema, pp. 191–204.

40   'Reviews of Licensed Films', NYDM, December 20, 1911, p. 34, and 'Films Worth Seeing', CL, December 24, 1911, B7. The Battle was praised in this very same column.

41   C. H. Claudy 'Modern Melodrama', MPW, January 13, 1912, p. 112. This criticism of In the Grip of Alcohol immediately followed Claudy's 'Hurrah' for The Battle.

42   The quote actually comes from a review of the second film in the Zigomar series – 'Zigomar contre Nick Carter', Ciné-Journal, March 9, 1912, p. 57.

43   'Reviews of Notable Films', MPW, October 14, 1911, p. 108; and 'Zigomar: Thrilling Detective Story', Photoplay, February 1912, pp. 56–7. Zigomar was the only French film other than Queen Elizabeth to appear in Photoplay.

44   Feature & Educational Film ad., CL, December 3, 1911, S5; 'Zigomar a Great Success', CL, December 17, 1911, S7; 'At the Leading Theaters', CL, January 7, 1912, B7, January 14, 1912, S5, and January 21, 1911, S6; and the Knickerbocker ad., CL, April 7, 1912, S8. See also the Éclair ad., Billboard, December 9, 1911, p. 99.

45   Rex ad., YV, December 31, 1911, p. 16, and Park ad., YV, January 7, 1912, p. 17.

46   For an analysis of Zigomar, see Richard Abel The Ciné Goes to Town: French Cinema, 1896–1914, Berkeley: University of California Press, 1994, pp. 358–9.

47   Wallace Irwin 'Colonel Crowe of Cripple Creek: A Word for Moving Picture Shows', Chicago Daily News, December 2, 1911, p. 7.

48   W. Stephen Bush 'Do Longer Films Make Better Shows', MPW, October 28, 1911, p. 275.

49   'Bison Gets 101 Ranch', NYDM, December 6, 1911, p. 29; 'Western Spectacles', Billboard, December 9, 1911, p. 46; and 'What Bison Wants', MPW, January 13, 1912, p. 119. A solid appraisal of Bison-101 and Thomas Ince can be found in Kevin Brownlow The War, the West, and the Wilderness, New York: Knopf, 1978, pp. 253–62. For a thorough, well-told story of the Miller Brothers' 101 Ranch, see Michael Wallis The Real Wild West: The 101 Ranch and the Creation of the American West, New York: St. Martin's, 1999.

50   'Bison-101 Feature Pictures', MPW, January 27, 1912, p. 28. The Golden Wedding had received the gold medal at the 1911 Cinematograph Exposition in Turin, Italy – 'Reviews of Notable Films', MPW, December 9, 1911, p. 799.

51   Louis Reeves Harrison 'The Indian Massacre', MPW, March 9, 1912, pp. 854–6; '"Spectator's" Comments', NYDM, April 17, 1912, pp. 24–5; 'Reviews of Special Feature Subjects', NYDM, April 24, 1912, p. 27; 'The "Bison-101" Headliners', MPW, April 27, 1912, pp. 320–2; and 'Reviews of Special Features', NYDM, May 8, 1912, p. 34, and May 22, 1912, pp. 27, 34.

52   'Programs of Leading Theaters', CL, March 17, 1912, S6, March 24, 1912, S6, and April 21, 1912, W8; 'From Religious to Wild West, Range of Weeks' Films', CL, April 7, 1912, S8; and the rare Family Theatre ad. in the DMN, April 21, 1912, p. 6.

53   This contractual dispute eventually forced NYMP to change the names of its production units to Kay-Bee, Broncho, and Keystone and to distribute them through Mutual. New York Motion Picture ads, MPW, July 6, 1912, p. 59, and July 27, 1912, p. 371; 'Mutual Gets Empire Film Exchanges', MPW, August 10, 1912, p. 525; the Mutual ad., MPN, August 10, 1912, p. 38; 'Universal Wins Point', MPW, October 5, 1912, p. 51; and Brownlow The War, the West, and the Wilderness, p. 257.

54  'Custer Film at Oxford', *CL*, October 13, 1912, W8, and 'Preliminary Peeps at the Peep Shows' and the Colonial Theater ad., *CL*, October 27, 1912, M3, M4. *NYMP* began promoting *Custer's Last Fight* in the trade press as early as May and continued that promotion throughout the summer and fall, making it one of the first American films to receive a sustained publicity campaign. Louis Reeves Harrison reviewed the film in *MPW*, June 22, 1912, pp. 1116–18. For a perceptive analysis of this and other early films of Custer, see Roberta Pearson, 'The Revenge of Rain-in-the-Face? or, Custers and Indians on the Silent Screen' in Daniel Bernardi (ed.) *The Birth of Whiteness: Race and the Emergence of U.S. Cinema*, New Brunswick, NJ: Rutgers University Press, 1996, pp. 273–99.

55  Louis Reeves Harrison 'The Invaders', *MPW*, November 9, 1912, p. 542; 'Big Holiday Bills at Local Theaters', *CL*, December 22, 1912, S5; 'Where Best Shows Are Found Today', *CL*, January 12, 1913, M5; and 'Latest Film Snapshots Local and Worldwide', *CL*, March 2, 1913, M11. See also the Unique ads for its Mutual programs, *DMN*, January 21, 1913, p. 5, and January 26, 1913, p. 6.

56  'Doings in Los Angeles', *MPW*, July 6, 1912, p. 35; Louis Reeves Harrison 'Two Strong Kay-Bee Subjects', *MPW*, November 23, 1912, p. 754; and Louis Reeves Harrison 'The Pride of the South', *MPW*, March 15, 1913, p. 1086.

57  'Sheridan's Ride Seen by Local Exhibitors' and 'Many Big Features in Week's Program', *CL*, January 26, 1913, W8. See also C. H. Judson 'The Battle of Bull Run', *MPW*, March 15, 1913, p. 1107.

58  'Feature Films', *NYDM*, June 11, 1913, p. 27.

59  New York Motion Picture ads, *MPW*, June 21, 1913, p. 1327, and July 12, 1913, p. 113; and the Alhambra Theater ads, *CN*, June 29, 1913, p. 12, July 3, 1913, p. 3, August 3, 1913, p. 16, and August 7, 1913, p. 3.

60  James S. McQuade 'Kings of the Forest', *MPW*, September 28, 1912, p. 1254; the Selig ad., *MPW*, November 2, 1912, p. 417; and James S. McQuade 'Alone in the Jungle', *MPW*, June 7, 1913, p. 1006.

61  'Genuine African Jungle', *CL*, November 10, 1912, B5; and 'Doings in Los Angeles', *MPW*, December 7, 1912, p. 969.

62  Gaumont ad., *MPN*, May 4, 1912, p. 3; and 'Reviews of Supply Co. Films', *NYDM*, July 10, 1912, p. 32.

63  Gaumont ad., *MPN*, August 31, 1912, p. 5; 'In the Land of the Lions', *MPW*, September 21, 1912, p. 1164; and the Columbia Theatre ads, *CRR*, October 31, 1912, p. 3, and November 3, 1912, p. 3.

64  General Film ad., *MPW*, November 16, 1912, p. 682; the Knickerbocker ad., *CL*, November 17, 1912, M5; as well as various theater listings in the *Leader* throughout December.

65  'The Margrave's Daughter', *MPW*, March 9, 1912, pp. 875–6; W. Stephen Bush 'The Margrave's Daughter', *MPW*, March 30, 1912, p. 1156; and Virginia West 'The Margrave's Daughter', *MPN*, April 27, 1912, pp. 12–13.

66  'Blanche Walsh a Success', *NYDM*, July 24, 1912, p. 27.

67  'Auto Bandits Terrorize Paris, Rivaling the Exploits of Most Notorious Westerners', *DMN*, April 13, 1912, p. 4, and 'The Phantom Bandits: Paris, Ever the Home of the Unusual, Furnishes the World Its Very First Automobile Ghost Story', *San Francisco Sunday Chronicle*, April 21, 1912, magazine section, 2.

68  Maurice Le Blanc 'Bonnot, Tiger Bandit', *CL*, May 12, 1912, C1–2.

69  'The Auto Cracksman Loots – Sometimes Slays – and Is Off Like a Flash', *New York Sunday Tribune*, September 3, 1911, 2: 1.

70  W. Stephen Bush 'Advertising and Criticizing', *MPW*, November 23, 1912, p. 750, and Bush 'Avoid Crime and Carrion', *MPW*, January 4, 1913, pp. 24–5.

71  Louis Reeves Harrison 'Gar-El-Hama', *MPW*, November 2, 1912, p. 436; 'In the Grip of the Vampire', *MPW*, December 31, 1912, p. 1308; 'Supply Co. Films', *NYDM*, January 1, 1913, p. 33; 'The White Glove Band', *MPW*, January 18, 1913, p. 266; and 'Feature Films on the Market', *NYDM*, April 9, 1913, p. 28.

72   'Supply Co. Films', *NYDM*, January 29, 1913, p. 38.

73   Louis Reeves Harrison 'The Fascinating Criminal', *MPW*, April 26, 1913, p. 356. For his scathing attack on 'rotten realism', see Harrison 'Red-Light Films', *MPW*, October 11, 1913, p. 133.

74   Palace ad., *CRR*, July 4, 1912, p. 3; the Princess ad., *CL*, August 18, 1912, W5; the Auditorium ad., *CN*, November 10, 1912, p. 17; and the Princess ad., *YV*, January 19, 1913.

75   Alpha ads, *Cleveland Gazette*, September 14, 1912, p. 3, and October 19, 1912, p. 3; and the Norwood ad., *CL*, November 17, 1912, B5. The Princess was one of only two downtown theaters to advertise in the city's labor weekly – the Princess ad., *Cleveland Citizen*, January 18, 1913, p. 2.

76   See the Princess ads for largely French crime thrillers in the *Youngstown Vindicator*, from January 19, 1913, p. 20, to March 23, 1913, p. 24.

77   Airdome ads, *CN*, July 9, 1913, p. 3, and July 31, 1913, p. 3.

78   Gaumont ads, *NYDM*, July 2, 1913, p. 34, and *MPW*, July 12, 1913, p. 119.

79   'Feature Films on the Market', *NYDM*, June 25, 1913, p. 25.

80   '*Fantomas*', *MPW*, July 26, 1913, p. 438; and Bush '*Fantomas, or The Man in Black*', *MPW*, November 8, 1913, p. 594.

81   Frank E. Woods 'Pictures Divided into Three Grades', *NYDM*, July 9, 1913, p. 25.

82   Hanford C. Judson '*Fantomas III*', *MPW*, December 22, 1913, p. 1531.

83   Orpheum ads, *CN*, October 16, 1913, p. 3, and December 11, 1913, p. 12.

84   Orpheum ad., *YV*, December 7, 1913, p. 58.

85   'Feature Films at Local Playhouses', *CL*, August 31, 1913, C4.

86   Gaumont ad., *MPN*, July 18, 1914, p. 72.

87   George Blaisdell '*Traffic in Souls*', *MPW*, November 22, 1913, p. 849.

88   'Feature Films on the Market', *NYDM*, November 19, 1913, p. 33.

89   Shelley Stamp *Movie-Struck Girls: Women and Motion Picture Culture After the Nickelodeon*, Princeton, NJ: Princeton University Press, 2000, pp. 52–3.

90   '*Traffic in Souls* Here This Week', *CL*, December 14, 1913, S11; and 'Cleveland Enjoys *Traffic in Souls*', *CL*, December 21, 1913, S10. In February, the film also played for four days to 'big crowds' at the Grand Opera House in Youngstown – see *Traffic in Souls* and the Grand Opera House ad., *YV*, February 1, 1914, p. 56.

91   Ben Brewster '*Traffic in Souls*: An Experiment in Feature-Length Narrative Construction', *Cinema Journal*, 31: 1, Fall 1991, pp. 37–56; Janet Staiger *Bad Women: Regulating Sexuality in Early American Cinema*, Minneapolis: University of Minnesota Press, 1995, pp. 116–46; and Stamp *Movie-Struck Girls*, pp. 70–82.

92   'Detective Burns in Vivid Kalem Drama', *NYDM*, March 19, 1913, p. 29. Indeed, during *Traffic in Souls*' run, the *Leader* called attention to the detective series in which Baggot starred – 'Baggot Appears in Mystery Play', *CL*, December 21, 1913, S10.

93   'Reviews of Feature Films', *NYDM*, March 5, 1913, p. 31; and Hugo Hoffman '*The Rajah's Casket*', *MPW*, May 17, 1913, p. 686.

94   For an insightful analysis of serial queen melodramas and of the heroine as an American middle-class figure of the active 'New Woman', see Singer, 'Power and Peril in the Serial-Queen Melodrama', *Melodrama and Modernity*, pp. 221–62.

95   These installments were written by Harold McGrath, the first of which I have seen in the Sunday Magazine section, *YV*, January 4, 1914, p. 8. They allegedly appeared in more than fifty newspapers across the country – 'Selig Resources for "Kathlyn" Series', *MPN*, January 31, 1914, p. 20.

96   Bowser *The Transformation of Cinema*, p. 186. In her chapter on genre films, Bowser does not take up crime films in relation to detective films – another indication of their 'foreignness' that has persisted in histories of early cinema.

97   '*The Adventures of Kathlyn*', *YV*, January 4, 1914, p. 56; and James S. McQuade '*The Adventures of Kathlyn*', *MPW*, January 17, 1914, p. 266.

98    McQuade 'The Adventures of Kathlyn', p. 266.

99    'Personality – Box Office Magnet', NYDM, January 14, 1914, p. 52; and 'Feature Films of the Week', NYDM, January 21, 1914, n.p.

100    Barbara Wilinsky 'Flirting With Kathlyn: Creating the Mass Audience', in David Desser and Garth S. Jowett (eds) Hollywood Goes Shopping, Minneapolis: University of Minnesota Press, 2000, pp. 34–56. See also a clipping, 'Selig to Undertake Wide Exploitation of Great Animal Pictures', from the Waterloo Reporter, September 6, 1913, Selig Collection, folder 13, Margaret Herrick Library, Beverly Hills, California.

101    Lauren Rabinovitz 'Temptations of Pleasure: Nickelodeons, Amusement Parks, and the Sights of Female Sexuality', Camera Obscura, 23, May 1990, p. 73. See also Rabinovitz's account of the Tribune's attack on Chicago nickelodeons in 1907 in For the Love of Pleasure: Women, Movies, and Pleasure in Turn-of-the-Century Chicago, New Brunswick, NJ: Rutgers University Press, 1998, pp. 122–8.

102    Wilinsky 'Flirting With Kathlyn', pp. 34, 41, 44.

103    The sentence comes from a review of Éclair's The Ingrate, one of the few French melodrama thrillers judged 'acceptable' by late 1913 – 'Feature Films', NYDM, October 8, 1913, p. 34.

104    'Feature Films on the Market', NYDM, October 15, 1913, p. 32. See also 'Protea', MPW, October 11, 1913, p. 137. Protea was advertised prominently in all of the cities whose newspapers I have researched; in fact, in Cleveland, it first appeared at a legitimate theater before moving to the downtown Orpheum – Knickerbocker ads, CL, November 23, 1913, S10 and S11; and the Orpheum ad., CL, December 7, 1913, S12.

105    Robert E. Welsh 'Where American Films Are Strangers', NYDM, January 14, 1914, p. 51. Arthur Lang was referring specifically to the 'fifty-three hundred' theaters in Latin America, but the demand seemed just as high in Europe.

## Chapter 3

## BEN SINGER

# 'CHILD OF COMMERCE! BASTARD OF ART!'
## Early film melodrama*

**D**URING THE NICKELODEON BOOM OF 1907–9, popular melodrama entered a new phase, a phase of unprecedented mass distribution by means of a modern technology of mechanical reproduction. Repackaged in a new medium – silent, black-and-white, canned – sensational melodrama was transformed. More striking, however, was the degree to which it remained the same.

Whatever the stylistic and structural differences between stage melodrama and film melodrama, there is no question that movies succeeded in capturing the essence of sensational melodrama. Movies delivered abundant rapid action, stimulating violence, spectacular sights, thrills of physical peril, abductions, and suspenseful rescues. On a narrative level, film melodramas relied on very similar stories emphasizing pure villainy and heroism catalyzed by the villain's jealousy and/or greed and often relying on extraordinary coincidences and sudden revelations and twists of circumstance. In what follows I offer a small sampling of one- and two-reel films between 1901 and 1913 before turning to a more detailed discussion of serial films between 1914 and around 1920. The survey does not purport to be systematic, comprehensive or studio-balanced; it simply presents some typical examples conveying the close intertextual connections between sensational stage melodramas and the films that took their place.

The earliest film melodramas were too brief to allow developed stories, but nevertheless they emulated stage melodrama in their use of artificial stagecraft to render sensation scenes. [. . .] Edwin S. Porter's *Life of an American Fireman* (Edison, 1901) may be regarded as a melodrama since it was built around two sensation scenes – a thrilling race of fire trucks and a treacherous rescue of a woman and child trapped in a burning building. *The Great Train Robbery*, produced two years later, expanded on the motifs of sensational melodrama by showing a violent binding-and-gagging, a daring robbery, three shocking murders, a racing locomotive, a hot pursuit on horseback, and a final gunfight killing all the bandits. Porter's 1906 film *The Trainer's Daughter; Or, A Race for Love* moved even closer to the classic melodramatic form, employing the conventional triangle of ingenue, favored beau, and jealous villain, and climaxing in a thrilling scene involving the young woman's courageousness. Jack owns a racehorse; wealthy Delmar owns the entire stable. Jack and Delmar wager on the next day's race. The ingenue, whom both men desire, overhears and pledges to give her hand in marriage to the winner. Delmar soon realizes that his horse has no chance against Jack's. That night, Delmar and a henchman try to drug Jack's horse but they are interrupted by Jack's jockey. Delmar beats the jockey and hides him in a deserted house. The next day it appears that Delmar will win by default since Jack's horse has no one to ride it. At the last minute, the jockey staggers in and reveals Delmar's villainy. The ingenue, still bound by her promise, decides to ride in the jockey's place to avoid an awful matrimonial fate. The race provides an opportunity for both suspense and thrilling action. She rides fearlessly and beats Delmar's horse by a nose. Racetrack melodramas were a common subgenre of sensational stage melodrama on both sides of the Atlantic in the decades around the turn of the century. The plot of Porter's film closely resembles that of *A Race for Life*, a 10–20–30 melodrama by Theodore Kremer that toured for several years beginning in 1904. An identical narrative was used in 1911 in a film entitled *The Girl and the Motor Boat*, the only difference being that the race involved speed boats instead of horses.[1]

According to a review in *Variety*, Pathé's 1907 film *The Female Spy* showed 'unlimited action', but was 'chaotic in its development'. Echoing a familiar complaint against melodrama, the critic stated that: 'The situations do not hold together in an easily followed line, but are scattered, what book reviewers call "episodic".' The review does not include a synopsis, but does mention a melodramatic sensation 'in which the captured woman spy is dragged by her hair across the fields behind a wild horse'.[2] Richard Abel's description, based on a surviving print, adds that the female spy is the daughter of a Cossack chieftain. She gives vital information to her lover, a young Tartar leader. For this treason, the father has her stabbed to death by a half-dozen men and then dragged back to the Tartar's encampment. In a failed attempt at a last-minute rescue, the lover chases after the body across the fields.

*Variety*'s review of a 1907 western melodrama entitled *The Bad Man* also mentions a 'wealth of incident'. After being defeating by a 'tenderfoot' (i.e. an Easterner) in a fight over the favors of a pretty railroad-station clerk, the villain, bent on robbery, attacks the romantic couple. In classic melodramatic form:

> The tenderfoot is tied to the railroad track, while the woman is bound hand
> and foot to the table within the telegraph office. She escapes in time to effect
> her lover's release and the two embrace as the express rushes past.[3]

D. W. Griffith is widely regarded as probably the finest director of melodramas in the feature-film era. *The Birth of a Nation*, *The Mother and the Law*, *Broken Blossoms*, *Way Down East*, *Orphans of the Storm*, *Hearts of the World*, and other films are extraordinary in their mastery of the mechanics of melodramatic pathos, moral injustice, and sensationalism. Griffith honed his skills as a melodrama specialist during the first phase of his career at Biograph. Perusing the plot synopses published in *Biograph Bulletins*, it is evident that his earliest films, from his directorial debut in July 1908 to about February 1909, gravitated heavily towards blood-and-thunder melodrama. Although one would have to view the actual films to confirm their sensational quality, the synopses suggest that of the roughly seventy films released during those seven months, about half (or two-thirds if one excludes comedies) contained some combination of extreme moral polarity, abduction, assault, brawling, brutality, binding-and-gagging, murder, and 'infernal machines' (intricate death-delaying contraptions used to prolong suspense). The third film of Griffith's career, *The Black Viper* (released in July 1908), illustrates this blood-and-thunder orientation. Its narrative contains brutality against a woman, a brawl, a binding-and-gagging, an attempted murder, two rushes-to-the-rescue, hazardous rolling boulders, another brawl, a fall off a roof, and a stabbing death. [. . .] Biograph's synopsis clearly conveys Griffith's reliance on a pre-existing intertextual reservoir of thrilling incidents familiar from 10–20–30 melodramas and dime novels.

In a similar vein, *The Fatal Hour* (August 1908), described as 'a stirring incident of the Chinese White Slave Traffic' and 'exceedingly thrilling', contains two violent abductions of women by a Chinese villain and his henchman, the binding and gagging of a female detective, an infernal machine (the pistol in front of which the detective is tied will fire when the hands of a clock reach twelve), and a 'wild ride' to the rescue. It should also be noted that, in typical melodramatic fashion, the story hinges on a chance occurrence: the police apprehend the henchman and learn the location of the imperiled detective after the henchman is injured in a streetcar accident.[4]

One of Griffith's most suspenseful melodramas is *The Cord of Life*, released in late January 1909. A Sicilian 'worthless good-for-nothing scoundrel' demands money from his cousin but is emphatically rebuffed. Determined to get back at him, the villain waits until the cousin and his wife briefly leave their baby unattended in their fifth-floor tenement room. Darting into the apartment, he puts the baby in a basket, ties a rope to it, dangles the basket out the window and closes the window on the rope so that when anyone opens it the baby will fall to its death. He then goes off to track down the husband. Just as he is about to stab him in the back, a policemen grabs the villain and places him under arrest. Indignant, and eager to agitate his cousin, the malefactor boasts about what he has done with the baby. Griffith creates powerful suspense by crosscutting between the husband racing home and the wife, who has returned and repeatedly approaches the window to hang out some clothes to dry but gets distracted each time. The husband finally bursts in, needless to say, just as the wife is starting to open the window. They are in a quandary as to how to rescue the baby without opening the window. Eventually, the husband lowers the upper panel of the window and precariously hangs head down, held by the feet, to lift the baby back inside. The *Bulletin* assures us that 'while the subject is intensely thrilling, it is totally devoid of gruesomeness'. This disclaimer is significant, for it signals a policy change at Biograph that almost certainly resulted from the launching of the Motion Pictures Patents Company (MPPC) in late December 1908, and the institution of the National Board of

Censorship in March 1909. Biograph sought both to avoid censorship problems and to make good on the MPPC's rhetoric about the cinema's moral 'uplift'. After releasing in January and February a few blood-and-thunder films that had already been in production, Griffith shifted his focus to sentimental and didactic melodramas about noble sacrifice and moral reawakening, in addition to pastoral romances, comedies and other dramas palatable to censors, reformers, and multiclass audiences. Race-to-the-rescue thrillers like *The Drive For A Life* (April 1909) and *The Lonely Villa* (June 1909) occasionally were thrown into the mix, but the films were never vulgar or sordid and seldom violent. If violence was depicted, it was carefully framed as part of a moral lesson.[5]

The Kalem Company, with its heavy emphasis on railroad westerns and Civil War stories, had something close to an all melodrama production policy (although it did make comedies, too). Kalem is particularly notable as the first studio to build virtually all of its melodramas on the heroics of courageous young women, thus setting a precedent for the 'serial queens' that I discuss in detail elsewhere.[6] The studio produced a Girl Spy series in 1909, and dozens upon dozens of one- and two-reel weekly releases followed, all adhering to the plucky girl formula, before Kalem went out of business in early 1917. *The Open Switch*, released in March 1913, typifies Kalem's railroad melodramas in its simple moral polarity, graphic action, and female agency:

> Grace Lane, the daughter of the operator at Ferndale, is in love with Billy Warren, the engineer on the local train. Jim West, a rough character employed as section foreman in the yards, endeavors to force his attentions on Grace and is roundly thrashed by Billy. West plans to ditch Billy's train. Grace discovers him tampering with the switch and runs for help, but he overtakes her and ties her near the tracks. During the struggle his revolver slips from his pocket unnoticed and when he leaves to watch Billy's train dash to destruction, Grace struggles with her bonds, secures the revolver and fires at the telegraph wires. She succeeds in breaking one of the glass insulators and a broken wire falls within her reach. With her hands still tied, she taps the end of the wire on the rail, crossing the circuit that operates the telegraph instrument in her father's station. Grace's father, receiving the warning, flags Billy's train in the nick of time and releases the girl, none the worse for her harrowing experience. After a desperate struggle with West, Billy leads him off to jail.[7]

Beginning in November, 1914, Kalem streamlined its marketing of railroad thrillers by incorporating them all within the *Hazards of Helen* series, which ran for 119 weekly episodes until March 1917.

Kalem's Civil War melodramas (and some set during the Mexican Revolution and Boer War) were very similar, showcasing various kinds of thrilling spectacle and female stunt work. *War's Havoc*, released two weeks after *The Open Switch*, is representative of this subgenre. The young heroine serves as a spy for the Confederate army (adhering to a curious convention in silent Civil War films that the protagonist side with the Confederacy). Inside enemy territory, she cuts the wires of a Federalists' telegraphy station and shoots its operator. She then hijacks a train and puts it on a collision course with a train carrying Federalist troops amassing for an attack. The trains collide on a bridge with a spectacular explosion. The heroine jumps off the train into river below. In all of this, she is assisted by a faithful slave (fighting for the Confederacy).[8]

Kalem also made numerous melodramas showcasing the courage and wit of 'girl detectives' and 'girl reporters', such as *The Girl Reporter's Big Scoop* (September 1912) in which the heroine goes undercover as a maid to spy on a band of robbers. She masters flash-photography chemistry to catch them in the act. Some of Kalem's films translated into film the most classic chestnuts of 10–20–30 melodrama, such as *Saved By the Telephone* (June 1912), *A Sawmill Hazard* (December 1912), and *The Wheel of Death* (June 1912) in which villains strap the hero to the massive paddle wheel of a Mississippi Riverboat.

Sensational melodrama remained a prominent genre as the feature film emerged in the early Teens (a fact that should be borne in mind in light of the tendency to oversimplify the feature film as an emblem of the film industry's gentrification). But it was in serial films that the genre really flourished. While sensational melodrama was just one genre among many in regular short subjects and feature films, with serials it was the *only* genre. With few, if any, exceptions all film serials were sensational melodramas. They covered a range of subgenres (such as Detective, Western, Gothic, Patriotic, and Working-girl melodramas), but they all concentrated on violence and intense action – abductions, entrapments, brawls, hazardous chase sequences, and last minute rescues – in narratively stark conflicts between a heroine or hero–heroine team and a villain and his criminal accomplices. Film serials represent an immediately recognizable and iconographically faithful descendant of the 10–20–30 and its literary cousins.

As early titles like *The Perils of Pauline* (1914), *The Exploits of Elaine* (1915), *The House of Hate* (1918), *The Lurking Peril* (1920), and *The Screaming Shadow* (1920) make obvious, serials promised thrills. Ellis Oberholtzer, Pennsylvania's cranky head censor in the Teens, described the serial as, 'In the main made up of shooting, knifing, binding and gagging, drowning, wrecking and fighting . . . It is crime, violence, blood-and-thunder, and always obtruding and outstanding is the idea of sex'.[9] A 1919 article in *Photoplay* stressed the melodramatic dynamism of serials and remarked on their connection to lowbrow literary antecedents:

> Action, action and yet more action! Situations if they come along, yes, but never worked out! . . . A famous serial writer said recently that serials consisted of action without psychology. It might be stated more simply by calling them action without padding. Something is always happening in a serial. Often the direct motive is lacking for this action, but serial audiences do not mind. They are not analytical. They want conflict and the serial producers feed it to them in reel lengths. . . . Serials are The Modern

Dime Novels! They supply the demand that was once filled by those blood curdling thrillers . . . Melodrama! Of course it's melodrama.[10]

In a similar vein, the *New York Dramatic Mirror* described an episode of Universal's 1914 serial *Lucille Love: Girl of Mystery* as 'a melodramatic melodrama, or otherwise a melodrama to the second degree'.[11] About another episode, the reviewer stated:

> It is, of course, improbable, impossible, out of the question, and any other synonyms that stand for 'can't be done,' but the film disregards these questions of credence lightly in its more ardent quest for action – constant action . . . The plot is one of those 'tear up the cheee-ild' affairs. Knowing that an assault on an unprotected girl is likely to provoke the attention; realizing that a strenuous brawl will please a large number of people . . . the producers have proceeded to picture it. . . . The result is a selection of hysterical action bound together by loose ties of unity.

'Tear up the cheee-ild' alludes to a stock parody of popular stage melodrama spoofing the acting as being so bad that the villain flubs the line 'give me the child or I'll tear up the papers!' The reference indicates the degree to which contemporary viewers recognized serials as a reincarnation of earlier stage melodrama.

[. . .] As one might expect, guardians of social propriety tended to regard sensational serials as the lowest form of cheap amusement. Ellis Oberholtzer insisted in 1920:

> The most hurtful and the most noxious and altogether objectionable kind of a crime picture that we have on the screen at the present is the serial picture – there is no question about it. The serial is the old dime novel made into a picture . . . There is nothing more deplorable than those crime serials, and yet I do not know how to get rid of them.[12]

Just how low was the serial's low cultural status is conveyed by instances in which even producers who specialized in serials spoke of them in a demeaning way. Carl Laemmle, whose Universal studio invested very heavily in serial production, saw fit to reassure exhibitors that his studio's feature-film offerings were 'not marred by a "serial-ish tone"'.[13]

An even more remarkable instance came from George B. Seitz, Pathé's serial czar, in a curious 1916 trade journal article entitled 'The Serial Speaks'. It opened with these lines:

> I am the serial. I am the black sheep of the picture family and the reviled of critics. I am the soulless one with no moral, no character, no uplift. I am ashamed. . . . Ah me, if only I could be respectable. If only the hair of the great critic would not rise whenever I pass by and if only he would not cry, 'Shame! Child of commerce! Bastard of art!'[14]

It is rare indeed for a promotional article in the Teens to lapse, however briefly, from the film industry's perennial mantra, 'We are attracting the better classes; we are uplifting the cinema; we are preserving the highest moral and artistic standards'. Probably few readers ever took such affirmations as anything more than perfunctory reassurances to a cultural establishment that approached the cinema with an unpredictable mixture of hostility and meddlesome paternalism. Nevertheless, it is unusual, and telling, that a studio mouthpiece should see fit to abandon the 'uplift' conceit altogether. Clearly, it was impossible to even pretend that the serial played any part in the cinema's putative rehabilitation. The serial's intertextual background doomed it to disrepute.

Serials stood out as 'the black sheep of the picture family' at a time when mainstream elements in the film industry were trying to broaden its market by making innocuous middlebrow films suitable for heterogeneous audiences in the larger theaters being built at the time. Rather than catering to 'the mass' – a supposedly classless general audience fancied by the emerging Hollywood institution – serials were made for 'the masses', the predominantly working and lower-middle class and immigrant audience that had supported the incredible nickelodeon boom. Oberholtzer again offered a sharp assessment of the serial's milieu and reputation:

> The crime serial is meant for the most ignorant class of the population with the grossest tastes, and it principally flourishes in the picture halls in mill villages and in the thickly settled tenement houses and low foreign-speaking neighborhoods in large cities. Not a producer, I believe, but is ashamed of such an output, yet not more than one or two of the large manufacturing companies have had the courage to repel the temptation to thus swell their balances at the end of the fiscal year.[15]

Oberholtzer's characterization of serials as dangerous rabble trash was obviously motivated by the classist snobbery of the conservative bourgeoisie to which he belonged. He undoubtedly pigeon-holed serials and their audience too narrowly. Serials were probably seen, at some time or another, by spectators from all classes, and their sensationalism may have appealed to disparate audiences.

Nevertheless, there is little question that the intertextual field of sensational melodrama to which serials belonged was most closely tied to the working-class audience. As a critic in *Variety* noted about the 1916 serial *The Yellow Menace*, 'The impression that these installments create is that the picture was produced with an idea of catering to the popular taste. The story thus far is "mellerdrammer" of the most rabid type.'[16] Almost never screened in large first-run theaters, serials were a staple of small neighborhood theaters and cheap second-run downtown houses. Some of these theaters, clinging to the less expensive 'variety program' well after the ascendance of the feature film, showed episodes from as many as five different serials each week, usually along with slapstick comedies and westerns.[17] Serials evidently were associated with cheap theaters and working-class audiences in England as well the United States. A writer in *The New Statesman* in 1918, observing that British moviegoers paid much higher ticket prices than Americans, noted an exception to this rule: 'Only in those ramshackle "halls" of our poorer streets, where noisy urchins await the next episode of some long since antiquated "Transatlantic Serial" does one notice the proletarian invitation of twopenny and fourpenny seats.'[18]

On both sides of the Atlantic, 'noisy urchins' raised hell during serials screenings. As Oberholtzer stated with chagrin, 'The very announcement that such and such a picture, such as *The Brass Bullet*, "will be shown in this house next Tuesday" has been enough to set young America wild – to howl and shout.'[19] This vocal, rowdy mode of spectatorship, particularly among youths, resembled the rambunctiousness of 10–20–30 audiences. The 'gallery gods' had found a new stomping ground. The resulting clamor, so anathema to highbrow sensibilities because of its association with a long tradition of disorderly working-class conduct in popular amusements, was in fact one of the serial's selling points. A trade journal advertisement for a 1917 Pearl White serial reprinted a telegram that the Pathé Exchange had received from the manager of the Bijou Theatre in Wilmington, North Carolina. It read: 'Showing *Fatal Ring* Here Today – Audience cheering so loud can be heard on tenth floor of Murchison Building and at a distance of one block down the street!'[20] This was a far cry from the tame decorum that contemporary scholars describe as the earmark of a new 'homogenized' audience in the early Teens, a time when the film industry was attempting in various ways to create a mass audience in which differences in class, ethnicity, and community no longer affected the film-viewing experience.[21] Although the rowdiness associated with serials was probably primarily a function of juvenile (as opposed to class or ethnic) identity, it reminds us that the paradigm of homogenized spectatorship never prevailed entirely.

Serial producers were perennially on the defensive. One fairly common rhetorical strategy was to maintain that those who scoffed at serials were actually closet serial-lovers. The 1919 *Photoplay* article illustrates this tack:

> There are some picture fans who will dish up for you all the old arguments about serials. They will tell you that they are silly, ridiculous, illogical, make a fool out of the audience, and stretch the imagination way beyond its proper degree of elasticity. They want to see good features with one thousand feet out of the allotted 5000 devoted to close-ups of the star smiling, or crying, or admiring a rose. Then they sneak over to Third Avenue or Main Street and sit enthralled through an episode of the latest serial.[22]

The reference to Main Street pointed to neighborhood theaters. 'Third Avenue' suggested the low-rent locale of second or third run houses, but more specifically, it alluded to a bastion of 10–20–30 melodrama. New York's Third Avenue theater was a famous popular-priced melodrama house. Sensational melodrama in general often was called simply 'Third Avenue melodrama'.

A more common defensive strategy employed by serial producers was to disavow the connection between their films and the lowbrow address of other serial melodramas. A trade-journal advertisement for Vitagraph's 1916 serial *The Secret*

*Kingdom*, for example, announced in bold print that it was 'The only serial ever offered that meets the taste of all classes – a delight to audiences that heretofore have refused to accept serial productions'. The claim was motivated by a desire to attract booking beyond the usual neighborhood theaters, and perhaps also by an upwardly mobile social mindset among producers. At the same time, the ad. reassured small-theater exhibitors that the serial's supposed refinement in no way dampened 'all the thrills, the tense interest, the mystery, the death-taunting situations that crowd adventure-lovers into your theater'.[23] It is doubtful that this serial, or any others (with a few exceptions), managed to break through the social and theatrical barriers. As a Pathé executive recalled, 'At the time when the pioneer serials like *The Perils of Pauline*, *The Adventures of Kathlyn*, and *The Million Dollar Mystery* were being issued, the attitude of the majority of the larger theaters was one of undisguised contempt'.[24]

A third strategy employed by serial producers to defend their product and woo theater owners involved a display of earnest self-criticism. In this rhetorical ploy, producers would admit that the films had not been as respectable as they should have been and promised that serials would shape up right away, or at the very least adhere more closely to basic conventions of narrative logic. A glance at statements by serial producers and distributors in the 1919–20 and 1920–21 editions of *Wid's Year Book* reveals how rote this rhetoric became:

The serial must, is and will change for the Better.

Sidney Reynolds, Supreme Pictures

We have passed through the era of cheap melodramatic serials with inconsistent plots and impossible situations.

Joe Brandt, National Film Corp.

I feel certain that the time has come for a breaking away from the old standards and the elevation of this class of films to a higher level.

William Fox

Today the serial is playing in better class houses than heretofore . . . [When serials are well made] then and only then will the best theaters who have never run serials before be willing to show serials.

Harry Grossman, Grossman Pictures

Serials will be better and higher class. They will have to be, because they are going into the big theaters which heretofore thought serials were not the proper diet for their patrons.

Carl Laemmle, Universal

We have consistently improved the quality of our serial stories and their production to the point where the product is thoroughly acceptable in the best class of theaters today. [But our] serials have just as big an appeal to the popular-priced houses as has the former type of blood-and-thunder serials.

Paul Brunet, Pathé Exchange

I long ago ceased to make serials as they are commonly known. In the past, the serial has been a series of sensational incidents strung together by the thinnest sort of plot which was constructed merely as a background for stunts and thrills. In the future, I shall make continued stories with the accent on the story. In the final analysis, the story is the thing. . . . We are just at the beginning of the serial era in motion pictures and the field we are entering has limitless possibilities.

Theodore Wharton, Wharton Inc.

Theodore Wharton (whose Ithaca, New York studio had made *The Exploits of Elaine* for Pathé, along with two Elaine sequels and a number of other serials sponsored by Hearst's International Film Service and released by Pathé) went out of business just weeks after this outlook statement was printed, suggesting the degree to which the prediction of a bright future for serials was pie-in-the-sky rhetoric.[25]

Like the stage melodramas they replaced, American serials were an extraordinarily formulaic product. With few exceptions, the conflict between the heroine–hero team and the villain expressed itself in a back-and-forth struggle for the physical possession of the heroine (whom the villain constantly kidnaps or tries to kill) and also the physical possession of a highly prized object – what Pearl White, Pathé's preeminent serial queen, called the 'weenie' (thus, perhaps unknowingly, becoming the world's first psychoanalytic film critic). None of the other words one could use for this object seems terribly apt – the talisman, the thing, the big object, the fetish, the MacGuffin, the commodity – and so, for the sake of convenience, I will keep Pearl White's term. The weenie took many forms: an ebony idol containing the key to a treasure trove; a blueprint for a new torpedo; a code book needed to decipher the location of a hidden fortune; a secret document outlining the defense of the Panama Canal; a special fuel to power a machine that disintegrates people; the chemical formula for turning dirt into diamonds; and so on. Basing narrative conflict around a weenie was a convention carried over from stage melodrama. A 1909 column satirizing the 10–20–30 formula refers to 'the Papahs' ('papers' spoken with a working-class or histrionic accent):

Now, The Papahs may be the old man's will and testament, stolen by the principal bad man in order that he may substitute a forgery, or they may merely be the purloined real estate deed that will make the heroine rich beyond the dreams of avarice if only she can lay hands on it. But Papahs of some description there must be.[26]

In the serial-queen melodrama, the weenie is invariably associated with a father figure, since in almost every serial the heroine is the daughter (for some reason, often an adopted one) of a powerful man (millionaire industrialist, newspaper mogul, ambassador, attorney general, etc.) who, in the first episode, is robbed of the weenie and murdered by the villain, or in a few cases just abducted and black-mailed. With the father dead or powerless, the daughter fights for the weenie in order to gain her inheritance or to rescue her father and clear his name. This stand-ard scenario is, needless to say, ripe for Freudian interpretation. The only exception to the formula that I have found is Mutual's *A Lass of the Lumberlands* (1916), which substitutes the Evil Father for the Good Father. Ruthless logging mogul Dollar Holmes abuses his wife for giving birth to a girl instead of a boy. When the wife later witnesses her husband murder a man, she fears for her life and flees with her baby girl. The serial picks up twenty years later: the girl, who for some reason controls huge tracts of timber, becomes her father's business nemesis. The father, not realizing he is battling his own daughter, orchestrates the requisite abductions, murder attempts, and weenie snatchings.[27]

The serial's bare-bones narrative structure – the repeated capture and re-capture of the weenie, along with the entrapment and liberation of the heroine – afforded a sufficiently simple, predictable, and extensible framework on which to hang a series of thrills over fifteen weeks. Like earlier forms of melodrama, serials were distinguished by the simplicity and reliability of their two-stroke narra-tive engine, the back and forth movement of virtue and villainy. But the engine, to belabor the metaphor, was also intricate and peculiar in its inner design. Although simple in their basic premise of the struggle between good characters and bad char-acters, serial plots tended to become highly convoluted as they progressed over the weeks. An overarching narrative unmappability characterizes many serial melo-dramas. As a review of the 1917 serial *The Seven Pearls* stated, 'There are so many conflicting parties, and so many pearls in this latest serial of Pathé's that there are times when the observer is completely mystified as to who is who, which is which, and what is what'.[28] This sort of narrative unwieldiness probably resulted from several factors: from the inherent difficulty of setting up so many different situa-tions of melodramatic crisis; from the relatively slapdash production process of early pulp cinema; and from the generic legacy of melodrama, which tolerated a high degree of narrative intricacy and discontinuity.

Although its chaotic, non-classical structure disconcerted bourgeois critics, and studio publicity men were at pains to deny it, producers and audiences recognized as a matter of course that popular melodrama was not in the business of narrative elegance and continuity, but rather the business of graphic thrills. It has been suggested that film serials served as a kind of training ground for feature films, an intermediate step on the path towards extended stories and detailed characters.[29] While it merits further inquiry, I think the idea is essentially misleading, since the serial's characters were purely stock and the causal continuity associated with clas-sical narratives were more or less absent in both the stories contained within individual episodes and the overarching story linking the episodes. [. . .]

*What Happened to Mary*, generally considered the first film serial, was released in twelve monthly 'chapters', beginning in July 1912. The serial centers on the adventures of a country girl (and unknowing heiress) as she discovers the pleasures and perils of big city life while at the same time eluding an evil uncle and sundry other villains. The story was serialized simultaneously with numerous stills from the screen version, in *The Ladies' World*, a mass-market women's magazine with the third largest circulation of all monthlies in the country and a primarily working-class readership.[30] This serial was very popular at the box office, making the actress Mary Fuller (in the role of Mary Dangerfield) one of American cinema's first really big, if rather ephemeral, stars.[31] (In one of the industry's first marketing tie-ins, the back cover of *Photoplay* in September 1914 advertised Mary Fuller Perfume, 'a caress from the screen'.) *The New York Dramatic Mirror*'s reviewer complained that although the serial had begun with a degree of 'human naturalness' and sympathetic characterization, it quickly degenerated into an 'overdrawn thriller', 'mere melodrama' reminiscent of the 10–20–30:

> The pictures have developed into melodramas of action rather than dramas of characterization. Mary has become a mere puppet. Mary Fuller does all that is possible for the role, but, at best, Mary Dangerfield isn't very human. She is reminiscent of the heroine of the old-fashioned melodrama where the 'villain still pursued her' to the final curtain.[32]

The commercial success of *What Happened to Mary* prompted the Selig Polyscope Co. and the *Chicago Tribune* syndicate to team up in the production and promotion of *The Adventures of Kathlyn*, exhibited and published fortnightly throughout the first half of 1914. In keeping with the early star system's trope of eponymous protagonists, Kathlyn Williams played Kathlyn Hare, a fetching American girl who, in order to save her kidnapped father, reluctantly becomes the Queen of Allahah, a principality in India. When it became clear that the Kathlyn series was a big hit, virtually every important studio at the time (with the notable exception of Biograph) started making action series and 12–15 chapter serials, running one or two reels per episode. Almost all were connected to prose-version newspaper tie-ins.

Thanhouser had one of the silent era's biggest commercial successes with *The Million Dollar Mystery* (1914). Terry Ramsaye reported:

> *The Million Dollar Mystery* swept through the motion picture theaters with a success without precedent or parallel. The twenty-three chapters of *The Mystery* played in about seven thousand motion picture theaters in a period when there were probably about eighteen thousand such houses. Production costs of *The Mystery* were in the vicinity of $125,000 [about $2,000,000 today], and the gross receipts for the picture were nearly $1,500,000 [about $25,000,000 today].[33]

However, Thanhouser's follow-up, *Zudora (The Twenty Million Dollar Mystery)* was reportedly a huge flop. It had advance bookings totaling $750,000 (almost $12 million today), but once it was released, 'exhibitors fell over each other canceling their bookings'. One problem (other than narrative awkwardness) was that

Thanhouser made the mistake of casting the hero of *The Million Dollar Mystery* as an evil Oriental villain.[34]

By far the biggest producers of serials in the Teens were Universal, Mutual, Vitagraph, and the American branch of Pathé, which dubbed itself as 'the house of serials' and 'the small exhibitor's friend'.[35] Pathé relied heavily on its successful Pearl White vehicles, almost all written and directed by George B. Seitz. *The Perils of Pauline* (1914) reportedly grossed nearly a million dollars, no doubt aided by its Hearst tie-in. *The Exploits of Elaine* (1915) (which was stretched out to thirty-six episodes by two immediate sequels, or extenders, *The Romance of Elaine* and *The New Exploits of Elaine*) reportedly was also 'a tremendous money maker', again with massive Hearst publicity. Renamed *The Mysteries of New York*, the Elaine series enjoyed excellent business in Europe and other parts of the world, as well.[36] Other White/Seitz Pathé serials included *The Iron Claw* (1916), *Pearl of the Army* (1916) (a 'preparedness' serial that capitalized on the First World War as melodramatic fodder), *The Fatal Ring* (1917), *The House of Hate* (1918) (which Eisenstein cited as an influence),[37] *The Black Secret* (1919), *The Lightning Raider* (1919), and *Plunder* (1923). In a publicity war with Mutual, which had claimed Helen Holmes was the biggest box office draw, Pathé carted out statistics indicating that the first four of these serials garnered $24,570,000 in ticket sales (the equivalent of about $320 million today).[38] However inflated that figure, there is no question that the Pearl White serials were highly successful. In a late 1916 mail-in popularity contest conducted by *Motion Picture Magazine*, Pearl White got 155,685 votes, making her the most popular female star in the business, and the second most popular star of all (Warren Kerrigan received 186,895 votes). By comparison, Lillian Gish received only 54,365 votes making her the twenty-first most popular female star – a fact that highlights the degree to which our reliance on 'the canon' has skewed our conception of early film history. In the same contest two years later, Pearl White again did well, coming in third, behind Mary Pickford and Marguerite Clark. Lillian Gish came in thirty-fifth. Two years after that, in late 1920, Pearl White was third again, although the margin between her and Pickford, who was still number one, had increased dramatically. Gish fared considerably better, coming in eighth, but the curve was steep: Pearl White got five times as many votes as Gish, and Pickford got twenty-one times as many.[39]

Throughout the Teens, Pathé also promoted other 'serial queens' – Ruth Roland, Grace Darmond, Mollie King, among others – since the studio almost always had another serial running alongside whatever Pearl White vehicle was out. *Neil of the Navy* (1915) privileged the hero in the title, rather than the heroine played by Lillian Lorraine, but the narrative situations were probably not very different in their gender dynamic. *Patria* (1917), another preparedness serial, starred Irene Castle, a fashionable ballroom dancer (with her partner husband Vernon Castle) billed as 'America's best known woman' and 'New York's best dressed woman'. The choice of this star suggests that Pathé was interested in the possibility of raising the serial's intertextual associations above 10–20–30 and dime-novel melodramatics. The studio insisted that 'there is no audience in the country too "high class" for the right kind of picture'. Trade-journal publicity claimed that *Patria* could play for 'one-dollar and two-dollar audiences', and that it was 'booked solid' over the Proctor circuit of picture palaces. The patriotic theme, capitalizing on the country's expectancy that it would soon enter the European war, may have helped legitimize what was, for all intents and purposes, just a typical blood-and-thunder thriller, albeit with a somewhat more ladylike heroine. The plot, presumably reflecting the politics of William Randolph Hearst (whose International Film Service sponsored the production, and whose newspapers published the tie-in), centered on an attack on the United States by an allied Mexican and Japanese army. According to Kalton Lahue, after those governments protested, President Wilson asked Pathé-Hearst to eliminate the most belligerent scenes (for example, by removing shots of the flags of Mexico and Japan in order to dissimulate the enemy's identity).[40]

In a slightly different vein, Pathé also experimented with a few fourteen-episode series that, like *Patria*, covered stock melodrama with a veneer of highbrow pretense. *Who Pays?* (1915), *Who's Guilty?* (1916), and *The Grip of Evil* (1916) presented moderately lurid thrillers under the guise of edifying 'problem plays that present a terrific indictment of certain present-day habits and conventions of society'. These three series are distinct from the others, and from American film in general, in their consistently unhappy endings.[41]

Universal, like Pathé, had at least two serials running at any time throughout the Teens. In the late Teens, serials reportedly made more money for Universal than any other branch of production, although the studio may not have been proud of that fact. A number of Universal serials were directed by Francis Ford (John Ford's older brother) and starred the duo of Ford and Grace Cunard: *Lucille Love, Girl of Mystery* (1914) (one of the first films Luis Bunuel recalled ever seeing); *The Broken Coin* (1915); *The Adventures of Peg O' The Ring* (1916); and *The Purple Mask* (1916).[42] Among other Universal releases were: *The Pursuit of Patricia* (1914 – a series); *The Trey o' Hearts* (1914); *The Black Box* (1915); *The Master Key* (1914–15); *Graft* (1915); *Peg of the Ring* (1916); *The Mystery Ship* (1917); *The Gray Ghost* (1917) (another serial Eisenstein mentioned); *The Red Ace* (1917); and *Liberty, A Daughter of the U.S.A.* (1916). *The Red Ace*, which began in February, 1917, represents a milestone of sorts: it is the first serial, as far as I know, that began showing profuse amounts of blood during fight scenes. All previous serials were bloodless (although one does not notice the absence when watching them). The blood greatly intensified the graphic violence critics of sensational melodrama found so objectionable.

Mutual's first venture into series melodrama was with *Our Mutual Girl*, made for Mutual by the Reliance studio. It was released for 52 consecutive weeks beginning in 1914. Although some episodes followed the star (Norma Phillips, later Carolyn Wells) on shopping trips, or meeting famous people, many incorporated typical melodrama stories. In 1916, Mutual lured away Kalem's popular stunt actress Helen Holmes (of *Hazards of Helen* fame), along with her director, J. P. McGowan. Their subsequent serials continued in the vein of railroad stunt thrillers with *The Girl and the Game* (1916), *A Lass of the Lumberlands* (1916–17), *The Lost Express* (1917), *The Railroad Raiders* (1917), and others. As Kalem had done with the original *Hazards of Helen*, Mutual generally made its serials relatively inexpensive for exhibitors to rent – a maximum of $15 a day [$195 in today's dollars]. The price was tailored, as was the serial's melodramatic content, to small, neighborhood theaters and second- or third-run downtown houses.

Vitagraph invested in serials from early on. At first, the studio claimed it was offering a 'better grade' of serials for a 'better class of audience'. Its first serial, *The Goddess*, directed by Ralph Ince in 1915, was pitched as 'The Serial Beautiful', something 'light, airy, angelic, kindly, mystic – an idyllic rhapsody'. The story concerns a beautiful waif raised on a desert island by rich industrialists who aim to use her as a tool for molding public opinion in favor of their self-consciously exploitative capitalist ideology. The plan goes awry when the girl, who has been raised to think she was a prophet sent from Heaven (presumably on the assumption that the rabble would therefore accept her as one), instead went about preaching the gospel of kindness and love as 'she faces the problems of anarchists, of socialists, labor questions, modern Christianity'. The producers evidently aspired to some degree of highbrow appeal through the serial's sociological pretensions, as well as its 'many opportunities for charming woodland settings'. Unfortunately, no episodes are extant, so it is hard to know to what extent this was all window dressing for just another melodramatic thriller. Vitagraph's later serials, such as *The Fighting Trail* (1917), *The Secret Kingdom* (1917), *A Fight for Millions* (1918), *Man of Might* (1919), *The Perils of Thunder Mountain* (1919), and *Smashing Barriers* (1919), were no more refined than those of its competitors.[43]

Paramount, a studio specializing in feature films for first-run theaters, put out a serial in late 1917, entitled *Who is Number One?* Apparently, the experiment was not as successful as Paramount had hoped, since the studio never made another serial. Strangely enough, Edison and Selig, the two studios that had pioneered the film-serial form, steered clear of serials despite their initial hits. However, after making a Mary sequel entitled *Who Will Marry Mary?* (1914), Edison went in big for weekly and monthly detective and plucky-girl series such as *The Chronicles of Cleek* (1913–14), *Dolly of the Dailies* (1914), *The Girl Who Earns Her Own Living* (1915), *Below the Deadline* (1915), and *Young Lord Stanleigh* (1915), along with numerous comic series. Throughout 1914, series films constituted about one-third of Edison's monthly output (generally about 8 of 24 releases per month). But the series policy did not go well for Edison, and by early 1915 the studio had dropped series altogether. The studio's executives realized that only series and serials backed by massive publicity campaigns would succeed, and Edison was not able or willing to invest in such heavy advertising. Also, exhibitors made it very clear that they did not want Edison series films, in part because it was felt that they were poorly made and lacked adequate 'thrill punches'.[44]

Kalem made no serials, but, as mentioned earlier, after 1914 it specialized in series films, more so than any other studio. The most famous is *The Hazards of Helen*, whose success impelled the studio to launch at least five series in 1915, including *The Girl Detective*; *Mysteries of the Grand Hotel*; *The Ventures of Marguerite*; *Stingaree* (an equestrian melodrama), and a series built around the actress Alice Joyce and simply referred to as *The Alice Joyce Series*. Kalem's 1916 series included *The Girl from Frisco*; *Grant, Police Reporter*; and *The Scarlet Runner*. The studio continued its short-subject policy into 1917, making another Helen Gibson series, *A Daughter of Daring*, along

with The American Girl series. Soon thereafter, however, Kalem ceased production, rather than braving the financial risks of producing feature films. There was
still a market for shorts, to be shown before the feature, but evidently it was difficult
for studios to stay afloat making only shorts.

Although when they hit they hit big, American serials had an erratic commercial history. Information on box office receipts is hard to come by, but trade-journal
surveys of film exchanges (rental offices) may tell us something about the serial's
popularity among audiences. Between 1914 and 1917, *The Motion Picture News*
conducted a number of in-depth polls of 'exchangemen'. In October, 1914, to the
question 'Do serials continue popular?' 60 percent said 'yes', while about 20 percent
said 'no' (the rest saying 'fairly'). A year later, however, the no's had swelled to
70 percent. But a year after that, at the end of 1916, the serial's popularity had
rallied again, with about a 65/35 percent split between yes and no responses. By
the summer of 1917, the responses had leveled out to exactly fifty/fifty. One should
stress that these polls are not very reliable. For example, in all eight surveys, the
respondent from Canton, Ohio, reported that serials were not popular, but the
respondent from St Louis reported each time that they were very popular. As
tempting as it is to hypothesize regional differences in audience taste, the individual
biases of particular exchange managers was probably a much stronger factor.[45]

If, in fact, serials did have mixed popularity among exhibitors and audiences,
a number of factors probably came into play. At least in part, it may have reflected
the growing rift between a residual 'nickelodeon' cinema, geared toward small-
time exhibitors and primarily lower class audiences, and an emergent Hollywood
model of middlebrow mass entertainment. It is also likely that some audiences
simply tired of the serial's highly formulaic stories, not-always-so-thrilling thrills,
and relatively low production values resulting from their hurried weekly release
schedule.

Nevertheless, despite the fact that they represented only a fraction of the films
produced every year, and despite their ambiguous commercial success, serial melodramas were commercially and culturally important in the Teens. They were
extremely widespread, they represented the most coherent descendant of a popular
tradition of sensational melodrama, they were controversial with respect to their
lowbrow cultural status, they ushered in a new era of mass publicity, and, on a
broader scale, they epitomized a new, or at least newly accentuated, cultural
appetite for powerful stimulus.[46] Perhaps above all, as I have explored at length
elsewhere,[47] they were significant as expressions of a new destabilization of traditional ideologies of gender. Serials were energized by the excitement and anxiety
prompted by the emergence of the New Woman.

## Notes

\*    This is an abridged version of the chapter of the same title in Ben Singer *Melodrama and
     Modernity: Early Sensational Cinema and Its Contexts*, New York: Columbia University Press,
     2001.
1    On the popularity of 'turf melodramas', see Frank Rahill *The World of Melodrama*, University
     Park: Pennsylvania State University Press, 1967, p. 218. Nicholas A. Vardac mentions the

play *A Race For Life* (but not Porter's film) in *Stage to Screen: Theatrical Origins of Early Film – David Garrick to D. W. Griffith*, Cambridge, MA: Harvard University Press, 1949, p. 57. Subsequent editions by De Capo Press and the University of California Press; Charles Musser notes the connection between the play and the film in *Before the Nickelodeon: Edwin S. Porter and the Edison Manufacturing Company*, Berkeley: University of California Press, 1991, p. 407, but mistitles the play as *A Race for a Wife*. That title was used for a 1906 Vitagraph parody.

2   *Variety*, February 2, 1907. Unless page numbers to specific issues of *Variety* are provided, the reference can be found in a comprehensive chronological collection entitled *Variety Film Reviews*, New York: Garland Press, 1983, vol. 1 (1907–20).

3   *Variety*, April 27, 1907. The review does not identify the producer.

4   *Biograph Bulletins, 1908–1912*, introduction by Eileen Bowser, New York: Octagon Books, 1973, p. 11.

5   Tom Gunning *D. W. Griffith and the Origins of the American Narrative Film*, Urbana: University of Illinois Press, 1991, pp. 143–62.

6   See Singer *Melodrama and Modernity*, chapter 8.

7   *Kalem Kalendar*, March 1, 1913, p. 3. Similar films include: *The Pony Express Girl* (released November 6, 1912); *A Race With Time* (December 7, 1912); *A Desperate Chance* (January 18, 1913); *The Flying Switch* (July 14, 1913); *The Railroad Inspector's Peril* (October 1, 1913); *The Railroad Detective's Dilemma* (October 1, 1913).

8   Similar titles include: *The Girl Scout* (released November 6, 1909); *The Tide of Battle* (March 7, 1912); *The Drummer Girl of Vicksburg* (May 15, 1912); *The Colonel's Escape* (June 1, 1912); *The Soldier Brothers of Susanna* (July 1, 1912); *Saved From Court Martial* (August 30, 1912); *The Darling of the C.S.A.* (September 6, 1912); *The Filibusters* (June 15, 1912).

9   Ellis Oberholtzer *The Morals of the Movies*, Philadelphia: Penn Publishing Co., 1922, p. 57.

10  Frank Bruner 'The Modern Dime Novel', *Photoplay*, 16: 48–9, June 1919, p. 118.

11  'Pictures Need No Censoring', *New York Dramatic Mirror* (hereafter *NYDM*), 64: 1651, August 13, 1910, p. 25.

12  'Statement of Mr. Ellis P. Oberholtzer', *Report of the Chicago Motion Picture Commission*, Chicago, September 1920, tenth session, p. 106.

13  The assertion that serials were Universal's most lucrative product appeared in Alfred A. Cohn 'Harvesting the Serial', *Photoplay*, 11: 3, February 1917, p. 25 (one should treat this skeptically without further research); 'Laemmle Explains "Diploma System" for His Directors and Cameramen', *Moving Picture World* (hereafter *MPW*), 43: 7, February 14, 1920, p. 1104.

14  George B. Seitz 'The Serial Speaks', *NYDM*, August 19, 1916, p. 21.

15  Oberholtzer *Morals of the Movies*, p. 55.

16  *Variety*, August 18, 1916. *The Yellow Menace* was an independent production by the Edwin Sales Corporation.

17  In his excellent study of early film exhibition in Lexington, Kentucky, Gregory Waller discusses three theaters that relied quite heavily on serials. [. . .] *Main Street Amusements: Movies and Commercial Entertainment in a Southern City, 1896–1930*, Washington, DC: Smithsonian Institution Press, 1995, pp. 86–95, 197–8.

18  Ernest A. Boyd 'The "Movie Fan"', *The New Statesman*, 10, March 30, 1918, p. 617.

19  'Statement of Mr. Ellis P. Oberholtzer', p. 106.

20  Ad for *The Fatal Ring*, *Motion Picture News* (hereafter *MPN*), October 27, 1917, p. 2838.

21  Miriam Hansen has suggested, for example, that the spectator's sense of belonging to a specific communal audience was diminished by the rise of classical narration, since the feature film 'mandated prolonged attention and absorption' and was therefore 'an effective step in minimizing awareness of the theater space'. This is a compelling argument, but the serials highlight a need for further qualification. Hansen *Babel and Babylon*, Cambridge, MA: Harvard University Press, 1991, chapter 2.

22  Bruner 'Modern Dime Novel', p. 48.

23  *MPN*, 14: 22, December 2, 1916, p. 3379.

24  Fred C. Quimby 'A Standard Feature', *Wid's Year Book*, 1919–20, p. 71.

25  'What of the Serial?', *Wid's Year Book*, 1919–20, pp. 67–71; 'Outlook for Serials', *Wid's Year Book*, 1920–1, pp. 72–3. On Kalem, see entry in Anthony Slide *The American Film Industry: a Historical Dictionary*, Westport, CT: Greenwood Press, 1986.

26  Anon. 'Downfall of Melodrama', *New York Sun*, February 10, 1909, p. 7.

27  Synopses of *A Lass of the Lumberlands* can be found in Mutual's publicity magazine *Reel Life*, beginning October 14, 1916.

28  Peter Milne 'The Seven Pearls', *MPN*, 16: 18, November 3, 1917, p. 3132.

29  For example, Kristin Thompson and David Bordwell *Film History: an Introduction*, New York: McGraw-Hill, 1994, p. 61.

30  Circulation figures in *American Newspaper Annual and Directory*. Characterization of *Ladies' World* readership in Ellen Gruber Garvey *The Adman in the Parlor: Magazines and the Gendering of Consumer Culture, 1880s to 1910s*, New York: Oxford University Press, 1996, p. 9.

31  The serial's popularity was indicated in comments by exhibitors that were gathered by Edison agents who visited about 150 theaters across the country. '1914 Moving Picture General (4 of 6)', Edison archives, Edison National Historic Site, West Orange, New Jersey.

32  Reviews of episodes 'A Will and a Way', *NYDM*, March 12, 1913, p. 32, and 'The High Tide of Misfortune', *NYDM*, May 7, 1913, p. 30.

33  Terry Ramsaye *A Million and One Nights: a History of the Motion Picture Through 1925*, New York: Simon and Schuster, 1926, p. 666.

34  Cohn 'Harvesting the Serials', p. 22.

35  In the survey of titles that follows, I have chosen not to provide narrative synopses. Unless otherwise noted, they all follow the melodramatic plucky-heroine-and-weenie formula discussed above. Kalton Lahue provides a somewhat random overview of a number of serial narratives, along with release dates, casts, and episode titles, in *Continued Next Week: A History of the Moving Picture Serial*, Norman: University of Oklahoma Press, 1964.

36  Financial successes of Pauline and Elaine mentioned in Cohn 'Harvesting the Serials'. Also, 'Pathé's Own Convention', *NYDM*, July 14, 1915, p. 21, reports on a banquet 'to celebrate the reaching of $1 million mark for Elaine'.

37  Sergei Eisenstein 'Dickens, Griffith, and Film Today', in *Film Form*, New York: Harcourt Brace Jovanovich, 1949, p. 203.

38  'Pathé Claims Pearl White Greatest Drawing Card', *MPN*, 15: 17, April 28, 1917, p. 2655.

39  *Motion Picture Magazine*, 12: 11, December 1916, p. 15; *MPN*, 16: 11, December 1918, p. 12; *MPN*, 20: 11, December 1920, p. 94.

40  Publicity articles and reviews of *Patria* in *MPN*, December 2, 1916 p. 40; December 9, 1916, p. 3668; February 3, 1917, p. 735; February 17, 1917, p. 1061 and p. 1075; March 19, 1917, p. 1363; April 14, 1917, p. 2365.

41  Publicity articles and reviews in *MPW*, May 13, 1916, p. 1146; July 8, 1916, p. 262; *NYDM*, July 22, 1916, p. 27; November 4, 1916, p. 34; *MPN*, June 10, 1916, p. 3549; July 1, 1916, p. 4033.

42  On Francis Ford: Tag Gallagher 'Brother Feeney', *Film Comment*, 12: 6, November/December 1976, pp. 12–18; Luis Bunuel *My Last Sigh*, New York: Vintage Books, 1984, p. 32. Bunuel gets things a bit mixed up. He refers to 'Lucilla Love . . . pronounced Lové in Spanish', as a popular actress, rather than as a character.

43  'Vitagraph's First Serial', *MPW*, 24: 5, May 1, 1915, p. 710; advertisement, *MPW*, 24: 7, May 15, 1915, p. 1042.

44  Studio memos and reports, '1914 Moving Pictures General (4 of 6)'; 'Moving Picture Info' files A–C, box 1; '1915 Moving Pictures – General (1 of 3)', Edison archives, Edison National Historic Site, West Orange, New Jersey.

45   'The Motion Picture News Chart of National Film Trade Conditions', *MPN*, 10: 17, October 31, 1914, pp. 21–2; 11: 10, March 13, 1915, pp. 32–5; 11: 20, May 22, 1915, pp. 38–41; 12: 8, August 28, 1915, pp. 39–40; 12: 22, December 4, 1916; 13: 23, June 10, 1916, pp. 3356–7; 14: 26, December 30, 1916, p. 4192; 16: 4, July 28, 1917, pp. 656–7.

46   For a concise history of serial films from 1913 to the mid-1950s, when their production ceased, and of serials made by non-American studios, see my entry simply entitled 'Serials' in Geoffrey Nowell-Smith (ed.) *The Oxford History of World Cinema*, Oxford: Oxford University Press, 1996, pp. 105–111.

47   Singer *Melodrama and Modernity*, chapter 8.

## Chapter 4

# STEVE NEALE

# ACTION-ADVENTURE AS HOLLYWOOD GENRE*

THE TERM 'ACTION-ADVENTURE' is nowadays mainly used to describe what was perceived in the 1980s and 1990s to be a new and dominant trend in Hollywood's output, a trend exemplified by the *Alien* films (1979, 1986, 1993), the *Indiana Jones* films (1981, 1984, 1993), the *Rambo* films (1982, 1985, 1988), the *Die Hard* films (1988, 1990, 1995) and the *Terminator* films (1984, 1991), as well as by films like *Total Recall* (1990), *Point Break* (1991), *The Last of the Mohicans* (1992) and *Braveheart* (1995). This trend encompasses a range of films and genres – from swashbucklers to science fiction films, from thrillers to westerns to war films – and is thus a clear instance of Hollywood's propensity for generic hybridity and overlap. The term 'action-adventure' has been used, though, to pinpoint a number of obvious characteristics common to these genres and films: a propensity for spectacular physical action, a narrative structure involving fights, chases and explosions, and in addition to the deployment of state-of-the-art special effects, an emphasis in performance on athletic feats and stunts. The hyperbolic nature of this emphasis has often been accompanied by an emphasis on the 'hyperbolic bodies' and physical skills of the stars involved: Arnold Schwarzenegger, Sylvester Stallone, Dolph Lundgren, Bruce Willis, Brigitte Nielson, Linda Hamilton and others. It is thus not surprising that the two major books published to date on these films – *Hard Bodies: Hollywood Masculinity in the Reagan Era* by Jeffords[1] and *Spectacular Bodies: Gender, Genre and the Action Cinema* by Tasker[2] – both focus on the ideological implications of this emphasis and both contain the word 'bodies' in their titles.

In the wake of her previous book, *The Remasculinization of America: Gender and the Vietnam War*,[3] Jeffords' aim is:

> on the one hand to argue for the centrality of the masculine body to popular culture and national identity while, on the other, to articulate how the polarizations of the body altered during the years of the Reagan and Bush presidencies.[4]

Her argument in essence is that

> whereas the Reagan years offered the image of a 'hard body' to contrast
> directly to the 'soft body' of the Carter years, the late 1980s and early
> 1990s saw a reevaluation of that hard body, not for a return to the soft
> body but for a rearticulation of masculine strength and power through
> internal, personal, and family-oriented values. Both of these predominant
> models . . . are overlapping components of the Reagan Revolution,
> comprising on the one hand a strong militaristic foreign-policy position and
> on the other hand a domestic regime of an economy and a set of values
> dependent on the centrality of fatherhood.[5]

In arguing her case, Jeffords links a reading of the narrative structure of the
films she discusses to the policy statements of Reagan, Bush and their spokespeople.
However, she does not specify a mechanism through which the presidential ideologies she discusses find their way into the films. She is therefore forced to rely on
analogy. This is a procedure – and a problem – common to numerous ideological
analyses of genres and cycles as we shall see, though it should be said that in this
case Jeffords's analysis dovetails with arguments made about 1980s action films by
Britton, Ryan and Kellner, Sartelle, Traube and Wood.[6] However, others have
taken a different view, both about the ideological significance and scope of 1980s
action films, and about their aesthetic characteristics and values. Pfeil, for instance,
argues that the category of 'white, heterosexual masculinity' that often underpins
these analyses is not as monolithic as is often implied, that the films as a whole are
often multivalent (combining appeals to the populist Left as well as the Right), and
that distinctions need to be made among and between the films themselves, particularly between those produced by Joel Silver at Warners and Fox – the first two
*Die Hard* films and the first two *Lethal Weapon* films – and others like *Batman* (1989)
and *Total Recall*.[7] For Pfeil the former are sites in which 'fantasies of class- and
gender-based resistance to the advent of a post-feminist/post-Fordist world keep
turning over, queasily, deliriously, into accommodations',[8] in which, within a 'very
specifically white/male/hetero American capitalist dreamscape, inter- and/or
multi-national at the top and multiracial at the bottom', 'all the old lines of force
and division between races, classes and genders are both transgressed and redrawn'.[9]
While 'the rhythms of excitation and satisfaction in these films' assert male violence,
'their own speeded-up processes of gratification undermine any claim to male
authority'.[10] The repeated spectacle of 'torn but still beautifully exposed slick-
muscled bodies' raises rather than answers a number of questions: 'how do we
distinguish between their (re)assertion of gendered difference and their submission
to the camera . . . as objects of its gaze and our own? What, likewise, is the
boundary line between the diehard assertion of rugged male individualism and its
simultaneous feminization and spectacularization?'.[11]

Similar points are made by Willis[12] and also by Tasker. Tasker points to the
ambivalent populism of many of these action films, and to the fact that the muscular
hero within them is often literally 'out of place': 'Increasingly . . . the powerful

white hero is a figure who operates in the margins, while in many senses continuing to represent dominance. This is an important trait in many action pictures and is central to the pleasures of the text'.[13] Equally central are style, spectacle, atmosphere and tone. Tasker is particularly interested in the knowing visual excess and the tongue-in-cheek humour characteristic of these films. She is therefore particularly insistent that ideological readings based solely on an analysis of their plots may be reductive, misleading, or both. As an example, she cites *Red Sonja* (1985), a sword-and-sorcery follow-up to Schwarzenegger's *Conan* films (1982 and 1984). Early on in *Red Sonja*, we learn that Sonja herself (Brigitte Nielsen) has rejected the sexual advances of Queen Gedren. She becomes a swordswoman, and it is in this guise that she encounters Schwarzenegger as Kalidor:

> An analysis of the ideological terms at work in a film like *Red Sonja* is not difficult – the film follows Sonja's journey to a 'normal' sexual identity, or at least the rejection of lesbian desire. After the initial 'threat' of lesbianism, Sonja becomes a masculinised swordswoman who refuses Kalidor/Schwarzenegger until he can beat her in a 'fair fight'.[14]

However, the comedy and the excess permeating the presentation of the fight and the 'texture' of the film as a whole 'call into question the very terms deployed – the "normal" sexual identity to which Sonja is led'.[15] Tasker continues, noting the extent to which exaggeration and parody are involved in the presentation of the body in these films. For her this means that the body and the terms of its gender can become the site of transgression and play, the focus of an attention that can make strange as well as reinforce norms of gender and sexual identity. Similar points are made by Holmlund in an article on *Lock Up* (1989) and *Tango and Cash* (1989), though while stressing the extent to which in these films heterosexual masculinity is presented as 'masquerade', she concludes by noting that 'Masculinity may be only a fantasy, but as the success of Sylvester Stallone's films, including their invocation by rightwing politicians like Reagan and Bush, so amply demonstrates, masquerades of masculinity are eminently popular, and undeniably potent'.[16] Her conclusion thus dovetails as much with Jeffords's position as it does with Tasker's.

Related issues and disagreements are raised by the 'women warrior' films discussed by Tasker, films like *Fatal Beauty* (1987), *China O'Brien* (1988) and the *Alien* trilogy, and by what Brown (1996) and Willis[17] see as an increasing trend towards 'hardbody heroines' and 'combative femininity' in action films in the 1990s. An additional complication here is the fact that *Fatal Beauty* centres on a black female star, Whoopi Goldberg, and thus constitutes an exception to what most commentators have perceived not just as an ethnic bias in action-adventure, but as a systematic project of marginalization, demonization and subordination *vis-à-vis* non-whites whose immediate roots lie in the racist and imperialist policies of Reagan and Bush.[18]

One way to contextualize, if not necessarily to resolve, these issues and debates is to contextualize the films themselves by locating them within a tradition.

'Action-adventure' is not a new term. It was used by *Film Daily* in 1927 to describe a Douglas Fairbanks film called *The Gaucho* (1927).[19] And it was used, among others, to categorize 'The New Season Product' in the *Motion Picture Herald* in 1939.[20] Used separately, the terms 'action' and 'adventure' have an even longer history, and films in the action-adventure tradition have been a staple in Hollywood's output since the 1910s.[21] With its immediate roots in nineteenth-century melodrama and in a principal strand of popular fiction, action-adventure has always encompassed an array of genres and sub-types: westerns, swashbucklers, war films, disaster films, space operas, epics, safari films, jungle films, and so on. As Thomas Sobchack points out, 'Although these groups of films may appear a disparate lot, their patterns of action and character relationships display characteristics which clearly link them together and distinguish them from other genres'.[22] 'In a sense,' he continues, echoing Cawelti:[23]

> all non-comic genre films are based on the structure of the romance of medieval literature: a protagonist either has or develops great and special skills and overcomes insurmountable obstacles in extraordinary situations to successfully achieve some desired goal, usually the restitution of order to the world invoked by the narrative. The protagonists confront the human, natural, or supernatural powers that have improperly assumed control over the world and eventually defeat them.[24]

Set 'in the romantic past or in an inhospitable place in the present', the exotic milieux and the 'flamboyant actions of the characters' in the adventure film afford numerous opportunities for filmic spectacle.[25] Its basic narrative structure, meanwhile, gives rise to two characteristic variations. 'One focuses on the lone hero — the swashbuckler, the explorer who searches for the golden idol, the great hunter who leads the expedition, the lord of the jungle.' The other, the 'survival' form, most apparent in war films, prison films and disaster films, 'focuses on a hero interacting with a microcosmic group, the sergeant of a patrol, the leader of a squadron, the person who leads a group of castaways out of danger and back to civilization'.[26] As Marchetti points out, the plots in adventure films of all kinds are usually episodic, 'allowing for wide variations in tone, the inclusion of different locations and incidentally introduced characters, and moments of spectacle, generally involving fights, explosions, or other types of violence'.[27] It might be noted that among the variations in tone to which Marchetti refers, tongue-in-cheek humour and tongue-in-cheek knowingness are as common in swashbucklers as they are in modern action-adventure films. And it might also be noted that even where locations are restricted, as they often are in prison and submarine films, space, the control of space, and the ability to move freely through space or from one space to another are always important.[28]

In his discussion of the swashbuckler, Sobchack notes that the hero is 'defined as much by his physical expressiveness as by his good deeds'.[29] He also argues that in the survival genres, 'women play a decisive role in the success or failure of the group', thus returning us to issues of gender and the body within the context of the adventure film as a whole. Displays of the male body and of the hero's physical prowess are traditional in all kinds of adventure films, especially those of the lone-hero variety. Swashbucklers themselves tend to rely on costumes and *coiffeur* rather than muscles (though as Richards[30] points out, displays of the naked male torso – often in scenes of torture or violence – are a regular feature of such films). But the reverse is the case in the Tarzan films and in epics like *Samson and Delilah* (1949). And just as modern performers like Schwarzenegger and Stallone are well-known for their physique, so too were Victor Mature, Burt Lancaster (who trained as an acrobat) and Johnny Weissmuller (who played Tarzan at MGM and Columbia, and who was once an Olympic swimmer).

These displays reach back beyond Elmo Lincoln's performances as Tarzan in the late 1910s and early 1920s and Douglas Fairbanks's performances in films like *The Three Musketeers* (1921), *Robin Hood* (1922) and *The Thief of Bagdad* (1924).[31] They include the performances of such muscular stars as House Peters, Richard Talmadge, Jack Tunney and Joe Boromo in the numerous adventure serials, 'railroad melodramas' and circus films that pervaded the 1920s, as well as those of Tom Mix, Ken Maynard and others in stunt-oriented westerns like *Riders of the Purple Sage* (1924) and *The Glorious Trail* (1928).[32] They also include performances of various kinds in the stunt-based aviation films of the late 1920s and early 1930s, the Errol Flynn films made at Warners in the mid-to-late 1930s and early 1940s, the Tyrone Power films made at Fox in the late 1940s, the post-war cycle of adventure films featuring the likes of Robert Taylor, Burt Lancaster, Alan Ladd and Cornell Wilde, such subsequent post-war epics as *Spartacus* (1960), *Ben-Hur* (1959) and *El Cid* (1961), and the numerous adventure serials, Tarzan films and jungle melodramas that appeared throughout the 1930s, the 1940s and the 1950s.[33]

Hence, as Tasker points out, 'the appearance of . . . "muscular cinema" during the 1980s calls on a much longer tradition of representation'.[34] The same might also be said of women warriors. The 1910s were marked by the serial queens; and even if 'the character of most successful serials after the war shifted to emphasize male heroics',[35] women warriors are by no means impossible to find. Texas Guinan, 'The Female "Bill Hart"',[36] starred in a number of two-reel westerns in the late 1910s and early 1920s, successors to such earlier films as *Queen of the Prairies* (1910) and *A Girl of the West* (1911) and contemporaries of films like *The Girl Who Wouldn't Quit* (1918) and *The Crimson Challenge* (1922). In the early 1940s, Republic and Universal began to make westerns with Kay Aldridge and Jennifer Holt, and traces of these new roles for women were evident in a number of post-war B westerns as well.[37] The adventure films of the 1920s included *Adventure* (1925), with Joan Lackland, and *Flaming Barriers* (1924), in which 'the heroine is required to play chauffeur to a fire truck'.[38] The aviation cycle included such films as *Flying Hostess* (1936), *Wings in the Dark* (1935), *Tail Spin* (1939) and *Women in the Wind* (1939).[39] And the post-war adventure cycle included *At Sword's Point* (1952) and *Anne of the Indies* (1952).[40]

There were specific contextual factors at work in each case. The female-centred adventure films of the 1910s were influenced by the advent of New Womanhood.

The female-centred westerns of the 1910s and the 1920s were influenced in addition by the notion that women in the west were 'free and untrammeled by the conventions of society',[41] and by a cultural tradition that included dime novel heroines, cowgirls and female performers in Wild West Shows and in rodeos.[42] The reappearance of the western heroine in the 1940s was due in part to the departure of male stars like Gene Autry and Tim McCoy for military duty during the war.[43] And the advent of female-centred aviation films was partly due to the promotion by the aviation industry of an association between women and flying as a means of assuring the public that flying was safe.[44] However, as Taves points out, 'the traits and activities of the adventurer are possible for members of either race and either sex'.[45] In other words, there is nothing inherent in the structure and the stereotypes of the adventure film to specify its central protagonists as either male or female.

The same is arguably true when it comes to ethnicity and race. As Nerlich has pointed out, the word 'adventure' originally meant simply an unexpected or extraordinary event.[46] However, as he himself goes on to argue, the ideology of adventure in its modern sense — its association with the active seeking out of such events — was developed in conjunction first with the medieval cult of the courtly knight, second with merchant adventuring (and state-sponsored piracy) in the early modern period, and third with the spread of empire during the course of the nineteenth century. Hence its links with colonialism, imperialism and racism, as well as with traditional ideals of masculinity, run very deep. These links have been explored in numerous books and articles on adventure films and adventure fiction.[47] They traverse an array of survivalist and lone hero genres, and are readily apparent in safari and jungle films, in 'lost world' adventure films, and in films about European empires and European imperial heroes as well as in westerns and war films.

However, they do so unevenly, and sometimes in contradictory and tension-filled ways. The connections between prison films and imperialism are tenuous to say the least, though they are clearly far less tenuous in prisoner-of-war films. The same is true of disaster films. Rhona Berenstein argues that the 'interstitial' role played by white women in many 1930s jungle films means that while the films themselves:

> are complicit with the larger mappings of racist attitudes that punctuated the era as a whole . . . the racial mobility of heroines suggests that dominant culture's investment in a racial hierarchy, in asserting the primacy of whiteness and the mastery of white masculinity, is also tenuous at best.[48]

And in his book on the historical adventure film, Brian Taves has argued that while imperial, colonial and ethnocentric assumptions underlie the genre as a whole, its commitment to an ethos of altruism, liberty and justice, to 'the valiant fight for freedom and a just form of government'[49] can generate all kinds of ideological contortions and an array of quite distinct political positions.

To an extent these positions correspond to those of the four major cycles Taves identifies as marking the genre's history, and to those of the five major sub-types he sees as comprising the genre as a whole. Following the production of early versions of *The Count of Monte Cristo* (1912) and *The Prisoner of Zenda* (1913), he argues that the first major cycle begins with the Douglas Fairbanks version of *The Mark of Zorro* in 1920. This cycle includes other Fairbanks films, like *The Iron Mask* (1929) and *Robin Hood* (1922), and a series of adaptations of the novels of Rafael Sabatini – *Scaramouche* (1923), *The Sea Hawk* (1924), *Captain Blood* (1924) and *Bardelys the Magnificent* (1926). It sets the pattern for a number of sub-types. A second cycle begins in 1934, with the release of *Treasure Island*, *The Lost Patrol* and *The Count of Monte Cristo*. It includes *Captain Blood* (1935), *The Adventures of Robin Hood* (1938), *The Mark of Zorro* (1940) and *The Sea Wolf* (1941), and although some of these films clearly deal in a displaced manner with the growth of fascism and the outbreak of the Second World War in Europe, America's entry into the war at the end of 1941 saw the end of the cycle. A third cycle begins in 1944 with the release of *Frenchman's Creek* and *The Princess and the Pirate*. Using the resources of colour much more frequently – and, after 1953, the resources of CinemaScope and other widescreen processes as well – the cycle encompasses such films as *Ivanhoe* (1952), *Moby Dick* (1956), *The Vikings* (1958) and *55 Days at Peking* (1963). It is marked as a whole by a 'loss of optimism',[50] by more flawed and less virtuous heroes, and by an increase in the level of torment, torture and violence. The fourth cycle – whose films are often more cynical or tongue-in-cheek in tone, and which Taves describes as 'revisionist'[51] – begins with *The Three Musketeers* in 1974, and includes *Crossed Swords* (1977) and *Robin and Marian* (1976). (Arguably the success of *Robin Hood – Prince of Thieves* in 1991 inaugurated a fifth cycle, a cycle which includes *Rob Roy* (1995), *1492 – Conquest of Paradise* (1992) and *Braveheart* (1995).)

The sub-types Taves identifies are the swashbuckler, the pirate film, 'the sea adventure film', 'the empire adventure film', and 'the fortune hunter adventure film'. These sub-types vary not only in setting – from the castles of medieval Europe via the Spanish Main to colonial India and Africa – but also in the way they handle the topics of oppression, revolt and 'proper governance'.[52] Thus while some swashbucklers, including most of versions of *The Three Musketeers*, are conservative in implication, most, like *The Adventures of Robin Hood* and *The Mark of Zorro*, oppose what they characterize as tyranny, and often portray just – if limited – rebellions and struggles for freedom. By contrast, rebellions in empire adventure films, in films like *The Lives of a Bengal Lancer* (1935) and *Gunga Din* (1939), tend to emanate from the struggles of native populations against white colonial rule, and to be portrayed both as unjustified and as destructive, as far more tyrannical than any act or form of colonial government.

The politics of the other sub-groups tend to vary much more from film to film. Taves notes, though, that while in gender terms most historical adventure films tend to be firmly male-centred, the pirate film 'permits some of the most important roles for women in the adventure genre':

The pirate adventure brings together diametrically opposed types of women, fellow adventurers and those who become objects and remain basically passive. The form is rife with women who occupy a background role, often abducted and won over by the pirate captain (*Raiders of the Seven Seas*). Yet the ranks of pirates also include unusually large numbers of fiery women of the sea who take active roles as the equal or superior of men (*Frenchman's Creek*; *Buccaneers Girl*; *Anne of the Indies*; *Against All Flags*).[53]

He goes on to argue that 'the independence of such characters is frequently undercut through their portrayals in situations where they become largely dependent on men'.[54] Here, the contradictions of the sub-group are as apparent as they are in the genre as a whole, where male codes of honour and dominance tend to rub shoulders with appeals to universal liberty and self-determination, where acts of rebellion tend to result in the institutionalization of benign but unelected regimes of authority,[55] and where 'while revolutionary movements are often valorized, many adventurers are also imperialists, who justify exploration and colonialism in the belief that they spread the benefits of their civilization to supposedly unenlightened lands'.[56] Only occasionally have such contradictions been brought to the fore. But in that regard, as in its inherently contradictory (and ethnocentric) stance, the historical adventure film is no different from most other Hollywood genres.

## Notes

\* This essay originally appeared in Steve Neale *Genre and Hollywood*, London: Routledge, 2000.

1 S. Jeffords *Hard Bodies: Hollywood Masculinity in the Reagan Era*, New Brunswick, NJ: Rutgers University Press, 1994.
2 Y. Tasker *Spectacular Bodies: Gender, Genre and the Action Cinema*, London: Routledge, 1993.
3 S. Jeffords *The Remasculinization of America: Gender and the Vietnam War*, Bloomington: Indiana University Press, 1989.
4 Jeffords *Hard Bodies*, p. 13.
5 Ibid.
6 A. Britton 'Blissing Out: The Politics of Reaganite Entertainment', *Movie*, 31: 2, 1986, pp. 1–42; M. Ryan and D. Kellner *Camera Politica: The Politics and Ideology of Contemporary Hollywood Film*, Bloomington: Indiana University Press, 1988, pp. 217–43; J. Sartelle 'Dreams and Nightmares in the Hollywood Blockbuster' in G. Nowell-Smith (ed.) *The Oxford History of World Cinema*, Oxford: Oxford University Press, 1996, pp. 516–26; E.G. Traube *Dreaming Identities: Class, Gender and Generation in 1980s Hollywood Movies*, Boulder, CO: Westview Press, 1992, pp. 28–66; R. Wood *Hollywood from Vietnam to Reagan*, New York, Columbia University Press, 1986, pp. 162–88.
7 F. Pfeil *White Guys: Studies in Postmodern Domination and Difference*, New York: Verso, 1995, pp. 1–36.
8 Ibid., p. 28.
9 Ibid., p. 32.
10 Ibid.
11 Ibid., p. 29.

12  S. Willis *High Contrast: Race and Gender in Contemporary Hollywood Film*, Durham, NC: Duke University Press, 1997, pp. 27–59.

13  Tasker *Spectacular Bodies*, p. 98.

14  Ibid., p. 30.

15  Ibid.

16  C. Holmlund 'Masculinity as Multiple Masquerade: The "Mature" Stallone and the Stallone Clone', in Cohan and Hark (eds) *Screening the Male: Exploring Masculinities in Hollywood Cinema*, London: Routledge, 1993, pp. 225–6.

17  J.A. Brown 'Gender and the Action Heroine: Hardbodies and *The Point of No Return*', *Cinema Journal*, 35: 3, 1996, pp. 52–71; Willis *High Contrast*, pp 98–128.

18  In addition to those already cited, see G. Marchetti 'Action-Adventure as Ideology' in I. Angus and S. Jhally (eds) *Cultural Politics in Contemporary America*, New York: Routledge, 1989, pp. 182–97; A. Ross 'Cowboys, Cadillacs and Cosmonauts: Families, Film Genres, and Technoculture', in J.A. Boone and M. Cadden (eds) *Engendering Men: The Question of Male Feminist Criticism*, New York: Routledge, 1990, pp. 87–101 (especially pp. 94–101.)

19  *Film Daily*, 27 November 1927, p. 6.

20  *Motion Picture Herald*, 3 June 1939, p. 17.

21  One reason for this was audience preference, particularly in foreign markets, and particularly in the era of sound. As Maltby and Vasey point out: 'it was an influential truism of foreign distribution that movies reliant on dialogue to explain their plot and develop their story, known in the industry as 'walk and talk' pictures, fared substantially less well in the non-English-speaking market than did action pictures'. ('The International Language Problem: European Reactions to Hollywood's Conversion to Sound', in D.W. Ellwood and R. Kroes (eds) *Hollywood in Europe: Experiences of a Cultural Hegemony*, Amsterdam: VU University Press, 1994, pp. 68–93: p. 90). See also Justin Wyatt *High Concept: Movies and Marketing in Hollywood*, Austin: University of Texas Press, 1994, p. 80.

22  T. Sobchack 'The Adventure Film', in W.D. Gehring *Handbook of American Film Genres*, Westport: Greenwood Press, 1988, p. 9.

23  J. Cawelti *Adventure, Mystery and Romance: Formula Stories as Art and Popular Culture*, Chicago: Chicago University Press, 1976, pp. 39–41.

24  Sobchack 'The Adventure Film', p. 9.

25  Ibid., p. 10.

26  Ibid., p. 12.

27  Marchetti 'Action-Adventure as Ideology', p. 188.

28  It is no accident that spaces and locations, in particular 'open' and 'closed' spaces and locations, often form the basis of systematic patterns in action-adventure films. In *Red Heat* (1988), for example, the hero is vulnerable to attack in interior spaces, but either safe or victorious out of doors; the first and the second halves of *The Great Escape* (1963) take place respectively inside and outside the prison camp; and *Silverado* is founded structurally on a repeated motif of imprisonment, confinement and escape into an open natural landscape.

It is tempting to map this preoccupation with space onto the preoccupation in many adventure films and stories with what Phillips has called 'The geography of adventure, a cultural space opened up by European encounters with the non-European world' during the era of colonialist and imperialist expansion (R. Phillips *Mapping Men and Empire: A Geography of Adventure*, London: Routledge, 1997, p. 13). While there are connections in numerous instances, it is probably best to avoid collapsing the one into the other. For the particular significance of geography, landscape and space in the western, see J. Basinger *American Cinema: One Hundred Years of Filmmaking*, New York: Rizzoli, 1994, pp. 116–20; E. Buscombe 'Inventing Monument Valley, Nineteenth-Century Landscape Photography and the Western Film', in P. Petro (ed.) *Fugitive Images: From Photography to Video*,

Bloomington: Indiana University Press, 1995; C. Bush 'Landscape', in Buscombe (ed.) *The BFI Companion to the Western,* London: Andre Deutsch/BFI, 1988; P. French *Westerns,* London: Secker and Warburg, 1973, pp. 100–12; J. Mauduy and G. Henriet *Géographies du Western,* Paris: Nathan, 1989; L.C. Mitchell *Westerns: Making the Man in Fiction and Film,* Chicago: Chicago University Press, 1996; C. Saxton *Illusions of Grandeur: The Representation of Space in the American Western Film,* University of California Berkeley, Ph.D. thesis, 1985, Ann Arbor: UMI Dissertation Information Service, 1988; E. Shohat and R. Stam *Unthinking Eurocentrism: Multiculturalism and the Media,* London: Routledge, 1994, pp. 116–18; J.R. Short *Imagined Country: Society, Country and the Environment,* London: Routledge, 1991, pp. 178–96; G. Szanto *Narrative Taste and Social Perspectives: The Matter of Quality,* Houndsmill: Macmillan, 1987, pp. 23–39; V.W. Wexman *Creating the Couple: Love, Marriage and Hollywood Performance,* Princeton, NJ: Princeton University Press, 1993, pp. 109–11; and the discussions of landscape in the reviews of *Dead Man* (1996) by K. Jones 'Dead Man', *Cineaste,* 22: 2, 1996, pp. 45–6: p. 46; and J. Levich 'Western Auguries: Jim Jarmusch's *Dead Man*', *Film Comment,* 32: 3, 1996, pp. 39–41.

29   Sobchack 'The Adventure Film', 1988, p. 13.

30   J. Richards *Swordsmen of the Screen: From Douglas Fairbanks to Michael York,* London: Routledge and Kegan Paul, 1977, pp. 15, 40.

31   On the Fairbanks films see Richards *Swordsmen of the Screen,* pp. 12–13, 25–26; R. Koszarski *An Evening's Entertainment: The Age of the Silent Feature Picture, 1915–1928,* New York: Scribner's, 1990, pp. 270–1; B. Taves *The Romance of Adventure: The Genre of Historical Adventure Movies,* Jackson: University of Mississippi Press, 1993, pp. 67–8.

32   On the serials in particular, see I.G. Edmonds *Big U: Universal in the Silent Days,* South Brunswick, NJ: A.S. Barnes, 1977; Koszarski *An Evening's Entertainment,* pp. 164–6; K.C. Lahue, *Continued Next Week: A History of the Moving Picture Serial,* Norman: University of Oklahoma Press, 1964, pp. 70–152 and *Bound and Gagged: The Story of the Silent Serials,* New York: Castle Books, 1968. On the westerns, see Buscombe 'The Western: A Short History' in *BFI Companion to the Western,* pp. 30–3; W.K. Everson *The Hollywood Western: 90 Years of Cowboys, Indians, Trainrobbers, Sheriffs and Gunslingers, and Assorted Heroes and Desperados,* New York: Citadel, [1969] 1992, pp. 84–7, 103–26 and Koszarski *An Evening's Entertainment,* pp. 288–91.

33   On the aviation films see M. Paris *From the Wright Brothers to* Top Gun: *Aviation, Nationalism and Popular Cinema,* Manchester: Manchester University Press, 1995, pp. 55–83 and S. Pendo *Aviation in the Cinema,* Metuchen, NJ: Scarecrow Press, 1985, pp. 1–150. On the Errol Flynn films, see T. Balio *Grand Design: Hollywood as a Modern Business Enterprise, 1990–1939,* New York: Scribner's, 1993, pp. 203–5; Richards *Swordsmen of the Screen,* pp. 18, 26–7; N. Roddick *A New Deal in Entertainment: Warner Brothers in the 1930s,* London: British Film Institute, 1983, pp. 235–47; T. Schatz *The Genius of the System: Hollywood Filmmaking in the Studio Era,* New York: Pantheon, 1988, pp. 208–10, and Taves *The Romance of Adventure,* pp. 69–72. On the Tyrone Power films, see Richards *Swordsmen of the Screen,* pp. 18, 30–1. On the post-war adventure films, see Richards *Swordsmen of the Screen,* pp. 18–24, and Taves *The Romance of Adventure,* pp. 72–4. On the male body and masculinity in the post-war epic, and in these films in particular, see S. Cohan *Masked Men: Masculinity and the Movies in the Fifties,* Bloomington, Indiana University Press, 1997, pp. 141–63; I.R. Hark 'Animals or Romans: Looking at Masculinity in *Spartacus*' in S. Cohan and I.R. Hark (eds) *Screening the Male;* L. Hunt 'What are Big Boys Made Of?: *Spartacus, El Cid* and the Male Epic', in P. Kirkham and J. Thumin (eds) *You Tarzan: Masculinity, Movies and Men,* London, Lawrence and Wishart, 1993; S. Neale 'Masculinity as Spectacle: Reflections on Men and Mainstream Cinema' in Cohan and Hark (eds) *Screening the Male,* p. 18, and P. Willemen 'Anthony Mann: Looking at the Male', *Framework,* nos 15/16/17, 1981, p. 16. On the adventure serials and the Tarzan films, see A. Barbour *Days of Thrills and Adventure,* London: Collier Books, 1970, pp. 11–156; D. Cheatwood 'The Tarzan

Films: An Analysis of Determinants of Maintenance and Change in Conventions', *Journal of Popular Culture*, 16: 2, 1982, pp. 127–42; W.C. Cline *In the Nick of Time: Motion Picture Sound Serials*, Jefferson, NC: McFarland, 1984; G. Essoe *Tarzan of the Movies*, Syracuse, NJ: Citadel Press, 1979; P. Lehman ' "What no red-blooded man needs lessons in doing", Gender and Race in *Tarzan of the Apes*', *Griffithiana*, 40: 1, 1991, pp. 124–9; and W. Morton 'Tracking the Signs of Tarzan: Trans-media Representations of a Pop-culture Icon', in Kirkham and Thumin (eds) *You Tarzan*. For further general discussion of adventure and the white male body, see R. Dyer *White*, London: Routledge, 1997, pp. 145–83.

34   Tasker *Spectacular Bodies*, p. 1.

35   Koszarski *An Evening's Entertainment*, p. 166.

36   *Exhibitors Herald and Motography*, 14 June 1919, p. 15.

37   R. White 'The Good Guys Wore White Hats: The B Western in American Culture', in R. Aquila (ed.) *Wanted Dead or Alive: The American West in Popular Culture*, Urbana: University of Illinois Press, 1996, pp. 135–59 (especially pp. 148–150).

38   *Film Daily*, 3 February 1929, p. 8.

39   R. Parks *The Western Hero in Film and Television: Mass Media Mythology*, Ann Arbor: University of Michigan Research Press, 1982, pp. 114–16; Pendo, *Aviation in the Cinema*, pp. 143–7.

40   Richards *Swordsmen of the Screen*, pp. 18, 38; Taves, *The Romance of Adventure*, pp. 29, 129–30.

41   'Western Dramas Win Patrons' *Exhibitors Herald and Motography*, 4 January 1919, p. 89.

42   S. Armitage 'Rawhide Heroines: The Evolution of the Cowgirl and the Myth of America', in S. Girgus (ed.) *The American Self, Myth, Ideology and Popular Culture*, Albuquerque: University of New Mexico, 1981, pp. 166–81; D.E. Jones 'Blood 'N' Thunder: Virgins, Villains and Violence in the Dime Western Novel', *Journal of Popular Culture*, 4: 2, 1970, pp. 507–17; C. Savage *Cowgirls*, London: Bloomsbury, 1996, pp. 86–93.

43   'Lady on Hossback Newest Fad In Westerns, But Will Fans Go For It?', *Variety*, 14 October 1942, pp. 1, 55.

44   M. Cadogan *Women with Wings: Female Fliers in Fact and Fiction*, Houndsmill: Macmillan, 1992, p. 87; J.J. Corn 'Making Flying "Thinkable": Women Pilots and the Selling of Aviation, 1927–1940', *American Quarterly*, 32: 4, 1979, pp. 556–71.

45   Taves *The Romance of Adventure*, p. 122.

46   M. Nerlich *Ideology of Adventure: Studies in Modern Consciousness, 1100–1750*, 2 vols, trans R. Crowley, Minneapolis: University of Minnesota Press, [1977] 1987, pp. 3–4.

47   Aside from those cited already, see G. Bederman *Manliness and Civilization: A Cultural History of Gender and Race in the United States, 1880–1917*, Chicago: Chicago University Press, 1995, pp. 170–239; J. Bristow *Empire Boys: Adventures in a Man's World*, London: HarperCollins, 1991; E. Cheyfitz '*Tarzan of the Apes*: US Foreign Policy in the Twentieth Century', *American Literary History*, 1: 2, 1989, pp. 339–60; G. Dawson *Soldier Heroes: British Adventure, Empire and the Imaginary of Masculinities*, London: Routledge, 1994; M. Denning *Mechanic Accents: Dime Novels and Working-Class Culture in America*, New York: Verso, 1987; R.M. Drinnon *Facing West: The Metaphysics of Indian-Hating and Empire Building*, Minneapolis: University of Minnesota Press, 1981; T. Engelhardt *The End of Victory Culture: Cold War America and the Disillusion of a Generation*, New York: Basic Books, 1995; L. Fiedler *The Return of the Vanishing American*, New York: Stein and Day, 1968; M. Green *Dreams of Adventure, Deeds of Empire*, New York: Basic Books, 1979. *The Great American Adventure*, Boston: Beacon Press, 1984; A. Kaplan 'Romancing the Empire: The Embodiment of American Masculinity in the Popular Historical Novel of the 1890s', *American Literary History*, 2: 3, 1990, pp. 659–90; A. Kolodny *The Lay of the Land: Metaphor as Experience and History in American Life and Letters*, Chapel Hill: University of North Carolina Press, 1975, and *The Land Before Her: Fantasy and Experience of the American Frontiers, 1630–1860*, Chapel Hill: University of North Carolina Press, 1984; T.J.J. Lears *No Place of Grace: Antimodernism*

*and the Transformation of American Culture, 1880–1920*, New York: Pantheon, 1981;
D. Leverenz 'The Last Real Man in America: From Natty Bumppo to Batman', *American
Literary History*, 3: 4, 1991, pp. 735–81; A. Saxton *The Rise and Fall of the White Republic:
Class, Politics and Mass Culture in Nineteenth-Century America*, London: Verso, 1990; E. Shohat
'Gender and the Culture of Empire: Towards a Feminist Ethnogaphy of the Cinema', in
M. Bernstein and G. Studlar (eds) *Visions of the East: Orientalism in Film*, London: I.B. Tauris,
[1991] 1997; E. Shohat and R. Stam *Unthinking Eurocentrism*, pp. 55–177; R. Slotkin
*Regeneration Through Violence: The Mythology of the American Frontier*, Middletown, CT:
Wesleyan University Press, 1973, *The Fatal Environment: The Myth of the Frontier in the Age
of Industrialization*, Middletown, CT: Wesleyan University Press, 1985 and *Gunfighter
Nation: The Myth of the Frontier in Twentieth-Century America*, New York: Atheneum, 1992;
J. Tompkins *Sensational Designs: The Cultural Work of American Fiction, 1790–1860*, New
York: Oxford University Press, 1985; M. Torgovnick *Gone Primitive: Savage Intellects, Modern
Lives*, Chicago: University of Chicago Press, 1990, pp. 42–72 and G.E. White *The Eastern
Establishment and the Western Experience: The West of Fredric Remington, Theodore Roosevelt, and
Owen Wister*, New Haven: Yale University Press, 1968. Engelhardt's thesis is particularly
interesting, and demonstrates the merits of grouping various kinds of adventure films
together. He argues that a 'national war story' common to westerns, war films and other
tales of adventure, whose basic motifs and whose fundamental ideological framework date
back several centuries, reached a peak in the 1950s and early 1960s. Shattered by the
Vietnam war, it was revived by *Star Wars* in 1977 and by 1980s war and adventure films
set in Vietnam itself. However, he goes on to argue that by then the motifs of the war
story had become detached both from their ideological and historical moorings and from
their place within a cohesive – and triumphant – political narrative. In consequence, the
'new war story . . . had only a mocking relationship to a national story, for all "war" now
inhabited the same unearthly, ahistorical commercial space. Even Rambo, transformed into
an action-figure team for children, found himself locked in television combat with General
Terror and his S.A.V.A.G.E. terrorist group . . . and everywhere the boundary lines
between us and the enemy, the good team and the bad team, threatened to collapse into
a desperate sameness' (*The End of Victory Culture*, p. 284).

48   R.J. Berenstein *Attack of the Leading Ladies: Gender, Sexuality and Spectatorship in Classic Horror
Cinema*, New York: Columbia University Press, 1996, p. 197.

49   Taves *The Romance of Adventure*, p. 4.

50   Ibid., p. 73.

51   Ibid., p. 83.

52   Ibid., p. 13.

53   Ibid., p. 29.

54   Ibid., p. 29.

55   Another way of reading these scenarios is in terms of the Oedipal fantasies they stage
and exemplify, fantasies in which an unjust paternal regime is replaced by a just one, and
in which in the process the central protagonist is granted status and recognition (often
marked in royal or noble terms). For male protagonists, the fantasy is often further marked
by eventual – and officially sanctioned – marriage to an aristocratic heroine whom the
hero has rescued or captured from the unjust regime. Fantasies like this bear a marked
similarity to the 'family romances' described by Freud ('A Special Type of Choice of
Object Made by Men (Contributions to the Psychology of Love 1)', trans J. Strachey, in
*On Sexuality: Three Essays on Sexuality and Other Works*, The Pelican Freud Library, vol. 7,
Harmondsworth, Penguin, [1910] 1977, pp. 239–42). Their origins in childhood, and
their appeal to children, are perhaps echoed in the putative juvenile appeal and status of
adventure films themselves. Within this context, female-centred adventure films –
and perhaps pirate films in particular – can be seen as engaging the 'tomboy pleasures'
discussed by Laura Mulvey in her 'Afterthoughts on "Visual Pleasure and Narrative Cinema"

Inspired by *Duel in the Sun*', *Framework*, nos 15/16/17, 1981, pp. 12–15). Either way, the social and political themes of historical adventure films in particular might in this light perhaps best be viewed as material for the activation and articulation of the fantasies and pleasures concerned.
56   Taves *The Romance of Adventure*, p. 222.

## Chapter 5

## MARK JANCOVICH

# DWIGHT MACDONALD AND THE HISTORICAL EPIC

FACED WITH DECLINING AUDIENCES in the years after the Second World War, the Hollywood film industry responded with the block-buster[1] and, between the late 1940s and the early 1960s, one of its key forms was the historical epic. These films were sold as events: magnificent cinematic achievements that were supposed to have recreated the magnitude and splendour of ancient times. It was for this reason that they were also referred to 'Spectaculars'. They were films that offered momentous sights such as the parting of the Red Sea, the battles of Spartacus and his armies and the fall of the Roman Empire.

In this way, the films were sold on the promise that they presented action of fantastic proportions: battles, earthquakes and floods. However, it is one of the ironies of these films that they are not only attacked on the grounds that their action was too excessive but also for simply being dull. Many critics have complained about their length (a running time of between three and four hours was not uncommon), and have also claimed that their focus on spectacle makes these films very slow moving; that they endlessly fetishise the details of the past that the studios had so painstakingly and expensively reconstructed.

In other words, this group of films are simultaneously criticised for having too much and too little action, and here the very term spectacular is central. On one hand, the term is associated with excessive action and on the other with inaction. Nor is this problem unique to the historical epics of this period; it is a problem that can be found more generally in work on the blockbuster. For example, in his excellent history of the blockbuster, Thomas Schatz employs both criticisms through the claim that the blockbuster is overly 'kinetic' and that the focus on spectacle is privileged over narrative movement.[2] On the one hand, the blockbuster is attacked for being too action centred and, on the other, the focus on spectacle is supposed to be incompatible with narrative drive. In this way, such criticisms relate back to more general concerns within film studies about the relationship between narrative and spectacle in which the two are seen as opposed terms so that narrative is about forward drive and spectacle is seen as something that threatens to freeze the action and disrupt its logic.[3]

Some critics have tried to address this problem; Steve Neale, for example, has tried to compare the historical epic to the musical in terms of their organisation around numbers and routines.[4] However, this position still tends to evade the problem. The implication remains that these moments of spectacle freeze the action, when in fact they are often precisely moments of action. The problem is thus not really about how one thinks about the relationship between spectacle and narrative but how the third term of action relates to these two terms, and threatens the clear distinction between them.

Furthermore, if we return to the historical epic itself, the criticism that it is too action centred and that it is too slow moving share one central concern: they see the films as not simply excessive but pompous. Indeed, it is the preoccupation with pomp and circumstance – battles, pageants, arenas and other staged spectacles – which is often the focus of concern. In this way, both criticisms share a common concern with cultural status in which the term 'pompous' is simply a synonym for pretentious. These films are thus attacked for their cultural aspirations, aspirations that identify them as central examples of middlebrow culture.

The following essay will therefore concentrate on one of the key critics of the middlebrow – Dwight Macdonald. Macdonald not only produced one of the most developed oppositions to the middlebrow, but also devoted a whole section of his 1969 book, *Dwight Macdonald on Movies*, to 'The Biblical Spectacular'. Indeed, Macdonald's dislike of the historical epic was so great that references to the cycle crop up throughout the rest of the book.[5] Though Macdonald's attack on the middlebrow was part of a more general post-war concern with totalitarianism and mass society, he should not simply be dismissed as anticommunist. Macdonald's concerns with totalitarianism were as much directed at developments within American society as they were with the threat of fascism and Stalinism from abroad. Indeed, his presentation of the middlebrow was heavily influenced by Marxist thought, and he identified himself as an American radical throughout his career.[6]

For Macdonald, the problem with the middlebrow is precisely that it is a 'peculiar hybrid bred from [high culture's] unnatural intercourse with [mass culture]'. As a result, it leads not only to a 'blurring of the line' between the two, but even threatens to 'absorb' them both into itself.[7] In other words, the middlebrow poses a threat to the cultural authority of intellectuals, such as Macdonald, for whom it represents a virtual 'revolt of the masses'. However, this threat is not an intentional one. The petite bourgeoisie, whose tastes are addressed by the middlebrow, pose a threat precisely because of their reverence for legitimate culture. Faced with exclusion from legitimate culture, the petite bourgeoisie threaten to blur the distinction between high and low culture, and so undermine the authority of the cultural bourgeoisie, precisely due to their desire to obtain legitimacy. As Pierre Bourdieu puts it, 'This petite bourgeoisie of consumers [is one] which means to acquire on credit, i.e., before its due time, the attributes of the legitimate life-style'.[8]

The following essay will therefore examine the way in which Macdonald himself condemns these films for being both too active and too static, before moving on to show how this is related to a more general criticism of their middlebrow status. It will then illustrate the ways in which this concern with the middlebrow depended on notions of authenticity and cultural authority that were deeply classed and gendered. In other words, his attack on the middlebrow is directly related to a concern with the growth of a new petite bourgeoisie and the changing sexual relations to which they were related.

## Action and stasis

Macdonald's objections to the pace of the historical epic is probably best summed up by his description of *Ben-Hur*, a film for which he had particular contempt and which he found 'bloody boring': 'Watching it is like waiting at a railroad crossing while an interminable freight train lumbers past, often stopping completely for a while.'[9] Here Macdonald captures the dual sense of movement and stasis, the feeling that something is moving relentlessly while still seemingly going nowhere. He also conveys the sense of its size and weight as it 'lumbers past' for what seems to be an 'interminable' period.

   This passage also stresses Macdonald's sense of impatience, exacerbated by both the continual stopping and starting, but also by the sheer sense of length. Indeed, the length of these films is a feature about which Macdonald complains on a number of occasions, most notably in his discussion of *Cleopatra*, which, he claims, he 'finally caught . . . at a narborhood theatre at a merciful narborhood price ($1.25) and length (three hours)'.[10] Not content with seeing an abridged version of *Cleopatra*, he even went so far as to walk out of *The Greatest Story Ever Told*, although he still felt qualified to review it: 'I then decided I had spent a reasonable amount of time, two hours, on *The Greatest Story* and that after this the Crucifixion could only be an anticlimax. So I left.'[11] Ironically, Macdonald himself is usually a staunch opponent of editing or abridging. He complains bitterly about Joe Levine, producer of *Hercules* and *Hercules Unchained*, who had decided to cut an hour from the film version of Eugene O'Neill's *Long Day's Journey into Night*,[12] and he also objects that most epics feel the need to popularise the gospels rather than 'use the original script'.[13]

   If Macdonald justifies his decisions to walk out of epics or to opt for the abridged versions with the claim that they bore him, he also suggests that they even bore themselves. Commenting on *The Greatest Story Ever Told* again, he claims that during the Sermon on the Mount, 'the bored camera moves off and we get some more mountain scenery'.[14] Here, however, the fault is with the film, and with Hollywood filmmaking more generally. For Macdonald, the problem is that these films exhibit the worst excesses of cinematic exhibitionism in which the scale of the story is an excuse for the Hollywood system's self-promotion. Like many others, he argues that these films were exercises through which Hollywood enhanced its power and prestige by displaying the sense of spectacle that only it could achieve.

   Rather than simply present the story, the camera gets bored due to an obsession with scale and size, a feature that Macdonald overtly condemns. He states, as one of his 'rules for success' in making a biblical film:

Keep it small. In spirit: no dramatics, sparing use of emphatic close-ups and photography, no underlining of a story that still moves us because it is not underlined; Jesus was a throw-it-away prophet, direct and unrhetorical even in a speech like the Sermon on the Mount. Also keep it small literally: no wide screen, no stereophonic sound, no swelling-sobbing mood music (maybe no music at all), no gigantic sets or vast landscapes or thousands of extras milling around with staves, palm branches and other picturesque impedimenta.[15]

Similarly he further objects to the colour photography in *Ben-Hur* which is 'the glaring kind that makes people stand out like waxworks, with no relation to the background',[16] and claims that the major problem with the film is its will to depict.

In other words, Macdonald accuses the film of 'pornographic realism' in which it is not simply images of suffering that are condemned but more generally the film's desire to visually represent everything and to leave nothing to the imagination.

We are treated to close-ups of the galled ankles of galley slaves, of their writhings under the lash of their overseers, of their gasping struggles as they drown. We are left in no doubt as to what a leper's face looks like on a Panavision Screen. We see exactly what happens when a man is run over in the chariot race, and we are treated to a good ten minutes of stimulating close-ups of Messala's bloody, crusted, broken face and torso while he is dying after being dragged face down in such an accident, in full colour and all suggesting a most insanitary butcher shop.[17]

Here it is not just the violence that is criticised but the obsession with 'showing': the supposed refusal of these films to define certain things as 'obscene'; as that which should be 'off scene' or unavailable for representation.[18]

Macdonald's concern about spectacle within the historical epic does not simply define them as boring due to a lack of action. On the contrary, he clearly objects to their inability to be quiet and reflective. The reason Macdonald walked out of *The Greatest Story Ever Told* was, we recall, an excess of action:

For the finale of Part One, Handel's *Hallelujah Chorus* was belted out with such deafening *brio* that, what with Lazarus rising from the dead and the extras running around like grand-opera peasants telling each other, needlessly since we and they had seen it happen, 'Lazarus has risen. He is *alive!*' and Ed Wynn recovering his sight (*I think*, but there was so much confusion) and tottering up to Herod's palace to shout triumphantly up to the guards on the high Babylonian ramparts that Lazarus has risen . . . is *alive*, etc.[19]

A similar claim is made about *Ben-Hur* in which, 'Misdirected by Wyler, Heston throws all his punches in the first ten minutes (three grimaces and two intonations) so that he has nothing left four hours later when he has to react to the Crucifixion'.[20]

McDonald's objection is that these films are overstated. It is not that there is no action but, on the contrary, that the action verges on hysteria, is so overblown that it simply becomes tiresome. The action is therefore supposed to appear ridiculous and to become alienating. In *Cleopatra*, for example, the action sequences 'were confused and oddly minuscule'.[21] The problem here is not the lack of scale but rather the opposite. The action is on such a large scale that the human actors seem dwarfed and distant:

> the battle of Actium seemed to have been staged in a bathtub, and the great processions in Rome also looked miniaturized although they must have been enacted by actual full-size people – unless they've developed some very life-like three-inch puppets out there.[22]

In order to compensate, Macdonald suggests that the players are forced to turn in ridiculously melodramatic performances. Hurd Hatfield's Pilate in *King of Kings* is supposed to give a performance that is 'right out of Grand Guignol, and Frank Thring's acting . . . out-Herod's Herod'.[23] Here the actors are castigated for being too animated and emphatic, while elsewhere he complains that in *Ben-Hur*: 'The tender passages between Heston and Miss Harareet make Joan Crawford's love scenes look animated.'[24]

## Middlebrow culture and the problem of cultural authority

Of course, Macdonald does not have to worry that he will be accused of being contradictory for claiming that the historical epic was/is both too action oriented and too static. On the contrary, it is their very condition of being neither one thing nor the other that he associates with the middlebrow, and he is at pains to emphasise that it is their status as middlebrow films to which he is centrally opposed. As he claims: 'Nicholas Ray's *King of Kings* is lowbrow kitsch, Pier Pasolini's *The Gospel According to St. Matthew* is highbrow kitsch, and [*The Greatest Story Ever Told*] is the full middlebrow, or Hallmark Hall of Fame treatment.'[25]

Thus while he marvels at 'the aggressive tastelessness of the sets, costumes and colors' in *Cleopatra*, he does not see this tastelessness as the product of harmless naivety. Instead it is seen as the product of these films' cultural aspirations. In his discussion of *The Greatest Story Ever Told*, for example, Macdonald refers to director George Stevens as 'pretentious'[26] and his major criticism of Joe Levine is that he 'aspires to more than profits'. Despite being 'the distributor of two fantastically profitable movies, *Hercules* and *Hercules Unchained*', two 'quickie spectaculars that make *Ben-Hur* look like *Citizen Kane*', Levine is attacked for his desire 'to make the art scene too':

> His ambitions, nourished by the millions he made out of Hercules-Reeves, are now flowering like some exotic plant, say the Venus Fly Trap. Among the films that his Embassy Picture has now in hand are: *Seven Capital Sins* (episodes directed by Godard, De Broca, Chabrol, among others); *Love at*

*Twenty* (Truffaut and Wajda among others); *Boccaccio '70* (Fellini, Visconti, De Sica); a new version of the Brecht-Weill *Threepenny Opera*; and a movie based on Henry Miller's *Tropic of Cancer*.[27]

Here the objection is precisely that cultural legitimacy is supposed to be free of economic conditions, and Levine's ambitions threaten to reveal that which Macdonald's whole position seeks to deny: that the art cinema is not outside the political economy of culture.[28]

It is therefore important to remember that while historical epics are often seen as kitsch, lowbrow fare today, they had considerable cultural respectability in their own period. They were prestige pictures, frequently winning some of the industry's highest awards. They often showcased fairly considerable talents from both Hollywood itself and the more legitimate arts. As Macdonald comments in relation to *Ben-Hur*, 'Wyler has made some not-bad movies, and the script was worked on by, among others, Maxwell Anderson, Gore Vidal, Christopher Fry, and S. N. Behrman. Quite a galaxy to produce this sputtering little Roman candle.'[29] Furthermore, as Bruce Babbington and Peter Evans argue:

> We should not forget – leaving aside the genre's many nominations in most fields – that *Ben-Hur* and *Spartacus* won Best Picture Awards, that Charlton Heston and Hugh Griffith gained acting awards for their performances in *Ben-Hur* and Peter Ustinov for his in *Quo Vadis*, and that Wyler was given Best Director award for *Ben-Hur*.[30]

Indeed, Macdonald's attack on historical epics is clearly presented as a counter-blast against the 'bellows of approval' with which *Ben-Hur* and other films were greeted by reviewers. As Macdonald puts it, 'what no one knows who hasn't seen it is that [*Ben-Hur*] is lousy' and the reason for this is that 'the secret was well-kept by the New York newspaper critics' who showered it with praise.[31]

McDonald is therefore keen to point out that his objection is not to the spectacular itself, but to the middlebrow spectacular, which he attempts to distance from the 'art-spectacular': '*Ben-Hur* is a "spectacle" and so, one gathers from the critics, must be judged by modest aesthetic standards. (Though, come to think of it, *Intolerance*, *Birth of a Nation*, and *Potemkin* were also "spectacles".)'[32] His real complaint is therefore that these films pose a threat to the very standards that establish his position of authority and superiority as a cultural intellectual, a position that is also being eroded by media such as 'the New York newspaper critics'. He therefore assumes the mantle of the person with the taste and authority to authenticate art and scripture, although this move got him into a major debate.

Reviewing *Ben-Hur*, McDonald accuses the film of misrepresenting the Bible and of presenting the Romans, and not the Jews, as responsible for the Crucifixion. This inevitably led to accusations of anti-Semitism, which he roundly dismissed: 'I won't insist that I am not a racist bigot any more than I will insist I am not a liar.'[33] However, he not only continued to maintain that these films made the Romans 'the fall guys',[34] but he even saw the attack on him as part of the problem.

For Macdonald, middlebrow culture was a product of a 'democratization of values' in which everyone has a right to their own opinion; this 'process destroys all values, since value judgments require discrimination, an ugly word in liberal-democratic America. Masscult is very, very democratic; it refuses to discriminate against anything or between anything or anybody.'[35] Thus, according to Macdonald, while democracy may be 'desirable politically',[36] it is a disaster for culture. He therefore argued that the issue was not his racism but rather that:

> We live in a time when the pendulum of social justice has swung back too far, when certain racial groups are sacrosanct, so that when one states, depending on the New Testament, that certain Jews two thousand years ago wanted Jesus killed, one is accused of denouncing all Jews today as 'Christ killers.' I daresay that if one referred to what Sitting Bull did to General Custer, some Indian Protective League would jump into action. And in fact several letters have come in accusing me of being anti-Negro because I wrote that Harry Belafonte is not a genius and because I criticized the acting in *Come Back, Africa* and the music in *The Cry of Jazz*.[37]

Published in March 1962, Macdonald's claim that 'the pendulum of social justice has swung back too far' is clearly preposterous. However, his concern is not primarily about racial politics but cultural politics more generally: he was strongly opposed to the notion that one could be democratic about cultural matters, maintaining that there were universal standards of taste and truth to which only the cultural elite had access.

## Authenticity and cultural authority

This opposition to democracy in culture therefore required him to establish a ground for the legitimacy and authority for his judgements and, in this instance, he repeatedly turns to the Bible as the authentic record. Thus he disparages George Stevens' claims to authenticity, quoting at length from 'the vellum-paper programme':

> The film moves to excite the imagination of the audience by rendering before it the beauty and the extraordinary nature of Him who represents many things, and one thing . . . To recall, or is it to challenge, one's own image of Christ – an image derived from a word, a panel of stain glass, a Gothic-lettered Christmas card, a burst of organ music, an inner exaltation, an experience.[38]

Macdonald's response to this passage is clear and direct: 'You can get an image of Christ, it seems, from practically anything, including a Hallmark greeting card, except the writings of Matthew, Mark, Luke and John.'[39] He also pours scorn on the labours of those involved in *King of Kings*:

> Well, no one can say they didn't try. Mr Samuel Bronston, the producer, discussed the script with the Pope. ('Now the way we see it here, your

holiness, where He does the Sermon on the Mount we figure it needs action so we have Him walk around and answer questions from the audience like Jack Paar does only more reverential.') Mr. Nicholas Ray, the director spent a year visiting 'Europe's art museums, cathedrals and libraries.' . . . Mr. Philip Yordan, who wrote the screenplay, 'availed himself of the counsel of religious advisers of all faiths, seeking as nearly a nondenominational viewpoint as possible.' You can say that again. Dr. Miklos Rozsa, 'world-famous composer' whose last *chef d'oeuvre* was the score for *Ben-Hur*, also did his homework, diligently haunting 'Europe's cathedrals and cultural centres seeking themes of ecclesiastical inspiration.'[40]

Here the aspirations of these filmmakers are dismissed as pretensions to authority that are simply bogus. However, it is not the assumption of such authority that is challenged, but the claims to it made by these individuals. Their presumption is presented as ridiculous precisely because Macdonald assumes this authority for himself.[41] It is he who has the right to declare that *Ben-Hur* is 'a falsification of the Bible';[42] it is he who is 'depending on the New Testament' when he claims 'that certain Jews two thousand years ago wanted Jesus killed'; and it is he who can claim that, in *King of Kings*, the 'story of Christ, so moving and tender in the Gospels, is . . . drowned in the brutal sensationalism that is considered necessary to interest a mass audience'.[43]

He is also equipped to claim that biblical epics are not only a falsification of the Bible but a perversion of history. These films, he claims, fail to present an authentic vision of the past, offering instead exoticised spectacle. They 'look back at the past from the present, inflating it into the grandiose and the picturesque and insulating it in its own dreamworld – which, since it is jerry-built by architects who can only think in terms of the present, is banal and phoney'.[44] For this reason, he complains that *Ben-Hur*'s sets 'are glossily new; the galleys look as if they were built yesterday, as indeed they were; the armor and helmets are shiny tin foil, and the columns of ancient Rome are of sleekest plastic'.[45] He therefore counsels film-makers that they should 'realize that the past was once a present, as everyday and confused and banal as the present present, and that Jesus and the people of his time didn't know they were picturesque any more than the builders of Chartres knew they were making Gothic architecture'.[46]

It is for this reason that Macdonald is particularly scathing about Stevens' locations in *The Greatest Story Ever Told*. According to Macdonald, despite months in the Holy Land, Stevens decided that it 'looked worn, beat up, mingy, *small*', and hence 'not worthy of the greatest story ever told'. As a result, 'he returned to the U.S.A. and shot the film in Utah, Nevada and California, where vistas are quite large'. Stevens is ridiculed for his claim that 'our own West is a "far more authentic" locale for filming the life of Christ "than is the modern Holy Land"'.[47] However, while Stevens is made to sound ridiculous, Macdonald legitimates Pasolini's use of southern Italy as a stand-in for the Holy Land, claiming to have been 'delighted with this kind of realism, by the authentic look of the landscape', a landscape that 'looks much like *photographs* of the Holy Land'.[48] While Stevens is ridiculed for dismissing the Holy Land as a location after visiting it, Macdonald is able to authenticate Pasolini's choice on the basis of photographs!

While Macdonald suggests that it is the authenticity of these texts that he is concerned to contest, he is clearly challenging their politics, and this is most clearly evident in his criticism of Pasolini. *The Gospel According to St Matthew* avoids many of the things that Macdonald identifies in the Hollywood spectaculars, but it fails to meet Macdonald's approval on ideological grounds. While the Hollywood spectaculars are castigated for their sentimental conception of Jesus, Pasolini is indicted for the opposite:

> his Jesus is an unsmiling fanatic, a reserved bureaucrat, combining the worst features of Trotsky and Stalin; his message of peace and goodwill and brotherhood is delivered with authoritarian firmness at best and at worst with something approaching an hysterical snarl; his attitude towards his disciples is distant, towards sympathetic outsiders, like the sick he heals, condescending, and towards hostile outsiders, contemptuous. Granted that the nineteenth-century idea of Jesus was often sentimental, I think that Pasolini's revised unstandard version has erred in the other direction.[49]

In other words, as we have already seen, his objection to these films is that they are 'kitsch', a term which carried specific resonances for Macdonald. By kitsch he does not mean that they simply have a trashy or camp quality since he uses the term in the sense that it was coined by Clement Greenberg, a fellow mass culture critic.[50] For Greenberg and Macdonald, kitsch was a quality of mass culture whether in its American capitalist or its Soviet Stalinist form. In this sense, kitsch is not simply meant to suggest the use of cliché but involves a thoroughgoing aesthetic and political critique.

For Macdonald, mass culture (whether capitalist or communist) addresses its audience as a mass, rather than as individuals. In the process, it requires its audience to focus on that which is common to all rather than unique and particular to themselves as individuals. It addresses its audience in such a way that they are forced to repress their individuality. This culture may give people the sense of being part of a large collectivity (the masses) but it is also supposed to eradicate communal interaction. People are not 'related to one another as individuals nor as members of a community' but rather they are organised as a mass through an 'impersonal, abstract, crystallizing factor':[51] the abstract image of the 'common man' or 'The Party'. In other words, Macdonald sees the masses as a 'lonely crowd' of atomised individuals, organised and controlled by centres of power. The masses are taught not to value their own individuality but to conform to some abstract ideal, surrendering their own judgements to others who supposedly speak for and represent the collective.[52]

The difference between the Hollywood Biblical spectacular and Pasolini's version of the Christ story is the difference between capitalism and Stalinism. Both involve the 'total subjection of the spectator' who is not required to think for themselves, but to simply conform to the demands of the film. However, while one is motivated by commercial considerations, the other is simply propagandist.

## Conformity, class and femininity

Despite claims to the contrary, this critique of kitsch is not directed against the centre of power in the Soviet Union – the Party – and in the US – the capitalist class: it is directed against the masses themselves.[53] Macdonald does provide a detailed critique of the commercial organisation of mass culture but his greatest scorn – and even disgust – is reserved for the supposed 'victims' of mass culture, the conformist, petite bourgeois, suburbanite and particularly its primary representative, the housewife.

Macdonald repeatedly emphasises the tastelessness of these consumers, as can be clearly seen in his recurrent references to Hallmark Greetings cards. This mass brand comes to stand for the clichéd expression of sentiment that is supposed to distinguish this class and particularly their feminised qualities. For example, Macdonald comments on *The Greatest Story Ever Told*:

> Picturesque effects are unremitting, beginning with the star that guides the three wise men to the manger. It is a very large star, gleaming in the shape of a Hallmark cross in the dark-blue Panavision sky, and the wise men would have to be extremely nearsighted to miss it.[54]

Here is the 'built-in reaction' writ large: an image with such a clear and obvious meaning that one would need to be nearly blind to miss it.

This association with the suburban middle-classes becomes even more overt in Macdonald's comments about *King of Kings*, where he complains that it reduced 'The Last Supper to a suburban cookout with picnic tables and bowls of tossed salad'.[55] These remarks not only condemn the films for a lack of imagination that supposedly prevents them from being able to represent another period, and only equips them to conceive of the past as a replica of the present, but they also work to present the suburban cookout – one of the key social rituals of suburban communities – as inherently banal and trivial.[56]

This association of the suburban world with blandness and triviality is also deeply gendered, and it is the suburban housewife who comes to bare the brunt of this attack. As Barbara Ehrenreich has pointed out, mass culture theorists' concerns with conformity were often bound up with concerns about gender.[57] Philip Wylie, for example, identified conformity as a 'womanisation of America'.[58] For many mass culture theorists, independence and autonomy were masculine traits and hence women were not only the ideal conformists, but were often also seen as the key instruments through which men were emasculated and controlled.[59] As Ehrenreich argues, conformity was usually equated with emasculation.

The housewife as a figure of revulsion and disgust is most clearly in evidence in Macdonald's account of *Cleopatra*, where he claims that 'Miss Taylor has attempted, and I think, achieved, nothing less than the unsexing and deglamorizing of the Queen of the Nile – Claudette Colbert couldn't quite make it, though it was a good try – and her reduction to a suburban matron of impeccable morals and peccable diction'.[60] Here the suburban woman comes to stand for conformity through her association with respectability and morality. She is the embodiment of supposedly conservative values.

In the process, she is also presented in opposition to healthy sexuality, and it is therefore interesting how often Macdonald makes Taylor's body the focus of his criticisms. Taylor had enjoyed a long career as a sex symbol. It was for this reason that *Cleopatra* was not only centred on her star status as one of the most beautiful women in the world, but was able to command one of the largest budgets of all time up to that point. By focusing on her body, Macdonald therefore challenged specific constructions of sexuality, woman coming to stand for all that was wrong with mass culture and suburban America.

Taylor's body is also contrasted with her voice, both of which are used to suggest her problematic status. The voice is presented as shrill and is clearly used to place her as a demanding middle-class American woman, while her body is presented as bloated with over-indulgence:

> A less confident actress might have taken voice lessons, might have dieted, but not Mrs. Richard Burton. Her matronly whine, as flat as her matronly figure was not, pulled us down to twentieth-century American terra firma on the rare occasions when Mr. Mankiewicz's script gave us the illusion we were in ancient Egypt or Rome.[61]

Similar points are made about costume. For example, he refers to a 'hostess-type wraparound bodice and skirt', in which she is 'all set to seduce the conqueror of the world with her Bronxville wiles'. In the process, then, her female body becomes an object of fear and repulsion. He comments that it is 'just as well' that she is 'fully clad' in one scene 'considering a later glimpse of her rump as she is massaged'.[62] On the one hand, Taylor's body is made to signify both middle-class lack of imagination and female avarice. But on the other it is not only presented as crudely sexually manipulative but also as a castrating body, a body that threatens masculine independence and autonomy.

## Masculinity, display and sexuality

Macdonald states that he would 'back Miss Taylor against Mr. Reeves any day',[63] a statement with several implications. First, as indicated above, Macdonald suggests that Steve Reeves, muscle man star of the Hercules films, would be no match for the feminine wiles of Taylor but, second, there is the implication that Reeves himself is a puny and even ridiculous figure.

Nor is this the only reference to Reeves. Macdonald seems to have a pathological hatred of the man and what he represents, much as he also seems to dislike Charlton Heston. Like his clear loathing for Elizabeth Taylor, Macdonald's distaste for these male stars is focused on their bodies and what they represent. Both stars are, as Yvonne Tasker has called them, spectacular bodies, performers whose films often operate around the display of their physicality; for many, this display raises anxieties.[64] The assumption is often that there is something unmanly about this display of the body; that display is appropriate to the female, but not the male, body. There is also the sense that the emphatic masculinity of these bodies 'protests too much'.

These responses can be seen as the product of a homophobic reaction, in which the image of the male body is just too uncomfortable for the critic. It is therefore not insignificant that, as his biographer notes, in his teenage years, Macdonald displayed a series of 'sexual anxieties that persisted into adulthood'.[65] Most significantly, he developed a series of 'crushes' on other boys but felt compelled to strongly to deny any homosexuality:

> I am in love and not with a girl either . . . It's largely a matter of looks as it was with [Vernon] . . . He is the most enchanting boy I have ever known . . . except Vernon . . . the added attraction is his intelligence, culture and breeding . . . If you think I am a homosexualist, please disburden yourself. My amatory feelings are not physical and I would also hate to have little boys like you at Oxford Street [Cambridge] think about such things. It's just not manly that's all.[66]

However, Macdonald's relationships to boys were more 'physical' than this letter might suggest. For example, Wreszin writes of Macdonald's relationship to Vernon:

> Dwight became Vernon's literary mentor. They took long walks in the countryside, discussing books and their own literary aspirations. One event, riding the rapids of the Exeter River, Dwight recorded as an exciting sensual experience. He 'stripped to the buff,' hauling the boat up the river against the roaring current, the water rushing by as high as his knees, 'the sun beaming on my bare body!' The ride down was 'like being borne on the wind.' The trip was 'good – very good. Partly to be alone with each other, partly on account of the river and woody banks, partly because of the adventure of it, and the sunny day.'[67]

This is, of course, more a homosocial than a homosexual experience, but it clearly indicates the more 'physical' aspects of this relationship.

It would also be unfair to simply dismiss Macdonald as a straightforward homophobe, since he was actually far more confused and contradictory about these issues. On the one hand, he had 'a fear and unease concerning homosexuality and was not averse to referring to gay men in the vernacular of the day as "pansies" and "fairies"',[68] but he also gave space to homosexual writers in *Politics*, a political periodical that he edited:

> Even more socially avant-garde was Dwight's publication of the poet and writer Robert Duncan's essay 'The Homosexual in Society.' Duncan, a friend of Allen Ginsberg and other Beats, was forever grateful to Dwight for offering him the opportunity to make a case for homosexuals . . . In

the 1940s such an open and frank discussion of homosexuality was an unusual occurrence.[69]

Like many of intellectuals of his generation, Macdonald saw an association between political and aesthetic avant-gardism on the one hand and sexual avant-gardism on the other. He therefore felt able to be sympathetic to homosexuality when it could be seen as a transgressive activity, but this position was necessarily based on an opposition to normal, mainstream and conformist sexualities[70] – specifically those associated with the petite bourgeois respectability that he in turn associated with Taylor's Cleopatra and the suburban housewife more generally.

Macdonald's revulsion at the male body stars was also part of a more general criticism of the sexual politics of the Biblical Epic. Like others after him, he claimed that these films displayed a sadistic obsession with the male body precisely because the American middle classes had a problem with sex and sexuality. Commenting on Ben-Hur, for example, he complains: 'There is not even a decent, or indecent, Roman orgy, the only valid excuse for making a Biblical picture.'[71] Here he suggests a hypocrisy at the heart of Hollywood's earlier cycle of Biblical pictures, in which their piousness was simply a cover for the display of the sexual decadence they purported to condemn. But he also suggests that the hypocrisy of the post-war cycle of historical epics was even greater:

> Instead of sex, Ben-Hur gives us sadism. As G. Legman demonstrated long ago in Love and Death . . . our mass culture compensates for its prudery about sex by the broadest licence in portraying violence. Ben-Hur carries this principle to its extreme – De Mille, after all, gave us both orgies and bloodshed – omitting Roman eroticism but dwelling on Roman brutality with pornographic realism.[72]

In this film, he claims, there 'is blood blood blood',[73] a quality that makes the film 'bloody in every way – bloody bloody and bloody boring'.[74]

## Conclusion

This dismissal of violent action as boring returns us to the original problem – the continued and apparently contradictory claims that the historical epic is both too action centred and too static. It is significant that these films are still criticised for their lack of narrative drive, historical authenticity or psychological realism by intellectuals who have made their careers by condemning these very features as ideological and opposing them to the values of the avant-garde. These contradictory claims reveal an ongoing concern with the cultural status of the historical epic, in which it is precisely through the claim that they are 'neither one thing or the other' that they are defined as middlebrow products: products despised by cultural intellectuals due to the ways in which they 'blur the line' between low and high culture, popular and legitimate taste. Indeed, as Leon Hunt has argued, rather than the popular itself, 'it is the "middlebrow" – arguably always the real set of easy pleasures, in Bourdieu's terms – which [cultural intellectuals have seen] as the low and indefensible'.[75] As Bourdieu has pointed out, cultural intellectuals often display a preference for the popular over the middlebrow, in part a result of the fact that 'aesthetic choices are in fact often constituted in opposition to the choices of groups closest in social space, with whom competition is most direct and immediate'.[76] In other words, the middlebrow threatens the authority of the cultural bourgeoisie more directly than does the popular. Indeed, the cultural bourgeoisie often celebrates the popular precisely because it 'prefers naivety to "pretentiousness". The essential merit of the "common people" is that they have none of the pretensions to art (or power) which inspire the ambitions of the "petite bourgeois".'[77] In short, while popular taste knows its place, the middlebrow does not.

## Notes

1   See Thomas Schatz 'The New Hollywood', in Jim Collins, Hilary Radner, and Ava Preacher Collins, (eds) *Film Theory Goes to the Movies*, New York: Routledge, 1993. See also Julian Stringer (ed.) *Movie Blockbusters*, London: Routledge, 2003.

2   Henry Jenkins 'Historical Poetics', in Joanne Hollows and Mark Jancovich (eds) *Approaches to Popular Film*, Manchester: Manchester University Press, 1995; Peter Krämer 'The New Hollywood', in John Hill and Pamela Church Gibson (eds) *The Oxford Guide to Film Studies*, Oxford: Oxford University Press, 1998; Schatz 'The New Hollywood'.

3   Laura Mulvey 'Visual Pleasure and Narrative Cinema', in Bill Nichols (ed.) *Movies and Methods*, vol. 2, Berkeley: University of California Press, 1986.

4   Steve Neale *Genre*, London: British Film Institute, 1980.

5   Dwight Macdonald *Dwight Macdonald On Movies*, Englewood Cliffs, NJ: Prentice-Hall, 1969.

6   For a discussion of Macdonald within the context of mass culture theory, see Joanne Hollows 'Mass Culture Theory and Political Economy' in Hollows and Jancovich *Approaches to Popular Film*.

7   Dwight Macdonald *Against the American Grain: Essays on the Effects of Mass Culture*, New York: Random House, 1962, p. 54.

8   Pierre Bourdieu *Distinction: A Social Critique of the Judgement of Taste*, London: Routledge, 1984, p. 271.

9   Macdonald 'On Movies', p. 424.

10  Ibid., p. 301.

11  Ibid., p. 435.

12  Ibid., p. 130.

13  Ibid., p. 430.

14  Ibid., p. 436.

15  Ibid., p. 431.

16  Ibid., p. 425.

17  Ibid., p. 425.

18  Linda Williams 'Second Thoughts on *Hard Core*: American Obscenity Law and the Scapegoating of Deviance', in Pamela Church Gibson and Roma Gibson (eds) *Dirty Looks: Women, Pornography, Power*, London: British Film Institute, 1993.

19  Macdonald 'On Movies', p. 435.

20  Ibid., p. 425.

21  Ibid., p. 302.

22  Ibid., pp. 301–2.

23  Ibid., p. 428.

24  Ibid., p. 424.

25   Ibid., p. 431.
26   Ibid.
27   Ibid., p. 131.
28   See, for example, Bourdieu *Distinction*; Nicholas Garnham *Capitalism and Communication: Global Culture and the Economics of Information*, London: Sage, 1990; Hollows 'Mass Culture Theory and Political Economy'.
29   Macdonald 'On Movies', p. 426.
30   Bruce Babbington and Peter Evans *Biblical Epics: Sacred Narrative in Hollywood Cinema*, Manchester: Manchester University Press, 1993, p. 7.
31   Macdonald 'On Movies', p. 424.
32   Ibid., p. 425.
33   Ibid., p. 429.
34   Ibid., p. 428.
35   Macdonald 'American Grain', p. 12.
36   Ibid., p. 34.
37   Macdonald 'On Movies', p. 429.
38   Ibid., pp. 436–7.
39   Ibid., p. 437.
40   Ibid., p. 427.
41   A similar attack is made on Demille in Alan Nadel *Containment Culture: American Narratives, Postmodernism, and the Atomic Age*, Durham, NC: Duke University Press, 1995.
42   Macdonald 'On Movies', p. 426.
43   Ibid., p. 427.
44   Ibid., p. 437.
45   Ibid., p. 425.
46   Ibid., pp. 430–1.
47   Ibid., p. 435.
48   Ibid., p. 439. My emphasis.
49   Ibid., p. 440.
50   Clement Greenberg 'Avant-Garde and Kitsch', in B. Rosenberg and D. M. White (eds) *Mass Culture: The Popular Arts in America*, New York: Free Press, 1957.
51   Macdonald 'American Grain', p. 8.
52   A similar argument was constructed by C. Wright Mills *The Power Elite*, New York: Oxford University Press, 1956, and David Reisman, who coined the phrase, 'the lonely crowd': *The Lonely Crowd: A Study of the Changing American Character*, New Haven: Yale University Press, 1961.
53   Mark Jancovich 'Othering Conformity in Post-War America: Intellectuals, the New Middle Classes and the Problem of Cultural Distinctions', in Nathan Abrams and Julie Hughes (eds) *Containing America*, Birmingham: Birmingham University Press, 2000.
54   Macdonald 'On Movies', p. 969.
55   Ibid., p. 428.
56   For an analysis of another equally derided suburban ritual of the 1950s, the Tupperware party, that challenges its presentation as simply banal and trivial, see Alison J. Clarke, 'Tupperware: Suburbia, Sociality and Mass Consumption', in Roger Silverstone (ed.) *Visions of Suburbia*, London: Routledge, 1997.
57   Barbara Ehrenreich *The Hearts of Men: American Dreams and the Flight from Commitment*, London: Pluto, 1983.
58   Philip Wylie 'The Womanization of America: an embattled male takes a look at what was once a man's world', *Playboy*, September 1958.
59   Philip Wylie 'Abdicating Male . . . and How the Gray Flannel Mind Exploits Him Through His Women', *Playboy*, November 1956.
60   Macdonald 'On Movies', p. 302.

61   Ibid.
62   Ibid.
63   Ibid.
64   Yvonne Tasker *Spectacular Bodies: Gender, Genre and the Action Cinema*, London: Routledge, 1993; Mark Jancovich 'Charlton Heston is an Axiom: Spectacle and Performance in the Development of the Blockbuster', in Andy Willis (ed.) *Film Stars: Hollywood and Beyond*, Manchester: Manchester University Press, forthcoming.
65   Michael Wreszin *A Rebel in Defense of Tradition: The Life and Politics of Dwight Macdonald*, New York: Basic Books, no. 7, 1994.
66   Letter from Macdonald to Dinsmore Wheeler, quoted in Wreszin *A Rebel in Defense of Tradition*, p. 9.
67   Ibid., p. 8.
68   Ibid., p. 9.
69   Wreszin *A Rebel in Defense of Tradition: The Life and Politics of Dwight Macdonald*, pp. 139–40.
70   For an analysis of the problems involved in this kind of sexual politics, see Mark Jancovich 'Naked Ambition: Taste, Pornography and the Middlebrow', in *Scope: An Online Journal of Film Studies*, June 2001.
71   Macdonald 'On Movies', p. 425.
72   Ibid.
73   Ibid., p. 426.
74   Ibid., p. 424.
75   Leon Hunt *British Low Culture*, London: Routledge, 1998, p. 160.
76   Bourdieu *Distinction*, p. 60.
77   Ibid., p. 62.

## PART II

# Theorising action aesthetics

## MARTIN FLANAGAN

## 'GET READY FOR RUSH HOUR'
## The chronotope in action

It is because cinema as the art of space and time is the contrary of painting that it has something to add to it.

André Bazin[1]

In literature and art itself, temporal and spatial determinations are inseparable from one another, and always colored by emotions and values.

Mikhail Bakhtin[2]

FOR SCREENWRITER LARRY GROSS, the 'Big Loud Action Movie' has been 'a central economic fact, structuring all life, thought and practice in Hollywood' since the mid-1970s, when Steven Spielberg and George Lucas steered the comic-book and B-movie inspired visions of *Jaws* (1975) and *Star Wars* (1977) to unprecedented box-office success.[3] Although the unstable commercial foundations of early 1970s Hollywood were revitalised by these films, which introduced a new set of aesthetic formulae linked to ruthlessly efficient business practices, the period came to be regarded by critics as the beginning of the end of mainstream Hollywood as art form.[4] Today, the cultural implications and global omnipresence of the action movie receive widespread attention within the discipline of film studies. From a perspective informed by the work of the Russian cultural theorist Mikhail Bakhtin, originator of the theories of dialogism and the carnivalesque, any text that can reach and connect with the mass audience to which a blockbuster action film typically plays – cutting across the barriers of age, class, sex, ethnicity and nationality that many other genres fail to negotiate – is certainly deserving of critical scrutiny.

Bakhtin's work prizes social and historical value above all else. The concept of dialogism, which states that any utterance depends on the anticipated response of another speaker for the determination of its meaning, stresses the centrality of social context to communication and interpretation.[5] Dialogic communities are formed through this semantic dependence of the utterance upon the word of an 'other' (or, in the case of the textual utterance, the response of a reader/viewer). Bakhtin seems fascinated by the novel – which he deems the pre-eminent dialogic mode of textual representation – at least partly because it was the dominant literary form of the era. He realises that there is something intrinsic to the novel form that sustains the ability to connect with a huge, popular audience (as writers like Rabelais and Dostoevsky certainly did). However, there are other vital elements in novelistic discourse, elements that provide the very grounds for dialogic representation in art. The academically overlooked form of the Greek adventure narrative provides the platform for examining modes of temporal and spatial construction in the novel. Bakhtin utilises the building-brick simplicity of the genre – which, with apologies to Gross, we might dub the 'Big Loud Action Novel' – to lay out terms for the wider-ranging discussion to follow.

Bakhtin's chronotope is a device not only for analysing the methods of narrative construction but also for evaluating the relationship between text and reader: how the world of the reader '*creates* the text' and how the text completes the dialogic circuit by feeding back into the world of the reader.[6] The action film can be used as a crucible for examining the relationships that obtain between text and viewer at the commercial heart of popular American cinema, and for studying the question of how these relationships become embedded over time in narrative formulas. Why do we flock in droves to the action movie, making it the most commercially potent of all Hollywood forms? And what does the textual representation of time and space have to do with this success? Each of the films chosen to illustrate my argument is centrally placed within the popular 'action' tradition. John McTiernan's *Die Hard* (1988) and Jan De Bont's *Speed* (1994) exemplify Gross's definition of the post-1977 block-buster. Both are narratively lean, structurally simplistic adventures, prioritising action over dialogue, characterisation or emotion. They are formulaic, visually excit-ing, conceptually shallow entertainment machines, and each definitively represents the state of Hollywood's art at the time of production.

## Forms of the chronotope

Bakhtin's term 'chronotope' translates as 'time-space', and taking the concept at this literal level, it may be suggested that film is the artform which most thoroughly expresses chronotopic activity. The processes of transmission and reception of film are centred on the manipulation of time and space; at a particular place and a specific time, a visual representation of spatial reality unfolds at around twenty-four frames per second, projected onto a screen with definite spatial parameters. It is in its ability to show spatial changes through time, the capacity to represent motion figu-ratively, that film is set apart from other forms of expression, such as the novel or painting. However, as Christian Metz notes, film's 'impression of reality' has an ambiguous basis. The cinema is no closer to a direct expression of unmediated reality than any other art form. In fact, in a material sense, film is considerably less 'substantial' than, for instance, theatrical presentation, in that the content of the frame is never really present. The medium, however, turns this insubstantiality to its advantage. The illusion of proximity that film creates is more suggestive of life precisely because it expresses a lack, which the diegesis fills. Hence, according to Metz, the cinema spectator invests onscreen elements with diegetic value to a greater degree than he or she would the actors in stage drama, whose reality is all too apparent to sustain the same illusion. Metz postulates movement, which is purely visual and therefore as authentic in cinematic reproduction as in the original moment of inscription, as the crucial factor in this process. The great illusion of the apparatus is founded on the 'real presence of motion'.[7] Time and space coalesce in the filmic presentation of motion, enabling the medium to appear animated and thus more lifelike than other visually static means of expression (still photography, painting, sculpture). The most innovative practitioners of film art, however, have derived powerful effects from a deformation of this verisimilitude, developing a range of techniques (slow motion, freeze frame, time-lapse photography) that self-consciously acknowledge the artificiality of filmic time and space. The device of the jump cut so prevalent in the early work of the French 'Nouvelle Vague', and later adopted in Hollywood by acolytes such as Arthur Penn, director of *Bonnie and Clyde* (1967), is a notable example.

Time and space, then, are the main constituents of film form, indicating the central role that the chronotope could play in any study of how cinema creates narrative effects. The chronotope is possibly the Bakhtinian concept most oriented towards filmic application, yet there are difficulties involved in giving a straightforward definition of the term. This ambiguity stems from Bakhtin's own explication of the concept in 'Forms of Time and of the Chronotope in the Novel'. In the essay, the main body of which was composed between 1937 and 1938, the term is prone to mutation between three apparently distinct meanings. The first sense in which 'chronotope' is used is to demarcate stable generic forms which are classified according to methods of representing time and space, such as the 'folkloric chronotope'.[8] Second, the term can signify a more localised rendering of time and space within the diegesis. Bakhtin refers to elements that fall into this second category as 'chronotopic motifs' (for example, the motifs of 'meeting' or 'the road').[9] A third level of meaning is introduced in the 'Concluding Remarks' (added in 1973), where Bakhtin draws the chronotope together with the theory of dialogism in postulating a chronotopic element in reading. Here, Bakhtin contends that the representational elements of the text emerge '[o]ut of the actual chronotopes of our world'.[10] It would thus seem possible to theorise a chronotope of reception, or at least a way in which real and represented time/space configurations are linked via the operations of chronotopes.

In the 'Concluding Remarks' Bakhtin seems to realise that the theoretical basis of his device requires further clarification, and here he 'fleshes out' his idea, defining chronotopes as 'the organizing centers for the fundamental narrative events of the novel [. . .] the place where the knots of the narrative are tied and untied'. The integral role played by the chronotope within all levels of the text is underlined: chronotopes not only link disparate parts of narrative material together and play a part in how we experience the text, but provide the very 'ground essential for the showing-forth, the representability of events'. Without chronotopes there would presumably be no narrative; for they make possible the combination of temporal and spatial co-ordinates that make narrative events 'visible . . . [and] concrete, makes them take on flesh, causes blood to flow in their veins'.[11]

These are the main ways in which Bakhtin seems to intend the chronotope to be defined. However, complex interrelations can exist *between* chronotopes, and Bakhtin characterises these relationships as 'dialogical'. As if to emphasise the different orders and functions of the chronotope, Bakhtin stresses that the 'relationships [. . .] that exist *among* chronotopes cannot enter into any of the relationships contained *within* chronotopes'.[12] This statement is never properly clarified, conveying some of the confusion that is an inevitable by-product of such a potentially all-encompassing term. Sue Vice notes that the chronotope 'seems omnipresent to the point either of invisibility or of extreme obviousness'.[13] Bakhtin cites Kant's claim that space and time are prerequisite categories of all forms of perception. The same criteria apply to the literary text, and accordingly all textual events must take place within time and space, even if these parameters are immaterial (for instance, in a character's memory or in the verbal account of a narrator).

Chronotopic value is not defined merely by the presence of spatial and temporal indicators in the work – other devices have evolved in textual systems for this kind of purely formal designation. The borders of the 'scene' (in the sense of a block of dramatic narrative with pre-determined markers) may often coincide with those of the chronotope, but we must take care not to confuse the two. Similarly, the chronotope can be manifested as a physical motif and locus of action within the text – Bakhtin offers examples such as 'the road' and the 'castle' – but not every concrete object in the work should be considered a discrete, self-contained chronotope.[14] If we take a scene from the early stages of *Die Hard*, where the central character John McClane (Bruce Willis) is conveyed through Los Angeles in a limousine, it might seem fair to speak of the vehicle as a chronotope, in the sense that the physical properties of the car determine the spatial parameters of the sequence and the brevity of the scene. However, the limousine is not narratively central to *Die Hard*, despite the fact that it performs the necessary time–space manoeuvre that results in McClane arriving at Nakatomi Plaza, where his adventures will begin. It would be more proper to talk of the car as contributing to a minor chronotope of *travel* or *arrival* in the film, one that underlines McClane's status as an 'outsider' in Los Angeles. The passenger bus featured in *Speed* plays a more significant role in that text; it is the major location, and can be referred to as a dominant chronotope because it is involved with the spatio-temporal organisation of the film on a level other than the purely mechanical. The *narrative* properties of that vehicle constitute its chronotopic character, not its physical ones – although the physical nature of the vehicle does have implications for its significance within both time and space patterns. The nearest equivalent to this category of chronotope in *Die Hard* is the Nakatomi Tower, which provides a major locus for the action and shapes the way in which events are presented, necessitating a narrow time scheme (McClane cannot evade capture in a building forever) and a compressed spatial context (related to the physical dimensions of a real building).

Reference to Bakhtin's own textual examples may help in clarifying our definition. He discusses the chronotope of the 'threshold' in the novels of Dostoevsky, arguing that stairways, foyers and landings all contribute to this central signifier. The chronotopic value of these motifs is derived from a combination of their *physical* functions and characteristics – their enabling of meetings, encounters and so on; and their *symbolic* associations – they represent the point where '*crisis*, radical change, an unexpected turn of fate takes place'.[15] A third reason why thresholds are loaded with chronotopic value is because they facilitate a certain type of formal spatio-temporal construction. Narratives are formed from the combination of different varieties of these spatio-temporal modalities. Bakhtin demonstrates this by surveying many different types of literary narrative. He discovers that, for instance, the pre-novelistic 'adventure' text relies heavily on a certain pattern encompassing motifs such as long journeys, shipwrecks and so on, while the 'idyllic' text utilises very different configurations (valleys, rivers, cyclical rhythms of time). The centrality of chronotopes to generic classification is hinted at here, but our main concern is the emphasis on the structural importance of chronotopes. Bakhtin argues that thresholds are the 'fundamental "points" of action' in Dostoevsky, in the same way that the bus is the fundamental point of action in *Speed*, or the highway takes narrative precedence in the road movie genre.[16]

This chapter will employ the three main senses of 'chronotope' in an interconnected way. The 'action' genre is delineated by a certain method of representing time, much as the Greek adventure narrative in Bakhtin's analysis. Within this mode of representation there are various chronotopic motifs of interest, corresponding with important time/space locales (the tower in *Die Hard*, the bus in *Speed*) or recurrent textual signifiers (for example, the iconic male hero). Having constructed itself along these lines, the cinematic text '*faces outward away from itself*' and attempts to interact with the temporal and spatial environment of the spectator, invoking Bakhtin's formulation of the relationship between the worlds of the real and the represented.[17] Thus, we will find that our contemplation of the chronotope will eventually return us to the fundamental equation of Bakhtinian theory: the dialogic relation between utterance (film text) and response (viewer).

## Adventure-time in Ancient Greece and Hollywood

In 'Forms of Time and of the Chronotope in the Novel', Bakhtin analyses several genres, from pre-novelistic antiquity to the works of Tolstoy and Flaubert, in order to determine the chronotopic patterns therein. For my purpose, the most pertinent of these is the Greek romance or 'Adventure Novel of Ordeal', in which Bakhtin identifies a special kind of temporal construction influencing every aspect of the text, from character to plot. The characteristics of what Bakhtin terms 'Adventure-time' include: a 'broad and varied geographical background' against which the adventures take place; a lack of everyday cyclical, biographically or historically bound time, which is replaced by an elastic, extratemporal order which has no 'internal limits' and therefore 'leaves no *trace*' in the personalities of the heroes; and the heroes themselves, who are not realised in a psychologically complex way, or connected to real social or historical patterns, but have a purely physical, schematic function of 'enforced movement through space'.[18] Adventure-time does not adhere to principles of realism, but rather 'possesses its own peculiar consistency and unity . . . its own ineluctable logic'.[19] The world of the adventure chronotope is thus ruled by chance and coincidence, structured around wild detours from reality that despite their infeasibility are perfectly acceptable within the self-determined logic of the genre.

There are many correspondences between the kind of narrative that Bakhtin identifies in the works of Heliodorus, Achilles Tatius and others, and the Hollywood action tradition. These parallels are especially noticeable in a sub-category that we might call 'action-adventure' or 'action-fantasy'. To deal with the first principle of adventure-time, many texts in this category employ a 'broad and varied geographical background'. The Bond films have a tradition of using exotic locations, and have even come to market themselves on this premise; a 'teaser' advertisement for *Tomorrow Never Dies* (1997), designed to whet the appetites of fans while the film was still in production, carried the legend 'Now shooting around the world'. Similarly, the Indiana Jones films reflect the mysterious foreign environments of the Saturday morning serials so beloved of co-creator George Lucas: Tunisia, Sri Lanka, Petra, Venice, remade by studio hands to look every inch the paradigmatic middle-eastern casbah or European city of intrigue. However, in achieving archetypicality, the locations often sacrifice geographical verisimilitude, as is demonstrated in *Indiana Jones and the Last Crusade* (1989) where Almeria, Spain, stands in for Jordan.[20] This unstable relation of what we might term 'adventure-space' to its real geographical equivalent denotes a trend that, usually sanctioned by political or economic factors, has become embedded in film production, and as such has important implications for chronotopic studies. Sue Vice suggests that the primary role of the chronotope is 'its mediation between real historical events and their appearance in the text'.[21] If this formulation were to be extrapolated to encompass spatial concerns, the role of the chronotope in the relationship between 'actual' space and its textual equivalent could also be explored. The central issue would be whether such distortions as those outlined above undermine the capacity of the chronotope to be a 'bridge [. . .] between the two worlds' of real and represented.[22] Although this aspect of chronotopic function is not a major concern in the present study, we will return to the issue of geographical accuracy in the chronotope later. For the time being, it should be noted that the 'action' movie of the *Die Hard* or *Speed* lineage, while taking its 'blockbuster' scale from *Star Wars* and many narrative elements from the Bond series, does not necessarily adhere to the same geographical premise. The 'spanner-in-the-works' sub-genre that those two films exemplify is actually predicated upon a rather more limited spatial axis. However, those texts do follow many of the other structural and characterological principles of adventure-time.

The kind of time in which the action hero exists represents a variant of the 'extratemporal hiatus between two moments of biographical time' that Bakhtin identifies in the Greek adventure narrative.[23] The action hero is invariably a blue-collar, 'everyman' figure, exemplified by the plain-talking east coast cop John McClane in *Die Hard*. This archetype often displays a distrust of authority figures and/or 'maverick' tendencies, the latter trope being best demonstrated by Mel Gibson's attractively psychotic Martin Riggs in the *Lethal Weapon* series (1987–98). At the outset of the action narrative, the protagonist is wrenched from normality and inserted into a chain of events over which he has little control. John McClane is visiting his estranged family in Los Angeles when he becomes embroiled in a corporate siege discharged by a group who claim to be terrorists but whose motive is subsequently revealed to be mere robbery. Jack Traven (Keanu Reeves) in *Speed* has no sooner received a commendation for his part in foiling psychopathic bomber Howard Payne (Dennis Hopper) than, next morning, he finds that Payne has engineered another plan to hold the city to ransom, in which he must play a central part. Very little running time, in either film, is devoted to showing the heroes doing 'normal' things; the arrival at LA airport of McClane and a quick visit to a coffee shop for Traven amount to the only moments of everyday life in which we see the heroes engaged. The only routine known to the action hero is that of random contingency and wild plot deviations; the unpredictable can always be relied upon. Individual texts often play on this unwritten rule of the genre, as in *Lethal Weapon 3* (1992), where Riggs' peaceful enjoyment of a cigarette is disturbed so often by the exigencies of the plot that it becomes a running joke, or in *Die Hard 2* (1990), where McClane, involved in another terrorist situation, exclaims, 'How can the same shit happen to the same guy *twice*?'

Like the archetypal hero of the Greek romance, the action protagonist does not undergo any real biographical or maturational adjustment over the course of their adventures; in other words, adventure-time 'is not registered in the slightest way in the age of the heroes'.[24] The most accurate analogy for this characteristic of the novel of ordeal can be found in James Bond, who has hardly aged over the course of twenty releases spanning four decades. Heroes arrive fully formed and change little in the action film, thus precluding any real sense of spiritual or ideological development. Despite the pretensions of McClane and Traven to normality, we are in no doubt as to their heroic credentials as soon as we are introduced to them. The first appearances of the heroes in their respective texts confirm this supposition. McClane startles a fellow air traveller who notices his firearm and receives a seductive glance from a cabin attendant, accentuating his toughness and sexual appeal. In *Speed*, Traven's maverick streak is revealed from the outset when he volunteers for the most dangerous assignment in the opening rescue sequence. They do not become heroes as a result of their exploits in the course of the narrative; they are *already* heroes, the only men who could measure up to the requirements of the situation. Their adventures do not alter their personalities, they merely facilitate changes in their romantic status. Traven ends *Speed* linked to the female lead character Annie, and McClane is reunited with his wife at the conclusion of *Die Hard*; moreover, it is suggested that both women are won over precisely because of the brave exploits of the heroes (in fact, such feats are inevitable as their characterological status as 'heroes' would not allow for any other response). This rather one-dimensional treatment of gender relations, along with the tendency to portray American institutions at the mercy of Middle-Eastern zealots or European nihilists, highlights the political conservatism that frequently pervades the form.

The Bond films' evasion of the issue of the age of the lead actor can be interpreted as part of a wider policy within the series to avoid, as far as possible, the incorporation of external historical or political developments. When such references do come, as in the storyline of *Goldeneye* (1995) which draws upon the dissolution of the Soviet Union, they invariably represent a shallow co-opting of historical signifiers designed to give audiences a ready-made reference point that can be quickly assimilated and forgotten, enabling them to return to the basic business of attending to the action. Films in the blockbuster action tradition rarely engage with a 'real' historical register, instead supplementing or conjoining historical allusion with self-conscious cinematic reference. The action film incorporates historical reality in a mechanical fashion, in much the same way as the ancient biography as described by Bakhtin. In the characteristic chronotope of that form, historical reality serves as 'an arena for the disclosing and unfolding of human characters – nothing more'.[25] In cinematic terms, this process of de-historicisation can be identified in, for instance, the manner in which the Vietnam War is used as a sort of cinematic shorthand signifying 'troubled male psyche' in productions like *Rambo: First Blood Part II* (1985) and *Lethal Weapon*. The Gulf War has recently undergone the same reductive treatment (*The Rock*, 1996).

## Action heroes and their worlds

Having addressed the temporal aspect, we must now determine the nature of the 'space' in which action films take place. As with time, abstraction is the dominant tone. These are static, 'finished' worlds, broadly drawn, non-specific backdrops constructed according to the purely physical requirements of the action.[26] This is not to say that action films take place in completely unfamiliar settings. In *Speed*, the iconography of 'actual' Los Angeles (Mann's Chinese Theater, Sunset Boulevard) is certainly intended to imbue the film with a degree of geographical credibility. However, the city does not become a major character in the text as it does in *Chinatown* (1974) or *LA Confidential* (1997), both of which draw deeply on civic history for their themes of corruption. In De Bont's film, the signifiers of 'Los Angeles' merely embellish the 'everycity' model with a little local colour. Here is a less extreme version of the geographical distortion mentioned earlier in reference to Indiana Jones; in a sense, it does not matter where or when the road in *Speed* is located, as its function is purely structural. That function is to enable the movement of the bus, and by extension the progression of the narrative, to continue unabated. To answer John McClane's rhetorical question, the same shit can happen to the same guy twice because the world of the action film, as expressed in time and space, is essentially *always the same*. The action world is a state of spatial organisation, a certain configuration of things, rather than a concrete place; in this it more resembles a temporal modality (a state of being) than a spatial one. The LA depicted in *Speed* and *Die Hard* is not a place where people work and live their lives, but an action movie simulation lifted from the template of the real city. The nature of cities in these films as sites of cinematic spectacle rather than quotidian existence is adumbrated in the identity of the building used to represent Nakatomi Plaza in *Die Hard* – the Century City headquarters of Twentieth Century Fox, the studio that funded and distributed the movie. McClane is constantly characterised as an outsider, bemused by the behaviour of LA denizens, a motif that reinforces the suggestion that Los Angeles, and by extension its most famous district Hollywood, is a place at once familiar yet somehow unreal.

Action movies display the same '*interchangeability* in space' that Bakhtin notes with reference to the Greek romance. In those texts, the abstract quality of space and time has a specific narrative motivation as catalyst for the work of chance: 'any concretization [. . .] would fetter the freedom and flexibility of the adventures and limit the absolute power of chance'.[27] The description holds well for the action film; unlikely things *always* happen in these places which are at once strange and strangely familiar, and as such evoke Christian Metz's formulation of the primal space in which film unfolds, 'that simultaneously very close and definitively inaccessible "elsewhere"'.[28] Thus, a combination of abstract time and space provides the crucial foundation for the type of plot construction preferred in both the Greek novel of ordeal and the modern action film.

The logic of chance and contingency in the action film can be illustrated using a scene from *Speed*. In Greek romance, the textual cues for the intervention of fate or chance are phrases such as 'suddenly' or 'at just that moment'.[29] The equivalent in cinematic grammar of these intrusions of irrational forces occurs in *Speed* when the bus (rigged by Payne to explode if its speed drops below fifty miles per hour) hurtles into the path of a woman crossing the road with a pram. The sequence is primed by two cuts from the speeding bus to shots of the woman with the pram saying farewell to a friend and starting to cross the road. Knowledge of the genre tells us that the bus is soon going to enter the same spatial context as the woman. However, we instinctively anticipate disaster to be averted, as children rarely come to harm in mainstream Hollywood movies. De Bont then completely undercuts our pre-emptive reading by having the bus smash into the pram, sending it flying into the air and away from the horrified woman, a moment that is extremely shocking on first viewing. However, the pram turns out to be filled with aluminium cans and our initial reaction of horror turns to relief and then embarrassment that such a contrivance could catch us out. The set-piece is structured around two instances of chance. The first coincidence is that the woman should be crossing the road 'at just that moment' when the bus intersects her path; the second, irrational coincidence is that the pram conveys cans rather than a child. Yet in the 'ineluctable logic' of the action film, the wildly unlikely occurrence fits perfectly.[30]

The nature of the hero in action texts, and their interaction with temporal and spatial elements, is also characterised by abstraction and non-specificity. In reference to the novel of ordeal, Bakhtin writes of the purely physical properties of adventure heroes. They must be as 'abstract' as the space in which they exist; details of individual psychology could expose a complex of socio-historical relations and tie the narrative down to a moment that could have 'really' happened. Character traits are given at the start of the narrative, from which there is little evolution; individuals are 'completely *passive*, completely *unchanging*'.[31] Bakhtin refines this model in the description of the Rabelaisian hero as 'completely external [. . .] All that a man is finds expression in actions and in dialogue'.[32] The hero of the action film is traditionally constructed along similar lines. Physique supersedes psychology and broad sentimentality replaces emotional complexity or depth. A prime example of the cinematic hero with no discernible interior life is James Bond who, especially in Sean Connery's incarnation, is almost cruelly physical and emotionally sterile. John Wayne, a figure whose connotations of masculinity seem 'absolutely fixed',[33] is an iconic precursor of the action star, while the borderline fascist heroes played by Clint Eastwood and Charles Bronson in *Dirty Harry* (1971) and *Death Wish* (1974) can also be included. The method of constructing the hero as a combat machine, purely defined by their physical characteristics, reaches its apotheosis in the cyborg protagonists of *Robocop* (1987), *Terminator 2: Judgement Day* (1991) and *Universal Soldier* (1992).

The 'Rambo' archetype that held sway in the 1980s is now unfashionably associated with the hard-line Reaganite policies of that decade, but despite efforts to update action heroes for more caring times, the kind of purely physical narrative tasks assigned to the protagonist continue to define him (the action hero is still too infrequently female) in terms of body rather than mind or personality. The stereotypical image of the muscles-for-brains protagonist, best embodied by Stallone's Rambo or the heroes played by Schwarzenegger in *Commando* (1985) and *Raw Deal* (1986) is fading, but continues to inflect perceptions of the genre. The image of the body in the 1980s work of such stars became another abstract space, a pumped-up, finely tuned locus of spectacle detached from most people's experience of a 'real' masculine body. Yvonne Tasker notes that in the action movie the presentation of the body is absorbed into the landscape of the film as a whole, the hero operating as a 'key aspect of the more general visual excess that this particular form of Hollywood production offers to its audience'.[34] Or, as Bakhtin puts it (in reference to chivalric romance): 'the hero and the miraculous world in which he acts are of a piece, there is no separation between the two.'[35] The aestheticised male body is so central to the economy of image in the action film that it may be possible to speak of a chronotope of the body, and one can certainly extract temporal data from the spatial codes of the physique. One way of measuring narrative progress in an action film is to monitor the state of dress of the male lead – as in *Die Hard* and *Speed*, they will invariably start the film fully clothed and end it in a grubby vest or blood-soaked t-shirt. Action films require broadly physical performances, and this is reflected in the type of actor that usually prospers in the genre. The acting burden often falls on the more technically gifted performers who are cast as villains – Alan Rickman in *Die Hard*, Jeremy Irons in *Die Hard With a Vengeance* (1995), Dennis Hopper in *Speed*.

As action narratives have become progressively more self-conscious, however, the macho archetype has undergone a subtle deconstruction. In 1988, *Die Hard*'s John McClane represented a movement away from the model of the cruel, intractable hero, aligning the character with the wisecracking star persona of Bruce Willis and shifting the emphasis slightly from body to voice.[36] The film ironically plays with the loaded associations of the action hero by alternately linking the character with John Wayne (as he is labelled by arch-villain Hans Gruber) and the distinctly less masculine Roy Rogers (as McClane refers to himself). The innovations made by Willis and director John McTiernan around the archetype of the action hero were soon followed by the introduction of more idiosyncratic actors like Nicolas Cage (*Con Air*, 1997) and Denzel Washington (*Crimson Tide*, 1995) to the genre, a development that served to break up the monopoly of 1980s 'tough guy' action stars.

## Space and plot

Although the action hero bears the outward signs of strength and self-control, he is characteristically powerless in the face of the irrational forces that dictate plot. In another correspondence between action films and the Greek novels of ordeal, Bakhtin characterises the generic hero as 'a person to whom something happens' rather than the driving force of narrative progression: 'He himself is deprived of any initiative. He is merely the physical subject of the action. And it follows that his actions will be by and large of an elementary-spatial sort. In essence, all the character's actions in Greek romance are reduced to *enforced movement through space* (escape, persecution, quests).'[37] These spatial manoeuvres tend to be epic in scale in Greek adventure narratives, encompassing whole countries and expansive timelines. The progress of the contemporary action hero also takes the form of movement through abstract time and space, albeit commonly within drastically compressed markers. The events in *Die Hard* take place within a single night, while *Speed* is structured around just two days separated by an elided period of a few weeks. In spatial terms, McClane spends mere minutes of the running time of *Die Hard* outside the environs of the Nakatomi Tower, while Traven is most often depicted on the speeding bus. There is further compression within these already narrow parameters; at one point, John McClane is forced to crawl through a tiny air vent to evade capture. A static camera witnesses his inexorable progress, as he quips 'Now I know what a TV dinner feels like'. This is a quintessential example of 'enforced movement through space', the hero compelled by the exigencies of plot through a minimal spatial context, robbed of any degree of initiative and forced to survive on wit alone.

In the 'Concluding Remarks', Bakhtin describes how time interacts with space to make 'narrative events concrete'.[38] Another way of putting this is to say that in the text, space is time waiting to happen. This principle informs the entire visual style and spatial presentation of *Die Hard*. The film's typical spaces – office areas on the deserted, unfinished floors of the Nakatomi building, lift-shafts, basements – all have the necessary physical attributes to make interesting settings for combat. These spaces seem to wait for the inevitable burst of action which will activate their potential; they resemble the characteristic spaces of the Greek romance, 'congealed "suddenlys", adventures turned into things', events waiting to be set into motion.[39] Space is constructed, via production design and shot composition, in a way that complements the action. The interaction of the hero with the spaces around him drives the narrative, although it must be stressed that this is a very mechanical, physical relationship, and not one that affords any change in the broader, abstract world of the narrative. McClane evades capture by achieving an instinctive, intimate understanding of the layout of the building, using its secondary structures

(access tunnels, air vents) to move around in. Surfaces and objects become potential allies; McClane uses a table to protect himself from a hail of bullets while he
positions himself to return fire. Another scene sees the hero defeat an opponent by
exploiting the space of an empty office area (creating a noise that draws the terrorist
into his sights). In terms of design within the frame, cinematographer Jan De Bont
(later director of *Speed*) frequently elects to let the camera focus on empty spaces,
generating the impression that the building is a major character; it is as if the hi-
tech Nakatomi Tower has a consciousness of its own, entwined with that of the
wilful, wandering camera. Occasionally these empty spaces will be transgressed by
the entrance of a character into the frame, for instance when the camera is positioned at the top of a flight of stairs where McClane will eventually enter into focus.
This technique plays with the assumptions surrounding space that is traditionally
offscreen, exploiting Noël Burch's observation that 'offscreen space has only an
intermittent or, rather, *fluctuating* existence during any film, and structuring this
fluctuation can become a powerful tool in the filmmaker's hands'.[40] In accordance
with Burch's classical prescription, the empty frame in *Die Hard* is used to define
spatial areas as three-dimensional, making us more aware of offscreen space as we
wait for something to fill the frame.

    Plot in the contemporary action film is deployed as a series of narrative hurdles
the hero must overcome, a structure that parallels the trope of 'testing' identified
by Bakhtin in the Greek romance. This is a category devoid of any experiential
value; '[n]o changes of any consequence occur, internal or external, as a result of
the events recounted'. The tests are purely 'external and formal' in character,
a method of plot structuration rather than anything with deeper social or psychological resonances.[41] *Speed* and *Die Hard* are constructed around a string of set-piece
sequences, each of which must trump the last for intensity, rising to a climactic
crescendo. This type of structure resembles nothing so much as the linear, level-
by-level construction of the computer 'platform' game. *Die Hard* is explicitly
modelled on this kind of physical arrangement, as its promotional tag-line suggests:
'Suspense. Excitement. Adventure on every level!' As in the computer game, the
obstacles placed in the path of the hero become more challenging as time goes on.
Bakhtin's description of basic adventure-time as breaking down into 'a sequence
of adventure-fragments' accurately conveys the mechanical division of plot in
the action film.[42] The frequency with which action films borrow the structural
motif of the 'game' suggests that this is a strong contender for a characteristic
chronotope of the genre. Payne, the villain in *Speed*, explicitly refers to his blackmail campaign as a game, quipping that his manipulation of Traven, observed on
close-circuit monitors, is like 'interactive TV'. It is perhaps unsurprising that *Speed*
and the three Die Hard films have all been successfully adapted to the computer
game format.

## The movie as 'ride'

The promotion of the Hollywood action film as an 'interactive' experience in
merchandising offshoots such as computer games reflects a broader institutional

strategy to involve the viewer in the events on the screen. The action genre represents the legacy of film's first experiments in scale and spectacle, and defines itself by its capacity to offer new and incredible visual treats in lieu of narrative innovation. Studios accentuate this aspect of action films by marketing them as thrilling, visceral experiences that physically grip the viewer. Recent technological developments have enabled Hollywood to market the action film, alongside its sometime hybrid partner science-fiction, through a procession of media, culminating, inevitably, in the physical experience of the theme park ride.[43] However, the physical embodiment of film narrative has provided a promotional angle since at least the 1950s. Kitsch experiments such as 3D or William Castle's *The Tingler* (1959), a horror movie where cinema seats were wired to electrical buzzers, capitalised on this idea of film as all-embracing visceral experience. Indeed, we can trace the roots of this aspect of pseudo-interactivity even further back in American cinema history. Charles Musser describes how the earliest film shows utilised motifs such as railway travel, creating a 'railway subgenre' where the spectator was led to assume the role of passenger. Railroad scenarios were ideally suited to promote a medium whose main selling point was the impression of movement through time and space, and a company called Hale's Tours took this analogous relationship to its logical conclusion, 'using a simulated railway carriage as a movie theater, with the audience sitting in the passenger seats and the screen replacing the view from the front or rear window'.[44] Here we can see an obvious precursor of the movie experience as defined by the modern blockbuster and its commercial spin-offs such as the theme park ride, as well as a literalisation of film's chronotopic capacity to 'move' the viewer.

The 'Cinema of Attractions' that these early film shows constituted represented the first flowering of a philosophy of action, spectacle and audience participation from which Hollywood cinema has rarely deviated. In contemporary cinema, the latest impresarios may employ 'virtual' technologies and computer enhancement, but the impulse to give the audience a thrilling 'ride' remains central. Exemplifying this, the irresistibly chronotopic tag-line of *Speed* – 'Get Ready For Rush Hour!' – fuses the temporal ('rush hour') with the spatio-physical (we are told to 'get ready', because something is going to happen to us). That the film successfully translates this impression is conveyed by one of its reviewers, Marshall Julius:

> The story is uncomplicated because what matters is the action [. . .] the movie delivers in full: imaginative, exhilarating and brilliantly executed, it tears along faster than a speeding bullet and passes two hours in what seems like a couple of minutes [. . .] The edge of your seat doesn't have a chance.[45]

These comments reveal much about how the action film is habitually viewed. Julius is caught up in the conflation of time and plot in the metaphor of speed. The pace of the narrative and the nature of its contents (speeding buses and subway trains) combine to give the impression that the experience of the text *itself* is fast. In an interpretation such as this, boundaries between chronotopic categories – motifs, genres, modes of reception – are dissolved. The bus *is* the film and vice versa.

And what is more, we are part of the process, physically incarnated in the action ('The edge of your seat doesn't have a chance'). The association between the chronotopic motifs within the text and the act of reception evokes Bakhtin's conception of the relationship between real and represented. We are beckoned into the text, invited to exploit the function of the chronotope as a 'bridge [. . .] between the two worlds'.[46] This idea is explicitly incorporated into the narrative of *Speed*. When Traven ploughs the runaway subway train through the end of the line and onto Sunset Boulevard, the vehicle comes to rest with a gentle bump against a tourbus offering views of Hollywood landmarks (an echo of 'Hale's Tours'?). Its passengers disembark and immediately commence taking photographs of Annie and Jack as they clinch romantically. The starstruck tourists represent us, the audience, our desire for spectacle satiated and the conventional happy ending firmly in place. It cannot be a coincidence that the train emerges right outside Hollywood's famous Chinese Theater, where *2001: A Space Odyssey* (1968) is playing. Kubrick's film is another 'journey' narrative, albeit one where the space voyage is a metaphor for an interior exploration of humanity. The gleefully unpretentious *Speed* cites these metaphysical concerns ironically.

## Conclusion

The successful action film usually combines a small amount of innovation with a much greater degree of emulation of the genre classics (among which *Speed* and *Die Hard* can surely be counted). Although the narrative configuration of the action movie often seems impervious to change, even such an avowedly populist and schematic form is never in creative stasis; as Bakhtin says, '[g]enre is reborn and renewed at every new stage of the development of literature and in every individual work in a given genre'.[47] The action genre, a narrative form absolutely central to the continuing industrial pre-eminence of Hollywood, will remake itself for many years to come, enjoying a lifespan unattainable to more historically bound genres such as the Western. Bakhtin discusses the lack of 'internal limits' in the Greek romance, which allows adventures to be extended indefinitely; the action film is spun from the same fabric.[48] Series such as the Bond films or *Die Hard* can endlessly propagate themselves because their form, the very time and space of which they are constituted and within which their adventures unfold, is so adaptable, elastic, abstract. Such qualities of archetypicality and ubiquity make the action film a suitable generic platform for the articulation of critical ideas about cinematic space and time, giving us a basic template against which to test formal hypotheses. The chronotope can play a valuable role in this process.

## Notes

1  André Bazin *What Is Cinema? Volume II*, trans. by Hugh Gray, London: University of California Press, 1972, p. 143.
2  Mikhail Bakhtin 'Forms of Time and of the Chronotope in the Novel', in Michael Holquist (ed.) *The Dialogic Imagination: Four Essays*, trans. by Caryl Emerson and Michael Holquist, Austin: University of Texas Press, 1994, p. 243.

3   Larry Gross 'Big and Loud', *Sight and Sound*, 5: 8, August 1995, p. 7.
4   For a consideration of the repercussions, both positive and negative, of the mid-70s rebirth of the 'blockbuster', see Thomas Schatz 'The New Hollywood', in Jim Collins, Hilary Radner and Ava Preacher Collins (eds) *Film Theory Goes to the Movies*, London: Routledge, 1993, pp. 8–36. The economic and institutional dimensions of this transition are further discussed in Richard Maltby 'Nobody Knows Everything: Post-Classical Historiographies and Consolidated Entertainment', in Steve Neale and Murray Smith (eds) *Contemporary Hollywood Cinema*, London: Routledge, 2000, pp. 21–44.
5   See Mikhail Bakhtin 'Discourse in the Novel', in *The Dialogic Imagination*, pp. 259–422.
6   Bakhtin 'Forms', pp. 253–7.
7   Christian Metz *Film Language: A Semiotics of the Cinema*, trans. by Michael Taylor, New York: Oxford University Press, 1974, p. 9.
8   Bakhtin 'Forms', p. 146.
9   Ibid., p. 98.
10  Ibid., p. 253.
11  Ibid., p. 250.
12  Ibid., p. 252. Italics in original.
13  Sue Vice *Introducing Bakhtin*, Manchester: Manchester University Press, 1997, p. 201.
14  For a discussion of how Bakhtin's chronotopic category of the road can be applied to cinema, and specifically the road movie genre, see Vice *Introducing Bakhtin*, pp. 210–18.
15  M. M. Bakhtin *Problems of Dostoevsky's Poetics*, ed. and trans. by Caryl Emerson, Minneapolis: University of Minnesota Press, 1997, p. 169.
16  Ibid., p. 170.
17  Bakhtin 'Forms', p. 257. Italics in original.
18  Bakhtin 'Forms', pp. 88, 90, 94, 105. Italics in original.
19  Ibid., p. 102.
20  John Baxter *Steven Spielberg: The Unauthorized Biography*, London: Harper Collins, 1997, p. 343.
21  Ibid., p. 218.
22  Katerina Clark and Michael Holquist *Mikhail Bakhtin*, Cambridge, MA: Belknap Press, 1984, p. 279.
23  Bakhtin 'Forms', p. 90.
24  Ibid.
25  Ibid., p. 141.
26  Ibid., p. 110.
27  Ibid., p. 100.
28  Christian Metz *Psychoanalysis and Cinema*, trans. by Celia Britton, Annwyl Williams, Ben Brewster and Alfred Guzzetti, London: Macmillan, 1994, p. 64.
29  Bakhtin 'Forms', p. 95.
30  Ibid., p. 102.
31  Ibid., p. 105.
32  Ibid., p. 239.
33  Yvonne Tasker 'Dumb Movies for Dumb People: Masculinity, the Body and the Voice in Contemporary Action Cinema', in Steven Cohan and Ina Rae Hark (eds) *Screening the Male*, London: Routledge, 1995, p. 234.
34  Tasker 'Dumb Movies', p. 233.
35  Bakhtin 'Forms', p. 153.
36  See Tasker 'Dumb Movies', p. 239.
37  Bakhtin 'Forms', pp. 95, 105. Italics in original.
38  Ibid., p. 250.
39  Ibid., p. 102.
40  Noël Burch *Theory of Film Practice*, London: Secker and Warburg, 1973, p. 21. Italics in original.

41   Bakhtin 'Forms', p. 106.
42   Ibid., p. 151.
43   Attractions based on the action/sci-fi hybrid texts *Robocop*, *Terminator 2: Judgement Day* and *Aliens* are now established in theme parks in the US and Europe.
44   Charles Musser *Before the Nickelodeon: Edwin S. Porter and the Edison Manufacturing Company*, Oxford: University of California Press, 1991, pp. 260–4.
45   Marshall Julius *Action! The Action Movie A-Z*, London: B. T. Batsford, 1996, pp. 192–3.
46   Clark and Holquist *Mikhail Bakhtin*, p. 279.
47   Bakhtin *Problems of Dostoevsky's Poetics*, p. 106.
48   Bakhtin 'Forms', p. 94.

## Chapter 7

## AYLISH WOOD

# THE COLLAPSE OF REALITY AND ILLUSION IN *THE MATRIX*

**I**S *THE MATRIX* (1999, Wachowski Brothers) a film about emancipation from the tyranny of machines, of freeing reality from the captivity of illusion; or, is it about being captured by the illusion of such an emancipatory tale? I argue here that *The Matrix* plays these two possibilities off against one another. In many ways it looks like a conventional kick-ass/machine action movie, although one whose special effects are undeniably impressive. However, in other ways the film is full of gaps and uncertainties, making it difficult to decide what it is really about. Whilst this may lead towards a view of the film as insubstantial, my contention is that *The Matrix* is about the possibility of playing the role of a hero. It plays a game with both its characters and its viewers, a game in which reality and illusion are equally open to question.

One of the central structuring devices of *The Matrix* is an exploration of the relationship between humans and technologies, a concern common to many science-fiction (SF) films. Indeed many initial responses to the release of *The Matrix* noted the opposition between alienating technology and the emancipatory struggles of the human figures. Frequently, the resolution of this conflict has been perceived as a relatively straightforward reassertion of human freedom over the restrictions of a fully technologised environment.[1] Such a perception of *The Matrix* assumes a version of humanism, or at least a view of the human as a being that retains the capacity to fight for freedom and autonomy. This in turn fits with Scott Bukatman's suggestion that in spite of the increased blurring of the human and the technological, a number of SF films retain the vision of a human figure that can resist the challenge to definitions: '[T]he utopian promise of the science fiction film – the superiority of the human – may be battered and beleaguered, but it is still there, fighting for validation.'[2]

David Lavery's analysis of *The Matrix* relies on a version of this argument; he suggests that Neo's role within the narrative is to dissolve the illusion of the Matrix, to give the humans back the possibility of their freedom by re-establishing and validating the real world through the actions of the Resistance.[3] In generating this analysis, Lavery compares *The Matrix* unfavourably to *eXistenZ* (1999, David Cronenberg) on the grounds that the latter film maintains an uncertainty about the status of the reality in which the characters find themselves. In the absence of a real Real World, *eXistenZ* 'while it does imagine seemingly heroic realists fighting against the triumph of illusion, has no such faith [about the possibility of knowing the real world]. For even they cannot escape from the ever-recursive game of eXistenZ and TransCendenZ.'[4] Lavery's position, like several reviews of *The Matrix*, not only gives Neo the status of a human who can vanquish machines and be a Messiah, but also assumes that within *The Matrix* the status of the Real World is certain. In contrast, I argue that *The Matrix*, whilst very different to *eXistenZ*, is as full of gaps and uncertainties, and that these gaps and uncertainties lead to a mistrust of the reality status of *both* the Matrix and the Real World. In *The Matrix*, the extent of the illusion, or the depth of the rabbit hole, is not the only thing in doubt; so too is the question of where it begins and ends.

In order to think about the uncertainties of *The Matrix* I draw on the idea of paraspaces. In *Terminal Identity* Scott Bukatman uses science fiction writer and critic Samuel R. Delaney's notion of paraspaces to introduce the idea of juxtaposed alternative worlds. As two worlds (or more) are aligned with each other, the events occurring in one world produce a commentary on events in the other(s). Delaney (quoted in Bukatman) suggests that a number of science fiction writers 'posit a normal world – a recognizable future – and then an alternate space, sometimes largely mental, but always materially manifested, that sits behind the real world, and in which language is raised to an extraordinarily lyric level'.[5] Delaney argues further that the conflicts beginning in the real world can be resolved within the paraspace. Although Delaney is primarily concerned with literature, Bukatman extends the idea of paraspaces to include SF films on the grounds that the spectacular elements of many such films raise the imagery to an extraordinary level.[6] There exist numerous SF films that incorporate within their narratives competing alternative realities. In some texts the spaces remain distinct, as the paraspace is a place where problems are safely resolved, but which nonetheless have implications for actions in the alternative space. Examples include *Tron* (1982, Steven Lisberger), *Virtuosity* (1995, Brett Leonard) and more recently *The Cell* (2000, Tarsem Singh). In other texts, the boundaries between the two spaces are blurred, as for instance in *Total Recall* (1990, Paul Verhoeven), and also *eXistenZ*. In films where the boundaries are indistinct, the movement between the spaces engenders not so much the possibility for the resolution of a conflict in an apparently safe place, but instead leads to a questioning of the certainties of each space. In *eXistenZ*, for example, as the difference between the game world and the real world is increasingly collapsed, the identities of the characters that potentially inhabit those worlds are made uncertain. Whilst such uncertainties lead to the exclusion of the possibility of a humanist ego, it does not, however, lead to the destruction of identity. Instead, it leads to a reconstitution of identity, one that takes into account the paradigms offered by the alternative realities.[7]

Like *eXistenZ*, *The Matrix* is a film that plays off two competing paraspaces, but it does so in two different ways. On the one hand it establishes two distinct worlds, the paraspaces of the Matrix and the Real World. But on the other hand, it frequently undermines the idea that the Real World is anything other than an illusion as potent as the Matrix. If each paraspace is as real or unreal as the other, then the identities of the characters are equally open to question.

## 'What is real?'

*The Matrix* works hard to establish the suggestion that the Matrix and the Real World are distinct. Although only evident through a series of brief sequences, the urban spaces of the Matrix conform to conventional images of a major US city in the late 1990s. By day the city streets are busy, full of people going somewhere, and by night the city is a place of dark corners, clubs and degrees of paranoia. Although this space bears the marks of exaggeration, as everything is a little too busy or too perfectly dark and dank (and a touch too green to be entirely enticing),[8] it is the actions of certain characters that finally establish the strangeness of this place. At the first time of seeing, the opening sequence may seem just to be a showcase for the cutting edge special effects that the publicity surrounding the release of the film would have led many viewers to expect – special effects in which time, space and gravity are defied. The use of 'bullet-time' photography allows Trinity to hang in the air as the policeman, also suspended in inaction, simply gapes at her unwinding kick, which sends him at speed into the wall.[9] The photography of this sequence gives the impression of time appearing to be both slowed down and speeded up – the brief stillness of Trinity in mid-air is followed by the speed of her unwinding kick. The subsequent chase scene over the rooftops is captured in a series of shots that accentuate movement, an effect that adds to the vibrancy of the opening sequence. For example, 'collision shots' in which the figures run towards a camera that seems to be moving towards them, rapid cuts on movement, and tracking shots of running figures, alongside the frankly improbable leaps, give this sequence an energy that is underscored by the beat of the music. Only with the revelation of Trinity's disappearance from the demolished phone box does it become fully apparent that this is a world where conventions of time and space can be disturbed. And although this disturbance is embedded in the chase sequence, it is only as the image lingers over the rubble of the phone booth, and the absence of a body, that the strangeness of the paraspace called the Matrix becomes inescapable.

A spectator might attribute the extraordinariness of the Matrix to Trinity as some kind of superhero, and suppose the inexplicability of her actions to be the result of special powers. It soon becomes apparent through the Neophyte Neo, however, that it is the space of the Matrix which is strange. What makes Trinity, and other members of the Resistance, different is not any special power but their ability to recognise and manipulate this strangeness.[10] Neo, as he learns to recognise and manipulate this strangeness, also introduces and explains the Matrix for the viewer. And whilst the Trinity sequence presents the Matrix as a place of spectacular possibilities, this proves to be something of a teaser. For as Neo begins to experience the powers behind the Matrix, the US cityscape is shown to be an illusion, a virtual construction. Initially, the illusory nature of the Matrix is only hinted at – such as the computer that seems to communicate with Neo, or the mobile phone that hangs in the air ever so briefly before it falls to the ground when Neo drops it whilst standing on the outside ledge of a skyscraper. But once he has been arrested, the flip-side of this world begins to emerge. The three agents (Smith, Jones and Brown), almost identical in their dark grey suits, dark hair and dark glasses, not only act as the representatives of a hitherto invisible presence, but also inaugurate a series of nightmarish events. But before these begin, a seamless movement through a set of monitor screens, along with the shot-reverse-shot sequence between Agent Smith and Neo, which unconventionally includes a sequence of elbow, as well as the more usual over-the-shoulder-shots, creates a slight disturbance in expectations. This disturbance becomes full-blown when mediated by Neo's reaction to the horror of his mouth sealing over, an event that is followed by the insertion of a 'bug' through his navel. In the world of the Matrix, the physical body is as open to manipulation as the physical space itself.

The end of the arrest sequence also explicitly suggests that the beginnings and ends of dreams are not always clear. As Neo wakens from what he initially takes as a nightmare, he finds that he is still inside the world of that nightmare. It is significant that just at the moment Neo might seem to be spiralling into an irrational fantasy he is offered a way out of his dilemma. This 'way out' both secures his relative sanity and introduces the paraspace to the Matrix – the so-called Real World, a place that acts to finally reveal the illusory and enslaving nature of the Matrix. At first this paraspace seems to be fully distinct from that of the Matrix, as Neo has to take a pill in order for him to make the transition, a transition marked by his passage through a liminal space. The existence of a liminal space, established through a shot of Neo's tonsils that morphs into a passage leading to a different version of reality, further emphasises the existence of distinct spaces. Here the gloom of the place is as exaggerated as the exhilaration and horror of the Matrix, and the rhetorical status of the Real World is as hyped as that of the Matrix. As Neo re-wakens, metaphorically reborn as he breaks through a membrane, the confusion of this breaking out, the violence of a suddenly encountered new environment is captured in the subsequent close-up sequence. Unlike most close-ups, which are anchored by framing a specific element of the image, in this sequence there is a jumble of tubes, dripping pink fluid and the motion of Neo's grasping hands, all of which move across the screen. In contrast to the disorienting motion of these unanchored fragments, Neo's location is then established through a pair of linked shots. In longer-held medium close-ups, Neo looks over the side and front edges of his capsule. The reverse shots of these two separate looks provide the co-ordinates of Neo's location, as the capsules seemingly extend into infinity both horizontally and vertically. As the vastness of this construction is accentuated by the rising note of the score, its awesomeness is rapidly displaced into terror as Neo, whose naked vulnerability is enhanced by the absence of hair, is detached and flushed away as waste in another series of rapidly edited shots.

In the following sequences, the substance of this other world becomes more apparent. In itself this world is not a terrifying place; instead, the terror belongs to the revelation of the extent of the illusory nature of the Matrix as the two para-spaces, that of the Real World and that of the Matrix, generate a commentary upon each other. The Real World is evidently a grungy space of cobbled together and battered machines, old clothing and food that is nutritional but looks like gruel.[11] However, subsequently there is a return to spectacle as the quotidian existence of the Resistance fighters is exchanged for a revelation of the extent of this alternative reality. The images and verbal descriptions, 'the desert of the real', reverberate with ideas of both apocalypse and environmental catastrophe, not to mention late twentieth century cultural criticism. The full awfulness of the Matrix is finally encapsulated in a digitised and seamless sequence showing humans grown in endless fields.[12] Accompanied by the resonant voice-over of Morpheus describing his own discovery of the 'truth', the machines are shown harvesting human babies. As insect-like metallic creatures 'buzz' around, as cable coils tighten menacingly and babies pass through conveyor tubes, the movement within the image pauses to allow the rows of capsules to be seen stretching into infinity.

This revelation sequence can be seen as the source of the Resistance's motivation for the remainder of *The Matrix*, as its hero, and viewers, are taken down to the depths of the ravaged world in order to ensure that they understand the difference between the opposing spaces. Whilst the Real World may be cold and grungy, it exists in opposition to the Matrix, where humans are reduced to batteries that enable machines to function. Given this scenario it seems to make sense that humans will want to release themselves from tyranny, and that Morpheus is persuasive and utterly believable as a figure whose intentions are honourable in ensuring that Neo will fulfil his potential to be the One. The Real World as a paraspace to the Matrix establishes the latter as a place of enslavement and exploitation. And in contesting the technological ascendancy of the Matrix, the Resistance seems to suggest that the Real World is the better place. Further, the rationale for the position of the Resistance rests on establishing the Matrix as an illusion that is fully distinct from the reality of the Real World. Essentially, the very possibility for humans to transcend the machines of the Matrix relies on ensuring that the reality of one world is secured against the illusion of the other.

Within the narrative of *The Matrix*, then, it is the existence of the paraspaces that apparently establishes a set of oppositions, the Real World as opposed to the Matrix, reality as opposed to illusion, freedom as opposed to enslavement. However, in each case the meaning of each term in these oppositions takes its meaning from its difference from its other. In other words, for the characters within the text the reality of the Real World is dependent on a belief that the Matrix is an illusion. If the Matrix is an illusion, then the Real World must be real. And given no third space to consider, it seems as though the characters have little difficulty in accepting this scenario. Once the characters accept this, their identity as Resistance fighters is also secured. Taking Neo as an example, once he believes in the reality of the Real World, it follows that he is free in this world, and furthermore, that he is the emancipatory hero who can release other humans from their enslavement.

## 'The Matrix can be more real than this world'

As I have already said, in order for the characters within the film to believe, the reality of the Real World must be secured by ensuring the illusory status of the Matrix. Similarly, in order to describe *The Matrix* as a rather straightforward (though admittedly technologically sophisticated) story in which humans transcend the alienating power of technology, it is necessary to believe in the characters' belief in the reality of the Real World. But given the number of games played within *The Matrix*, is there any reason to sustain such a distinction?

There are several ways of blurring the distinction between the Real World and the Matrix. One of these is to think about how the spaces of the Matrix and the Real World have equally uncertain claims to reality. On an overt level within *The Matrix*, the competition between the machines and the resistance is played out through the fight and chase sequences between Morpheus, Trinity and Neo, and the representatives of the machines –the Agents, the sentinels and also Cypher. This conflict, which seems to further establish the distinction between the realities, is not only evident at the level of the action of the characters, as it is also played out across the rhythms of the narrative – the machinic rhythm is constantly in tension with that of the resistance. One example of this is Agent's Smith slow-paced speech. His slow enunciation establishes one pattern of progression that seems out of step with the more rapid speech patterns of the human characters. This tension is especially evident in the two interrogation sequences, the first with Neo and the second with Morpheus.

The competition between humans and machines is also played out in terms of who controls the status and rhythm of time and space throughout *The Matrix*. As viewers, we are given the knowledge (via the interchanges between Morpheus and Neo) that Matrix time is machine set, dislocated from the human tradition of dates, or at least the date system of the western world. Yet the Matrix is recognisable as a representation of a US city from the late 1990s. Whilst this cityspace is only ever seen through a series of glimpses (when Neo is in the MegaCortex building, and during the visit to the Oracle), as an audience we are meant to come to this understanding through the ways in which the spatio-temporal dimensions of the Matrix are constantly broken. The shifting of the phases of space-time is most apparent in the slowing, stretching and warping of space-time evident in most of the major set pieces of the film. Take the opening sequence of *The Matrix*: during the Trinity chase, some of the possibilities of this spatio-temporal manipulation are demonstrated – here is a figure who can hang in the air, leap across impossibly wide spaces and vanish into thin cable, via the electronic signal of a phone line. All these feats are flamboyantly created through the use of digitising effects, wire-work and bullet-time. This latter technique captures most fully the disruption of time and space. It enables the filmmakers to slow or speed the sequence of shots, holding on some whilst accelerating through others. Bullet-time gives, in an already fast moving and edited film, a kind of whiplash effect that accentuates at the level of the progression of the frames the conflict being worked out through the physical actions of the characters. In both Neo's roof-top bullet-dodging scene and his fight with Agent

Smith, his unexpected actions are re-iterated by the unexpected movement through space. Similarly, a sense of spatio-temporal disruption is visible when Morpheus breaks free of his chains and runs towards Neo in the helicopter. As he runs across the room, the trajectory of the bullets from Agent's Smith weapon are marked in the splashes of water. Very briefly, there is a disjuncture between the movement of Morpheus and the movement of the bullets. Although Morpheus and the bullets are within the same location, inhabiting what should be the same spatio-temporal dimension, one is moving and the other is not. Morpheus is frozen, at first in the background which becomes the foreground, as the images trace the fired bullet as it travels towards Morpheus's ankle, finally giving Morpheus motion just at the moment he is shot.

This spatio-temporal disruption is typical of the ripple effects that run through *The Matrix*, a ripple that demonstrates a dissonance in the organisation of the competing spatio-temporal worlds at the basis of the narrative of *The Matrix*. That is, the machine-time of the Matrix is under siege from a second organisation, that of the Resistance movement. But this pattern of dissonance does not culminate in a complete fracturing of time; instead, it is more of a flexing of that time – at the end of *The Matrix* Neo bends the space-time of the machine world, demonstrating that he knows how to interfere with it, manipulate and control it.[13] However, it does not therefore follow that *The Matrix* is about human time transcending machine time, that the Resistance provides the possibility of a natural order transcending an unnatural one, or the restoration of reality after an illusion. As many critics have pointed out, there is nothing natural about our representations of time.[14] Whether they take the form of calendars, clocks or narratives, all representations of time are impositions, each attempting to establish order or coherency. From this perspective, *The Matrix* involves a conflict between two opposing forces that seek to control and order the space-time dimensions of the world. In the light of this discussion, the paraspaces of the Real World and the Matrix are no more or less real than each other.

This blurring of the distinction between the two paraspaces can be taken further by thinking about the actions of the characters within them. If we take first the notion of humans as able to transcend technologies, both the Real World and the Matrix are technologised environments, so the actions of the characters always involve some degree of dependency on technology; even at this level *The Matrix* does not rely on a simplistic opposition between human and technology. The Resistance must exploit technology in order to battle with the machines and their emissaries, the Agents, as well as needing the hovercraft to maintain their day-to-day living. However, the virtual spaces, the site of many of the actual conflicts, emerge as the Wonderland of the film. In a paradox evident in many SF films, the capacities of the alienating technologies are shown through a demonstration of the capacities of cinema technologies, which in turn effects a double articulation of technology. On the one hand, technology is meant to be understood as alienating and exploitative. On the other hand, the spectacular sequences of the second half of *The Matrix* make the technologised environment a fascinating and even seductive space. Such sequences tend to counter the more negative images of the

Matrix seen during Neo's induction into the Real World. The ambiguity of these two dimensions of the text, the context provided by the plot, and the construction of the images, splits the potential points of identification for the viewer. This effect is furthered through the actions of the characters; they function simultaneously as narrative agents that enable a story about alienating technologies, and as figures that act as vehicles to display the virtuosity of cinematographers and special effects (SFX) teams.

The idea of characters having a split function within *The Matrix* is also relevant to their actions within the story-world of the film. As narrative agents, or characters, that operate to enable the progression of a story, they not only serve to heighten the split content of the film and its mode of production, as they also act as agents across more than one of the paraspaces. As a result, their identities can themselves be seen to be split, or to put it another way, distributed across the two paraspaces. Neo is the central character within the narrative of *The Matrix*, making him a key agent through which the story progresses. When first encountered he is shown to have a split persona: he is Thomas Anderson, program writer for MegaCortex, and Neo, a hacker who is seeking the answer to a question. Once he has been 'liberated' from the Matrix by Morpheus, he fully assumes the identity of Neo, though this identity is different from hacker Neo. That is, Neo becomes the point through which the illusion of the Matrix is revealed, and he takes up this position at the moment his identity is stabilised into that of the One – the messianic figure who will show reality to the sleeping humans. However, Neo Version 2.0 has a distributed identity; his existence as the saviour emerges in both the Real World and the Matrix, through his ability to move between the two paraspaces, and to exert control over the Matrix.

The idea of distributed identity is informed by the work of N. Katherine Hayles in *How We Became Posthuman*. In her discussion of the posthuman, Hayles develops the idea of distributed cognitive environments, environments that involve technologised intersections of humans with their environment. Rather than knowing the world through a position centred solely through the various human organs of perception, humans know the world through a more distributed network that can include technologies acting as channels for what can be told and known about the world. In other words, human organs of perception work in connection with non-human objects in the world, and it is this combination that makes possible cognition and actions. As Hayles remarks: '[E]very day we participate in systems whose total cognitive capacity exceeds our individual knowledge . . . Modern humans are capable of more sophisticated cognition than cavemen not because moderns are smarter . . . but because they have constructed smarter environments.'[15] Hayles also makes clear that it is not simply a question of humans controlling an array of technologies, and so extending themselves into the world in increasingly sophisticated ways. Instead of humans simply using technology for their own devices, the extent of cognition, and hence the ways humans extend themselves within the world, is contingent on the possibilities or limits generated in the combinations of human and non-human elements of any distributed network. This argument can be taken further to include questions of identity – if cognition can be distributed then a sense of identity that arises from cognition is similarly distributed. Equally, if actions are distributed, then an identity that emerges in relation to those actions is also distributed. For example Tank, a 'genuine child of Zion', cannot move between the two paraspaces because he does not have a port through which he can jack-in.[16] Yet he knows about the machines, in part because of the attacks of the sentinels, but also through his use of the computer system that is integral to the functioning of the *Nebuchadnezzar*. His knowledge of the machine world is distributed through his direct experience of the sentinels, and by his technologically mediated knowledge of the world of the Matrix and the Agents. What he knows of the Matrix is contingent on what the available technologies enable him to know. Tank's identity as a member of the Resistance emerges through a distribution across two paraspaces. And since both are essential to his identity, is either more or less real than the other? A similar situation holds for all the characters that can pass between the two spaces, the difference being that their extension into the technologically enhanced virtual Matrix is at a different level of experience. Within the story-world of *The Matrix*, when they enter the Matrix they do so fully cognisant; physical and presumably emotional damage is felt, and has very real effects on the characters' actual and virtual bodies; severe trauma leads to death in both worlds. Similarly, their actions in each paraspace have very real consequences in both places. Neo as the One can be leader of the Resistance because of the ways in which he operates within the Matrix. Neo's own belief in this identity is also dependent on his ability to manipulate the world of the Matrix when his identity is distributed through human and non-human objects.

Thus *The Matrix*, even though it seems to promote the possibility of humans transcending alienating technologies, never provides a space in which such a proposition can occur. Whilst the two paraspaces are presented as distinct, one actual and the other virtual, one apparently real the other apparently an illusion, such a distinction itself turns out to be something of an illusion.

## 'You're waiting for something, your next life maybe'

The potential for illusion or delusion is not only evident in the collapsed distinction between the Real World and the Matrix, as this is a possibility that runs riot within *The Matrix*. Not only are the identities of the characters distributed across the paraspaces of the text, but the identity of the text is equally distributed across a myriad of intertextual allusions. *The Matrix* includes allusions to the Old and New Testaments, and the narratives of enslavement and emancipation that could encompass Israelites, Rastafarians and African-Americans. There are references to numerous other texts and/or films, not least *Alice in Wonderland* and *The Wizard of Oz*. These two particular texts introduce the idea of fantasy or dreaming, a theme that emerges in *The Matrix* most explicitly in the figure of Morpheus, the King of Dreams and son of Hypnos, the God of Sleep. And whilst it might just be that the Wachowski Brothers were profligate to a point that approaches indiscriminate in their selection of allusions, intertexts suggestive of delusions and dreams predominate. The incessant reiteration of this point makes it hard to ignore the possibility that *The Matrix* is not about a man who is the saviour, but a man who is enjoying the fantasy/dream/trip or even game of being the saviour. After all it is Morpheus who sends Neo on a trip down the rabbit hole, and at the end of the rabbit hole is Morpheus' ship, the *Nebuchadnezzar*.

The name Nebuchadnezzar conjures up a whole other set of possibilities. In the Book of Daniel, Nebuchadnezzar was a Babylonian king who enslaved children from Israel. Amongst them was a child known by his captors as Belteshazzar, but who refused this name, preferring instead Daniel. The parallels with Neo are clear: Daniel, a man who changed his own name, became a prophet, and could read 'the writing on the wall', much like Neo can come to see the Matrix walls as computer code. Daniel also had a revelation in which he was told that there would, at the end of days, be an apocalypse in which the people would wake from their sleep (in the dust), and that this awakening would allow the multitude to understand. Only some, however, would be saved.[17] Although the correspondences with *The Matrix* are strong, my intention here in invoking some of the stories from the Book of Daniel is not to suggest that *The Matrix* is in any sense a version of those stories. Rather, it is to suggest that the biblical references within the film do not only lead towards Neo as a saviour. They equally lead towards him being a captive figure, though also a prophet who receives a dream that there will, in time, be an apocalypse.

Where does any of this leave us with *The Matrix*? It is a film that is full of gaps and contradictions, packed with allusions to the extent than it feels overburdened, and perhaps even empty because of that. But instead of thinking of *The Matrix* as a conventional film text that tells a narrative with a straightforward hero figure, perhaps it is more useful to think of *The Matrix* as equivalent to working through levels of a video game. And rather than thinking of Neo as 'really' being a saviour figure, or a prophet, or that his whole experience is merely a dream, a drug-induced fantasy trip, think of him as a locus through which an audience can watch a series of scenarios unfold. Seeing the film in this way might make sense of some of the repetitions of the film. For instance, Neo gets two 'next lives' within *The Matrix*, and each time he is re-animated, either re-born or resurrected, he ascends to a different level of the game. The action of *The Matrix* also has a circularity as Neo ends up in Room 303, exactly where the whole game began with the police chasing Trinity. But the game does not end with watching Neo, and the other characters of the plot; it also involves us as viewers making decisions about the reality or illusions of the film. When reality and illusion collapse into each other, as viewers we are left to make a decision about what we think is going on: Is Neo a digital prophet or a digital dupe? A prophet who can foresee emancipation, or a dupe who wants to believe, to play along with a scenario of being a saviour? The Oracle, a key figure for the Resistance and a notoriously duplicitous figure in mythology, allows Neo to believe what he wants to believe, and we as the audience can also believe what we want to believe.

## Notes

1  See, for instance, Kim Newman 'Rubber Reality', *Sight and Sound*, 9: 6, June 1999, p. 6. Whilst this article meets many of the games of *The Matrix* on their own terms, Newman does suggest that Neo wakes up the world.

2  Scott Bukatman *Terminal Identity: The Virtual Subject in Postmodern Science Fiction*, Durham, NC and London: Duke University Press, 1993, p. 17.

3  David Lavery 'From Cinescape to Cyberspace: Zionists and Agents, Realists and Gamers in *The Matrix* and *eXistenZ*', *Journal of Popular Film and Television*, 28: 4, Winter 2001, pp. 150–7.

4  Ibid., p. 156.

5  Samuel Delaney as cited by Scott Bukatman *Terminal Identity*, p. 157.

6  Indeed, it is possible to argue that SF films (and books) that involve alternative realities constitute in themselves a paraspace, since they exist in distinction to the viewer/reader's more mundane reality. Scott Bukatman *Terminal Identity*, p. 174.

7  Scott Bukatman *Terminal Identity*, pp. 174–80.

8  Several reviewers have commented on the greenness of the world inside the Matrix. This is most evident in the sequence of Neo's interrogation by Agent Smith. Here the greenness of the Matrix world first looks to be a consequence of the screen, or more accurately, the array of screens through which Neo is seen. However, as the image crosses through the liminal space of the screen, the green hue continues. This moment captures the collapse of boundaries that is central to *The Matrix*.

9  As described at the end of the VHS tape and the DVD, bullet time involves the use of still photography. A number of stills are taken in a complex sequence, digitised and then further manipulated to enable to filmmakers to produce moving images in which time is expanded or compressed within the spatial dimensions defined by the original sequence of still images.

10  This makes *The Matrix* different from *Dark City* (1998, Alex Proyas). In this latter film John Murdoch is the saviour figure of the film because, unlike the other humans, he has the special powers of the aliens and so can compete with them. In *The Matrix* all humans have the capacity to learn the apparently special powers of the Resistance.

11  Geoff King comments that given the dystopic vision of the real world in *The Matrix*, Cypher's decision to return to the comforts of the Matrix does not seem unreasonable. Geoff King *Spectacular Narratives: Hollywood in the Age of the Blockbuster*, London and New York: I. B. Tauris Publishers, 2000.

12  This particular scene has strong echoes of the centre of the alien hive in *Aliens* (1986, dir. James Cameron).

13  Neo is also an anagram of Eon, a variant of the word aeon meaning the chronological period of a 'power existing from eternity; an emanation, generation, or phase of the supreme deity, taking part in the creation and government of the universe' (Oxford English Dictionary). Whatever the reality status of the film, as well as being the One, Neo introduces a new Eon, a period when control is open to contestation.

14  I am thinking here of the ideas of Henri Bergson, Hayden White and Paul Ricouer.

15  N. Katherine Hayles *How We Became Posthuman: Virtual Bodies in Cybernetics, Literature and Informatics*, Chicago and London: The University of Chicago Press, 1999, p. 289.

16  The naming of the two genuine children of Zion as 'Tank' and 'Dozer' again plays up the uncertain boundaries between humans and technology.

17  John J. Collins *Daniel: A Commentary on the Book of Daniel*, Minneapolis: Fortress Press, 1993.

## Chapter 8

## TICO ROMAO

# GUNS AND GAS
## Investigating the 1970s car chase film[1]

Surely, goodness, mercy and high octane will triumph over villainy with lead in their guns, if not in their gas.[2]

**L**IKE THE SONG AND DANCE NUMBERS of musicals or the gun-fights in westerns, car chase sequences are one of the most readily recognizable elements of action films. Even though car chases, or pursuit sequences more generally, are not universal features of contemporary action films, their status as 'action' spectacles can be traced back to the origins of the American cinema. The capacity of pursuit sequences to engage audiences was used as early as *The Great Train Robbery* (1903) with its crosscutting from pursued bandits to pursuing posse contributing to the film's dynamism. Later, the 'chase' film became one of the earliest templates for narrative construction with films such as *Personal* (1904), *The Lost Child* (1904), *Jack the Kisser* (1907), and D. W. Griffith's *The Curtain Pole* (1909) exploiting the pursuit structure's additional comedic potential.[3] In the 1910s, the distinct thrills deriving from the car chase would become one of the trademark elements of Mack Sennett's Keystone films. As Douglas Riblet has observed, one of the chief sources of appeal of Keystone productions was their unique combination of the conventions of slapstick comedy with elements derived from 'action melodrama' in an attempt to provide 'purely visceral pleasures'.[4] Many Keystone films often highlighted these automotive moments in their very titles with *Barney Oldfield's Race for a Life* (1913), *Mabel at the Wheel* (1914), and *Love, Speed and Thrills* (1915) indicative of such promotional techniques. During the classical period, genres that were widely identified by audiences on the basis of their action sequences – namely westerns and crime films – often counted upon pursuit sequences to deliver the action goods. Countless westerns have at least one pursuit sequence built into their narratives. Crime films, such as *High Sierra* (1941), *The Big Steal* (1949), *Side Street* (1950), and *The Racket* (1951), true to their modern milieu, would replace the horseback sequences of the western with car chases as the preferred means of depicting high speed pursuits.

Despite this reliance upon the pursuit sequence over the history of the Hollywood cinema, it is only in the 1970s that the car chase became Hollywood's action sequence *par excellence*. Even the briefest sampling of Hollywood movies frequently identified as 'action' films can demonstrate the pervasiveness of this form of action sequence. Within the police/crime thriller one can cite *Bullitt* (1968), *The French Connection* (1971), *The Seven-Ups* (1973), *White Lightning* (1973), '*McQ*' (1974), *Mr. Majestyk* (1974), and *The Driver* (1978). In terms of the 'pursuit' films that structure large sections or the entirety of their narratives as a car chase, one could refer to *Vanishing Point* (1971), *Dirty Mary, Crazy Larry* (1974), *Gone in 60 Seconds* (1974), *The Sugarland Express* (1974), *Eat My Dust* (1976), and the entire Smokey and the Bandit series (1977, 1980, 1983). One can additionally point to those comedies that portray races taking place on the nation's highways and which are thematically and stylistically related to more conventional car chase films. These would include *Death Race 2000* (1975), *The Gumball Rally* (1976), *Cannonball* (1976), and *Cannonball Run* and *Cannonball Run II* (1980, 1983). The extent of Hollywood's enthusiasm for car chases is best expressed in a *Variety* review of *The Seven-Ups* in which the author complains that virtually every film in production at the time appeared to include 'some sort of auto carnage'.[5] As the Smokey and the Bandit and the Cannonball Run series attest, car chase films could prove enormously successful at the box office. The revenues to be gained by films with prolonged car chase sequences was made clear to the industry when *Bullitt* yielded $19 million in rentals to be only topped a few years later when *The French Connection* went on to earn $26 million. The full box office potential of such films was eventually mined by the Smokey and the Bandit series, with the first installment generating over $61 million in rentals, while its sequel, *Smokey and the Bandit II*, brought in $37 million. Even at the tail end of the cycle, *Cannonball Run* yielded a respectable $36 million at the box office.[6]

Given the ubiquity of car chases and their perceived commercial value in the industry, one would expect to discover some form of extended analysis of this historically significant production cycle. Yet, apart from Julian Smith's and Andrew Horton's contemporaneous writings,[7] film scholars have generally overlooked the 1970s car chase film. While recent texts attempt to redress the broader scholastic neglect of the action film,[8] these works are primarily concerned with the 1990s action cinema as opposed to tracing its recent, post-classical history. Similarly, although many 1970s car chase films are clearly subsumable under the road movie heading, such films receive little attention in David Laderman's *Driving Visions* or *The Road Movie Book* and *Lost Highways*, recent collections on the road movie.[9]

In this chapter, I will identify the institutional and social factors that gave rise to the car chase film and sustained its prominence as a production cycle through the 1970s and early 1980s. As I shall argue, the 1970s car chase film has its most proximate origins in a realist aesthetic that was renovating the police thrillers at the time and in the film industry's attempt to exploit the automobile, and its cultural connotations of rebellion, as a means to tap the lucrative youth market. Finally, no discussion of the car chase would be complete without an examination of the specific techniques by which they solicit such strong emotional responses from the spectator.

Through a stylistic analysis of car chase sequences in *The Seven-Ups*, *Smokey and the Bandit*, and *The French Connection*, I shall show that the emotional power of these sequences derive as much from their narrative aspects, as from their spectacular character.

## Taking it to the streets: character placement, realism, and the technological apparatus of the non-processed car chase

> The theater is in the streets, where the people are. You can't stage
> it. You have to be there.[10]

If one were to identify the most significant formal development in the techniques of filming car chases that occurred during the late 1960s and early 1970s, then it would have to be the tendency to film actors in actual moving vehicles instead of resorting to staging such scenes in a studio using rear screen projection (see Figure 8.1). While both techniques serve the same underlying function of depicting characters in cars, a crucial difference exists in terms of their respective abilities to situate, at the purely perceptual level, the characters within the context of the chase.

An effective way to illustrate these differences would be to compare the car chase in *Bonnie and Clyde* (1967) that immediately follows the Barrow Gang's first bank robbery with the way the pursuit sequence is staged in *Bullitt* made only a year later. Despite obvious differences in tone and length, both car chases share a number of significant similarities.[11] Both sequences, for instance, evince a conventional pursuit structure in which shots of the pursued alternate with that of the pursuer. Both chases use moving camera shots, taken from a camera vehicle, to film the speeding automobiles. Moving POV shots that represent the optical view points of the occupants/vehicles are to be found in both sequences as well. But where the *Bonnie and Clyde* sequence differs pivotally from the car chase in *Bullitt* is with respect to the former's recourse to rear screen projection. Interspersed throughout the sequence are interior, frontal shots of the Barrow Gang's vehicle in which rear screen projection is used to depict the view from the rear window of one of the pursuing police cars. Not surprisingly, the flatness and decreased definition of these views contrasts sharply with the exterior, location shots of the chase. It is not just these image properties that contribute to the evident artificiality of the process shots used in the sequence. Also detracting from the authenticity of the chase are the simulation shots of the policemen inside their car that depict the vehicle's movement along the road by exaggerating its rollicking motion. The net effect of these discrepancies between studio and location work is a failure to compellingly place the characters in the context of the action.

The pursuit sequence in *Bullitt*, on the other hand, has been explicitly designed to showcase its ability to situate characters in their respective vehicles without relying upon rear screen projection. For one thing, a high proportion of the shots depicting the car chase are taken from the interior perspectives of the vehicles. In addition, these interior views are not restricted to a limited number of camera

*Figure 8.1* Stage mounted action: rear screen projection in *Bonnie and Clyde* (1967)

positions, but are taken from a range of different camera setups, once again reinforcing the placement of characters in the midst of the action (see Figures 8.2, 8.3, and 8.4). Further enhancing the credibility of the chase are the shots that enable the spectator to identify characters/actors on the basis of facial recognition. Such shots tend to discourage spectatorial speculation of whether stunt doubles were used during the filming of dangerous scenes. For example, the recognition of characters in certain long shots in the *Bonnie and Clyde* chase is restricted to the identification of members of the Barrow Gang on the basis of their costume, suggesting the probable use of stunt doubles. In contrast, many shots in the car chase in *Bullitt* actively seek to facilitate character identification through facial recognition. The fact that Steve McQueen did his own stunt driving in several scenes is highlighted in a number of interior shots in which his face is rendered partially visible through the angling of the vehicle's rearview mirror (see Figure 8.5).[12] Facial recognition is even more effectively deployed towards the end of the chase. When Frank Bullitt attempts to force the assailants' Charger off the road, a series of shot/reverse shots depicts the exchange such that all of the actors' faces remain clearly discernible (see Figures 8.6 and 8.7).

These contrasts would have been all the more apparent to audiences when Warner Brothers re-released *Bonnie and Clyde* and *Bullitt* together in 1968 as a double-bill.[13] Not surprisingly, such differences were also evident to the industry's trade press. In *Variety*'s appraisal of *Bullitt*, the reviewer specifically highlights the 'non-process lensing' of the pursuit, a phrasing suggesting that the use of rear screen projection in the filming of car chases was standard industry practice at the time.[14] One way to begin to explain this stylistic development is to recognize that the differences between the two techniques cannot be completely captured in terms of narrative function. Narratalogical concepts that delineate the ways by which a film's narrative depicts the spatial context in which a character is situated, such as Edward Branigan's account of focalization[15] or Murray Smith's more precise notion of spatio-temporal attachment,[16] while useful in other applications cannot be used in this instance as a means to differentiate the two techniques; after all, both methods share the same underlying purpose of depicting characters in moving vehicles. What is at stake then is not narrative function but the very credibility of the stagings. Car chases that include process work do not successfully place characters in the context of the pursuit for the simple reason that the spectator can easily detect the presence of such studio-bound shots. Conversely, car chases that film actors in actual moving vehicles, or employ special effects that yield such an impression, are credible with respect to the spectator's standards of perceptual realism.[17] I shall label this ability to credibly situate characters in dangerous narrative contexts, be it car chases or other perilous scenarios, as *character placement*.

On initial reflection, the desire for a more realistic means of rendering character placement when filming car chases seems to provide sufficient reasons as to the abandonment of process shots. But like most stylistic shifts, such a limited answer cannot tell the whole story. As David Bordwell and Janet Staiger have argued, accounts of stylistic change must also provide explanations concerning the timing of such developments.[18] For one thing, the development of camera rigs for interior car shots predates the late 1960s, a point clearly illustrated by the famous sequence-shot of the Hampton robbery in *Gun Crazy* (1950). For another, any perceived benefits of enhanced character placement would have been offset then by increased production costs, the technical difficulties associated with filming sync dialogue shots in a moving vehicle, and by the inevitable risks that actors and technicians faced when staging such scenes. To explain this change one must therefore proceed beyond local stylistic considerations to address how realism, as a particular aesthetic discourse, was revamping the police genre in the late 1960s and early 1970s.

The significance of this realist aesthetic can be demonstrated by noting its impact upon the production of *Bullitt*. According to its director Peter Yates, the primary reason that the film was shot on location was to differentiate itself from the studio 'look' of television programming and previous detective films, a goal corroborated by McQueen's demand to shoot *Bullitt* 'in the streets'.[19] Equally indicative of this realist impulse was McQueen's and Don Gordon's background work with the San Francisco police as a means to heighten the authenticity of their roles.[20] But perhaps the most revealing way in which the realist aesthetic discloses itself is in a promotional short made at the time of the film's release. Entitled *'Bullitt': Steve McQueen's Commitment to Reality*, the short plugs not only the realism of the car chase but also the location work of the hospital and airport scenes, and the film's fidelity to these locations through its use of non-actors as extras.

While *Bullitt* set a precedent for subsequent 1970s police thrillers, it was *The French Connection* that truly established the realist aesthetic as a way to revitalize the genre. This renovation was achieved in a number of ways. As is well known, the film's director William Friedkin (widely recognized in the industry for his previous

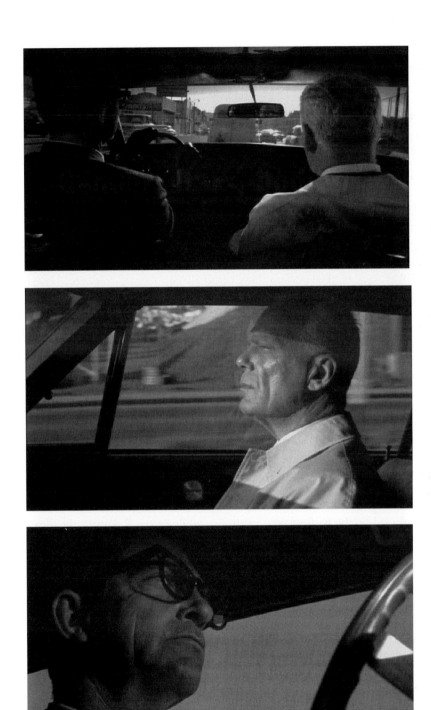

*Figure 8.2–4* Camera set up and the reinforcement of character placement in *Bullitt* (1968)

*Figure 8.5* Steve McQueen as stunt driver in *Bullitt* (1968)

documentary work) researched the story extensively by accompanying Eddie Egan and Sonny Grosso, the two policemen who made the original drug bust and who would be eventually portrayed in the film by Gene Hackman and Roy Scheider, on their patrols.[21] Along with Friedkin's research to ensure the credibility of the story material was his selection of Ernest Tidyman to write the script due to Tidyman's ability to craft street-wise dialogue, a skill derived from his previous experience as a crime reporter for the *New York Times*.[22] Yet where *The French Connection* ultimately surpasses *Bullitt* in terms of its realist aspirations is with respect to its choice of locations and cinematography. In the desire to portray the underbelly of New York, locations were selected on the basis of their grittiness, while Owen Roizman, the film's cinematographer, emphasized this look by purposely underexposing the film to make the image grayer when it was forced-developed in the lab.[23] The formula 'grittiness equals realism' established by *The French Connection* became one of the defining features of the 1970s police thriller, with films such as *Dirty Harry* (1971), *The New Centurions* (1972), *Busting* (1973), and *McQ* exploring different varieties of moral degeneracy in the city.

   Given this context of generic revitalization through the application of realist techniques, it is understandable that filmmakers judged the use of process shots as antithetical to such a sensibility. In *American Cinematographer*, Ralph Woolsey, the director of photography for *The New Centurions*, directly expresses this view within a wider discussion of the film's realist style: 'It has become standard, for daytime running shots, to make them in the actual moving vehicles, because nobody wants to shoot process anymore.'[24] The increased demands for realism in the staging of car chases did not end, however, with the abandonment of process work; also considered stylistically inappropriate were flagrant instances of increasing the

*Figure 8.6–7* Facial recognition and character placement in *Bullitt* (1968)

appearance of a vehicle's speed through undercranking. When preparing for the car chase in *Bullitt*, McQueen informed the film's stunt coordinator, Carey Loftin, that he wanted to ensure the authenticity of the chase by capturing it at normal camera speed.[25] In addition to filming car chases at actual speed, filmmakers also sought to depict authentic city traffic as the backdrop for such pursuits. To obtain POV shots for the car chase in *The French Connection*, a camera was mounted on the front bumper of the car as Bill Hickman, the film's stunt coordinator, sped through uncontrolled city traffic as a means to obtain realistic footage.[26] With the augmented sense of excitement derived through character placement, the heightened standards of realism introduced by these practices, and the resultant increase in audience discernment toward the staging of car chases, filmmakers, in all likelihood, would have found it extremely difficult to return to rear screen projection.

This shift from processed work to filming car chases in moving vehicles resulted in a veritable reconfiguration of a sector of the film industry's technological apparatus. To film extended car chases, camera cars had to be outfitted to specifically capture the requisite moving camera shots. While most camera cars did not have to meet the rigorous, technical demands of the Ford GT-40 used to film the high speed races in *Grand Prix* (1966), special vehicles were nonetheless constructed and re-employed on different shoots; the camera car built for the car chase in *Bullitt* was reused for the chase sequences in *The Sugarland Express*.[27] Camera cars were not the only vehicles that had to be redesigned; often automobiles had to be reconstructed to perform spectacular stunts since stock vehicles were incapable of withstanding such punishment. Both the Mustang and the Charger in *Bullitt* had extra suspension installed for the hill jumping scenes, as did the white Challenger in *Vanishing Point* for it to perform its leap over a creek.[28] But in terms of character placement, the most significant technological development was the car-rig tow. By having a car towed by a camera vehicle, actors were no longer required to undertake dangerous driving, as had McQueen and Hackman, and were free to focus exclusively upon acting and dialogue delivery. Car-rig tows facilitated character placement in that any actor could be made to appear an expert driver capable of adeptly maneuvering a vehicle during a high speed chase.

Technological changes were not limited to the redesign of vehicles; new camera equipment had to be developed as well. One such development was the 'dynalens', an anti-vibration lens invented to produce fluid moving camera shots taken from vehicles, an accessory that was used to film the chase sequence in *The New Centurions* when the cars were required to speed through uneven back streets.[29] Yet the main technical problem connected with filming car chases remained the difficulties associated with shooting synch dialogue shots within a moving vehicle. This problem was eventually surmounted with the arrival of the Panaflex camera in 1973 that was sufficiently small and silent enough to film synch dialogue scenes in close quarters. It was first used in *The Sugarland Express* where it performed a remarkable 360° pan within the hijacked police car, augmenting the sense of character placement of the actors inside the vehicle.[30] With the return of lengthy dialogue scenes in vehicles, car chases could now be explored for their dramatic possibilities as opposed to strictly functioning as virtually dialogueless, action spectacles.

All these technological advances necessitated a redefinition of institutional roles. Of course, stunt coordinators had existed prior to the 1970s car chase film, but their role had been largely restricted to staging battle sequences and horse stunts in historical epics and westerns.[31] However, as the action spectacles of previous years began to be eclipsed by contemporary automotive stunt work, stunt coordinators' technical expertise became increasingly focused upon the ability to stage complicated car chases. Carey Loftin had been performing motorcycle and car stunts since the 1930s, but it was only in the 1960s and 1970s that his career as a stunt coordinator began to truly take off. Following his supervision of stunt work in *It's a Mad, Mad, Mad, Mad World* (1963), he would act as stunt coordinator of the car chases in *Bullitt*, *Vanishing Point*, *Duel* (1971), and *Fear is the Key* (1972). As the production of car chase films became primarily a matter of managing elaborate stunt sequences, stunt coordinators were called upon to make the move into film direction. Hal Needham's career development is illustrative. Initially performing horse and fight stunts in film and television westerns, Needham shifted his skills to second unit direction and stunt coordination for *White Lightning*, before directing the first two Smokey and the Bandit installments and the Cannonball Run films. Needham's shift from stuntman to director of comedic, automotive mayhem nicely parallels the industry's own commitment to produce car chase spectacles as one of its primary forms of entertainment.

## The cinema of distractions: youth culture, the automobile, and the drive-in aesthetic

> Rise up. Break away from the everyday. Rebellious Dodge Coronet 500 will show you how.[32]

While it is important to recognize the ways in which realist considerations revitalized car chases within the police and crime thriller, such aesthetic factors alone cannot wholly explain the sheer pervasiveness of this form of action spectacle. To understand the prevalence of car chases in this decade, one must situate them within the broader production practices through which Hollywood attempted to cater to the youth market. That Hollywood would follow other industries in exploiting this market can be made apparent once one acknowledges the economic significance of this age group. As has been well documented, discretionary spending by teenagers and young adults comprised a significant proportion of the consumer-based economy. It has been estimated that this age group spent $10 billion a year in the late 1950s, a figure that increased to $13 billion by the mid 1960s, and continued to expand during the 1970s.[33] Just as significant as the size of the youth market were the advertising strategies employed to entice teenagers and young adults to purchase consumer goods and services. As the social historian Thomas Frank observes, one of chief advertisement techniques employed in the 1960s and early 1970s was to invoke the vernacular and symbolism of the counterculture as a means to address the youth market.[34] One common theme continually reiterated in magazine and television adverts was that of rebellion, usually configured by opposing a nonconformist rebel against some figure of the establishment.[35] In a 1969 television commercial for the Dodge Challenger cited by Frank, a southern police officer is pitted against a young hipster, tellingly presaging the dominant dramatic conflict of the pursuit film.[36] It should be underscored that such appeals to the image of the rebel were not aimed simply at the youth demographic. As Frank convincingly demonstrates, being 'young in spirit' and rebellious was an attitude available to all, so long as one embraced the counterculture's rejection of social conformity, and more importantly, adopted the acquisitiveness that characterized youth culture at the time.[37]

It is in this wider social context that Hollywood's targeting of the youth audience is to be understood. In attempting to exploit the youth market in its most inclusive form, the youth-oriented film of the 1970s came to adopt the mode of address of those advertisements that had made accessible the themes and symbols of the counterculture to an older generation. Given the aims of such production practices, references to automotive culture in youth-oriented films were eminently sensible. Since the Second World War, there has been a strong connection between youth culture and the automobile. The illegal street racing of hot rods was, and continues to be, primarily a white male youth practice that began to attract media attention in the 1940s.[38] Such activities contrasted with the legally sanctioned drag meets conducted by professional hot rod associations whose members were older and who sought to project an image of social responsibility onto the activity.[39] Despite such legitimizing efforts, hot rodding remained coupled, in the popular imagination at least, with the mystique of the outlaw. In true exploitation style, the 1950s hot rod film would select the more sensationalist aspects of hot rodding, focusing on its illegal dimensions that were dramatically played out in a narrative derived from the juvenile delinquent film. As Doherty notes, films such as *Hot Rod Girl* (1956), *Teen Age Thunder* (1957), and *Dragstrip Riot* (1958) depicted adults in conflict with adolescents who used drag racing as a means to express their rebellion against parent culture.[40]

By the mid 1960s the cultural status of the automobile underwent modification as advertising firms employed the vernacular of the counterculture to extend the parameters of the youth market. The image of the outlaw rebel in a speeding automobile did not just symbolize a (white male) teenager's revolt against parental constraints but came to express a wider resistance towards social regimentation of any kind. In a 1968 advertising campaign for Oldsmobiles, the cars were rechristened 'Youngmobiles'.[41] Automobile manufactures also began to produce in the 1960s and 1970s 'muscle cars' – such as the Mustang, Charger, and Challenger – that were designed to compete with the hot rods built by auto enthusiasts. Such muscle cars projected a youthful, rebellious image onto their owners, irrespective of their age, by having virtually the same high performance specifications as their hot rod counterparts. Given such cultural connotations, it is not surprising that the muscle car became the preferred vehicle of the 1970s car chase film.[42]

Yet if one is searching for the most substantial connection between youth culture, the automobile, and the 1970s car chase film, then that connection is to be found in the drive-in. To say this is to not simply state the obvious fact that at drive-ins spectators viewed films from the comfort of their cars but to point toward a more significant relation; namely, that the form and content of certain films screened at drive-ins was shaped by the exhibition circumstances of the theaters and the interests of the youth audience that attended them. While teenagers were certainly not the only people attending drive-ins, they composed a lucrative segment of that audience, especially when one considers their repeat viewing habits.[43] Further, the very existence of exploitation specialists such as American International Pictures (AIP) and Allied Artists depended upon their ability to attune themselves to the shifting tastes of the teen market, an aptitude reinforced by the fact that such production houses were the principal suppliers of product to drive-in exhibitors during the 1950s and 1960s.[44] That 1970s car chase films, such as *Vanishing Point*, *Dirty Mary, Crazy Larry*, and *Gone in 60 Seconds* have been heralded as drive-in classics can be taken as a measure of the continued popularity of depictions of automobile culture amongst the decade's youth audience.[45]

Yet it was not just the interests of the drive-in youth audience that determined the shape of the 1970s car chase film; the circumstances of drive-in reception also impacted upon the form of these films, constituting what I describe as its drive-in aesthetic. Mary Cohen contends that previous studies of drive-in theatres have neglected their unique circumstances of reception, a social context that was similar, in many respects, to the turn of the century fairground attraction from which the cinema began.[46] At many drive-ins a film had to compete with a host of other activities such as fireworks, dare-devil stunts, beauty contests, and last but not least, the possibility of interaction with other patrons.[47] Aware of these distractions, it is likely that the producers of exploitation films tried to create a type of film that could hold its own in a competitive environment. The formula that they came up with was a film that interspersed its narrative with spectacles, such that a spectator could enter into the fictional world when the spectacular moments were imminent. Such a description not only fits the main variants of the teenpic – rock 'n' roll films showcased musical numbers, sci-fi and horror films emphasized the scenes in which the monsters and aliens appeared, etc. – but is also consonant with the ways by which later exploitation fare traded upon their spectacles of sex and violence. Seen from this perspective, the alteration between dramatic moments and automotive mayhem that characterize the 1970s car chase film derives from the drive-in aesthetic that inflected the majority of exploitation films.

As the 1970s car chase cycle developed, its mode of narrative address to the youth audience shifted from the suspense thriller of the police/crime film to the comedies that typified the pursuit and race films of the late 1970s and early 80s. Along with this change in tone went a modification in the countercultural stance of the cycle. Many early car chase films aligned themselves to the counterculture, while later instances, on the whole, refrained from engaging in social critique. In *Bullitt*, Steve McQueen's depiction of a hip policeman possessing integrity is played against the Walter Chalmers character, portrayed by Robert Vaughn, an untrustworthy and self-serving representative of the establishment. Early 1970s pursuit films provide even clearer examples. Kowalski, the protagonist of *Vanishing Point*, incarnates the counterculture's version of the outlaw. Through flashbacks, the spectator is informed of his failed attempts at happiness as a race driver, a police officer, and as a lover. Unable to find fulfillment in mainstream society, Kowalski, on a bet, resolves to deliver a White Challenger from Denver, Colorado to San Francisco within two days, a pointless resolution that initiates the police pursuit and brings about his eventual death. Towards the end of the cycle, this countercultural impetus was dissipated in the race films that manifest mere resentment toward energy conservation measures. Michael Bannon, the organizer of the coast to coast race in *The Gumball Rally*, opens the competition by declaring that participants will have the pleasure of racing 'flat out against the red line, with no catalytic converter, and no 55 mile an hour speed limit!'. The same theme is reiterated in the gags in the opening credit sequences of the Cannonball Run films. In the first installment, a Lamborghini stops at a 55 mile per hour speed limit sign to have one of its occupants cross it out with spray paint; the sequel repeats the gag, replacing the numbers '55' with '155'. At the close of the decade, defiance toward highway statutes was seen as a more viable and non-politicized means of representing vehicular lawlessness, a gesture stripped of any true countercultural significance.

## Narrativizing the spectacle: suspense, stunts, and the POV shot

> The secret is to have a story that is so based in reality that when you reach the chase, you get caught up in them emotionally and accept them as reality.[48]

Analyzing the relations between the youth market and automobile culture is necessary when constructing explanations of the general popularity of the car chase cycle during the 1970s. However, when one wishes to investigate how a specific car chase in a given film attempts to engage spectators, one must inevitably narrow analytical focus to the mechanics of film style. In writings on the action cinema, the main explanatory concept advanced has been the notion of spectacle, usually understood in relation to Tom Gunning's influential discussion of the cinema of attractions. According to Gunning, the first decade of the cinema was characterized by a form of filmmaking that prioritized the presentation of visual spectacles over the construction of a compelling narrative world.[49] While Gunning admits that the cinema of attractions was eventually superseded by the feature length narrative film, he maintains that such attractions have persisted over the course of film history and remain an indelible element of the contemporary cinema.[50] Gunning's notion of spectacle as non-narrative attraction has been taken up by Richard Maltby in his analysis of the spectacle of movement manifested in Hollywood action films.[51] Maltby claims that the spectacle of movement afforded by the moving camera shots in *Bullitt* are designed to directly address the spectator and that the sequence 'emphasizes the general impression of speed for its own sake, rather than developing the narrational possibilities of the scene'.[52] Here I want to question this tendency to treat car chases, and action spectacles more generally, as if they were the logical antithesis of narrative. While research on spectacle has profitably extended our understanding of the Hollywood film by identifying other aesthetic impulses at work in the cinema, notably with respect to the study of comedy and the musical,[53] there has been a propensity, nonetheless, to overstate the non-narrative case by overlooking the inherent narrative dimensions of action spectacles.[54]

A profitable way to advance this debate is to sharpen the distinction between narrative and spectacle by noting how these two concepts have been conceptually distinguished in recent cognitive writings on the emotions and the cinema. Dirk Eitzen[55] and Greg Smith[56] maintain that emotional responses that have characters as their principal foci are to be differentiated from those that react to non-narrative elements such as gags, spectacles, and the visceral dimensions of horror. These non-narrative elements, they argue, make a direct appeal to the spectator's emotional response to the events depicted on screen, responses that are not necessarily filtered through the reactions that characters exhibit towards such narrative occurrences. The distinction is useful in that it follows the theoretical precedent set by Gunning of defining the spectacle in terms of the notion of direct spectatorial address, enriching the concept by connecting it with the issue of the generation of spectatorial emotions. More important, one can use the distinction to identify the character and non-character centered aspects of car chases to provide a finer grained account as to the manners by which narrative and spectacle intermesh in action sequences.

One way one can begin to discuss car chases in relation to the notion of narrative is to situate these sequences within the broader narrative structures in which they appear. The car chase in *Bullitt*, for instance, does not suspend narrative development as Maltby suggests, but constitutes an instance of plot advancement that introduces, in turn, specific narrative ramifications. Frank Bullitt's chase of the assailants brings an end to their monitoring of his investigations while their deaths exacerbate Bullitt's strained relations with his superiors. And as the opening quote from the film's producer, Philip D'Antoni, suggests, the emotional effectiveness of the car chase depends upon its anchorage in a wider, compelling narrative. Yet it is not only in this manner that one can demonstrate the narrative significance of pursuit sequences; the case can be taken one step further by speaking of the inherent narrative dimension of the pursuit structure itself and its ability to generate the emotional experience of suspense. Most pursuit sequences in police/crime thrillers manifest those characteristics that Noël Carroll has claimed are central to the production of suspense.[57] Carroll claims that for suspense to be produced in a film, a spectator must care for a character who is involved in a certain course of action. This course of action, in addition, must have two logically opposed outcomes in which the morally correct outcome is perceived less likely to eventuate.[58] Suspense then refers to this narrational process by which a film sets up expectations and tacit speculations as to future narrative outcomes concerning the actions of characters who solicit spectatorial allegiance.[59] While Carroll's account can be productively applied to the pursuit sequences of numerous police/crime thrillers, an analysis of the car chase in *The Seven-Ups* can illustrate the specific means by which the generation of suspense is linked to narration.

The narrative context out of which the pursuit sequence in *The Seven-Ups* arises has the characters Moon and Bo shoot an undercover police officer concealed in the trunk of a car. The shots attract Buddy, a fellow policeman portrayed by Roy Scheider, to the scene of the crime, who then takes pursuit after the assailants. From the start, the narration introduces a tacit question in the spectator's mind as to the final narrative outcome of the chase: will Buddy be capable of overtaking Moon and Bo? The assailants' head start constitutes the first impediment to Buddy's attempt to capture Moon and Bo, an indication that the morally correct outcome is already in doubt at this stage. The first phase of the chase depicts how both pursued and pursuer negotiate city traffic. Crucially, the manner by which these stunt scenes are narratively constructed at the local level follows the question and answer model of suspense proposed by Carroll. Each time Bo, the driver of the assailants' vehicle, performs a risky driving maneuver – speeding down a one way street against traffic, negotiating a difficult corner, etc. – the narrative sets up spectatorial curiosity as to how Buddy will be able to execute the same action. In addition, certain stunt scenes instill interest by presenting shots of obstacles before the speeding vehicles are in their vicinity. For instance, when another police car enters into the pursuit, Buddy instructs them through the radio to have the bridge ahead closed off. Shortly after this, a shot of the police blockade is presented. Through dialogue and image, the spectator is made aware of a forthcoming narrative situation – namely, the assailants' impeding collision with the police blockade – a narrational strategy that generates anticipation as to how the event is to be actually played out.

So far, the pursuit sequence in *The Seven-Ups* conforms to the well-worn conventions of the car chase. Where the filmmakers endeavored to introduce novelty is by heightening the suspense of the stunt scenes presented at the end of the chase. After managing to bust through the blockade, the assailants leave the city and enter into an open freeway, with Buddy still in pursuit. In an attempt to finally shake Buddy off their tail, Bo conceals their vehicle from Buddy's view by positioning the car directly in front of a moving bus (see Figure 8.8). Moon then loads his sawed off shotgun, preparing to blast Buddy as he passes in the next lane. The narrational perspective

*Figure 8.8* Narration and suspense: concealment of vehicle in *The Seven-Ups* (1973)

shifts to the optical vantage point of Buddy in an over-the-shoulder shot that presents his tentative approach of the bus (see Figure 8.9). This alternation of narrational per-spective creates suspense by providing, once again, information to the spectator that provokes the formulation of expectations as to the way in which events will proceed. Warned by the bus driver's honking of the imminent gun-blast, Buddy is able to break in time such that the spray of bullets onto his vehicle only temporarily detains him. Emboldened by the gunfire, Buddy tries to force their vehicle off the road. As the two vehicles ricochet violently off each other, they approach a bend in a freeway in which a parked truck is situated, obstructing Buddy's path. The spectator is presented with a quick glimpse of Buddy as he dives under the dashboard, just moments before his vehicle impacts into the back of the truck. The initial narrative question pertaining to Buddy's overtaking of the assailants is finally answered in the negative with the demo-lition of his vehicle. Yet the chase poses one last question as to Buddy's condition: has he survived the impact? As the truck driver picks through the wreckage, Buddy is eventually assisted out of the vehicle, appearing, for the most part, unscathed.

Two points need to be raised with respect to the character and non-character centered emotions generated by this sequence. First, by applying Carroll's account of suspense to the analysis of this car chase, the relations between the film's narra-tion and character are made apparent. It is through the spectator's allegiance with

*Figure 8.9* Narration and suspense: narrational perspective in *The Seven-Ups* (1973)

Buddy that the narration of the more local plot developments of the chase acquire significance. Each difficulty Buddy encounters when performing a risky driving maneuver is inflected by the larger narrative question underlying the chase. Second, these narrative aspects of the pursuit should not obscure the elements of spectacle that are also present. The assailants' crash through the police blockade, the gun-blast onto Buddy's vehicle, and the final collision are all moments of spectacle whose emotional force derives equally from non-character centered stimuli.

At a more general theoretical level, then, one can distinguish the stunt as an instance of local spectacle from narration as the process in which different stunts are interlinked into a broader narrative chain. That stunts form the building blocks of car chases is demonstrated in Friedkin's account of the production history of the pursuit sequence in *The French Connection*, in which he claims that during the planning stage of the sequence, five stunts were envisioned to form the principal events of the chase.[60] Significantly, all of the stunts he describes involve placing some form of obstacle in the way of Jimmy Doyle's vehicle. Indeed, one could maintain that the main type of stunt in car chase films consists of a vehicle either avoiding, crashing or leaping over some obstacle placed in its path. While the car chases in the police/crime thriller often have their stunts integrated narratively into an overall architecture of suspense, the chase sequences in pursuit films, particularly of the comedic variant, tend to possess weaker narrative linkages. As such, car chases in pursuit films are more episodic in nature with the stunts functioning in a greater capacity as spectacle. For instance, at one point in the chase in *Smokey and the Bandit*, Carrie is at the wheel of the Trans Am with Sheriff Buford T. Justice and his jilted son in 'hot pursuit' of her and the Bandit. As she and the Bandit attempt to trade places, a tractor trailer appears ahead of them, blocking the entire highway. At the last moment, the Trans Am veers safely off the road while Buford T. Justice's car slides underneath the carriage of the trailer, sheering off the top of the vehicle. The spectacular dimension of the stunt is emphasized by having the action captured in a slow motion insert that accentuates the formal properties of the collision (see Figure 8.10).[61] Still, the stunt is not completely abstracted from the flow of the narrative. Like the narration of the stunt scenes in the pursuit sequence in *The Seven-Ups*, a shot of the tractor trailer is presented to the spectator before the vehicles are in its immediate vicinity. Spectators are therefore cued to formulate rough expectations as to how Carrie and the Bandit will successfully negotiate the obstacle while anticipating that Buford T. Justice will not, given the history of his past ineptitude.

Despite the spectacular function that stunts perform, they are not the only type of spectacle in car chases. Just as significant are the moving POV shots that represent the optical perspective of the occupant/vehicle. David Bordwell has claimed that one of the functions of camera movement is the presentation of a visual field such that it yields a strong impression of subjective movement on the part of the spectator.[62] Moving POV shots in car chases are clear instances of the production of this effect, especially when the camera is mounted on the front bumper of a speeding vehicle. More important, given the strong phenomenological effect that

*Figure 8.10* The slow motion insert and the spectacularization of the stunt in *Smokey and the Bandit* (1977)

such shots produce, they can be readily understood in terms of the notion of direct spectatorial address that characterize spectacles. Nonetheless, it is necessary to recognize that the function of moving POV shots can also operate in character centered ways to present the spatial context in which a particular character is situated. The character and non-character centered functions of moving POV shots, then, can either operate in tandem or in opposition.

The moving camera shots taken from the front bumper of Jimmy Doyle's vehicle in the pursuit sequence of *The French Connection* can illustrate these points. On the one hand, these front bumper shots are designed to induce in the viewer a sensation of movement through narrative space. To maximize the sensation of speed, the camera was placed nearer to the ground, rather than maintaining the camera positions of the over-the-shoulder and POV shots taken from the interior of the vehicle. On the other hand, these front bumper views are edited in typical shot/reverse shot style that is routinely used to represent the optical perspective of a character. Bumper views are followed by shots of Jimmy Doyle's facial expressions as he reacts to the oncoming traffic (see Figure 8.11). Despite the fact that these front bumper shots are not, strictly speaking, the perceptual equivalent of the optical field of the driver, the editing structure prompts the spectator to interpret them in character centered ways.

These tensions suggest that the moving POV shots appearing in car chase films should be situated conceptually along a continuum that has character centered functions at one end of the spectrum with non-character centered functions placed at the other. Any given moving POV shot in a car chase will usually employ both functions. For instance, the opening POV shot used for the credit sequence in *Duel*

*Figure 8.11* Facial expression and the character centered functions of POV shots in *The French Connection* (1971)

presents the optical vantage point of a car as it pulls out of a drive way and travels along city and country thoroughfares. The character centered function of the shot is suppressed until the credit sequence is over, at which point the spectator is finally presented with an interior shot of the driver of the vehicle. In contrast, the opening POV shot in *Eat My Dust* (clearly inspired by the credit sequence of *Duel*) is anomalous since its character centered function is barely operative. The spectator is presented with an undercranked, bumper mounted, POV spectacle of a winding country road; the only clue as to the identity of the driver of the vehicle is provided in a brief insert shot of a hand shifting gears. As a prefiguration of the joy ride that structures most of the narrative of *Eat My Dust*, this POV sequence uses the spectacle of movement as a means to promote the teenage, entertainment value of the film.

One could speculate on the various factors that contributed to exhaustion of the car chase cycle in the early 1980s. No doubt the endless recycling of car chases in film and television programs of every variety hastened its demise. One could also point to the arrival of a new type of action hero, exemplified by the popularity of Arnold Schwarzenegger and Sylvester Stallone, in which fighting ability replaced driving skills as the preferred mode of representing masculinity. Yet if one is correct to chart the cycle's development from the suspense thriller to the comedy of the race films, then another factor may have also entered into the equation. The car chases in the comedy pursuit and race films have no place for suspense. By eliminating one of the primary enjoyments of the pursuit sequence, later instances of car chases lacked the capacity to fully engage audiences with respect to narration and character. Unremitting spectacle, then, is not an inherent feature of the car chase but a symptom of a lack of narrative imagination.

## Notes

1  A brief explanation is in order on the expression '1970s car chase film' as used in this chapter. While a more accurate periodization of this production cycle would run from 1968 to 1983, I shall refer to it as the 1970s car chase film since it is the films of this decade that have been routinely associated with car chases, unlike the films of the 1960s and 1980s.

2  *Variety* Review of *Cannonball*, July 21, 1976 in *Variety's Film Reviews, 1975–1977, Vol. 14*, New York: R. R. Bowker, 1983.

3  E. Bowser *The Transformation of the Cinema, 1907–1915*, Berkeley: University of California Press, 1990, pp. 56–7, 60; C. Musser *The Emergence of the Cinema: The American Screen to 1907*, Berkeley: University of California Press, 1990, pp. 377–8.

4  D. Riblet 'The Keystone Film Company and the Historiography of Early Slapstick' in K. Karnick and H. Jenkins (eds) *Classical Hollywood Comedy*, London: Routledge, 1995, p. 180.

5  *Variety*, December 26, 1973 in *Variety's Film Reviews, 1971–1974, Vol. 13*, New York: R. R. Bowker, 1983.

6  J. Finler *The Hollywood Story*, New York: Crown Publishers, 1988, pp. 277–8. All figures refer to domestic rental income.

7  J. Smith 'What Mad Pursuit: Car Culture in Film', *American Film*, 1: 2, 1976, pp. 30–2, 49–53; 'The Secret of the Deserted Meadow: Car Culture in The Movies', *American Film*, 2: 1, 1976, pp. 50–5; 'Smash! Bang! Crash!', *American Film*, 2: 2, 1976, pp. 24–30; 'What's In It For Us?: Car Culture Invades the Cities', *American Film*, 2: 4, 1977, pp. 28–32, 49–51; A. Horton 'Hot Car Films and Cool Individualism', *Cinéaste*, 8: 4, 1978, pp. 12–15.

8  J. Arroyo (ed.) *Action/Spectacle Cinema: A Sight and Sound Reader*, London: BFI, 2000; G. King *Spectacular Narratives: Hollywood in the Age of the Blockbuster*, London: I. B. Tauris, 2000.

9  D. Laderman *Driving Visions: Exploring the Road Movie*, Austin: University of Texas Press, 2002; S. Cohan and I. Hark (eds) *The Road Movie Book*, London: Routledge, 1997; J. Sargeant and S. Watson (eds) *Lost Highways: An Illustrated History of Road Movies*, London: Creation Books, 1999.

10  Steve McQueen, cited in M. Terrill *Steve McQueen: Portrait of an American Rebel*, London: Plexus, 1993, p. 164.

11  For purposes of this analysis, I also set aside the fact that the pursuit sequence in *Bonnie and Clyde* is intercut with flashforward shots of a witness and a policeman before the press, reporting their encounters with the Barrow Gang.

12  It is worth noting that when McQueen's stunt double, Bud Ekins, was used to execute the more difficult and hazardous stunts, the rearview mirror is turned away in these shots. For an informative discussion of the technical details of the car chase in *Bullitt* see M. Nagda 'After 30 Years, The Real Truth Behind the "Bullitt" Chase', *Motor Trend*, December 1998.

13  Terrill *Steve McQueen*, p. 171.

14  *Variety*, October 16, 1968 in *Variety's Film Reviews, 1968–1970, Vol. 12*, New York: R. R. Bowker, 1983.

15  E. Branigan *Narrative Comprehension and Film*, London: Routledge, 1992, pp. 100–7.

16  M. Smith *Engaging Characters: Fiction, Emotion, and the Cinema*, Oxford: Clarendon Press, 1995, pp. 83, 146–8.

17  While it is not my intention to provide a full-blown account of perceptual realism here, I shall direct the reader to Gregory Currie's (*Image and Mind: Film, Philosophy and Cognitive Science*, Cambridge: Cambridge University Press, 1995, pp. 79–112) and Stephen Prince's ('True Lies: Perceptual Realism', *Film Quarterly*, 49: 3, Spring 1996, pp. 27–37) sophisticated defenses of the concept. According to Currie, perceptual realism refers to the ways in which 'the experience of film watching is similar to the ordinary perceptual experience of the world' ('Film Reality, and Illusion', in D. Bordwell and N. Carroll (eds) *Post-Theory: Reconstructing Film Studies*, Madison: University of Wisconsin Press, 1996, p. 329). On this account, process shots do not wholly match perceptual experience due to their inability to provide compelling depth cues and realistic depictions of vehicle movement.

18   D. Bordwell, J. Staiger and K. Thompson *The Classical Hollywood Cinema: Film Style and Mode of Production to 1960*, London: Routledge, 1985, pp. 248–9.

19   Terrill *Steve McQueen*, p. 164.

20   Ibid., pp. 160–2.

21   Significantly, Egan and Grosso also acted as the film's technical consultants and were even cast in the secondary roles of Simonson and Klien.

22   W. Friedkin 'Anatomy of a Chase', in R. Koszarski (ed.) *Hollywood Directors: 1941–1976*, New York: Oxford University Press, 1977, p. 394.

23   'Photographing "The French Connection"', *American Cinematographer*, 53: 2, 1972, pp. 158–61, 184–5, 211, 213–19: p. 161.

24   R. Woolsey 'The Photography of "The New Centurions"', *American Cinematographer*, 53: 9, 1972, pp. 1028–31, 1031–69: p. 1029.

25   S. Encinas 'The Greatest Chase of All', *Muscle Car Review*, March 1987. In his article on the production history of the film, Mike Nagda maintains that undercranking was still used in a few shots, most notably in the scene in which McQueen overshoots a corner in his Mustang (1987). Close inspection of this specific moment of the chase would appear to confirm Nagda's claim, especially when one attends to the over-rapidity of McQueen's arm movements. Such an example illustrates the broader reluctance within Hollywood of completely abandoning undercranking when filming car chases.

26   Friedkin 'Anatomy of a Chase', p. 402.

27   J. Stephens 'Photographing the Races for "Grand Prix"', *American Cinematographer*, 48: 1, 1967, pp. 30–3, 42–3, 56–7, 60–1: pp. 32–3, 42; Encinas 'The Greatest Chase of All'; H. Lightman 'The New Panaflex Camera Makes its Production Debut', *American Cinematographer*, 54: 5, 1973, pp. 564–7, 598–9, 611–20: p. 598.

28   J. Baxter *Stunt: The Story of the Great Movie Stuntmen*, London: McDonald, 1973, pp. 258–9; P. Zazarine 'Behind the Scenes of the Movie "Vanishing Point"', *Muscle Car Review*, March 1986.

29   'The Dynalens', *American Cinematographer*, 50: 5, 1969, pp. 476–8, 498; Woolsey 'The Photography of "The New Centurions"', p. 1067.

30   B. Salt *Film Style and Technology: History and Analysis*, 2nd edition, London: Starword, 1992, p. 276; Lightman The New Panaflex Camera', pp. 617–18.

31   Baxter *Stunt*, p. 16.

32   1965 Dodge Advert reproduced in T. Frank *The Conquest of Cool: Business Culture, Counterculture, and the Rise of Hip Consumerism*, Chicago: Chicago University Press, 1997.

33   T. Doherty *Teenagers and Teenpics: The Juvenilization of American Movies in the 1950s*, Boston: Unwin Hyman, 1988, p. 52.

34   Frank *Conquest of Cool*, pp. 26–33, 118–23.

35   Ibid., pp. 227–8.

36   Ibid., pp. 160–1.

37   Ibid., pp. 118–23.

38   S. Convoy 'Popular Technology and Youth Rebellion in America', *Journal of Popular Culture*, 16: 4, 1983, pp. 123–33: pp. 124–26; H. Moorhouse *Driving Ambitions: An Analysis of the American Hot Rod Enthusiasm*, Manchester: Manchester University Press, 1991, pp. 29–36.

39   Moorhouse *Driving Ambitions*, pp. 45–9; H. Moorhouse 'Racing for a Sign: Defining the "Hot Rod" 1945–1960', *Journal of Popular Culture*, 20: 2, 1986, pp. 83–96.

40   Doherty *Teenagers and Teenpics*, pp. 108–9.

41   Ibid., p. 158.

42   Hollywood's exploitation of the cultural connotations of the automobile did not end with the inclusion of muscle cars in high speed pursuits; other films explore different aspects of automobile culture, usually set in some form of youth context. *Two-Lane Blacktop* (1971), for instance, explores the subculture of illegal dragstrip racing; *American Graffiti* (1973) depicts the relationship between teenage courting rituals and automobiles in the early

1960s; while *Hollywood Knights* (1980) recreates the adolescent activities centering around a 1965 fast food drive-in.

43   C. Krinsky '"Passion Pits with Pix": Drive-In Movies and Ideologies of Youth in the Late 1950s', 1999 SCS conference paper; M. Cohen 'Forgotten Audiences in the Passion Pits: Drive-In Theatres and Changing Spectator Practices in Post-War America', *Film History*, 6: 4, 1994, pp. 470–86: p. 479.

44   Cohen 'Forgotten Audiences', p. 483.

45   The regional constitution of the drive-in youth audiences that were drawn to car chase films could stand for more precise specification. Denis Giles suggests that some of the most successful drive-in theatres operated in southern and midwestern states, areas known for their stock-car racing culture ('The Outdoor Economy: A Study of the Contemporary Drive-In', *Journal of the University Film and Video Association*, 35: 2, 1983, pp. 66–76: p. 69). Giles' hypothesis receives support in a comment made by Charles Griffith, the director of *Eat My Dust*, when he claims that the film was 'aimed directly at the market of country kids'(in Smith 'Smash! Bang! Crash!', p. 27). Whether such films were as popular amongst the urban youth audience is a question that warrants further investigation.

46   Cohen 'Forgotten Audiences in the Passion Pits', pp. 471–3.

47   Ibid., p. 472.

48   Philip D'Antoni cited in interview with C. Poggiali *Shock Cinema*, 17, 2000, pp. 26–7: p. 27.

49   T. Gunning 'The Cinema of Attractions: Early Film, Its Spectator and the Avant-Garde', in T. Elsaesser (ed.) *Early Cinema: Space, Frame, Narrative*, London: British Film Institute, 1990. pp. 58–9.

50   Ibid., p. 60.

51   R. Maltby *Hollywood Cinema: An Introduction*, Oxford: Blackwell, 1995, pp. 237–42.

52   Ibid., p. 239.

53   D. Crafton 'Pie and Chase: Gag, Spectacle and Narrative in Slapstick Comedy', in K. Karnick and H. Jenkins (eds) *Classical Hollywood Comedy*, London: Routledge, 1995; J. Feuer *The Hollywood Musical*, 2nd edition, London: Macmillan, 1993, pp. 35–42; H. Jenkins *What Made Pistachio Nuts?: Early Sound Comedy and the Vaudeville Aesthetic*, New York: Columbia University Press, 1992, pp. 1–25.

54   For convincing critiques of this tendency that are similar to the arguments that I raise here, see W. Buckland 'A Close Encounter with *Raiders of the Lost Ark*: Notes on Narrative Aspects of the New Hollywood Blockbuster', in S. Neale and M. Smith (eds) *Contemporary Hollywood Cinema*, London: Routledge, 1998; King *Spectacular Narratives*, pp. 1–17; and K. Thompson *Storytelling in the New Hollywood: Understanding Classical Narrative Technique*, Cambridge MA: Harvard University Press, 1999, pp. 344–52.

55   D. Eitzen 'The Emotional Basis of Film Comedy', in C. Plantinga and G. Smith (eds) *Passionate Views: Film, Cognition, and Emotion*, Baltimore: Johns Hopkins University Press, 1999, pp. 86–93.

56   G. Smith 'Local Emotions, Global Moods, and Film Structure', in Plantinga and Smith *Passionate Views*.

57   Carroll 'Toward a Theory of Film Suspense', in his *Theorizing the Moving Image*, Cambridge: Cambridge University Press, 1996, pp. 100–9.

58   Following Carroll, the notion of morality referred to is that of the moral system operating within the narrative world of a film as opposed to specific ethical precepts guiding a spectator's social behavior. Ibid., p. 105.

59   The notion of spectatorial allegiance invoked here derives from Murray Smith's discussion of the concept (Smith *Engaging Characters*, pp. 187–94). In Smith's account, allegiance refers to the processes by which the moral valence of a character solicits sympathy and emotional investment from the spectator.

60   Friedkin 'Anatomy of a Chase', pp. 398–400.

61   The utmost instance of the spectacularization of the stunt in the 1970s car chase film is the final leap in the original *Gone in 60 Seconds*. The jump, as narrative event, is presented three

times; the first two in slow motion and from different camera angles, while the last depicts the leap at normal speed. In addition, the first presentation of the jump is paused as the car is in mid-flight, then superimposed, in freeze-frame, onto the second presentation, then restarted after the second presentation ends. To cap it off, a significant discrepancy can be detected between the first and third presentations of the action. After the first presentation is restarted, the vehicle is shown performing a 360° spin, an action that does not occur in the third presentation. With the principles of spatial and temporal continuity thrown to the wind, this stunt represents the extreme end of the logic of the spectacle, a logic that few Hollywood car chase films would pursue in this unmitigated form.

62   D. Bordwell 'Camera Movement and Cinematic Space', in R. Burnett (ed.) *Explorations in Film Theory: Selected Essays from Ciné-Tracts*, Bloomington: Indiana University Press, 1991, pp. 233–4 (originally published in 1977 in *Ciné-Tracts*, 1: 2, pp. 19–26).

## Chapter 9

# MICHAEL HAMMOND

## *SAVING PRIVATE RYAN'S* 'SPECIAL AFFECT'

*S*AVING PRIVATE RYAN (1998) is probably not an action movie. It belongs in a discussion of war epics such as *The Big Parade* (1925), *Wings* (1927), *All Quiet on the Western Front* (1930), *They Were Expendable* (1945), *Paths of Glory* (1957), *The Longest Day* (1962), *Beach Red* (1967), *The Big Red One* (1980), or even *Apocalypse Now* (1979) or *Platoon* (1986). True, these films, like *Private Ryan*, contain all of the elements expected of an action movie; spectacles of violence, fast editing and/or camera movement, sweeping landscapes, heroics by the characters, dangerous foes and they were also accompanied by big soundtracks. Even the silent films such as *Wings* and *The Big Parade* had specially written scores (apparently the *Wings* premiere in London was accompanied by the sound of plane engines duplicated by running a whirring vacuum cleaner over a sheet of plywood). In comparison, action films such as *Speed* (1994), *Point Break* (1991), *Commando* (1985), *The Long Kiss Goodnight* (1996) or *True Lies* (1994) are 'simply entertainment'. While the accompanying soundtrack of action films are loud in your face Dolby Digital or THX aural spectacle, that of the epic war film, whether 'new Hollywood', 'classical Hollywood' or 'pre-classical spectacular', possesses an underlying obbligato of melancholy. This undertone exists not only in the musical score but in the tone of anguished voices and viscerally felt noises which heightens the consequence of weaponry and makes poignant fear, suffering and loss. In this regard *Saving Private Ryan* belongs firmly in the category of epic war film.

Yet consider the paradoxical nature of the film's reception. *Saving Private Ryan*'s nomination for the Peace Award by the Political Film Society sits rather strangely with its award for Best Action-Adventure-Thriller by the Academy of Science Fiction, Horror and Fantasy Films. Or the contrast between military historian John Keegan's statement in the *Daily Telegraph* that he 'felt ultimate reality several times'[1] with critic Anne Billson's assessment: 'In (Spielberg's) desire to put the audience through a virtual reality battle . . . he can't stop turning it into one of his cinematic rollercoaster rides.'[2] The oxymoron of a spectacular realism is apparent within most contemporary reviews. Writing within a British context, Billson adds that 'the technological exhilaration at the technical excellence of the filming is counterbalanced by the sobering awareness that our own fathers or grandfathers might have gone through a similar ordeal further on up the coast'. US critic Richard Goldstein writes in the *Village Voice*:

> Spielberg is our Rodgers and Hammerstein, infusing the clichés of show biz with a naturalism so unassailable that the most traditional ideas seem fresh and new. . . . If the mood of a postwar musical is bursting with optimism, Spielberg's affect is deeply melancholy. His view of tradition is one that leaves the present infinitely wanting.[3]

In a paraphrase of Frederic Jameson's 'nostalgia for the present' Goldstein attributes the power of the film to a naturalism which we must assume is made unassailable precisely by the advances in cinema technology.[4] This affect is apparent in the Norman Rockwell imagery of the home front where Mrs Ryan learns of her sons' deaths or the nostalgically rendered patriarchal hierarchy of a bureaucratic system sensitive enough, through a female clerk's attentive notice, to order the rescue of her remaining son. But it is also made visceral through the spectacular realism of the D-Day landing sequence. Goldstein does not concentrate his critique of what he terms 'World War II Chic' – represented by *Saving Private Ryan*, Tom Brokaw's best seller *The Greatest Generation*,[5] and the new craze for swing dancing in New York – on the film's opening. Implicitly he places the function of that scene as part of a formula for assuaging guilt-ridden baby boomers who 'feel the need to atone for the patricidal leanings of their youth'.[6] In this scenario Spielberg's hyperrealist reconstruction of the horror of warfare allows boomers to empathise with their now disappearing parents. Underlying this, Goldstein claims, is the boomer's 'idea that America is floundering in some radical disjunction with its heroic past'.[7]

In general, critics in the US and in Britain had a two-tiered response to the film; the astonishment and cathartic experience of the spectacle of death in the first twenty minutes set against the less than enthusiastic endorsement of the remainder. For John Keegan 'the improbabilities of the last hour remind the viewer that he [*sic*] is watching a film',[8] while Samuel Hynes writes in the *New Statesman*: 'In my view *Private Ryan* is 25 minutes of virtual D-Day followed by a conventional special unit story, a war movie made out of war movies with only high tech spectacles at the beginning and end to distinguish it.'[9] For the *Times Literary Supplement* Ben Shephard writes:

> the Omaha Beach sequence is overwhelming in its power and horror [but] . . . The whole of the lengthy second section . . . finds Spielberg struggling for coherence [and] . . . The last half-hour brings a tangible sense of relief. Back with the war as action adventure, Spielberg can forget character and concentrate on machinery . . . the scene stealer is a German flak-gun.[10]

Clearly then these critics give credence to the spectacular attraction of the realism achieved through state of the art special effects while pointing to considerable limitations in the Robert Rodat and Spielberg script. This is not without some irony given the qualities of self-reflexivity inherent in the use of 'big and loud' special effects in blockbuster action films. For many critics the limitations of the script are of the general variety in what has become a central trope in Spielberg criticism; his over dependence on sentimentalism, his unerring attraction for the positive story, and his mechanical expertise as the cinematic master of summoning tears. Shephard cites David Thompson's labelling of Spielberg as 'the film director as junior mechanic'.[11] Firmly in this mould, Amy Taubin writes of *Private Ryan*:

> Between . . . two bravura sequences is merely a banal war movie with a forced premise and clichéd characters [in which] Spielberg tries too hard to overwhelm you emotionally. And he underestimates either his own powers or the intelligence of the audience. What other excuse could there be for John Williams's bathetic score?[12]

In these critiques 'realism' is afforded by the special effects. Further, the seamlessness of spectator involvement and suspension of disbelief is effected by state of the art cinematic technology which, in action adventure films, is both the measure of the quality of the film going experience and the point at which the cinematic apparatus is foregrounded. Conversely Taubin, Shephard and Hynes all point to the conventional 'war movie narrative' as the site of their displeasure, the moment when they are reminded that it is only a movie. The 'classical narrative style' of the middle section is one normally attributed to seamless subject positioning, yet here it functions in the opposite manner thus highlighting an undercurrent in David Bordwell's description of the classical style as 'an excessively obvious cinema'.[13]

The paradox of the spectacular depiction of slaughter based on a somewhat vague consensus among critics as to what constitutes realism becomes even more complicated in relation to the term 'disturb'. The 'disturbing' images do not 'disturb' the realist project of the text but disturb the viewer, perhaps even meeting the criteria of a cinema of unpleasure. Indeed Taubin describes the opening sequence in terms which recall Laura Mulvey's clarion call for the disruption of the visual pleasure of narrative cinema:

> The Omaha Beach scene has more gore and a higher body count than any movie ever made. It runs on a castration anxiety inspired by the close-ups of all those bloody stumps and mutilated torsos and Spielberg's astonishing ability to drive an action forward through space and time. And it's all the more impressive for being both terrifyingly visceral and impersonal to the point of abstraction.[14]

In identifying the overall affect as physical, impacting on the body through images of evisceration and, although she does not explicitly mention it, the aural impact of the soundtrack in combination with the empathetic disorientation through the anonymity of the characters, Taubin tacitly endorses Spielberg's own description of the confusion of combat as abstract expressionism.[15] Even Taubin, who ends her article arguing that the film is 'meretricious' and that it 'creeped her out', testifies to the 'realism' of the opening scene. The film's physical impact and the emphasis on realism in these reviews recall another older form of cinematic affect, the visceral astonishment of the cinema of attractions, perhaps most emphatic in the stories (probably apocryphal) of the audience's terrified response to the Lumières' demonstration of the cinema with *Arrival of a Train* (1895). Tom Gunning has recently drawn attention to the technology of the cinematic apparatus as a source of horror and fear rooted in nineteenth century visual forms and technology. Gunning points to an element of the fantasy of producing animated bodies or technological simulacrum of life in which the result is the reproduction of animated corpses rather than living beings.[16] This fantasy 'stops halfway' toward fulfilment and yields nightmare. Such an affect of terror combines with the cinema's explicit associations with amusement (and the amusement industry) producing critical responses caught between the realistic, and therefore worthy, depiction of historical events and the spectacular sensations normally associated with the 'lower' genres such as action films and body horror. This in turn results in the almost unanimous assessment amongst film journalists of *Private Ryan*'s first twenty minutes as unique in the history of cinema, a catharsis for the audience: in short a 'special affect'.

## Special affect

This 'special affect' of the film's first twenty minutes hinges on its status as trauma. In a televised interview with Spielberg Mark Cousins sets up the issue thus: 'It is as if the world's most famous filmmaker has tapped into (the audience's) nervous system and taken them back to the blood stained beaches themselves'.[17] Spielberg himself describes his intent to:

> create a kinship between the audience and the citizen soldier . . . to put the audience inside those landing craft . . . [so that the audience] . . . anonymous to each other and the soldier equally anonymous are shoveled onto those beaches [and experience] what the soldiers experienced in time 54 years ago.[18]

Putting the audience through the same trauma as the soldiers is intended to achieve catharsis. The result is that 'people are coming out with more respect than they had for what those kids did for us 54 years ago'. Spielberg's words here remind me of the public discourse on realism and war developed in British cinema during the Great War. With few exceptions, public reception of the Official War Film *Battle of the Somme* (1916) celebrated the film as showing the people at home what the boys were going through. The film features a sequence, purported to be real, of British soldiers going over the top: two fall, one slumping back into the trench and the second a few yards ahead into the barbed wire. *Battle of the Somme* also showed the bodies of dead British soldiers in the field and a burial detail. Though these images were shocking for the audience, they were also seen as necessary for the morale of the nation. Spielberg's statement above assumes a similar therapeutic function. In this context we might consider a medical film made during the First World War entitled *War Neuroses: Netley 1917, Seale Hayne Military Hospital 1918*.[19] This film employs a before and after structure to depict shell shock victims at various stages. The final sequence depicts the patients reconstructing the Battle of the Somme for the cameras in the fields outside their hospital as evidence of their cure. The 'cure' is demonstrated by their re-enactment which ostensibly demonstrates their fitness for return to duty but also a process of psychic inoculation against the terrors of warfare.

For *Saving Private Ryan* British critics, as we have seen, reinforced an expectation of catharsis through trauma. Not without tongue in cheek, the *Independent*'s John Walsh describes the moment before the press screening thus:

> Film critics, novelists, style-mag smart alecs and assorted media harlots hung around outside smoking like beagles, waiting for the 6.30 balloon to go up. Nick Hornby was there and Gerald Kaufman, Tom Shone, Anne Billson, John Lyttle, Alexander Walker, Richard Williams . . . It was a nervy occasion, 'You're sure you're ready for this' asked one. 'See the *New Yorker* piece?' asked another and we all shivered. . . . 'It's the Fear . . .' said Tony Quinn. We nodded solemnly and fell silent. Some lit cigarettes with shaking fingers. It was amazing that nobody vomited with apprehension, or started playing a harmonica. Two guys from a listings magazine came up. 'Okay', they said, white with apprehension, 'We're going in . . .'[20]

Here Walsh uses irony to temper claims for the overwhelming special affect of the opening scene, pointing to what he regards as the film's formulaic and manipulative construction (the 'only thing that stops you from fleeing the cinema'). Yet however humorous, Walsh's emphasis on shaking fingers, shivering and 'falling silent' draws not only on the generic conventions of the war film but also on the popular language used to describe battle fatigue or post-traumatic stress disorder.

Public discourse about the cinema, whether 'unofficial' in the form of journalism or the 'official' regulatory regime of censorship, has long involved concerns about the physical effects of the cinema.[21] Recent scholarship on early cinema has made links between the impact of technologies and the neurological experience, or effects, of modernity.[22] Ben Singer and Lynne Kirby draw variously on the work of Benjamin, Kracauer, Simmel and Freud as evidence of attempts to understand the public need for stimuli represented by the popularity of thrilling and sensational entertainments and amusements. Singer notes how for both Simmel and Kracauer 'Popular sensationalism both compensated for and mimicked the frenzied, disjointed texture of modern life'.[23] Kirby works to associate the cinema with the railroad as overlapping 'paradigms of perception', arguing that with the railroad, the experience of shock was emblematised by the accident, both real and anticipated, which gave rise to a condition known as 'railway spine', later called 'traumatic neurosis'.[24] Both remark that these theories around the 'shocks' of modernity either lead or refer to Freud's discussion of shell shock in 'Beyond the Pleasure Principle'. Here Freud suggests that the function of rehearsing anxiety was to prepare the soldier for violent events in small doses in order to prepare for the shocks of battle and to avoid major breakdowns.[25] Singer quotes Benjamin's use of Freud to connect this phenomena with the cinema: 'The film is the art form in keeping with the increased threat to his life which modern man has to face.'[26]

Such a prophylactic function of the cinema is clearly apparent in Spielberg's intentions for *Saving Private Ryan*, forming part of his formula for the film's didactic purpose. Spielberg points to the problem of knowing precisely what happened in these battles, of understanding what the soldiers went through. He refers to the axiom that those who did not see the worst can talk about it, while those who saw the worst are condemned to silence, or to muteness: 'So many veterans who went through [this] kind of hell . . . have not been able to speak openly about it without causing terrible pain.' Spielberg places the cinema of the past in the position of errant spokesman for these veterans. Veterans told him there were two wars, 'Hollywood's and ours . . . [they asked him] can you find it in your heart to tell the story of our war?'[27] This is not simply a standing-in for the veterans, or a hubristic gesture towards the representability of these events. Rather it is an attempt to create an affect that literally approximates shell shock in order to memorialise 'what those kids did for us' but also to make manifest those experiences for the audience so that the catharsis of the experience is not only the soldiers' but also theirs. This intent was successfully conveyed to the press on the film's release, mobilising popular conceptions of shell shock or the more contemporary term post-traumatic stress disorder. John Hancock in Los Angeles reporting for the *Daily Telegraph* frames his impressions in the language of trauma: 'The film . . . is an emotional experience and many cinema goers have been leaving the cinemas in tears or unable to speak.'[28]

These affective qualities are picked up on in the reports of the film 'reawakening veteran's fears'. British national papers ran stories of US veterans experiencing flashbacks with special phone lines being set up to help them. The *Guardian* quoted William Weitz, a clinical psychologist at the veterans' affairs department in Palm Beach, as saying: 'Seeing that movie opens up the emotional floodgates'.[29] Popular British film journal *Empire* opened their 16 page feature with the account that D-Day veteran and military historian Stephen E. Ambrose lasted only the first twenty minutes before calling for the projectionist to stop the film. He is described as striding 'purposefully for daylight. He needed to compose himself, to gather the storm of memories that swirled around his head. Then he returned and watched the rest of the film without a break.'[30] In both publicity and reviews the line between spectating and experiencing, distance and involvement are blurred. The affect is one of traumatic experience followed by delayed and uncontrolled reaction. In describing his purpose in inducing audience response Spielberg talks in the terms associated with delayed stress syndrome:

> Audiences don't need to consume and process every moment as they are experiencing it. If a film is going to make a lasting impact you'll be thinking about it later. . . . (the moral) might come to you later. I'm not asking you to try to find those values as you are trying to survive the mission.[31]

Both the Ambrose story and Spielberg's comments offer a directive for audience response.

## The (big and loud) silence of memory

Suspicion of Spielberg's use of melodramatic dramaturgy was central to the *Shoah/Schindler's List* debate in 1994. Tracing the terms of this debate Thomas Elsaesser notes that criticism of the filmmaker ranged from the modernist position of distrust of any '"mimetic" affective engagement' such as that associated with melodrama to specific charges of the manipulation of spectator empathy and iden-tification. He suggests that while Spielberg does 'tilt the narrative' of *Schindler's List* toward Schlinder's story he is careful to draw attention to the mass executions in 'the background'. Yet for Elsaesser it is also arguably the case 'that a mode (such as melodrama) that encompasses the oblique, the unstated, along with the explic-itly horrific, requires a story told "against the grain" of all the narratives we have in our head about the Holocaust'.[32] In *Saving Private Ryan* Spielberg again employs a melodramatic dramaturgy – how could he not – to try to express the ineffable experience of combat. Yet because he is on less sensitive terrain here, he can attempt to achieve an erasure of distance through visceral affect in the first twenty minutes but also through a conflation of point of view and memory in the chief witness Ryan. This conflation not only expresses the muteness, the silence of memory but also maintains it. It simultaneously (re)articulates the traumatic event and at the same time suspends the symptom 'stopping halfway' or just short of catharsis.

To explore how this works it is necessary to look at the opening shots of the film. The film begins with a black screen as the credits appear and the low solemn tones of John Williams' score. A shot of an American flag in the breeze with the diffuse sun-light behind it gives it a translucence, a faded quality. The next shot is a low angle moving camera of a pair of shuffling feet which then pans up to reveal the back of the old Ryan walking. This first shot is a point of view shot and the next shot is a reverse shot of his family, again a moving camera. The third shot is a cut in to Ryan's son who lifts his camera and takes a photograph, a shot of his father's back, the first shot of the film. He lets the camera drop and exchanges a knowing look with his wife: a surrep-titious photograph perhaps, the kind taken at an inappropriate moment, or just a rather uninteresting snapshot. Nevertheless the gesture underscores a generational viewing position. One is tempted to suggest that the photograph taken by the son privileges the film's address to baby boomer males, reinforcing Richard Goldstein's hunch that *Private Ryan*'s 'mourning work' is towards a post-60s rapprochement with 'the establishment'. However the second shot reveals a cross-generational viewing position which marks out a descending level of empathy with the elder Ryan. His wife knows his silence but not his experience, which as we find out at the end of the film he has never talked about. The son and daughter-in-law know the history but not the personal experience. The granddaughters walk arm in arm and seem curious, perhaps feigning interest and are holding what looks to be a guide to the cemetery while the grandson holding his mother's hand is just simply too young to understand or more importantly, too young to get in to see this movie.

The shot (5) which follows is from behind the whole family with the elder Ryan at the centre of the frame. This is the first omniscient position and helps to set up the system of point of view which is characterised by an alternation of concealment and revelation. It seems to place the family as spectators, as the family in the row in front of the viewer at the cinema. The next shot (6) is a reverse angle which pans to centre on the wife. The dynamic here is to centre the already established position of a family watching the exterior signs of a man experiencing a traumatic memory. The next shot (7) however is a long shot as the moving camera picks up the family, with Ryan at the front. Between the camera and the family are the trees that form the boundary of the cemetery. This is what Warren Buckland has identified as an 'offscreen presence', 'an external norm . . . that . . . dominates a large number of contemporary films, and is consistently used to structure Spielberg's films'.[33] Buckland goes on to suggest that these 'agents or presences' are not necessarily fixed. The camera position in this instance suggests the unseen presence of history, or more specifically the spiritual presence of the dead, witnesses who cannot speak. These are the agents who, in this visit to an American cemetery in Europe will demand a voice, a retelling. As he turns to enter the cemetery the camera and Ryan move towards each other. Ryan stops and leans his hand on a tree. His family moves up behind him. The next two shots (8 and 9) are of the US flag and the French tricolour but they are unattributable in terms of point of view. The next shot returns to Ryan at the tree; he moves slowly onto the cemetery grass and his face gradually fills the screen. The next shot (10) is a long shot, an unseen presence again as it tracks him on his walk on the grass from the level of the graves. A drum signals the interruption of the frame by a white cross in the foreground as Ryan passes a grave in the shape of a Star of David. Spielberg uses such interruptions to set up the significance and potential dangers held in off-screen space in *Jaws* or the Indiana Jones films. Here, however the interruption is the spectre of history and memory. This aesthetic device of interrupting the frame will have its equivalent in the tank obstacles during the D-Day landing sequence. The camera then moves with him and begins to rise, revealing the vast field of graves. This poignant spectacle recalls the rising camera shot of Scarlett emerging from the hospital to reveal a landscape of the dead and the dying in *Gone With the Wind*. The next shot is again from the level of the graves as it tracks around to face Ryan. He looks then, crying, drops to his knees and his family rushes to him. The next three shots are unattributed point of view shots of diagonal rows of graves, the last focused enough to clearly mark out the names, a first identification in a sea of anonymity, including the film's initial characters.

The next shot is a tableaux vivants. The camera tracks in to the family, Ryan's son on screen left and his wife on the right, but its movement drifts slightly to the left to get a three-quarter close up of Ryan's face and then tighter into his eyes, eyes that we assume are looking into his own traumatic memory. A wave crashes and the next shot looks out onto the sea, the view partially obstructed by a tank obstacle, a visual icon of the D-Day landings with the titles 'Dog Green Sector, Omaha Beach, June 6, 1944'. Another wave crash signals a high angle shot of a Higgins boat. An unattributed point of view, that is later revealed as that of the

German machine gunners. A side shot of the Higgins boats is the first of the shaking, hand held camera shots that sets up the kind of restricted vision and use of off-screen space on which the sequence depends for its power. The next shot is a cut to Miller's hand shaking; he steadies it with his canteen and the camera follows it up as he drinks from it. He puts his head down into the dark safety of the boat and then slowly raises it, looking off to screen right in the same way that the elder Ryan has. The implication of similarity is clear. The long shot of movement and then a slow revealing of the face, Tom Hanks the star, are the narrative codes of the intro-duction of character. In a reversal of the tracking-in shot onto the elder Ryan the camera tracks back to reveal faces of other men. Tom Sizemore puts tobacco in his mouth, a gesture which reveals character as the camera pulls back further to reveal the number of men in the boat.

In these sequences of shots there is a play on the convention of the introduc-tion of characters, the restricted narration sets up the D-Day landing sequence by implying that the old Ryan is the young Miller. The introduction of Hanks and, of lesser significance, Sizemore provides an anchor of stability in terms of providing audiences with a point of empathy. That focus of empathy is the centrepoint in the creation of the special affect, but rather than being dependent on a non-specific set of realistic special effects, sound and editing it is crucially dependent on the levels of empathy that those particular elements encourage. I am purposely avoiding the term identification but rather find that the term empathy is most appropriate here. Alex Neill has described empathy as differing from sympathy, the emotion of feeling *for* someone, in that it is an experiencing of the same feelings as another being, a feeling *with* someone.[34] The circumstantial proof is the limit case of *Saving Private Ryan*'s critical reception and the unanimous endorsement of the '*realité*' of the D-Day landing sequence.[35] In their consistent reference to the D-Day sequence as the pinnacle of the cinematic depiction of the experience of battle, these critics, in Neill's terms, recall the special affect of the sequence as creating feelings that are new to them. The deliberate confusion of the identities of the main characters is not made manifest until the end of the film. The beginning serves to provide the viewer with a sense of anchorage based on the well-established codes of contem-porary mainstream narrative film practice. It is on this empathetic base that the film's use of the stylised techniques of '*realité*' builds its 'special affect'.

## Nervy camera: approximating war neurosis

Spielberg describes the techniques he and cameraman Janusz Kaminski used in making the film 'nervous to look at'. They used a 45 per cent and a 95 per cent camera shutter which de-glamourised the sequences by getting rid of out of focus blurring, thus allowing every frame to be in focus (on regular 24 fps film move-ment is slightly blurred within each frame). Spielberg also employed a shaker lens that could be activated by the push of a button (used to simulate the shock of the explosions). In *Schindler's List* and *Saving Private Ryan* hand-held work was utilised to 'get rid of the distance between historical horror and the audiences perception of it'. Spielberg aimed to achieve the texture of the famous Robert Capa photographs of the actual landing. At the same time he tried to approximate the kind of camera work seen in John Huston's documentary *Battle of San Pietro* (the work, according to Spielberg, of cameramen who 'wanted to get back to their wives and children':[36] the camera stays low to the ground and near cover).

In the D-Day landing sequence, point of view alternates between a 'sidelong position' and that of the Hanks character Miller, giving the impression at first viewing of chaos. The camera often follows alongside Miller from the time he orders the men who are still alive over the side of the Higgins boat to the point where they rally at the sea wall. These two points, from the dropping of the ramps to when the unit reaches the sea wall, mark out the extreme confusion and disorientation of the sequence. From there the unit that we follow through the rest of the movie is fighting together. The alternation of positions takes place at times at the level of the soundtrack. When the first soldiers go underwater, the camera and soundtrack goes under with them. The underwater sound offers a kind of refuge from the overwhelming aural onslaught of the gunfire and explosions. Later this muffled sound is replayed as an interior sound, a visceral escape from the madness that approximates a symptom of shell shock. Interestingly these instances are each sparked by an explosion, twice in the D-Day sequence and once in the last set piece battle of the film. In all three cases the explosion sparks an interior, muffled soundtrack and the 45 per cent to 95 per cent shutter effect.[37]

The first of these shifts takes place as Miller struggles to the beach. The comrade he saved from drowning is shot out from under him and as he moves toward the beach an explosion knocks him to the ground. There is then a shot from the beach of an explosion that renders a man legless. As the sand clears, the hand held camera picks out Miller in the background and moves toward him into a close up and it is here that the soundtrack becomes muffled and dreamlike, the image takes on the stylised process of the special shuttering. After three point of view shots of the carnage the camera then sits alongside Miller with a Higgins boat and the men inside in flames in the background. Here the soundtrack works in opposition to the image and at times the viewer is both inside and outside the character. There is another section of the landing sequence where we are clearly seeing things from Miller's point of view. It is later in the sequence and it is the second time the approximation of what I will call 'the escape symptom' occurs where the soundtrack becomes muffled. The sound of explosions and his breathing is matched with the moving camera. His (i.e. the camera's) vision is jerky and at one moment focuses on a screaming wounded man but then turns away. The sequence works between the sidelong camera, the point of view of Miller and the shot from behind the German machine gunners. This effectively places the viewer in the firing line close to the ground and often seeking out Miller. It is an evocation of a frightened unseen presence. At the end of the sequence after Miller takes a drink from his canteen, Horvath (Sizemore) says off camera, 'What a view.' Miller responds: 'Yeah, what a view.' The camera repeats the move into his eyes as it moved into those of the elder Ryan at the beginning of the film. Then the camera in a reverse from the earlier rising shot revealing the graves hovers over the debris and bodies on the beach and then onto S. Ryan, a name amongst the anonymous dead.

I want to raise two concluding points in relation to this sequence. The first concerns the position of the viewer. The placing of the viewer is crucial to the narrative project of the film and the intended affect of approximating war neurosis. The transition from present to past brings to mind Hans Blumenberg's essay 'Shipwreck With Spectator: Paradigm of a Metaphor for Existence' in which he traces philosophers' use of the shipwreck/seafaring metaphor to imagine their relation to the object 'knowledge'. In the middle of his essay he picks up on Voltaire's use of this metaphor in *L'A B C ou Dialogues entre A B C*, noting that here the spectator: 'No longer represents the exceptional existence of the sage, on the edge of reality; rather, he has himself become an exponent of one of those passions that both move and endanger life'. For Voltaire, 'people hasten to witness such a drama out of curiosity (not secret pleasure)'.[38] A drama of imperilment need not draw attention to the safety of one's own position. 'I was curious and sensitive' wrote Voltaire; later, after almost losing his life in an actual shipwreck he began to question 'whether there is any safe haven in this world'.[39] A sensitive curiosity becomes empathy. In *Saving Private Ryan* Spielberg's narrative construction around a shifting point of view, a point of view which requires a retro-interpretation at the end of the film, seems to have arrived at Voltaire's conclusion. Spielberg will not allow Voltaire's 'sensitive curiosity'; we must look and feel, arriving with Ryan at the end of the film. We have survived the mission and we must, with Ryan, empathise. In shifting point of view at the end of the film Spielberg intensifies affect, playing on the assumption that the elder Ryan is remembering his own experience. As I have shown, this is achieved by keeping the camera with or near Miller throughout the traumatic events of the D-Day sequence. This combination of point of view construction and the almost overwhelming visceral impact in this sequence, by a number of accounts, manages to 'disturb' viewers.

An afterword: in a response to Voltaire the Abbé Galiani states that 'curiosity is a form of sensibility from which the slightest danger tears us away, forcing us to be concerned with ourselves alone'.[40] As if to anticipate the cinema viewer Blumenberg goes on to state that:

> For this reason, theatre illustrates the human situation in its purest form, according to Galiani. Only when the spectators have been shown to their secure places can the drama of human imperilment be played out for them. The more safely the spectator sits there and the greater the danger he witnesses, the more intense his interest in the drama. This is the key to the secrets of tragic, comic and epic art.[41]

This seems an appropriate response to Spielberg's apparent hubris in assuming that the cinema experience can be indistinguishable from actual experience.

My second concluding point concerns the modern sections which bookend the film. Spielberg's narration in *Saving Private Ryan* seems to work to effect a distance through the motif of the flashback and the safe distance in history and then to close that distance throughout the presentation of seven days from June 6 to June 13, 1944. In interview Spielberg recalls his father's friend coming over and how at the beginning of the evening they would be laughing and later they would be sobbing: 'We know that today as an intervention – when you help someone over a difficult and traumatic emotion'. The narrative of the film could be stated like this. A man takes his family to visit the cemetery in Europe where he fought and where many of his fellow soldiers are buried. He is also looking for a particular soldier's grave, unbeknownst to his family. He is overcome with emotion when he finds it. The memories flood back; his family leaves him alone to spend time with his own thoughts. He speaks to the gravestone; 'I brought my family here with me today. To tell you the truth I didn't know how I would feel coming back here . . .'. He stands and his wife rejoins him, she speaks the name on the gravestone. He asks if he has led a good life, stands back and salutes.

The film we see is a film of Ryan's silence. The intervention has been a silent one for him but a narrativisation of history for the film viewer. The film rehearses, through action and special effects the external causes and the interior conditions of shell shock. The empathetic attachment is revealed to us not to be an attachment to Miller but empathy, a feeling with. Ryan's empathy with Miller at the end of the film is, for the viewer, the beginning of its affect, a kind of cinematic delayed stress syndrome. Ryan is a witness for another witness, a witness who wasn't there. His flashback, the film we see, the silence his family observes, are symptoms of war neurosis. Peter Krämer has written of the therapeutic 'family work' of Spielberg's adventure films.[42] It is not surprising then that *Saving Private Ryan* has reportedly been used by therapists to work through 'survivor guilt'.[43] The 'intervention', Spielberg's own term, occurs in the shifting point of view and achieves its 'mourning work'. The older generation has been spoken for and at the same time is allowed to remain silent. Spielberg has said of this movie: 'I didn't write a love letter, I wrote a letter home.' In that sense *Saving Private Ryan* is an epic family adventure film that depends upon big and loud action for its special, emotional affect.

## Notes

1   John Keegan 'Is This How it Was?', *Weekend Daily Telegraph*, August 8, 1998, p. 2.
2   Anne Billson 'Cinema', *Sunday Telegraph*, September 13, 1998, p. 9.
3   Richard Goldstein 'World War II Chic', *The Village Voice*, January 19, 1999, pp. 143–4 and p. 147.
4   Frederic Jameson 'Nostalgia For the Present', in *Classical Hollywood Narrative: The Paradigm Wars*, Durham, NC and London: Duke University Press, 1992, pp. 252–74.
5   Tom Brokaw *The Greatest Generation*, New York: Random House, 1998.
6   Goldstein 'World War II Chic', p. 47.
7   Ibid.
8   Keegan 'Is This How it Was?', p. 3. Keegan goes on to state that he has used the male pronoun deliberately because 'Although the women in whose company I saw the film were moved and disturbed by its unrolling, they were able quite soon to discuss it as a dramatic experience'. Implying that the film's traumatic affect is gender specific Keegan offers no further explanation. Presumably the crucible of war is a male domain.
9   Samuel Hynes 'The Thin Red Line', *New Statesman*, February 26, 1999, p. 42.
10  Ben Shephard 'The Doughboy's D-Day', *Times Literary Supplement*, September 18, 1998, p. 23.
11  Ibid.

12  Amy Taubin 'War Torn', *The Village Voice*, January 28, 1998, p. 113.
13  David Bordwell, Janet Staiger and Kristin Thompson *The Classical Hollywood Cinema, Film Style and Mode of Production to 1960*, London: Routledge & Kegan Paul, 1985, p. 3.
14  Taubin, 'War Torn'.
15  I am attributing the term 'affect' here to both Taubin and Spielberg in the Freudian sense of the term, that is, a phenomenon of a release of psychic energy in response to either the repetition of a traumatic event or something similar enough to provoke such a response.
16  From a paper 'Early Cinema and the Attractions of Modernity' given at the Literature, Cinema and Modernity Conference held at Senate House, University College London, by the English Society, January, 2000.
17  *War Stories: Mark Cousins Talks to Steven Spielberg*, BBC2 documentary, broadcast September 13, 1998.
18  Ibid.
19  A copy of the film can be viewed at the National Film and Television Archive in London.
20  John Walsh '*Saving Private Ryan*', *Independent Review*, July 27, 1998, p. 5.
21  And of course recently it has been necessary to warn the audience of the possibility that the strobe effect of some films, often action cinema (e.g. *Titanic*, 1997), could trigger epileptic fits.
22  Ben Singer 'Modernity, Hyperstimulus, and the Rise of Popular Sensationalism', in Leo Charney and Vanessa R. Schwarz (eds) *Cinema and the Invention of Modern Life*, Berkeley, Los Angeles, London: University of California Press, 1995. See also Singer *Melodrama and Modernity: Early Sensational Cinema and its Contexts*, New York: Columbia University Press, 2001. Lynne Kirby *Parallel Tracks: The Railroad and Silent Cinema*, Exeter: University of Exeter Press, 1997.
23  Singer 'Modernity, Hyperstimulus and the Rise of Popular Sensationalism', p. 93.
24  Kirby *Parallel Tracks*, pp. 57–8.
25  Sigmund Freud 'Beyond the Pleasure Principle' in *On Metapsychology*, Penguin Freud Library, vol. 11, London: Penguin Books, 1991, pp. 269–339.
26  Singer 'Modernity, Hyperstimulus and the Rise of Popular Sensationalism', p. 94. The reference to Walter Benjamin is from 'Some Motifs in Baudelaire', in Hannah Arendt (ed.) *Illuminations*, New York: Harcourt Brace, 1968, p. 175.
27  *War Stories: Mark Cousins Talks to Steven Spielberg*.
28  John Hancock 'Latest Spielberg Fills Cinemas', *Daily Telgraph*, July 28, 1998, p. 16.
29  Joanna Coles 'Spielberg Film Revives Trauma for War Veterans', *The Guardian*, July 29, 1998, p. 13.
30  Ian Nathan 'Apocalypse Then', *Empire*, October, 1998, p. 102.
31  *War Stories: Mark Cousins Talks to Steven Spielberg*.
32  Thomas Elsaesser 'Subject Positions, Speaking Positions: From *Holocaust*, *Our Hitler* and *Heimat* to *Shoah* and *Schindler's List*', in Vivan Sobchack (ed.) *The Persistence of History: Cinema, Television and the Modern Event*, London: Routledge, 1996, p. 163.
33  Warren Buckland 'A Close Encounter with *Raiders of the Lost Ark*: Notes on Narrative Aspects of the New Hollywood Blockbuster', in Steve Neale and Murray Smith (eds) *Contemporary Hollywood Cinema*, London and New York: Routledge, 1998, p. 172.
34  Alex Neill 'Empathy and (Film) Fiction', in David Bordwell and Noël Carroll (eds) *Post Theory: Reconstructing Film Studies*, Madison: University of Wisconsin Press, 1996, pp. 175–6.
35  In *War Stories* (see note 17), Spielberg uses the term *realité* to describe the style of realism employed in *Schindler's List* and *Saving Private Ryan*.
36  Ibid.
37  It is worth remarking here that this is a visual expression of the general tendency of soldiers in the Great War to attribute the source of their war neuroses to having been near an explosion. In this sense it exteriorises and localises the cause of the malady and moves it away from the cumulative effect of combat experiences, or more seriously a charge of hysteria. For a full discussion of this see Joanna Bourke *Dismembering the Male: Men's Bodies, Britain and the Great War*, London: Reaktion Books, 1996, p. 115.

38   Hans Blumenberg *Shipwreck With Spectator: Paradigm of A Metaphor for Existence*, Cambridge, MA: MIT Press, 1997, p. 35.

39   Ibid., p. 36.

40   Ibid., p. 39. From a letter written by the Abbé Galiani to Madame d'Épinay on August 31, 1771.

41   Ibid.

42   Peter Krämer 'Would You Take Your Child To See This Film?: The Cultural and Social Work of the Family Adventure Movie', in Neale and Smith *Contemporary Hollywood Cinema*, pp. 294–311.

43   This claim is made in an article entitled 'Film Therapy' by Joanna Rahim in the British Airways in-flight magazine *Highlife*, pp. 52–4. In this article she notes therapist Maggie Roux, of Leeds University recommends *Saving Private Ryan* as it 'addresses the issue of survivor guilt'. The use of film as a therapeutic device is more thoroughly explored in Shannon B. Dermer and Jennifer B. Hutchings 'Utilizing Movies in Family Therapy: Applications for Individuals, Couples and Families', *The American Journal of Family Therapy*, 28: 163, 2000, pp. 163–79.

## PART III

# Gender, stars, bodies

## Chapter 10

# LINDA RUTH WILLIAMS

## READY FOR ACTION
### *G.I. Jane,* Demi Moore's body and the female combat movie

**A** **PARTICULAR PHENOMENON** characterized many a Hollywood star's role choices in the late 1980s and throughout the 1990s, one played out against the backdrop of action cinema. It had a male form and a female form. Male stars who had cut their teeth in action and fantasy movies began to take on 'sensitive' roles foregrounding nurturing (nursery teacher Schwarzenegger in *Kindergarten Cop*), introspection (brain damaged Harrison Ford in *Regarding Henry*) and even procreation (a pregnant Schwarzenegger in *Junior*). The wise-cracking action star Bruce Willis gave voice to a baby in *Look Who's Talking*, and *Mad Max/Lethal Weapon* star Mel Gibson played Hamlet. Whilst this broadening of an actorly portfolio functioned as insurance against aging and a bid for a wider range of offers, the comedic effect, particularly in Schwarzenegger's choices, was predicated on his established profile as *the* prototype action star. The idea – and indeed the image – of a pregnant Arnie gleaned its marvellous absurdity from the relief posed by his apparently assured masculinity: only one so utterly male could risk becoming so precariously female.

The female counterpart to this male move ran, predictably, in the opposite direction. If we saw muscleman Arnie with a fecund bump, we then saw ditsy vanilla heroine of the decade's most successful romantic comedies, Meg Ryan, piloting a Huey in *Courage Under Fire*. If we saw Stallone as country singer in *Rhinestone*, we saw Hollywood's most cerebral of thespians, Meryl Streep, shooting the rapids in *A River Wild*. Both *Courage Under Fire* and *A River Wild* were serious dramas. Neither gained comic relief from the star's more usual actorly choices. These women were also extending their portfolios, but with the serious intent of demonstrating adaptability through work within unfamiliar genres. Even Laura Dern's palaeobotanist Dr Ellie Sattler in *Jurassic Park* leaves behind academic pursuits in order to weigh in and do her bit for the film's action, such as it is, eschewing Richard Attenborough's chivalry with a line objecting to 'sexism in survival situations'. Jamie Lee Curtis in *Blue Steel* and Angela Bassett in *Strange Days* both won their spurs from collaboration with action's prime female auteur Kathryn Bigelow, Curtis developing this with her work on Cameron's *True Lies*. Both Curtis's Helen Tasker and Geena Davis's amnesiac CIA assassin in *The Long Kiss Goodnight* metamorphose into kick-ass heroines from an initial position of apple pie domesticity, and much of the comedy as well as the power of their new images comes from the contrast between domestic drudgery and dangerous derring-do. Curtis does the action equivalent of the bespectacled secretary who turns man-eater as she loosens her hair with one hand and discards her glasses with the other; more interestingly, Davis's action character emerges through the cracks of memory flashes which reveal a forgotten past career.[1] This backstory of violence is remembered through the symptoms of her body – she finds she can chop carrots at an extraordinary pace, and defends her home from an attacker with revelatory skill. The work of the film, then, is to expose the action woman underneath the layers of motherhood (though when defending her daughter protectiveness and aggression are complementary). Read together, these films might serve as images of the female star's move from more traditional roles into action in the 1990s: reveal to yourself and your audience a previously unexploited talent, and your portfolio of possibilities will extend far beyond the limits of the usual female (screen) roles.

The most prominent female stars have dipped into but then moved back from action roles, remaining at the top of their game through a diversity which includes a spell demonstrating their physical prowess, but which finally avoids full identification of star with genre. Sharon Stone moved from B to A list with her fighting role in Verhoeven's *Total Recall*, but has rarely worked up a sweat since (save one turn as a gunfighter in *The Quick and the Dead*). Most recently, Carrie-Anne Moss has tempered her star-forming action turn in *The Matrix* with a more cerebral role in *Chocolat*; Angelina Jolie's role as Lara Croft was preceded by the more actorly performance of *Girl, Interrupted*; whilst the action sequences of *Charlie's Angels* were tempered by the reputation of the film as an audience-pleasing spectacle of fashionable female flesh. Sandra Bullock may have cut her cinematic teeth with the exemplary action-piece *Speed*, but her physical skills were limited to bus driving, and she is unlikely to be remembered as an action heroine. Even the iconic Linda Hamilton and Sigourney Weaver, have actually only tooled-up and muscled-up for one (albeit high profile) role apiece. Though Weaver is the nearest we have to an A list female action star, she has in fact worked far more outside of action. Ripley's weary line to the alien in *Alien 3* – 'You've been part of my life so long, I can't remember anything else' – is no reflection of Weaver's broader portfolio.

This desire to commute in and out of – as it were – 'foreign' genres (for women, into action; for men, into comedy or softer, character-focused drama), has not generally been accompanied by radical bodily transformation. This is particularly interesting since one thing which has characterized action genres has been a focus on the body. How, then, has arguably the most overtly and traditionally 'embodied' cinematic sex – women – been capable of breezing in and out of action adventure films or Gulf War combat movies or boot camp dramas with the only significant physical makeover being a tough new wardrobe? Despite the association of action with muscles, few women dipping into the genre seemed to feel much of a need to engage in radical physical transformation: body formations are fairly static across and between films. Schwarzenegger's body changes little; it is a built up (though now late middle-aged) monolith, less sculpted perhaps than in the days of *Pumping Iron*, but not requiring the ups and downs of reinvention between shoots (his family films frequently offer the opportunity for action sequences). The same might be said of Meg Ryan, who slipped into US Army combat fatigues for *Courage Under Fire* and black biker leather for *Addicted to Love* as easily as she slips into elegant femininity for a Nora Ephram romantic comedy, though little about her body apart from her haircut changes.

Demi Moore is different. Who or what constitutes Moore's body as a star body became particularly interesting at that point when she took on the title role in *G.I. Jane*; for one moment in 1997, Demi Moore (never before identified as an action star) constructed and inhabited *the* exemplary female action body. Directed by Ridley Scott, *G.I. Jane* is neither *Alien* nor *Thelma and Louise* (though film critics compared it to both),[2] but still it touches on some crucial debates about how women deal with male-minted power, and what is required of their bodies in the combat genre. A Schwarzenegger or a Meg Ryan might remain fairly immovable in body type across and between different film forms, but this is not true of Moore – a comparison might be made between Moore in *G.I. Jane* and Linda Hamilton before, during and after *Terminator 2*, tooling and muscling up for one particular role, but working down to a more traditionally feminine type soon after the shooting closed, a blank canvas ready for the next job. Whilst her most recent re-invention as the villainous former angel in *Charlie's Angels: Full Throttle* showcases the star in an action role, it also represents a return to the dangerous sexiness with which she was associated in *Disclosure*. Moore's work in the 1990s was characterized by a series of self-masquerades, transformative acts through which she managed to bring off a curiously paradoxical coup: like the obsessively self-transformative Madonna, disguising, masking or completely making herself over only served to clarify Moore's star image, a singular sameness paradoxically constructed through the vacillations of physical difference. Moore's corporeal shape-shifting was predicated on a peculiarly late-twentieth century notion of the body as a thing to be moulded, worked on, worked out, and which, through suitable customized transformations, was able to take her in a range of different generic directions. Indeed, Moore claims that she openly embraced 'the opportunity to deal . . . with the enormous physical demands of the action genre'.[3] In the 'opposition between star bodies and star performances' upon which 'discourses surrounding Hollywood cinema' rest, Yvonne Tasker aligns Moore with body rather than performance,[4] not least because it constitutes the prime commodity (worth $1 million for a single night to Robert Redford) in *Indecent Proposal*. Moore, as one critic put it, chooses 'big, brazen, high-concept pieces in which she and/or her physique are the concept'.[5] Making herself busty and lithe, and with the aid of some dance training, she was able to 'bare all' (as the publicity had it) in *Striptease*. By growing her hair and hitting the stairmaster she was able to exemplify the corporate *femme fatale* in *Disclosure*. But most dramatic of all, training alongside the Marines and building herself up to the point of being capable of one-armed press-ups, she could take on the Cinderella-role of Jordan

O'Neil, the first female participant in the tough Navy SEAL training programme, and undergo a particular bodily transformation which fulfilled both the requirements of genre and the needs of Moore's career trajectory. The demands of a particular generic form for a particular bodily form, and the impact of this on Moore's wider star image, are the subjects of this chapter.

## Boot camp babes: the military makeover narrative

*G.I. Jane* is a body work, but it is also a genre work; Moore's Jordan sits (albeit uneasily) alongside Ryan's Karen Walden at the centre of a woman-in-combat film which – in Jordan's case – focuses first on the rigors and physical indignities of training, also endured by Goldie Hawn's Judy Benjamin in the 1980 comedy *Private Benjamin* and the TV series which followed. Although there is a long tradition of women in the celluloid military, fetishized by their phallic-female association with weapons and uniform, by the 1990s this had become only one of the ways in which women tackled action as a wider umbrella of genres. The boot camp narrative is a particularly interesting subgenre of the war film where gender is concerned. These are essentially transformation stories, the *Now Voyagers* of the war genre with a narrative arc which functions rather like those 'before and after' beauty product advertisements: the naive, wet-behind-the-ears rookie soldier (or airman or marine) enters training like a lamb to the slaughter, endures the bullying demoralization of a sociopathic Sergeant Major figure (Viggo Mortensen as Master Chief in *G.I. Jane*; Eileen Brennan as Captain Lewis in *Private Benjamin*; Lou Gossett Jr as Sergeant Foley in *An Officer and a Gentleman*), either grows (literally, physically putting on the bulk the job requires) or falls, then graduates to a spell in a real warfare situation, which may turn out to be less harrowing than the preparation which led up to it. In *G.I. Jane* Jordan is plucked from her job as a smart naval intelligence officer and plunged into a form of training for which there is a '60 per cent drop out rate' (even her boyfriend says 'These guys are world class warriors . . . they'll eat corn-flakes out of your skull'). But Jordan makes it, surviving first the torture and near-rape of the Master Chief in a military exercise, then a set-up lesbian scandal, followed by the political manipulations of Texan Senator Lillian DeHaven (Anne Bancroft). But when she proceeds to a real war situation on the Libyan coast the film loses the courage of its convictions. Unlike *Courage under Fire*, we are spared the sight of a woman actually killing the enemy, and Jordan proceeds to graduate with tears in her eyes (Scott's original ending saw her shot dead in Libya, but test audiences objected).[6] Though *Sight and Sound* read *G.I. Jane* as battling with 'our preconceptions of the military recruitment movie',[7] essentially it is a female-focused reworking of venerable male boot camp stories such as *Full Metal Jacket*, *An Officer and a Gentleman* and *Tigerland*, its prime focus being the overhaul of rigorous physical preparation. In its male form, such films see men fashioned from mice in readiness for the combat sequence, which sometimes the film never even bothers to cover, so action-packed is the training itself: Schumacher's *Tigerland*, for instance, never reaches Vietnam; the Advanced Infantry Training camp in a Louisiana swamp is represented as even worse than Nam itself. Kubrick's film does eventually arrive in a real conflict, but, like *G.I. Jane*'s Libya, *Full Metal Jacket*'s Vietnam sequence seems an afterthought following the harrowing training drama which constitutes the most 'active' body of the film. Yet whilst both Meg Ryan and Moore help the USA to fight Islam in Desert Storm and the Libya skirmish respectively, for both the primary conflict is with nation and self.

This is focused in *G.I Jane* through the hard battle Jordan wages and wins first with her own body and second with fellow countrymen of a different gender over the issue of her body. The threat of your body letting you down is particularly acute when that body is female. Whilst Moore's Jordan is only finally vindicated once she shines in the front-line, the film's central action spectacle is played on the simulated battlefield of training, where Scott loses no opportunity to equate the sex war with real war, and the perceived physical weaknesses of femininity with the dangers of betrayal by one's own side in the line of fire, suggesting that the female body might prove to be America's most dangerous fifth columnist. The main mystery of *Courage Under Fire* as unpicked by Denzel Washington's military investigator Lieutenant Colonel Sterling rests on the possibility that the now-dead Walden was a coward and does not deserve her posthumous Medal of Honor. Though the film exposes guilt in Sterling's past and vindicates Walden, it still relies for much of its duration on the presupposition of women's culpability. In the boot camp story, this guilt – the traditional manifestation of the castration anxiety women evoke, for which their whole bodies formed a fetishistic icon of disavowal in classical Hollywood – is figured through the spectre of feminine physical unreliability pitched against the certainty of muscular prowess. Women's struggles to cope with physical hardship and succeed in a physical landscape designed to test men underpins much of the drama or the comedy of this subgenre: Jewish princess Judy Benjamin survives the rigors of her Mississippi training camp by marshaling the attributes of femininity in innovative ways (using her electric toothbrush to clean out the latrine; deploying sexy red underwear to mimic the enemy's red armbands in a training manoeuvre). Judy thus moves from hopeless recruit to successful graduate, and is assigned to an elite paratroop regiment which has hitherto taken no women.[8] When she is sexually harassed she is transferred to a fictional version of NATO, at which point *Private Benjamin* ceases to be a military movie and pursues a soft feminist line about the loss of self in marriage. Another narrative of female self-overcoming against a backdrop of military hardship is the story of Casey Seeger, lone female recruit in the officer's training school joined by Richard Gere's Zack Mayo in *An Officer and a Gentleman*. Seeger can do everything except 'walk the wall' on the assault course, but on receiving private tuition from Mayo she is able to graduate to pilot training with her male peers. It is as if *G.I. Jane* has taken these training vignettes and blown them up to full-length movie proportions, making physical struggle emblematic of sexual struggle.

Yet any story which foregrounds the physical preparatory action which precedes the combat action might make women a more interesting focus for this particular subgenre than men. Where combat sequences involve action *with* the body, training sequences involve action *on* the body, an emphasis women are arguably more geared up to due to their social propensity for, or willingness to indulge in, the makeover in its various forms. If psychoanalytically women have embodied guilt, socially they have been seen as the sex most open to physical transformation, the one perhaps masking the other.[9] That the body can and must be perfected (your comrades' lives depend on it) suggests its potential for radical improvement and overhaul as well as its original weakness. For men, enlarged muscles are a sign of the natural and – as it were – the super-natural or the extra-natural. Dyer argues that muscles signal both a natural 'physical strength that women do not generally match' and a process of cultivation:

> developed muscularity – muscles that show – is not in truth natural at all, but is rather achieved. The muscle man is the end product of his own activity of muscle-building. . . . Conversely, a man's muscles constantly bespeak this achievement of his beauty/power.[10]

But Dyer also argues that the sex most associated with physical making-up is also the sex which fails to show the process in the end result:

> As always, the comparison with the female body beautiful is revealing. Rationally, we know that the beauty queen has dieted, exercised, used cleansing creams, solariums and cosmetics – but none of this really shows in her appearance, and is anyway generally construed as something that has been done to the woman.[11]

The paradox here is that the to-be-looked-at sex displays herself as natural though artificial, whilst the sex associated with the look displays an exaggerated body replete with the power of labour and effort. Nevertheless, few male training narratives choose to display a *changed* male body in the way that *G.I. Jane* displays Moore's: for all the homoerotic fetishization of Richard Gere or Tom Cruise, neither *An Officer and a Gentleman* nor *Top Gun* would dare to show its heroes in a state of pre-training puniness. Moore/Jordan thus manifests the hard body as a locus of change, achieved through work. Indeed, films which feature women in preparation for or participating in combat situations may also constitute a persuasive argument for their innate suitability for it. If Davis's CIA background makes her more able to defend her daughter, motherhood has prepared Ryan's character for battle: the pain of being shot is prefigured by that of labour: 'I gave birth to a nine pound baby, asshole' she snaps, 'I can handle it!' This machismo borne of childbirth is especially fascinating in the light of Moore's star motherhood which I will discuss later. But physical experience also offers a forum for gender transformations which Tasker has termed 'musculinity':

> The masculinisation of the female body, which is effected most visibly through her muscles, can be understood in terms of a notion of 'musculinity'. That is, some of the qualities associated with masculinity are written over the muscular female body. 'Musculinity' indicates the way in which the signifiers of strength are not limited to male characters.[12]

This scenario is literalized and dramatized in *G.I. Jane*. If physical modification is most overtly emblematized by shape-shifters such as Moore, then the women-in-training story proves an exemplary narrative of transformation. Tasker argues that body-building serves to destabilize gender in that it displays the body as manufactured, feminizing men whilst it masculinizes women – a perverse practice which 'transgresses supposedly 'normal' gendered behaviour'.[13] So how does the effort of physical transformation impact on Moore as a female star? Jordan's demonstration of mettle coincides with Demi Moore's, producing a case history of physical self-overcoming and engendered mythmaking.

## Demi Moore's star body

What is a star in 1990s Hollywood? Since the decline and fall of the studio system's controlling machines, how do we mark our icons? If the star persona of classical Hollywood was brought into being through the detailed Machiavellian authority of studios, perhaps now it is the strength of control which the star herself wields which constitutes contemporary Hollywood's guarantee of stellar celebrity. Around the mid-1990s Demi Moore embodied the notion that female star quality was synony-mous with $12 million pay cheques, final-cut control and the ability to open a movie. In 1995, *Premiere* magazine voted Moore America's most powerful actress, placing her at number 9 in their Power Top 25 (which judges 'actors with the most ability to exert their will on the making of movies in Hollywood'), higher than her co-star in *Indecent Proposal*, Robert Redford, and a clear ten places ahead of her (then) action-hero husband Bruce Willis. As Tasker has noted, the *Striptease* fee made Moore both 'the highest paid female star of the day and foreground[ed] the extent to which the success of the female star is frequently linked to a physical performance of sexuality'.[14] *Striptease* failed to deliver in either box office or crit-ical terms what was promised by its star's fee. But in *G.I. Jane* Moore chose to follow it with a different kind of performance piece, consolidating her high profile as a body talent rather than an actorly one.

Moore's stardom rests on a classic public–private ambivalence: though occasionally a subtle and persuasive actor, she is perhaps more famous for her stroppy on-set demands (her soubriquet is 'Gimme Moore'), her propensity for self-publicity, her willingness to shape-shift, than for her actorly profile, yet the substance of her roles has served as a kind of strange commentary on her stardom. Star studies remind us that stars are for the industry the central commodities in the marketing of the film product as well as being pleasurable 'organising presences in cinematic fictions':

> Just as a commodity is defined as having both exchange value (it can be bought and sold) and use value, so the two circuits of stardom are separ-able only analytically. For the profit to be realised, there must be at least a promise of pleasure. Enjoyment of the star has to be paid for.[15]

Moore grasps this in its most corporeal sense, but poses the question on her own terms. The trading of body for money, and the ability to provide the right kind of body if the fee is big enough, is a story played out in the narrative of *Striptease* as well as in the contract Moore signed in order to appear in it. The actress as whore is an old image, and one which Moore seems comfortable with: like her character in *Indecent Proposal*, as well as any number of female actors whose physical work has aligned them with prostitution, she took the money in exchange for her body. The difference is that in publicly celebrating her high fees she also confidently advertises the amount of pleasure she promises to her audience. If enjoyment of the star must be paid for, then payment is also an index of enjoyment, the higher the fee the headier the pleasure.[16] The frenzy of publicity which surrounded her in the mid-1990s when she was Hollywood's foremost star body because she was also its most expensive, was part of a self-generating loop which saw Moore's stock rising fast.

Moore is in many ways the perfect 1990s multiplex product, maximizing audiences across gender lines through her equal marketability to men and women. Though she is one of the few survivors of the seminal 1980s brat pack vehicle *St Elmo's Fire*, by the time she made it she had long been an established regular on *General Hospital*, which she followed with a range of relatively non-cheesecake, tough roles, including models and hookers in *No Small Affair* and *We're No Angels*. It was her role as Patrick Swayze's bereaved sculptor girlfriend in the massive 1990 hit *Ghost* which established the 1990s Moore, breaking through into leading roles and talking-point parts: the broke wife who sells herself to Robert Redford in *Indecent Proposal*, the rookie military lawyer supporting Tom Cruise in *A Few Good Men*, the sexual harasser in *Disclosure*, the improbably feisty Hester Prynne in *The Scarlet Letter*, the 'sexy mother' of *Striptease*. Neither is she averse to quirky cameos: a perkily boyish shelf-stacking supermarket shlub in the 'coming out' episode of American sitcom *Ellen* preceded a stint as the voice of Esmeralda in Disney's *Hunchback of Notre Dame*, exposing her to younger audiences (Moore's trademark voice – gravely rasping, perhaps as iconic an auditory 'body' as is her visual body – merits further work; it is interesting that possibly her most masculine quality has lent itself to such a feminine incarnation). Perhaps only in the underrated *Mortal Thoughts* did we begin to see Moore open up that potential just glimpsed – albeit insistently – in her other work: the sense that she can be a subtle and surprising actress as well as a bankable star. Sadly, intelligent roles in small films do little to cement one's position as an ongoing Hollywood power-broker. After *Mortal Thoughts*, she traded the possibility of small, challenging, and artistically risky roles, for huge salaries and tight image control. She has also developed work through her production company, notably the 1996 portmanteau drama *If These Walls Could Talk*, the woman's film *Now and Then*, and all three Austin Powers movies. Moore also has a producer credit on *G.I. Jane*.

Threaded through this filmographic biography is another story – another fiction, perhaps – of how Moore's 'real' self is publicly displayed, of what we think we know and what we are allowed to see. Dyer has famously read the star as a polysemic entity, whose multiple meanings are created by the multiple contradictory elements brought to bear on a single identity by forces both inside and outside of the film text. As most star theorists verify,[17] stars never exist solely inside films; they are forged in the interrelationship between a number of different textual and extra-textual elements. As a star, Moore's persona exceeds, overlaps and colludes in the individual demands of the role; if in *Gentlemen Prefer Blondes* we are watching 'not just Lorelei Lee but also Marilyn Monroe',[18] in *G.I. Jane* we are not just watching Jordan O'Neil but responding to a particular repackaging of the Demi Moore commodity, drawing fragments of meaning from those disparate details of a colourful life we have hitherto been privileged to glimpse: the early marriage to an English rock musician, the engagement to Emilio Estevez, the celebrated wedding (and subsequent divorce) of Bruce and Demi conducted by Little Richard – these are the basic romantic co-ordinates. Mix in a solid handful of female support (neighbour Nastassja Kinski encouraged her teenage talent; her production company is female-headed), a scattering of scandal (her battle with drink and drugs, rumours of cosmetic surgery, nude magazine covers), some intriguing character details (Demi as devoted mother against Demi as tough cookie on set), and you have a public–personal profile which brilliantly builds upon the star commodity developed through the films. An image of her life has partly become the product of herself – her passion for collecting dolls, for instance, was read by Zoe Heller as key to those physical reinventions: 'it is as if she is playing real-life Barbie with herself: Demi the babe, Demi the sensual earth mother, Demi the exotic dancer, Demi goes to war.'[19] Heller's interview draws from Moore some surprisingly revealing insights on the practice of 'autosculpture' which seems to breach the starry rift of public and private (before suggesting that this is just another ironically postmodern veil): Moore's personal investment in the endless moulding and remoulding of her own looks has less to do with movie-star self-infatuation, she says, than with standard female insecurity:

> What's so funny is that, from where I sit, I am much more like the women who are trying to work out the answers to the issue of body image than some kind of expert or example. I've always used photography and film as my opportunity to work through my own stuff about image . . .[20]

The interplay between the prosaic and the stellar, the way in which Moore is like us and not like us (like us she has babies; unlike us she shows off her bump on magazine covers; like us she has had trouble in love; unlike us her marriage was one of the most famous on the planet), confirms John Ellis's image of stars as simultaneously available and utterly separate:

> Stars are incomplete images outside the cinema: the performance of the film is the moment of completion of images in subsidiary circulation, in newspapers, fanzines, etc. Further, a paradox is present in these subsidiary forms. The star is at once ordinary and extraordinary, available for desire and unattainable.[21]

For Ellis each of these incomplete and incoherent elements – voice, face, still photos – is completed (or so we are promised) in the cinema: 'the star image . . . functions as an invitation to cinema . . . It proposes cinema as the completion of its lacks, the synthesis of its separate fragments'.[22] *G.I. Jane* must thus promise the delivery of Moore, making sense of the incoherence of star fragments which orbit around her name at the edges of the film. Watching the ordinary/extraordinary Jordan O'Neil, one would expect to understand a bit more about the ordinary/ extraordinary Moore, especially since the body on display is Moore's real one as well as O'Neil's fictional one. Moore's consummate stardom is partly rooted in the way she has manipulated the boundary between screen and private self, so reminiscent of the old studio system's exploitation of the 'real' self-as-commodity used, adjacent to the film persona, to market, model, advertise. Moore is a quick-change artiste whose famously naked flesh is only one of her cloaks. Diverse as her film performances are, the dominant view of her persona is that of a powerful star who has managed to maintain a close identification of self with body whilst escaping objectification and exploitation.

*G.I. Jane* adds another texture to this story of embodied stardom and manipulated flesh, which has been played out through a number of incarnations which both contradict and reinforce each other by turns: the muscular woman, the pregnant and mothering woman, the woman-with-a-dick. In *Disclosure* her character, an executive involved in developing virtual reality technology, promises a future in which humans can attain 'freedom from the physical body, freedom from race and gender . . . we can relate to each other as pure consciousness' (in fact the carnal Meredith wants none of this for herself, even though she eventually appears in cyberspace as a virtual body resembling a suit of armour with her face pasted on it). The speech resonates beyond the scope of this particular film, since it is the context of cinema which has given Moore the opportunity to embrace bodily transformation and put physical femininity to the test; in *G.I. Jane* Moore 'puts on' far more than she takes off. If she undid in *Striptease*, she builds up in Scott's film. The director's trademark look, that lustrous widescreen low-angle precision which can impart a monumental slo-mo glamour to the most prosaic of objects, has had no more fitting a subject than the vest-clad Moore in the film's highly fetishistic working-out sequence (and no body doubles here – she did the one-handed press-ups on David Letterman to prove it). That Moore endured what Jordan endured is at the root of the star/role ambivalence; press reports emphasize Moore's hard work, her willingness to endure the real discomforts of the shoot, her physical courage.[23]

In the reception of *G.I. Jane*, Moore's body also became the site of profound confusion about attitudes to feminism. The physicality of the role provoked a remarkably incoherent critical response, which swung between ecstatic celebration of the film's feminism (despite Jordan's own plea that she doesn't become 'some poster girl for women's rights') and anger at its failure to present a coherent gender case. *G.I. Jane*'s gauntlet to feminism was taken up from different quarters in a confusion of ideological response. On its release in America some critics claimed that it was an insult to women, whilst in interview in Britain Scott tried to separate the strands of debate: 'I really wanted to avoid making this a film about women's rights and all that nonsense. I've done one of them. It's really more about a woman trying to do a man's job',[24] he told *Empire*, responding to another interviewer's question about this not being feminism but 'a misogynistic exercise in "turning women into men"' with 'people who say that have just never met a strong woman'.[25] Some saw stardom, glamour and feminism as at odds,[26] whilst Ryan Gilbey in *The Independent* noted the film's potential for activating the collision of the iconic and the historic, writing that *G.I. Jane* shows 'how the woman's movement might have turned out if the suffragettes had been commandeered by Emma Peel'.[27] Ambivalence about Jordan's/Moore's gender was central to this confusion. Whilst many critics were dismayed by the masculinization of Jordan, others chivalrously saw her brutalization as an attack on women. For Alexander Walker, Jordan is unnatural in her physicality, a regression from Scott's *Alien*. 'Now it's the woman who's the monstrous mutant' in a film which charts 'the progressive surrender' of gender (Demi is gotten into shape, Walker wrote, 'by every mutilation imaginable short of an actual penis graft').[28] Critical confusion over whether Jordan is a man or a woman means that across the spectrum of reception she/he is both: man enough to constitute a betrayal of feminism and femininity, but woman enough to be deemed hormone-driven,[29] masochistic,[30] and brutalized.[31] Amy Taubin pointed out that this ambivalence is focused through the iconography of violence inscribed on the body but with a shifting locus of aggression:

> Eyes blackened, lips split, cheeks bloody, she would be a perfect victim were it not for her muscled upper torso, her tight jaw, her defiant gaze, her stiff-legged swagger . . . This is woman as spectacle, but the spectacle is a gender bender that scrambles the iconography of top and bottom, butch and femme, exploding male and female identities in the process.[32]

*G.I. Jane*'s reception thus reveals Moore's body as anxiously sliding not just from masculine to feminine identifications, but from sadist to masochist, from political pawn to crack-killer, from feminist icon to gender betrayer to damaged victim.

Moore's star body also ensures that the film is haunted by images of maternity established in earlier photoshoots and her previous star role. Early in her SEAL initiation, Jordan overhears a conversation between the male trainees, in which they exclaim with disgust 'the average woman is 25 per cent body fat. That's a quarter fat!' Not so Jordan – or Demi, who has not been 'the average woman' since work-outs and alleged liposuction put paid to 'the average man's' objections. Rather than challenge the disgust of this prevailing misogyny, she instead reworks the canvas of herself and dispenses with the fat. But this must be set against the image of Moore's heavily pregnant body on the cover of *Vanity Fair* in 1991. Whatever the trans-forming iconography her physique represents at different moments, she has insisted that each incarnation be read in the context of a personal/public maternal story which has woven in and out through her publicity stunts and fictional narratives. Tasker notes that one element in the confused androgynous image of the muscular but femininely sexualized Brigitte Nielson was reports of her unfitness for mother-hood.[33] Moore has been careful to protect herself (and her daughters) from such aspersions despite the apparently unmotherly roles she accepted (and her public nanny-scandals), trying to ensure that the 'unmotherly' potential of her filmic body (sex icon, combat soldier) has never undermined her public images as a very 'fit' mother. A film which might seem to be most problematic for this issue is *Striptease*, released in the wake of Paul Verhoeven's porno-musical *Showgirls*, and initially seen as part of the wave of lap-dancing chic which created a mild frisson in celebrity circles in the mid-1990s. But like Ice Cube's rather more interesting *The Player's Club*, *Striptease* uses the sex industry as a platform to propound decent family values, though underpinned by an ambivalence about the sexual-maternal body. Here the mother strips not in contradiction of motherliness but *as a sign of* her devotion (she needs the money to win custody of her daughter again) – Moore's character epitomizes the tart with a (mother's) heart. Indeed, Moore's career has extended the meaning of the 'sexy mother', two forms of embodied femininity traditionally seen as contradictory. Jordan is not a mother but viewers read her worked-out body against the backdrop of these earlier images of the pregnant and maternal body. By contrast, *Courage under Fire* smooths over the apparent contradiction of the maternal and the military with a montage of Karen's mothering skills, as she multitasks press-ups practice and child care simultaneously.

## Moore dick: the body as battlefield

This shadow of maternity cast by Moore's presence in the film is rendered more unsettling by the spectre of phallic femininity made explicit in Jordan's rally cry 'Suck my dick', which ignited America's Southern Baptist moral majority in a frenzy of vitriol against Walt Disney Studios, *G.I. Jane*'s backers.[34] Echoing Thelma's line to the rapist in *Thelma and Louise*, for Amy Taubin 'Suck my dick' 'lays claim to the crucial male body part, neatly severing anatomy from destiny'.[35] Liberated from a strict anatomical context, Moore's utterance suggests that we might all have enough of a dick to make it available for the purposes of insult: you do not necessarily have to actually *have* one to be able tell someone what they can do with it. Yet to grasp the position from which 'dick' can be spoken and then, in words, to throw it back at your assailant makes the speaker the better endowed of both of them at this point in the film. We might also remember that Meredith the boardroom bitch of *Disclosure* is animated by such sexual and corporate aggression that a rumour goes around that 'she was once a man'. In 1992, another *Vanity Fair* cover featured a naked Moore body-painted in a male business suit.[36] *G.I. Jane* builds on this, switching playfully between differently gendered ways of naming the phenomenon of Demi-as-Jordan, whose calibre as top notch SEAL material is underlined when Anne Bancroft proclaims that she 'really is top drawer – with silk stockings inside'. Indeed, Jordan was chosen over more butch candidates (including a 'holder of several records for female power lifting') *because* of the PR value of her demure feminine qualities.[37] This propensity for straddling the extremes of embodied womanhood is suggested when she is called 'Joan of Arc meets Supergirl', a female articulation of traditionally male forms of self-sacrifice and heroism. Even her name – Jordan – is ambivalently androgynous, currently both one of the top ten names given to baby boys in Britain and the single moniker of a celebrated busty (female) glamour model, pin-up to a generation of heterosexual youths; her surname – O'Neil – incorporates another male moniker. Scott said tellingly in interview that masculinization was a prerequisite of SEAL training: 'She'd earned, if you like, her dick. It takes balls to do that job and she has balls.'[38] No wonder that critics saw the film as a story of G.I. Jane becoming G.I. Joe.[39]

Feminine musculinity is only one manifestation of this gender meld. It also functions indelibly to identify star image with the demands of a role. Another question is then raised, that of how we read what *Moore* does to herself through our reading of what *Jordan* does to herself, since it is so hard to distinguish Jordan's self-change from Moore's transformation. One moment of anxious collision between Demi the star and Jordan the role exemplifies this. Breaking into the buzz shop after finally losing patience with her impractically flowing locks, Jordan appropriates a razor and shaves off her hair, right there, for real, in view, to the tune of Chrissie Hynde singing 'The bitch is gone'. There could be no retakes, as Scott's multiple camera-positions testify. What we see is not just Lt Jordan O'Neil taking control of her career by taking control of her body, but Demi Moore giving herself a Number One, reversing those years of growing-out we have tracked through her screen history. The 'mondo'-pleasure of the scene lies in this latter impression that what the scene says about the star is as important as how the character develops in the film. Even a haircut which seems like a form of disrobing is primarily a stage in bodily costuming: like acting whilst nude, taking off one's hair has a particular performative agenda, further blurring the line between Jordan the role and Moore the star. More of Jordan there may be as the film proceeds, but this worked-on, worked-out, built-up body is still Moore. It may seem an obvious point, but if Jordan shaves, Demi does too; if Jordan's pecs swell, so do Demi's. This begs the question, is the Moore we see any more real than Jordan? The body of Demi Moore is a costume, a mask, a masquerade which conveys Jordan's development, but which Moore too carries through into all those photocalls with Bruce and the kids, those chat show appearances, those shock-spreads in the *National Enquirer*. However much she takes off or builds up, the possibility that we are really seeing *her* is as big an illusion as those coy publicity shots of Judy Garland with her tennis racket, or Susan Hayward persuading us to use Lux soap.[40] None of these faces, these voices, these actions, are real; only the products marketed by these illusions of genuineness are different. Moore strips and shows a pregnant body, a painted body, a glamour-body, and whilst all of these bodies are hers, they are also part of the skin-flick which is her ever-changing public self. Showing all, she actually shows very little, since all are part of the show.

Demi Moore has long recognized that what women do to their bodies they do, in the eyes of the world, to themselves. Female self and body image are inextricably intertwined, and she has chosen to exploit this in a set of unshrinkingly headline- and cover-grasping moves. But what is the difference between this bodily transformation and a male actor's manipulation of personal flesh in fulfilment of the demands of a role (De Niro's weight gain for *Raging Bull*, for instance)? Why is one seen as the act of a literally selfless method actor, subsuming the personal into the professional, whilst the other is seen as at worst the move of a pushy self-publicist? Moore, after all, put on 25 pounds – albeit of muscle – for the role.[41] In her battle to control the inevitable link between the body of the role and her bodily public image Moore has risked the possibility of at least one of her parts sticking – *Disclosure*'s manipulative harpy, whose heart, it is said, is 'made of that plastic they use for football helmets'.

Compare, then, that central image of Meredith, scheming whilst treading her stairmaster in *Disclosure*, with Jordan's one armed press-ups sequence. Earlier in *Disclosure* the worried male victim, familiarly played by Michael Douglas, had exclaimed to a colleague, 'That woman's probably on a stairmaster an hour a day – she can kick the shit out of both of us!' The time-honoured tradition of Hollywood show-and-tell ensures that in due course we *do* see Meredith on her stairmaster, Douglas' words enforcing the view that this is no prudent act of physical fitness, but a *femme fatale* forging her weapon. Jordan's press-ups also highlight the woman's body as weapon, except that here it's a weapon in service of the nation.[42] Nevertheless until they are forced to see otherwise, both women labour under the crucial misapprehension that honing the self into a singular trajectory of ambition will bring real public power. Meredith's final words, the bitter bile of the defeated bitch, in another context, in another film (*G.I. Jane* perhaps), would be the enlightened speech of a woman grasping the truth. Jordan could equally say, as Meredith does, 'I'm only playing the game the way you guys set it up – and I'm being punished for it. That's fine.' Bitch-monster or action-heroine, the force of Moore's roles lies in their exposure of the hypocrisies of power to which women are subject, combined with a refusal to let go of that power just because it is flawed.

If a number of films show Moore trying to reconcile female body image with this power, perhaps only *G.I. Jane* highlights what is at the heart of Moore's stardom. *G.I. Jane* is in the end *not* primarily a film about a solitary woman trying to forge a path for other women to follow in a sexist institution. It is about Jordan's (mythically American) war with her personal weakness. It is thus also not a film which finally posits men, or even Islam, as the enemy. Woman's body, and Jordan's ability to control its involuntary failures and responses, become the film's prime battlefield. Thus the manufacture of the body which is inherent in bodybuilding might serve as a key to the manufacture of self which is inherent in star-making. Tasker argues that 'Bodybuilding offers the possibility of self-creation, in which the intimate space of the body is produced as raw material to be worked on and worked over, ultimately for display on a public stage'.[43] The same might be said of Demi Moore herself. The closer you look at her star biography, the more it seems to be modelled on the myths of fame woven around the icons of classical Hollywood. Moore might easily be read as the trailer-trash daughter of a Joan Crawford or a Lana Turner, rising from a tough childhood of extreme poverty and broken marriages to immense wealth and a conspicuously luxurious public life. 'Hard work' is the lauded quality which rings out through the biographies of each of these women, the drivenness of self-overcoming which makes individual glamour the all-American reward for a sufficiently motivated rise. But in the age of the musculine action heroine, hard work is no longer most visibly manifest in consumer rewards – the designer wardrobe of a forties icon, or the Malibu villa. If it is to be seen anywhere now, 'hard work' must be demonstrated, enshrined, lived out *first* in the body. Now that the show girl must have more to show for her efforts than a gown by Adrian, Moore meets the challenge by revealing not just those allegedly augmented breasts but a whole worked-on physique. Hard work must have its corporeal manifestation. And just as in Crawford's day the star's rise from poverty to an opulence 'earned' by personal graft was at the same time remote *and* attainable for viewers (a Butterick version of those Adrian frocks could be run-up at home), so Moore's worked-on star body is something we could all achieve, if we only had that singular personal quality. She may have had $15,000 worth of gym equipment at her disposal when training for *Striptease*, but Demi also ran on the beach before dawn and did two hours of yoga each day, the publicity tells us – activities free and available to us all. As ever, then, stars are like us and not like us, attainable role models and remote glamour icons, excessive versions of the fans who buy the tickets. That Demi Moore does so little to disguise her thirst for control makes her, like Jordan, a hard but compelling female icon.

## Notes

1   Both stars had explored action in different forms before: Curtis as prototype 'final girl' in *Halloween*, Davis as swashbuckler in *Cutthroat Island*. Davis's transformation from dippy wife to gun-toting revenger in *Thelma and Louise* tracks a similar trajectory to her role in *The Long Kiss Goodnight*.

2   Most reviewers saw *G.I. Jane* as latest in an honourable line of feisty feminist vehicles, reminding us of the director's prior 'gender fuck' films (Amy Taubin 'Dicks and Jane', *Village Voice*, August 26, 1997, p. 73); one headline quipped that this propensity for strong women was 'Heroine Addiction' (Gary Dauphin *Village Voice*, August 26, 1997, p. 80), whilst Erica Wagner wrote 'O'Neil and Alien's Ripley would probably get on like a house on fire. And what a night out they'd both have with Thelma and Louise' (Wagner 'Great Scott', *The Times*, metro section, 1997, p. 6); one even compared Scott to George Cukor as a generous and empathetic director of strong women (Dennis Lim 'He's not a feminist, but . . .', *Independent on Sunday*, October 26, 1997, p. 27). Tom Charity called him 'the most macho feminist in town' (Tom Charity 'G.I. Jane', *Time Out*, November 19, 1997, p. 87). See also Matthew Sweet 'G.I. Jane' in *Independent on Sunday*, November 16, 1997, section 2, p. 12; Geoff Brown 'Me Tarzan, Says Jane', *The Times*, November 13, 1997, p. 34; Quentin Curtis 'A Movie That Fights With Itself', *Daily Telegraph*, November 14, 1997, p. 28).

3   'Soldier Blue', *Film Review*, December 1997, pp. 52–4: p. 53.

4   Yvonne Tasker *Working Girls: Gender and Sexuality in Popular Cinema*, London: Routledge, 1998, p. 8

5   Zoe Heller 'The Prisoner of Gender', *Sunday Times* magazine, October 12, 1997, pp. 40–2, 44, 46: p. 42.

6   Dauphin 'Heroine Addiction'.

7   Robert Ashley 'G.I. Jane', *Sight and Sound*, 7: 11, November 1997, pp. 42–3: p. 42.

8   All of these women are isolated by being military pioneers: Jordan, Judy and Casey Seegar in *An Officer and a Gentleman* are singled out as the first or only women in their troop; Walden is the first woman to win the Medal of Honor.

9   Tasker puts this the other way around, arguing that bodybuilding culture 'plays on male insecurities in a form that could be seen as analogous to the ways in which women are addressed by beauty culture' (*Spectacular Bodies*, London: Routledge, 1993, p. 79).

10   Richard Dyer 'Don't Look Now', *Screen*, 32: 3–4, 1982, pp. 61–73: p. 71.

11   Ibid.

12   Tasker *Spectacular Bodies*, p. 149.

13   Ibid., p. 78
14   Tasker *Working Girls*, p. 8.
15   James Donald 'Stars' in Pam Cook and Mieke Bernink (eds) *The Cinema Book*, 2nd edition, London: BFI, 1999, pp. 33–9: p. 34.
16   This makes it sometimes hard to extrapolate one from the other: of *G.I. Jane, Empire* critic Deborah Brown wrote, 'Physically, at least, Mrs Willis certainly earns her fee' ('G.I. Jane', *Empire*, 102, December 1997, p. 43).
17   See Richard Dyer *Heavenly Bodies: Film Stars and Society*, Basingstoke: Macmillan, 1986; Christine Gledhill (ed.) *Stardom: Industry of Desire*, London: Routledge, 1991; Jackie Stacey *Star Gazing: Hollywood cinema and female spectatorship*, London: Routledge, 1994.
18   Donald 'Stars', p. 38.
19   Heller 'The Prisoner of Gender', p. 44.
20   Ibid.
21   John Ellis *Visible fictions: Cinema: television: video*, London: Routledge, 1982, p. 91.
22   Ibid., p. 93
23   See *Film Review* (see note 3); Dauphin 'Heroine Addiction'; Gene Siskel 'Siskel on Screen', *T.V. Guide*, September 26, 1998, p. 16.
24   Adam Smith 'Action' (interview with Ridley Scott), *Empire*, 102, December 1997, pp. 110–18: p. 112.
25   Lim 'He's not a feminist'.
26   Richard Williams 'Moore is hell', *The Guardian*, section 2, November 14, 1997, p. 6; Geoff Brown 'Me Tarzan, Says Jane'.
27   Ryan Gilbey 'Corporal punishment', *The Independent*, eye section, November 14, 1997, p. 7.
28   Alexander Walker 'G.I. Jane', *Evening Standard*, November 13, 1997, p. 28.
29   Mark Steyn 'America's Secret Weapon: A Bomb called Demi', *Asian Age*, November 25, 1997, p. 13; Anne Billson 'Review of *G.I. Jane*', *Sunday Telegraph*, review section, November 16, 1997.
30   Ed Vulliamy 'Take it like a man', *The Guardian*, section 2, August 26, 1997, pp. 2–3; Alexander Walker 'The War on Womanhood', *Evening Standard*, June 30, 1997, p. 9.
31   Sweet 'G.I. Jane'; Walker 'G.I. Jane'.
32   Taubin 'Dicks and Jane'.
33   Tasker *Spectacular Bodies*, p. 14.
34   See Philip Finn 'Demi the 'Dirty' GI Comes Under Fire from the Baptist Church', *Evening Standard*, August 12, 1997, p. 31; David Sapsted 'Baptists Turn on Disney Film Venture', *Daily Telegraph*, August 13, 1997, p. 13; Catherine Scroop 'Mouse Trap', *Premiere*, 5: 9, October 1997, p. 16.
35   Taubin 'Dicks and Jane'.
36   As Michael Medved reports, 'Moore helpfully explained: "What clearer way can you say that you're not afraid to be a woman operating in a man's world?"' ('Demi's Monde', *Sunday Times* magazine, June 27, 1993, pp. 24–6: p. 28).
37   Alan Rudolph, who directed her in *Mortal Thoughts*, likened her to 'a beautiful ballerina who can also kickbox' (Lesley O'Toole 'Moore Moore Moore', *The Guardian*, section 2, April 30, 1996, pp. 6–7: p. 7)
38   Smith 'Action', p. 114
39   Philip French 'She Only Asked for a Cut 'n' blow-dry . . .', *The Observer*, review section, November 16, 1997, p. 12. Tasker prefaces her central definition of musculinity with a meditation on the 'ball busting' bitch figure as a woman succeeding in a male team, 'ball busting' thus producing a kind of consequent ball-acquisition (*Spectacular Bodies*, p. 149).
40   Dyer (*Heavenly Bodies*, p. 157) includes the tennis image of Garland, whilst Jackie Stacey discusses and includes the image of Hayward (*Star Gazing*, p. 4).
41   Ridley Scott 'Ridley Scott on . . . G.I. Jane', *Evening Standard*, hot tickets, November 13, 1997, p. 11.

42   Interestingly, one reviewer of *Striptease* had already identified Moore's breasts as instruments of aggression: 'Moore exposes her breasts. They jut out, firm and proud, like weapons, like John Wayne's gun, which was an extension of his body, too' (William Leith 'Boom to Bust', *The Observer*, review section, September 22, 1996, p. 20).

43   Tasker *Spectacular Bodies*, p. 78

## Chapter 11

# MARY BELTRÁN

## *MÁS MACHA*
## The new Latina action hero

A RECENT DEVELOPMENT in the evolution of the Hollywood action genre is the rise of the Latina protagonist. In *Anaconda* (1997), Nuyorican actress Jennifer Lopez portrays documentary director Terri Flores, who adeptly avoids being made into a meal by a series of monstrous snakes in the Brazilian jungle. As Karen Sisco in *Out of Sight* (1998), she is an intrepid federal marshal, albeit with a romantic weakness for bank robbers, who wields weapons with skill and aplomb. Lopez has since portrayed a tomboyish police officer in *Angel Eyes* (2001) and a woman who trains in a deadly martial art to fight her abusive ex-husband in *Enough* (2002). Dominican-Puerto Rican actress Michelle Rodriguez in turn came into the public eye as a tough teenager who learns to box in *Girlfight* (2000). She has followed this role in turns as similarly ballsy and physically active characters, including an illegal street racer in *The Fast and the Furious* (2001) and a paramilitary commando in the futuristic thriller *Resident Evil* (2002). Action is such an integral element of the characters she portrays that she has thrown a punch in almost every one of her films.

And let's not forget Alexa Vega, who, as Carmen Cortez, discovers early in Robert Rodriguez's *Spy Kids* saga that it is her full name, Carmen Elizabeth Juanita y Costa Brava Cortez, and thus indirectly her Latin heritage that is the key that unlocks the Cortez family safe house after her parents are kidnapped. Similarly, she and her brother discover as they come into their own as young spies (highlighting how one can *learn* to become an action hero), 'what's so great about being a Cortez' (*Spy Kids*, 2001). By the opening of the second installment in the series, Carmen is fully recognized as one of the top 'spy kids' in the nation, a young Latina action hero on whom the nation's security depends.

Given the existence of these portrayals among the still relatively small cadre of female action protagonists, Latinas have become prominently visible icons within the genre. While verbally assertive Hispanic female characters have appeared through-out the history of US film – note the history of Latina representation as documented by Charles Ramírez Berg, Carlos E. Cortés, and others,[1] and the occasional appearance of the physically capable Latina in films such as *Total Recall* (1990) and *Aliens* (1986) – Latina protagonists with a sense of physical purpose that puts them among the ranks of the action hero embody a new trend on the rise since the late 1990s.

In light of the history of the action genre as what Yvonne Tasker, Susan Jeffords and others have described as a traditionally white and male-centered domain,[2] it is important to interrogate the emergence of the *más macha* action hero, Latina protagonists who resolve conflicts through physical force, their ability to use weapons and to hone their bodies into weapons, and their bravery in the face of danger, as well as intelligence and skill. In this essay I examine the narrative construction and ideological implications of this new heroine, with a particular focus on characters portrayed by Jennifer Lopez in *Anaconda* and *Out of Sight* and by Michelle Rodriguez in *Girlfight* and *Resident Evil*. In addition, I contextualize this exploration with respect to the history of Latina representation in the Hollywood action genre and in assertive and physically active roles in general.[3] Such a consideration necessarily builds upon and problematizes previous scholarship on action cinema, particularly with respect to the impact of ethnicity and gender in the construction of Latina action protagonists as both active agents and 'spectacular bodies'. Given that Latina stars typically have been constructed as flamboyant, excessive bodies in both film roles and star publicity, as scholars such as Chris Holmlund and I have documented,[4] the interplay of this racialized star function and of the aesthetics and politics of the Hollywood action hero when portrayed by a Latina is fruitful to explore.

## Gender, race, and the evolution of the Latina action hero

In my review of literature exploring the action genre and Latina film representation, no reference was found to the Latina action protagonist, although a few of her predecessors have warranted brief mention, such that this study necessitates piecing together incongruent scholarship to illuminate this new trend. Particularly useful is Rosa Linda Fregoso's insightful explication of the *pachuca-chola*-homegirl and her positioning within the realm of Hollywood drama, which highlights the long-term presence and power of the assertive and socially transgressive Latina in US Latino (and the broader 'American') culture, as well as in Hollywood film.[5] In this essay I stretch Fregoso's discussion to examine the elevation of the *pachuca* in the role of the action heroine in more recent years. In addition, I build on Tasker's foundational work on gender, race, and the spectacle of the body in Hollywood action cinema. I set out in particular to interrogate Tasker's explication of the action heroine as 'distanced from a classed and raced "femininity" which is defined by passivity and hysteria'.[6] I aim in this respect to account for the complexities of the construction of the Latina action hero, given that Latinas traditionally are already distanced from a classed and raced (white) femininity in Hollywood film, as I have discussed elsewhere with respect to Latina star images.[7]

What qualities elevate a protagonist to the status of action hero? From the action film's legacy in the Western and adventure genres of prior decades, we have come to expect action heroes and heroines to be defined by their physicality and their fight against an evil figure and/or corrupt system. In this regard the body is of prime importance, the ultimate iconographic element of many action films. As Tasker notes, 'in the action cinemas of both Hong Kong and America, the body of the hero or heroine is their ultimate, and often their only, weapon'.[8] Until fairly recently, however, not just any body would do. The persona of the physically active Hollywood protagonist has been tied to 'freedom of movement, confidence in the body' and 'engagement with the material world', notions previously and often still associated with white, male, and straight bodies in the public imagination, as Richard Dyer asserts.[9] Given this history, the nascent presence of the Latina action hero challenges many preconceptions of the genre.

Similarly, the iconography associated with the action film is telling with respect to the relative invisibility of Latina protagonists before the late 1990s. The public sphere of the street historically has been underscored as the social – and cinematic – domain of men, particularly when Latinas are considered, as Fregoso asserts. Fregoso notes that *pachucas*, the predecessor of the *chola* in the Latino community, were known in her hometown in Texas as '*muchachas corrientes y callejeras* (cheap, street-roaming girls)' because they refused to abide by cultural prohibitions regarding socially proscribed male and female territory.[10] The action genre, similarly, outlined its traditional landscapes as male-only turf until recent decades, when strong and active female protagonists began to be included in substantial roles. This was the case particularly in films that blended action genre conventions with those of science fiction, resulting in diegetic worlds that offered narrative detours from contemporary realities. Even in such fantastic realms Latina heroines were few and far between before the late 1990s, however.

Even so, a Latina legacy in this regard can be traced back to the classic Western. Carlos E. Cortés discusses the rise of strong and assertive Latina characters, such as Chihuahua (played by Anglo actress Linda Darnell) in *My Darling Clementine* (1946) and Helen Ramirez as portrayed by Katy Jurado in *High Noon* (1952), in Westerns of the 1940s to 1960s. These were strong figures, although they were marginal to the storyline of the white leads. Less positive versions of the *cantinera* or cantina girl appeared in such low-budget Westerns as *The Alamo* (1960) and *The Professionals* (1966), as Frank Javier Garcia Berumen notes.[11] As might be assumed from Berumen's descriptor, most were prostitutes or otherwise socially transgressive women, fitting Fregoso's description of the *pachuca* as a woman of taboo sexual knowledge who transgressed the confines of the patriarchal home (although also without a place of acceptance within Chicano or Anglo cultures).

Such characters predate the physically active and assertive women, typically Anglo but occasionally African American or Latina, that began appearing in low-budget film cycles of the 1960s and 1970s such as urban gang films, teen delinquency films, and women-in-prison films. Such films were freer of constraints than studio fare and in fact often capitalized on the sensationalism of tough women battling with confidence and aggression, as in the extreme case of the violent anti-hero Varla, played by Tura Satana in Russ Meyer's *Faster Pussycat, Kill! Kill!* (1965). Latinas began to be featured in the limited, girl gang-member role in urban dramas in particular. Rita Moreno's role as Anita in *West Side Story* (1961) is one of the best known and most sanitized examples. In later decades such images were recycled in urban dramas that featured Latino gangs; a more notorious version is the part of Louisa played by Maria Conchita Alonso in *Colors* (1988). Such films, similarly to Westerns of previous decades, often posited Latina characters as untrustworthy, sexually promiscuous, potentially violent, and inherently fiery in personality, 'harlots' as described by Charles Ramírez Berg in his scholarship.[12]

The 1980s brought physically assertive and generally Anglo female characters into the bigger budget and thus more mainstream 'muscular cinema' of the decade.[13] Female police officers and other physically assertive female characters began to appear in this formerly all-male terrain in such films as *Raiders of the Lost Ark* (1981) and *Robocop* (1987), but generally were relegated to the role of marginal sidekick or love interest. A few Latina actresses were among their ranks in lower budget films, as was the case for then-rising stars Elpidia Carrillo in *Predator* (1987) and Maria Conchita Alonso in *The Running Man* (1987) and *Predator 2* (1990).

By the late 1980s and early 1990s, physically assertive female characters rose to the level of protagonists in their own right. The melding of science fiction and action genres also offered up female protagonists who 'combine[d] musculature and military skills' at the safe remove of fantasy, as Carol M. Dole argues[14]; notable examples include the characters portrayed by Linda Hamilton in *Terminator 2* (1991) and Sigourney Weaver in the *Alien* series. While there were occasional, powerful Latinas in the sci-fi/action hybrids of this period, including the role of Private Vasquez (played by non-Latina Jenette Goldstein) in *Aliens* and of Melina (Rachel Ticotín) in *Total Recall*, these characters were ultimately subservient to the white lead characters' storylines. In the case of Private Vasquez in *Aliens*, moreover, Kathleen Newman's assertion of the trope of sacrifice demanded of Latinos in multicultural ensemble films of the 1980s also applied: If a strong Latina's ethnicity was foregrounded, she was going to die in the name of the protagonist's cause before the story ended.[15]

Such ethnic-specific patterns began to change as the racial mix of Hollywood action film protagonists shifted in the mid to late 1990s, however. African American, Latino, Asian, and other non-white characters, both men and women, began entering the ranks of the Hollywood action protagonist at this juncture, as Yvonne Tasker, Ed Guerrero, and others have noted.[16] Recent roles portrayed by Wesley Snipes, Angela Bassett, Jet Li, Keanu Reeves, Michelle Rodriguez, and Lucy Liu are among these new icons. This rise in Hollywood cops, saviors of the world, and vampire slayers of color arguably reflects not only diegetic revolution, but also industry developments and shifting cultural preoccupations.

For one thing, the rise of Latino-produced feature films in the 1980s and 1990s provided more fully dimensional versions of former *pachuca* characters that arguably have informed the representation of assertive and physically capable Latinas in studio-backed films since. Films such as Gregory Nava's *El Norte* (1983) and *My Family/Mi Familia* (1995) and Luis Valdez's *Zoot Suit* (1981) included fully narrativized Latinas who could hold their own in the face of societal and personal obstacles that included poverty and racism. Such characters still often served the storylines of male protagonists, however. More recent films have furthered developed Latina subjectivity. Allison Anders' *Mi Vida Loca/My Crazy Life* (1993) was a revelation in this regard with respect to moving such characters from the periphery to the fulcrum of the narrative and endowing protagonists Mousie, Sad Girl, and their friends with subjectivity and purpose. Given this history of representations, the casting of Jennifer Lopez in such roles as that of Karen Sisco in *Out of Sight* and of Michelle Rodriguez in *Girlfight* are milestones in an ongoing progression.

In addition, the evolution of the cinematic action hero has resulted from industrial developments in the 'New' New Hollywood. Aside from bigger budgets and thus the need for bigger profits, in essence a boost from B-list to A-list status for many action films, these shifts include the increasing hybridity of film genres, what José Arroyo refers to as a rising 'slippage . . . between contemporary Hollywood cinema, action/spectacle, high concept, and the blockbuster'.[17] This blending of the action genre with romantic comedy, science fiction, urban gang films and so on arguably challenges the policing of the prototypical terrain of the action narrative as primarily male or white turf, calling into question the definition of the action hero and who can be described as such. The film industry also has become increasingly aware of the growing economic power and influence of female and ethnic audiences and of the need to appeal to both while still drawing in its former target audience of young, white, and male moviegoers. Latinos now comprise more than 12 percent of the population, making us the largest non-white ethnic group in the US, and are more likely than any other ethnic group to go to the movies.[18] Meanwhile, non-whites as a whole now comprise approximately 30 percent of the total population. Female moviegoers, in turn, are seen as 'driving' the film audience, as former Fox Film Chairman Bill Mechanic noted during his tenure in the mid-1990s.[19] These shifts are reflected in the rise of protagonists meant to appeal to an increasingly diverse audience with respect to ethnicity and gender; the entrance of the Latina action hero can be seen as a natural reflection of such shifts. In addition, the growing popularity and box office success of actors such as Jennifer Lopez, Michelle Rodriguez, and Benicio Del Toro, in both domestic and international markets, has spurred an interest in casting and promoting Latinas and Latinos in bigger budget films, as producers such as Moctesuma Esparza attest.[20] Such actors are part of a growing 'Latinowood' of bankable Hollywood actors, particularly in comparison to a decade ago.

## Jennifer Lopez holds her own: *Anaconda* and *Out of Sight*

The action film roles of Jennifer Lopez serve as apt illustrations of these developments. When Lopez starred in Luis Llosa's *Anaconda* in 1997, her role in *Selena* the same year overshadowed this portrayal with respect to both critical acclaim and mainstream attention. Downplayed by critics as B-film fare showcasing an animatronic snake, *Anaconda* nevertheless made a healthy profit that contributed to Lopez's growing stardom. The film grossed almost $70 million in domestic release alone from its $35 million budget.[21] Lopez's lead role also distinctly challenged previous patterns of Latina representation, setting the stage for future Latina action protagonists.

In this horror-action exploitation film sendup, Lopez (see Figure 11.1) stars as an assertive documentary director who must face down a Brazilian jungle full of killer anacondas and an equally deadly snake poacher, played by Jon Voight. Despite the multiple dangers, Terri proves capable of protecting herself – with a little help from her friend and cameraman, Danny (Ice Cube) – even while most of her crew is eventually felled (some even eaten whole). While competently rising to such challenges as the temporary poisoning of her love interest, expedition leader Professor Cale (Eric Stoltz), she also livens the jungle setting with her clingy, though expedition-appropriate ensembles. Terri as embodied by Lopez in fact can be seen as one prototype of the distinctly Latina action protagonist in her dual construction as both a particularly sexy woman and a capable fighter when she must protect herself or her charges.

This duality is established in Terri's introduction in the narrative. She is alone in her hotel room, wearing only a short nightgown, using a laptop computer to research the indigenous tribe that they are hoping to record on film in the jungle. Professor Cale arrives; Terri puts on a robe but does not close it, establishing both her intimacy with Cale and one aspect of her role in the film, as eye candy in the B-movie tradition. Llosa's camera in particular fetishizes Lopez's body in its framing and tendency to linger throughout the film. Despite this visual 'tease', Terri does not respond fully to Cale's flirting, however; she is intent on the job at hand. Moreover, the next scene establishes that Terri is more than a sexy body and thus will survive the onslaught of horror to follow. As their boat is being prepared, Terri

*Figure 11.1* Ice Cube and Jennifer Lopez in *Anaconda* (1997). Courtesy of the Kobal Collection

welcomes her friend Danny. We learn that they met in film school at 'SC', the University of Southern California, which is situated in a working-class neighborhood in downtown Los Angeles. From this background Lopez's street credibility and thus ability to take care of herself in rough circumstances are established, which arguably is buttressed by her aesthetic appearance as a visible Latina and associations of the urban Latina with the *pachuca-chola*-homegirl. Moreover, despite Terri's role as a 'spectacular body' (in a different respect than I believe Tasker intended), she also abstains from a focus on sex and otherwise displays androgynous traits, establishing her Final Girl role within the narrative. In her discussion with Danny, Terri states, 'You know me, I don't mix business with pleasure'. While the unconscious state of her potential boyfriend through much of the narrative aids in this construction, Terri focuses on the job at hand, and later the crew's safety, rather than romance or sex. (A few of her crew are not so lucky, seeing as, as one of them says, 'the jungle makes you really horny'.)

In addition, Lopez's characterization illustrates how at times age-old stereotypes are skewered in the construction of the Latina action protagonist. In one notable scene, Terri manages to convince the evil poacher Paul, who had commandeered their boat to take it into anaconda territory, to let down his guard through performing the harlot role. He kisses her, thinking she is vulnerable and sexually available to him; in this moment the rest of the crew are able to overcome him. On the other hand, other long-term stereotypes are still foundational to the characterization of Terri Flores. For instance, while limited by her physical abilities, the narrative poses Terri as easily able to throw a punch or use a weapon. She does not hesitate to use a shotgun to save her friend from an anaconda, although she presumably has never used one. And when Terri discovers that the tragedies her crew has experienced have been engineered by Paul, now tied up on the boat's deck, she is quick to confront him angrily and to punch him. Such action arguably is made believable in part because of her Latina and presumably urban background, which establishes expectations of her ability to fight and be stoic in the face of danger. These expectations paint Terri as a survivor, an urban and raced Final Girl who also happens to serve in the role of the beautiful spectacle.

Lopez experiences a similar, and similarly dual construction as Karen Sisco in her next film, *Out of Sight*. This duality is aided greatly by the genre hybridity of the film. In combining the genres of the cop film, crime caper, and romantic comedy, expectations of Hollywood femininity are melded with traditional expectations of the action hero in the narrative. In this manner, director Steven Soderbergh positions Karen Sisco simultaneously as 'tough cop and soft hearted lover', as Carol M. Dole asserts.[22] Again, these expectations are quickly established in the scene in which Karen Sisco is introduced in the narrative. It opens on Karen dining out with an older man, presumably her boyfriend. She is dressed in a feminine dress ensemble and lit in a manner that highlights her beauty. The man presents her with a gift; Karen opens the box and we see her pure pleasure at its contents. When the camera finally reveals the nature of the gift, it becomes clear that Karen is not what she first appears, or rather she is that and much more. It is not a piece of jewelry, as traditional gender expectations would lead us to believe, but a gun, and, we learn quickly, a tool she will use in her job as a federal marshal. The man presenting the gift also is not an older boyfriend but her father, who fully supports her potentially dangerous choice to work in law enforcement. Karen is established in this scene as attractive, but even more so as assertive, proficient with weapons, and capable of protecting herself.

Throughout the narrative Soderbergh reinforces this dual construction of Karen Sisco as sexy, yet extremely physically capable, a 'feisty woman' heroine by Tasker's description. She is shown in interactions with her law enforcement peers that establish her experience, grit, and comfort going against the grain, while her first encounter with Jack Foley and his associates illustrate that she is brave and capable with a weapon. Karen's strong subjectivity also is established by Soderbergh through her separate story line and POV scenes, such as her dream of a romantic liaison with Jack before they actually meet up again. Simultaneously, through a number of cinematic strategies Karen is visually constructed as possessing what can be termed a 'spectacular heterosexuality'. For instance, Soderbergh's lighting and use of frequent close-ups emphasize both Lopez and Clooney's attractiveness and the sexual tension in the film. Camerawork that focuses on Lopez as an attractive female also serves the cop caper storyline, however. For instance, while the camera lingers on Lopez's body and briefly on her rear end in a few scenes, this is often in moments immediately before Karen takes decisive and strong action; such is the case when the camera focuses concertedly on Lopez's rear end before she pulls her shotgun out of the trunk of her car upon seeing the prison escapees.

While Karen Sisco's full ethnic background is in fact difficult to determine, given that her father appears to be Italian and her mother is deceased, she arguably takes on a Latina – or usefully indeterminate – ethnic identity with respect to her ability to connect with characters of various ethnic and socioeconomic backgrounds in order to fulfill her police work. She also quite easily protects herself from the physical advances of a sexually predatory (and notably, African American) informant in Detroit. This scene serves as an illustration of Karen Sisco's innate ability to calmly protect herself. Again, Lopez's Latin ethnicity and thus association with 'urban' street smarts arguably makes this construction more believable. Problematically, it also elevates her character in relation to an African American character and what is constructed as black criminality.

## Michelle Rodriguez: a new *macha* heroine for a new era?

Michelle Rodriguez, in contrast, is unique among Latina stars in that she experienced her feature film *debut* in an extremely physical role that showcased her intensity and ability to fight and was fully centered on her subjectivity. As Diana Guzman in *Girlfight* (see Figure 11.2), Rodriguez portrays a teenager who acts out her disappointment over an unhappy home life through violence, who ultimately gains discipline and self-esteem through training to become a boxer. Along the way, the character of Diana, while engaging in physicality primarily in the boxing ring, undergoes many of the spiritual and physical trials that we expect of the action hero.

*Figure 11.2* Michelle Rodriguez and Jaime Tirelli in *Girlfight* (2000). Courtesy of the Kobal Collection

Rodriguez, ironically, was a screenwriting hopeful making ends meet through work as a film extra when she decided to take a chance on auditioning for the role of Diana.[23] The film's director, Karyn Kusama, expresses in the DVD commentary that she wanted to tell the story of an anti-hero 'who also happened to be a woman', and that Rodriguez won the role with her ability to bring the character to life with raw energy. Having trained as an amateur boxer herself, Kusama also was intent on shaping a narrative about a female protagonist who bettered her life through engaging in the physicality of the sport. She describes that there is 'something powerful about women in motion . . . [who are] after merely their own dignity . . . and goal setting'.[24] As such *Girlfight* challenges gender typing with respect to the physical and mental training and qualities we associate with heroism. As film critic Roger Ebert commented in his review, 'This is a story about a girl growing up in a macho society and, far from being threatened by its values, discovering that she has a nature probably more macho than the men around her'.[25] In this regard, *Girlfight* comments on the qualities associated with masculinity in US culture, and the tradition of resistance to women demonstrating such so-called 'masculine' traits.

One of the chief messages of the film is that a girl perceived by society as 'nothing but trouble' in fact has the potential to become a champion through determination, discipline, and encouragement. The uncouth, aggressive woman that is Diana Guzman at the onset of the narrative is shown to also be the (untrained) action protagonist. As Kusama notes in the director's commentary, it is powerful to see a girl respected enough to be *taught* to fight. Crudely drawn signs tacked up around the run-down boxing club where Diana trains, emblazoned with such sayings as 'Champions are made not born', and 'It's not the size of the dog, it's the size of the fight of the dog', further reiterate the sentiment that everyone, regardless of gender or ethnic background, can train to become powerful if they struggle and persevere. In this and other respects, the narrative and its characters challenge traditional cinematic definitions of both heroic action and of the action protagonist.

Even today Hollywood does not easily translate such complexities, however. An apparent uncertainly about what to do with a strongly subjective and highly physical Latina within narrative storyworlds is evident in Rodriguez's next decided action role, in *Resident Evil*. The role of Rain Ocampo as portrayed by Rodriguez in the film provides an interesting counterpoint to the more heterosexually framed, feisty women played by Jennifer Lopez. Rain, like several other roles portrayed by Rodriguez, is a tomboy character, a natural fighter who demonstrates almost no traditionally feminine qualities or romantic interest in the opposite sex. She in fact is almost a parodic character in this regard, with lines like 'Blow me' and a penchant for cleaning her nails with her knife before using it to do battle with a zombie. The futuristic, over-the-top storyline calls for such extreme behavior, however. *Resident Evil* is based on a video game of the same name: Rain is part of a paramilitary team that must contain a deadly virus in a secret research facility before it infects the rest of the world, fighting zombies and mutating creatures along the way. The film adaptation poses Milla Jovovich and Rodriguez as leaders of the team, although Jovovich is the brain to Rodriguez's brawn within the strategic scheme of things.

The character is perhaps Rodriguez's most stoical to date, again illustrating the typical construction of Latina action protagonists as inherently fierce and fearless. She is described by reviewers as 'the tough-talking, attitude-throwing veteran of *The Fast and the Furious*',[26] 'always spunky',[27] and as 'radiat[ing] enough bad-ass attitude to intimidate even a couple of flesh-eating zombies'.[28] Rodriguez's limited character development, however, confirms that Hollywood creatives do not quite know what to do with the physically capable Latina action protagonist after she's handily escaped a catacomb full of zombies, particularly when she is paired with a white female. *Resident Evil* in this respect illustrates that Hollywood narrative traditions that historically gave primacy to white characters at the expense of Hispanics die hard, even while there is a growing interest in Hispanic stars and general appeal to ethnically diverse audiences. Even while Jovovich and Rodriguez are both capable fighters in the film, it is the character of Alice, portrayed by Jovovich, who is endowed with a more nuanced subjectivity. The story opens on Alice waking up in the Umbrella complex, stricken with amnesia even while paramilitary commandos, including Rain, break in to help her contain the deadly virus and escape the complex. Much of the ensuing storyline focuses on Alice regaining her memory about the role she had played that set the stage for this crisis. Alongside this narrative emphasis on Alice's mental state and emotions, Rain is relegated to 'assertive sidekick' status. Additionally, just as Private Vasquez was marked as distinctly different from Ripley in *Aliens*, contemptuously referring to her as 'Snow White' upon their first meeting, Rain's characterization is built in large measure on how she is distinct from Alice. She is a fighting machine, willing to lay down her life for their mission, but without demonstration of this commitment springing from a deeper sense of humanity. In this regard, Alice is elevated as the most natural leader of the two.

Ultimately Rodriguez turns into a zombie herself, a tragedy that the surviving Anglo action heroine must bear. Rain arguably would have been killed off much earlier in the narrative a decade ago, however, a Latina sacrifice in the name of citizenship, to draw on Newman's work. The fact that she lives until almost the end of the narrative arguably is a sign not only of Rodriguez's current star status but also of the rising status of the Latino audience in the eyes of Hollywood film producers. Living almost until the end is a sign of progress in a genre in which Latinas formerly were only included as victims to be saved by heroic white male counterparts, or as ensemble members created almost solely for the sacrifice they would offer to the cause held by the (white) survivors.

## The mojo of the *macha* Latina

Given these examples of the new, physically commanding Latina heroines, what can we make of the *más macha* action hero, particularly in light of the scholarship of Thomas Schatz and others that posits that the preoccupations and evolution of cinematic genres, including their typical heroes and iconography, reflect the cultural concerns of a given era?[29]

Scholars and cultural critics have generally disagreed regarding how to interpret the physical aggression of non-white female protagonists, in a debate that also illuminates this critique. Some argue that black action heroines of the 1970s, for example, are based on associations of African American women with 'vulgarity, violence, and vanity', as the Reverend Jesse Jackson asserted in 1972.[30] Richie Pérez has made a similar assertion with respect to the portrayal of Puerto Rican gang members as 'oversexed' and inherently violent in films of the 1960s.[31] According to such interpretations, the violence of non-white females is often constructed as due to innate, animalistic aggression. As Kimberly Springer argues, 'the violence of Black women always seems a result of their being Black, [while] the violence of white women is often celebrated as liberatory'.[32] Such dichotomies, part and parcel of the nation's post-colonial imaginary and Hollywood's related 'pigmentocracy' of racial and ethnic status,[33] are beginning to be challenged in contemporary representations, however.

Springer underscores the interplay of class discourses in such constructions in her assertion that contemporary films portray the violence of black female characters as coming in part from 'a devilish "Sapphire" within'.[34] As she describes, referring to this legacy of representation:

> [The Sapphire] is not afraid to be loud and speak her mind. Her danger lies within her words and only *home training* constrains her violence. Most African Americans are familiar with the concept: 'That girl ain't got no home training.' A lack of home training marks a deficiency in breeding.

> Home training is about being well mannered in public, being a lady, and being middle class or working toward that class status.[35]

Springer thus highlights 'the mediating influence of money' in the establishment of narrative expectations for physically active and assertive ethnic female characters.[36] The mediating influence of money is apparent, for instance, in the construction of the Latina action hero, in this analysis most notably with respect to the characters of Terri Flores, Diana Guzman, and presumably Rain Ocampo. All three are characterized as having come from a working-class background, hinting at – and in the case of Diana Guzman, quite literally embodying – the presence of a Sapphire within.

In addition, and as alluded to earlier, the association of Latina action protagonists with urban environments contributes to the construction of these characters as more formidable than their Anglo female counterparts. In the case of the roles played by Michelle Rodriguez and of Terri Flores as portrayed by Jennifer Lopez, these are characters who have not had the luxury of being protected from the street and thus have gained strength and mastery over it. This connection arguably is made more easily because both actresses are Latina. In addition, as Deena J. Gonzalez asserts, centuries-old imagery of the sexually available Latina and the related threat of sexual harassment have been all-too-real issues that contemporary Latinas, not protected by wealth and related trappings of whiteness, have had to face.[37] Thus for Chicanas and other Latinas in the US, it has been vital to be seemingly unafraid and able to defend themselves in order not to be earmarked as victims. It is no coincidence then that the related, automatic 'street credibility' of Latina cinematic protagonists presupposes their ability to fight, diminishing the need for such characters to prove their physical prowess through musculature or other 1980s-era action heroine paraphernalia.

Moreover, the aggression of Latinas is often 'excused' to a great extent by the actual or presumed social context in Hollywood films, similarly to how the physically aggressive responses of non-white characters in Blaxploitation films and other urban dramas have often been posed as the natural and just response to racism, sexism, or other forms of discrimination. This argument can be extrapolated from Judith Halberstam's discussion of the 'different stakes different people might have in rhetorics of retaliation, revenge, and violent response' in film narratives.[38] From this perspective, social problems such as poverty, racism, and a failing public education system that obstruct some Latinas from bettering their lives can be viewed by audiences as just rationale for aggressive or criminal behavior in film narratives, as Roger Ebert argued was the case for the African American protagonists of *Set It Off* (1996).[39] *Girlfight* in particular provides such a rationale for Diana Guzman's explosive aggression at the onset of the narrative.

The rise of the Latina hero within the action genre has relevance with respect to contemporary cultural concerns in more general terms as well. Considering that the US is at a crossroads with respect to rapidly changing ethnic demographics and notions of 'race' and race relations at the onset of the twenty-first century, as numerous scholars and critics assert,[40] Latina action protagonists, whether read as Latina and thus of mixed racial heritage or as ethnically ambiguous, arguably provide a visual and ideological referent that is compelling to audiences today. Embodying cultural concerns and related schisms in a manner reminiscent to (and overlapping with) the function of star images as described by Richard Dyer, Joshua Gamson and others,[41] the *más macha* heroine is both an of-the-moment cinematic role model symbolizing Latina and national progress on a number of fronts, and a smokescreen in relation to inequities that continue to prevent many Latinas from gaining power in real life.

In addition, previous patterns of Latina star promotion also have assisted in the construction and palatability of the contemporary Latina action hero. I refer elsewhere to the historical tendency within Hollywood film and star publicity for Latina actresses to be promoted as hypersexual, innately inviting bodies or in relation to metaphors of tropicalism, such as allusions to heat and spice.[42] For instance, emphasis on the body and what has been constructed as inordinate physical attractiveness has been key to the marketing of Jennifer Lopez as a rising star. Given this Hollywood treatment of Latinas, femininity and physicality are typically not placed at opposite poles for the Latina action protagonist. This duality can contribute to the construction of a Latina action heroine who is powerful, but viewed as sexier than the average woman, so that the transgression of aggression is more palatable. In essence, these characteristics of the *más macha* protagonist disrupt the risk of displaced femininity with which Anglo action heroines have had to contend. By extension, many assumptions of previous critical scholarship on the action heroine are called into question in relation to the Latina protagonist. Take Jennifer Lopez, for example, who has been the most successful Latina at the box office in action roles. She demonstrates in her action roles, rather than a compromised femininity, what could be termed a *spectacular heterosexuality* – including wardrobes and camera framing that highlight her body prominently at multiple points – that arguably softens these characterizations and contributes to their appeal.

While Jennifer Lopez has moved on to bigger budget films since *Anaconda* and *Out of Sight*, physicality continues to be a primary feature of many of her roles, as was the case in the films *Angel Eyes* and *Enough*. *Enough* in particular evolved from melodramatic domestic drama to full-out action film in scenes that showcased Lopez's character, formerly a battered wife, training in the martial art Krav Maga in order to battle her abusive and obsessive ex-husband in a *mano a mano* fight to the death. Michelle Rodriguez, in turn, continues to actively pursue action film roles over other offers, noting in interviews that in this way she aims to enjoy herself and to be a positive female role model. It will be important to follow the implications of the physicality of the characters that both actresses and that other Latinas portray in future roles with respect to the challenge these developments represent to Hollywood, as well as in regard to how such scholarship promises to interrogate previous assumptions of feminist critical work on gender and the action film.

## Notes

1  See for example Charles Ramírez Berg *Latino Images in Film: Stereotypes, Subversion, & Resistance*, Austin: University of Texas Press, 2002; Carlos E Cortés 'Chicanas in Film: History of an Image', in Clara E. Rodríguez (ed.) *Latin Looks: Images of Latinas and Latinos in the U.S. Media*, Boulder, CO: Westview, 1997, pp. 121–41; Ana M. López 'Are All Latins

from Manhattan?: Hollywood, Ethnography, and Cultural Colonialism', in Lester D. Friedman (ed.) *Unspeakable Images: Ethnicity and the American Cinema*, Urbana: University of Illinois Press, 1991, pp. 404–24.

2   See for example Yvonne Tasker *Spectacular Bodies: Gender, Genre and the Action Cinema*, London: Routledge, 1993, and *Working Girls: Gender and Sexuality in Popular Cinema*, London: Routledge, 1998; Susan Jeffords *Hard Bodies: Hollywood Masculinity in the Reagan Era*, New Brunswick, NJ: Rutgers University Press, 1994; and Martha McCaughey and Neal King (eds) *Reel Knockouts: Violent Women in the Movies*, Austin: University of Texas Press, 2001.

3   I would like to thank my friend Lee Sparks, *más macho* independent scholar, for sharing his extensive knowledge of the history of the action genre as I was researching this aspect of the study.

4   Christine Holmlund *Impossible Bodies: Femininity and Masculinity at the Movies*, London: Routledge, 2002; Mary C. Beltrán *Bronze Seduction: The Shaping of Latina Stardom in Hollywood Film and Star Publicity*, Dissertation, University of Texas at Austin, 2002, and 'The Holly-wood Latina Body as Site of Social Struggle: Media Constructions of Stardom and Jennifer Lopez's "Cross-over Butt"', *Quarterly Review of Film and Video*, 19: 1–13, 2002, pp. 71–86.

5   Fregoso 'Homegirls, *Cholas*, and *Pachucas* in Cinema: Taking Over the Public Sphere', *California History*, Fall 1995, pp. 317–27.

6   Tasker *Working Girls*, p. 69.

7   See Beltrán *Bronze Seduction*.

8   'Fists of Fury: Discourses of Race and Masculinity in the Martial Arts Cinema', in Harry Stecopoulos and Michael Uebel (eds) *Race and the Subject of Masculinities*, Durham, NC: Duke University Press, 1997, pp. 315–36: p. 316.

9   'Action!' in José Arroyo (ed.) *Action/Spectacle Cinema*, London: British Film Institute, pp. 17–21: p. 18

10  Fregoso, 'Homegirls, *Cholas*, and *Pachucas* in Cinema: Taking Over the Public Sphere', *California History*, Fall 1995, p. 318.

11  Frank Javier Garcia Berumen *The Chicano/Hispanic Image in American Film*, New York: Vantage, 1995.

12  Berg's explication of the Hispanic harlot first appeared in 'Stereotyping in Films in General and of the Hispanic in Particular', *Howard Journal of Communications*, 2: 3, Summer 1990, pp. 286–300. A revised version of this essay can be found in Chapter Three, 'A Crash Course in Latino Imagery,' in Berg *Latino Images in Film*.

13  Tasker *Spectacular Bodies*, p. 1

14  Carol M. Dole 'The Gun and the Badge: Hollywood and the Female Lawman', in McCaughey and King (eds) *Reel Knockouts*, p. 78.

15  Kathleen Newman 'Latino Sacrifice in the Discourse of Citizenship: Acting Against the "Mainstream," 1985–1988', in Chon A. Noriega (ed.) *Chicanos and Film: Representation and Resistance*, Minneapolis: University of Minnesota Press, 1992, pp. 59–73.

16  Tasker *Spectacular Bodies: Gender, Genre and the Action Cinema*, 1993 and *Working Girls: Gender and Sexuality in Popular Cinema*, 1998; Ed Guerrero 'The Black Image in Protective Custody: Hollywood's Biracial Buddy Films of the Eighties', in Manthia Diawara (ed.) *Black American Cinema*, London: Routledge, 1993, pp. 237–46, and Ed Guerrero *Framing Blackness: The African American Image in Film*, Philadelphia: Temple University Press, 1993.

17  Arroyo 'Preface', in Arroyo (ed.) *Action/Spectacle Cinema*, p. v.

18  As concluded by a Tomás Rivera Policy Institute study. Harry Pachon, Luis DiSipio, Rudolfo de la Garza and Chon Noriega 'Missing in Action: Latinos In and Out of Hollywood', reprinted in Chon Noriega (ed.) *The Future of Latino Independent Media: A NALIP Sourcebook*, Los Angeles: UCLA Chicano Studies Research Center, 1999, pp. 15–58.

19  McCaughey and King 'What's a Mean Woman Like You Doing in a Movie Like This?', in McCaughey and King (eds) *Reel Knockouts*, pp. 1–24: p. 19.

20  Esparza produced such films as *The Milagro Beanfield War* (1988) and *Selena* (1997). He has noted in interviews that studios were more receptive to Latino-oriented film projects and to promoting Latina and Latino actors in lead roles after the financial success of *Selena*.

21   Elysa Gardner 'How Lopez Fills Out Her Career', *USA Today,* August 11, 2000, Life pp. 2E.
22   Carol M. Dole, 'The Gun and The Badge', p. 99.
23   Désiree Guzetta 'Michelle Rodriguez: The Girl Fights On', *Estylo,* June/July 2001, pp. 56–63: p. 57.
24   Karyn Kusama, audio commentary, *Girlfight,* Columbia Tri-Star, 2001.
25   *Chicago Sun-Times,* September 29, 2000. Available at http://www.suntimes.com/ebert/ebert_reviews/2000/09/092903.html, accessed March 2, 2003.
26   Jan Stuart '*Resident Evil*'s Gore is Guilty Fun', *New York Newsday,* March 15, 2002. Available at http://www.calendarlife.com/movies/reviews/cl-movie000018886mar15.story, accessed March 2, 2003.
27   Mick LaSalle 'Resident Evil', *San Francisco Chronicle,* March 15, 2002. Available at http://www.sfgate.com/cgi-bun/article.cgi?f=/c/a/2002/03/15/DD162364.DTL, accessed March 2, 2003.
28   Joe Leydon 'Game Over', *San Francisco Examiner,* March 15, 2002. Available at http://www.examiner.com/sfx/templates/printer.jsp?story=X0315RESIDENTw., accessed March 2, 2003.
29   Thomas Schatz *Hollywood Genres: Formulas, Filmmaking, and the Studio System,* Philadelphia: Temple University Press, 1981.
30   Quoted in Guerrero *Framing Blackness*, p. 100.
31   Pérez 'From Assimilation to Annihilation: Puerto Rican Images in US Films', in Rodríguez *Latin Looks*, pp. 142–63: p. 146.
32   Kimberly Springer 'Waiting to Set It Off: African American Women and the Sapphire Fixation', in McCaughey and King *Reel Knockouts*, pp. 172–99: p. 173.
33   Alejandro Lipshutz quoted in Robert Stam *Tropical Multiculturalism: A Comparative History of Race in Brazilian Cinema and Culture,* Durham, NC: Duke University Press, 1997, p. 47.
34   McCaughey and King 'What's a Mean Woman Like You Doing in a Movie Like This?', p. 8.
35   Springer 'Waiting to Set It Off', p. 176.
36   Ibid., p. 173.
37   Deena J. Gonzalez 'Lupe's Song: On the Origins of Mexican/Woman-Hating in the United States', in Curtis Stokes, Theresa Meléndez and Genise Rhodes-Reed (eds) *Race in 21st Century America,* East Lansing: Michigan State University Press, 2001, pp. 143–58.
38   Judith Halberstam 'Imagined Violence/Queer Violence: Representations of Rage and Resistance', in McCaughey and King (eds) *Reel Knockouts*, p. 245.
39   Quoted in Springer 'Waiting to Set It Off', p. 181.
40   See for example the various authors in Stokes, Meléndez and Rhodes-Reed (eds) *Race in 21st Century America,* based on a national conference of the same title held at Michigan State University in April 1999.
41   Richard Dyer *Heavenly Bodies: Film Stars and Society*, Basingstoke: Macmillan, 1986; Joshua Gamson *Claims to Fame: Celebrity in Contemporary America*, Berkeley: University of California Press, 1994; Christine Gledhill (ed.) *Stardom: Industry of Desire*, London: Routledge, 1991.
42   Beltrán *Bronze Seduction.*

## Chapter 12

# MARC O'DAY

## BEAUTY IN MOTION
## Gender, spectacle and action babe cinema

### The contemporary action babe cinema phenomenon

ONE OF THE MOST STRIKING DEVELOPMENTS in recent popular cinema has been the wave of action-adventure films featuring attractive women stars as hugely capable heroines 'kicking ass' in a range of fantasy-oriented screen worlds. These movies trade in the fare of contemporary 'high concept' cinema – elevated 'B' movie genre materials, episodic plots, breathtaking visual spectacle of the post-*Matrix* combat stunts, amazing digital effects and computer generated imagery variety and tie-in friendly musical soundtracks – but what marks them out in the field are the beautiful, sexy and tough heroines who command their narratives, invariably driving vehicles, shooting guns, wielding weapons or fighting in hand-to-hand combat better than their (frequently male) adversaries.[1]

Undoubtedly the most iconic of these is Angelina Jolie's potent incarnation of the world's most famous video game character, Lara Croft, in 2001's adventure thriller *Tomb Raider*. In 2000 the comic-strip mutants of *X-Men* included stunning superheroine X-women played by Famke Janssen, Halle Berry and Rebecca Romijn-Stamos; Drew Barrymore, Cameron Diaz and Lucy Liu teamed up as glamorous private detectives in the big screen *Charlie's Angels*; and a dutiful Michelle Yeoh locked swords with mysterious Zhang Ziyi in the martial arts chivalry film *Crouching Tiger, Hidden Dragon*. We can add to this list the tomboy-ish Milla Jovovich and butch Michelle Rodriguez as commandos in the survival horror picture *Resident Evil* (2002), and the digital perfection of computer-generated scientist Dr Aki Ross in the epic science fiction *Final Fantasy: The Spirits Within* (2001) (voiced by Ming-Na). In their shared concern with showcasing female stars as beautiful action heroines in beautiful fantasy action spectacles, these movies comprise an interesting category for critical analysis. In the argot of contemporary popular culture, through their combinations of 'eye candy' and 'the ride', those elements of cinematic spectacle which make us go 'wow!', these movies constitute what I shall term the contemporary action babe cinema.[2]

The figure of the beautiful action heroine with amazing combat skills has long been a staple of Hong Kong martial arts and sword-fighting movies, and has surfaced periodically – in a variety of costumes, body shapes and action spectacles – in Hollywood genres, from 1960s spy movies and 1970s blaxploitation through to westerns, science fiction, fantasy, sword and sorcery, police thrillers and rape revenge narratives in which the heroine's beauty makeover becomes part of her seductive armoury as a female avenger. Although often in a more pathologised or deviant context, the figures of the vampire and the Final Girl of horror and the femme fatales of 1990s neo-noirs and erotic thrillers also have affinities with the action babe heroine to be discussed here; they are often beautiful, active, sexy and dangerous.[3]

However, in the era of Girl Power, ladettes, lesbian chic and commodity feminism for all ages, the most immediate reference points for the action babe cinema come from representations in television, comics and video games; indeed, it is no surprise that five out of the six films in my proposed action babe corpus are adapted from one or another of these media (even *Crouching Tiger* comes from a novelistic source). In television, *Buffy the Vampire Slayer* and *Xena Warrior Princess*, starring Sarah Michelle Gellar and Lucy Lawless respectively, have been major successes, introducing hugely influential wirework-based stunts into their fantasy action worlds and heading a TV-based action babe cycle which includes *Charmed*, *Cleopatra 2525*, *Dark Angel* and *Alias*, as well as the animation-based *Aeon Flux* and *Xcalibur*. In comics and video games, action babe heroines have been among the most memorable characters created, from the unruly *Tank Girl* and erotic *Barb Wire* (adapted into the mid-1990s movies starring Lori Petty and Pamela Anderson Lee) through to the female game protagonists inspired by Lara Croft, such as Druuna, Cate Archer (*No One Lives Forever*), Joanna Dark (*Perfect Dark*) and D'Arcy Stern (*Urban Chaos*).[4] The franchise-led and synergistic cross-media borrowing of iconic comic strip, video game and martial arts/fantasy-based aesthetics – in which the imagery, montage and music of MTV have also been crucial – clearly marks out the stylistic territory of the recent action babe cinema.

## Propositions: gender exchanges, gendered spectacles and mobile identifications

Action babe cinema raises issues highly pertinent to critical discussion of the relationship between gender and spectacle in action-adventure cinema. In particular, three interrelated propositions in the field are replayed and, indeed, re-worked through the figure of the action babe heroine operating in the effects-laden fantasy worlds of these recent movies.

The first is that a defining feature of action-adventure cinema, not least since it entered its Hollywood blockbuster era from the late 1970s onwards, is its simultaneous re-inscription and questioning of the binary oppositions which structure common-sense understanding of gender in patriarchal consumer culture. Beginning from a more or less overt set of patriarchally defined traits and qualities equating men and masculinity with hardness, strength, muscles, activity, rationality, decisiveness and power, and women and femininity, in opposition, with softness, weakness, curves, passivity, intuition, indecisiveness and powerlessness, criticism of the action cinema has proceeded to demonstrate how representations of paradigmatic action heroes and heroines are not only exaggerated and often parodic stereotypes of the 'manly' or 'womanly' but are also invariably marked by meanings associated with the gender which they are 'not'.[5]

In the action-adventure cinema, therefore, a series of gender transactions and, sometimes, gender thefts can be seen to take place, as qualities of masculinity and femininity, activity and passivity, are traded over the bodies of action heroes and heroines. Thus, for instance, the hyperbolically masculine eighties bodybuilder action heroes played by Arnold Schwarzenegger and Sylvester Stallone are also repeatedly figured as soft, vulnerable, weak and feminised, in a host of spectacle scenarios where they ultimately triumph. Over against this, the new action heroines of the period, epitomised by Sigourney Weaver in the Alien cycle and Linda Hamilton in the Terminator movies, embody what Yvonne Tasker calls 'musculinity',[6] a conventionally masculine strength most obviously signified by their muscular yet clearly female bodies. The musculinity trend perhaps reaches its zenith to date in Demi Moore's famous, one-armed press-ups workout in G.I. Jane (1997). It is, however, as we shall see, not particularly significant in the action babe movies, where the emphasis is on beautiful feminine bodies combined with active masculine strength.

Closely associated with and partly developing this line of argument is a second proposition: the action-adventure cinema breaks open, or rather doubles up, Laura Mulvey's dictum that in the classic Hollywood movie the active male protagonist operates as the 'figure in the landscape', the subject who advances the narrative, while 'woman' connotes 'to-be-looked-at-ness', freezing the narrative as the passive object of eroticised visual spectacle.[7] In the action-adventure film, by contrast, with the movement of women into medium and even big budget starring roles, increasingly both the central hero and/or heroine – albeit in different ways and with differing emphases, relating to the operation of power in a patriarchal society – can be seen to function simultaneously as the action subject of the narrative and the erotic object of visual spectacle. As Tasker, drawing on the work of Richard Dyer, argues, in a patriarchal culture typically representations of the action hero which put his body on show allay the erotic and feminine qualities of his 'to-be-looked-at-ness' by stressing his activity. By contrast, representations of the action heroine as the figure in the landscape allay their active masculine connotations by stressing the heroine's sexuality and availability in conventional feminine terms.[8] While it remains the case that in patriarchy it is often men who look at women and women who are looked at, both the action hero and heroine can increasingly be viewed as simultaneously active and passive, both in action and on display. It follows that Mulvey's opposition between narrative and spectacle finds little favour among action-adventure critics, who view both narrative and visual elements as part of the overall filmic spectacle. Hence the much used copula action/spectacle implies that

the action narrative itself is as much excessive spectacle as those lingering close ups
of the hero/ine's beautiful body traditionally described by the term.

The third related proposition, which arises from the convergence of psychoanalytic and sociological approaches to film spectatorship, is that cinematic identification is a complex and fluid process. Just as the action hero and heroine can
be seen to embody and problematise elements of masculinity and femininity, and
to occupy both the position of (narrative) subject and (erotic) object, so too it is
now commonly argued that spectator identifications are not necessarily locked
within the Mulvey dynamic of the active, sadistic 'male' gaze and the passive,
masochistic 'female' gaze. Cinema spectators are, of course, positioned in time and
space by gender, class, ethnicity, age, sexuality, object choice and many other variables but criticism of popular cinematic genres has by now successfully demonstrated
that, at any given moment, each of us is capable of making a range of fantasy identifications in relation to any given film. Such identifications can, for instance, both
confirm and question our gendered identities and they may be, however fleetingly,
sadistic *and* masochistic, cross-gendered, and moving through a range of alignments
and allegiances in relation to the unfolding filmic spectacle.

A detailed example of such processes, argued from within a psychoanalytic
perspective, is Carol Clover's analysis of the ways in which teenage boys and young
men can identify across gender with the Final Girl in slasher horror, a figure combining feminine and masculine traits in ways partly comparable to the action babe
heroine.[9] However, the institutional context of the high concept cinema demands
that, in the commercial jargon, movies are made and marketed to the broadest
possible demographic, and in such a context it is more or less common sense to
assume that the pleasures on offer will target diverse audience constituencies. The
action babe cinema provides an illuminating example of such processes, since it is
clearly designed to appeal to both (mainly young) men and women. Along the have
me/be me axes of desire, the action babe heroine can be seen most obviously to
appeal not only to heterosexual boys and men, who desire to 'have' her in fantasy
but also to heterosexual girls and women, who desire to 'be' her in fantasy. As Famke
Janssen puts it: 'We've always been ready for female superheroes. Because women
want to be them and men want to do them.'[10] However, while in general it is true
that the action babe films stress the heroines' heterosexual object choices, there are
occasional moments and scenes in these films which offer the potential of a range of
lesbian, gay and/or queer identifications. For instance, men who identify as either
heterosexual or gay may cross-identify with either or both the feminine and/or
masculine characteristics of the empowered action babe heroine, exploring in fantasy
the 'be me' aspects of cross-gender identification. There is also plenty of evidence –
in mainstream as well as lesbian media – that several of the action babe stars, and
notably Angelina Jolie, appeal strongly to lesbians, who may identify simultaneously
along the 'have me' and 'be me' axes. Similarly, who is to say that women who
identify as heterosexual may not in fantasy experiment with identifications along
the 'have me' axis? Or that they may not enjoy watching the action babe heroine as
eroticised spectacle even if they do not desire her as a fantasy sexual object choice?
Though these examples are false in so far as they attempt to fix and label psychic

and bodily processes which are partial and fluid, it is clear that the action babe cinema offers pleasures to a wide audience.[11]

The contemporary action babe cinema is an entertaining and at times, literally breathtaking, example of these trends in the action-adventure cinema. On the one hand, the physical beauty and alluring sexuality of the female stars and the characters they play embody traditional, patriarchally defined qualities of femininity. These qualities, however, which the Mulvey thesis links to passivity, vulnerability, sexual availability and to-be-looked-at-ness, can also be seen as a source of active feminine strength, and one by which heterosexual men in particular (including male spectators) are all too easily seduced, as the case of the eroticised female avenger powerfully illustrates, albeit in a very different dramatic context. On the other hand, in their function as central protagonists in the action narrative, these heroines are undoubtedly coded as masculine, active and physically strong and can clearly be seen to constitute the figure in the landscape, the position traditionally occupied by the male hero in classical cinema. In crude terms, the action babe heroine is simultaneously and, quite brazenly, both the erotic object of visual spectacle and the action subject of narrative spectacle, the two of course being combined in the movie experience itself. She combines elements of the 'soft body' of 'woman' and the 'hard body' of 'man', as well as traits of successful hegemonic patriarchal femininity and masculinity, for instance, intuition and charm with toughness and decisiveness, to emerge as an emblematic fantasy icon among contemporary representations. It is this 'soft-hard' combination, as Kate Stables identifies it in her discussion of *Tomb Raider*,[12] which we can now explore further.

## Babes and action: the discursive framing of the action babe heroine

The term 'action babe heroine' is intended to capture the yoking together of the 'soft' and 'hard' elements which comprise this fantasy figure. She is at once – to draw on the contemporary popular cultural lexicon for describing beautiful young women – a 'babe' and, equally importantly, she is 'fit'. 'Babe' is, of course, a term of endearment in personal relationships but its current hegemony stems from its wide circulation in media representations and everyday conversation. While its infantilising and sexist connotations are undoubtedly present in the lads' culture of men's style magazines, soft pornography and internet sites, nevertheless it is a term used quite unselfconsciously by many people, particularly the young. Similarly, the use of the term 'fit' to designate physical attractiveness has emerged from commercialised sport and body culture into mainstream usage, stressing the idea of the body beautiful as the healthy, exercising, worked-on, athletic body.

The circulation of extra-textual publicity and behind-the-scenes materials on the action babe stars, characters and movies draws pervasively on this 'fit babe' discourse, highlighting the ways in which the gendered body of both the star and the action babe heroine are processed through the twin lens of eroticisation and active strength. Representational gatekeeping in the action babe arena demands an actress who is 'young' (usually in her twenties or early thirties), slim, shapely, often (though by no means exclusively) white and marketed as of primarily (though not necessarily wholly) heterosexual orientation, who repeatedly undergoes the celebrity makeover of the beauty and gossip industries and is willing to undergo what we can call 'the action makeover' to prepare her for the rigours of fights and stunts in the action babe spectacle.[13]

That the action babe stars are among the beauties of the contemporary entertainment industry is undeniable. Several started out as models (Berry, Diaz and Jovovich among them) or came to prominence as beauty queens (Yeoh, Berry again) and all undertake fashion, advertising and promotional work of various kinds (Jovovich, for instance, was the face of L'Oréal and is reputedly Miuccia Prada's muse). Their erotic glamour and aura of sexual availability – key ingredients in Hollywood love goddess assembly lines since the star system emerged – are regularly promoted in the on-the-edge-of-soft-porn pin-up articles which populate men's style magazines, playing on the soft and feminine visual aspects of the stars as they answer questions riddled with double entendres and suggestive 'inside' details. Thus, to take the magazine *FHM* as exemplar: Angelina Jolie and Rebecca Romijn-Stamos feature in the portmanteau 'American Beauties',[14] consisting of large, well-lit colour photographs of each in various states of undress and insights such as Jolie remarking: 'I'm just a big softie.'

The epitome of the pin-up babe discourse can perhaps be found in the *SFX* magazine Babes Specials, which comprise cover-to-cover photos and features on the beautiful young actresses appearing in sci-fi and fantasy films and TV. In 2002's edition we discover that the female assistants in the long-running *Doctor Who* TV series were babes all along, encounter 'Strange Attractions' in the forms of 'Robot Babes', 'Comic Book Babes', 'Alien Babes' and 'Cartoon Babes' and find an image of *Final Fantasy*'s Aki Ross in a skimpy purple bikini.[15] Dr Ross, by far the least overtly eroticised of the action babe heroines in the filmic text itself, is not immune to extra-textual eroticisation, and indeed the movie's DVD extras include the 'Aki Photo Shoot', where this fantasy digital beauty is literally stripped down to her bare essentials, transformed in a variety of poses into an erotic fantasy machine.[16]

We should not forget, however, that in the promotion of the action babe movies considerable emphasis is also laid on the star's 'fitness' and preparation for her role through the action makeover. A pervasive theme in recent Hollywood-centric cinema has been the focus on the stars' willingness to diet, exercise, train, go through pain and learn a range of action-based and combat skills to shape up for their roles. Though Zhang Ziyi comments that she knows nothing about kung fu[17] and Cameron Diaz admits that the Angels copy moves which they can sustain for about three seconds (the length of a take),[18] nevertheless the process of authenticating stars by showing that they really do lots of their own combat stunts (albeit with the aid of wire-work and effects) has gathered pace since *The Matrix*'s success kicked off the trend.

Following the Wachowski Brothers' employment of Hong Kong auteur choreographer Yuen Wo-Ping, *Charlie's Angels* followed suit when his brother Cheung-Yan Yuen was hired to train the actresses in running, kicking, basic kung fu skills and specific sequences for the movie. A similar process is recorded in relation to

Angelina Jolie's preparation for the role of Lara Croft: a special diet, meditation and yoga, gymnastics, fights and weapons training, motorbike riding and husky racing are all mentioned in the DVD behind-the-scenes documentary. Special emphasis is laid on Jolie's lack of fear, on her mission as 'an actor training to be an Olympic athlete' and on her apparent identification with the character she plays. A different, and more painful, inflection is given to the 'fitness' narrative in Michelle Yeoh's account of her role in *Crouching Tiger*. Yeoh has an impressive action pedigree, having learned her trade in 1980s 'girls and guns' movies and 1990s martial arts fantasies, before reaching a wide audience in the Jackie Chan vehicle *Police Story III* and the Bond movie *Tomorrow Never Dies*, but she has also suffered several serious injuries throughout her career, including knee ligament damage during the filming of *Tiger*. If the real danger to the stars inherent in the history of Hong Kong action filmmaking hasn't quite been replicated in Hollywood, nevertheless the commitment to the action makeover and the pain it entails, if we are to believe the stories, necessitates a degree of genuine physical determination and hardness on the part of the action babe stars. It's all part of a contemporary working portfolio.

## Babes in action: the action babe heroine and cinematic spectacle

The spectacle of the action babe heroine functions as the central visual and narrative driver within the overall audio-visual feast which contemporary action-adventure aims to offer its audience. As José Arroyo suggests, at one level the action star operates as an integral production value, while the digital and other computer generated effects which deliver the requisite number of set-piece thrills in the action-adventure entertainment package can be seen as forms of product differentiation.[19] Arroyo argues that at certain moments in the action spectacle the human body functions as an almost abstract graphic element within the overall orchestration of non-representational signs such as colour, motion and music, an orchestration which at its most successful is not only obviously artistic but also an affecting contemporary representation of the sublime.[20] All this is true but at the same time as recognising the commercial language of product and the aesthetic language of the impulse to represent the unrepresentable, it is equally important to stress, from a phenomenological perspective, the unique ontological, photogenic and – lest it be forgotten – acting qualities of each of the action babe actresses.[21] A brief application of the commutation test to the stars in these films suggests, for instance, how different *Charlie's Angels* would have been if, as was mooted, Angelina Jolie had played the third Angel, or if Liz Hurley 'was' Lara Croft. And, for all the wire-work and post-production effects, we are invited to believe that this is, for example, Cameron Diaz – not a body double or a digital simulation – who floors the male opponent who is attempting to assassinate her. The fact that (we believe) this *is* Cameron Diaz *matters*.

In considering the relationship between gender and spectacle in action babe movies, we can note initially that each shares common modal, structural and thematic features. Though drawing individually on a wide variety of genres and intertexts, all combine elements of action, romance/soap and (in very varying degrees) comedy and operate within the traditional structure of the literary medieval romance. As Thomas Sobchack explains, in this foundational mode a protagonist with special skills confronts human, natural or supernatural powers which have brought disorder to the world of the narrative and overcomes them to achieve a specific goal, usually the restoration of order.[22] It is noteworthy that, in terms of special skills, the action babe heroines are all professionals of one kind or another and, with the possible exception of Jen in *Crouching Tiger*, are not pathologised or motivated by personal revenge or gain (as in the rape revengers, noirs and erotic thrillers). Rather they are motivated by doing their job well.

Whether set in the present (*Charlie's Angels*, *Tomb Raider*), the future (*X-Men*, *Resident Evil*, *Final Fantasy*) or the past (*Crouching Tiger*), the romance quests of these movies are structured around the drive to acquire and control what we can call, after Hitchcock, the action MacGuffin – usually a hi-tech fetish or an object with magical qualities. In *X-Men* this is Magneto's marvellous mutating machine, which threatens humans and requires the energy of the teenage Rogue (Anna Paquin) to power it. In *Charlie's Angels*, it is the voice decoder, which Knox (Sam Rockwell) steals in order to get to Charlie and which (apparently) threatens global privacy. In *Tomb Raider*, it is the two halves of the mystical Triangle of Light which, when put back together, enable the bearer to control time and change the course of history; in *Resident Evil*, the lethal T-Virus and its Anti-Virus; in *Crouching Tiger*, the antique sword Green Destiny; and in *Final Fantasy*, the eight spirits which Aki seeks in order to rid the Earth of the alien phantoms.

Slightly more tendentiously, it may also be argued that each of these films is set in a society where the institutional structures of patriarchy and/or, more directly, sick patriarchal men, prove to be the villains of the piece. In *X-Men*, for instance, the paternal trilogy of the good Xavier (Patrick Stewart, X-Men), the bad Magneto (Ian McKellen, Brotherhood) and the just plain wicked Senator Kelly (Bruce Davison, repressive State forces) preside over the action, while the Angels, of course, work for Charlie and end up saving him. The action plot of *Tomb Raider* concerns Lara's battle with the evil Manfred Powell (Ian Glen) but the (more important?) psychic plot concerns her quest to make peace with her father (played by Jolie's real-life father Jon Voight), the success of her transition from adolescent tomboy to adult woman being signified in the final scene by the conventional white summer dress and hat which she wears at his memorial (don't worry, she goes for the guns again in the final freeze frame). In *Resident Evil*, the patriarchal force behind the plot is the multinational Umbrella Corporation and the sick man is Alice's operative partner and mercenary sell-out Spence (James Purefoy), while *Crouching Tiger* is set in nineteenth-century Qing Dynasty China and the conflicts between the characters stem from their differing relationships to the patriarchal Wudan orthodoxy. *Final Fantasy* is slightly more ambiguous, in that the Council ruling the future United States is composed of a black man and a woman and the enemy appears to be the alien phantoms. However, it soon becomes clear that both these functions (State and enemy) are conflated in the figure of the twisted military fascist General Hein.

The soft-hard combination which informs the representation of the action babe heroine figure is brilliantly demonstrated in the Marvel comic-strip adaptation

*X-Men*, a film in which, although they are not the central narrative drivers, the characters of Jean Grey (aka Marvel Girl, Famke Janssen), Storm (aka Ororo Monroe, Halle Berry) and Mystique (aka Raven Darkholme, Rebecca Romijn-Stamos) strikingly embody the erotic and heroic aspects of the action babe. Although the franchise arrangement determines that the comic title be retained, the cinematic adaptation offers the same number of male and female mutants within the opposing teams, placing Jean Grey and Storm with the goodies and Mystique with the baddies.

The leaders may be men but a kind of gender democracy prevails within the mutant communities and, by virtue of the genetic evolution which is the franchise's narrative premise, there is also a democracy of superpowers among the characters. The representational (and commercial) potency of the simple iconic comic-strip images is brilliantly adapted to the screen and, while there is a common, if not at all explicit, eroticised emphasis on the superheroines' breasts and cleavage, each is carefully delineated by her costumes and powers. Thus the white-skinned Jean Grey is the clever psychokinetic brunette – her cleverness coded in her erudite-looking glasses – who sports a smart red skirt suit while lecturing the Senate and a white medical coat while treating Logan/Wolverine (Hugh Jackman). In contrast, the mixed-race Storm is the icy blonde with a penchant for hippy, ethnic and exotic outfits and the ability to control the elements; and the blue scaly-skinned shape-shifter Mystique is the apparently (but not really) nude reptilian redhead with yellow eyes and amazing martial arts skills.

Within the overall story arc each is showcased in moments of fantastic spectacle which demonstrate their (literally) superhuman strengths. During the prolonged final face off, for instance, with the X-Men clad in their black leather X-suits ('It was a little sexy, but something you could still wear for battle', opines Berry),[23] Jean Grey telekinetically suspends Toad (Ray Park) in mid-air as he attacks her; Storm floats forward through the air in a Christ-like pose, her cape flowing behind her, lightning emanating from her white eyeballs, and despatches Toad into the river below; and Mystique confuses opponents by morphing into them. At one point it appears that Mystique, disguised as Logan, stabs Storm in the belly with 'her' adamantine claws but it transpires that this is Logan stabbing Mystique disguised as Storm. It looks much more fascinating than it sounds.

If *X-Men* foregrounds bold costuming and superhuman combat effects, then the distinctly soft and girlie *Charlie's Angels* virtually elevates the opportunity for costume changes to its structuring principle. Like their TV predecessors, the cinematic Angels are Californian sunshine babes for whom the pop glam aesthetic of dressing up to complete each adventure is a fabulously taken-for-granted norm and the notion of performing femininities to charm and seduce their (mainly male) opponents is an unqualified given. Exemplifying Naomi Klein's argument that 'the mantra of retro entertainment seems to be "Once more with synergy!"'[24] the movie nevertheless adds two contemporary ingredients to the original formula: broad sexual comedy (which earned it a UK 15 certificate) and big action sequences. In the 1970s and 1980s, as women's roles in the action cinema and television gradually developed, there was a tendency to use comedy to undermine the woman's position in the action scenario. However, in an era where, as Chris Holmlund points out, mainstream Hollywood female stars tend to display 'openness and brash indepen-dence',[25] assertive comedy becomes a mode of self-empowerment and a knowing compact with the audience. Alongside this, as a big budget action movie seeking a wide teen and young adult cross-gender audience, the movie must deliver its quotient of exhilarating set pieces within a representational regime which is not *too* violent. In short, the Angels have spectacular fun playing with femininity as masquerade, operating mesmerising hi-tech gadgets and running rings around their opponents as they save Knox, Bosley (Bill Murray) and Charlie in succession.

The opening 'skydive' sequence, modelled on *Mission: Impossible 2*, sees former rock chick Dylan Sanders (Drew Barrymore), improbably dressed across gender, race and size as Mr Jones (LL Cool J), foiling a bomber on a commercial flight with the assistance of classy, raven-haired Alex Munday (Lucy Liu) and, anchoring the sequence in gorgeous, blonde, bikini'd femininity, kooky speedboat-piloting Natalie Cook (Cameron Diaz), all to a searing rock guitar score. 'You crazy bastard!' screams the paradigmatically dorkish male villain Pasqual (Sean Whales) at Mr Jones as he lands on the boat. 'I think you mean crazy bitch' retorts Dylan as she removes her mask and flicks her flowing red tresses. This combination of cheeky, eroticised costuming, brash comedy, in-your-face action and loud popular music provides the template for the film's style.

The 1970s television series was branded as 'jiggle TV' for its high bikini quotient, the film playing up to these expectations with a succession of teasing moments, including Diaz's now famous bottom-wiggling 'wake up' dance in pink T-shirt and panties, Barrymore's cleavage rolling out of her blue mechanic's outfit as she distracts a chauffeur, Liu's whip-cracking, leather bondage corporate effi-ciency expert and close-up split-screen lip fetishism as the Angels consider how to break into the mainframe room at Red Star. And there is more: in the course of the narrative the Angels transform miraculously into a host of feminine avatars, including masseuses, geisha girls, waiters, beauties in evening gowns, exotic belly dancers, kinky Fraulein dancers, seventies disco babes, slacker 'boy' babes and drag kings, the latter very much of the men's style magazine type dismissed by Del LaGrace Volcano and Judith 'Jack' Halberstam as 'supermodels in moustaches'.[26]

However, as the movie's promotional strapline – 'Charlie's Angels: Get Some Action!' – makes clear, it is the representation of the beautiful action babe heroine within the action spectacle which completes the contract promised by the movie. As the brief account above of the training provided by Cheung-Yan Yuen suggests, *Charlie's Angels* fits squarely within the trend to incorporate wire-work based Hong Kong style martial arts combat sequences into Hollywood action. Alongside the FX led top and tail airborne sequences, the racing car chase and face-off and big fireball explosion moments which any self-respecting Hollywood action movie must feature, therefore, we find the spectacular Chinese Alley fight. This pits the Angels against the creepy fetishistic Thin Man (Crispin Glover), showcasing soaring aerial kicks and iconic poses.

Comedy and product placement are injected into the final martial arts battle between Natalie and Knox's sidekick Vivian (Kelly Lynch), the former becoming seriously annoyed when the latter interrupts her mid-fight cell phone conversation with new (dorkish) boyfriend Pete (Luke Wilson) ('D'you know how hard it is to find a quality man in Los Angeles?'). And, in a tour de force scene which works a variation on the one-woman-defeats-several-men-and-secures-them-with-a-single-pair-of-handcuffs routines in the eighties Hong Kong movies *Above the Law* and *Righting Wrongs*, Dylan escapes from a situation in which she is trapped in a chair with her hands tied behind her back, executes a towering backward somersault and proceeds to trounce three of Knox's henchmen, still with her hands tied together, before moonwalking off to the sound of Michael Jackson as she delivers the mantra of the action babe cinema: 'And that's kicking your ass!' Angel Power rules.

*Charlie's Angels* imports Eastern martial arts into a Hollywood scenario; *Crouching Tiger, Hidden Dragon*, by contrast, re-works the traditional Hong Kong martial arts genre by investing it with Yuen Wo-Ping's post-*Matrix* style action choreography and crossing it with Western intertexts from Jane Austen's *Sense and Sensibility* to Hollywood suffering lovers melodramas and musicals. William Leung[27] demonstrates how the adaptation from Wang Du-Lu's 1940s popular novels shifts the Confucian masculine focus of the wuxia pian into a Taoist feminine one of a nuxia pian. In this process, the psychological and emotional conflicts of Zhang Ziyi's soft–hard action babe heroine Jen – who is probably both the Crouching Tiger and the Hidden Dragon of the film's title – are in some respects elevated over the unrequited love melodrama of the characters played by the established stars, Michelle Yeoh's swordswoman Shu Lien and Chow Yun Fat's Wudan master swordsman Li Mu Bai. Leung further explains how the film's feminine and feminist slant is enhanced by making Shu Lien more important than Li, by feminising the character of Li himself, by adding the older female character Jade Fox (Cheng Pei-Pei), who killed Li's master and is Jen's secret teacher in stolen Wudan martial arts and by giving the women most of the spectacular fights.

Jen is by far the most psychologically complex of the recent action babe heroines. On the surface the obedient daughter of the aristocratic patriarch Governor Wu, she appears at the outset to be a model of sumptuously attired and submissive femininity, about to be consigned to a convenient arranged marriage, though she makes no secret of her daydreams about the imagined freedoms of the warrior's life when she first meets Shu Lien. However, under the tutelage of Jade Fox, whose powers she has long outgrown, she has in reality become a sword-fighting rebel against patriarchal norms, taken the bandit Lo (Chang Chen) as her secret lover and is unable to resist stealing Li's sword Green Destiny, a potent symbol of patriarchal power, when Shu Lien brings it to Beijing for safekeeping. While Jen's abilities undoubtedly qualify her as a professional warrior (albeit an unrecognised one), unlike the other recent action babe heroines her personal motivation to escape patriarchal repression and find freedom place her as a wronged woman, part female avenger (Jade Fox is wholly a female avenger), part femme fatale (in her ambivalent seduction of Li) and also, however ambiguously, the film's villain.[28] As Ang Lee observes in the DVD director's commentary, while Shu Lien and Li fight only to contain Jen's rebellious energy, she fights for real, though she cannot bring herself to kill either of them when she has the opportunity.

With Ziyi/Jen at its centre, the orchestration of action and romantic spectacle in *Crouching Tiger* – its blend of gorgeous natural scenery, superb action choreography, heartbreaking love scenes, disciplined energy and moving pathos (conveyed not least in Yo-Yo Ma's melancholy cello solos) – is arguably unrivalled in recent action cinema. At the screening where I first saw the film, when Shu Lien and the sword thief (Jen) leap, float and fly across the night-time Beijing rooftops in the first big action sequence, the (western) audience's awe and amazement was palpable in the theatre. The feminine and inward-looking Wudan martial arts techniques lend a grace and beauty to the combat sequences, whether hand-to-hand or sword-fighting, at once expressing the conflicting relationships between the characters and offering that rarely achieved sublime spectacle of the human body in motion comparable to musical numbers at their best. In the Hong Kong martial arts tradition, of course, female to male cross-dressing is an unremarked convention and so Jen on the run is able to pass as Young Master Long without comment, though her possession of Green Destiny provides the occasion for the film's show-stopping set piece, as she takes on and defeats a host of men, albeit with some obvious wire-work and digital assistance, in the kind of inn scene made famous in King Hu movies, uttering comic one liners as she overcomes each opponent. The film's version of the more *is* more action principle features in Jen and Shu Lien's final confrontation, as Shu Lien fights with a series of increasingly large swords, while the duel which follows between Li and Jen among the uppermost branches of a bamboo forest (similar to that in the classic *A Touch of Zen*) conveys the repressed eroticism of their unfulfilled Master-Pupil relationship, as they swing back and forth towards and away from one another, in a languorous and dreamily melancholic spectacle. This repression is almost lifted when, shortly before Li dies, the drugged Jen, with her nipples briefly visible through her wet clothes in one of the movie's very few obviously eroticised moments, asks him: 'Is it me or the sword you want?'[29]

*Crouching Tiger* integrates character, plot and action to a degree highly unusual in contemporary action-adventure cinema, no doubt partly because of the talented personnel working on it and its unusual straddling of Eastern and Western traditions (and finance). The remaining three action babe films under discussion all derive from video game franchises: Eidos's *Tomb Raider*, Capcom's *Resident Evil* and Square's *Final Fantasy*, though the action babe heroines in the latter two, Alice (Milla Jovovich) and Aki Ross, do not appear in a prior game. Each of these films showcases the soft-hard figure of the action babe heroine but, partly in contrast to the fantasy martial arts trend, here the emphasis is as much (or more) on guns as the weaponry of choice. Lara (see Figure 12.1) and Alice handle guns confidently, wielding the power of life and death which shooting entails. And, while Aki doesn't fight physically at all, she is nevertheless immersed in a testosterone-fuelled *Aliens*-type future world where those around her have armoured bodies and massive firearms.

If Lady Lara Croft is the Cool Britannia babe of the action babe cinema, with her inestimable personal wealth and upper class English accent, then Alice is the off-the-wall transatlantic Euro babe with one of those American accents still clearly marked by immigrant origins (Jovovich's father and mother hailed from Yugoslavia and Russia respectively). Both are given signature costumes which highlight their

*Figure 12.1* Angelina Jolie as Lara Croft in *Lara Croft: Tomb Raider* (2001). Courtesy of the Kobal Collection

femininity but enable them to leap easily into action. Jolie's Lara outfit is modelled on her game avatar, comprising a close-fitting black vest and shorts which emphasise her rangy form and padded breasts, black boots with combat lace-ups and fetishistic straps and her trademark pistols strapped to each thigh. Jovovich as Alice boasts the strangest action babe costume, a long red cocktail dress held up by the tiniest of shoulder straps and diagonally slashed at the left waist to reveal a short black mini skirt underneath, with plain black Prada boots for footwear. Strongly suggestive of outerwear as underwear, the outfit draws attention to her female and boyish body and, uniquely for these films, she wears it throughout most of her ordeal, as the plot does not allow for costume changes, except when she borrows the black leather jacket of Spence – her lover and enemy.

Both the films play knowingly with the eroticisation of the action babe figure. Each includes an early teaser shower scene in which the heroine is unrobed, Lara turning coquettishly to one side to reveal the outline of her left breast, Alice placed in a more *Psycho*-like scenario as we first encounter her naked and wrapped in the shower curtain which she pulled down as she fell unconscious when the Red Queen released gas into the gothic mansion above the Hive. *Resident Evil*, however, with its 15 UK certificate and US R rating, takes this eroticisation further, making sure that Alice gets wet in the laboratory so that her nipples show through her dress and, in the film's denouement, returning us to her naked body as she wakes alone in the Racoon City hospital. Jovovich is very arch about this, remarking: 'It's fun to objectify beautiful women. I objectify beautiful women as much as anybody, and I am a beautiful woman.'[30] And, in the DVD making-of documentary: 'And to see me in a wet mini dress and a gun [*sic*]. I mean, come on, what more can you ask of *Resident Evil*?'

The answer perhaps is, quite a lot. Though *Tomb Raider* is somewhat hamstrung by externally imposed requirements to replicate the games' moves and scenes, especially in the tomb set pieces, as a cinematic action babe spectacle it does have some specifically cinematic virtues. Jolie's largely monochromatic wardrobe is beautifully varied to suit each action scenario.[31] The movie's most successful action set piece, too, the attack by Manfred Powell's forces on Croft Manor to steal the clock which Lara has discovered, is prefaced by the extraordinarily beautiful and feminine bungee ballet sequence, in which Lara jumps from the balcony to rock back and forth on her bungee ropes before literally using them to swing into prolonged action, mixing *Matrix*-like moments with elaborate bike stunts.

Lara may be a masculine tomboy in search of Daddy but she is also feminine and vulnerable. In however corny a fashion, the movie's aura of spirituality and mysticism, captured wonderfully in Lara's encounters with her ethnic girl Other avatars as she approaches the tombs and especially in her *Rambo*-like retreat at Angkor Wat (Jolie/Lara sports an orange silk designer sari), is affecting, as is the quest to make peace with her lost father. Critical rejection of these moments perhaps stems partly from the judgement that their incursion of the feminine and the mystical into the action scenario is alien and mistaken. The mysticism may be shallow and the daughter-father reunion sentimental – though, as I have hinted, the male-centred action narrative can access such realms too – but nevertheless these melodramatic elements are among the film's more distinctive achievements.

Lara Croft as cinematic action babe heroine echoes many iconic figures from the action-adventure tradition: she is a bit James Bond (neo-imperialist agent), Indiana Jones (archaeologist adventurer), Batman (has an estate and an eccentric butler) and Tarzan (swings from ropes and dives off waterfalls), and a bit Modesty Blaise, Barbarella and Tank Girl. In the rush to replicate the Lara formula, however, Alice in *Resident Evil* has considerably less resonance. Her amnesiac outsiderness recalls Ripley in *Aliens* but she appears as an almost fairytale-like anomaly – the movie could be called *Alice's Adventures in Zombieland* – in the film's masculine jumps-and-shocks horror world, which offers the 'hardest' violence in the recent action babe cinema. The movie delivers its quotient of action spectacle but the glass corridor laser sequence, which slices up half the commando team, is the only real stand out and compared to the other action babe movies, it is thin on meaningful relationships, too.

In this respect, its most promising aspect is its revival, in the developing relationship between Alice and the muscular commando Rain (Michelle Rodriguez from the independent boxing picture *Girlfight*), of the feminine tomboy/masculine butch opposition most famously represented in *Aliens*' counterpointing of Ripley and Vasquez (Jenette Goldstein). Rain is the first of the team to be bitten by a zombie and the plot, such as it is, partly concerns Alice's attempts to secure the antidote in order to save her. Rain makes Alice promise to shoot her before she is transformed into one of the flesh-eating Undead but, as Alice is about to do so, she grabs her gun, looks up at her with her Marlon Brando-like eyes and declares: 'I'm not dead yet.' 'I could kiss you you bitch.' Alice responds, in a moment which explicitly opens up a lesbian reading, though spectators familiar with the tradition will no doubt have been pursuing such a reading since Rain barked at Matt (Eric Mabius), as she first removes her mask near the beginning of the film to reveal that she is a woman, 'Blow me.'[32] Moments later, as the gruesome Licker attacks the train, Rain transforms, Matt blows her – away – and any trace of overt lesbian desire is summarily expelled from the text.[33]

## Conclusion: the trend continues

As I write the action babe cinema trend continues apace. The *X-Men* sequel *X 2* has just been released, giving more screen time and space than the original to Jean Grey, Storm and, especially, Mystique. The *Charlie's Angels*, *Tomb Raider* and *Resident Evil* sequels are beginning to appear though, for artistic and financial reasons respectively, *Crouching Tiger* and *Final Fantasy* appear to have been one-offs. Among the seminal classics, *The Matrix* and, after a long gap, *Terminator* sequels are also due, the summer season will see Uma Thurman as an action babe heroine in *Kill Bill* and TV action babe heroines have continued to arrive in series such as *Birds of Prey* (a Batman spin-off), *She-Spies* (a *Charlie's Angels* clone) and *Witchblade*. More pervasively, the search for the perfect action babe form in the purely fantasy comic strip, video game and digital arenas is growing prodigiously, as many of the portfolios in Julius Wiedemann's collection of *Digital Beauties* illustrate.[34]

Writing against the patriarchal regulation of desirable femininity in *The Beauty Myth* a dozen or so years ago, Naomi Wolf complained of the impossible burden being placed on young women (for which read middle-class, College-educated professional women in the United States) who were increasingly 'expected to act like "real men" and look like "real women"',[35] that is, to be tough, aggressive and competitive in the workplace while simultaneously grooming themselves to be slim and attractive. She imagined a dystopian future in which women would be robots; bred for beauty and passivity; or created with adjustable breast implants. She even noted the existence of a Japanese lifelike geisha with artificial skin.[36] The action babe phenomenon which has flourished since she wrote this attack seems directly to address both the reality and the fantasy of her statements. The action babe heroine does indeed combine elements of successful patriarchal femininity and masculinity and we may not always like the traits and qualities she embodies. Albeit in an overt fantasy context, the action babes are, in the main, professionals doing their job, who have to be competitive and violent in order to survive and win. The figure of the action babe heroine demonstrates how the 'built' female body is no longer the masculinised muscular body but rather the slim yet strong body, which may be excessively feminised or boyish. It's also the case that the figure of the ontologically unique female star, however beautiful she may be, is increasingly haunted by the body made over by special effects or the digitally created 'perfect' female body (whether as alien, robot, animal, girl . . .).

Such assertions, however, are by no means the whole story of the action babe cinema phenomenon. Clearly responding and contributing to changing gender representations and relationships, these films take refreshingly for granted the ideological givens of patriarchal consumer culture – yes, beautiful, well-qualified women are sometimes best placed to succeed in a competitive, individualist, appearance-obsessed meritocracy – to produce potent fantasies of female empowerment with a strong appeal to both girls/women and boys/men. Virtually unmarked by the rape or patriarchal abuse motifs which underpin the figure of the avenging heroine and less obsessed with rage, resistance and fighting back against white male oppression than much woman-centred action cinema, these films *assume that women are powerful*, offering heroines who are both vulnerable and strong and, above all, who survive and win, often in great style. In however a restricted and limited way, therefore, they help us to both think through and fantasise about the meanings of gender in our culture and, on occasion, offer those forms of utopian expression which popular culture arguably does best. When the elements of the action babe spectacle are orchestrated to produce those great wow moments, with the body of the action babe heroine evoking, in David Bordwell's words, 'elemental and universal events like striking, swinging, twisting, leaping [and] rolling',[37] they are indeed luminous examples of the cinema's ability to create beauty in motion.

## Notes

Thanks to Judy O'Day for talks about the movies, Lewis and Steve Rouse for information on the games, and Yvonne Tasker for seeing the essay through to completion.

1   See Steve Neale in this volume and 'Action-Adventure' in Pam Cook and Mieke Bernick (eds) *The Cinema Book*, 2nd edition, London: British Film Institute, 1999, pp. 228–31;

Justin Wyatt *High Concept: Movies and Marketing in Hollywood*, Austin: University of Texas, 1994; Jose Arroyo (ed.) *Action/Spectacle Cinema: A 'Sight and Sound' Reader*, London: British Film Institute, 2000.

2   The pervasiveness of the action babe figure is signalled by its migration into the children's animation fantasy *Shrek* (2001), with its high-kicking heroine Princess Fiona (voiced by Cameron Diaz).

3   See Martha McCaughey and Neal King (eds) *Reel Knockouts: Violent Women in the Movies*, Austin: University of Texas, 2000; Sherrie A. Inness *Tough Girls: Women Warriors and Wonder Women in Popular Culture*, Philadelphia: University of Pennsylvania Press, 1999; Christine Holmlund 'A Decade of Deadly Dolls: Hollywood and the Woman Killer', in Helen Birch (ed.) *Moving Targets: Women, Murder and Representation*, London: Virago, 1993, pp. 127–51; Jacinda Read *The New Avengers: Feminism, Femininity and the Rape-Revenge Cycle*, Manchester: Manchester University Press, 2000; Barbara Creed *The Monstrous Feminine: Film, Feminism, Psychoanalysis*, London: Routledge, 1993; Carol J. Clover *Men, Women and Chainsaws: Gender in the Modern Horror Film*, London: British Film Institute, 1992; Kate Stables 'The Postmodern Always Rings Twice: Constructing the Femme Fatale in 90s Cinema', in E. Ann Kaplan (ed.) *Women and Film Noir*, 2nd edition, London: British Film Institute, 1998, pp. 164–82.

4   On female game protagonists, see the symptomatically named 'Sexy Heroes' section in David Choquet (ed.) *1000 Game Heroes*, Köln and London: Taschen, 2002, pp. 504–41.

5   See Susan Jeffords *Hard Bodies: Hollywood Masculinity in the Reagan Era*, New Brunswick, NJ: Rutgers University Press, 1994, on the hard and soft bodies of 1980s Hollywood action cinema and Christine Holmlund *Impossible Bodies: Femininity and Masculinity at the Movies*, London: Routledge, 2002, on the shapes of gendered star bodies in contemporary Hollywood cinema.

6   Yvonne Tasker *Spectacular Bodies: Gender, Genre and the Action Cinema*, London: Routledge, 1993, p. 3.

7   Laura Mulvey *Visual and Other Pleasures*, London: Macmillan, 1989, pp. 19, 20.

8   Tasker *Spectacular Bodies*, p. 19.

9   Clover *Men, Women and Chainsaws*, pp. 21–64.

10  Biography for Famke Janssen, http://www.US.imdb.com/Bio?Janssen,+Famke, accessed 4 September, 2002.

11  Identifications, of course, proceed across race and ethnicity, class and age and many other categories.

12  Kate Stables 'Run Lara Run', *Sight and Sound*, 11: 8, August 2001, pp. 18–20: p. 20.

13  The celebrity makeover involves the 'built' body as much as the action makeover. Diaz: 'I want girls to realise that nobody looks like the women in the photos without the help of a load of talented people' (Jan Masters 'Sweet and Lowdown', *Elle*, UK edition, February 2003, pp. 74–80, p. 80).

14  *FHM*, September 2000, pp. 196–222.

15  *'SFX' Babes Special 2002*, Bath: Future Publications, 2002, pp. 16–19, 24–8, 55.

16  Publicity featuring the star in her action babe costume/s constitutes the mediating instance between the general circulation of the female stars as babes and specific filmic texts. See, for instance, the *Tomb Raider* images in Mark Dinning '*Tomb Raider*', *Empire*, 146, August 2001, pp. 69–77.

17  Derek Yu 'Zhung Ziyi' *The Girls of 'FHM'*, London: EMAP, pp. 26–8: p. 28.

18  Masters 'Sweet and Lowdown', p. 77.

19  Arroyo *Action/Spectacle Cinema*, p. xiii.

20  Ibid., pp. 23–5.

21  See Stanley Cavell 'From *The World Viewed*', in Gerald Mast, Marshall Cohen and Leo Braudy (eds) *Film Theory and Criticism*, 4th edition, New York and Oxford: Oxford University Press, 1992, pp. 291–301.

22  Cited in Neale 'Action-Adventure', p. 230.

23   Mike Peake 'SUPERGIRL!', *FHM*, April 2001, pp. 201–17, p. 212.

24   Naomi Klein *No Logo*, London: Flamingo, 2001, p. 79.

25   Holmlund *Impossible Bodies*, p. 7.

26   Del LaGrace Volcano and Judith 'Jack' Halberstam *The Drag King Book*, London: Serpent's Tail, 1999, p. 2.

27   William Leung 'Crouching Sensibility, Hidden Sense', *Film Criticism*, V: I, 2001.

28   Jen is, accordingly, the only action babe heroine who is not overtly triumphant. *Crouching Tiger*'s mystical and transcendent closure is thoroughly polysemic, leaving her literally in suspension, an interesting variant on the death-denying freeze frame which ends *Thelma and Louise* and Ripley's Christ-like fall as she gives birth to the alien in *Alien 3*.

29   Jen is also eroticised in the bathing scene during the long, Western-style flashback in which she fights and falls in love with Lo.

30   Michelle Manelis 'Closet Queen', http://www.millaj.com/art/nova0301.shtml, accessed 30 August, 2003.

31   See Alan Jones *'Lara Croft Tomb Raider': The Official Film Companion*, London: Carlton, 2001, pp. 75–6, and S. Hamilton *The Official Tomb Raider Files*, London: Carlton, 2001, pp. 14–15, 30–1.

32   Reminiscent, of course, of Vasquez's reference to the male testicles in *Aliens* and G.I. Jane's invitation to 'Suck my dick'.

33   Jovovich plays up the femme/butch lesbian reading in interview: 'I'm a real girl. I like to shoot guns, but I like to wear lipstick, and Michelle is just more of the shooting guns type' (Chuck Wagner 'Milla Jovovich', *SFX*, July 2002, pp. 40–1: p. 40).

34   Julius Wiedemann *Digital Beauties*, Köln and London: Taschen, 2001.

35   Naomi Wolf *The Beauty Myth*, London: Vintage, 1991, p. 211.

36   Ibid., pp. 267–8.

37   David Bordwell *Planet Hong Kong: Popular Cinema and the Art of Entertainment*, Cambridge, MA and London: Harvard University Press, 2000, p. 244.

## Chapter 13

# SUSAN JEFFORDS

## *BREAKDOWN*
## White masculinity, class, and US action-adventure films

I'm looking for my wife. She's wearing a white Benetton sweater.

A white *what*?

IN THEIR INTRODUCTION to a special journal issue on cities, James Holsten and Arjun Appadurai argue that the globalization of capital and its consequent transnationalization of products and production 'tend to drive a deeper wedge between national space and its urban centers' in postcolonial societies.[1] In the US, as identities are defined increasingly in relation to patterns of consumption and shared product references rather than to historic affiliations with concepts of region and nation, a similar disjunction is occurring in the relations between national space and urban centers. From the time that Thomas Jefferson declared that 'our cities . . . exhibit specimens of London only; our country is a different nation', there has been a tension in the US between the ways in which urban and rural spaces are constructed in relation to the nation. While capital has largely defined the growth of urban centers (linked to tropes of 'progress', 'growth', etc.), pastoral mythologies have long held sway in defining the American imaginary.

However, as demographers such as William Frey are pointing out, demographic shifts in the US are challenging much traditional thinking about urban and non-urban spaces. Distinctions are now, according to Frey, less between city and country than between one region and another:

> The old 1950s distinctions between cities and suburbs could soon be rendered obsolete, supplanted by a new regional division: the old metropolitan areas, increasingly multiethnic, vs. new white-dominated population centers, mainly in the Southeast and Rocky Mountain West.[2]

It is a distinction that, as Frey argues, is taking place along racial lines. 'On a national scale', Frey concludes, such migration 'portends a pattern of demographic balkanisation rather than an even increase in racial and ethnic diversity across all regions and metropolitan areas'.[3]

As Frey's examination of recent census data suggests, it is no longer simply a question of prioritizing urban versus rural spaces as the essence of a 'true' America, but a question, as Larry Grossberg points out, of the very definition of space itself and how individual, communal, and national notions of space are redefining 'America'. Grossberg argues for a more complex reading of what is called the global and the local and the critical tools we employ in their analysis:

> This entails asking what it means to be situated in particular places, what it means to belong, and what different ways (or modalities) of belonging are possible in the contemporary milieu. It is no longer a question of globality (as homelessness) and locality (as the identification of place and identity), but of the various ways people are attached and attach themselves (affectively) into the world.[4]

The distinction, then, is less about urban versus rural than about the relationship between place and space, i.e. the relationship between a particular location – place – and the process of conceptualizing subjectivities as they relate to that location – space. Local, regional, or national discourses about space can, consequently, offer insights into how the process of redefinition is taking place, what is at stake in that defining, and who stands to profit in the process.

There is, arguably, a battle in the US under way about how those spaces are being defined and who gets to define them. It is a battle that is being fought, I would like to suggest, not simply over rural places but over the very definition of what is perceived as and understood to be 'rural' and, more importantly, the people who live in and are affiliated with 'rural spaces'. It is as well a debate about redefining the relationship that determines both how the 'rural' and how what have traditionally been seen as rural places are positioned in the American imaginary. As Frey's data suggest, one of the most heated and important of those battles is taking place in relation to the West and Southeast, i.e. in relation to those places that have been the most recent repositories of the notion of the 'rural' as white out-migration from metropolitan areas increases.

The radical economic and social restructuring that is taking place in the US results from both changing population demographics – principally through immigration, coded as 'race' – and changing economic structures – principally through globalization, coded as class. Because of the historic grounding of the American imaginary in spatial terms, there is, consequently, a parallel restructuring of the American imaginary through a rearticulation of space. The history of this country shows the profound and intimate connections between definitions of space in the US and constructions of identity. As a result, it is important to examine how the rearticulations of space that are taking place under the guise of 'globalization' are implicated in the reconstruction of ideas of identity.

In this essay, I want to focus on a specific aspect of how US identity is being rearticulated in relation to space, and that is through the interconnections between masculinity and class as Hollywood films have narrativized the restructuring of rural spaces and the kinds of people who inhabit them. While there are numerous recent films that are important sites for such a discussion (including *The Postman* (1997), *Phenomenon* (1996), *Last Man Standing* (1996), *To Wong Foo* (1995), *Armageddon* (1998), *Cast Away* (2000), *Gladiator* (2000), *The Perfect Storm* (2000), and many others), I want to focus here on *Breakdown*, a 1997 thriller about a yuppie urban couple stranded in the middle of an undesignated remote Southwest (the scene of many John Ford Westerns)[5] when their Jeep Grand Cherokee breaks down. On their way from Boston to San Diego to start new jobs, Jeff and Amy Taylor (Kurt Russell and Kathleen Quinlan) find themselves, as one reviewer puts it, thrown 'into the vast open spaces where the law does not reach'. As director Jonathan Mostow conceptualized the film, 'I wanted to explore the universal feeling of unease that people get when they're out in the middle of no place, far from home, far from civilized society, far from a place where rules and cops protect you'. In this film about tourism, class, job restructuring, and consumerism, the open spaces of the West are the spaces not only in which but about which the movie's narrative is structured. The levels of violence that qualify this film for the action-adventure genre are expressions of the intensity of the struggle over who can lay claim to these spaces. That the protagonists and antagonists are all white is a reflection of the value of the terrain and the stakes of the struggle, for these discourses are finally about the reconfiguration of white America.

*Breakdown*'s depiction of class conflicts among whites positions this film as embedded in the broad social, economic, and political shifts that are taking place in the US as a result of the global reconfiguration of capitalism, a reconfiguration that is resulting in the loss as well as the reconstruction of US jobs, as employment moves increasingly from the industrial to the service sector. Through its use of the action-adventure genre, *Breakdown* finally legitimizes violence against working-class whites by positioning them as members of obsolescent and useless economies and communities. The film's narrative implies that the only recourse of such a class of people is to prey upon the class above them, using whatever means of violence are necessary to eke out an income. In such a scenario, the film legitimizes the violence that is used in response to a predatory white working class. What begins as a battle over property quickly becomes a struggle for survival, thereby eliding the distinction between consumer possessions, class position, and life itself; in other words, this narrative implies, violent self-defense is the middle-class's only refuge against a predatory working class's efforts to take its possessions – its life – at all costs.

As they are re-locating from Boston to San Diego, Jeff and Amy Taylor decide to take the 'scenic route' through the Southwest, establishing themselves as tourists from the film's opening scenes. After stopping at a gas station along the way, their new Jeep Cherokee breaks down on the road. With no one in sight, they flag down the driver of an eighteen-wheeler who offers to give them a ride to the nearest phone (having 'roamed' too far, their car phone is inoperable). The suspense begins when Jeff decides to stay with their car and belongings and Amy hitches a ride from the trucker. To Jeff's surprise, he discovers that the car has not really broken down at all, but that a piece of wiring has merely come undone (we discover later in the film that the wire was deliberately loosened at the gas station by the kidnappers). When Jeff is able to re-start the car and drives to the diner where he is supposed to meet Amy, he finds that no one claims to have seen her or the trucker. In a take-off of Roman Polanski's 1988 *Frantic*, Jeff finds that his wife has been kidnapped and is being held for ransom by a gang led by the Good Samaritan trucker who gave Amy a ride. Jeff Taylor must rise out of his pastel-shirted urbanity to fight off this gang of rural misfits who supplement their low-paying jobs by hijacking and killing unsuspecting tourists.

*Breakdown* is marked by class conflict throughout its narrative. The Taylors are marked as upper middle-class urbanites from the moment we see them, driving their bright red new Jeep Cherokee, cell phone in hand, expensive belongings spilling out of their back seat. While Jeff's career is never specified (does it matter?), the fact that he is moving from Boston to San Diego for a better job suggests that his work can be done only in urban centers. When, early in the story, he side-swipes a pick-up, he is targeted for pursuit, since it turns out that the driver is part of a robbery and murder ring that targets tourists. While the film makes it clear that the members of this gang are 'locals', the film's reviewers also make it clear that they interpret those local signifiers as not simply ones of region but of class as well. The driver of the pick-up, Earl (M. C. Gainey), is labeled a 'stringy-haired goon' by Roger Ebert, someone who 'looks like he belongs back home in the swamps of *Deliverance*'. Lisa Schwarzbaum of *Entertainment Weekly* calls the same character a 'menacing-looking hillbilly',[6] while Peter Stack of the *San Francisco Chronicle* labels one of Earl's accomplices as 'a simple-minded sagebrush slug'.[7] Mike Clark of *USA Today* refers to the patrons of the diner as a 'flannel-shirt culture' of 'testy locals who haven't spent much time at the health club'.[8] The blandest referent is used by Paramount itself in its production information web-site, when they call the gang of hijackers 'the unsavory people one might run into at a roadside diner or small-town bar while on the road'.

While Taylor's job is never clear and his economic status is suggested only through the numbers of expensive items piled into the Jeep, the kidnap gang is clearly marked as working class (Red, played by J. T. Walsh, drives an eighteen-wheeler) or unemployed (Earl and Billy (Jack Noseworthy) seem not to have jobs to worry about). Whatever their legal sources of income, they have decided to supplement that income through robbing tourists. But even that enterprise, the film makes clear, is not a lucrative one. Though they have been doing this for some time (as the card-board boxes of stolen cameras stashed in Red's barn would attest), they seem not to have improved their economic position. If this is their business, then they are not very good businessmen. Thus, while they are marked by class, their class status is itself unmarked, i.e. their class position is not historicized in a way that would lead viewers to understand why these men cannot improve their incomes in any other way or why other types of work are not available to them. (The numbers of 'flannel-shirted' patrons at the diner at mid-day would suggest that there are more than Red and Earl who are underemployed.) The only conclusion that viewers are left to draw is that they are too 'lazy' to seek other work or to work harder, i.e. that there is an individual or possibly even a genetic[9] explanation for their class status. These impressions are reinforced by the labels placed on these characters by film reviewers: Ebert's reference to *Deliverance*, Schwarzbaum's use of 'hillbilly,' even Stack's use of 'simple-minded' (which turns out to be a mis-label in the film, as Billy reveals himself to be playing the simple-minded role in order to fool Taylor).

As they are presented in *Breakdown*, Red and his fellow hijackers are examples of what Evan Watkins has called 'throwaways':

> relics . . . isolated groups of the population who haven't moved with the times, and who now litter the social landscape and require the moral attention of cleanup crews, the containing apparatus of police and prisons, the financial drain of 'safety nets,' the immense maintenance bureaucracies of the state.[10]

While the hijackers' obsolescence is shown in numerous ways in the film – their clothing (this is not Ralph Lauren western style); the age of their pick-up trucks; their use of CBs instead of cell phones; and so on – there are three primary ways in which their obsolescence is made palpable: gender, nationalism, and consumer objects, chiefly the cars they drive. These are what Pierre Bourdieu labels the 'classifying practices' of 'taste':

> Taste is the practical operator of the transmutation of things into distinct and distinctive signs, of continuous distributions into discontinuous oppositions; it raises the differences inscribed in the physical order of bodies to the symbolic order of significant distinctions. It transforms objectively classified practices . . . into classifying practices, that is, into a symbolic expression of class position, by perceiving them in their mutual relations and in terms of social classificatory schemes. Taste is thus the source of the system of distinctive features which cannot fail to be perceived as a systematic expression of a particular class of conditions of existence, i.e. as a distinctive life-style.[11]

While 'taste' has been defined in relation to place throughout the history of this country, it is nonetheless important to understand the ways in which it is being structured now in relation to the reconfiguration of the 'rural'.

Red's traditional gendered household and his treatment of his wife mark him as out-of-step with the advertised social consciousness of the American corporate workplace. More specifically, the structures of masculinity that typify Red and his cohorts signify an outdated model of manhood, one that is tied to notions of nationalism and patriarchal providership. When the hijackers confront Jeff with their ransom demands, their comments about Amy are explicitly sexist. After Earl calls her a 'slut', Red begins to describe the 'object' they have that would be of interest to Jeff: 'it's about 5'5", 115 pounds, 3 or 4 of that just pure tit; nice curly brown hair, upstairs and down'. When Red and his accomplices arrive at his house, with Amy's body and the Taylors' belongings in the back of the trucks, his wife comes out to meet him. She clearly has no knowledge of the hijackings and does not want his friends to be there – 'Can't they come some other time?' Red dismisses her and clarifies her place in their relationship by saying, 'Why don't you go and make breakfast?'

More than marking their obsolescence, the attention drawn to the hijackers' 'outdated' sexism distracts from the gender dynamics of the film. While both Jeff and Amy are traveling to San Diego to start new careers, and while she is portrayed as 'feisty' enough to fight her kidnappers, it is clear that the film's hero is Jeff Taylor alone. It is Jeff who must rise above his urban masculinity to rescue his wife, and Jeff who defeats her kidnappers. For most of the violent conflict scenes, she is hidden in a truck or locked in a freezer below the barn. Even in the final, climactic scene in which Red is using his eighteen-wheeler to push their pick-up off a bridge, she is kept from the fight by having her leg pinned under the dashboard of the pick-up, leaving Jeff to do all the work of defeating their last and most vicious enemy. Only at the film's end, when Jeff has thrown Red over the side of the bridge into a riverbed below and has rescued Amy, does Amy take an active role in the fight. Reinforcing the gender-typing maintained throughout the film, rather than fight Red directly, Amy's only action is to release the parking brake on the pick-up, the only thing keeping the massive cab of the eighteen-wheeler from falling over the side of the bridge; when she releases the brake, the truck falls onto Red's still-conscious body, crushing him. Unlike Jeff's violence, which is motivated by the necessity of saving his wife, hers is unnecessary and gratuitous, motivated by revenge. Thus, while Red's outdated sexism marks his obsolescence, Jeff's masculinity is marked as up-to-date, 'modern', and, finally, more effective. While gender equity may be the rhetorical façade of the modern corporate economy, *Breakdown*'s narrative suggests that beneath that façade lies a continuing need for gender distinctions and gendered roles, if the corporate urban class is to keep apace of its own obsolescence.

An equally important mark of obsolescence is the hijacker's nationalism. Though there is never an explicit discussion of the US, there are numerous and clear references to a patriotic Americanism that is affiliated only with the hijackers. When Red first steps out of his truck to offer assistance to the Taylors, he is wearing a cap with a US flag on the front; he later changes this hat for another, this time with a 'USA' logo. Later, when Jeff and Amy seek refuge from Red's attacks in a dilapidated mobile home on his land, Red chases them with his eighteen-wheeler, running right through the middle of the trailer.[12] As the trailer breaks in half, Amy and Jeff are thrown back onto an old couch above which a US flag is prominently displayed. These symbols are subtle but not unnoticeable; their consistent affiliation with Red marks his obsolescent economy, gender, and culture as grounded in a US patriotism that is identified, not with an American capitalism, but with an American imaginary that is itself shown to be outdated. Because it is a nationalism affiliated with a class-based obsolescence, this country-centered patriotism is seen to be not simply inoperative but defunct.

But more than this, the hijackers are obsolescent because they manage their 'business' in an outdated way, with little productivity and no growth. It is clear from the plot that the Taylors are not the first tourists that these men have robbed and killed. While it is not stated, it is probable that Red, Earl, and Billy may use these hijackings as their primary if not sole source of financial support. Both Earl and Billy are available in the middle of the day to set up the deal,[13] while Red's eighteen-wheeler is always empty. However, besides their availability during the day, there is little to suggest that these hijackings have been profitable; only the glimpse of a large-screen TV and video-game setup in Red's house would indicate any financial benefits that have accrued to these men from their labors. They are also, of course, somewhat constrained by their choice of targets for robbery. Since they rob only tourists, they are in a position of having to be reactive to the driving plans of travelers, awaiting those who choose to take the less direct, more 'scenic' route. Consequently, while this may be their 'business', these men seem to have failed to develop or benefit from it in any but the most mundane ways. They operate a business that is truly local, limited by terrain, and unable to connect to larger enterprises. They are, in other words, incapable of moving into a global market.

In contrast, the Taylors are clearly part of an urban class that is mobile and flexible. They are relocating from Boston to San Diego for new jobs. While their jobs are never identified, their 'style' suggests that of a professional class, marked by the trappings of expensive automobile, cell phones, CD players, Polo and Benetton clothing, and possessions that they do not wish to leave unattended in the desert. In a particular sense, their jobs are less important than their style, for it is precisely that style that gets them marked by the hijackers in the first place. As Earl says to Jeff:

> Do you think we just picked you out of the clear blue? Shiny new car, Massachusetts plates – probably be a week before anybody misses you. Should've got the bumper sticker that goes with that car: 'Rich asshole looking for trouble.'

They assume that, because of this style, the Taylors are wealthy. When Jeff protests that he does not have the $90,000 in ransom money that the hijackers have asked for, Billy shouts at Jeff, 'If some hot-shot fuck like you ain't watching the bottom line, it'd be the first time in history!'

This is the style of the class that Masao Miyoshi identifies as the 'transnational elite':

> The rapid formation of the transnational class is likely to develop a certain homogeneity among its members. . . . Everywhere commodities are invented, consumed, and discarded. And they are the cultural products of the transnational class. The members of such a class are the leaders, the role models, of the 1990s and beyond; their one gist is, needs to be, an ability to converse and communicate with each other.[14]

While neither Jeff nor Amy Taylor is identified as a member of a transnational corporation or is leaving Boston to relocate outside the US, it is clear that their lives are situated in transnational urban centers and that they perceive themselves as 'tourists' in their own country, when they travel outside the boundaries of cities. In addition, they are identified almost exclusively with and through consumer products. When Jeff is first trying to find Amy at Belle's Diner, he asks a man behind the lunch counter if he has seen a woman 'wearing a white Benetton sweater'. The man's response – 'A white what?' – and later misdesignation of the label – 'Has anyone here seen a woman with a white button-down sweater?' – marks the Taylors as living in another world, one in which a familiarity with consumer labels is an assumed token of the everyday, of 'home'. When Jeff is first kidnapped by the hijackers and hears their ransom demand, he protests that they do not have $90,000. It is only when Earl calls him the 'Donut King' that he realizes that the $90,000 figure came, not from Red and Earl, but from Amy, and that she was sending him a message. Earlier in the film, when the Taylors first left the gas station where they saw Earl, Amy purchased a bag of junk food, including some Hostess donuts that offer a contest prize of $90,000. Their mode of communication, then, and a means of deceiving the hijackers, is through consumer products. Finally, Jeff's own sense of work and employment is shown when he asks the bartender at Belle's, 'Do you think that she [Amy] could have left a message with one of your other employees?' The response – 'I don't think that's possible. You see, I'm the only one that works here' – shows the radical disjunction between Jeff's sense of labor – layers of workers, hierarchies, employees – and that of the men who hang out at Belle's.

One of the key ways in which the hijackers' outdated nationalism and obsolescent industrial capitalism is shown is through the vehicles they drive. Red's eighteen-wheeler signifies a certain era of American growth, a nationally centered capitalism, and a transportation system that emphasizes interstate highways and geographic contiguity. It is also a vehicle that signifies a certain brand of unionism, a culture of independence, and an ethic of communality. Automobile workers are also those around whom large portions of a narrative about the loss of US-based high-wage industrial jobs have been centered. Al drives a paneled truck that boasts the slogan 'Country Wide' on its side, emblazoned across a map of the US. Earl drives a used black Ford F150 pick-up.

In contrast, the Taylors drive a new bright red Jeep Cherokee. The Jeep Grand Cherokee was named *Peterson's 4-Wheel and Off-Road Magazine*'s '4 × 4 of the year', receiving this title six times in sixteen years. The Jeep has also been the car that brought the Chrysler Corporation back to its current levels of profitability, leading the company in sales, both nationally and internationally. (Jeeps were among the cars responsible for Chrysler's significant leap in profit between 1995 and 1996, with the company increasing its earnings by 77 percent in that year.) With international sales around the world and with an assembly plant in Thailand, Jeep has been the vehicle that has led international sales for Chrysler. Its advertising campaign has been noted by *Advertising Age* to promote Jeep as one of many 'lifestyle products' that can utilize 'universal ad[s], in which the product and the image become one'[15] in global ad. campaigns.

Earl's vehicle, the Ford F150, has been the best-selling truck in the US for nineteen years and was *Motor Trend*'s 1997 'truck of the year'. Placed second on the Fortune 500 list, the Ford Motor Company has sales that are more than twice those of Chrysler, with Ford also being the leading US exporter of vehicles. However, Ford's international line of cars does not include the F150 truck or other pick-up trucks, focusing instead on passenger cars. The company celebrates itself as 'the Company that revolutionized transportation of livery and goods to help build this great country' (Ford recently sold its heavy truck line to Freightliner).

While the pick-up truck is affiliated primarily with independent rural labor, the Jeep is sold as the vehicle of recreation and adventure:

> For over 50 years, Jeep vehicles have been modern beasts of burden in the quest for adventure and discovery. Check out the 1998 Wrangler, Cherokee, and Grand Cherokee, vehicles with a heritage of four-wheel drive excellence and a hunger for freedom and open places.[16]

In this distinction, the Taylor's choice of vehicle is symbolic not only of a certain economic status but of a certain *style*, one that seems to fit with global marketing campaigns, new definitions of 'adventure' and 'discovery' that are defined less by territorial expansion than by a frame-of-mind that defines itself in global rather than regional terms. While Ford's web-site celebrates its long history and recounts the 'Ford story' from Henry Ford's first plant to the new CXZ model that is being marketed as the global 'model T', Chrysler offers only the logo: 'Even our history looks forward.'

The Jeep (flashing back here to the cars featured in Steven Spielberg's 1995 blockbuster *Jurassic Park*) – affiliated with tourism, exploration, adventure, and disposable wealth – is the vehicle-of-choice for a class that views rural spaces through the lens of adventure, leisure, and a departure from labor. Its 'go-anywhere' imagery suggests that these forms of tourism and adventure are unbounded, not limited by road systems or boundaries. It symbolizes an urbanized consumer class that balks at barriers to its enactment of its chosen forms of consumption. Ford trucks, on the other hand, are marketed as working vehicles for American workers. As country-western star Alan Jackson's theme song for Ford trucks suggests, these trucks are purchased, not by the wealthy or by those having the expendable income to afford weekend 'adventures', but by working Americans whose incomes are limited. Leaning against the side of a Ford pick-up, Jackson sings, 'If I had money, tell you what I'd do – go downtown and buy a Ford truck or two.' The opening premise of the song – '*if* I had money' – seems to say it all.

While *Breakdown* is clearly about a class conflict, the film evades class specificity by regionalizing sites of working class status. The use by reviewers of terms such as 'hillbilly', 'the swamps of *Deliverance*', or 'cowboy' to describe the members of the gang suggests – along with names such as 'Red', 'Earl', or 'Billy' – regional markings that have historically been used to identify poor whites living in partic- ular regions of the US, whether the South, Appalachia, or the West. The fact that these characters are read by reviewers as fitting these regional stereotypes suggests, however, that their regional specificity has been evacuated to now refer to any poor, rural, non-urbanized whites. (I say non-urbanized to distinguish this group from those whites, largely middle-class, who have 'escaped' to rural areas in recent years in order to avoid city life, a theme seen in such films as *For Richer or Poorer*). *Breakdown* presents rural areas of the US as sites of fear for its viewing audiences, audiences that it assumes will identify more with urbanized, middle class Jeff Taylor as hero than with regionalized, working class Red Barr. But unlike the flurry of urban white anxiety films of the early 1990s (such as *Grand Canyon* (1991) or *Falling Down* (1993)), in which whites expressed fears about urban minority populations, *Breakdown* exhibits a fear that is specifically associated with white, working-class antagonists.

Certainly, *Breakdown* is not the first Hollywood film to narrativize white middle-class fears of the white lower classes. The classic film in this category – which Roger Ebert predictably spotted – is *Deliverance* (1972). But *Breakdown* is not *Deliverance*, and the distinctions are important for understanding how rural spaces are being configured in relation to white ethnicities. First and foremost, *Deliverance* is a film that laments the disappearance of a 'true' pastoral, the river that is about to disappear as part of an expansive development scheme that includes the building of a huge dam. The territories of *Breakdown*, however, are tourist spaces, places that have come in the American imaginary to be synonymous with the genre of Western films (particularly the panoramic vistas of John Ford films) or with the 'See America First' tourism movement. While Jeff and Amy Taylor seem isolated in the midst of Monument Valley, their isolation is very much a constructed one that is self-consciously troped as a desire for what has been manufactured through consumer tourism (in an extension of the imperial gaze) as the 'scenic'. In contrast to *Deliverance*, which touts its rural landscape as an escape from the world of business and consumerism, the landscape in *Breakdown* is always and already seen through a lens of consumption.

Perhaps more importantly, the antagonists in *Deliverance* – the white mountain men who sodomize Bobby Trippe – are typed as genetically different from the group of white urban men canoeing down the river for a weekend adventure. Though the mountain people are also white, the suggestions of the population's decline as the result of advanced inbreeding place them as almost a race apart from the middle-class white men who are the film's protagonists. The possibilities that one group could become the other are beyond consideration. In contrast, the white antagonists in *Breakdown* are distinguished from the Taylors only through their class affiliations – through their choices in lifestyle and employment.

The threat that the Taylors could become the hijackers is not beyond comprehension. Without their Benetton sweaters and their Jeep, the Taylors could find themselves drinking Budweisers at Belle's diner. At a time when more than 43 million jobs have been lost in the US since 1979, and when the US is experiencing its 'most acute job insecurity since the Depression',[17] approximately 72 percent of people claim to be either personally affected by a layoff or to know someone close to them who has been laid off. The jobs that are being lost are increasingly those held by white-collar workers like the Taylors. And, most importantly of all, the Taylors do not have the $90,000 that is being demanded for Amy's ransom. Jeff can at best have money advanced from his credit cards, but they clearly do not have the kinds of resources that their 'style' suggests. In such a context, it is their style and a few consumer possessions that stand between the Taylors and the hijackers. The titles of the two films are perhaps clearest in articulating the shifts that have taken place between 1972 and 1997: while the male-bonding buddies have been 'delivered' from the shadow of their whiteness, Jeff and Amy Taylor are living in a society in which such categories have 'broken down', as it were, and in which such a deliverance is no longer possible, even in a Jeep.

While *Deliverance* provides important referents, especially for *Breakdown*'s reviewers, the film whose plot is most closely copied by *Breakdown* is Polanski's suspense drama, *Frantic*, the story of a fairly nondescript upper-middle class American doctor in Paris on a business-vacation trip whose wife is kidnapped and held for ransom when she mistakenly picks up a suitcase that contains stolen American military technology. Like Taylor, Richard Walker (Harrison Ford) gets no assistance from police or state authorities and must abandon his everydayness and discover some internal resources that will enable him to get his wife back safely. Like Taylor, Walker must discover his potential for violence in order to combat the kidnappers. But for all of the similarities in plot, the films differ in significant ways. First and foremost, *Frantic* takes place in Paris, a large international urban center, rather than the unpopulated rural areas of the desert Southwest. Though Walker is effectively isolated because of the lack of police support and his inability to speak French, the film's anxieties rest, not on the dilemma of being 'stranded out in the middle of nowhere', but on the more 1980s problem of being anonymous in the midst of a crowded city. Second, Ford's character is given assistance in this movie, suggesting that his isolation is more situational than absolute. He meets a young Frenchwoman, Michelle (Emmanuel Seigner), courier for the stolen goods, who then helps to guide him through Paris, suggesting that the stakes here of international espionage affect people of different nationalities, classes, etc. The fact that Russell's character has no such ally makes his triumph over his own urbanity more heroic and underscores the fact that his battles foreground rather than overcome boundaries of nation and class. *Frantic* ends up emphasizing Walker's resourcefulness, persistence, and potential for violence as part of his 'Americanness', celebrating his national identity in ways that are distinct from *Breakdown*, a film that celebrates Taylor's 'Americanness' only inasmuch as it makes him the inheritor of a global consumer culture. Third, there is a detailed motivation for the kidnapping, one that places the film securely in a late Cold War context. Ford's wife mistakenly takes from the airport a suitcase that contains a piece of top-secret military hardware; spies have stolen it and are putting it up for sale on the international market. Finally, because the villains are international spies and the bidders for the military hardware are wealthy businessmen, the element of class conflict is eliminated in favor of a national one, as the American hero both rescues his wife and foils the spies.

This shift from foreign enemies to local 'hillbillies' is suggestive of the ways in which a post-Cold War American imaginary is being constructed. Since it is precisely the Cold War enemies who are becoming some of the US's largest trading partners, narratives that target foreign nationals as sources of US fears are no longer as economically profitable as they once were. While Cold War films suggested that difference should be seen in terms of US/non-US distinctions, films such as

*Breakdown* indicate that difference can now be marked in terms of types of market economies and labor structures, economies that are coded as 'global' and 'local', 'new' and 'obsolescent', professional and working class, or – more to the point of this essay – mobile and place-bound. Jeff Taylor's defeat of the hijacking gang shows not only the ability of the middle-class hero to defeat working-class efforts to redefine income but also his ability to reclaim ownership of the American 'Heartland' through restoring the safety of tourism as the urban middle class's mode of access to the mythologies of American national spaces.

Historian Susan Rhoades Neel comments: 'Over and over again, America has (re)formulated its national identity from the stuff of the mythic West.'[18] *Breakdown*, set in Hollywood's backdrop for that mythic West, is about nothing less than this: the reformulation of American national identity in a transnational era. Because the 'mythic West' has been the site for such reformulations for so much of US history, and because that space has been mythologized precisely through its rurality – its separateness from urban centers, industrialization, and change – a film such as *Breakdown* can be read as indicative of how the reformulation of American identity is being articulated as a reconstruction of rural spaces. Lisa Schwarzbaum's review of *Breakdown* characterizes one of the key ways in which that redefinition is taking shape:

> The American West has always been our final frontier – an untamed swath of continent big enough for those who don't socialize well to find a suitable address and romantic enough to let a million moviemakers' imaginations bloom. But the kind of behavioral wildness inspired by all that brutal vastness has changed with the times. Where Butch Cassidy types once hid in the hills and made it a point of honor not to kill the gentry they robbed, now angry militia groups and more psychopathic stick-em-up types have moved into the neighborhood, threatening our highly prized sense of neighborliness. Today's mythic West is still a place to drive fast and free. But it's also an anxiety-provoking territory that can turn creepily alien with just one bad close encounter – you wouldn't want to get stranded there.

Schwarzbaum puts her finger on both how the 'West' has changed and why that change is so fearful: while 'Butch Cassidy types' did not kill the 'gentry' they robbed, Red Barr and his partners do. Those who once lived on the margins of social wealth were, according to Schwarzbaum, more 'polite' than their contemporary compatriots. The escalation of fear – of having that 'one bad encounter' – is related specifically to an escalation in perceived violence, a violence committed, for Schwarzbaum, by 'angry militia groups' and 'psychopaths'. Both *Breakdown* and Schwarzbaum explain the perceived increasing violence in rural spaces – and, by extension, the increasing violence in the US – through the individual emotional shortcomings of marginalized groups – 'angry' militias and psychopaths.

The slippage here is important: those psychopaths and angry warriors turn out, in *Breakdown*, to be nothing other than working-class white men, who, like 'psychopaths', seem to have no rational explanation for their anger and the violence that results from it. Let there be no mistake: many working-class white men *are* angry. And while, according to Michelle Fine *et al.*, who have studied working-class white men, they target their anger at women, people of color, and gays and lesbians, the source of their anger is more critically the very movements towards globalization that *Breakdown* takes for granted.

> In our interviews with poor and working-class males . . . we hear a mantra of losses that they narrate, angrily, bitterly, with pointed fingers. From days gone by, they have lost wives whom they thought would stay home and cater to them, good jobs in the public sector and those protected by labor unions. Their schools and communities have been 'invaded' by people of color. Their monopoly on power and privilege has been pierced. They are not happy. Their stories of loss are voiced in a discourse of property rights. While it is the case that they have been dethroned, re-gendered, and re-raced in the past two decades, they feel only mugged. Not by the global treachery of late capitalism, the flight of manufacturing jobs from the United States, or the erosion of strong labor unions, all of which are the real cause of their present circumstances. Instead, they feel erased by white women, men of color, gays and lesbians.[19]

Because it heroizes those who profit from the economic forces that are the source of that anger, *Breakdown* must show these working-class men as impolite, as predators, and as violators of the West through which a new American identity is being defined.

In contrast to those who are presented as extremists – the militia members and psychopaths – Jeff Taylor is presented as middle class, not simply in the sense of his income but also in the sense that he can be seen as a middling or average man. Roger Ebert refers to Taylor as the new 'Everyman'. The production materials are explicit here, both producers and the director referring to Taylor as an 'ordinary man'. Martha De Laurentiis comments that Russell was selected because:

> Kurt is every man's actor. He's vulnerable so that men can relate to him and he's handsome so that women like him. The emotion he brings to this character is perfect for this story about a situation that could happen to anybody.

Writer-director Mostow is clear about how he envisions the 'ordinariness' of his story: 'This is a story that could happen to anybody,' he says, 'anybody who has ever driven a car and had a breakdown or run out of gas or anything.' Mostow continues:

> When I wrote this story, I wanted to explore the *universal* feeling of unease that people get when they're out in the middle of no place, far from home, far from civilized society, far from a place where rules and cops protect you (emphasis added).

From whom, one might ask, does one need protection when in these remote places? While the film offers only the three kidnappers – Red, Earl, and Billy – the film's reviewers fill in whatever gaps the depictions of these characters may leave behind. Through references to *Deliverance*, militias, hillbillies, or psychopaths, reviewers have constructed a character who inhabits these rural areas of America. What little we know about them is that they are white, male, unpredictable, and violent, and that their greatest threat is posed, not to their rural neighbors, but to the 'gentry' that is passing through. And while many viewers may have more reason to sympathize with Red, Earl, and Billy as being out of work and desperate to find a source of income, the film's producers and director guide viewer identifications towards Taylor, the 'Everyman' tourist whose consumer goods and lifestyle are threatened by those who challenge his class's possession of new cars, new technologies, and new jobs. As the producers emphasize repeatedly, 'the story could happen to anyone . . . When the audience sees this picture, they will be able to see that they could be in a similar situation tomorrow if they're driving while on vacation.'

In a recent article, Pico Iyer describes what he calls the new 'Global Man', a member of 'The New Business Class' who lives 'everywhere at once, inhabiting a growing community of the air that is responsible to no nation or governing body but only to the imperatives of commerce'.[20] For such global citizens, Iyer declares, 'The practical assumption is that everyone's passing through.' Like Jeff and Amy Taylor, such 'Global Men' have no real tie to a location or place but instead inhabit the new spaces of global commerce, showing clearly the extent to which upward mobility in a global economic regime requires a separation from historical affiliations with land as nation or territory. In such a scheme, those who maintain ties to historically determined definitions of space are marked as outmoded and, more pointedly, possible threats to those who are operating in the new global spaces, especially if, as in the case of the Taylors, those who adhere to obsolescent definitions of space attempt to interfere with the 'passing through' of those engaged in displaced commerce.

In such a framework, not only does the fact of Red's, Earl's, and Billy's obsolescence become significant, but the terms in which their obsolescence is articulated become even more powerful. That the kidnappers are white, male, and violent is important but not sufficient to make these men threatening (in the way that it would be, for example, for characters who were young, male, and black; after all, violent white men still serve as big box office draws when they are cast as heroes). But that they are bad businessmen, sexists, and nationalist patriots does. They are not, like Iyer's 'Global Men', participating in a 'global marketplace', but are instead dependent upon the random and unpredictable leavings of a mobile consumer class. The significance of bad business practices being associated with American patriotism cannot be lost here; that both are marked as obsolescent and threatening to middle class Americans should give us some indication of where *Breakdown*'s fears really lie, i.e. as targeting those who have failed to adjust to the economic terms of the new 'global marketplace'.

The historic regional affiliations that marked earlier periods in this nation's history – the South, the West, the mid-West – are collapsed in *Breakdown* to form a homogenous category of 'hillbillies' and 'cowboys' who stand in stark contrast to the mobile (both regionally and economically) Taylors, whose histories have affiliations only with consumer products and not with a nation or region. *Breakdown* pits the upwardly mobile Taylors against the economically battered inhabitants of the rural West in terms that suggest that being tied to a region or to land is not only counterproductive economically but threatening to the very lifestyle the Taylors represent. The beauty of *Breakdown*'s narrative is that it manages to make the style of Iyer's corporate consumer class stand in as the 'everyman' of US global restructuring, in striking opposition to the rural laborer who was the foundation of the Jeffersonian pastoral ideal. *Breakdown* is constructing, then, an 'everyman' that is identified as a white, urban, consumer who lives in urban centers and only 'vacations' in rural areas. While the film begins with an assumption of urban tourism as the 'universal' experience and emotional vehicle for the narrative, it quickly moves to ownership of and access to rural spaces as the mark, not simply of an urban, but of a *global* consumerism that depends for its profitability on unrestrained access to sites for consumer production and development.

Films such as *Breakdown* narrate what geographer Neil Smith calls a 'spatial shift' that prefaces the kinds of significant cultural and economic changes that took place at the beginning of the twentieth century and again at the end of the Second World War. As we move closer to 'globalization', films about rural places help us to see both how that shift is being articulated and who will be affected by it.

## Notes

I would like to thank the following people for their excellent feedback on an earlier draft of this essay: Ann Anagnost, Lucy Jarosz, Vicky Lawson, Lorna Rhodes, Laurie Sears, and Priscilla Wald.

1   James Holsten and Arjun Appadurai 'Cities and Citizenship', *Public Culture*, 8: 2, Winter 1996, p. 189.
2   William H. Frey 'Demographics of cities, suburbs becoming similar', *Seattle Post-Intelligencer,* March 26, 1998, p. A15.
3   William H. Frey 'Immigration and Internal Migration "Flight" from US Metropolitan Areas: Toward a New Demographic Balkanisation', *Urban Studies*, 32: 4–5, 1995, p. 755.
4   Larry Grossberg 'The Space of Culture, the Power of Space', in Iain Chambers and Lidia Curtis (eds) *The Post-Colonial Question*, New York: Routledge, 1996, pp. 185–6.
5   *Breakdown* was filmed in Barstow, California (also the location for *Broken Arrow* (1996) and *Courage Under Fire* (1996)), Templin Highway, Los Angeles, California (also the location for *The Net* (1995)), Moab, Utah (also the location for *City Slickers II* (1994) and *The Sunchaser* (1996)), and Victorville, Mojave Desert, California (also the location for *Contact* (1997), *Face/Off* (1997), and *My Favorite Martian* (1998)). While there is not adequate time to discuss these locations here, the consistent use of these sites as backgrounds for films about class, conspiracies, and violence should not be overlooked.
6   Lisa Schwarzbaum 'Review', *Entertainment Weekly*, May 1997.
7   Peter Stack 'The Call of the Wild Ride', *San Francisco Chronicle*, May 2, 1997.
8   Mike Clark 'Well-crafted *Breakdown* revels in suspense', *USA Today*, May 2, 1997.
9   Roger Ebert's quick reference to *Deliverance* makes this inference explicit, but the characterizations utilized by the film tap into the kinds of historical imageries popularized by *Deliverance*. For a further discussion of the country/city dynamic in *Deliverance*, see Carol Clover's chapter on this film in her book *Men, Women, and Chainsaws*, London: British Film Institute, 1992.

10   It is not, of course, accidental that the factor of time would become a mechanism for distin-
     guishing between classes. As Pierre Bourdieu points out, the 'mark of time' is itself one
     of the fundamental factors in the functioning of the dominant classes as it is played out in
     terms of generational differences in jobs, access to employment, etc. See Pierre Bourdieu
     *Distinction: A Social Critique of the Judgment of Taste*, trans. Richard Nice, New York:
     Routledge, 1984, pp. 295–6.
11   Bourdieu *Distinction*, pp. 174–5.
12   The use of the trailer here is yet another subtle marking of obsolescence as class- and not
     individually-based. To show that this is about rural spaces and not just about Red, there is
     a scene earlier in the film in which the sheriff is distracted from helping Jeff find his wife
     by a radio call: 'Mrs. Gilbert's locked out of her trailer again.' Even those who could help
     Taylor are kept from doing so by the demands of a class of people that live in trailers.
13   While it is certainly the case that being free during the day does not necessarily lead to a
     conclusion of not being in a wage-earning job, as Raymond Williams reminds us, these
     kinds of assumptions are products of capitalism as a shaping force of what constitutes the
     day-to-day sense of 'reality': 'When we have lived long enough with such a system it is
     difficult not to mistake it for a necessary and practical reality.' Raymond Williams *The
     Country and The City*, London: The Hogarth Press, [1973] 1985, p. 295.
14   Masao Miyoshi 'A Borderless World? From Colonialism to Transnationalism and the
     Decline of the Nation-State', *Critical Inquiry*, 19, Summer 1993, p. 747.
15   Jay Schulberg 'Successful global ads need simplicity, clarity', *Advertising Age*, June 30, 1997,
     p. 17.
16   Official Jeep web-site: http://www.jeepunpaved.com/nav/fsmaster.html.
17   *The Downsizing of America*, New York: *The New York Times*, 1996, p. 6.
18   Susan Rhoades Neel 'Tourism and the American West: New Departures', *Pacific Historical
     Review*, 65: 4, p. 519.
19   Michelle Fine, Lois Weis, Judi Anderson and Julia Marusza 'White Loss', in Maxine Seller
     and Lois Weis (eds) *Beyond Black and White: New Faces and Voices in US Schools*, Albany, NY:
     SUNY Press, 1998, p. 283.
20   Pico Iyer 'The New Business Class', *The New York Times Magazine*, March 8, 1998, pp. 37ff.

## Chapter 14

## MARTIN FRADLEY

# MAXIMUS MELODRAMATICUS
## Masculinity, masochism and white male paranoia in contemporary Hollywood cinema

Paranoia *n* 1. A mental disorder characterised by any of several types of delusions, as of grandeur or persecution. 2. *Inf.* Intense fear or suspicion, esp. when unfounded.

. . . delusions of persecution are unpleasant, but they are acceptable in so far as the ego remains the focus of attention.[1]

THE UNDOUBTED HIGHLIGHT of the typically uneventful 73rd Annual Academy Awards in Los Angeles was the sight of Russell Crowe – the star of Ridley Scott's Oscar-magnet *Gladiator* (2000) – sneering and pouting his way through the ceremony. As host Steve Martin cracked gag after gag at the star's expense, Crowe's sullen features refused to budge, his steadfast scowl threatening to crack the lens of the camera inspecting the actor in leering close-up. Such unflinching disdain remained even when the actor's performance was hailed as the year's best by Hollywood's *glitterati*, his terse acceptance 'speech' indicating little more than scarcely concealed contempt. Despite his entertainingly grumpy refusal to grin and bear it, this was still a *performance*; indeed, it was an almost generic turn in a gendered role in which Hollywood has invested much time, money and ideological angst in recent years: that of the angry, beleaguered white male.

This chapter examines how white masculinity has represented itself within the utopian masculine sphere of the Hollywood imaginary. In particular, I explore here the aesthetics, narratives and rhetorical strategies of the Hollywood action movie as it stands today, reading *Gladiator* as a high-profile, near-canonical and – I would argue – symptomatic Hollywood take on what has been dubbed the so-called 'crisis of masculinity'. Whilst focusing on this revivalist epic, I will also propose that the masochistic narratives and tortured *mise-en-scène* that typify the contemporary action film have their basis in wider cultural narratives characterised by a form of paranoia which is itself mobilised and soothed by a somewhat paradoxical emphasis on a *narcissistic* and performative masculine angst. By looking at the fantasy space of contemporary Hollywood – the popular bastion, as Robyn Wiegman points out, of US culture's 'historic reliance on the ideological supremacy of everything white, heterosexual, and male'[2] – I will argue that broad but historically contingent fears, desires, fantasies and anxieties can be read, interpreted and critiqued.

It is widely alleged that the average American male – and, more specifically, the average *white* male – has been having a tough time of it lately. In a cultural discourse which has grown louder and more prominent since the so-called liberationist era of the 1960s, the decentring, disenfranchisement, disempowerment and (more melodramatically) even the *death* of the Great White American Male has been frequently pronounced. Indeed, what with the usual roll-call of supposed post-1960s advancements by, amongst (structuring) others, feminists (read: women), civil rights activists, the ideologues of identity politics, the gay and lesbian rights movement, not forgetting the slow-but-growing acceptance of multi-culturalism and postmodern celebration of difference(s), white guys are apparently on the ropes and in danger of going out for the count.[3] A 1993 *USA Today* piece entitled 'The End of the Great White Male' typifies this trend. Here, John Graham rhetorically asks:

> [w]hat about the future of the Great White Male? . . . There will be pitiful efforts to restore his feathers, to prop up his prowess and power. Nevertheless, the great white male's day has passed, along with his un-limited, unilateral power and influence . . . From now on the great white male will be one of many.[4]

The death of the Great White Male has surely been greatly exaggerated. Nonetheless, Graham raises some pertinent questions; how exactly, we may ask, have white American men, and by extension Hollywood cinema, interpreted, responded to and represented these shifts in contemporary American culture and society?[5]

The answer is, of course, with a great deal of complaint, hysteria and no little paranoia; a potent combination resulting in a dubious appropriation of victim status. The same year that Graham's provocative article appeared, Joel Schumacher's *Falling Down* (1993) – perhaps *the* Ur-text in Hollywood's take on the angsty, angry white male – was released to a mass of controversy and critical debate. The film has been widely represented as an important popular text in this emergent discourse, both deeply symptomatic and highly problematic. *Falling Down* has been thoroughly analysed and extensively critiqued, and is – alongside David Fincher's ambivalent and darkly comic *Fight Club* (1999) – probably the most explicit cinematic take on the much-vaunted 'crisis of masculinity' in post-industrial American culture. This narrative of (so-called) crisis reached its zenith in the 1990s, a decade neatly framed by two key texts: Robert Bly's hysterical tome of essentialist masculine 'mythopoeticism', the bible of the so-called 'men's movement' *Iron John*;[6] and high-profile feminist Susan Faludi's entertainingly sensationalistic *Stiffed: The Betrayal of the Modern Man*.

Faludi's impressionistic, quasi-ethnographic survey of America and its male discontents focuses upon the baby-boomer generation's angst and alleged patrimonial burden (or, indeed, the *lack* of such a gendered encumbrance). Faludi's rhetoric of – real or symbolic – 'paternal desertion' is typified by a nostalgia for the past and the invocation of abundance and wholeness which came in the wake of the Second World War:

> Never, or so their sons were told, did fathers have so much to pass on as at the peak of the American Century. And conversely, never was there such a burden on the sons to learn how to run a world they would inherit. Yet the fathers, with all the force of fresh victory and moral virtue behind them, seemingly unfettered in their paternal power and authority, failed to pass the mantle, the knowledge, all that power and authority, on to their sons.[7]

The overdetermined rhetorical tropes Faludi employs here – abundance/lack, presence/absence – culminate in a quasi-Lacanian metaphor: in the introjective relay of the eternal masculine, the phallus-baton has been dropped somewhere along the way. If this narrative verges on 'mythopoeticism', Faludi's increasingly mixed metaphors merely add to the melodramatic storm-in-a-teacup. Thus, 'paternal betrayal' becomes the 'artichoke's bitter heart' of masculine angst. 'The fathers had made a promise,' suggests Faludi, 'and then had not made good on it. They had lied'.[8] Employing liquid metaphors of natural disaster, *Stiffed* suggests the emasculating swamp of contemporary American culture whose 'tsunami force' drowns 'fathers as well as sons':

> Its surge had washed all of the men of the American Century into a swirling ocean of larger-than-life, ever-transmitting images in which usefulness to society meant less and less and celebrityhood ever more, where even one's appearance proved an unstable currency. The ever-prying, ever-invasive beam reducing men to objects comes not from women's inspection but from the larger culture. Cast into the gladiatorial arena of ornament, men sense their own diminishment in women's strength . . . The femininity that has hurt men the most is an artificial femininity manufactured and marketed by commercial interests . . . Truly, men . . . have arrived at their ornamental imprisonment.[9]

Faludi here draws upon and reiterates a series of contemporary (male) paranoia's favoured tropes: Schreberian 'beams'; the abject horror of penetration; the triad of emasculation, commodification and feminisation; homosocial betrayal; objectification and diminished/extinguished utilitarianism, as well as alluding in an intriguing and fortuitously prescient way to one of the biggest Hollywood hits of recent years, *Gladiator*. However, the overt anxiety about the state of masculinity, individualism, identity and its unstable basis in consumer culture evident here can also be found in cultural sites as confused and contradictory as *Fight Club*,

Naomi Klein's best-selling *No Logo* and the recent outbreaks of direct-action protests over the iniquities of global capitalism.[10] The point I wish to make here is less that Faludi is somehow 'wrong' in a broadly sociological sense, but that the argument she forwards is both symptomatic and representative of the social perceptions and frustrations of many white American men.[11]

Of course, in many ways this is yesterday's news: a rhetorically compelling and suitably angst-filled narrative of white male decentring and decline has become one of *the* master narratives in post-1960s American culture. As Liam Kennedy has pointed out, '[o]ne notable feature of this paranoia is that it has led to a growing recognition of whiteness as a social category and more particularly of white male selfhood as a fragile and besieged identity'.[12] However, this discourse has become especially pronounced in the 1990s. The anguished howl of Bly's 'wild men' testifies to the perceived displacement of normative – that is, white, middle-class and heterosexual – masculinity by a series of racially and sexually determinate others. Indeed, one key symptom of this sense of victimisation is a powerful nostalgia for a prelapsarian homosocial economy of white male centrality. This is then invariably accompanied by a mourning and/or longing for a 'lost', mythic national wholeness and plentitude. To this end, such masculinist desires have recently manifested themselves in a cycle of high-profile Second World War movies, Oedipal hymns to the 'greatest generation' such as *Saving Private Ryan* (1998), *U-571* (2000), *Pearl Harbor* (2001) and *Windtalkers* (2002).

Paranoia is, needless to say, a fundamentally *narcissistic* delusion, a regressive construction of the self as the external world's object-choice. If we posit that power and paranoia are little more than *noir*ish mirrorings of each other, delusions of persecution thus structure the identity of the male subject: paranoid counter-narratives make connections and (re-)order their universe, anxiously re-cohering the world, quite literally, around it*self*. As such, the grandiose narcissism of the paranoiac can be seen as a form of (over-) compensation for displaced feelings of (personal, cultural and/or socio-economic) worthlessness and inadequacy. Paranoia thus works in a cyclical double bind, staging various masochistic fantasies in order to master them through what Dana Polan dubs a reactionary 'aggressive surety'[13] wherein anxiety and neurosis manifest themselves in (self-)aggrandisement and unambiguous certitude. As normative masculinity is itself defined largely by negation, dependant upon passified structuring of others for its own ontological (and hegemonic) security, it is inevitable that 'th[is] process of passifying the other generates the fear of retaliation, hence anxiety, and hence more aggressiveness'.[14] The male paranoiac is a reader of *signs*, and his paranoia functions both to make sense of the world and as an ever-vigilant border patrol, forever placing his own tenuous, fragile masculine identity at the centre of a beleaguered narrative of suffering, victimisation and white plight. For Patrick O'Donnell, cultural paranoia operates, like the myth of the phallus, as a 'compensatory fiction', a narcissistic process which sates the desire for 'absolute centeredness, immediacy, transparency and control'.[15] Such narratives serve as a phantasmic corrective to the perceived displacement of normative masculinity as the putative centre of 'America'; at the same time they expose the performativity of masculinity, the need to continually reassert and reiterate the centrality of that supposed normalcy and the fundamental conservatism it seeks to uphold. Paranoid strategies thus inadvertently reveal the work of white masculinity and its ceaselessly narcissistic operations, a process made clear in the spectacular hegemonic investments of the action cinema.

To be sure, America has a well-established paranoid tradition – faithfully mirrored by Hollywood – from the Salem witch trials through to more pervasive contemporary manifestations, from UFO theorists and anti-government conspiracists, though events at Ruby Ridge and Waco, to Timothy McVeigh's righteous individualist zeal and nightmarish intimations of the (invariably 'Zionist') New World Order. Yet the paranoid spectacle of white masculinity as the 'victim' of progressive social change is perhaps *the* key element – however displaced or obliquely registered – in spectacular narratives of male crisis. This siege mentality and the concurrent fantasies of victimisation which white masculinity has adopted can be explained in several ways. Both O'Donnell and Timothy Melley ascribe the omnipresence of paranoid narratives in contemporary culture to what they see as the abjection of the postmodern condition. Arguing that paranoia and fantasies of persecution are 'symptoms of a more pervasive anxiety about social control',[16] Melley suggests that given America's cultural and historical investment in the nationalist–masculinist fantasy of rugged individualism, such anxieties are particularly acute, with white male paranoia functioning 'less as a defence of some clear political position than as a defence of individualism, abstractly perceived'.[17] As he argues, such anxieties – and the aggressive response(s) they provoke – 'are all part of the paradox by which a supposedly individualist culture conserves its individualism by continually imagining it to be in peril'.[18] The anxious counterblast to this 'pomophobia'[19] is *hyperindividualism*, a near-hysterical (hyper)masculine response to the perceived 'feminisation' of men within postmodernity; a narcissistic fantasy which works 'by seeing the self as only its truest self when standing in opposition to a hostile social order'.[20]

'Masochistic' spectacles of heroically suffering white men have become perhaps the key trope in recent Hollywood action cinema. For Paul Smith, the cyclical narrative triad of eroticisation of the male body, through physical punishment and near-destruction (both synonymous – at least within the relentlessly binaristic terms of the masculine symbolic – with *feminisation*) and eventually towards a process of regeneration and remasculinisation, forms 'the orthodox structuring code'[21] of contemporary Hollywood action movies. The 'temporary masochising' of the male body is, in Smith's schemata, merely a stepping stone *en route* to the re-emergence of an inviolable phallic masculinity displaced by the first two stages of the triad. Using the metaphor of 'the thrill of the chase' to explain the attraction of such narratives/spectacles, Smith argues that the sadomasochistic allure of male powerlessness is not subversive of the paternal law of the masculine symbolic (as Frank Krutnik or Kaja Silverman argue),[22] but a mythic, ritualised and recuperative strategy based on the double-bind of disavowal: the hero knows he will get his ball(s) back, but chooses to believe, albeit briefly, that the lost object is irretrievable.

These cinematic rituals are similarly theorised by Rick Altman as, in his terms, the cyclical pleasures of 'generic economy':

> [G]eneric reversals produce pleasure in proportion to the distance that must
> be traversed in order to restore order . . . The greater the risk, the greater
> the pleasure of the return to safety. The greater the wrong, the greater the
> pleasure taken in righting it. The greater the chaos, the greater the pleasure
> of restoring it.[23]

Thus, the narrative drive towards remasculinisation is structured on a prior
feminisation; for David Savran, the suffering white hero requires the gaze of an
audience:

> prov[ing] his masculinity only by letting it go momentarily . . . and
> allowing himself to be hurt . . . Only by temporarily relinquishing the
> phallus can the [hero] make himself an imitation of Christ and [acquire]
> the moral authority (and sympathy) to win hearts and minds.[24]

White male suffering, like white male crisis, is thus deeply narcissistic, overtly
performative and rhetorically forceful; the fantasy of victimisation which structures
the crisis-discourse of white masculinity is, in Sally Robinson's terms, 'governed
by a narrative economy that privileges infinitely deferred release, theatricality and
display'.[25] She continues:

> The rhetorical power of 'crisis' depends on a sense of prolonged tension;
> the announcements of crisis are inseparable from the crisis itself, *as the
> rhetoric of crisis performs the cultural work of centring attention on dominant
> masculinity* . . . Masochistic narratives, structured so as to defer closure or
> resolution, often feature white men displaying their wounds as evidence of
> disempowerment, and finding a pleasure in explorations of pain.[26]

Perhaps, then, it is safe to argue that white masculine crisis has become – to borrow
Kaja Silverman's phrase – the 'dominant fiction' of the US cultural imaginary in
recent years.

Surely, therefore, it is more apt to posit that normative masculinity is *always
already* in crisis, always under negotiation, dependant as it is upon the anxious
defences of projection, disavowal and the myth of the phallus. Indeed, the sheer
*banality* of masculine crisis is both managed and refuted through the prolonged melodramatic spectacles of white male suffering – on one level, epic bouts of *fort/da* –
that populate contemporary Hollywood representations. For if the hegemonic
power of white masculinity has always depended upon its structuring *invisibility*,
then it also has a considerable investment in temporary hypervisibility: normative
folks doing their (cultural) work before riding off into the sunset, the ordinarily-
extraordinary, extraordinarily-ordinary white man. Mobilising a distinctly phallic
metaphor, Hollywood action cinema enacts the fall, abjection and subsequent rise
of white masculinity through the metonym of the wounded white hero. Thus, white
male *ressentiment*[27] is expressed cyclically through a masochistic aestheticisation of
physical wounding and bodily punishment of the white protagonist; as Robinson

again points out, this rhetorical socio-somatic process 'materializes the crisis of white masculinity, makes it more *real*', while the spectacular melodramatic excess evidences 'the impossibility of recuperating the [national-masculinist] fiction of abstract individualism'.[28] For while white masculinity becomes (hyper)visible through bodily trauma, the performative individualisation and paranoid projections of social trauma – the way 'articulations of white men as victimizers slide almost imperceptibly into constructions of white men as victims'[29] – has no little ideological investment:

> While it is true that 'crisis' might signify a trembling of the edifice of white and male power, it is also true that there is much symbolic power to be reaped from occupying the social and discursive position of subject-in-crisis.[30]

It is in this way that we can read the grandiosity of gendered action spectacles in terms of *melodrama*; as Nina Baym has pointed out, it is possible to explain the broad history of American fictional representation(s) of masculinity as, to paraphrase, 'melodramas of beset manhood'.[31] Indeed, recent work on so-called 'trauma theory' has suggested that melodrama is *the* generic form for representing the psychological and emotional detritus of social upheaval. As E. Ann Kaplan explains: 'It makes sense that personal and social traumas caused by political and social transition [are] displaced into fictional melodrama forms where they could be more safely approached or remembered but also forgotten, in the peculiar manner of trauma.'[32] She goes on:

> [O]ne might argue that at certain historical moments aesthetic forms emerge to accommodate fears and fantasies related to suppressed histor-ical events. In repeating the traumas of both class and gender struggle, melodrama would, in its very generic formation, constitute a traumatic cultural symptom . . . Rather than focusing upon traumatic cultural symp-toms, independent cinematic techniques show paralysis, repetition, circularity – all aspects of the non-representability of trauma and yet of the search to figure its pain.[33]

The parallels between the compulsively ritualistic allure of melodrama described here and the generically sadomasochistic aesthetic of the contemporary Hollywood action film are easy to draw. Indeed, the generic iconicity of tortured white male bodies as the displaced register of social angst would certainly seem to cohere with Kaplan's criteria. Action cinema's generic tropes – character archetypes, moral polarisation, transparency of legibility, spectacular and excessive *mise-en-scène* – further link such movies with the structural elements of melodrama.

As such, white male paranoia has registered itself in various ways in Hollywood representation though the 1990s. The anxious re-centring of the world around Average White Guys was perhaps *the* structuring trait (as it was in their 1970s antecedents) of the recent cycle of disaster movies such as *Daylight* (1997), *Dante's*

*Peak* (1997), *Volcano* (1997), *Deep Impact* and *Armageddon* (1998). Key Hollywood stars have also taken on distinctly paranoid roles: Tom Cruise in *The Firm* (1993), *Mission Impossible* (1996), *Vanilla Sky* (2001), *Minority Report* (2002) and *Eyes Wide Shut* (1999); Clint Eastwood in *In the Line of Fire* (1993) and *Absolute Power* (1997); Harrison Ford as the saintly, persecuted Dr Kimbel in *The Fugitive* (1993) and hysterical president in *Air Force One* (1997)[34]; Nicholas Cage in *Snake Eyes* and *8MM* (both 1998); Kurt Russell in *Breakdown* (1997); Bruce Willis in *12 Monkeys* (1995), *The Sixth Sense* (1999) and *Unbreakable* (2001); Keanu Reeves in *Johnny Mnemonic* (1995), *Devil's Advocate* (1997) and *The Matrix* (1999); not to mention *uber*-paranoid Mel Gibson in the likes of *Ransom* (1996), *Conspiracy Theory* (1997), *The Patriot* (2000), *Signs* (2002) and per-haps even *What Women Want* (2001); and, of course, the iconic Michael Douglas in *Fatal Attraction* (1987), *Basic Instinct* (1992), the aforementioned *Falling Down*, *Disclosure* (1994), *Don't Say a Word* (2001) and the convoluted, self-mocking yuppie nightmare of *The Game* (1997). Meanwhile, Tom Hanks – 1990s Hollywood's Ameri-can Everyman *par excellence* – has embarked on a series of quasi-revisionist projects – most notably *Forrest Gump* (1994) and *Apollo 13* (1995) – which either place the white protagonist as the unwitting victim of bewildering (and invariably negative) social forces, or as the modest unwilling hero in a notably Caucasian universe. In the survivalist mythopoeticism of *Cast Away* (2000), for example, Hanks's bloated, over-worked and undersexed corporate everyguy finds himself stranded on a desert island, forced to shed (indeed, 'cast away') pounds of compromised flabby flesh and rediscover the toned, muscle-bound and essentialised hunter-gatherer that lurks within; an overt narrative of remasculinisation which concludes with Hanks at a (literal) crossroads of quasi-frontiersman opportunity, abundance and (hetero)sexual adventure. Even more extravagantly, both the Baudrillardian nightmare of *The Matrix* and super hero art-flick *Unbreakable* – apparently without irony – forward unwary white chaps as the literal embodiment of the phallus: inviolable, all-powerful, and in the case of the former's Neo, 'the One' (who, presumably, will make good America's lack). And then, of course, there is Russell Crowe in *Gladiator*.

The grandiosity and emphasis on spectacle which characterises the Hollywood action-adventure blockbuster is, as Steve Neale has suggested, the direct descend-ant and contemporary heir to the epic genre. The Hollywood epic itself has long been interpreted in allegorical terms as an historical displacement of contempora-neous fears, desires and discourses.[35] *Gladiator* itself is fairly self-evidently allegorical in its depiction of 'American' imperial might, political corruption and depthless cultural entropy. It is also an 'epic' of populist-masculinist American mythology: the film's portentous promotional tag-line – 'The general who became a slave . . . the slave who became a gladiator . . . the gladiator who defied an empire' – is hardly ambiguous in its comfortingly ritualistic promises of masochistic, individualistic adventures and populist masculine anti-authoritarian defiance. Furthermore, few genres have been quite so closely associated with spectacle, and, in particular, the spectacle of the male body. Here, the film's warrior-hero, Maximus[36] (Crowe), is the archetypal self-made man, his masculinity shored up by a potent combination of professional prowess (he is, we understand, 'Rome's Greatest General'), a litany of military conquests and, perhaps most significantly, the pastoral idyll of fecundity and self-sufficiency that is the American Dream-homestead to which he longs to return. If the film depicts Rome as the locus of corruption, greed and decadence, then it is the etherealised, isolated soft-focus abundance found in the idealised triad of 'a wife, a son, the harvest' for which Maximus pines that is evidently its moral and ethical structuring other.

Maximus/Crowe's star body was the focus of much critical attention during *Gladiator*'s pre-release marketing campaign. Much was made of the disciplining of Crowe's body following the considerable weight gain required for his previous role in Michael Mann's *The Insider* (1999). Like so many recent paranoid narratives, *The Insider* dramatised homosocial corporate seduction,[37] and as with Hanks in *Cast Away*, the flabby body of Crowe's protagonist figured as a visual metaphor for a compromised phallic masculinity and the perceived 'feminisation' of subjugation to a hierarchical corporate structure. As Steve Cohan explains, the heroic body in the epic is always metonymic and symbolic, a visual metaphor for an idealised national body.[38] As such, it is easy to understand the interpretation of Maximus/Crowe's muscles in terms of a collective male nostalgia for a more authentic, less performative and/or consumerised and commodified nation. This extratextual narrative of Crowe's ability to control and discipline his body after a 'masochistic' (but temporary) loss of self-mastery itself serves as a microcosmic synopsis of *Gladiator*'s narrative.

Crowe's masculine 'presence' was eulogised over when the film was released. *Sight and Sound*, for example, breathlessly suggested that Crowe 'commands the movie magisterially, never more so than when hacking down opponents with a casual economy of movement, barely breaking into sweat'.[39] More than a year later, the same journal bemoaned the absence of Crowe's 'stoical masculine gravitas' in subsequent Hollywood productions.[40] *The Observer* nostalgically compared Crowe to the youthful Mr Universe, Sean Connery.[41] *Empire*'s similarly hyperbolic (and distinctly homoerotic) awe was hardly atypical: 'Russell Crowe was clearly born in a hard month, in a hard year during a freak outbreak of total hardness. The man exudes the physicality of a wild animal. Shifting testosterone like a pre-bloated Brando, he holds the screen with such assuredness you simply can't rip your eyes away from him.'[42] The same magazine also featured an on-set profile of Crowe, expending many words rhetorically asserting the authenticity of Crowe's unreconstructed masculine charisma:

> The credentials of Russell Crowe . . . look impressive. This is, after all, a man who lives on a 560-acre farm, in a remote corner of New South Wales, which he likes to walk – that's *walk* – around . . . Let's be clear from the start, Russell Crowe is not a Starbuck's cappuccino man. 'Rugged' is the word.[43]

Clearly, such journalistic hyperbole is part and parcel of the promotion and construction of a star's public persona, but the insistence upon Crowe's all-too-real *un*reconstructed masculinity is striking; it builds upon previous 'tough' roles in *Romper Stomper* (1992), *L.A. Confidential* (1997) and the aforementioned *The Insider*, helping to elide the gap between masculine presence and masculine performativity. The terms used to both construct and help audiences understand Crowe are also significant: he is portrayed as a quasi-frontiersman (albeit the Australian out-back), unpampered by Hollywood wealth and glamour, whilst the nostalgia for a pre-commodified masculinity can hardly be missed in the reference to Starbuck's coffee. This distinctly fetishistic adulation surrounding Maximus/Crowe's quasi-bestial masculine persona belies a return of the repressed: a nostalgic longing for a mythic masculine essence, a phallic presence rather than a *bricolage* of 'decorative' and commodified signifiers. Of course, this is exacerbated by the generic throwback to the 1950s epic and the national-masculine certitude it worked to represent. *Gladiator*'s disingenuous contempt for 'the mob' and 'feminine' mass culture, whilst wholly contradictory (though arguably self-mocking) given the hyper-commercial basis of Hollywood entertainment, also help structure Crowe/Maximus's masculinity, whilst simultaneously disavowing the feminising construction of Crowe/Maximus as object of the gaze and mass-culture's commodified star.[44] The anxious insistence on real, corporeal physical presence is exacerbated by the visible 'truth' of Crowe/Maximus's muscles amidst the hyperreal CGI *mise-en-scène*. Maximus not only does battle with a corrupt, shallow and feminised world; he also, apparently, casually vanquishes the so-called 'Adonis complex': a muscle-bound ego-ideal, and then some.

If one incredulous colleague who witnesses Maximus's fury and proficiency in battle has trouble imagining 'Maximus the farmer', so does *Gladiator* itself. As in *The Patriot*, the family in *Gladiator* functions primarily as a structuring absence, their demise granting Maximus's quest 'rooting interest' in the terms of generic economy. Karen Schneider has argued that Hollywood action-adventure movies have become 'hysterical about families', suggesting that many 'seem hell-bent on the spectacular rearticulation of the traditional – white, bourgeois, patriarchal – family':

> the action hero's story is the story of the family, tortured and triumphant. These narratives violently enact the centrality of the family to the struc-turing of contemporary American experience . . . reveal[ing] a desperate attempt to rescue and reassert the hegemonic family, widely perceived as under siege.[45]

Schneider is right, I think, to point out the anxiously overdetermined investment in the patriarchal family that is evident in many recent action movies, but conversely I would suggest that the threatened family largely functions to motivate and struc-ture the white hero's masochistic, hyperindividual exploits. However, Maximus's slain wife and son enable the film to conveniently resolve the tension between masculine man-of-action and domesticated husband-father, while the true (melo)drama is the suitably epic confrontation between corrupt state and righteous individual subject. Maximus's nuclear family unit barely exist as a presence within the film except as either corpses or as etherealised phantasms within our hero's fevered and traumatised imagination. In this way, *Gladiator* almost seems to fold under its contradictory strategies and structuring tropes. For example, the family serve to structure Maximus's heterosexual normativity, but their absence also underlines the impossibility of the nuclear unit in the homosocial universe of the diegesis. As Cohan points out:

> the dualism of freedom and slavery [in the epic] . . . expose[s] the contradictions inhering within both the United States' own domestic operations as a modern national-security state and the traditional imbrication of masculinity in the nationalistic myth of rugged American male individualism.[46]

That is, the true focus of *Gladiator* is homosocial conflict and the postmodern 'agency panic' of Melley's diagnosis.

*Gladiator* is, in effect, an Oedipal melodrama of beleaguered white masculinity, with a narrative revolving around the relationship(s) between 'fathers' and 'sons', patrimony and homosocial inheritance. Indeed, the central drama of the film gravitates around the issue of an authentic patrimonial line murderously interrupted when benevolent Emperor Marcus Aurelius (Richard Harris) opts to leave the Empire in the capable-but-unwilling hands of Maximus rather than bitter and estranged biological son Commodus (Joaquin Phoenix): issue is not the issue, as it were; 'authentic' masculinity, patriarchal authority and the egalitarian meritocratic democracy of 'American' society clearly is ('You,' the Emperor informs Maximus, 'are the son I *should* have had'). If the masculine angst evident in the overdetermined exchanges between Marcus Aurelius and Commodus unintentionally lapse into camp ('Your faults as a son,' weeps the former, 'is my failure as a father!'), *Gladiator* has a considerable investment in the insistence upon righteous patrimonial inheritance. Maximus is clearly Rome/America's true son, fit to cleanse the culture of its 'fallen' decadence, his aptitude for the task demonstrated when he deferentially prays to the (all male) ancestors: a willingly introjective subject of a conservative patriarchal lineage. And if the film's posters attempt to interpellate their audiences into the grandiose mythology of individualism ('What we do in life,' we are ponderously informed, 'echoes in eternity'), it is surely no coincidence that it is a *white*, unmistakably middle-class male who, *Gladiator* suggests, can recuperate America's democratic utopia.

For *Gladiator* – like the men in Faludi's scattershot analysis of America's masculine crisis – is almost obsessed with the question of who is fit to inherit 'Rome'. From the quasi-paternal relationship between Maximus and Marcus Aurelius, through the murder of the former's son (and, therefore, heir), to the restoration of order with the reinstatement of Graccus (Derek Jacobi), on to the film's evident anxiety over the fate of Lucius (Spencer Treat Clark), the young son of Lucilla (Connie Nielson), and his positive (and, again, quasi-paternal) bond with Maximus. Of course, the threat to this white masculine hegemony lies in both engulfment by the fickle ebb and flow of 'feminising' mass culture – as signified by the notably passive proletarian lumpen hordes in Rome – and more specifically by Maximus's wildly overdetermined nemesis Commodus. If masculine anxieties can already be detected in the excessive musculature and phallic potency of Crowe's star body – what Cohan has dubbed male 'drag' – it seems that abs, pecs and 'ceps are simply not enough to secure your manly credentials: your structuring arch-rival must also be a sexually ambiguous, cowardly, narcissistic, morally corrupt, effeminate, affluent, decadent (and, therefore – note how his flamboyant costumes contrast sharply with Maximus's no-nonsense tunic – more consumerised), incestuous and patricidal inverse of the Oedipal ideal. Not only does Commodus murder his own father (perhaps the ultimate crime, given *Gladiator*'s unrelenting Oedipal logic), he also has sexual designs on his sister, alongside indeterminate but doubtless sinister plans for his male nephew, and a notably obsessive relationship with Maximus. Indeed, Commodus's incestuous desire(s) for his sibling seems to be largely motivated (and, indeed, triangulated) by her one-time affair with former lover Maximus. Commodus's 'queerness' – rendered in wholly negative terms – is exacerbated by the film's knowing discourse concerning the 'decadence' of Rome's higher echelons. Amidst the homosocial environs of the Roman Senate, the fear of 'backstabbing' takes on an unmistakably homophobic taint. Finally, a scantily clad, chained Maximus (in an overtly sadomasochistic-style crucifixion-pose) is literally stabbed in the back by Commodus in an echo of the embrace of *amour fou* with which he earlier despatched his benevolent father.[47] Just as *Gladiator* proposes a man like Maximus as the antidote to an ideologically emasculated, spiritually diseased and commercially feminised culture, Commodus acts as a metonym for all that Crowe/Maximus is *not*: the phallus, in other words, as bad object.

This Schreberian take on homosocial paranoia subsequently serves to disavow the overtly homoerotic bonding between the enslaved gladiators. These 'real' men, with their taut, glistening bodies are structured as the antithesis of the pampered ruling elite with their silk togas and horticultural pursuits. And this textual paranoia is made all the more acute by *Gladiator*'s almost exclusively male focus. Marcus Aurelius earnestly wishes out loud to his daughter Lucilla: 'If only you had been born a man!' Similarly, Maximus's murdered child is a boy, and later – knowing how to *really* hurt his usually stoic nemesis – Commodus gloats that Maximus's first born did not take it like a man, but in fact 'squealed *like a girl*'. Women are thus almost entirely marginal to this phallocentric melodrama. Leading lady Lucilla's role is essentially a structuring one, relevant only in relation to other men: she gives birth to a son, and structures both Maximus's heterosexuality *and* Commodus's ambi-sexual perversity. Maximus's wife's rape, meanwhile, is represented primarily as a violation of the white hero, her presence in the text a fleeting, etherealised one. Conversely, it is the homosocial bonds between men in the film that dominate *Gladiator*'s melodramatic emotional core, and alongside the strenuously disavowed eroticism of these bonds there is a significant narrative thrust towards the casually naturalised re-centring of white masculinity.

*Gladiator* is, above all else, the story of the fall and rise of Maximus Decimus Meridus. Following the murder of his family, Maximus is cast into an abyss of bodily punishment, *literal* commodification and an abject universe of racial and ethnic otherdom. Upon finding his wife and child slain, Maximus reveals the first of his hysterical symptoms: he *faints*. Awakening later (the trauma has clearly been considerable), our hero finds himself passively nursed by a benevolent African slave, surrounded by a disorienting, diverse (and menacing) collective of disenfranchised racial others. This abject condition finds its socio-somatic bodily metonym in the bloody trauma marked on his arm – a wound stuffed with writhing maggots. Advised by his saintly comrade to allow the pupae to 'cleanse' his wound, Maximus begins the quest for purification and re-birth which structures many action narratives, and the classical *rite de passage* structure which underpins this male tale. Having fallen from privileged middle-class professional and institutional security to the level of 'stock', Maximus must perform his way back to the political and ideological centre in the gladiatorial arena. The film's glib rhetorical attempt at racial relativism – both Maximus and his black comrade Juba (Djimon Hounsou) are enslaved, equals in their subaltern status, longing to return to their families/homelands – is on particularly dubious ground when, in an emotional exchange, Maximus reveals that *he* actually has it worse since he has no family or home to return to. This masochistic one-upmanship and casual co-option of a race-based victim-discourse *by* a land-owning, middle-class professional white male and *from* a disenfranchised black slave is both profoundly overdetermined and, needless to say, astonishingly crass given the painful history behind the African-American presence in the US. No matter how displaced in terms of history and geography *Gladiator*'s allegory is, Maximus's appropriation of a discourse of enslavement, upheaval and emancipation here is symptomatic of the deeply problematic workings of the paranoid white imaginary as represented through the melodramatic prism of mainstream Hollywood representation. That Juba is eventually freed by Maximus's righteous actions (the former offering grateful thanks to the martyred hero in the film's elegiac closing moments) merely highlights his status as racial fetish in *Gladiator*'s troubling ideological schemata.

Nevertheless, such homosocial bonding works, like Maximus himself, extremely hard to naturalise the re-centring of normative masculinity. *Gladiator*'s emphasis on homosocial bonds almost inevitably collapses into a celebration of homoerotics which at times is almost beyond disavowal. Such pleasures are hardly alien to the genre, of course: one of the key pleasures of the genre is precisely the overt display of the male body as part of the spectacular pleasures of the text. In *Gladiator*, however, part of Maximus's masochistic journey towards remasculinisation is the abject experience of becoming a commodified, objectified spectacle. While Crowe/Maximus's sneering defiance and stoical suffering affirms his status as epic hero, it is the reverse psychology of his angsty masculine *performance* in the gladiatorial arena which paradoxically/strategically encourages the gaze whilst the ultraviolent action serves to disavow threatening notions of passivity or 'feminisation' which such aggressive narcissism may suggest. Maximus despatches opponents with a strutting, athletic surety whilst at the same time sneering at the cultural dupes who cheer him on, his masochistic ordeal requiring the adoring gaze of the masses he treats with such contempt. In this way, Crowe's visible contempt at the Oscars ceremony is a precise echo of his performance as Maximus: the 'manly' disdain is registered only by way of a petulant, pouting narcissism. The rhetoric of the mutinous and martyred body encourages and desires the collective gaze ('win the crowd' Maximus is continually told) just as he paradoxically asserts his indifference/defiance towards it.

The performance of the hero-martyr is a reflexive one, for sure: but the gaze that Maximus's body and manly essence attracts is primarily *male*. Indeed, *Gladiator* is positively bursting at the seams with adoring, awestruck reaction shots whenever Maximus is in action, often a slow zoom to close-up intercut with reverse shots registering the move from admiration to adoration. Certainly, Maximus has no shortage of male admirers: from his ever-loyal troops, through his new-found gladiatorial comrades, to his adoring manservant Cicero (Tommy Flanagan) and the youthful Lucius's introjective fandom, Maximus's homosocial magnetism is reflexively asserted throughout the film's formal and narrative strategies; but this overdetermined animal magnetism has its dangers, with the ever-tenuous distinction between identification and desire threatening to erode completely. If, as I would argue, the film serves as a melodramatic treatise on who is fit to inherit 'America' and its masculinist traditions, *Gladiator* calmly suggests that the remasculinisation of the nation is the only authentic (or, indeed, viable) way forward; in this sense the film is distinctly millennial. Progression from the entropy and abjection of post-modernity here requires the collective introjection of Maximus's brand of masculine certitude. Furthermore, it is entirely in keeping with the film's populist agenda that Maximus comes to lead the slave revolt ostensibly because of his professional skill and experience, rather than, say, his hardly insignificant ethnic or social status. Maximus is so clearly the centre of the film both diegetically and extratextually, his cause so 'obviously' righteous that all his (largely proletarian) comrades – even the selfish and cynical slave trader Proximo (Oliver Reed) – are more than willing to give up their lives for him for the greater good: a narcissistic wish-fulfilment fantasy (and, perhaps, even a form of displaced aggression) if ever there was one.

*Gladiator* thus operates around a rhetorical binary discourse of authentic/inauthentic national-masculine ideals, metonymically represented by the key opposition of Maximus–Commodus. Yet this structuring relationship, rhetorically over-determined as it is, effectively collapses under the weight of its own anxious signification. 'We are not so different, you and I,' gloats Commodus as he leers over the glistening, bound body of his gladiatorial nemesis. While both Maximus and the film struggle to disavow this possibility, to emphasise Commodus's *mis*recognition, the homosocial paranoia that drives the narrative becomes wildly apparent. As such, Commodus figures as a monstrous doppelganger for the idealised masculinity that *Gladiator* fetishises: a melodramatic, gothicised projection of all that normative masculinity must reject in order to stabilise, purify and affirm it*self*. Just as Maximus physically rejects the interpellation of a (now-)corrupt homosocial regime literally inscribed on his body in the form of a regimental tattoo, there is a considerable contradiction between his own hyperindividual exploits and the utopian, 'democratic' homosocial collective restored at the film's conclusion. Similarly, Maximus's phallic and inflexibly rigid individualism is contrasted with the cultural dupery of the crowd and Commodus's own polymorphous openness to the fickle ebb and flow of the masses' desires. Here, the former's gladiatorial narcissism and ability to 'win the crowd', to both resist *and* revel in his commodification as spectacle supposedly outweighs the Emperor's lack of integrity and commitment to shallow populism. Again, Commodus's diabolical queerness functions as an overt disavowal of the erotics at work in *Gladiator*'s excessive display of muscular male bodies and its near-obsession with homosociality. There is, after all, a thin line between fear and desire, and nowhere is this more evident than in the antithetical structuring relationship between the phoney Emperor and the 'real' man.

And it is here that *Gladiator*'s certitude comes undone. As Maximus cleanses this allegorical America of its sins with his final commandments, casually restoring a legitimate social order in his own image as he does so, the film seems to concede its own excess(es) with the necessity of the re-centralised hero's demise. First, given their structuring interdependence, we must question whether Maximus could possibly survive narrative closure following Commodus's death. Second, Maximus is, in Robinson's terms, a *marked man*[48]; 'You have a great name', he is sagely informed at one point. While the film flexes all its muscles in an effort to emphasise individualist ideology and a utopian version of social mobility, Maximus's privileged social standing problematises such populist dogma. Maximus both is and is not the film's *eponymous* hero; both the warrior-phallus and simply 'a' gladiator. Recall the scene in which Commodus requests that the gladiator-hero remove his mask and reveal his identity: Maximus refuses, ostensibly because he wants Commodus to believe he is dead, but on another level it is precisely because he wishes to maintain his *invisibility* as a hegemonic male; Maximus/Crowe's central speech ('I *am* Maximus Decimus Meridus') melodramatically and rhetorically points out the incongruity of his great white *name* and his degraded position. Clearly, then, Maximus suffers from a peculiar brand of white man's burden; but if *Gladiator* suggests that our hero is an entirely self-made 'great man' – as opposed to one 'burdened' with socio-economic privilege by his very normativity – it also admits the impossibility of that phallic masculine essence in its ultimate etherealisation. Similarly, it is this essence – the phallus in all but name – which is destabilised by its narcissistic performativity in the gladiatorial arena. Indeed, *Gladiator*'s cultural work strains precisely *to* stabilise and recuperate a masculinity perceived to be under threat, victimised – improbably – by virtue *of* its virtue. Furthermore, these anxieties (and even longings) are also unmistakably evident in the excess of Crowe's body/performance, and the rapturous (even *hysterical*) critical reception it received. *Gladiator*'s melodramatic excess, in a grand Hollywood tradition is, like Maximus, simply too much, a phantasmic and impossible ideal; something which the film appears to admit with the reluctant, remasculinised hero's departure, death-driven (with all of Rome's eyes upon him, of course) back to ordinarily domestic, yet phantasmically mythic wholeness: a spiritual return to the insular bosom of his family which gently disavows any social or political stake in his spectacular wrong-righting.

And so here is the white man, a weight on his shoulders. And yet for all its cultural work, all its sombre and elegiac *gravitas*, the masculine utopia of *Gladiator* – and, by extension, the Hollywood action film *per se* – flaunts its paranoia, renders its symptomatic hysteria as visibly as Maximus's wounded body. In effect, these fantasies of white plight and the rhetorical masochistic scenarios of the likes of *Gladiator* protest *too much*. By giving the game away through their overwrought, melodramatic angst they unravel the populist, conservative agenda in play. For if the prevalence of the tortured white hero in contemporary American cinematic representation belies anxieties simmering underneath utopian national ideologies, then it is precisely their basis in the narratives of the Hollywood imaginary which suggest that this is an outlet for strategically masochistic/narcissistic white male fantasies of being beaten. As such, it is perhaps safest to posit that only those secure enough and assured of their continued hegemonic centrality that can afford to play so regularly and so melodramatically with 'epic' fantasies and mournfully paranoid delusions of disempowerment, displacement and degradation. As the surly Maximus would doubtless concur, albeit with a sneer, sometimes it hurts so, *so* good.

## Notes

1   Teresa Brennan *History after Lacan*, London: Routledge, 1993, p. 34.
2   Robyn Wiegman *American Anatomies: Theorizing Race and Gender*, Durham, NC: Duke University Press, 1995, p. 131.
3   Richard Dyer *White*, London: Routledge, 1997; David Savran *Taking It Like a Man: White Masculinity, Masochism and Contemporary American Culture*, Princeton, NJ: Princeton University Press, 1998; S. Robinson *Marked Men: White Masculinity in Crisis*, New York: Columbia University Press, 2000.
4   John Graham 'The End of the Great White Male', in Richard Delgado and Jean Stefanic (eds) *Critical White Studies: Looking behind the Mirror*, Philadelphia: Temple University Press, 1997, pp. 3–5.
5   As Robyn Wiegman points out, the synergy between Hollywood representations and notions of American identity are far from trivial, *American Anatomies*, p. 131.
6   Robert Bly *Iron John: A Book About Men*, New York: Addison-Wesley, 1990.
7   Susan Faludi *Stiffed: The Betrayal of the Modern Man*, London: Chatto & Windus, 1999, p. 597.
8   Ibid., p. 598.
9   Ibid., pp. 598–9.
10  Naomi Klein *No Logo*, London: Flamingo, 2000.
11  Although Faludi's survey does not focus exclusively on white males, the 'crisis of masculinity' more generically seems to be dominated by the complaints of white men.
12  Liam Kennedy 'Alien Nation: White Male Paranoia and Imperial Culture in the United States', *Journal of American Studies*, 30: 1, 1996, pp. 87–100.
13  Dana Polan *Power and Paranoia*, New York: Columbia University Press, 1986, p. 14
14  Brennan *History after Lacan*, p. 75. This process is all-too-evident in American culture's attitude towards so-called 'rogue states' in the wake of the astonishing events of 11 September, 2001; one only has to watch the news to see how vulnerability and paranoia find their mirror image in the aggressive surety which seeks to place such uncertain objects under passifying control.
15  Patrick O'Donnell *Latent Destinies: Cultural Paranoia and Contemporary U.S. Narrative*, London: Routledge, 2000, p. 7.
16  Timothy Melley, *Empire of Conspiracy: The Culture of Paranoia in Postwar America*, London: Cornell University Press, 2000, p. vii.
17  Ibid., p. 11.
18  Ibid., p. 6.
19  I borrow the term 'pomophobia' from Thomas Byer's insightful essay 'Terminating the Postmodern: Masculinity and Pomophobia', *Modern Fiction Studies*, 41, 1994, pp. 5–34: p. 12.
20  Melley *Empire of Conspiracy*, p. 25. Donald Pease has outlined the fundamentally paranoid structure of US national identity and interpellation of national subjects, in his essay 'National Narratives, Postnational Narration', *Modern Fiction Studies*, 43, 1997, pp. 1–23.

21  Paul Smith *Clint Eastwood: A Cultural Production*, Minneapolis: University of Minnesota Press, 1993, p. 156.

22  Frank Krutnik *In a Lonely Place: Film Noir, Genre, Masculinity*, London: Routledge, 1991; Kaja Silverman *Male Subjectivity at the Margins*, London: Routledge, 1992.

23  Rick Altman *Film/Genre*, London: BFI, 1999, pp. 155–6.

24  David Savran *Taking it Like a Man: White Masculinity, Masochism and Contemporary American Culture*, Princeton, NJ: Princeton University Press, 1998, pp. 147–8.

25  Robinson *Marked Men*, p. 13.

26  Robinson *Marked Men*, p. 11, emphasis added.

27  See Wendy Brown 'Injury, Identity, Politics', in A. F. Gordon and C. Newfield (eds) *Mapping Multiculturalism*, Minneapolis: University of Minnesota Press, 1996, pp. 149–66.

28  Robinson *Marked Men*, p. 9.

29  Ibid., p. 5.

30  Ibid., p. 9.

31  Nina Baym 'Melodramas of Beset Manhood: How Theories of American Fiction Exclude Women Authors', in Elaine Showalter (ed.) *The New Feminist Criticism: Essays on Women, Literature and Theory*, London: Virago, 1986, pp. 63–80.

32  E. A. Kaplan 'Melodrama, Cinema and Trauma', *Screen*, 42: 2, 2001, pp. 201–5: p. 202.

33  Ibid., pp. 203–4.

34  In a reversal of this trend, Ford played the menacing 'other' of *female* paranoia in *What Lies Beneath* (2000).

35  Steve Cohan *Masked Men: Masculinity and Movies in the 1950s*, Bloomington: Indiana University Press, 1997; Steve Neale *Genre and Hollywood*, London: Routledge, 2000; Lesley Felperin 'Decline and Brawl', *Sight and Sound*, 10: 6, June 2000, pp. 34–5.

36  Revealingly, early versions of *Gladiator*'s script named the lead Narcissus.

37  Other films which follow this pattern include *Wall Street* (1987), *The Firm* (1993), *Devil's Advocate* (1997) and *Antitrust* (2001). The homophobic metaphor of corrupt homosocial 'seduction' serves to structure their paranoid schemata.

38  Cohan *Masked Men*.

39  Felperin 'Decline and Brawl', p. 35.

40  A. O'Hehir 'Gorilla Warfare', *Sight and Sound*, September 2001, p. 13.

41  P. Kane 'Hero today, but gone tomorrow?', *The Observer Review*, 25 June, 2000, p. 5.

42  I. Nathan 'Gladiator', *Empire*, 132, June 2000, pp. 46–7: p. 46.

43  M. Palmer 'Grrrrr . . .', *Empire*, 132, June 2000, pp. 76–80: p. 77.

44  This process of male bodily display/eroticisation, action and disavowal is analysed in Steve Neale's classic article 'Masculinity as Spectacle', *Screen*, 24: 6, 1983, pp. 2–16.

45  Karen Schneider 'With Violence if Necessary: Rearticulating the Family in the Contemporary Action-Thriller', *Journal of Popular Film and Television*, 27: 1, 1999, p. 4.

46  Cohan *Masked Men*, p. 133.

47  For more on the homophobic structure of the male epic (and its contradictions), see Leon Hunt 'What Are Big Boys Made Of? *Spartacus, El Cid* and the Male Epic', in Pat Kirkham and Janet Thumin (eds) *You Tarzan: Masculinity, Movies and Men*, London: Lawrence and Wishart, 1993, pp. 65–83.

48  Robinson argues that 'in a post-liberationist America . . . white men have been "marked" as the bearers of power, privilege, and a violent sexuality' (*Marked Men*, p. 180).

## Chapter 15

## YVONNE TASKER

# THE FAMILY IN ACTION

T HE LAST TEN YEARS have seen the mapping and re-mapping of the family in both high-profile action films with prohibitive certificates and those adventure movies geared to a 'family' audience. Karen Schneider argues that while 'the lone action hero has not altogether disappeared, the action-thriller of the late 1990s has in the main become obsessed with, not to say hysterical about, families'.[1] Similarly Mark Gallagher contends that 'action films in the 1990s have increasingly constructed stories around threats to domesticity, marriage, and the nuclear family'.[2] It is clear not only that families are more central to the contemporary action film – the films of the 1980s were indeed more typically (though by no means exclusively) preoccupied with the figure of the veteran/cop as alienated loner – but that familial concerns are also thematically more central. Fatherhood, mothering, and child/parent relationships all play an important part in recent films as diverse as *Independence Day* (1996), *Twister* (1996), *Contact* (1997), *Armageddon* (1998) *Mercury Rising* (1998) and *Lara Croft: Tomb Raider* (2001). Developing ideas about feminism, gender and sexuality clearly inform such narratives.

The familial themes foregrounded in the films considered here do not, I argue, serve a straightforwardly recuperative function as some critics suggest. Moreover, we can identify a source for these themes within the conventions of action-adventure itself. That is, there is a clear continuity between contemporary familial relationships in action and the thematics of nurturing and mutual support played out in the most prominent on-screen relationships seen in 1980s action films: those which constitute colleagues (and sometimes bystanders) as comrades. Just as families are thrown together by chance as much as choice, the shared experience of adventure helps to forge unlikely but intense alliances. Thus I would like to suggest that the inclusion of family groups within action-adventure is in many ways an extension of the genre's logic rather than a significant departure from it. Equally, while I agree with both Schneider and Gallagher that an emphasis on familial relationships, both biological and otherwise, became increasingly evident in 1990s action and adventure narratives it is also the case that the family film more generally has thrived in recent years. With its strategic capacity to address different generations the family film is a distinct phenomenon drawing on diverse genres and storytelling traditions, some aimed primarily at adults, others directed at children.

A renewed cinematic interest in the family has attracted corresponding levels of attention from film and cultural critics who suggest that a re-negotiation of the figure of the father can be seen at work across diverse Hollywood genres. However, with its reputation as a masculine if not a male genre, action-adventure has something of an over-determined position in these debates. Susan Jeffords has influentially argued that the American action picture first elevated a hard-bodied muscular hero in the films of the 1980s, then qualified that enactment of toughness with a new softness centred on a nurturing paternity during the 1990s. Jeffords points to the transformation in Arnold Schwarzenegger's persona as he moves from the embodiment of a disturbing de-humanised and violent masculinity as the relentless cyborg of *The Terminator* (1984) to his cuddly reprise of that role in the 1991 sequel. For Jeffords the slightly earlier Schwarzenegger comedy *Kindergarten Cop* (1990), is indicative of precisely what is at stake in this seeming shift. The film's message, she writes, is that '[t]he emotionally whole and physically healed man of the eighties wants nothing more than to be a father, not a warrior/cop, after all'.[3] In turn the transformation is understood as part of a wider cinematic phenomenon: Jeffords views 1991 as 'the year of the transformed U.S. man', centred on an idea that 'the hard-fighting, weapon-wielding, independent, muscular, and heroic men of the eighties [. . .] have disappeared and are being replaced by the more sensitive, loving, nurturing, protective family men of the nineties'.[4] Similarly Fred Pfeil explores what he regards as a new emphasis on fatherhood in films including *Regarding Henry* and *Hook*, dubbing 1991 Hollywood's 'Year of Living Sensitively'. [5]

Family is the key narrative device in the films that Jeffords analyses, providing 'both the motivation for and the resolution of changing masculine heroisms'.[6] It is not only the *form* that male transformation narratives take – for example, how often this is achieved through the mediating figures of men who are 'less empowered or authorized'[7] – but their impact on women that has preoccupied critics. From a feminist perspective an emphasis on family is potentially troubling – after all, conservative political rhetoric has long employed the family as a rallying cry associated with an attempt to reposition women both economically and culturally. In 'Three Men and Baby M', Tania Modleski's discussion of the 1987 hit *Three Men and a Baby* a male appropriation of woman's nurturing role is analysed as underpinned by a fearful misogyny.[8]

Though adopting different tones and critical methods, Jeffords, Modleski and Pfeil all suggest that movies in which men are shown to turn to their families and to 'learn' the language of emotions enact a transformation that is achieved at the expense of women. Jeffords reads *Terminator 2*, for example, as a movie in which Schwarzenegger's character usurps the role of mother/carer, relegating Connor/Hamilton to the sidelines. From this perspective, films which seem on one level to be indicating the need for shifts in masculinity actually function to shore up hierarchical structures of race, class and gender within which screen masculinities are produced and inscribed. However, as Steven Cohan contends, none of this means 'that the rhetoric of a "masculinity crisis", which implicates men and women alike in representations of sexual difference, is not without its significance for feminism'.[9]

While action movies in general are often dismissed as the extended enactment of (male) adolescent fantasy, their box-office ascendance associated with a supposed juvenilisation of the US cinema, the presence of actual juveniles within the diegesis is something else. And it is this factor in particular that has, it seems to me, triggered the critical attention given to families in action. Action and adventure films – including Steven Spielberg's *Indiana Jones and the Temple of Doom* (1984) and *Jurassic Park* (1993), George Lucas's *Star Wars* series (1977, 1980, 1983, 1999, 2002), the Schwarzenegger vehicles *Terminator 2* (1991) and *Last Action Hero* (1993), TV series adaptation *Lost in Space* (1998) and perhaps most successfully Robert Rodriguez's *Spy Kids* (2001) and *Spy Kids 2: Island of Lost Dreams* (2002) – all feature child or teenage protagonists-in-action whose relationship to parental (and even grandparental) figures is at issue within the narrative.

I aim here to explore differing figurations of the family and familial relations across diverse examples of action and adventure films. The films I discuss draw on a range of generic sources – including spy fictions, science-fiction, horror and crime – and operate across different modes – comedy and melodrama amongst them – but all centrally involve familial relationships. Moreover it is clear – and indeed should come as no surprise – that involvement in the action, being part of the adventure functions differently not only for men and women, but for adults and parents on the one hand, children and adolescents on the other. The scene-setting work of *Spy Kids*, for instance, suggests a desire on the part of Carmen and Juni for their parents to be cooler than they seem to be, but also the yearning of Gregorio (Antonio Banderas) and Ingrid Cortez (Carla Gugino) for the thrills and excitement of their former lives as spies.[10] At issue in action and adventure's staging of familial and other bonds of loyalty is an insistent and intense opposition between the perils and pleasures of freedom (physical exhilaration; potential isolation) on one hand and responsibility (limits placed on physical activity; the intensity of romantic love or comradeship) on the other.

## The child protagonist of action-adventure

Schwarzenegger's 1993 comedy *Last Action Hero*, a fantasy satire about movie heroism, attempts to manage the contradictions of the more child-friendly action Arnold suggested by his quasi-paternal role in *Terminator 2*. Schwarzenegger plays Jack Slater – a tough fictional cop idolised by lonely New York kid, Danny Madigan (Austin O'Brien). At a sneak preview of 'Jack Slater IV', Danny finds himself – via a magic ticket – taking part in the movie. Initially unable to convince Slater that he is actually a fictional character, both Danny and his hero ultimately follow the arch-villain Benedict (Charles Dance) back into Danny's world. Whilst making familial themes central, *Last Action Hero* takes a comical approach to conventional movie heroism and to the developing Schwarzenegger persona.

Danny lives with his widowed mother, and seems to have no friends other than the ageing projectionist Nick (Robert Prosky) with whom he spends time when he should be in school. The movies, it seems, are Danny's life. In its elaboration of the differences between movies and real life, the film ultimately suggests that Danny needs to accept his circumstances, to return to reality. It is made clear that he is destined for parental responsibility himself when, at the end of the film Ian McKellen's Death (accidentally liberated from a screening of Bergman's *The Seventh Seal*) tells Danny that he will 'die a grandfather'. The movie world offers no safe, idealised version of family life to contrast with Danny's insecurity and uncertainty. Slater is divorced, has lost his son to a psycho axe murderer (at the climax of 'Jack Slater III') and bemoans his daughter Whitney's preference for weapons over boys ('on prom night she stays home and field strips her AK47'). Though the movie opens with Danny watching the scene in which Slater's son is killed, the film goes out of focus at the crucial moment. Replayed later in Slater's memory (in black and white, signalling the emotional significance of the moment), the scene is subsequently restaged in New York with Danny taking Andy's place. The repetition underscores the extent to which the relationship between Danny and his hero is both that of sidekick and (surrogate) son.

*Last Action Hero* exemplifies two concerns that have figured large in many of Schwarzenegger's star vehicles: familial themes and his own developing star image. Since the success of *Twins* (1988) Schwarzenegger has tended to appear in either solid action vehicles – such as *Eraser* (1996) – and family-themed comedies. These include *Kindergarten Cop*, discussed above, *Junior* (1994), in which he plays an austere scientist who becomes pregnant and learns the value of human life, and *Jingle All the Way*, (1996), in which he plays a neglectful father attempting to buy a popular toy for his son at Christmas. The implication of Jeffords' work is that 1990s movies such as *Terminator 2* are in effect 'having it all'. If there are contradictions between the strength and violence that is associated with heroic masculinity in the cinema, and the very different nurturing qualities needed to manage family life, these are not apparent. It is interesting to note in this context not only that Schwarzenegger's movies in general are concerned with both fatherhood/family life and the possibilities and pleasures of spectacular destruction, but that *Last Action Hero*'s explicit project is to construct a parody of heroic masculinity in the action cinema which centres on the Schwarzenegger persona. Of course this strategy represents an intensification of rather than a departure from the star's self-reflexive persona. Indeed for Pfeil the star's tendency to parody precisely what he represents is little more than an invitation 'to respond to his ridiculous implacability, obscene violence, and hulking insensitivity with a sneer that then permits the qualities sneered at to be embraced and enjoyed'.[11] Perhaps the climactic setpiece of *Last Action Hero* is the sort of thing Pfeil has in mind. The villainous Benedict decides to kill Slater off by assassinating the actor who plays him (Schwarzenegger) at the premiere of 'Jack Slater IV'. Here Slater confronts Schwarzenegger, represented as a promotion-hungry buffoon: 'I don't really like you. You've brought me nothing but pain', Slater tells the star, a newly humanised action hero rebuking the performer who produced him. This moment is quickly succeeded by rooftop confrontations, first

with the Ripper (brought back from another movie) and then with Benedict. Jack
saves Danny, proving his skills in the real world – however, Slater has been injured
and Danny must return him to the movies, to a place 'where this is just a flesh
wound'. In this way, Danny is forced to relinquish the fantasy father figure with
which the cinema has so helpfully provided him, accepting the reality and the limits
of his life.

Although a clever film, with some spectacular sequences it is worth considering why *Last Action Hero* may have fared so badly at the box office (domestic video
is a different matter). Perhaps the laughs are too often at the expense of the action
audience? Or perhaps, from Danny's point of view the fantasy is not particularly
satisfying? Danny is explicitly shown to be ineffectual in the real world (he is
tempted but ultimately fails to confront the man who breaks into his apartment),
something of a sadistic spectator in the cinema and, upon entry to the movie world,
rather smug. Learning that your hero is vulnerable, that you need to grow up and
accept that life just is not like the movies may not be too appealing when you are
small, friendless, and the world is scary. Moreover, the deliberate flattening out of
the image accentuates the cartoon rather than emotional aspects of the picture.[12]
Thus while the film's narrative focuses on learning about (and coming to accept)
loss, the parodic tone tends to undercut this.

*Lost in Space*, by way of contrast, takes the child's fantasy – or at any rate, a
child's point of view – much more seriously. That is to say, the narrative explicitly acts out the wishes of the young male protagonist. In terms of both theme and
plot the key innovation of *Lost in Space* – a moderately successful, expensive movie
based on a cheap, camp 1960s television series – involved placing the dysfunctional
family centre-stage. The opening sequences set the scene: remote father, young
genius son and two daughters, the elder of whom, Dr Judy Robinson (Heather
Graham) is smart but distant ('a ghost' according to her mother), while the younger,
Penny, is rebellious and lonely. This bickering family, traumatised children and
distant father update the squeaky-clean Space Family Robinson of the 1960s. The
characterisation of Professor Maureen Robinson as a calm and capable professional
woman clearly reflects the desire to bring the script up to date in terms of contemporary gender politics.[13] She demonstrates presence and authority when she rebukes
both her husband, John Robinson (William Hurt) and pilot Don West (Matt
LeBlanc) for their macho stubbornness. All this was very self-conscious, squarely
centred in the promotion of the movie as thoroughly modern. Mimi Rogers spells
this out for the readers of *Film Review*:

> As Maureen Robinson, I set only one table and I prepare no meals! June
> Lockhart didn't do much in the show apart from that. What's great about
> Akiva's script is Maureen is a fully modern woman, a professor on a level
> with her husband John. She's an integral part of the space mission and
> spends a great deal of time trying to keep her family together. Unlike in
> the series, Maureen is a well-rounded character with no artificial housewife
> restrictions in operation.[14]

Note that the mission and preserving the family unit are presented as tasks of equal importance for the 'fully modern woman' here.

Set in 2058, *Lost in Space* follows the journey of the Robinson family and pilot Don West into deep space. Their mission is to construct a hypergate that will allow Earth's population to flee the planet they have devastated and colonise a suitable replacement, Alpha Prime (the environmental message is actually a little underplayed and receives little of the significance or screen time accorded to the family narrative). For three years training and preparation have occupied the family – patriarch John Robinson in particular – who have become distant from each other. Paid to sabotage the mission, evil Dr Smith (Gary Oldman) reprograms the ship's high-tech robot to destroy both the family and the on-board navigational systems. Forced to enter hyperspace at random, they encounter a distortion in time which, it transpires, has been created by a disaffected adult version of the young Will Robinson provoked in part by Dr Smith in the role of monstrous parental surrogate. This glitch in time also allows the crew to encounter the Proteus, a deserted ship that has been sent, years later, to search space for them – and thus acquire the updated charts needed to regain their course – as well as a species of metal-eating space spider. Father and son are finally reconciled in this alternate dimension, and the adult Will uses his time machine to return John Robinson to the waiting family and indeed to his child self. As he does so Will makes a plea that is also a rebuke: 'Don't make me wait another lifetime to know how you feel.'

Rather as Slater/Schwarzenegger must convince Danny to trust him in *Last Action Hero*, a key scene in *Lost in Space* involves John Robinson attempting to convince the adult Will to believe in the depth of his paternal love. It is when Will can see 'how much [his father] cared' that he softens. In acknowledging the tensions within the 'modern' family, but centring the movie on the need for reconciliation and understanding between father and son, the themes, narrative and publicity for *Lost in Space* dovetail neatly with the debates touched on above in critical work on gender in the 1990s. The crisis in the family is largely to do with men and masculinity, while the ways in which these issues are developed and resolved leaves gender hierarchies untouched.

Peter Krämer suggests that what he terms the 'family-adventure film' – of which both *Last Action Hero* and *Lost in Space* might be considered a variant – offers itself as a 'temporary relief from the real-life problems which their stories focus on but can never solve'. The emotional experience of this type of film is characterised by Krämer as follows:

> These films are imbued with sentimentality, spectacle and a sense of wonder, telling stories about the pain and longing caused by dysfunctional or incomplete families (usually with dead or absent fathers), about childish wishes and nightmares magically coming true and the responsibilities that go along with this, about the power of shared adventures to unite the young male protagonist with other members of his family and community beyond the boundaries of the family, and about the irrevocability of loss and separation (the family remains incomplete, the father does not return).[15]

In *Lost in Space* the father does return of course, recalling those early 1990s features in which men learn to be good fathers and in the process save themselves.

The re-worked *Lost in Space* cleverly brings the TV series into 1990s terrain. In a very real way it is crucial that fathers learn to speak with their sons. Daughters, it seems, are rather more dispensable. Penny has long got used to 'apology videos' from her father and the film does not seem particularly interested in exploring how either she or her sister feels about it.[16] Will is 'starved for attention' and his father never has enough time for him: this is the problem at the heart of the narrative. Perhaps it is no surprise then that Will's 'brilliant mind' fixates on two projects in particular: first, reconstructing the robot whose revised primary directive is to destroy the Robinson family and, second, building a time machine. Will's ideas about time travel are raised early on – the first prize he wins at the science fair (which his father fails to attend) is part of his ongoing experiments. Even when confronted with the distortion in time, John rejects Will's claims that this might be generated by an individual as 'flights of fancy' for which there is 'no time'. Of course as we have seen, Will's time machine eventually allows him to forcibly grab his father's attention. Not only do Will's experiments with time allow him to save his family, they also allow Will to meet his adult self and marvel narcissistically at his own future achievements.

Each child has a role onboard – Will's is robotics and he is systematically aligned with the robot. It is Will who uses his expertise to disarm the robot when it is destroying the ship in the first part of the film, for instance. As they are preparing to board the deserted Proteus, Will startles his father by reviving the robot. Will has it advance menacingly declaring its intent to 'destroy Robinson family' before explaining to his father (and the audience) that he has bypassed its systems and is operating it via remote control. Switching from this destructive impulse, Will enjoins the robot to take care of his father. This is an unnecessary command since Will controls and then becomes quite literally *embodied as* the robot – first operating it via remote control and then via a 'holographic interface', a sort of gaming device that explicitly positions the robot as an extension of Will. When the robot body has to be left behind, Will downloads as much of its 'personality' as he can, rebuilding it (when it finally assumes something akin to the homespun shape familiar from the TV series) by incorporating his own traits. Finally, Will is able to appeal (as if by magic) to the future robot to override its subsequent reprogramming and aid him and his family. His alignment with the robot nicely expresses his ambivalent relationship with his family, his father in particular – a desire to protect, to be acknowledged and to destroy.

The film's narrative trajectory of patching up the family is both 'fully modern' and very familiar. As with *Last Action Hero* what might previously have been discernible as a subtext – the importance of paternal love – becomes the central narrative concern of the film. All the characters but one (of which more below) undergo a transformation of some kind – even the robot. These transformations are along fairly conventional lines. John learns that he must show his emotions to his children. Judy and Don form a couple (she softens, he wises up, if only slightly), Penny settles for the animatronic female alien (accepting the responsibility of nurturing) and Will is reconciled to his father. In the future Dr Smith has also been transformed – into a monstrous man/spider hybrid as a result of being scratched by one of the alien creatures. This last transformation underlines Smith's role as monster within, an alternative, manipulative and self-serving father/protector for Will.

Ironically, because the film has taken such pains to portray her as a thoroughly modern, well-rounded woman, Professor Maureen Robinson is the only character who is not transformed through the course of the movie – she is more than capable from the outset and subsequently seems to fade to the margins of the narrative. This is not to dismiss Mimi Rogers' performance, more to note that however impressive her character, she is given nowhere to go.[17] Not even, or perhaps particularly not, the maternal, since that might compromise the film's evident intent to stress her modernity. Though we see two key scenes in which she tells her husband to listen to their son, we never see *her* speak to Will about her concerns. Moreover, it is remarkable that Maureen does not have a single scene alone with either of her daughters. Though John Robinson repeatedly lets his family down, there are more scenes between him and the three children (particularly, given the plot, between father and son) than between mother and children. That Maureen Robinson simultaneously has nowhere to go but is not sufficient for her children (and therefore implicitly requiring character development) echoes the portrayal of Danny's capable (but once again struggling/insufficient) mother in *Last Action Hero*. Perhaps this bland competence helps to frame the extent to which, within what we might in this context term the action film proper, we can discern a concomitant fantasy at work: a desire on the part of adult characters to escape the constriction of parenthood, home and domesticity. It is to this very different construction of familial tensions that we now turn.

## Mean mothers and distant dads

While *Lost in Space* may stage Robinson/Hurt's acknowledgement of the need to communicate with his son, *True Lies* adopts a simpler and more familiar strategy of placing daughter Dana in peril and having hero dad Harry Tasker (Arnold Schwarzenegger) rescue her. Maybe it is because she is a girl – or just because it is not that sort of movie – that they do not need to actually *talk*. Talk or no, a transformation nonetheless occurs: at the beginning of the film Dana is disaffected, tomboyish and dishonest (she steals money from her dad's buddy and CIA partner Gib, played by comic Tom Arnold). At the end she is a happily integrated family member and appropriately feminised young woman. Of course while preoccupied with family matters, particularly in its central section, *True Lies* was in many senses not a family film.[18]

In *True Lies* Schwarzenegger's Harry Tasker is an international spy who lives under the cover of an everyday job as sales rep for a computer company. After the spectacular action sequence that opens the film, perhaps it is no surprise that he returns to his suburban house with such evident reluctance. Dropped at the door by Gib he pauses before going in, bracing himself and looking up at the house with a sigh. It is Gib who provides Harry with a gift for his daughter – 'y'know . . . the dad thing' — and who reminds him to replace his wedding ring. The morning after in the Tasker home, the film sketches a domestic scene of dysfunctional family life. Harry drones on about his job, while only pretending to listen to his wife Helen (Jamie Lee Curtis). She slips a joke into the conversation about the cost of some work on the house — 'I slept with him and he said he'd knock off a hundred dollars' — to which Harry's only response is 'that's good thinking' and a kiss on the cheek.

While Harry approaches the family home with trepidation, Helen is simply bored by her husband: 'Whenever I can't sleep, I just ask him to tell me about his day' she confides to a female colleague. It is thus the project of the film's narrative not only to defeat a terrorist plot, but to bring the family back together — to inject some spice into married/family life with a bit of action. Helen's desire for adventure leads her to take up with Simon, a used car salesman played by Bill Paxton. Simon has an angle on what women want — the 'promise of adventure, a hint of danger'. 'You gotta work on their dreams', he tells Harry. Though he fantasises about killing him with one blow, Harry settles for first reducing Simon to a gibbering wreck and second taking his advice about women. 'She wants a little adventure — I'm going to give her one', vows Harry, setting himself up in a ritzy hotel suite and casting Helen as a prostitute. The sleazy second honeymoon scenario Harry has planned is disrupted by the terrorists, and he is unmasked. Despite his best efforts to contain her fantasies to a hotel room, Helen becomes involved in Harry's work, a part of his alternative existence — first as someone to be rescued and protected and, ultimately, as a partner.

Unsurprisingly, more than a few critics found the film's central section, in which Curtis's character is deceived and humiliated, not only implicitly conservative in its punishment of Helen but disturbing and cruel. *True Lies*, writes José Arroyo, 'perpetuates astonishing emotional violence in the name of the traditional nuclear family', violence he regards as directed primarily at Helen (although the cardboard cut-out Arab antagonists have an equally problematic position).[19] It would be hard to disagree with Arroyo's assertion that the movie 'affirms traditional gender roles'. Yet Harry's pursuit of his wife is *so* extreme, so evidently out of proportion that it attracts expressions of disbelief not only from reviewers and critics but from other characters within the diegesis. Against this, Krämer's summary of the action's 'peculiar *raison d'être*' seems somehow too reasoned, calm:

> the hero and his wife have to learn to understand, and interact with, each other in a new way so as to revive their marriage, and once this is achieved the action-hero has to go through the motions all over again to overcome the alienation of his daughter.[20]

To me this doesn't really convey the excess that critics found so unsettling, the extent to which the film offers not only a re-working of the family that integrates a sexier version of Helen and a less troublesome Dana, but also a (male) fantasy of retribution against the family and domesticity. This fantasy of retribution seems to me to be of a rather different order to the use of the kidnapped daughter as motivation in *Commando*, a 1985 Schwarzenegger vehicle, or the dead families that haunt his characters in *End of Days* (1999) and *Collateral Damage* (2002). Instead, the creepy pleasures of terrorising the family, even as Harry Tasker struggles to save it, recall for me the simultaneous sadism and sentimentality of a film like *Face/Off* (1997).

Fred Pfeil notes wryly how, despite their familial emphasis, the first two *Lethal Weapon* films 'wring the full ambiguity out of the domestic injunction to "keep the home fires burning"'.[21] In each film in the series the Murtaugh (Danny Glover) home, car and family are destroyed, damaged or threatened. The 'aggressive, even sadistic, and certainly anti-domestic' pleasures on offer have become a firm convention of the cycle – a Triad gang led by Jet Li set the house ablaze in the most recent, *Lethal Weapon 4* (1998). An ambivalent relationship to domesticity is reinforced by the recurrent Christmas setting – 'the time, symbolically, mythologically, of maximally happy domesticity' notes Pfeil[22] – allowing corny old tunes to be set against scenes of carnage and destruction. Studies of masculinity and action genres, the western in particular, have pointed to a recurrent structuring opposition between the hero and domesticity. Family bonds tie the hero down, making him vulnerable. Of course it is the work of popular films – and criticism – to problematise such an opposition, dramatically and visually enacting the tensions and contradictions between a desire for action and a desire for domesticity. In both *True Lies* and *The Long Kiss Goodnight* (1996) it is domesticity that is dull, set against the protagonists' more exciting double identity in the world of espionage. What is more, though perhaps unsurprisingly, it is clear that this disaffection with the domestic is inflected differently for men and for women. What then is at stake for the family when action movies explicitly (that is, not only via an identification with male protagonists) allow women, as well as men, to side-step responsibilities, to avoid growing up and to revel in the adolescent pleasures of action and destruction that the genre both stages and permits?

As in *Lethal Weapon* and *Die Hard*, the Christmas setting of *The Long Kiss Goodnight* operates as an ironic counterpoint to the film's familial themes. Geena Davis plays Samantha, a small-town teacher afflicted with amnesia. She has a forgotten past – and an alternative family – as a government assassin: her whole identity as Sam Caine is, it seems, a cover, a parodic fantasy invented by her former self, Charly Baltimore. As her old personality returns, Sam/Charly starts to views her new life differently and seeks to escape the restricting role of mother. The re-emergence of her secret agent identity is marked explicitly not only by a capacity for decisive, violent action, but by being mean to her daughter. 'I didn't ask for the kid,' Charly protests to P.I/buddy Mitch Hennesey (Samuel L. Jackson), 'Samantha had the kid, not me. Nobody asked me.'

In contrast to *True Lies*' Helen Tasker, Sam is not particularly unhappy at the start of the movie, not evidently in need of transformation. Her loss of memory makes her incomplete however. She functions as both child and mother: 'You might not believe it to look at me, but I was born only eight years ago on a beach in New Jersey' her voiceover tells us in the opening sequence. After she is involved in a car crash, Sam's past slowly begins to return with a vengeance. Recovering in hospital Charly visits Sam in her dreams, her words both a threat and a promise: 'I'm coming back. You know that don't you. The name's Charly by the way. You're gonna *love* me.'

Of course it would be wrong to suggest that *The Long Kiss Goodnight* simply offers a fantasy of escape from motherhood/domestic into action. Just as Charly's re-appearance is indicated through her attempts to toughen up daughter Caitlin, pushing her on when she is hurt, her developing identity is mapped through not only a physical transformation and the new abilities this brings, but a shifting attitude to her daughter. If Samantha gave birth to the child, Charly was already pregnant – the father is revealed as arch-villain Timothy (Craig Bierko) – so that Caitlin is a product of both worlds. Leaving Caitlin behind to find her true identity, Sam promises to return (Charly has a different idea). Charly returns to trash her daughter's bedroom in search of a key to a new life. This key, all that Sam retained from her past life, is described in the opening voice-over as 'blank and faceless, a fitting metaphor' for her condition. Neatly, it is revealed to be the key to a new identity in the form of hidden money and papers. Inconveniently however, Sam has left the key with her daughter, on a charm bracelet tied around her teddy bear's neck, thus taking her back home. From her daughter's bedroom, Charly looks down through her rifle's sights at Caitlin, dressed as an angel for a Christmas event (a nativity perhaps?), Hal crouched beside her in supportive paternal pose. One of the film's key thematic axes is represented here in the extreme juxtaposition of an intimate Christmas festivity, slow-motion and soft-focus, with Charly's image, hard and sharply drawn. If the image of Charly looking at her family through the gun suggests that she is divided between killing and caring, the soft music signals the return of maternal feelings. Moreover the camera first closes in on Charly's face and then pulls back into an image of loss and yearning familiar from the woman's picture – a woman framed in a medium shot looking out through the bars created by the window. Action – signalled by the sound of Mitch honking the horn to alert her to danger – disrupts the moment, but the scene paves the way for Charly to return to her daughter.

The reconciliation of these action and domestic space comes as Timothy takes Caitlin hostage and Charly/Mitch set out to rescue her. Like *True Lies*, *The Long Kiss Goodnight* ends with an idyllic family image (i.e. mom, daughter and step-dad) which is not the end of the story. I am not saying these images are ironic (actually they are more dreamlike) but that the movie expresses the kind of ambivalence in relation to children and domesticity that Modleski finds permeating *Three Men and a Baby*, read by her as cleverly disguised misogyny. Modleski's analysis is predicated in part on the fact that it is a female child who, in the symbolic economy of the film, is equated with shit (and cleaning up shit is work typically reserved for those lower in the hierarchy than the film's male protagonists). Interestingly, both Sam and Charly vent their aggression on a male child, the hapless Raymond (who, it is worth noting, becomes an acceptable target in Hollywood terms by being overweight).

The scenario suggested by *The Long Kiss Goodnight* is one in which women might speculate about a more exciting life than that offered by parenthood or suburbia, or by some boring office job like Helen Tasker's in *True Lies*. And isn't this the very fantasy that *True Lies* allows Harry and punishes Helen for wanting? Following Harry's discovery of Helen's 'affair', *True Lies* portrays the family home as a comically ominous place. Domestic scenes are accompanied by darkness, thunder and rain, with distorting shots from both high and low angles. The camera tracks in through a window as Helen demonstrates her ability to spin a line just as well as Harry. The rooms are somehow too small for the Schwarzenegger physique, which seems more at home in the grandiose settings with which the film opens and closes. Deceived by both husband and suitor, Helen is finally allowed into the action funhouse in the closing sequences. Yet, as with the ending of *Men in Black* (1997), in which Linda Fiorentino's pathologist is admitted to the MiB ranks, we can only speculate if this will generate a sequel in which a woman gets to do something from the off.[23]

## Buddies, comrades and other extended families

Finally I would like to return to the ways in which action and adventure movies employ familial metaphors in their staging of intense relationships between individuals and within groups. Clearly while many action movies express an ambivalence towards domesticity, this is not necessarily about the desire for a solitary existence. Rather it is framed by other allegiances, alternative families and, crucially, the community of work. And if 'the family' in its most traditional guise was not always at issue in 1980s action films, then kinship, attachment and loyalty most definitely were. Some 1980s movies emphasised the melodramatic (loved ones in peril), whilst the sentimentality of others clearly drew on an image of the patriarchal family as a moral anchor. Motivation in these films came not from simplistic patriotism, but from threats to loved ones. Though Jeffords acknowledges that the heroes of 1980s action movies were motivated by the needs of others, she is concerned more with the development of masculinity through fathering than the wider patterns of allegiance that this might suggest. Yet the success of the buddy format, with its trajectory of the attraction of opposites, and its thematic concerns with work-as-family remains one of the key features of 1980s movies to carry over into contemporary productions.

*True Lies* draws a sustained analogy between marriage and the buddy relationship. 'Honey, I'm home', Harry's first words in the film are addressed to Gib not Helen. Writing elsewhere about the film I suggested that 'it is not so much that the marriage overcomes the buddy relationship, but that Harry and Helen must *become buddies*'. While 'Helen and Harry are produced as a couple in terms of the homosocial codes of the buddy partnership', the relationship between Harry and Gib is displaced.[24] Yet in the context of the argument I am making here the relationship between buddies and families can perhaps be seen as complementary rather than in terms of substitution. The desired goal is a relationship characterised by honesty and transparency rather than deceit.

Buddy relationships are central to the *Lethal Weapon* series in which police work is cast as a largely male community defined by loyalty and mutual protection. It is perhaps the fact that she is a cop – and therefore part of this community – that allowed Martin Riggs' (Mel Gibson's) love interest Lorna Cole (Rene Russo) to survive *Lethal Weapon 3* (1992). Yet if this promised the kind of sequel in which men and women are buddies, *Lethal Weapon 4* manages to side-step that possibility by having her heavily pregnant for most of the action in a film that foregrounds themes of paternity and family even more centrally than its predecessors. The by now familiar setpiece opening – which has Riggs declaring that he has less to lose than Murtaugh and should therefore be the one to take the risks – brings the news that Riggs is to be a father and, by way of counter, that Murtaugh is to be a grandfather (the action neatly skipping to 'nearly nine months later'). These paternal plots are complemented by sub-plots to do with the fate of the Hong family and Rhianne Murtaugh's marriage to cop Lee Butters (played by Chris Rock), which is, for no clear reason, being kept a secret from her father. Russo's Lorna is pretty much sidelined – comically cranky, she has an insatiable appetite – with only one fight scene (in the Murtaugh family home, just before it gets torched). Unsurprisingly, the movie ends in the maternity ward, childbirth triggering not only last-minute marriage but a celebration of extended family: 'we're not friends, we're family' chants the disparate group including Joe Pesci's Leo Getz (a regular since the second film) and Captain Murphy. The photo for which they pose is then displayed in a family album which the camera ranges over during the closing credits, offering images of the film's cast and crew, together with scenes from some of the earlier films.

What is 'the family' in this context? Is it more than a hierarchical structure in which gender and paternity are legally inscribed, the family as institution rather than support system? I would like to emphasise the fantasy of living either outside or in reconfigured 'families'. While *The Long Kiss Goodnight* features a family or two, I am less convinced that '*the* family' is on display. Charly's life as a spy involves a series of marriage and familial related metaphors: the postcard that describes her fiancé is a codified way of registering the target for assassination; the plan that she and Mitch foil is codenamed Operation Honeymoon; Mr Perkins is revealed as a sort of CIA father to her, while Nathan (Brian Cox) functions as a mentor. Charly finds her alternative family via her developing buddy alliance with Mitch (himself estranged from his son) who in turn continually reminds her about her responsibilities to Caitlin. Charly's decision to rescue Caitlin follows a scene in which she first kicks Mitch out of the car and then comes back for him – a turning point of sorts (played for comedy) which acknowledges that self-sufficiency only goes so far.

Of course this discussion raises further questions about the definition of family: what types of groupings can be read as familial? What role does the presence of children play here? The ideological persistence of a particular familial norm in political rhetoric should not obscure the diversity of kinship and community structures in both social life and in popular culture. Arroyo writes that while Cameron's:

> previous movies have been critical of the established order . . . *True Lies* simply affirms it. For instance, the family is usually an impossible ideal in Cameron's work – much longed for and highly valued, but out of reach. His characters end up making their own 'families' the best way they can.[25]

Revisiting a much-discussed movie like *Aliens* (1986) in this context, it becomes significant that Newt is not Ripley's biological child, and that their bonding is framed by the closeness of the military team, for example.

The foregrounding of familial themes in recent action films is not simply a matter of revering a benevolent paternalism at the expense of women. Fantasies of escape and empowerment, which permeate and even structure so many action films, frame an increasingly explicit voicing of familial themes and concerns. These themes are articulated and resolved in different ways for men and women, for children and for the extended work-based families/communities so typical of the genre. Given that other Hollywood genres – musicals, war movies or gangster films, for instance – favour settings that foreground structures of support beyond the biological family, the examples discussed here further underline the diversity with which popular culture imagines families, as spaces of possibility as well as a place to escape from.

## Notes

1  Karen Schneider 'With Violence if Necessary: Rearticulating the Family in the Contemporary Action-Thriller', *Journal of Popular Film and Television*, 27: 1, 1999, p. 4.
2  Mark Gallagher 'I Married Rambo: Spectacle and Melodrama in the Hollywood Action Film', in Christopher Sharrett (ed.) *Mythologies of Violence in Postmodern Media*, Detroit: Wayne State University Press, 1999, p. 199.
3  Susan Jeffords 'The Big Switch: Hollywood Masculinity in the Nineties', in Jim Collins, Hilary Radner and Ava Preacher Collins (eds) *Film Theory Goes to the Movies*, London: Routledge, 1993, p. 200.
4  Ibid., p. 197.
5  Fred Pfeil *White Guys: Studies in Postmodern Domination and Difference*, London: Verso, 1995, p. 37.
6  Jeffords 'The Big Switch', p. 200.
7  Pfeil *White Guys*, p. 44.
8  Tania Modleski *Feminism Without Women: Culture and Criticism in a 'Postfeminist' Age*, London: Routledge, 1991.
9  Steven Cohan *Masked Men: Masculinity and the Movies in the Fifties*, Bloomington: Indiana University Press, 1997, p. xi.
10  The use of the in-laws/grandparents in *Spy Kids 2* comically emphasises how antagonistic–affectionate relations with parents continue into adult life.
11  Pfeil *White Guys*, p. 31.
12  Director John McTiernan notes: 'Everything is shot with long [telephoto] lenses, bringing the interesting elements into focus and eliminating the boring details. It compresses more action into the frame. The most exiting bits are done in slow motion. And every character is a giant figure photographed from slightly below because everyone needs to look like he's six-foot-eight. And moment to moment reality is completely manufactured by edits. In essence it's all a giant illusion, this giant fabrication up on a movie screen.' Steve Newman and Ed Marsh, *Last Action Hero: the Official Movie Book*, New York: Newmarket, 1993, p. 31.
13  And with the acknowledged aim of a sequel were the movie's success to warrant it (which it has not to date).
14  Alan Jones 'Spaced Out', *Film Review* Special, 23, 1998, p. 35.
15  Peter Krämer 'Would You Take Your Child to See This Film? The Cultural and Social Work of the Family-Adventure Movie', in Steve Neale and Murray Smith (eds) op. cit., p. 304.
16  While Krämer (ibid.) suggests that cross-sex identification is at work in these family films, it is still worth noting how rarely the child protagonist is female.
17  Whereas the emotional education of men is a common theme of mainstream cinema, including action-adventure, it seems that female characters are often assumed to be already

fully developed. Thus rites of passage narratives are staged far less frequently in relation to female protagonists (I discuss this in *The Silence of the Lambs*, London: BFI, 2002).

18  *True Lies* had an R rating in the US versus the PG-13 of *Lost in Space*. In the UK the film was edited for violence before release.

19  José Arroyo 'Cameron and the Comic', *Sight and Sound*, September 1994, pp. 26–8, p. 28. See also Barry Keith Grant's essay in this volume.

20  Krämer 'Would You Take Your Child', p. 294.

21  Pfeil *White Guys*, p. 16.

22  Ibid.

23  *Men in Black II* (2002) did not feature Fiorentino's Agent L, reviving Tommy Lee Jones's K to partner Will Smith's J.

24  Tasker *Working Girls*, p. 78.

25  Arroyo 'Cameron and the Comic', p. 28.

## PART IV

# Nation, ethnicity and stardom

# LEON HUNT

# THE HONG KONG/HOLLYWOOD CONNECTION
Stardom and spectacle in transnational action cinema

> I've seen a lot of Hong Kong cinema. I think it's very interesting,
> terrific stuff. It just doesn't have a chance in the United States.
> James Glickenhaus, director of *The Protector*[1]

A T THE TURN OF THE MILLENNIUM, two characteristics seem to
define state-of-the-art action films – the supremacy of digital special effects and
what David Bordwell calls the 'Hong-Kongification of American cinema'.[2] The two
converge most dramatically in *The Matrix* (Andy and Larry Wachowski, US 1999) and
those films that have been visibly influenced by it – *Romeo Must Die* (Andrzej
Bartkowiak, US 2000) and *Charlie's Angels* (McG, US/Germany 2000). The two-way
traffic between Hong Kong and Hollywood accounts for both the Hollywood careers
of Bruce Lee, John Woo and Jackie Chan, and the Hong Kong careers of George
Lazenby, Cynthia Rothrock, Jean-Claude Van Damme, Fred Weintraub and Robert
Clouse. Nowhere is this crossover more apparent than in martial arts action, which,
in Meaghan Morris's words, constitutes 'a fuzzy space between the critically visible
grandeurs of "Hollywood" and "Hong Kong"'.[3] This essay is concerned with the changing shape – and location – of that 'fuzzy space', the 'in-between-ness' of Hong Kong-
Hollywood action. If this has largely been a matter of stars working in both industries,
more recently there has also been a dialogue between different *action technologies* –
the very different regimes of the spectacular represented by CGI and wirework.

Hollywood has assimilated three kinds of 'Hong Kong action' – the high-octane
gunplay of John Woo, the stunt-filled action-comedy of Jackie Chan and Sammo
Hung, and the 'wire fu' of historical martial arts films like *Once Upon a Time in China*
(Tsui Hark, Hong Kong (HK) 1991). It is the second and the third which interest me
particularly here, because of their implications for how Hollywood films are made,
the valuing of certain types of cinematic labour (choreography) and for culturally
specific constructions of the 'real'. But spectacle does not exist in a vacuum, and I

shall also consider issues of representation. This provides another way of thinking about the 'in-between', because Hong Kong-Hollywood can be seen to be positioned precariously between 'Asiaphilia' – 'a deceptively benign ideological construct that naturalises and justifies the systematic appropriation of cultural property and expressive forms created by Yellow people'[4] – and Asiaphobia. Both are evident in the first and most successful Hong Kong-Hollywood co-production, *Enter the Dragon* (Robert Clouse, HK/US 1973), which both fetishises the 'Orient' and replays 'Yellow Peril' archetypes. To some extent, Hollywood's 'Hong Kongification' can be seen as the latest manifestation of America's 'Encounter with Asia'. And yet there are problems, too, with regarding certain cultural forms as off-limits, as the essential property of a particular group – Hong Kong cinema has, after all, had global aspirations for some time. Ding-Tzann Lii goes further by suggesting that Hong Kong cinema, at its peak, represented a form of 'Marginal Imperialism', which both reproduces the dynamics of traditional imperialism and poses a threat to it. On the one hand, Hong Kong's Asian expansionism contributed to the underdevelopment of Taiwanese cinema, just as Hollywood did to Hong Kong itself after 1993. But Lii also argues that there are significant (cultural if not economic) differences between 'core' and 'marginal' imperialism – the latter represents a 'rupture' in global capitalism 'where the peripheral "other" surfaces as a subject'[5] – in this case, Hong Kong's 'localised' media imperialism contributed to an 'Asianisation', blending into other Asian countries and 'creating a synthesis-form with a higher cognitive order'.[6] What happens when core imperialism seeks to incorporate its peripheral counterpart? Lii distinguishes between *incorporation*, where the 'other' is transformed by imperialism, and *yielding*, a 'synthesis which transcends both the self and the Other'.[7] Ackbar Abbas seemingly has something similar in mind for his hypothetical 'third space', where 'East and West are overcome and discredited as separate notions, and another space or a space of otherness is introduced'.[8] With this in mind, I shall be looking in particular at the Hollywood films of Jackie Chan and Jet Li, and the work of choreographer Yuen Wo-ping.

## Trans-Pacific traffic: a short history

Between mid-1972 and the end of 1973, Warner Brothers had distributed Shaw Brothers' *King Boxer/Five Fingers of Death* (Cheng Chang-ho, HK 1972) in Europe and North America, broadcast the early episodes of the *Kung Fu* TV series,[9] and co-produced Bruce Lee's final complete film, *Enter the Dragon*.[10] This short-lived period also saw a series of Hong Kong co-productions with Britain (*Legend of the Seven Golden Vampires, Shatter*), Italy (*Blood Money*) and Australia (*The Man From Hong Kong*), most of them attempts to break Hong Kong action stars (David Chiang/Jiang Dawei, Ti Lung/Di Long, Lo Lieh, Wang Yu) in the west. However, the division of labour on these films was strikingly consistent – written and directed by white westerners, fight scenes choreographed and performed by Hong Kong Chinese. The use of Chinese choreographers was short-lived – Jackie Chan had to work with American stunt co-ordinators in the 1980s – and no space existed for a Hong Kong director to have a Hollywood career.

Some interesting short- and long-term careers developed during this period. Producer Fred Weintraub and director Robert Clouse maintained their connection with Hong Kong cinema in a more low-rent capacity than the success of *Enter the Dragon* might have promised, but they anticipate the 'Gatekeeper' role Bordwell later attributes to producer Terence Chang.[11] Just as Chang facilitated the Hollywood debuts of John Woo, Chow Yun Fat and Michelle Yeoh, Weintraub and Clouse performed the same role for Bruce Lee, and, less successfully, Jackie Chan (*Battlecreek Brawl*, Clouse, 1980) and Cynthia Rothrock (*China O'Brien 1* and *2*, both Clouse, 1988).

Chuck Norris, meanwhile, had done some minor stuntwork in Hollywood, but first made his mark as Bruce Lee's opponent in *Way of the Dragon* (Lee, HK 1972). David Desser sees stars like Norris as indicative of America subsequently using the white martial arts star to 'co-opt the Asian martial arts for the American action hero', not infrequently operating in the Asian locale which had arguably contributed to a crisis in white American masculinity – Vietnam.[12] Most westerners (including Norris) who participated in Hong Kong films were martial artists hired to play heavies – only Cynthia Rothrock gravitated to leading roles – but George Lazenby is a notable exception, the closest Hong Kong came to enlisting a major western star.[13] In the 1970s, the former Bond was situated in a netherworld of dubbed international films, but was apparently set to raise his profile in Bruce Lee's incomplete *Game of Death*. After Lee's premature death, Golden Harvest cast Lazenby instead in *Stoner* (Huang Feng, HK 1974), *The Man from Hong Kong* (Brian Trenchard-Smith, HK/Australia 1975) and *Queen's Ransom* (Huang Feng, HK 1976), pairing him with Hong Kong stars like Wang Yu and Angela Mao-ying. Lazenby's Hong Kong 'acting' experience accords with stories told by other Western performers – 'They just asked me to move my mouth a certain number of times, and if I didn't do it enough, they'd ask me to say something else'.[14] But a crash course in martial arts and Sammo Hung's expert choreography transformed Lazenby into a creditable performer – in *The Man from Hong Kong,* he moves rather better than nominal leading man Wang Yu does. *Man* was Wang Yu's crack at English-speaking stardom, and the first film to play out the culture clash of a Hong Kong hero operating in the modern west. The film hinges on the image of a stereotypically brutal Far East, as Wang's bull-in-a-china-shop Hong Kong cop decimates Australia in his pursuit of Lazenby's drug baron. In contrast with the asexual mysticism of Lee in *Enter* and David Chiang in *Legend of the Seven Golden Vampires* (Roy Ward Baker, GB/HK 1974), Wang's Inspector Fang Sing-ling is a strikingly corporeal and libidinous presence – he even seduces two caucasian women, an interracial taboo rarely transgressed in Western films. Lazenby, meanwhile, is a villain with colonial overtones, even down to his kung fu skills: 'My business takes me to the East regularly. I find the Chinese make the best servants. I understand your culture, and your language, Inspector. And your martial arts – especially those.'

There seems to be a yawning chasm of western indifference between the brief 'kung fu craze' of the early 1970s and the exodus of Hong Kong talent to Hollywood in the mid-1990s – the failure to establish Jackie Chan outside Asia, the fact that Golden Harvest could only score global hits with 'Hollywood knock-offs . . .

movies bankrolled out of Hong Kong but filmed in the West, shot by and starring US-based talent, and distributed in the West by Hollywood-based companies'.[15] But some more modest successes suggest that the 'fuzzy space' could still command a cult following. Golden Harvest's *China O'Brien* films try to look as much like Hollywood films as possible, but Ng See-Yuen's *No Retreat, No Surrender* series (1986–7) sees some intriguingly converging traditions. As Meaghan Morris observes, the first *No Retreat* ('Corey' Yuen Kwai, HK/US 1986) draws on the pedagogic narrative structures which can be found in both Hong Kong-produced films and American offshoots like *The Karate Kid*.[16] It also draws on the Bruce Lee 'clone' films, which include not only vehicles for Bruce Li and Dragon Lee but also the posthumously completed *Game of Death* (Robert Clouse, HK 1978). Lee's double in *Game*, Kim Tai-chung, plays Lee's ghost in *No Retreat*, materialising to tutor the neophyte hero. The films are topped off with Western martial arts talent – Jean Claude Van Damme,[17] Cynthia Rothrock – and Yuen Kwai's high-impact choreography.

Since the mid-1990s, the Hong Kong movie diaspora has comprised three groups of people – stars (Jackie Chan, Chow Yun Fat, Jet Li, Michelle Yeoh, Sammo Hung), directors (John Woo, Tsui Hark, Ringo Lam, Stanley Tong, Ronny Yu, Kirk Wong) and choreographers (Yuen Wo-ping, Yuen Kwai, Yuen Cheung-yan). The directors, notwithstanding Woo's success, largely support Bordwell's suspicion that 'Hong Kong has served as a cheap source of directorial labour for second-rate productions'.[18] Steve Fore was (initially) more optimistic, likening the exodus to Hollywood's European émigrés of the 1930s and 1940s – he described them as 'transnational design professionals' belonging to 'image-projecting and consciousness-transforming industries'.[19] But there are not a lot of Asian faces in John Woo's American films, while *Double Team* (Tsui Hark, US 1997) places the questionable charms of Van Damme and Mickey Rourke centre stage while talented Xiong Xin-xin briefly dazzles as a silent heavy. Lii, like Fore, is hopeful that 'Hollywood movies will be changed dramatically' and that 'Jackie Chan . . . will definitely be of equal importance to Stallone and Schwarzenegger'.[20] Instead, Chan found himself 'of equal importance' to Chris Tucker and Owen Wilson – Chow Yun Fat's initial Hollywood films, *The Replacement Killers* (Antoine Fucqua, US 1998) and *The Corruptor* (James Foley, US 1999) also followed the interracial 'buddy' narrative. In any case, this was not Jackie's first experience of Hollywood.

## The trouble with Jackie: *The Protector* and *Shanghai Noon*

> That chink don't fight right. He fights foreign.
> *Battlecreek Brawl*

The failure of Jackie Chan to crack non-Asian markets prior to the crossover success of *Rumble in the Bronx* (Stanley Tong, HK 1995) has become symbolic of the west's incomprehension in the face of Hong Kong action. Chan made four English-language films in the 1980s – *Battlecreek Brawl, The Cannonball Run* (Hal Needham, US 1981),

*The Cannonball Run II* (Hal Needham, US 1983) and *The Protector* (James Glickenhaus, US/HK 1985). *Battlecreek Brawl* and *The Protector*, in particular, hold special places in the Chan mythology, even though the consensus is that they are 'substandard films directed by American hacks'.[21] First, they have come to symbolise the failure of 'American hacks' to recognise Chan's abilities as a filmmaker rather than simply a martial arts performer. Second, what little value they are grudgingly accorded lies not in their achievements but in indirectly inspiring superior films made by Chan in Hong Kong – *Brawl*'s 1930s gangster milieu becomes *Mr Canton and Lady Rose* (Jackie Chan, HK 1989) and *The Protector*'s rogue cop heroics become *Police Story* (Chan, HK 1985).[22] Chan has helped add fuel to this version of events:

> (Glickenhaus) told me I'm just an actor. For me, it's just say my lines and back to the motor home. After *The Protector* I decided it's back to Asia. I told Glickenhaus, 'You do *The Protector* and I'll do *Police Story*, and I'll show you what the action movie is all about.'[23]

Granted, *Battlecreek Brawl* and *The Protector* are less accomplished films than *Rush Hour* (Brett Ratner, US 1998) and *Shanghai Noon* (Tom Dey, US 2000), yet their 'failure' tells us as much as the later films' 'success'.

In his account of the American promotion of *Rumble in the Bronx*, Steve Fore suggests that Chan was sold primarily as a physical performer, while the less 'universal' aspects of his star persona were played down.[24] *Battlecreek Brawl* doesn't do a bad job with Chan's persona, which was still in the process of being fully formed even in his Hong Kong films. It incorporates (but does not develop) aspects of the master–pupil narratives of the kung fu comedies that made Chan a star. His uncle–teacher, played by Mako, recalls the dissolute rogue-masters played by Yuen Siu-tin in *Snake in the Eagle's Shadow* and *Drunken Master* (both Yuen Woo-ping, HK 1978), part sage, part mischievous roué, part sadistic tutor. It is Chan the performer who emerges less fully. He does backflips and handstands, delivers multiple kicks and punches, and skilfully wields a bench and pole against butterfly swords. But 'Jackie Chan' is arguably the sum of Chan and his stunt team, his mastery of camera placement and editing, the irresistible pace that subtle undercranking bestows on an elaborately composed fight. 'American stuntmen are so slow,' Chan has complained. 'I hit bam-bam-bam, and, by the third time, he will have blocked the first punch!'[25] But slow stuntmen are only part of the problem – barring a brief fight with two Chinese assassins, his opponents are overweight sluggers, and these speed-versus-strength confrontations are not conducive to the intricate rhythms of Hong Kong choreography.

'There's one thing you don't do to a protector, you don't make him mad,' warns the end-title song from *The Protector*. As the lyrics suggest, the film makes fewer concessions than *Brawl* to Chan's Hong Kong films, but they also inadvertently point to the aesthetic battle going on in the film. When Stephen Teo suggests that 'the film looks surprisingly like a made-to-order Hong Kong kung fu action movie',[26] one has to assume that he has seen the Asian-language version. In an interesting reversal of what later happened to *Rumble in the Bronx*, Chan re-shot, re-edited and redubbed the film for its Asian release. Some of the changes are to do with his 'family' image – there's no nudity and no swearing in the Hong Kong version (it *is* a shock to hear him say, 'Give me the fucking keys!'). But Chan also cranked up the action, adding a trademark comic scene in a gym, where he bounces off benches and uses weights machines as weapons, and re-shooting his climactic fight with kick-boxing champion Bill Wallace. For all his talk of slow American stuntmen, Chan is as fond of pounding *gwailo* martial arts champs as Bruce Lee was – he had had a memorable duel with Benny 'The Jet' Urquidez the previous year in *Wheels on Meals* (Sammo Hung, HK 1984), which was enough of a fan favourite to merit a rematch in *Dragons Forever* (Sammo Hung, HK 1987). In the US cut, the Chan–Wallace fight follows the 'realist' conventions of North American martial arts films – 'a blend of two-or-three-step sparring drills and barroom-brawl tactics'.[27] Interestingly, Wallace's flashy kicking comes out of this version quite well, captured in extended master shots, but Chan merely seems to flail ineffectually with unextended kicks and underpowered flurries of defensive blows. Chan's version varies the rhythm of the fight, the editing and the speed of the film – undercranking pumps the action up to twice the speed of the Glickenhaus version, and he slows down some of the moves retained from the original version. More use is made of props and environ-ment – twice Chan is bounced off a wire fence and each time turns it into a different hyperbolic stunt. Above all, the Hong Kong version uses what Bordwell calls 'expressive amplification' – exaggerated movements that lend 'a distinct, vivid emotional profile' to a fight.[28] After a powerful punch from Chan, Wallace (or at least his stunt double) performs a corkscrew spin before crashing to the ground. But does this really tell us about anything other than the respective merits of James Glickenhaus's and Jackie Chan's filmmaking, a straight-to-video hack and an expe-rienced, respected action director? Glickenhaus's aversion to 'undercranking'[29] is later echoed by Brett Ratner in his commentary for the *Rush Hour* DVD. Ratner's take on Chan is intriguing, a mixture of knowledgeable fanboy and expert on what will 'work' in an American film. Not unlike the Wachowski Brothers' use of Yuen Wo-ping on *The Matrix*, this was a combination of toning him down and having him 'quote' himself:

> I gave him ideas of things that he's done before in other movies or things that I've seen before . . . I felt like I knew what Jackie needed. I knew what to do to take a chopsocky star and put him into an American formula and make it work.

If Ratner's 'formula' finds a middle ground between *Beverley Hills Cop* and *Police Story*, *The Protector* has more in common with the films of Chuck Norris and other 'White Warriors'. The role of Jackie's 'buddies' in *Rush Hour* and *Shanghai Noon* is to 'Americanize' him, but Vietnam vet Danny Garroni (Danny Aiello) goes further by symbolically enlisting him in the conquest of Asia. Chan's New York cop Billy Wong accompanies Garroni to Hong Kong in a case mixing drug trafficking with kidnapping. Garroni's knowledge of Hong Kong derives from RnR during his Vietnam days, a connection which positions Asia as a space for sexual conquest as well as imperialist adventure – 'I never go anywhere in South East Asia without an Uzi', Garroni explains. The promise of 'adventure and forbidden pleasures' [30] is a central trope in Hollywood's 'Orient' – Garroni 'initiates' Billy by taking him to a massage parlour, where the women are both compliant and deadly. [31] Chan cut the scene extensively for the Asian version, removing the nudity and the blow jobs delivered from beneath massage tables, which suggests that there's more at stake here than action aesthetics and star personas. He also introduced a subplot involving actress/Cantopop star Sally Yeh, which goes some way towards locating him within the Chinese population of Hong Kong rather than simply appropriating him as colonialist aggressor.

In both *Battlecreek Brawl* and *The Protector*, Chan plays fully assimilated Asian-Americans – only the latter film specifies how long he has been in New York (ten years). Interestingly, it is a Hong Kong film, *Rumble in the Bronx*, which first drama-tises his cultural acclimatisation in North America. [32] As Tony Rayns observes, *Rush Hour* and *Shanghai Noon* have essentially the same narrative – 'it's about him "becoming American", with a little help and hindrance from a reluctant American sidekick'. [33] Indeed, the same plot device turns up in Sammo Hung's TV series *Martial Law* (CBS 1998–2000). But *Rumble* is part of a series of Hong Kong movies filmed and set in America which, as Julian Stringer suggests, can be seen to 'repre-sent Asian-American screen identities that are in the process of formation'. [34] While these action films explore the theme of hybrid identity formation less fully than dramas like *Comrades: Almost a Love Story* (Peter Chan, HK 1996), their treatment is very different from the 'melting pot' narratives of Hollywood. To borrow Lii's distinction, the Hong Kong films seem to be about *yielding* – 'the self goes out of oneself and blends into the "other"' [35] – while the Hollywood films are about *incorporation*.

Jackie Chan, Chow Yun Fat (*A Better Tomorrow II, An Autumn Tale*) and Jet Li (*Dragon Fight, The Master, Once Upon a Time in China and America*) each made films set (at least partly) in North America prior to their recent Hollywood films. *Dragon Fight* (Billy Tang, HK 1988) remains most closely focused on diasporic Chinese communities in America. Most of the action takes place amongst émigrés from Taiwan, China and Hong Kong, while America itself is implicitly corrupting and hostile. *The Master* (Tsui Hark, HK 1989) and *Once Upon a Time in China and America* (Sammo Hung, HK 1997) place the Southern Chinese folk hero Wong Fei-hung within an American setting – the latter film is part of Tsui Hark's profitable fran-chise starring Jet Li as Wong, while *The Master* earlier cast Li as a modern-day Wong figure (the film is also known as *Wong Fei-hung '92*). In both films, Li interacts with other 'peripheral' communities – a young Mexican street gang who idolise him as their *shifu* in *The Master* and Native Americans in *China and America*, whose loss of 'home' is implicitly linked to Hong Kong's own 'identity crisis' and impending handover to China. As most Chan aficionados know, *Once Upon a Time in China and America* was 'stolen' from Chan's cherished project about a Chinese hero who loses his memory in the 'Old West'. [36] Chan subsequently revamped his kung fu Western into *Shanghai Noon*. He plays Chon Wang – a running gag has his name misheard as 'John Wayne' – a Qing Dynasty Imperial Guard sent to America to negotiate the release of kidnapped Princess Pei Pei (Lucy Liu). His 'American Education' is at the hands of Roy O'Bannion (Owen Wilson), a kind of slacker-bandit, who articulates the exotic appeal of Chon's mission – 'Forbidden City? I like that. The Forbidden City, Princess, kidnap – it's so mysterious'. Chon must learn to lighten up – 'You're the most irritable guy I've ever met' – but otherwise he is as much 'Jackie Chan' as one could reasonably expect to see in a Hollywood film. Unlike in *Rush Hour*, there is an element of reciprocity in this cross-cultural education – Carter (Chris Tucker) teaches Inspector Lee (Chan) how to sing 'War' properly, while Chon Wang teaches Roy a Chinese drinking song. In the opening titles, the credit 'In Association with A Jackie Chan Films Production' suggests a heightened authorial control and the film in many ways bears this out. The knockabout tone and period setting seem to facilitate a more fully extended dose of Chan's trademark action-comedy. In an early scene, he dodges a couple of flying tomahawks, twirls them impressively and tosses them back at their owners, who promptly catch them and continue their pursuit. Yet a comparison with *Once Upon a Time in China and America* reminds us that there is a difference in Chan making his Eastern-Western *in* the west. Both films initiate their heroes into Native American tribes, both films feature a blonde cowboy who finds himself attracted to Chinese culture and both feature an exploitative Chinese turncoat (played by the same actor, Roger Yuan). When Chon Wang bonds over a 'Peace Pipe', it is only to accommodate some throwaway gags about 'powerful shit' and failing to cross language barriers. *China and America* is not the most reflective of the Wong Fei-hung series, but it is able to make something of Wong Fei-hung/Hong Kong's identity crisis – 'I envy you guys,' he tells the tribe who rename him 'Yellow', 'At least you know where your roots are. I don't even know where I come from.' The question of retaining one's identity is treated partly as a joke – Wong's audience falls asleep during his lengthy speech, but his sermon includes the salutary reminder that 'When they leave home, goods are worth more and people are worth less.' The film ends with the building of the first Chinatown, and the optimistic impression that the Chinese diaspora can both 'copy the merits of foreigners' and yet still 'know who you are'. *Shanghai Noon* opts instead for America-as-Melting-Pot, where cultural difference must be partially erased. Roy's earlier lesson – 'This isn't the East, this is the West. The sun doesn't rise here, it sets here' – is echoed by Chon as he defies the Imperial Decree and supports the Princess's desire to remain in the west. The villainous Lo Fang cuts off Chon's queue and insists that 'he will always be a slave' (like the indistinguishable railroad workers used to conjure images of Chinese servitude). He can only be free by being 'American'.

'No Fear. No Stuntman. No Equal' was the tagline for the English-language version of *Rumble in the Bronx*. Chan represents Hong-Kong-cinema-as-authenticity, a construction which can be traced back to Bruce Lee and other 1970s performers whose eschewal of cinematic trickery seemed to attest to a heightened investment in the 'real'. But the 'new' Hong Kong cinema fashioned by directors like Tsui Hark invested as much in technological and aesthetic modernity as the 'authenticity' of stuntwork and martial arts skills. *Zu: Warriors of the Magic Mountain* (Tsui Hark, HK 1982) was the first Hong Kong film to use digital effects, but CGI was not fully incorporated into Hong Kong cinema until recent 'blockbusters' like *Storm Riders* (Andrew Lau, HK 1998) and *Gen-X Cops* (Benny Chan, HK 1999). The flamboyant spectacle of films like the *Chinese Ghost Story* and *Once Upon a Time in China* series was light on postproduction effects and high in on-set technology like 'wirework'. Interestingly, this is currently the dominant strand in 'Hongkongified' Hollywood, as evident in Jet Li's recent films and Yuen Wo-ping's contribution to *The Matrix* and *Crouching Tiger, Hidden Dragon* (Ang Lee, US/China/Taiwan 2000).

## Downloading 'Hong Kong': Yuen Wo-ping and Jet Li

Trinity (Carrie Anne-Moss) has her hands full – she's been traced and surrounded by the police and by the dour virtual agents who patrol the 'computer-generated dreamworld' known as *The Matrix*. One hapless cop tries to put the cuffs on her, but has his arm painfully snapped. Trinity floats into the air and holds the pose as the camera circles her – look, no wires – until this suspended moment is broken by a disabling kick. She dodges bullets by running up and around the walls of the room, but the final *pièce de resistance* is an over-the-shoulder kick to the face of the officer who unwisely grabs her from behind. In *Romeo Must Die*, Han Sing (Jet Li) finds himself in a similarly tight spot, again surrounded by heavies. He leaps in the air and rotates horizontally in mid-air to kick each opponent in turn. When the gang produce guns, Han/Jet disarms them with a fire hose, but an axe cuts off his water supply and he has to think again. The spectacle shifts to a different level as he uses the severed hose as a rope dart, spinning in graceful, balletic circles and performing the kind of *wu shu* forms that made Beijing-born Jet Li a champion in the early 1970s.

Both of these films are sending out mixed messages about technological and physical spectacle, about the 'real' and the digital. According to Manohla Dargis, *The Matrix* created 'a new kind of action hero, one heavily predicated on digital effects', but if the plot reduces humans to 'wet-ware', the same is not necessarily true of the stars.[37] Carrie Anne-Moss really seems to deliver that over-the-shoulder kick – the kind of kick Hong Kong fans are accustomed to seeing Jet Li do – and it was common knowledge that choreographer Yuen Wo-ping insisted on the cast being trained intensively in martial arts. In Hong Kong, this is nothing new – many action stars, including Michelle Yeoh, acquired their fighting skills on film sets rather than in classes and in Shaw Brothers' heyday martial arts were built into actor-training programmes. But Hollywood stars have traditionally been rather less hands-on. *The Matrix* did not only set a new standard for special effects; it also appeared to initiate a trend for 'authenticating' Hollywood stars. Tom Cruise is equipped with martial arts skills in *Mission: Impossible 2* (John Woo, US 2000) and *Charlie's Angels* employed Yuen Wo-ping's brother Yuen Cheung-yan to bring wirework and kung fu training to its three stars. But if Hong Kong expertise could 'authenticate' Keanu Reeves, Tom Cruise and Cameron Diaz, technology can arguably undercut a 'real' martial artist like Jet Li, seemingly confirming the 'oft-repeated threat that (the) digital will eventually render the human actor superfluous'.[38] While Jet's firehose routine offered something that Hollywood stars simply could not do, most of *Romeo*'s fight scenes were computer-aided, an 'intrusion' which upset many fans – '(I was) really disappointed that CGI was used, and that it distracted from Jet Li's outstanding martial arts abilities'.[39]

'From the Acclaimed Action Director of *The Matrix* & *Crouching Tiger, Hidden Dragon*', reads the sticker on the DVD of *Iron Monkey* (Yuen Wo-ping, HK 1993). The choreographer-as-star is the most recent development in Hong Kong's infiltration of western cinema. And yet Yuen was significantly absent from *Crouching Tiger*'s Oscar nominations – no such category presently exists (unlike special effects), a telling indicator of how different kinds of cinematic labour (and spectacle) are valued. Yuen Wo-ping was part of the third generation of 'Dragon-Tiger Masters' in Hong Kong cinema, part of a large family of martial artists, Beijing Opera performers and, eventually, fight choreographers. Initially a stuntman, Yuen starting choreographing in the 1970s and made his directorial debut with Jackie Chan's *Snake in the Eagle's Shadow*. He was in the forefront of every major development in martial arts-based Hong Kong action – comedy (*Miracle Fighters*, *Dance of the Drunken Mantis*), films based on the intricacies of individual fighting styles (*Buddhist Fist, Legend of a Fighter*) and modern day action (the *Tiger Cage* and *In the Line of Duty* series). Yuen's career found a new lease of life in the 'New Wave' martial arts films of the early 1990s, particularly the first two episodes of *Once Upon a Time in China*, which set new standards in their fight choreography and use of wirework. According to Ackbar Abbas, the series marked a rupture in the 'authenticity' of the genre – 'what sets the series apart are not the authenticities of action or history but its mastery of *special effects* . . . there are no more authentic stars/heroes of the order of Bruce Lee'.[40] Abbas correctly identifies a shift even if he overstates it – performative skill did not by any means disappear, and Hong Kong wirework has largely remained a pro-filmic spectacle. Nevertheless, this points to the dialogue between different action technologies in recent Hollywood films. Hong Kong's representation of 'speed' – undercranked action – remains too low-tech for Hollywood, too reminiscent of silent cinema, however exciting it is when done well. Compare Donnie Yen's breakneck-speed 'invisible kicks' in *Iron Monkey* with *The Matrix*'s digital 'bullet-time' for two very different representations of martial arts velocity. But wirework and CGI could profitably converge – in Hong Kong, wires are 'lit out',[41] but *Crouching Tiger* used 300 digital wire-removals as well as effects like sky replacement in scenes like Chow Yun Fat's bamboo-treetop duel with Zhang Ziyi.[42] Jet Li's horizontal kicks in *Romeo* digitally combined three separate shots as well as suspending him on wires, although all the digital removals in the world cannot conceal just how bad the film's wirework is.

Hong Kong-style aerial combat is often dubbed 'Wire-fu' (sometimes affectionately, sometimes not), but *The Matrix* seemed to create a new genre, 'Cyber-fu'. Kung fu skills are downloaded from a computer program – 'I know kung fu!' Neo (Keanu Reeves) exclaims with a mixture of surprise and anticipation. If full-throttle Jackie Chan was both too 'real' (self-endangering) and insufficiently 'real' (too exaggerated) for Hollywood, how was wirework going to fare in American genre cinema? 'Our sense of reality is different from their sense of reality,' explains Richard Donner on the DVD commentary for *Lethal Weapon 4* (1998), Jet Li's show-stopping Hollywood debut. Li is offered as a spectacle to the protagonists – 'How the hell did he do that?' – as well as the audience, the film's exported piece of action technology as well as its 'inscrutable' Other. His villainous Triad is equipped with incongruous silk suits ('Nice pajamas') and a pigtail, and mocked as an implicitly emasculated 'Oriental' – 'Enter the Drag Queen'. Yet the film makes formidable use of Li the performer, and choreographer Yuen Kwai, deploying subtle wirework to allow Jet to bend gravity without defying it – no other film encapsulates the paradoxical collision of Asiaphilia and Asiaphobia quite so spectacularly.

Hollywood, Bordwell suggests, is 'unusually fastidious about realism of detail, restraint of emotion, and plausibility of plot',[43] By contrast, Hong Kong genre cinema's most characteristic modes are melodrama and (broad) comedy. Even so, it has its own hierarchies of 'realism' – wirework is much less extravagant in modern day films than period fantasies. In Hollywood, wirework initially came in through the fantasy door.[44] What *The Matrix* does is to download and authenticate Hong Kong 'reality', to reconstitute it as a virtual action space into which it can insert its protagonists. Morpheus (Lawrence Fishburne) explains to Neo that in the digital world, 'rules like gravity . . . are no different than the rules of the computer system. Some of them can be bent, others can be broken.' As some commentators have noted, *The Matrix* is only superficially dystopian and easily seduced by 'a world without rules and controls, without borders or boundaries, a world where anything is possible'.[45] By the end of the film, Neo and Trinity do not just 'do' John Woo – with the sort of limitless ammo usually enjoyed only by Lara Croft – they *outdo* him as they scale walls, performing cartwheels as countless spent shells litter the floor. *Romeo Must Die*'s interesting 'failure' lies precisely in its inability to negotiate a coherent 'reality' for its interfamilial/interracial crime drama and wired-up action – 'This isn't *The Matrix*, idiots!!!' commented one disgruntled viewer.[46]

But there's another narrative embedded in *The Matrix*, where the 'utopia' of Hollywood showcasing Hong Kong talent gives way to a 'dystopia' of appropriation and marginalisation – there was some hope of Jet Li appearing in the sequels, but Joel Silver clearly felt the money could be better spent. In any case, the film's downloading of 'Hong Kong' is almost a metaphor for the Wachowskis' use of Yuen Wo-ping. In Hong Kong, fight choreographers are like 2nd Unit directors, sometimes more – a film like *Fist of Legend* (1994), in effect, has two directors, its nominal one Gordon Chan and its 'action director' Yuen Wo-ping. Fight scenes are not storyboarded or scripted – action and camera angles are semi-improvised by the stunt director's team, pretty much 'edited' in camera with little coverage and no 'masters'. Hollywood's authorial discourses, however, work rather differently, with the deification of the director(s). According to Larry Wachowski:

> Wo(-ping) was the choreographer, but we were the ones who were in complete control at all times . . . He positioned the camera where he thought it should be – Hong Kong choreographers always pick out the camera angles – and then Andy and I would look at them. Some of them we liked, some of them we didn't like . . . Many times Wo's shots just didn't meet our criteria, so we added moving camera shots, dollies, stuff like that around sections that we wanted.[47]

Somewhere, James Glickenhaus is nodding in approval. Yuen was similarly, if more endearingly, frank about the process:

> In American movies, they're all storyboarded and they leave little room for inspiration on the set. It's good that everything's organised, but if I have any inspiration on the set, it's only good if the actors can follow. Jet Li and Jackie Chan can follow, but not these actors.[48]

Yet this is not to say that *The Matrix*'s fight choreography did not follow an interesting, if convoluted, process in its attempt to Xerox (but also 'improve') Hong Kong action. The fight scenes were scripted and storyboarded by the Wachowskis, based on scenes from Yuen's Hong Kong films – *Fist of Legend*, Jet Li's gritty reworking of Bruce Lee's *Fist of Fury*, was a particularly central reference point and several of its stunts find their way into *The Matrix*. They showed the storyboards to Yuen, who shot video footage using his stunt-team; the footage was shown to the Wachowskis, who approved and/or vetoed scenes. The cast were then 'taught' the moves from the videos so that they could perform them in the final film.[49] Spontaneity is not the only casualty in the martial arts scenes – postmodern appropriation can erase any sense of context or resonance. When Neo/Keanu mimics Bruce Lee (cockily thumbing his nose) and Wong Fei-hung's signature stance (arm extended, palm turned upwards in 'invitation'), he unwittingly exposes the limits of 'deterritorialised' images and commodities. *The Matrix* does not need Jet Li precisely because 'goods mean more and people mean less' in certain transnational image-flows.

## Postscript: 'Sense and Sensibility with Martial Arts'[50]

Jackie Chan, Jet Li, Michelle Yeoh and Chow Yun Fat arguably comprise the last generation of Hong Kong stars with global potential – the Cantopop idols of recent Hong Kong movies are geared more towards 'local' tastes. In some ways, *The Matrix* and *Charlie's Angels* offer worst-case scenarios for the future of diasporic Hong Kong action – Asian expertise used to bolster a cinema that continues to marginalise Asian performers. In 1997, Steve Fore envisioned a 'best-case scenario' with 'directors, cinematographers, actors and other personnel oscillating semi-permanently between hemispheres, working on a range of projects with different geolinguistic emphases'.[51] Until recently, only Jackie Chan displayed anything like this kind of mobility – *Rush Hour* was followed by the more 'local' *Gorgeous* (Vincent Kok, HK 1999), *Shanghai Noon* by *The Accidental Spy* (Benny Chan, HK 2001) – but Chan's increasing years and battered body must suggest an approaching sell-by date.[52] However, while it is impossible to predict its long-term influence and the significance of its global success, *Crouching Tiger, Hidden Dragon* seemed to realise precisely the kind of cinema Fore might have envisioned – an émigré Taiwanese director, a script produced by an ongoing process of translation between Chinese and American writers, two stars and a choreographer from Hong Kong, one Taiwanese and one Mainland Chinese star. Most importantly, it suggested that

Asian action had a broader range of options than simply being grafted onto variable Hollywood blockbusters until another 'fad' came along. *Crouching Tiger* finds its 'world where anything is possible' not in the virtual world but in the heroic narratives of *wu xia* (martial chivalry) fiction, and the classic swordplay films of King Hu and Zhang Che – stolen swords, 'Lady Knights', the transcendent powers of impossibly noble *wu dang* swordsmen. Seemingly conceived as a pan-Asian blockbuster, the film played in the west as what *Sight and Sound*'s December 2000 cover copy dubbed 'Martial Arthouse', seemingly bestowing cultural capital on a lowbrow genre (at least for critics whose exposure to the genre was narrow). At its worst, the film's western appeal could be construed as 'a visually and narratively exoticized representation of China's past that does not challenge white, Western stereotypes of the "Orient"'.[53] Yet its breathtaking action scenes confirm that there was more going on than a particularly sophisticated manifestation of neo-Orientalism – cult Asian-American magazine *Giant Robot* dubbed it 'the best kung fu movie ever.'[54] Yuen Wo-ping's choreography blends wirework, CGI and performative skill so artfully that Abbas's 'space of otherness' starts to materialise in bamboo forests, crowded taverns and across the rooftops of Qing-era Beijing – it is not just 'East' and 'West' which are overcome, but 'past' and 'future', technology and the performing body. I would like to end optimistically, then, seeing *Crouching Tiger* as a starting point, as opening a space where Asian and Hollywood action can yield deliriously to one another.

## Notes

1  Bey Logan *Hong Kong Action Cinema*, London: Titan, 1995, p. 70.
2  David Bordwell *Planet Hong Kong: Popular Cinema and the Art of Entertainment*, Cambridge, MA and London: Harvard University Press, 2000, p. 19.
3  Meaghan Morris 'Learning From Bruce Lee: Pedagogy and Political Correctness in Martial Arts Cinema', *Metro*, 11, 1998, pp. 6–15, p. 10.
4  Darrell Y. Hamamoto and Sandra Liu (eds) *Countervisions: Asian American Film Criticism*, Philadelphia: Temple University Press, 2000, p. 12.
5  Ding-Tzann Lii 'A Colonised Empire: Reflections on the Expansion of Hong Kong Films in Asian Countries', in Kuan-Hsing Chen (ed.) *Trajectories: Inter-Asia Cultural Studies*, London and New York: Routledge, 1998, pp. 122–41, p. 127.
6  Ibid., p. 128.
7  Ibid., p. 134.
8  Ackbar Abbas 'Cultural Studies in a Postculture', in Cary Nelson and Dilip Parameshwar Gaonkar (eds) *Disciplinarity and Dissent in Cultural Studies*, London and New York: Routledge, 1996, p. 300.
9  With its mixture of the Western and Chinese Shaolin mythology, *Kung Fu* is the genre's first 'Coming to America' narrative – it also anticipates many an 'Eastern-Western' to come.
10  David Desser 'The Kung Fu Craze: Hong Kong Cinema's First American Reception', in David Desser and Poshek Fu (eds) *The Cinema of Hong Kong: History, Arts, Identity*, Cambridge: Cambridge University Press, 2000, pp. 24, 43.
11  Bordwell *Planet Hong Kong*, p. 86.
12  Desser 'The Kung Fu Craze', p. 39.
13  By the time Lazenby went to Hong Kong in 1972, *On Her Majesty's Secret Service* (Peter Hunt, GB 1969) had only recently been released there. As the 'current' James Bond, he *was* effectively a star.

14  Bey Logan 'George Lazenby's Far Eastern Odyssey (Part Two)', *Impact*, 2000, pp. 36–7: p. 37.

15  Steve Fore 'Golden Harvest Films and the Hong Kong Movie Industry in the Realm of Globalization', *Velvet Light Trap*, 1994, pp. 34, 40–58, p. 51.

16  Morris 'Learning From Bruce Lee', pp. 9–10.

17  Van Damme, too, has sustained links with Hong Kong cinema. The production of a Van Damme film has virtually become *de rigeur* as an initiation for Hong Kong émigrés – John Woo, Ringo Lam and Tsui Hark, whose *Double Team* (1997) deploys Peter Pau's cinematography and Sammo Hung's choreography to make the most visually striking of the Muscles From Brussels films.

18  Bordwell *Planet Hong Kong*, p. 85.

19  Steve Fore 'Home, Migration, Identity: Hong Kong Film Workers Join the Chinese Diaspora', in Law Kar (ed.) *Fifty Years of Electric Shadows*, Hong Kong: Hong Kong International Film Festival/Urban Council, 1997, pp. 130–5: p. 133.

20  Lii 'A Colonised Empire', p. 136.

21  Fore 'Home, Migration, Identity: Hong Kong Film Workers Join the Chinese Diaspora', p. 137.

22  Logan *Hong Kong Action Cinema*, p. 66.

23  Rene Witterstaetter *Dying For Action: The Life and Films of Jackie Chan*, London: Ebury Press, 1997, p. 127.

24  Steve Fore 'Jackie Chan and the Cultural Dynamics of Global Entertainment', in Sheldon Hsiao-peng Lu (ed.) *Transnational Chinese Cinemas: Identity, Nationhood, Gender*, Honolulu: University of Hawaii Press, 1997, pp. 239–62: p. 250.

25  Logan *Hong Kong Action Cinema*, p. 66.

26  Stephen Teo *Hong Kong Cinema: The Extra Dimensions*, London: BFI, 1997, p. 130.

27  Craig Reid 'Fighting Without Fighting: Film Action Choreography', *Film Quarterly*, 47: 2, 1993–4, pp. 30–5: p. 32.

28  Bordwell *Planet Hong Kong*, p. 232.

29  Logan *Hong Kong Action Cinema*, p. 70.

30  Gina Marchetti *Romance and the 'Yellow Peril': Race, Sex, and Discursive Strategies in Hollywood Fiction*, Berkeley, Los Angeles and London: University of California Press, 1993, p. 1.

31  These scenes make for an interesting comparison with *Rush Hour 2* (Brett Ratner, US 2001), in which Chan initiates Chris Tucker into Hong Kong nightlife, including a visit to a massage parlour.

32  See Steve Fore for an interesting discussion of how Chan's later Hong Kong films 'disembed' him from local contexts and resonances in the process of transforming him into a more global commodity. 'Life Imitates Entertainment: Home and Dislocation in the Films of Jackie Chan', in Esther Yau (ed.) *At Full Speed: Hong Kong Cinema in a Borderless World*, Minneapolis and London: University of Minnesota Press, 2000, pp. 115–41.

33  Tony Rayns 'To Die in America', *Sight and Sound*, 11: 4, 2001, pp. 26–7: p. 26.

34  Julian Stringer 'Cultural Identity and Diaspora in Contemporary Hong Kong Cinema', in Hamamoto and Liu (eds) *Countervisions*, p. 298.

35  Lii 'A Colonised Empire', p. 133.

36  Jackie Chan and Jeff Yang *Jackie Chan: My Life in Action*, New York: Ballantine Books, 1998, pp. 348–50.

37  Manohla Dargis 'Ghost in the Machine', *Sight and Sound*, 10: 7, 2000, pp. 20–3: p. 23.

38  Ibid.

39  http://www.imdb.com/title/tt0165929/usercomments-192.

40  Abbas 'Cultural Studies in a Postculture', p. 298.

41  Josh Orick and Eric Matthews 'Wired Style: Wirework Special', *Giant Robot*, 16, 2000, pp. 57–62: p. 58.

42  Ang Lee and James Schamus *Crouching Tiger, Hidden Dragon: A Portrait of the Ang Lee Film*, London: Faber, 2000, p. 122.

43 Bordwell *Planet Hong Kong*, p. 19.

44 More specifically, it first appeared in fantasy *television*, giving flight to the superhuman exploits of *Xena – Warrior Princess* and *Buffy the Vampire Slayer* (both 1996). In both cases, the campy tone also seemed to license over-the-top wire-aided stunts.

45 Geoff King *Spectacular Narratives: Hollywood in the Age of the Blockbuster*, London and New York: I. B. Taurus, 2000, p. 191.

46 http://www.imdb.com/title/tt0165929/usercomments-192.

47 Mitch Persons '*Matrix*: The Wachowski Bros.', *Cinefantastique*, 31: 5, 1996, pp. 20–1: p. 21.

48 Dennis Fischer '*Matrix*: Martial Arts', *Cinefantastique*, 31: 5, 1999, p. 26.

49 Orick and Matthews 'Wired Style', pp. 58–9.

50 Allegedly Ang Lee's pitch to Michelle Yeoh (Lee and Schamus *Crouching Tiger, Hidden Dragon*, p. 10).

51 Steve Fore 'Home, Migration, Identity', p. 135.

52 At the time of writing, Jet Li, too, seems to be pursuing a degree of international mobility. *Kiss of the Dragon* (Chris Nahon, France/US 2001) was made in collaboration with Luc Besson, *The One* (James Wong, US 2001) is a Hollywood science fiction film, and he is currently working on Zhang Yimou's *Hero* with Maggie Cheung, Tony Leung and Zhang Ziyi. *Hero*, a Mandarin-language historical martial arts epic, suggests that *Crouching Tiger* is not an isolated phenomenon.

53 Steve Fore 'Jackie Chan', p. 248. In British cinemas, at least, the wire-and-CGI-aided scenes of flight seemed to inspire giggles as well as gasps, another way in which the film could be both enjoyed and marginalised. The 'exoticising' of *Crouching Tiger* can be partly attributed to what Fore calls 'semiotic rupture' ('Home, Migration, Identity', p. 134), one of the casualties of cultural translation. The martial arts film has often been seen as nostalgically (re)creating a mythical, idealised China, 'an emigrant cinema for an audience seeking not only its identity . . . but also its legitimization' (Roger Garcia 'Alive and Kicking: The Kung Fu Film is a Legend', *Bright Lights*, 13: 6–7, 1994, p. 48). According to Ang Lee, 'The film is a kind of dream of China, a China that probably never existed, except in my boyhood fantasies in Taiwan' (Lee and Schamus *Crouching Tiger, Hidden Dragon*, p. 7).

54 Claudine Ko '*Crouching Tiger*: It's the Best Kung Fu Movie Ever', *Giant Robot*, 20, 2001, pp. 20–1.

## Chapter 17

# CHRISTINE HOLMLUND

# EUROPEANS IN ACTION!

## 'To be or not to be'

Desperate, a woman teacher tries to coax a class of bored students into *Hamlet*, billing him as 'one of the first action heroes!' and showing a film clip with Laurence Olivier. The kids aren't buying it: 'Don't talk, just do it!' one prays . . .

ARNOLD, as action hero Jack Slater, takes over. RED-toned color seeps into, then replaces, grainy black and white footage. 'Hey, Claudius! You killed my father! BIG MISTAKE!' he shouts, then BLASTS Claudius through the window.

This is a trailer, for a film within the film *Last Action Hero* (John McTiernan, 1993). A male voice-over promises: 'Something is rotten in the state of Denmark, and Hamlet is taking out the trash!', then reassures, 'No one's going to tell this sweet Prince good night!' No siree! Arnold mutters 'To be or not to be?' and opts, 'NOT TO BE!' Explosions obliterate everyone and everything.

SELF-REFLEXIVE, BARELY VERBAL, spectacular set pieces characterize contemporary American action films. So too does the presence of European actors playing American-named characters like 'Jack Slater', though less has been made of the fact. Other characters may make fun of these big men's 'European-ness' (in *Last Action Hero*, Arnold-as-actor's last name is 'Braunsch-weiger'; others respond 'bless you', as if to a sneeze). Undaunted, continental actors stand ready for box office action: in the last two decades, Antonio Banderas, Dolph Lundgren, Rutger Hauer, Jeroen Krabbé, Christophe Lambert, and Jean-Claude Van Damme have appeared in scores of action extravaganzas.

Whiteness, Richard Dyer maintains, underpins most action appeal.[1] How do *European* accents add spice? Using Arnold and Antonio as touchstones, I here chart the American orbits of five other European action stars as they move through the Hollywood firmament. Given my choice of actors, I am obviously interested in how ethnicities and nationalities are performed and perceived; I also discuss sexual and class positioning, age and aging. I have lots of material to draw from since, from the early 1980s onwards, my five big men have made over 90 action films; I have studied roughly half.[2] Based on my survey, I comment on the success – or no – of my 'guys' and analyze the impact of their (often bipolar) casting as millionaires or workers, loners or lovers, hulks or hunks.

Unlike Schwarzenegger (who has never acted in a European film) but like Banderas (who has appeared in several) all five actors began their careers in European productions (Lambert and Krabbé continue to work both in the US and in Europe).[3] Yet professional options, even their differing ages (Hauer and Krabbé are slightly older than Arnold; Lundgren, Lambert, and Van Damme belong to Antonio's generation), have little impact on the identity tags or passports assigned their characters. Instead, each is distinguished in US 'actioners' by his ability to assume accents and pronounce English; anatomies and acting also count. All five are tanned, toned, and honed, but their bodies range from tall to small, bulky to boyish. Dolph is known for his stone face and massive 'movie' muscles (belly and buns); Rutger, for his piercing blue eyes and blond hair; Jeroen, for his dark hair and big nose; Christophe, for his sensual lips; Jean-Claude, for his amazing arms and saucy butt.

My discussion proceeds by size and, roughly, geographical origin, moving from huge blond Swede (Lundgren) to equally big and blond but less hulky Hollander (Hauer) to tall dark Dutchman (Krabbé) to lean 'Latin' lover (Lambert), to *the* 'Muscles from Brussels' (Van Damme). I alter geography slightly to begin with Lundgren and end with Van Damme because I want to sandwich those stars with more varied screen careers between two exclusively action heroes. Mindful of Sarah Kozloff's work on dialogue, dialect, and genre, building on Yvonne Tasker's work on body and voice,[4] in conclusion I review how national and ethnic markings shape this particular subset of films, and fantasize about the future of European accents, anatomies, and acting in action.

## Dolph Lundgren's 'pecs appeal'

Now married to a Swedish fashion designer, Dolph (né 'Hans') Lundgren was earlier famous for spectacular appearances with 'black panther' girlfriend Grace Jones. On screen or in public, his size draws attention: he is 6 foot 5 or 6 inches, and tips the scales between 230 and 240 pounds. Yet Lundgren is 'no Swedish meatball', but instead the 'perfect union of brains and brawn'.[5] He speaks five languages (Swedish, English, German, French, and Japanese) virtually without accent and holds a masters in engineering from the University of Sydney. Skinny and weak as a child, he became a skilled fighter in his late teens and early twenties, earning black belts and titles in karate.[6]

Lundgren's film career began with a bit part as a KGB agent in the British *A View to a Kill* (John Glen, 1985). At the time, he had had no acting training; since then he has worked with several coaches. Sadly, reviews are often negative, for

Lundgren is limited by his size and dead pan delivery: though often compared to Arnold, he has less range.[7] He wants to do romantic comedy; instead he nets roles in action films based on comic strips (*The Punisher*, Gary Goddard, 1987) or toy lines (*Masters of the Universe*, Mark Goldblatt, 1989).

His most successful roles are as villains. Critics and crowds cheered as Dolph went down to defeat playing Drago in *Rocky IV* (Sylvester Stallone, 1985). Audiences (if not reviewers) thrilled as Lundgren/Andrew Scott was mashed in a mincer by Jean-Claude Van Damme/Luc Devreux in *Universal Soldier* (Roland Emmerich, 1992). Audiences alone hurrahed as Dolph/Street Preacher was burned, then drowned in Newark opposite Keanu Reeves' *Johnny Mnemonic* (Robert Longo, 1995).

Usually, however, Lundgren plays the hero. Often he is American: Jack Caine (*I Come in Peace*, Craig Baxley, 1990), Frank Castle (*The Punisher*), Detective Chris Kenner (*Showdown in Little Tokyo*, Mark Lester, 1991), Michael Dane (*The Shooter*, Ted Kotcheff, 1994), Waxman/'Shooter' (*Silent Trigger*, Russell Mulcahy, 1996), Major Frank Cross (*The Peacekeeper*, Frédéric Forrestier, 1997), Jack Devlin (TV pilot *Blackjack*, John Woo, 1998). Sometimes he transforms himself into a Russian or Eastern European who champions democracy: in *Red Scorpion* (Joseph Zito, 1989) he plays rebellious Soviet lieutenant and defector Nikolai; in *Pentathlon* (Bruce Malmuth, 1995) he jumps to freedom as East German Olympic star Eric Brogar.

The majority of his action films are laden with ethnic clichés: in *The Punisher* Yakuza gangsters and Italian American mobsters figure as villains; in *Showdown in Little Tokyo*, Yakuza are again blood-thirsty bad guys. Lundgren always knows best. Raised in Japan, trained in flower-arranging as well as martial arts, in *Showdown* he is more conversant in things Japanese than Eurasian partner Brandon Lee. In *Red Scorpion* he learns survival skills from an African bushman, then leads African freedom fighters to victory against evil Soviets and Cubans. In *Pentathlon* he trades buddy banter with his coach, Creese (Roger E. Mosley), complaining, 'I live in a country run by people I don't understand who don't understand me'. Creese replies, 'You must be black'.

In general, Lundgren's heroic characters are monosyllabic, even a bit vulgar. His bass voice is so deep it seems expressionless. Dialogue and dialect combine western and gangster traits, blending regionally distinguished taciturnity with ethnically emphatic declaration.[8] In *Rocky IV* Drago's most notable speech comes as he adopts American individualist values and in his thick Russian accent bellows, 'I fight to win! For *me!*' In *Showdown in Little Tokyo* Brandon Lee teases Lundgren/Kenner after he has terminated a roomful of villains: 'It's like one of those video games, you just defeated the first wave.' Kenner growls, 'You know, there are moments when you're really an asshole'. In most films, Lundgren hefts guns and chucks grenades rather than executing kicks or performing jumps. In interviews, he explains: 'If you're my size it looks corny to throw all those high kicks.' 'It's better if you just throw a guy through a window and hit him with a $2 \times 4$ over the head.'[9] The $2 \times 4$s and the limited vocabulary double as class signifiers with costume reinforcing proletarian connections: most characters wear work boots, jeans, T-shirts, and/or sweat pants. Occasionally a certain fashion sense surfaces: Michael Musto aptly describes Lundgren's 1987 work-out video, *Maximum Potential* (John Langley), as 'sinew parade and fashion shoot'.[10]

Romance is rare: Lundgren is just too big, his voice too deep. In early films, he is never a lover: tersely, he explains, 'in *Universal Soldier* my romance is with my machine gun'.[11] Later films (e.g. *Showdown*, *Silent Trigger*) allow him some 'full contact' love scenes. Spectacle comes primarily from gun battles, explosions, and displays of Lundgren's own (occasionally naked) body. Always, at some point, he is tortured: as Tom Tunney says, 'Lundgren's image is organized around suffering'.[12] In *Red Scorpion*, Lundgren endures an extreme form of acupuncture; in *The Punisher*, he is chained on a rack; in *Showdown*, he is subjected to electric shocks; in *Blackjack*, he is temporarily blinded, then develops a severe phobia of things white triggered by childhood trauma. Not surprisingly, therefore, Dyer takes Lundgren as a prime example of his argument that transcendence and whiteness are linked. I agree, but would nonetheless underline that in these films the linkage often occurs in conjunction with 'ethnic' and/or national identity markers.[13]

And yellow-haired, blue-eyed Rutger Hauer provides yet another piece in the Europeans' action puzzle because, although *he* almost always plays Americans, his characters are more skilled at seduction than transfixed by transcendence, *plus* they are devils fully as often as gods.

## Rutger Hauer: the Netherlands' Paul Newman

Touted as 'a modern Dutch master', his 'charming arrogance' compared to that of Errol Flynn, Hauer is, like Lundgren and Schwarzenegger, quite large (between 6 foot 2 and 6 foot 4 inches, 220 or so pounds).[14] Like Banderas, however, Hauer is not bulky; tellingly, he refused Ridley Scott's request that he pump iron for his role as replicant Roy Batty in *Blade Runner* (1982), saying, 'as an actor, I don't think I should get into pumping up. It *harms* your looks. Your muscles block you . . . [I]n preparing for any part it's more important to get your thoughts together.'[15]

A thinking man's actor, Hauer relishes the chance to explore psychology. He is thus unafraid to play villains. Tri-lingual in Dutch, German, and English, with solid acting training, Hauer was critically acclaimed for performances in Dutch films like *Turkish Delight* (Paul Verhoeven, 1973), *Max Havelaar* (Fons Rademakers, 1976), *Soldier of Orange* (Verhoeven, 1977), and *Spetters* (Verhoeven, 1980) before coming to the US. In his first US film, *Nighthawks* (Bruce Malmuth, 1981), he plays a German terrorist named Wulfgar opposite Sylvester Stallone's and Billy Dee Williams' undercover cops.

Where Wulfgar addresses the diplomats that he is holding hostage in English, French, and German, if always with Dutch inflections, post *Nighthawks* Hauer spent one and a half years learning American speech patterns. He was so successful that in his next film, *The Osterman Weekend* (Sam Peckinpah, 1983), he plays a character who is described as 'more American than Americans'. From then on, he usually plays Americans. In *The Hitcher* (Robert Harmon, 1986) he embodies a 'peculiarly American species of psychopath: the serial killer';[16] in *Blind Fury* (Philip Noyce, 1989) he stars as Vietnam vet Nick Parker; in *Wanted: Dead or Alive* (Gary Sherman,

1987) he is ex-CIA agent Nick Randall. Occasionally (think: *Blade Runner* and *Buffy the Vampire Slayer*, Fran Rubel Kuzui, 1992), his characters have an 'alien' edge: like Dolph and Arnold, Hauer incarnates Aryan menace.

At times Hauer plays badly dressed drifters; in other roles he looks aristocratic. Renowned for his own dramatic dress (he showed up for a *New York Times* interview wearing 'black leather pants, suede boots, and a sweater with a large, furry appliquéd fox crawling over one shoulder . . . its fangs bared, its eyes wild, its mouth blood-red')[17] he brings his fashion flair to many characters. Post plastic surgery in *Nighthawks*, Wulfgar emerges as a fashion plate and lady killer. Hair New Wave white in *Blade Runner*, he makes a stylish punk. In *Buffy*, he sports spats, ascots, black capes, and evening gloves.

Unlike most male action stars, moreover – *pace* Arnold in *Junior* (Ivan Reitman, 1994) and Antonio in every Almodóvar film – Hauer specializes in sexually ambiguous roles. Although he occasionally protects children (an adoptive son in *Blind Fury*, his own son in *The Osterman Weekend*), he pleasures in stalking and seducing teens, cognizant that generational and size differences add perverse pep to screen romance. His relationship with the young Jim Halsey (C. Thomas Howell) in *The Hitcher* is overtly, viciously, homoerotic: from the first, Hauer/John Ryder gets physical, putting his big hand on Jim's leg as he drives. Startled, Jim asks, 'What do you want?' Ryder leers, 'That's what the other guy said. I cut off his legs and his arms and his head.' Jim crashes his car to get rid of Ryder but he always rematerializes to kiss or taunt the boy. Yet Ryder tempts and torments the pretty young waitress (Jennifer Jason Leigh) who befriends Jim, too, lacing her French fries with amputated fingers, then abducting and finally killing her, all to get Jim's attention and provoke his revenge. (Ryder wants to die but cannot kill himself.)

Androgyny and homoeroticism are evident in *Blade Runner* and *Buffy* as well. In the former, Hauer/Roy purses his lips, paints his face, struts, and prances. Yet when he tells William Sanderson/J. F. Sebastian 'we're not computers, we're physical', he proves his point by lustily kissing Darryl Hannah/Pris. In *Buffy*, he looks feminine next to Kristy Swanson/Buffy's post martial arts training 'butch'; he also delights in dallying with his flamboyantly punk subordinate (Paul Reubens).

Yet the sexual complexity Hauer brings to his roles is shrouded in ethnic clichés. Rescued and trained in martial arts by friendly Vietnamese when he loses his sight in Vietnam, *Blind Fury*'s Nick Parker returns stateside primed to take out silly Southerners, big blacks, thieving Latinos, huge Asians, fat cat white men, even martial arts movie star Sho Kosugi. Notoriously *sans* African Americans, with other racial and ethnic groups glimpsed only in crowd scenes, *Blade Runner* serves up a story wherein white replicants figure as both slaves and masters.[18]

Less voluble and less volatile, Hauer's compatriot, Jeroen Krabbé, is always cast in bit or supporting roles in US actioners. He is also most often a villain, in large part because *he* never loses his (Teutonic) foreign accent.

## Jeroen Krabbé: dark, Dutch, and dangerous

Like Hauer, Krabbé has worked in several genres both in Europe and the US; unlike Hauer, he has had few action roles. Originally he intended to be a painter but then studied acting; by age 20 he was appearing on stage. His first action credit is a bit part in *Jumpin' Jack Flash* (Penny Marshall, 1986); his latest and largest role is in *The Fugitive* (Andrew Davis, 1993).

The 'passports' assigned his action characters vary: he plays a Sicilian mafia mogul in *The Punisher*, a Mexican villain in *No Mercy* (Richard Pearce, 1986), a Russian general in *The Living Daylights* (John Glen, 1987), an unspecified American immigrant in *The Fugitive*. In *Jumpin' Jack Flash* he is, exceptionally, a good guy, a Dutch secret agent named Mark van Meter. With tousled brown hair and an attentive manner, Krabbé/van Meter is both attractive and reassuring to amateur agent Whoopi Goldberg/Terry Doolittle. Shortly after meeting her, however, he is killed.

All other action characters are high-ranking and/or wealthy villains. Hair slicked back, in military uniforms, tuxedos, and swimsuits, General Koskov embodies double-dealing in *The Living Daylights*. Hair slicked back, in designer suits and ties, drug dealer Gianni Franco's costume and coiffure constitute decided contrasts to Dolph Lundgren's disheveled leather look in *The Punisher*. Hair again slicked back but now in a tight pony tail, long leather coats or fancy raincoats atop expensive slacks and high-heeled boots, in black leather gloves, Losado towers over T-shirt and jean-clad Chicago cop Eddie Jillette (Richard Gere) in *No Mercy*. Hair slicked back but now *sans* pony tail, in fancy suits and functional lab coats, occasionally wearing reading glasses, Dr Charles Nichols cuts an imposing if somewhat less fit figure next to Harrison Ford/Dr Richard Kimble and Tommy Lee Jones/Samuel Gerard in *The Fugitive*.

Fortunately for action ethics, some weakness – typically protectiveness, greed, and/or jealousy – always ensures Krabbé's defeat. Yet since his villains are 'worthy' opponents, final struggles are protracted, full of blasts, blood, guns, and gore. In all three films, characters from other racial, ethnic, and/or national backgrounds fight with and often against Krabbé's 'foreigners': Afghani freedom fighters, Brits, and Russians oppose Koskov in *The Living Daylights*; Japanese gangs line up against Italian and Italian American mafioso in *The Punisher;* a few Latinos, and several Asian and African Americans appear in crowds and as cronies in *No Mercy*; African Americans serve as cops, prison guards, hospital patients, and medical technicians in *The Fugitive*. Women of all colors most typically side with 'Anglo' heroes *against* Krabbé's Italian, Mexican, Russian, and immigrant 'aliens'.

Younger, fairer, and less hulking, Christophe Lambert more frequently plays lovers in English-language actioners. Despite his (increasingly faint) French accent, he also often plays an American. Alternately vulnerable and invincible, with less acting range than either Krabbé or Hauer, Lambert plays heroes, never villains.

## Christophe Lambert: from chimp to champ

Some 5 foot 9 inches tall, sullen-faced, with full lips reminiscent of Jean-Paul Belmondo and a smoldering gaze attributable to near-sightedness, Lambert has starred in as many European as US productions. Born in New York in 1957, he holds dual US–French citizenship. Educated in Switzerland and France, by age 12 he knew he wanted to be an actor. An undistinguished student at the Paris Conservatory, he unexpectedly won the part of Tarzan in *Greystoke: The Legend of*

*Tarzan, Lord of the Apes* (Hugh Hudson, 1984): for it, he learned 'chimp'. The following year he won acclaim for his performance in *Subway* (Luc Besson, 1985); in 1986, playing immortal Connor McLeod/Russell Nash in *Highlander* (Russell Mulcahy) he became a cult 'champ'.

Active in several genres, Lambert's largest body of work is nonetheless in action. There, unfortunately, cheesy effects, porous plots, bad choreography, and his own wooden acting often ensure greater success on video than in theaters. Yet Lambert enjoys a certain reputation as a sex symbol; indeed, during the mid 1980s, the press wondered endlessly which lucky lady would bed and wed him.[19] His heroes are typically shy, sensitive, romantics who attract women in spite of themselves. As McLeod/Nash in *Highlander*, he squires two beauties, one Scottish, one American; as American businessman Paul Racine in *The Hunted* (J. F. Lawton, 1995) he also gets two 'girls', both now 'Japanese'. In *The Fortress*, in contrast, Lambert/John Brennick and his wife are prisoners of the fascist Men-Tel Corporation because they dared conceive a second child. Women prisoners bear their children only to see them turned into robots. Male prisoners are 'intestinated' with devices that cause intense pain and on command burst out through their stomachs, like so many nightmare visions of male C-section pregnancy.

Many films feature an assemblage of fighters. In *Highlander*, McLeod/Nash duels with a Spaniard (Sean Connery), an African, and a Russian, among others. In *The Fortress* Brennick leads a little Latino, an older black servant, a 'four-eyed' hippy, and a huge, no-good, cracker to dignified death or freedom. In *Mortal Kombat* (Paul Anderson, 1995) white-haired god of electricity Lambert/Lord Rayden guides three young fighters (one Chinese, two white Americans) to victory over bad 'Chinese' (Cary-Hiroyuki Tagawa), blacks, whites, a four-armed monster and other non-humans. Rarely does Lambert *bond* with his sidekicks: they are, after all, working class; he is a leader and/or aristocrat. The 'European-ness' of his accent hints at the panache his outfits underline. In *Highlander*, he wears rumpled raincoats and Armani suits; suspicious, cops ask him where he is from; softly, he replies 'lots of places'. In *The Hunted* he is Oriental robe- and again Armani-clad. Here no comments are made about his accent in English; instead he jokes gently about Grateful Dead concerts and laments his inability to speak Japanese.

Like Lundgren, Lambert typically suffers for his beliefs, though only in certain roles does he similarly transcend torture. In *Highlander* all immortals are repeatedly pierced and shot, without lingering effect. In *The Fortress*, it is always 'time for pain!': Brennick endures electric shocks, 'intestination', video surveillance, sleep- and motion-deprivation, and more. In *The Hunted*, Racine spends half the movie bleeding from a neck wound and suffering from hallucinations. In no film, however, is his body really on display as spectacle.

In decided contrast, fellow 'Latin lover' Jean-Claude Van Damme loses no opportunity to proffer his enormous arms and sculpted butt to other male and female characters, and to us. More than any other action hero, Van Damme works with multi-ethnic casts; he also plays more consciously to kids. Not surprisingly, then, he is the most financially successful of my European crew, surpassed in box office action only by Schwarzenegger, Stallone, and Seagal.

## Jean-Claude Van Damme: the muscles from Brussels

Compared in studio publicity to Baryshnikov and Belmondo, Van Damme *moves* far more than Schwarzenegger, Lambert, Lundgren or Krabbé. A fierce fighter (one press moniker is 'the Van Damminator'), because he is shorter (5 foot 9 inches) and smaller (185 pounds) than his opponents, he looks vulnerable. He believes his willingness to get roughed up *and* be emotional set him apart.[20]

Born 'Van Varenberg', Van Damme was a thin, sensitive child who studied both ballet and martial arts. After a small role in *Rue Barbare* (Gilles Béhat, 1984), at age 19 he headed for Hollywood, knowing no English. For five years he worked odd jobs. In 1984 he had a small part as a 'Gay Karate Man' in *Monaco Forever* (William A. Levey);[21] in 1985, Chuck Norris helped him get a part as a Russian villain in *No Retreat, No Surrender* (Corey Yuen). His big break came when he convinced action impresario Menahim Golem he had the action 'right stuff' by aiming well-placed kicks above Golem's head, then jumping into his trademark split. Golem offered him the starring role in the 1987 martial arts biopic *Bloodsport* (Newt Arnold). By 1993, he was working for major studios, earning $3 million per picture; today, he has nearly 30 actioners to his credit and is as big as Schwarzenegger in Europe and Asia.[22]

Conscious of his image, Van Damme is very involved in its creation. He choreographs most of his fight scenes, co-wrote *Lionheart* (Sheldon Lettich, 1991; UK title *A.W.O.L.*), co-wrote and helped produce *Double Impact* (Lettich, 1991), wrote and directed *The Quest* (1996). Since 1997, he has helmed his own production company. His notorious temper often makes for bad publicity, however. He has been married five times, his fourth marriage dissolved (post accusations of mutual abuse) in one of the largest child- and spousal-support awards in California divorce court history. A suit for willfully gouging the eyeball of an extra during the filming of *Cyborg* (Albert Pyun, 1989) was settled out of court; another fight with a stunt man resulted in $500,000 in damages. Now diagnosed as 'cyclo-manic depressive', from 1993 to 1996 Van Damme was addicted to cocaine, snorting up to 10 grams a day;[23] in 2000 he was arrested and convicted for drunk driving.

Never has he succeeded in losing his thick Belgian accent or correcting his ungrammatical English. Instead he and others often joke about his speech. In *Timecop* (Peter Hyams, 1994), Van Damme threatens a young thief's face with his boot; the kid returns the purse he had stolen. 'Smart kid, he read my mind!' he quips to his wife. 'With your accent, he didn't have much choice!' she teases back. Many roles are tailored to fit him: in *Nowhere to Run* (Robert Harmon, 1993) he plays a French Canadian; in *Universal Soldier* and *Hard Target* (John Woo, 1993), a Cajun; in *Lionheart*, *Maximum Risk* (Ringo Lam, 1996), and *Legionnaire* (Peter MacDonald, 1998), a Frenchman. As often, however, he plays 'Anglos': Jack Quinn in *Double Team* (Tsui Hark, 1992), Marcus Ray in *Knock Off* (Hark, 1998), Darren McCord in *Sudden Death* (Peter Hyams, 1995), 'Max Walker' in *Timecop*, Kurt Sloane in *Kickboxer* (Mark diSalle, 1989).

Like Lundgren and Lambert, Van Damme is well cast as comic book (*Timecop*) and video game (*Streetfighter II*, Steven E. de Souza, 1994) heroes. As Tunney says,

'Van Damme is a child's idea of what a grown-up should be: brave, loyal, stead-fast, and true.'[24] Kids (mostly boys) are often seen in his films: in *The Quest* he protects a band of teen-age boys in turn-of-the century New York; in *Nowhere to Run* he plays 'Shane' to Kieran Culkin's 'Joey'; in *Sudden Death* he rescues his daughter, the Vice-President, and local dignitaries from terrorists; at the end of *Timecop*, he meets his 10 year old son; at the end of *Double Team* he greets his new-born son ('it's me! Daddy!') after saving him from an evil Russian agent (Mickey Rourke), a tiger, and huge explosions. His broken, impassioned speech to the (sadistic, German) Foreign Legion commander in *Lionheart* captures the essence of Van Damme doctrine: 'I never give up my family, never!'

Mostly working class, Van Damme's characters are sometimes married, their wives pregnant (*Timecop*, *Double Team*). More often they become romantically involved (both *Universal Soldier* films, *Hard Target*, *The Quest*, *Bloodsport*, *Lionheart*, *Nowhere to Run*, *Maximum Risk*). Even playing the Russian villain in *Black Eagle* (Eric Karson, 1988), Van Damme has love scenes with a Soviet scientist girl-friend. Occasionally, there are male buddies – in *Knock Off* Van Damme/Marcus mopes because Rob Schneider/Tommy is mad at him; in *Double Team* he com-bines forces with Dennis Rodman/Yaz; in *Maximum Risk* he rescues partner Jean-Hugues Anglade/Sebastien; in *The Quest* he avenges a Siamese co-trainee's death, wearing his headband; in *Bloodsport*, he exchanges final 'I love you's' with hospitalized fellow American buddy Donald Gibb/Ray Jackson.

Usually, however, Van Damme fights alone: in martial arts competitions, as a secret agent or a cyborg. Nonetheless his films showcase ethnic mixes more than those of other action heroes because: first, they take place in locales that range from Europe to the US to Asia to Africa; second, several rely on a gathering-of-fighters plot; and third, others differently promote 'politically correct' line-ups (*Double Team*, *Lionheart*, *Timecop*, and *Hard Target* place black characters in substantial – if often expendable – partner roles; *Bloodsport*, *Knock Off*, and *The Quest* have Van Damme fight on behalf of – if not together with – Asian characters he feels are 'family'). Ethnic and national identities assigned to villains vary, although big whites, some of them wealthy, are usually the 'bad guys': in *Black Eagle*, *Double Team*, and *Maximum Risk*, they are Russians; in *Hard Target* and *Timecop* wealthy Europeans, South Africans, and Americans; in *Kickboxer*, the adversary is Thai; barbaric Chinese trick Van Damme's characters in *Bloodsport* and *The Quest*; and in *Lionheart*, *Bloodsport*, and *The Quest*, his characters square off against black fighters.

Sadism and masochism undergird much. The countless revenge plots provide ample opportunity for witnessing the excruciating training Van Damme undertakes and the ferocious punishment he undergoes. Subsequently (usually) audiences get the chance to glory in his determined comebacks, fierce counterattacks, and defin-itive victories. Another spectatorial sado-masochistic plus: martial arts contests are bloody. *Bloodsport* might easily be renamed *Blood Spurt*. In other films, Van Damme maims and kills waves of opponents. Those directed by John Woo, Ringo Lam, and Tsui Hark package explosive action and high energy movement with particular aplomb, using multiple camera set-ups, intricate camera movements, and rapid editing to enhance Van Damme's grace and speed. A few films (*Bloodsport*, *Kickboxer*,

*Double Team*) include lengthy training sequences which showcase his stunning physique. Always, however, his body is center screen, huge arms set off by tight or revealing clothing and/or by shackles, the better to show bulging biceps. *Universal Soldier* and *Lionheart* offer full rear nudity; more often Van Damme models jockey shorts (grey in *Timecop*, black in *Knock Off*, red in *Bloodsport*, white in *Lionheart*). He boasts: 'I've got the best body of all of them . . .. I can put a suit on, I look elegant. If I take my clothes off, I look enormous. I've got a very strong butt. It's like a horse butt. It's very powerful [for an audience] to see a guy with a strong butt.'[25]

Critics lament the lack of cerebral challenge afforded by Van Damme's combats: 'you don't have to be brain-dead to enjoy this one, but it sure helps' is a common response.[26] But action thrills and chills are visceral, rooted in 'brogue' and 'brawn' as much as in 'brain'. In the last two decades at least, therefore, accents, anatomies, and acting have all been key.

## European accents, anatomies, and acting in action

Together Lundgren, Hauer, Krabbé, Lambert, and Van Damme offer several variations on the *vivace* action theme. In each film, how they *sound*, look, and move shapes who they play and how they 'perform' with audiences. The biggest stars, Lundgren and Van Damme, may owe their success primarily to 'being' rather than to 'acting' (as Tunney says, 'what their characters are about is pure self-confidence').[27] Yet the opposition obscures the impact of accents, for combinations of an always perfect body and sometimes bad English temper the god-like status of the heroes and villains they play.

All five men are, of course, white. But certain national and ethnic markings repeat across sub-genres, throughout plots, and these repetitions merit attention.[28] Big blond Lundgren plays Americans, Germans, Eastern Europeans, and Soviets, but never Swedes.[29] As hero, he learns from but knows better than smaller African Americans, Asian Americans, Africans, and Asians. With no accent in English unless he so desires, Lundgren is nonetheless constrained by his size, condemned to act only in action. More articulate and mobile, the handsome Hauer appears in other genres as well; in action he excels at Americans, whether villains or heroes. Unlike Lundgren, he never plays an Eastern European or a Russian in action films, and once only appears as a German (with Teutonic accent roughly to match). Krabbé's appearance as a Russian in *The Living Daylights* would seem to confirm that casting agents of the 1980s onwards not only 'saw' German, Eastern European, and Soviet characters as big, solid, and stolid but also 'heard' them as (somehow) 'Teutonic'. (Of course Krabbé's dark hair and foreign accent mean he can also be cast as Mexicans and Italians who fight 'Anglo' heroes.)

Per Hollywood tradition, French accents alone are consistently associated with *amour*. Lambert's action appeal, in particular, is built on vulnerability and seduction. Limber but limited, he has a certain female fan base; more significant is his (straight) male following. Typically he romances and fights other whites and Asians; blacks appear in sidekick roles. In contrast, Jean-Claude Van Damme fights for as well as against Asians; with and against North Africans and Turks; but – save for

*Kickboxer* — he makes love only to white women. Casts in his films are multi-ethnic and multi-national, but there are few *bona fide* buddies. Of these five actors, therefore, Van Damme most typically moves, per Fred Pfeil on the *Lethal Weapon* and *Die Hard* films, in a 'capitalist dreamscape [which is] inter-and/or multinational at the top and multiracial at the bottom'.[30]

Admittedly, accents and anatomies afford tricky foundations for discussions of nationality and ethnicity: as Ian Jarvie comments, it is easy to confuse actor, character, and star.[31] Action films work hard to compound the confusion. Geographic locations are sketchy, with postcard backdrops providing directional pointers in films often shot in other locations.[32] Junks, dark alleys, and skyscrapers thus 'signify' Hong Kong; the Thames and double decker buses 'mean' London; Central Park, the Manhattan skyline, elevated trains 'say' New York; the Eiffel Tower and Notre Dame 'equal' Paris; the Coliseum 'is' Rome. Other locales (fortresses, islands, prisons, mansions) are archetypes. Heroes and villains travel constantly in space and time; all governments are somehow corrupt.[33] That 'Hollywood' imports directors, stories, editing patterns, and sound design from other film and literary traditions jumbles geography still more (think: Hong Kong 'actioneers' like Lam, Woo, and Hark; Japanese samurai films, Britain and Bond, France and Besson, Holland and Verhoeven).[34]

Nonetheless the examples of my five big men demonstrate, I think, the value of nuancing Richard Dyer's observation that action films 'ally the speed they offer with white male characters'.[35] Whether actual or imagined, *marked* ethnic and national flavorings play a decided part in the 'thrills' delivered primarily to and by 'straight white men' in many contemporary action films.

But what will the future hold? Though undeniably fit, all five of these men are aging, with two approaching 60, the other three in their mid 40s. Born in 1960, the youngest, Jean-Claude Van Damme, predicts he will be dead by 50, of a massive heart attack.[36] Under pressure from new — and old — immigrant groups seeking to see 'themselves' on screen as heroes, not just as sidekicks or villains, will other accents mark action? The Hollywood actioners my five star in are, on the whole, more preoccupied with 'domestic problems' than with foreign policy dilemmas, hence the presence of so many Latino, black, and Asian sidekicks and subordinates; hence, on the whole, the absence of Africans and Arabs. Will shifting political alliances of the future prompt Hollywood to identify new friends and target new foes, just as, post 1990 *glasnost* and *perestroika*, terrorists and drug dealers replaced Russians as villains?[37]

Because screen assignments of nationality, ethnicity, race, and gender are always over-determined and ambivalent, there can be no single or simple answers to these or other questions. It may not be easy to determine whether Arnold Schwarzenegger/Braunschweiger/Jack Slater's emphatic answer, 'NOT TO BE!', to Hamlet's famous query recapped in *Last Action Hero* accurately predicted the future of European accents in action. For action audiences, the spectacular *enactment* of the nihilistic response, 'NOT TO BE', matters more than any particular outcome: in action, especially, 'the play' is hyperbolically, hysterically, 'the thing'.

Yet post the September 11, 2001 World Trade Center attacks, I find it harder to watch action films with quite the same laid-back excitement. Although I remain skeptical of claims that action figures and films directly or unilaterally fuel violent acts, I worry about overly abstracting and aestheticizing action's appeal. What does it mean, for example, that a six year old girl tells her mother that the TV images of the collapsing World Trade towers are beautiful even as, crying, she insists she knows thousands died? Or that a younger boy, snatched from his Tribeca day care center to run with crowds up Broadway, understands the spectacle as 'just more Power Rangers', though he himself was *there*?

## Notes

1  R. Dyer 'Action!', in José Arroyo (ed.) *Action/Spectacle Cinema*, London: British Film Institute, 2000, pp. 17–20.

2  The label 'action' is somewhat fuzzy, since many films cross genres. My 'count' is based on (1) web labeling (in particular through http://www.imdb.com), (2) placement in local video store aisles, and (3) labeling used in critical reviews.

3  Lambert and Krabbé live in Europe; Lundgren moves back and forth between New York and Stockholm; Hauer and Van Damme reside in California.

4  See S. Kozloff *Overhearing Film Dialogue*, Berkeley: University of California Press, 2000, especially pp. 139–55 and 201–16, and Y. Tasker *Spectacular Bodies*, London: Routledge, 1993, especially pp. 73–90.

5  S. Saban 'The Action Man Who Fell to Earth,' *Movieline*, 6, July 1995, p. 48.

6  In 1981 Lundgren won the European Heavyweight Full-Contact Karate Championship, and in 1982, the Australian heavyweight division title.

7  Swedish reviewers are among the harshest, charging he is capable 'neither of mimicry nor gestural body language'. Bent Liholm 'Svensk filmstjärna med stenansikte', *Filmrutan*, 1993, 36: 1, p. 21. My translation.

8  See Kozloff *Overhearing Film Dialogue*, pp. 142–4 and 206–7.

9  Saban 'The Action Man Who Fell to Earth', p. 50, and N. Forde 'Universal Man', *Venice Magazine*, July 1992, n.p.

10  M. Musto 'Minimum Requirement', *Village Voice*, May 17, 1988, n.p.

11  J. Jerome and J. Yarbrough 'Eurohunk Dolph Lundgren Takes on America's Ultimate Tag Team: Sly Stallone and Grace Jones', *People Weekly*, 24: 9, December 1985, p. 156.

12  T. Tunney '*The Shooter*', *Sight and Sound*, 6: 1, January 1996, p. 51.

13  See R. Dyer *White*, London: Routledge, 1997, pp. 145–65. That Tasker specifically links Lundgren and Van Damme to 'Christian traditions of representation which offer up the white male body as spectacle' strengthens my suspicion that 'European-ness' matters. See Tasker *Spectacular Bodies*, p. 74.

14  W. Wilson 'A Modern Dutch Master', *GQ*, September 1982, p. 290.

15  Ibid., p. 325. Hauer also refuses stunt work, conscious that 'one scar is enough to end a career'. R. Long 'Rutger Hauer: Portraying Fantasy Characters', *Starlog*, February 1986, p. 48.

16  H. Johnson 'Going Dutch', *US Magazine*, April 7, 1986, p. 40.

17  Wilson 'A Modern Dutch Master', p. 326.

18  Kaja Silverman argues that Hauer's 'hyperbolic whiteness separates slavery and race, while also displacing the white male human from his normally privileged position within such hierarchies'. S. Bukatman *Blade Runner*, London: British Film Institute, 1997, p. 76; see further K. Silverman 'Back to the Future', *Camera Obscura*, 27, 1991, pp. 109–32. On the racial dynamics of the film, see also Dyer *White*, pp. 212–15.

19  Speculation ended in the late 1980s when Lambert married actress Diane Lane. The two are now divorced; he is remarried.

20  E. Hedegaard 'Van Damme Kicks Back', *Details*, September 1993, p. 167; A. Cahduhuri 'Damme Buster', *Time Out*, May 19–26, 1993, p. 23.

21  Van Damme repudiates the role. See J. Chetwood 'No Coming Out Party for First Van Damme Movie', *Hollywood Reporter*, November 10, 1997, n.p.

22  Together *Bloodsport*, *Cyborg*, and *Death Warrant* probably cost $5 million to make; they earned more than $150 million. Most films now cost between $15 and $40 million. Hedegaard 'Van Damme Kicks Back', p. 165.

23  P. Wilkinson 'Van Dammaged: The Trials of Jean-Claude Van Damme', *US*, October 1998, p. 56.

24  T. Tunney '*Sudden Death*', *Sight and Sound*, 6: 5, May 1996, p. 93. Compare Van Damme: 'The young people who are my fans identify with me for good reasons: they all have a little brother, a little sister, a girlfriend, a mother, a grandmother they want to protect.' I. Frain 'Jean-Claude Van Damme: "Les Femmes ont toujours envie de me protéger"', *Paris Match*, August 12, 1991, p. 18. My translation.

25  M. A. Lipton and J. Griffiths 'Jean-Claude Van Damme', *People*, August 3, 1992, p. 83. On Van Damme's gay fan base, see Tasker, *Spectacular Bodies*, p. 128.

26  G. Dwyer 'Soldier Returns from the Undead', *Daily Yomiuri*, September 30, 1999, Dow Jones interactive database, accessed July 20, 2001.

27  Tunney *Sudden Death*, p. 93.

28  As I wrote some years back, 'most of the model male murderers today – Sylvester Stallone and Arnold Schwarzenegger, Jean-Claude Van Damme, even Mel Gibson – are ethnic or foreign. Virility, once home-grown and Anglo-American, is now imported'. C. Holmlund 'A Decade of Deadly Dolls', in H. Burch (ed.) *Moving Targets: Women, Murder, and Representation,* Virago, 1988; reprinted Berkeley, University of California Press, 1994, p. 151. Today a separate study on Australian actors in action may well be in order, with emphasis on Mel Gibson and Russell Crowe. Thanks to Yvonne Tasker for this observation.

29  See further C. Holmlund *Impossible Bodies: Femininity and Masculinity at the Movies*, London: Routledge, 2001, especially pp. 91–107.

30  F. Pfeil *White Guys: Studies in Postmodern Domination and Difference,* London: Verso, 1995, p. 32.

31  I. Jarvie 'Stars and Ethnicity: Hollywood and the US, 1932–51', in L. Friedman (ed.) *Unspeakable Images: Ethnicity and the American Cinema*, Urbana: University of Illinois Press, 1991, p. 84.

32  *The Punisher* is set in New York, *The Fortress* in the Southwest, but both are shot in Australia. *Mortal Kombat* depends heavily on computer-generated sets.

33  Compare Arroyo on *Mission Impossible*: 'There is no longer any difference between the East and the West. What happens in Kiev and Prague or Washington and London is similar. All are corrupt places.' J. Arroyo '*Mission Impossible*', in Arroyo, *Action/Spectacle Cinema*, p. 23.

34  *Blind Fury* was adapted from a Japanese samurai series featuring blind character/hero Zato Ichi.

35  Dyer 'Action!', p. 20.

36  Wilkinson 'Van Dammaged', p. 58.

37  Van Damme's 1997 *Knock Off* reprises older patterns: here evil Russians reappear together with corrupt CIA-agents and money-grubbing triads.

Chapter 18

## LYDIA PAPADIMITRIOU

# GREEK WAR FILM AS MELODRAMA
## Women, female stars and the nation as victim

**T**O CONSIDER GREEK WAR FILMS AS melodramas and women's films sounds like a paradox: how can a quintessentially male genre like the war film be considered a female genre? And yet, the majority of Greek war films produced in the 1960s and early 1970s told stories of women, their sacrifices, their activities and their desires during war. How can we understand and explain this phenomenon?

Greek war films were produced predominantly in the period during which the country was ruled by the right-wing dictatorship of the Colonels (1967–74). This article will suggest that the melodramatic form of these films, and the centrality of female characters and their suffering in them, can be seen as expressing the Colonels' anthropomorphic vision of the nation as an ailing body in need of rescue. The main ideological tenet of the Colonels was stringent anti-communism – an ideology much more evident in the regime's torture and oppression of dissenting citizens than in the language used by its leaders to justify the regime. This, instead, was full of incoherent sentences and ideas, violent threats, empty moralistic statements and metaphors of illness.[1]

A brief initial presentation of the history, the politics and the generic characteristics of the Greek war film will set the background for analysis. Considering melodrama both as a male and a female genre, I will examine to what extent the Greek war films possess melodramatic features, and then focus specifically on the function of women and female stars in these films. I will then analyse four key war films in order to consider the extent to which the central female characters, performed by the two major female stars of the period, Aliki Vougiouklaki and Jenny Karezi, express a vision of the nation defined around the binary opposition victim/hero.

### The Greek war film

War films first appeared in Greece after the end of the Second World War.[2] The war films of the late 1940s introduced the two main features of the Greek film genre: heroic tone and melodramatic form. During the 1950s, very few war films were made in Greece. By the end of the decade the genre gradually re-emerged.[3] During the early and mid-1960s between one and four war films were produced annually.[4]

As noted above, the peak of production of Greek war films was the late 1960s and early 1970s, and especially the years 1967–74 when the Colonels were in power. The revival of the genre in this period is to a large extent the result of the dictators' provision of military equipment and personnel to assist the making of films which promoted their own military image and ethos.[5] In the late 1960s, the war film was one of the most popular genres of Greek cinema. By 1969–70 – that is, two years into the dictatorship – twelve new war films were released, four of which dominated the box office. In the following two years, production consisted of about eight war films annually, at least two of which reached the top ten each year. After the fall of the dictatorship in 1974 the genre practically disappeared. This sudden drop both in production and popularity suggests that there was a strong link between the genre and the repressive regime. It is also revealing in this respect: no war films have been produced since in Greek cinema.[6]

Like most war films, Greek war films projected nationalist feelings, and aimed to enhance national unity and coherence in the face of an unjust and heartless enemy.[7] The privileged conflict was the Second World War.[8] Told from the Greek perspective, this war offered the possibility of projecting a tale of both heroism and victimization; of national victory but also of suffering.

Brief reference to historical events will be useful here. Greeks fought World War Two on the side of the allies, entering the war on 28 October, 1940. For five months the Greek army were victorious against the Italians, managing to push them back into Albania. By April 1941, however, German troops invaded Greece and a three and a half-year period of Occupation began. Famine and inflation were severe. National strife took the form of guerrilla warfare, undertaken by various resistance groups – the most important of which were communist-led. In October 1944 the German army withdrew from Greece, but a civil war between communists and nationalists ensued, ending in 1949 after the intervention of British and American troops.[9]

The victorious war against the Italians, and the long and tough period of the Occupation, offered themselves for appropriation into narratives of both heroism and national victimization. Representations, however, excluded totally the period of the civil war. Evidence of internal conflict and national division, the civil war could not be used to sustain narratives of national pride.[10]

It is worth considering how a typical Greek war film narrates these events – and how it personalizes them. A Greek war film usually starts before the war – often on the eve of declaration, offering a glimpse of happiness during peace – a happiness symbolized by the union of a young couple, just married or engaged. Very soon afterwards, the war begins. The couple splits: the woman back home is worried, fearful but courageous; victory at the front brings hope and pride to all concerned, but the German Occupation ends this situation. Defeat and a sense of victimization come to dominate. The couple remains separate and, often, the woman believes that her man is dead. Following a period of mourning, she reacts and becomes involved with the resistance or some other act for the community. But, as we soon find out (usually before the heroine herself), the man is alive.[11] National liberation and the re-union of the couple concludes the narrative. Thus personal history and national history are brought together in a happy ending.

There is, in terms of narrative, a very clear structure of equilibrium, dis-equilibrium and restoration of equilibrium: the film begins in peace/the couple are unified); it is followed by the eruption of war/the separation of the couple; and it concludes with the restoration of peace and of the couple. There is also a very clear use of duality in the plot: the war and the Occupation separate the couple; the end of the war (assisted by the couple's actions) brings the couple back together. The public adventure (the war) and the private romance of the couple are closely intertwined. What distinguishes Greek war films from the majority of other war films is not the existence of such duality, but rather the prevalence of the romance, almost to the detriment of the adventure. In other words, the emphasis is on the woman's story, as opposed to the man's. It is no coincidence, therefore, that the most popular Greek war films were vehicles for female stars, particularly, Aliki Vougiouklaki and Jenny Karezi.[12]

## Greek war film as melodrama

The term 'melodrama', as applied to cinema, has at least two meanings which are not always reconcilable, though both are applicable in the case of Greek war films.

One meaning draws on the theatrical origins of the genre, and refers to the use of spectacle for the depiction of a world full of moral oppositions. Related to this meaning of melodrama are the notion of 'excess'; the use of sudden plot twists; the use of narrative devices such as false or mistaken identities; the schematic depiction of characters; and a didactic tone, associated with the final re-establishment of moral order. Music also plays a key expressive role in this type of melodrama.[13]

There is also a use of the term melodrama that coincides with 'the woman's film'. In this sense, the term refers to films which focus on a female protagonist, and have as their main location the home and the family. These films are addressed predominantly to female spectators. The conflicts expressed in women's films are not externalized through confrontation and action (as in the traditional male genres – the western, the detective, the war film); rather, conflicts are evaded by the characters, and 'displaced' onto gestures, unconscious actions and the overall *mise-en-scène* of the films.[14]

Greek war films fit the definition of melodrama in both senses. First, like theatrical and silent film melodrama, they present a Manichean moral world, where good and evil are clearly delineated and opposed. The nation and its enemies consti-tute the key binary opposition organizing these films. The moral message is clear: the ultimate value in this world is the defence of the nation, inextricably associated with the family. The films also make use of spectacle, typically including sequences involving tanks, warships, and planes, although these sequences are rarely fully orchestrated into meaningful action   instead they seem inserted into the plot for the sake of spectacle.[15] Furthermore, Greek war films are excessive. Their narratives are systematically organized around a series of coincidences, reversals of expectation, mistaken identities, recognitions, etc. Suspense and surprise are also extensively used. Finally, most scenes are accompanied by music, which strongly underlines and enhances their main emotional features.

The similarities between Greek war films and the woman's film consist mainly in the centrality of the female characters and the fact that the stories are told from a woman's perspective. Related to this is the key function of romance, and the family. In order to elaborate on the feminine aspects of the Greek war films, I will make direct reference to four case studies. Made between 1966 and 1971, these films were amongst the most popular of the period. The films are *I Daskala me ta Chryssa Mallia/The Teacher with Golden Hair* (1969–70) and *Ypolochagos Natasha/Lieutenant Natasha* (1970–1) starring Aliki Vougiouklaki; and *Kontserto gia Polyvola/Concert for Weapons* (1966–7) and *Mia Gynaika stin Andistasi/A Woman at Resistance* (1970–1), starring Jenny Karezi.[16] All their main characteristics illustrate that they can easily be considered as 'women's films'.

All four films tell war stories predominantly from the perspective of the women. In all cases the women are both victims and heroes. They are victims because they lose a beloved person – or they think they have lost him – and heroes because they show courage, perseverance and a deep belief in the national ideal. The heroines are totally committed to their husband/fiancé, remaining faithful despite his absence. Their passionate love is only briefly experienced, as the man leaves for war very soon after their union.[17] However, despite the woman's clear commitment to her man, romantic triangles are formed. The second contender, who fails in his attempts to win the woman over, is an enemy: a German (*Natasha*, *Gynaika*), or a traitor (*Daskala*).[18]

In three of the four films (*Kontserto*, *Daskala*, *Gynaika*) the woman experiences the war (and/or the Occupation), wrongly believing that her man is dead. This allows the script to devote more time to her perspective, to position her as a victim, and to manipulate our emotions through suspense and surprise. In all three cases, the man returns at the end (*Kontserto*, *Daskala*), or towards the end (*Gynaika*) of the film, and usually reverses the fate of the heroine: he saves her from suicide (*Kontserto*), or stops an unwanted second marriage (*Daskala*).[19] Again, in three of these films the woman works: she is a teacher (*Daskala*), an employee (*Kontserto*) or a singer (*Natasha*). When she does not work for money, she works for the resistance (*Natasha*, *Gynaika*). Work, however, is not seen as career, but either as a necessity for survival, or as voluntary work for the benefit of the community.[20] In half of the films, the woman undergoes a major psychological crisis as a result of her suffering: she loses her memory and her voice (*Natasha*); or she lapses into hysteria, refusing to accept the loss of her partner (*Gynaika*). In both cases she eventually regains her sanity through re-union with her man (*Gynaika*) or her son (*Natasha*).

Considering these war films as women's films highlights the ambivalent position of the female characters – as victims and heroes – but also suggests their ultimately subservient position to the (often absent) males. It is worth examining in more detail these women's ambivalent function, but also their relation to male power. To what extent do these women develop initiative and independence from their male partners or remain subservient and dependent on patriarchal rules? To put it differently, does the heroine's activity in these films result in her occupying a masculine role in the narrative (does she control the narrative), or are her actions determined by male will and values?

Analysis shows that the possibility for the woman to take on a masculine role through her actions is repeatedly contained by an emphasis on her feminine traits: the films locate the heroine within the context of romance, associating her with traditional feminine roles. Furthermore – and this is particularly evident in the case of star Aliki Vougiouklaki – they present her as an object of spectacle for the male gaze. Ultimately, the woman's actions do not challenge patriarchy – if anything, they serve to reinforce it.

The heroine's services for the nation are often dictated by a male-dominated hierarchy, in which the woman's position is subservient.[21] When she acts through her own initiative, her activity for the nation is also romantically motivated. In other words, her involvement with the resistance is motivated by her desire to help her man, or to keep his memory alive. The 'personal' is so closely interconnected with the 'national' that the heroine's actions ultimately become representative of the patriarchal expectations of what a 'good woman' should do and be like. Struggling to protect both the nation and her traditional place in society, she is an impersonation of ideal womanhood in patriarchy.

What is particularly interesting, especially with regard to metaphoric meanings of the nation, is the double association of these women with victimization and heroism. Sacrificial and suffering for their man and their country, on the one hand, they are also celebrated for enduring pain, and for being able to act despite it. Their lack of selfishness (a feature which, in part, victimizes them) is also the source of their heroic lack of self-pity which leads them to action. As such they become the perfect emblems of an ideology that sees the nation as a phoenix periodically resurrected from its ashes.

According to tradition, the phoenix was a legendary bird that consumed itself by fire every 500 years, while a new, young phoenix sprang from its ashes. Early Christian tradition adopted it as a symbol of immortality and resurrection.[22] The symbol has been adopted a number of times in the history of modern Greece to underline the ideology of national continuity between ancient, Byzantine and modern Greece, but the Colonels added a figure of a standing soldier in front of the bird, thus making it an emblem of their own right-wing, militaristic regime. The 'resurrection of the nation', for the Colonels, could only happen with the help of the military.

What I am suggesting here is that the figures of the victimized and heroic women of Greek war films made in the late 1960s and early 1970s represent a view of the nation concomitant to the militaristic ideology of the colonels. Both the women and the nation, in this vision, are victims (of the enemies) and heroes (because of their soldiers); they are both saved by the military, resurrected from their ashes.

## Women and the nation: victims or heroes?

I will now look in more detail at the four case studies, in order to explore the dynamic between victimization and heroism that is expressed through the female characters, and consider to what extent they could be seen as allegories of the nation. By looking at the plots and the extent to which they are informed by the female characters, I will examine the degree to which their activity and free will is contained by patriarchal discourses. I will also discuss the role played by star image in containing the characters' initiative and freedom, and reinforcing their traditional feminine role. The two war films starring Aliki Vougiouklaki provide a good starting point.

*I Daskala me ta Chryssa Mallia* (1969–70) focuses on a woman who goes to a remote village as a teacher, a few months before the war. There, she falls in love with a young man. On their wedding day, the war begins and he leaves to fight. Soon, news of his death reaches his wife. Despite her desperation, she stays in the village and continues to teach. Then, an old admirer joins her as a teacher. They work together throughout the Occupation. Just before liberation, her father-in-law urges them to marry. But her husband arrives unexpectedly, and stops this unwanted marriage. As he explains, he had been injured and kept hostage in an Italian concentration camp. The couple re-unites, the other man leaves, and everyone celebrates the liberation.

Myrto (Aliki Vougiouklaki) is depicted as an enthusiastic and keen teacher who loves children. An orphan herself, she prefers to work rather than marry without love. Myrto is strong not only because she continues to work after her husband's death, but also because, during the Occupation, she initiates a raid into the grocer's warehouse in order to help feed the children. She is generally presented as articulate and outspoken, but also respectful of the limitations that a traditional (read patriarchal) village society imposes. Thus she carefully preserves her virginal reputation before marriage, and remains faithful and committed to her husband, even after his death. She agrees to marry someone else, not because she wants to, but because of her promise to her father-in-law. Despite her apparent independence, Myrto relies extensively on father figures (her older colleague, her father-in-law) and follows closely their advice, particularly in personal matters.

Like most star-vehicles for Vougiouklaki, *Daskala* presents the heroine as an attractive and desirable woman. Even the title signals the importance of her looks, characterizing the teacher not through intelligence, courage or any other virtue, but through her beauty – her fetishized 'golden' hair, unmistakable star sign of Vougiouklaki.[23] This emphasis on her looks – and her sexual identity as a desirable, but virginal and subsequently monogamous figure – blocks any potential attempt to forget her feminine identity. It should be said that Myrto is probably the least 'masculine' of these heroines – and not only because of her specularization. Her activity as a teacher and her contribution to the community during the Occupation, fall into more conventional feminine roles than the other heroines' actions. Like them, however, Myrto is caught within the hero/victim dialectic: she suffers for the loss of her husband, but finds the courage to endure pain and to resist oppression.[24]

Vougiouklaki's other star-vehicle, *Ypolochagos Natasha* (1970–1) remains to this day the most popular Greek film ever made.[25] The story is narrated through a series of flashbacks as Natasha returns to Greece from Germany, after 20 years of capture and amnesia. During the journey she remembers the years of the Occupation, and her romance with Orestis, a resistance fighter. Her memories tell us her story until her capture by the Germans: how she met Orestis, and how their relationship grew; how they married despite persecution; how he left the following day, unaware that she was carrying his child; how she went to find him, became involved in the resistance, and was captured by the Germans; how he saved her from execution, and then was killed, by mistake; how finally she was sent to a concentration camp, where she was paralysed, and lost her memory, sense of identity and speech. Back in Greece, Natasha is honoured as a hero; and seeing her son again, after 20 years of separation, she finally regains her long-lost ability to speak.

As a melodrama, *Natasha* is very effective, particularly in its use of *mise-en-scène*. Its central scene – the marriage in blood – visually condenses the generic discourses of the war film and the romance: on their way to church, the young couple are persecuted by the Germans. A bullet hits the young bride whose dress turns from white to red. Determined to get married, the couple continue to church, and the wedding begins. The Germans catch up with them, joining them in church. But they do not kill them immediately, waiting for the ceremony to finish. On their way out, the resistance stops the Germans, allowing the couple to leave. Bells ring as the Greek fighters shoot them to mark the celebration.

The scene aims to convey the horror of the war and the Occupation through the symbolism of a marriage in blood, but ensures that this particular episode ends well – suggesting ultimate victory. This is a very good example of the way in which the genre personalizes national conflict. The suffering of the couple becomes emblematic of the suffering of the nation. But the national conflict is also expressed as a romantic triangle: the German leader who persecutes the couple is a previously rejected admirer of Natasha. His desire to stop the couple is not only the result of his national and ideological affiliations, but also of his personal envy. The conflict is not just between Germans and Greeks, but also between two men for the love of a woman.

As a heroine, Natasha is more active and more independently minded than Myrto. From her first encounter with the Germans, she marks her opposition by helping the Greeks pull a cart with wounded soldiers. But the director, again, underlines her essentially feminine presence: in her striking orange blouse, long blonde hair and high heels, she leaves no doubt as to her primary status as an object of desire. Interestingly, the scene follows immediately from her first encounter with the German leader: as such it is doubly coded as an act of national pride, but also of personal provocation.

Natasha's heroism is marked by the extent to which she takes risks: she hides Orestis in her house when he is persecuted; she works for the resistance; and, most significantly, she does not succumb to torture, even if she has to deny her mother and child. As usual, all her heroic actions involve a close association between her commitment to the nation and her love for her man. But as if the emphasis on romance and her specularization are not enough, Natasha's essentially feminine nature has to be marked through her loss of sanity. The use of hysteria victimizes her further, and allows the narrative to relegate her to a conventionally subservient role. It is interesting that her health is totally restored only when she meets her son, in a scene that is explicitly meant to remind her (and us) of her first meeting with her husband: it is the restoration of her role as a mother – a role sanctioned by patriarchy – that finally heals her hysteria.

In the roles played by Vougiouklaki, the fetishized body – the blonde hair, the strong make-up, the colourful clothes – is of the utmost importance in relegating her to a conventionally feminine role. In the case of Jenny Karezi, fetishization is evident, but not as pronounced: brunette (rather than blonde), and often playing middle-class, serious, educated women, Karezi did not serve as the object of the male gaze as emphatically as Vougiouklaki. Her films were therefore more careful in containing her potential threat to patriarchal order through narrative means.

*Kontserto gia Polyvola* (1966–7) tells the story of a woman who acts as a double agent between Italians and Greeks. Niki – whose name, significantly, means 'victory' (Jenny Karezi) – works for the Ministry of Defence. She becomes a double agent unwillingly: the Italians blackmail her into spying for them, while the Greeks employ her after discovering her involvement with the Italians. Niki loves Alexis (Kostas Kazakos), a colleague of hers. But, again unwillingly, she gets him into trouble and the Greeks condemn him to death. The war begins, Alexis is executed, and Niki prepares to commit suicide. Here, a sudden reversal occurs, as Alexis appears at the last minute. He explains that his capture and execution were faked for reasons of public opinion. The couple is joined, whilst the people celebrate the first victories against the Italians.

In *Kontserto* the heroine is victimized in at least two ways. First, she gets involved in spying unwillingly; second, she is led to feel (wrongly) responsible for the death of her beloved. The patriarchal structure at work in this film is very pronounced, as her actions are carefully dictated by others – mainly by the Greek underground leader, who also is responsible for a lot of her suffering. The heroine never questions the necessity to obey this 'law of the father', even if it means the destruction of both her man and herself.

In *Mia Gynaika stin Andistasi* the character played by Karezi is 'contained' mainly through mental illness. The story is as follows: a young woman loses her fiancé who goes to war on the day after their engagement. Refusing to accept the news of his death, she loses her mind. After a physical shock, however, she recovers, and starts working for the resistance. The narration initially misleads us into thinking that she is working for the Germans, but we soon discover her real affiliations. Reacting against the organization's decision that she should stop working for them, she goes to find its leader. To both her (and our) surprise, the leader is her fiancé, who was not, after all, dead – just injured. After their reunion, she continues to work for the resistance, but is caught during her last mission. The resistance saves her from the Germans, and the film ends with hope.

In this film, the woman's activity is evident through her involvement with the resistance (for which, however, she plays a traditionally feminine role, as an escort of the German commander). She is victimized through suffering for the death of her beloved, and through losing her sanity. In both cases, her suffering is the result of false information, given to her by men with the complicity of her beloved. Her victimization is almost intentional – a desire to test and 'break' her. And in both cases, her 'resurrection' is the result of her man appearing and telling the truth: she is thus saved by him.

In all four Greek war films examined, the activity of the heroine is strongly 'contained' by patriarchal discourse. This happens through recourse to both visual and narrative means: on the one hand, by excessively fetishizing the heroine's image; on the other, by 'punishing' and victimizing her through the narrative. Also, in all four films, a dialectic of heroism and victimization is at work. This, I would argue, plays two roles: on the one hand, it helps 'keep the woman in her place'; on the other, it creates metaphoric meanings that associate the nation with womanhood.

This needs further explanation: by victimizing the woman, and then saving her, patriarchal ideology asserts its superiority over women. By extension, it can also be argued that this expresses the dominant political ideology of the period of the films' production. Controlled by a paternalistic and authoritarian right-wing regime, the nation was addressed by the Colonels in their speeches through various metaphors concerning illness and near death.[26] The regime saw its function as that of a doctor who can resurrect his patient, and restore him/her to sanity. And, as noted earlier, underlining its military nature, the regime symbolized itself through a phoenix in front of which stood a soldier. The above reading of Greek war films, and especially of the function of women in them, points to an analogy between the female characters' subservient position, and the way in which the nation was imagined by the Colonels. As soldiers and military leaders – like the ones portrayed in the films – the Colonels saw themselves as saviours of the nation; of a nation ailing and victimized, acting in the service of its leaders, but ultimately saved only through their own intervention – like the women in the films. The melodramatic structure of Greek war films can thus be explained through their ideological function as instruments of a regime which saw its function as that of the 'saviour of the nation'.

This ultimately propagandist function of the films also helps explain why so many war films were made during the dictatorship. It does, however, leave unexplained the films' popularity. For, according to historians, the Colonels' regime did not have strong support among the people – rather it managed to impose itself because of popular passivity.[27] The student demonstrations of November 1973, which gained the wider support of the population, served as belated evidence of long brewing anti-regime feelings. It is possible, therefore, to suggest that the victim/hero dynamic evident in the war films was read by the audience 'against the grain'. The Occupation, in such a reading, could be seen as a metaphor for the Colonels' oppressive regime; the victimized and heroic women as the people who suffered in silence but also heroically endured these adverse times; and the final liberation and happy ending as a fantasy projection into the future that was yet to come – the Colonels' fall and the restoration of democracy.

Whether seen as ideological instruments of the repressive regime, or as ritualistic expressions of the repressed and silenced population, it is by no means a coincidence that the rise and fall of the Greek war film occurred during the Colonels' dictatorship.

## Notes

1  Meletis I. Meletopoulos *I Dictatoria ton Syndagmatarchon / The Colonels' Dictatorship*, Athens: Papazisi, 1996, pp. 155–256.

2  Prior to this period, only newsreels depicting the army and combat had appeared (dir. Joseph Hepp *Eisodos tou Ellinikou Stratou sti Thessaloniki / The Entry of the Greek Army in Thessaloniki*, 1912), as well as a few attempts to dramatize events from the nineteenth century national revolution against the Turks – which are not preserved (Yannis Soldatos *Istoria tou Ellinikou Kinimatographou / History of Greek Cinema*, vol. 1, Athens: Egokeros, 1988, pp. 30–1; Michel Demopoulos (ed.) *Le Cinema Grec*, Paris: Centre Georges Pompidou, 1995). War films of the mid to late 1940s include *Adoulotoi Sklavoi / Unslaved Slaves* (1946), *Katadromi sto Aigaio / Persecution in the Aegean* (1946), *I Kriti stis Floges / Crete in Flames* (1947), *Paidia tis Athinas / Children of Athens* (1947), *Anna Roditi* (1947), *Teleftea Apostoli? Las Mission* (1948–9), *Ochyro 27 / Fortress 27* (1948–9) and *Germaniki Peripolos stin Kriti I German Patrol in Crete* (1948–9). Note: Most films are dated according to the season of their release (on the basis of which annual box-office figures are arranged). This is a more reliable way of classification, because different sources attribute either the date of production or of release. When a single date is given, it refers to the year of release.

3  The production of *To Nisi ton Gennaion / The Island of the Brave* (1959–60), signalled the return of the genre (dir. Dimis Dadiras, with Jenny Karezi and Alekos Alexandrakis). The film was placed fourth in the season's box office.

4  Interestingly, the two most successful war films of the mid 1960s, *Prodosia / Betrayal* and *Diogmos / Persecution* were rather personal films, which offered innovations to the generic formula. Both films were made in 1964–5 and were offered awards at the Thessaloniki film festival. *Prodosia* (dir. Kostas Manousakis) focused on the love between a German and a Jew – a theme that has not been taken up before or since in Greek war films (440,000 tickets were sold, and it reached sixth position at the box office); *Diogmos* (dir. Grigoris Grigoriou) combined a story from the Second World War with references to the Asia Minor destruction (340,000 tickets, tenth position). Box-office information from Stathis Valoukos *Filmografia tou Ellinikou Kinimatographou / Filmography of Greek Cinema*, Athens: EES, 1984.

5  This practice was not unprecedented: *To Nisi ton Gennaion* (1959–60), produced before the dictatorship, explicitly acknowledges the support of the Greek army. During the dictatorship, however, this practice was revitalized and further reinforced.

6  This does not include films which deal with wars or other armed conflicts but are made in the context of the predominantly left-wing 'new Greek cinema'. These films aim at the critical reconsideration of these conflicts, rather than their celebration. Such films include Pandelis Voulgaris's *Petrina Chronia / Stone Years* (1985) which deals with the Greek civil war (1945–9) and Theo Angelopoulos's *Vlemma tou Odyssea / Ulysses' Gaze* (1995), which reflects on the Balkan conflicts of the 1990s.

7  Very few Greek war films portrayed a more complex view of the enemy. The most notable exception is Kostas Manousakis's *Prodosia* (1964–5).

8  Very few films do not deal with this war. Among the most successful exceptions were: *Papaflessas* (1971–2), *Mando Mavrogenous* (1971–2), which dealt with the nineteenth century Greek War of Independence and *To Nisi tis Afroditis / The Island of Afroditi* (1969–70), which addressed the conflict in Cyprus.

9  Richard Clogg *A Concise History of Greece*, Cambridge: Cambridge University Press, 1992, pp. 120–44.

10  Furthermore, reference to the civil war required acknowledgment of the existence of communists in Greece. But, from the early 1950s until the fall of the dictatorship in the

mid 1970s communism was a taboo subject, and its supporters were banned both from politics and from representation. See, among others, John O. Iatrides (ed.) *Greece in the 1940s: A Nation in Crisis*, Hanover and London: University Press of New England, 1981.

11   Needless to say, the resistance in Greek war films is portrayed as a unified movement, with undoubted nationalist aims: a continuation of the war, but with different means. There is never any mention of the fact that the resistance consisted of a range of different groups with different political agendas, and that the largest of these resistance groups, after the liberation, became the nucleus for the communist fight against nationalists. On the Greek civil war, see Iatridis *Greece in the 1940s*.

12   The emphasis on the romantic plot is not exclusive to war films with major female stars. In films like *Ochi/No* (1969–70) or *Ypovrychio Papanikolis/Submarine Papanikolis* (1971–2) both of which place more emphasis on the male story, and have no major female stars, the romance plot is still prevalent.

13   See Peter Brooks *The Melodramatic Imagination*, New Haven: Yale University Press, 1976; Christine Gledhill (ed.) *Home is where the heart is: Studies in Melodrama and the Woman's Film*, London: BFI, 1987; Jacky Bratton, Jim Cook and Christine Gledhill (eds) *Melodrama: Stage, Picture, Screen*, London: BFI, 1994.

14   Melodramas of this kind have been analysed extensively through feminist and psycho-analytic approaches. See Mary Ann Doane *The Desire to Desire*, London: Macmillan, 1987; Jackie Byars *All that Hollywood Allows: Re-reading Gender in 1950s Melodrama*, Chapel Hill and London: University of North Carolina Press, 1991.

15   Despite the fact that it fares poorly when compared to its American or European coun-terparts, the war film was, together with the musical, one of the most spectacular genres of Greek cinema. Note also, that this use of spectacle in war films contributes to the asso-ciation of melodrama with excitement and thrills. See Steve Neale 'Melo Talk: On the Meaning and Use of the Term "Melodrama" in the American Trade Press', *The Velvet Light Trap*, 32, 1993, pp. 66–89.

16   Vougiouklaki's two war films reached the top of the box office charts in the two consec-utive seasons when the genre was at the peak of its popularity: 1969–70 and 1970–1. *Daskala* sold 739,000 tickets; *Natasha* sold 751,000 tickets (the highest gross for any Greek film ever, during its first run). Jenny Karezi's war films did not lag far behind. *Kontserto* was the most successful war film of 1966–7 (it sold 427,698 tickets, reaching eighth place at the box office), while *Gynaika* was the second most successful war film, after Vougiouklaki's *Natasha* in 1970–1 (460,036 tickets; fourth place). Both these female stars regularly appeared on screen with their real-life husbands – Dimitris Papamichail and Kostas Kazakos respectively. The female stars, however, had greater star status than their husbands: they commanded top billing, played bigger parts, and were more successful in films in which they appeared separately.

17   Separation occurs on their wedding day (*Daskala*), the next day (*Natasha*), the day after their engagement (*Gynaika*), or during their period of courtship (*Kontserto*).

18   In *Kontserto* there is no third person, but the husband believes that there is.

19   In the case of *Gynaika*, the recognition only strengthens the heroine's determination. In the only case when the husband actually dies (*Natasha*), the reunion with the long lost son restores the equilibrium (the woman is thus emotionally 'completed' as a mother).

20   Women's work before marriage characterizes most Greek films of the period – especially films starring Vougiouklaki and Karezi (see Maria Paradeisi 'I Parousiasi tis Ginekas stis "Comedie" tou Ellinikou Kinimatographou'/'The Representation of Woman in the Comedies of Greek Cinema', in *To Vima ton Kinonikon Epistimon*, 3: 11, 1993, pp. 185–203.

21   Interestingly, *Natasha* has another woman playing a leading role in the resistance (played by Kakia Panagiotou); but the decision that ultimately leads Natasha as a victim to the Germans – the decision to 'sacrifice' her – is taken by the male hierarchy in the resistance.

22   See Encarta Encyclopedia, CD Rom.

23   For the concepts of fetishization and the male gaze see Laura Mulvey 'Visual Pleasure and Narrative Cinema', *Screen*, 16: 3, Autumn 1975.

24 Her heroic nature is clearly defined in the film. In reply to the question 'what is a hero?' the older teacher explains to the pupils: 'Hero is not just he who fights and dies for freedom; it is also she who can endure the pain of death and persevere in her work.'

25 See Valoukos *Filmografia tou Ellinikou Kinimatographou*.

26 See Meletopoulos *I Dictatoria*, pp. 165–68.

27 See Meletopoulos *I Dictatoria*, pp. 101–16; Clogg *A Concise History of Greece*, pp. 163–8.

## Chapter 19

# DIMITRIS ELEFTHERIOTIS

# SPAGHETTI WESTERN, GENRE CRITICISM AND NATIONAL CINEMA
Re-defining the frame of reference

**T**HIS ESSAY IS AN ATTEMPT TO re-define the frame of reference of critical approaches to the 'spaghetti western'. Trapped between unreflective 'cult' adoration and (equally unreflective) outright dismissal as an inferior sub-genre, the 'spaghetti' remains very much outside the mainstream of genre criticism, often seen as the eccentric product of an opportunist film industry. In the rare occasions that the textuality of the 'spaghetti' is addressed[1] this involves a close comparison with the American western, which *de facto* becomes the only appropriate frame of reference.

As the adjective 'spaghetti' suggests, this is not a neutral, descriptive designation. The term, coined by American critics,[2] is a hybrid *par excellence*, an impossible mixture of cooking and filmmaking. 'Spaghetti' not only connotes inferiority and foreignness but also contamination as a dangerous and degenerate impurity. In this way, merely as a generic classification, the Italian engagement with the American genre is precluded to be an inferior, impure and contaminating exercise.

Further attention to the ambiguity of the term 'hybrid' in genre criticism is required. A Ford western, a Sirk melodrama, a Hitchcock thriller, a Minnelli musical are all hybrids in the sense that they involve a transformation, a reworking of the formula, an intersection between creative impulse and long established tradition. The hybrid nature of these texts is celebrated, as the creative genius's intervention is not perceived as a contaminating destructive influence, but as an invigorating force which takes care of the renewal of the genre and of the successful balance between the new and the established. On the other hand, a Hong-Kong gangster movie, an Indian melodrama, a French comedy, a German spy film, are all hybrids of a different order. They exist as specific local or national transformations of Hollywood generic conventions, the latter perceived as simultaneously national and global/universal. The normative position that these conventions occupy in Anglo-US film theory effaces the cultural and historical specificity of their production.

However, the term 'spaghetti western' foregrounds in its ludicrous hybridity the absurdity of the norm and calls into question the fundamental classificatory activity of genre criticism. It is with that in mind that I shall continue to use the term 'spaghetti western' throughout this essay: such derogatory designation offers a rare glimpse of the 'violence' involved in generic classifications as well as an indication of the normative position that Hollywood cinema occupies in critical discourses.

Furthermore, the hybrid nature of the term invites critical/analytical approaches that conceptualize the genre in both national and transnational terms. Christopher Frayling's pioneering work clearly operates within such a framework but suffers from certain methodological and conceptual weaknesses. Frayling analyses spaghetti westerns in terms of an essential Italian-ness that he identifies in the themes of the films and which accounts for the transformation of the 'original' Hollywood forms and conventions. It is rather surprising that Frayling's detailed study of the genre relies almost exclusively on Luigi Barzini's *The Italians* (1964) for the analysis of the Italian part of the hybrid. While Frayling acknowledges that the stereotypes that Barzini offers 'cannot, of course, be treated as serious sociology', he is also quite happy to suggest that:

> if one accepts Barzini's account of these stereotypical themes at face value, one gets the unnerving (although not necessarily surprising) impression that contemporary Southern Italian society bears more than a superficial resemblance to the world of the Spaghetti Western . . . This is clearly an impressionistic, cavalier view of Italian life – which might explain why its emphases mirror so closely those of the Spaghetti Western.[3]

Equipped with this implicit endorsement of Barzini's essentialism, Frayling criticizes Will Wright's reading of Sergio Leone westerns[4] for failing to consider 'Italian values'. Frayling then proposes the 'Italian plot' as a separate category (with three 'narrative variants') that accounts not only for the narrative structure of spaghetti westerns but also reflects the historical development of the genre.[5] While this is a well-intended intervention that challenges naturalized notions of 'authenticity' and questions the Hollywood norm, it also offers a rather biological understanding of the spaghetti western as a hybrid/impure product of two pure primary entities. There is no doubt that the spaghetti western is the product of cultural interaction and exchange. It must be approached, nevertheless, in a way that accounts for the textual specificity of the genre and at the same time relates such forms to a dynamic field of power relations and to national and international historical contexts.

In what follows I shall first examine briefly the mode of production of the spaghetti, the position of Italy in the world film market and the dynamics of the relationship between Hollywood and Italy. The essay relies heavily on the close analysis of sequences from two films, *Johnny Oro/Ringo and His Golden Pistol* (Sergio Corbucci, 1966, Italy) and *Django il bastardo/Django the Bastard* (Sergio Garrone, 1969, Italy/Spain). The emphasis on 'lesser' known directors and texts is deliberate as it bypasses Sergio Leone whose films occupy a canonical position in Anglo-US film criticism enhanced by his subsequent career in Hollywood (as well as those of the other 'trademark' contributors, Clint Eastwood and Ennio Moricone). The analysis of the films will focus on the identification of key textual characteristics that demonstrate the eclectic engagement of the 'spaghetti' with the American western. I shall relate such textuality to a broader historical and industrial context, offer an alternative generic frame of reference and consider some of the key questions that the 'spaghetti' poses vis-à-vis notions of national cinema and identity.

## The Italian film industry and the international market in the 1960s

It is not my intention to discuss extensively the complex post-war history of the Italian film industry or to offer a convincing, insular narrative about the emergence and decline of the spaghetti western. Instead, I want to refer to selective events and processes that are, nevertheless, crucial for an understanding of the place of the spaghetti western in the volatile international market of the 1960s: the close (sometimes friendly, sometimes bitterly antagonistic) relationship between the Italian and the American film industries; the remarkable strength of the Italian industry from the mid 1950s to the mid 1970s; the conditions of production/distribution/exhibition of the spaghetti western as well as the international marketing strategies used for its promotion.

The strong American presence in all sectors of the Italian film industry in the post-war period is well documented, as is the Italian response to it.[6] Immediately after the end of the war American films flooded the Italian market, which in the late 1940s was completely dominated by distributors and exhibitors very keen to satisfy American interests. This was eventually countered by protectionist measures that 'blocked' American film earnings in Italy and encouraged domestic production and distribution. The American companies responded by establishing foreign branches, by co-producing with Italian and other partners, and by disguising films with major American financial interests as Italian.

Paradoxically, a side effect of the strong American involvement was that Italian producers and distributors gained access to the worldwide distribution networks of the Americans. The accessibility of the international markets was also facilitated by the success of the neorealist films of the late 1940s and 1950s, which opened a number of foreign markets to Italian distributors.

The remarkable strength of the Italian film industry in the 1950s, 1960s and 1970s is also well documented. In that period Italy produced more films and attracted more spectators in more cinemas than any other European country. In terms of number of films produced, in the 1960s and early 1970s Italy consistently outnumbered the US.[7] In Cinecittá, Italy possessed the most Hollywood-like complex of studios in Europe, with advanced technology and facilities used in the production of a vast number of different kinds of films from peplums and spaghettis to Fellini films.

Also crucial for understanding the spaghetti is the international orientation of Italian cinema since the mid 1950s. Co-productions account for more than half of the overall Italian production in the years that the spaghetti western was launched and consolidated: in 1963 there were 134 co-productions out of 241 films made, in 1964 153 out of 270, in 1965 126 out of 188, in 1966 145 out of 245, in 1967 125 out of 258, in 1968 123 out of 254.[8]

Additionally, since the mid 1950s the Italian film industry expanded in world markets and captured significant fractions of audiences in Europe, North Africa, the Middle and the Far East and Latin America. The number of total export permits granted to Italian films rose from 848 in 1950 to 3,947 in 1964,[9] while at the same time Italian films outnumbered European and in some cases Hollywood films in international markets.[10] The spaghetti spearheaded the expansionist orientation of Italian producers in the 1960s and 1970s and it was the most successful example of the strategy 'new genres for new markets'. From the early 1960s to the late 1970s over 400 spaghettis were produced, often in co-production with Spanish, French or German companies. Significantly, the emergence of the spaghetti coincides with the decline (in terms of production numbers) of the American western: while in 1958 Hollywood produced 54 westerns, in 1963 the number fell to 11.[11]

The timing of the appearance of the spaghetti western is interpreted by many as strong evidence of the opportunism of the Italian film producers and directors who identified and exploited the lack of 'supply' of westerns in the international markets. What seems to further support the accusation of opportunism is the fact that at least initially the producers of spaghetti westerns promoted and marketed their films disguised as 'genuine' American westerns. However, the Italians were by no means the first Europeans to make westerns. Indeed, there is a long history of international engagement with and production of such films. Over thirty westerns were made in Britain before 1920[12] and then again in the 1940s, 1950s and 1960s.[13] Germany produced westerns in the 1920s and 1930s[14] and just before the Italians in the early 1960s.[15]

Furthermore, the Italians were not the first to 'disguise' their films as those of a different nation. It is arguable that they were only imitating the established tradition of American producers and investors who developed very sophisticated ways of presenting their films as European in order to beat the protectionism of national governments – nowhere was that more evident than in Italy in the 1950s.

There is an essential ambivalence around the Italian expansion as exemplified by the spaghetti western. Italian producers, directors and actors were able to shake off Hollywood's domination and successfully produce and export their own work, but one of their strategies (for the early period of the genre at least) was to do so by pretending to be Americans. This is demonstrated by the massive operation of re-naming directors, actors and films, and by the importance given to an extremely complex and sophisticated system of dubbing. There is nothing of the confidence of Hollywood in the international expansion of Italian cinema. There are no battles against protectionist laws of national governments, not instantly recognized (or systematically introduced) system of genres or galaxy of stars and no acclaimed production values and standards. Instead there is marketing improvisation, low-risk investment strategies and unexpected success.

But the ambivalence goes deeper than that. In the process of re-naming the creative personnel of the spaghettis the Italians were clearly playful, ironic and even self-sarcastic. How else are we going to interpret the fact that the director Mario Costa, after a successful career in the industry since the 1930s, called himself John W. Fordson for the only western that he directed (*Buffalo Bill, L'Eroe del Far West*, Italy/France/Germany, 1964)? Or that the well-known actor Giuliano Gemma changed his name to Montgomery Wood and the less known actress Anna Miserocchi was re-named Helen Wart? It seems to me, that when critics ridicule the spaghettis for their perceived ineptitude in imitating the American westerns (so incontrovertibly demonstrated by the 'silly' names of the films, the actors and the directors) they overlook the playfulness and the self-consciousness of the genre as well as the complexity of the spaghetti as a process of transculturation.[16] It is crucial to recognize the deep ambivalence of the industrial context of the spaghetti: the growing confidence of the Italian film industry and the powerful presence of American companies and creative personnel in Italy, the strategic decision of the industry to export the genre masqueraded as American that goes hand-in-hand with an elaborate system of re-inventing and re-launching the careers of numerous Italian actors and directors, the fact that this necessitates a playful process of re-imagining and re-negotiating national identity; and finally, that there is no evidence that audiences around the world watched spaghetti westerns as if they were genuine American movies.

## Detached heroes and collapsed antinomies

On the level of the industry the relationship between the spaghetti and the American western is by no means simple and cannot be reduced to a conflict between the hegemonic power of Hollywood's global cinema and the flexible opportunism of a commercial national cinema. The textual relationship between the two reflects such complexity and dynamism that any attempt to understand the spaghetti as a 'counterfeit' or as a clumsy attempt to imitate Hollywood becomes fundamentally reductive and misleading. The textuality of the spaghetti involves an eclectic engagement with the American western that demonstrates both an awareness of the national specificity of the latter and a desire to overcome and evade national ideologies and histories. A brief analysis of *Ringo and His Golden Pistol* and *Django the Bastard* will identify textual characteristics of the spaghetti that inform the dynamics of such eclecticism.

This essay is not an attempt to offer a definitive and all-inclusive definition of the spaghetti western as a genre. Taking André Bazin's early theorizations of the western as a starting point, this section attempts to map textual aspects of the *relationship* between the spaghetti and the American western. When Bazin wrote his seminal essays on the western,[17] and for at least another decade, Hollywood was producing more westerns than any other kind of film and their global popularity clearly surprised him:

> Its world-wide appeal is even more astonishing than its historical survival. What can there possibly be to interest Arabs, Hindus, Latins, Germans or Anglo-Saxons, among whom the western has had an uninterrupted success,

about evocations of the birth of the United States of America, the struggle between Buffalo Bill and the Indians, the laying down of the railroad, or the Civil War![18]

This might sound a bit naïve today, given the understanding that we have of Hollywood as global cinema, but what Bazin seems to suggest in his essays is that the western is not just a form of film but the essence of American cinema. The western is the American film *par excellence* because it is linked to America in crucial ways. It is made in Hollywood and follows the formal conventions of its mode of production. It is also about American history, the re-working of that history through mythical and symbolic structures, and about the moral and cultural values attached to the binary wilderness/civilization that constitutes a certain powerful version of American national identity. Furthermore, Bazin suggests that the western is best understood as a relation:

> It would be hopeless to try to reduce the essence of the western to one or other of the manifest components . . . The western was born of an encounter between a mythology and a means of expression . . .[19]

While the considerable scholarship on the subject has explored many aspects of such an 'encounter' I want to focus here on two. First, the economic, smooth and efficient strategy of integrating cinematic codes with ideological and cultural values and the historical context – the powerful and all pervasive iconography of the 'West' is an obvious manifestation of that. Second, the (male) hero of the film is also fully integrated within such a structure. Despite the fact that usually the symbolic sphere and narrative space that he occupies are marked as different and in opposition to that of the 'community' the formal system of the American western creates unbreakable links between the two – particularly important here are modes of editing and point of view structures. No matter how individual films 'work' with (and possibly even explode) the contradictions of the relationship between the hero and the community, the two exist in mutual dependency and are only meaningful in relation to each other.

The hero of spaghetti westerns, on the other hand, is profoundly an outsider. Not only in the narrative sense of being somebody who comes from outside the community but more importantly because the cinematic codes position him in a relationship of profound exteriority with the community and the ideological values attached to it.

The opening sequence of *Ringo and His Golden Pistol* is a particularly interesting manifestation of this. Ringo (defined by the ballad that accompanies the credits as a cynical, ruthless bounty hunter who only 'loves gold') arrives at a small Mexican village where a travesty of a wedding between a bandit and a local woman takes place. At the end of the 'ceremony' and in a spectacular shootout Ringo kills several members of the gang and offers the woman her freedom while he claims the reward for the elimination of the outlaws.

The first shot (see Figure 19.1) is the longest of the sequence and one of the longest in the whole film. Ringo (Mark Damon) riding his horse moves slowly towards the camera with his eyes looking straight out. As Ringo's head 'floats' closer and closer we can see his dark eyes and hair, his perfect moustache, the golden chain on his jacket, in a soft focus shot that places Ringo's body and his immaculate black clothes against the simmering foliage of olive trees. As he approaches, the camera tilts to an extreme close up of his golden pistol and with a rapid 180° pan, punctuated in the soundtrack by a dramatic chord, Ringo (with his back to the camera) enters a dusty, deserted village. The shot places Ringo in two different narrative and symbolic spaces: the beginning shows Ringo in the 'wilderness' and the end in a village road as he enters 'civilization'. Effortlessly, without a cut or through the mediation of point of view, the film moves the hero from one pole of the binary to the other. Significantly, the two narrative spaces are not structured around a tension loaded with symbolic meaning and laboriously stylized through the *mise-en-scène* and editing, but are connected through a fast movement of the camera down and across Ringo's body that momentarily centralizes the golden pistol. Ringo's physical presence, the materiality of his body and weapon, offers the means of a visual transition that overcomes the antinomy civilization/wilderness that informs the formal system of the American western.

The two following shots (see Figure 19.2) are linked in a similar fashion. Inside the church a wedding is taking place and the camera pans right from the groom to

*Figure 19.1* The opening shot of *Ringo and His Golden Pistol* (1966)

*Figure 19.2* Shots from the opening sequence of *Ringo and His Golden Pistol* (1966)

his brother standing by the door while in the background Ringo appears and starts to dismount. There is an action-match cut to a long shot of Ringo dismounting and as he turns his head the camera zooms to offer a close up of his face and then pans right to follow him as he ties his horse. Once again it is Ringo's presence and the materiality of his body that offer a visual anchor connecting the two shots and dispelling the danger of disorientation inherent in cutting from inside to outside the church without altering the direction of the camera. Ringo's image (the immaculate black clothes against the dusty, white village) is a point of connection between the two shots, a bridge between two distinct narrative spaces (inside/outside, the space of Ringo and that of his enemies) which represents an alternative strategy to (potentially divisive) shot/reverse shot structures or the use of point of view shots.

Particularly interesting is the zoom-in that the camera performs in response to Ringo's direct look in the third shot (see Figure 19.2). The camera and Ringo exist in a relationship of mutual attraction so powerful that it overcomes formal conventions of economy and motivation of movement, so self-sufficient that it stretches beyond the barriers of ideological binaries. This is further facilitated by the systematic undermining of such binaries by the film. In the first shot the connotations of garden/desert, that underpin the fundamental civilization/wilderness opposition, are totally reversed as the village is a dusty deserted area marked by the ominous bell-ringing of the soundtrack, whereas 'wilderness' is overwhelmingly green and dominated by the confident, well-groomed Ringo. The rest of the sequence, furthermore, makes a mockery of the values of domesticity, the family and religion, as the church is used for the staging of a wedding that is a clear violation of the freedom and desires of the local woman.

Equally important is the way in which the opening sequence and the film in general work with objects. While in the American western clothes, guns and horses are key iconographic elements linking specific representations with cultural and historical contexts, in *Ringo and His Golden Pistol* objects are detached from such significance and presented purely for their visual qualities. In this sequence the black clothes against the white background, the glitter of gold, the reflectiveness of the horse's plates, become a 'visual effect'. They add glamour to the *mise-en-scène* but also function as points of reference for a mode of editing that does not depend on the interactive exchange of point of view shot between characters (see Figure 19.3). Indeed, there is a total absence of such shots in the sequence until the conclusion of the shootout when Ringo surveys the defeated bandits.

Let us examine a bit closer the golden pistol that is Ringo's 'trademark'. The emphasis placed on the gun's form (what the gun is made of and what it looks like) appears to detract from its function (to shoot and kill). In a sense such a pistol is very appropriate for a film that centralizes the hero's presentation and appearance and is expressive of his vanity and obsession with gold. But Ringo uses his gun excessively as his greed for gold can only be satisfied through the effective use of the pistol. In a sense, there is no subordination of function to form but a mutual dependence – as Ringo says about his gun, 'the more I shoot it the prettier it gets'. In this sense, the golden pistol links looks and actions: to be pretty is to shoot well and vice versa. The gun, then, becomes relatively independent of narrative function and of moral or ideological codes: its function is to shoot; if this looks good then everything is fine.

What *Ringo and His Golden Pistol* demonstrates is a different relationship between elements than the one that, according to Bazin, makes the western the American film *par excellence*. The film takes the mythical aspect of the West, as well as the legacy and the conventions of the American western, as 'raw' material, which it processes and transforms. This process is an act of transculturation that defines the spaghetti and shatters the particular relationship between historical events,

*Figure 19.3* Shots from the opening sequence of *Ringo and His Golden Pistol* (1966)

ideological operations, cultural meanings and aesthetic forms characteristic of the American genre. In many spaghettis this involves a weakening of the historical referent that is also facilitated by the presence in the films of unique heroes who transcend historical and cultural specificity. This is further reinforced by the disengagement of the *mise-en-scène* from the ideological and iconographic values of the American western and the detachment of the heroes from a point of view system that could place them in an interactive relationship with other characters.

For the purposes of the present argument, the most important effect of this process is the autonomy of the hero, his emotional, moral and visual separation from the values of the community and the defining antinomies of the American western. This is emphasized by the particular way in which cycles operate within the spaghetti western. There is clear emphasis on heroes whose names are used to construct series of films: Django, Ringo, Sartana and Trinita (Trinity) are the central characters in around one hundred films. The names of the heroes are used in order to market and sell spaghettis[20] but this is not accompanied by any consistency in the way that the heroes' identities are constructed and represented. The actors portraying Django, Ringo or Sartana vary from film to film: Django has been played by Franco Nero, Anthony Steffen/Antonio de Teffé, George Eastman/

*Figure 19.3* Continued

Luigi Montefiori, George Ardisson/Sean Todd, Terence Hill/Mario Girotti who later became famous as Trinita, George Hilton, Tomas Milian, and many others. Anthony Stephen's Django in *Django the Bastard* bears little physical resemblance to the 'original' Django of Franco Nero and has a completely different character background. The confusion around nationality and the difference in the physical appearance and the defining characteristics of the heroes renders them autonomous even within cycles constructed under their name.

The detachment of the hero from textually defined communities and relevant national and generic contexts is explored with interesting implications in *Django the Bastard*. A detail of the credits is indicative of the evasive qualities of the spaghetti: Anthony Steffen/Antonio de Teffé uses the American version of his name as an actor and the Italian version as a scriptwriter. But more significantly, Django's definition as an outsider is so extreme that his relationship with the community is devoid of any interactive characteristics. Such absolute detachment places Django in a position similar to that usually reserved for the 'monster' in horror films – in other words, in a position of complete 'otherness' in relation to the other characters.[21] As Christopher Frayling has noted, there is a clear ambiguity in the film whether the hero is a real man or a ghost.[22]

However, this apparent transcendence of generic boundaries (most evident in the 'supernatural' status of the hero) should not be seen as an aberrant or simply 'trashy' one-off but as a formal exploration of the textual characteristics of the spaghetti that places *Django the Bastard* firmly within the logic of the genre. As we noted in relation to *Ringo and His Golden Pistol* the rejection of an interactive and integrating point of view system is a key formal mechanism for the textual detachment of the hero and one that *Django the Bastard* explores in a variety of ways.

The opening sequence of the film (in typical fashion the entrance of the hero in the town) consists of shots that clearly deviate from the unobtrusive, invisible positions, angles and editing patterns characteristic of a third person omniscient cinematic narration (see Figure 19.4). Oblique or unusual angles are used (the first shot of Django comes directly from above his head, the camera often stays on ground level) and objects occupy the foreground obscuring the field of vision and limiting access to Django's image. Before providing a comprehensive establishing shot of the hero (whose face is carefully concealed throughout the opening shots) the film offers two subjective point of view shots (marked by the jerky movement of the hand-held camera) that, unmediated as they are by shots of the hero's face, appear to come from nowhere. As a result the opening sequence de-naturalizes the position of the camera and draws attention to a point of view system that disconnects rather than integrates the hero with the diegetic context. In many other instances the film destabilizes the point of view system by playfully and unpredictably withdrawing access to Django's image. Indeed, one of the editing patterns used (and the most obvious way in which Django is coded as a ghost) is the temporary establishment of shot/reverse shot patterns between Django and other characters which is disturbed by point of view shots that fail to locate the hero.

But the film deviates from the clear and unambiguous distinction between 'monster' and community/normality characteristic of many horror films. Although Django is placed within a cinematic point of view system that represents him as a threat to the community, the narrative point of view (through the use of flashbacks) constructs a background story that explains his motivation and actions and reveals the 'monstrosity' of the crimes of his enemies. This is paralleled by the shifting narrative function of the point of view structure: the systematic withdrawal of Django from the field of vision in the first half of the film places him in a 'monstrous' position while in the second half it becomes essential to his elusion of the 'monstrous' crowd who are hunting him down. Such ambiguity of the monster position is another clear manifestation of the collapse of any meaningful integration of the fundamental antinomies of the American western in the system of values of the spaghetti.

The eclecticism of both films raises issues about the spaghetti western that need to be placed within a more general theoretical framework that focuses on questions of genre and national identity and cinema.

## Spaghetti western, national identity and questions of genre

The important methodological and conceptual issue that requires clarification is the exact nature of the 'national' aspect of the spaghetti and where to locate it. With reference to European westerns, there have been less than a handful of critics who have attempted to address the issue. We have already discussed Christopher Frayling's attempt to discover 'Italian-ness' in the spaghetti westerns. Motivated by his admirable desire to challenge notions of authenticity and cultural superiority that surround the American western, Frayling discovers an Italian 'essence' in the themes, the plots and the characters of the spaghettis and the peculiarity of the studio production in Italy. On the other hand, Tassilo Schneider discovers a new *Heimat* in the German western of the early 1960s which, he argues, 'offers a neatly organized narrative and social Utopia where everything is out in the open, plain to see, and under control'.[23] Schneider, while still looking for and identifying a central core of distinctly German concerns in the films that he examines, is doing so with direct reference to both the American and the spaghetti western as well as the prevalent genres in Germany at the time. The comparison to the spaghetti is particularly interesting:

> Despite the similarities, the ironic or even parodic quality that this generic 'self-consciousness' (or self-reflexivity) takes on in many Italian Westerns is missing from the May adaptations. While the 'spaghetti Western' might be said to 'deconstruct' the genre, the German films may be said to *reconstruct* it. If the Italian films might be said to be interested in 'demythologisation', the May adaptations seem to pursue the opposite objective: to construct, or reconstruct, a viable generic mythology.[24]

Although this is probably an accurate account of the German westerns and their relationship with the spaghetti, which also offers a description of the latter that is reasonably compatible with the one suggested here, it relies on a conceptualization of the national that is problematic for the spaghettis. The latter are defined in negative terms ('deconstruction', 'demythologisation'), and in contrast with their German counterparts which in the process of 'reconstructing' the genre can be seen as expressive parts and constituent components of German nationhood. This leaves the spaghetti western's relationship to national identity marked by a similar negativity, or rather a gap, a place beyond the reach of the discourse of national cinema.

A way to overcome this impasse is by revising the conceptualization of the 'national' both in terms of identity and in relation to cinema. The spaghetti western involves a re-imagining of identity that takes place beyond the boundaries of the nation and must be conceptualized in terms of a transcultural and transnational understanding of national cinema. The 'Italian-ness' of the spaghettis does not reside in hidden national cultural references, plots, themes and underlying value systems, but in the very ability of this type of film to weaken the 'national' as its referent. Two of the most obvious ways in which this happens is through the erasure of the national identity of the heroes and in terms of co-production as the main mode of production of the spaghetti.

The heroes of the spaghettis are never Italian (although there could have been plausible historical grounds for that) and rarely American. In most cases they are 'transnational' either by defining themselves as 'half American, half Mexican' like

*Figure 19.4* Shots from the opening sequence of *Django the Bastard* (1969)

*Figure 19.4* Continued

Ringo, or by avoiding to commit themselves to a specific identity as is the case with Django. If one also adds the confusion around the identity of the actors portraying the heroes it becomes evident that it is very difficult to fix national identities for the heroes of the spaghetti. The disjuncture of the history/ideology/form compound and the mutual exclusivity between the hero and the community makes it impossible to have the Great American Hero in the centre of a spaghetti – but it also makes it impossible to have a Great Italian Hero or, indeed, any national hero. The spaghettis are fundamentally about men with no name, no place and no nation.

Co-production, on the other hand, is a mode of production that is clearly transnational but one that also challenges the constructed unity and narrative of a national cinema. In the context of popular European cinema in the 1950s and 1960s, Tim Bergfelder has explored the contradictions involved in the way that co-productions were viewed by critics and national and pan-European bodies.[25] Despite the ability to compete with Hollywood and to expand international markets, co-productions were often viewed with hostility as undermining 'the project of re-centering the definition of national cinemas through critical discourses and national film policy'.[26]

The erasure of the national in the spaghetti entails a re-thinking of the 'national' of national cinema. This must involve an understanding of national cinema that does not seek to discover ways in which film cultures are defined in unique national terms but explores the ways in which such cultures engage with and transform other film cultures. It also involves the realization that on a general, structural level such processes might characterize many different national film cultures. Indeed, the 'outward' orientation of the Italian film industry in the 1950s and 1960s is by no means unique to Italy as similar tendencies are also evident in Germany, France and Britain. However, it is important to identify the specific ways in which the spaghetti operates within this transnational framework of 'outward' look.

One can be intentionally iconoclastic and argue (following Charles Musser's pioneering work on the 'origins' of the American western)[27] that the spaghetti western is closely related to a genre historically prior to the American western. Like *The Great Train Robbery* (Edwin Porter, US, 1903) spaghettis make better sense examined in terms of their relationship to the 'travel genre'. Let us briefly reconsider the conclusions of the analysis of *Ringo and His Golden Pistol* and *Django the Bastard*. A number of textual characteristics of the films (such as the detachment of the hero from the community, the importance attached to the physical presence/absence of the hero rather than invested in the embodiment and resolution of ideological tensions and contradictions, the presentation of a system of objects detached from their cultural and historical specificity) can be interpreted as fundamental components of the 'travel genre'. The mythical setting of the West, the landscape, clothes, horses and guns, the characters and the stories, simply offer an exotic background and location for the travelling 'outsiders' of the spaghetti.

The suggestion that the spaghetti western as a generic category is more meaningful in its relation to the travel film is supported by examining closer the European and Italian context. As Bergfelder notes, a variety of popular European genres in the 1960s (all sub-categories of what he calls the 'adventure film') demonstrate a 'shrinking of the world' in their perception of space:

> Amidst increasingly international casts globe-trotting through convoluted global intrigues, the notions of national and cultural identity became dispersed or reduced to empty clichés . . . Despite their nostalgic references to old-fashioned narrative traditions, the popular genres of the 1960s suggested to their audiences the possibility of a cosmopolitan and classless identity in a new world, made accessible and commodified by tourism, leisure and lifestyle consumption.[28]

The disjuncture of the history/ideology/form compound makes it possible to approach the spaghetti western as a form of 'fantasy tourism' or 'pauper's travelling', where the non-American explores the mythical and exotic Wild West in an entertaining journey that pays no respect to local codes of authenticity. Importantly, a similar sense of travelling informs many of the popular Italian films and genres of the period and also the condition of the national film industry. The mythical adventures of the peplum are obvious examples of travelling in space and time. The exploitation documentaries of the *Europe by Night* (Alessandro Blasetti, Italy, 1958) type (with films such as *World by Night* and *World by Night II*, *America by Night*, and *Universe by Night*), the documentary series initiated by *Mondo Cane* (Paolo Cavara and Gualtiero Jacopetti, Italy, 1962), the comedies of Franco Franchi and Ciccio Ingrassia (with films such as *I Due della Legione Straniera*, 1962 and *Due Samurai per Cento Geishe*, 1964) and the various spy films all involve exotic locations and travelling around the world either as the setting for adventures or as material for (pseudo)documentaries.

On the other hand, the extreme detachment of Django suggests a structural similarity, clearly explored by *Django the Bastard*, of the spaghetti with the horror genre. Significantly, it is in the late 1960s that various versions of the Italian horror film become increasingly popular domestically and eventually take the place of the spaghetti as the main exportable genre in the mid 1970s. While Sergio Leone and Sergio Corbucci made a transition from the peplum to the spaghetti western, Sergio Garrone left the spaghetti behind him and continued his career in the 'genre of the 1970s', the horror film: *La mano che nutre la morte* (Italy/Turkey, 1973), *Le amanti del mostro* (Italy, 1974) – both starring Klaus Kinski – and *Dinero maldito* (Italy/Spain/Mexico, 1978).

The spaghetti western is marked by a profound 'homelessness' – textually of the hero, contextually of an industry that transcends its 'home' and playfully rejects a 'home' identity. Such 'homelessness' is deeply ambivalent and gives expression to often contrasting emotional registers. The escape from the constraints of a home (especially within a culture that so obsessively and passionately revolves around the family)[29] is celebrated in the autonomy of the (male) hero and the exciting encounters with other cultures in a striking similarity to the travel genre. On the other hand, such homelessness can give rise to anxiety and insecurity and can represent the encounter with the other culture in tropes consistent with the horror film.

It is possible, then, to construct a generic genealogy of the spaghetti western that places the genre in a context that is simultaneously national and transnational. Such positioning not only facilitates a better understanding of the dynamics involved in the hybrid nature of the spaghetti but also establishes a frame of reference that allows for an approach that goes beyond the offensive and reductive understanding of the genre as a poor relation to the American hegemonic model.

## Notes

1 Christopher Frayling *Spaghetti Westerns: Cowboys and Europeans from Karl May to Sergio Leone*, London: Routledge, 1981.
2 Ibid., p. xi.
3 Ibid., p. 42.
4 Will Wright *Sixguns and Society: A Structural Study of the Western*, Berkeley: University of California Press, 1975.
5 Frayling *Spaghetti Westerns*, especially pp. 39–53.
6 See, for example, Gian Piero Brunetta 'The Long March Of American Cinema in Italy from Fascism to the Cold War', in David Ellwood and Rob Kroes (eds) *Hollywood in Europe: Experiences of a Cultural Hegemony*, Amsterdam: University of Amsterdam Press, 1994; Thomas H. Ghuback 'Hollywood's international market', in Tino Balio (ed.) *The American Film Industry*, Madison: University of Wisconsin Press, 1985; Ian Jarvie 'The Postwar Economic Foreign Policy of the American Film Industry: Europe 1945–1950', *Film History*, 4, 1990; Pierre Sorlin *Italian National Cinema 1896–1996*, London and New York: Routledge, 1996.
7 *Statistics on Film and Cinema 1955–1977*, Paris: Unesco Press, 1981.
8 *Statistics on Film and Cinema 1955–1977*, Paris: Unesco Press, 1981.
9 Christopher Wagstaff 'Italian Genre Films in the World Market', in Geoffrey Nowell-Smith and Steven Ricci *Hollywood & Europe: Economics, Culture, National Identity 1945–95*, London: BFI, 1998.
10 For example Iraq, Algeria, Spain, Turkey, Greece, Portugal; see *Statistics on Film and Cinema 1955–1977*, Paris: Unesco Press, 1981.
11 Frayling *Spaghetti Westerns*, p. 50.
12 Edward Buscombe and Roberta E. Pearson 'Introduction', in Edward Buscombe and Roberta E. Pearson (eds) *Back in the Saddle Again: New Essays on the Western*, London: BFI, 1998, p. 5.
13 For example, the 'straight' western *The Singer not the Song* (Roy Ward Baker, UK, 1961) starring Dirk Bogarde, *Diamond City* (David MacDonald, UK, 1949) and *The Hellions* (Ken Annakin, UK, 1961), both set in the 'Wild South' of South Africa, the Australian set *Eureka Stockade* (Harry Watt, UK, 1949).
14 *Der Todescowboy/Cowboy of Death*, 1920, *Der Kaiser von Kalifornien* (Luis Trenker, Germany, 1936).
15 *Dar Schatz in Silberbese/The Treasure of the Silver Lake* (Harald Reinl, Germany, 1962) and the Winnetou series which started with *Winnetou the Warrior* (Harald Reinl, 1963, Germany).
16 For an analysis of transculturation see Mary Louise Pratt *Imperial Eyes: Travel Writing and Transculturation*, London and New York: Routledge, 1992.
17 André Bazin 'The Western: or the American Film *Par Excellence*' and 'The Evolution of the Western', both in Bazin's *What Is Cinema?*, vol. 2, Berkeley: University of California Press, 1971, written in 1953 and 1955 respectively.
18 Bazin 'The Western: or the American film *Par Excellence*', p. 141.
19 Ibid., p. 142; for the civilization/wilderness antinomy see Jim Kitses *Horizons West*, London: Secker & Warburg/BFI, 1969.

20  See Christopher Wagstaff 'Italian Genre Films in the World Market'.
21  See, for example: Philip Brophy 'Horrality: The Textuality Of Contemporary Horror Films', *Screen*, 27: 1, 1986; Barbara Creed 'Horror and the Monstrous Feminine: an Imaginary Abjection', *Screen*, 27: 1, 1986; Andrew Tudor *Monsters and Mad Scientists*, Oxford: Blackwell, 1989.
22  Frayling *Spaghetti Westerns*, pp. 85–6.
23  Tassilo Schneider 'Finding a New *Heimat* in the Wild West: Karl May and the German Western of the 1960s', in Edward Buscombe and Roberta E. Pearson (eds) *Back in the Saddle Again*, p. 155.
24  Ibid., p. 146.
25  Tim Bergfelder 'The Nation Vanishes: European Co-productions and Popular Genre Formula in the 1950s and 60s', in Mette Mjort and Scott MacKenzie (eds) *Cinema and Nation*, London: Routledge, 2000, pp. 139–52.
26  Ibid., p. 139.
27  Charles Musser 'The Travel Genre in 1903–04: Moving Toward Fictional Narratives', *Iris*, 2: 1, 1984; Musser's argument is also considered and developed by Rick Altman in *Film Genre*, London: BFI, 1999, and Steve Neale in 'Question of Genre', *Screen*, 31: 1, 1990.
28  Bergfelder, 'The Nation Vanishes: European Co-productions and Popular Genre Formula in the 1950s and 60s', p. 150.
29  See Marcia Landy *Italian Film*, Cambridge: Cambridge University Press, 2000, especially chapter 8 '*La Famiglia*: the Cinematic Family And The Nation', pp. 205–33.

## PART V

# Action, authorship and industry

## STEPHEN PRINCE

# GENRE AND VIOLENCE IN THE WORK OF KUROSAWA AND PECKINPAH

THE SAMURAI FILM AND THE WESTERN have been enduringly popular genres in the movie culture of Japan and the United States, and the work of Akira Kurosawa and Sam Peckinpah transformed these genres, breaking with past formulations and reconstituting their elements in a manner that subsequent filmmakers could not ignore. Following Kurosawa's demonstration in *Seven Samurai* (1954) of what the period film could achieve in its highest formulation, Japanese filmmakers found themselves constrained by the vitality and humanity of the medieval warriors Kurosawa had created. While formulaic period films would continue to be made, peopled with cardboard and stereotypically idealized warriors, Kurosawa had decisively shown how limited these lesser formulations were and had thereby consigned them to cinematic purgatory.

Peckinpah's *The Wild Bunch* (1969) achieved similar results. Its 'dirty' West, peopled with psychopaths and down-on-their-luck bad guys brought to life with the most elaborate and graphic violence yet filmed, exploded the boundaries of the Western, making it very difficult for subsequent filmmakers to work in the genre because of the enormity of Peckinpah's accomplishment. How could one make a Western after *The Wild Bunch*? Many did, of course, but that film cast a shadow upon their work, a set of standards by which it would be measured and judged.

The samurai film and the Western are genres of physical action – precisely coded rituals of conflict and combat are central to each. By virtue of their attraction to these genres, Kurosawa and Peckinpah were drawn to the possibilities of an action cinema, of a kinetic and visceral kind of filmmaking that, in their work, would also be used as a vehicle for ideas. In *Seven Samurai, The Wild Bunch*, and other pictures, Kurosawa and Peckinpah made some of cinema's supremely successful and most accomplished action films. As filmmakers they were thrilled by the sensuous pleasures they discovered through imposing the templates of style upon scenes of physical action, and yet, unlike lesser filmmakers for whom effect is all, they took the kinetic cinema they were practicing to new levels by making of it a means for examining ideas, specifically, the visions of history that the samurai film and the Western could be configured to offer.

This conjunction – of action and idea – might seem a strange one in light of what action has come to represent in many contemporary Hollywood films, namely the absence of ideas. Partly due to the bloated budgets of today's Hollywood spectaculars – the average production budget, with advertising and promotion costs added, now hovers around $100 million – action has devolved to an expression of pure form – explosions, car chases, stunts, gun violence, in which the physical expression furnishes its own reason for being and constitutes a marketing hook. When divorced from moral, thematic or sociological issues, action may be used to cover plot holes or other gaps in narrative logic and to demonstrate the money invested in a production. Although Hollywood churns out an unending supply of action films, most cannot sustain the kind of philosophical and historical frameworks that infuse *Seven Samurai*, *Yojimbo* (1961), *Stray Dog* (1949), *High and Low* (1963) or *The Wild Bunch* and *Straw Dogs* (1971). Good action films are hard to make. Harder still to inflect the action so that it can point beyond itself, becoming a form that incarnates essential qualities of the world outside the cinema. Kurosawa and Peckinpah, however, did precisely this, which is why their work must loom so large in the canons of action cinema.

I have written elsewhere, and at greater length, about both of these filmmakers, and I cannot hope here, in the span of a single chapter, to capture the breadth and complexity of their work.[1] I would like, instead, to show some of the commonalities in their use of genre and in their attraction to genre and the uses to which they put screen violence. In significant ways, these commonalities point to, and are symptoms of, the informal mentor relationship that existed between the two filmmakers. Kurosawa began work as a director in wartime Japan, with his first film, *Sanshiro Sugata*, released in 1943, a full generation before Peckinpah's first feature, *The Deadly Companions* (1961). As Peckinpah moved from television work to feature filmmaking, therefore, Kurosawa's career was already in full flower, and Peckinpah was keenly attracted to a number of his films. He cited *Rashomon*, for example, as a personal favorite, probably because its vision of the relativity of truth appealed to his own sense that things in life were always mixed – love and hate, pacifism and anger, truth and falsity.

Discussing his second feature, *Ride the High Country* (1962) with *Film Quarterly*'s Ernest Callenbach, Peckinpah said he wanted to make Westerns the way Kurosawa made Westerns, perceiving, in other words, an affinity between the samurai film and the Western and between the historical visions that both filmmakers would use these genres to create. *The Wild Bunch* would be Peckinpah's *Seven Samurai*, as much for its bravura technique and story of an all-male band of adventurers in changing times as for its detailed, sensuous evocation of historical period. When an admirer of *The Wild Bunch* compared Peckinpah's editing to Kurosawa's in *Seven Samurai*, Peckinpah proudly claimed that his was better.[2] When Peckinpah was wrapping *The Wild Bunch*, the star of Kurosawa's films, Toshiro Mifune, wrote to wish Peckinpah the best of luck with his new film, and Peckinpah replied just before the film went into release with the hope that Mifune would like it and that he thought it something special.[3]

Many years later, when Kurosawa had completed yet another samurai epic, *Kagemusha* (1980), he personally requested that Peckinpah travel to Japan to attend its premiere.[4] Among Peckinpah's crew members, the inspiration that Kurosawa held for Peckinpah was openly acknowledged. Production designer Ted Haworth described a visual effect in *Cross of Iron* (1975) as 'Kurosawa Peckinpah at his best'.[5]

When Peckinpah speaks of making Westerns in Kurosawa's manner, he implies a continuity of style and genre between samurai films and Westerns. Indeed, one popular view of Kurosawa sees him as a filmmaker greatly inspired by Hollywood, borrowing from its classic Westerns for pictures like *Seven Samurai*, *Yojimbo*, *Kagemusha* and others. As I have suggested elsewhere,[6] this perception of Kurosawa's work is singularly wrong-headed because it reverses the direction in which the influences have manifestly operated (Kurosawa has inspired far more work in Hollywood than the reverse) and because Westerns and samurai films are rooted in very different cultural traditions, despite some superficial similarities between these genres. Samurai and farmers, for example, belonged to distinct and separate classes, a culturally codified relationship that is not analogous to the situation of gunfighters and farmers in the American West. Thus, the network of class allegiances that is the true subject of *Seven Samurai* (which has a band of samurai making war on their own class on behalf of a village of farmers) does not translate to the American West and could not be straightforwardly adapted for the Hollywood remake, *The Magnificent Seven* (1960).

Despite these differences of cultural emphasis, however, Peckinpah was right in sensing an affinity between his work in the Western and Kurosawa's in the samurai film. This affinity is multifaceted, and it includes aspects of formal design (as we will see, the filmmakers shared significant commonalities of image design), personal temperament and the uses to which they put their respective genres. I will first examine these latter qualities and will then consider their shared visual style and its significance for action filmmaking.

Both Kurosawa and Peckinpah were artists of crisis. They owed their best work to conditions of social upheaval. The richest periods in their careers were tied to times of great historical volatility and uncertainty. For Kurosawa, it was the aftermath of the Second World War, when Japan emerged as a ruined nation, its industries in collapse, its cities burnt and uninhabitable, its population facing dire shortages of food, clothing, and shelter. Japan had rushed headlong into the war, the culture's tradition of respect for the social hierarchy, for Emperor and nation leading few to question the disastrous course on which the country had embarked. After 1945, the Allies occupied Japan, rewrote the constitution, and instigated a series of economic and political reforms intended to provide an opening for the growth of democratic institutions. As Western influences swept in, the culture was buffeted by the anxieties unleashed by change and by the evident fact that Japan was embarked on a course whose outcome could not be clearly envisioned but which would take it far from the relatively insular and xenophobic society of the Showa period.

Kurosawa began work as a director during the war and chafed under the wartime policies of censorship. After the war, by contrast, he felt an exhilarating freedom to grow as an artist and the excitement and challenge of responding as a filmmaker and citizen to the turmoil and destruction that were the war's legacies for his homeland. From *Drunken Angel* (1948) to *Red Beard* (1965), Kurosawa's films are responses to this national predicament, efforts through art to find a way of envisioning a forward path for Japan by which it might recover from the war's devastation.

Kurosawa, then, lived through a period of great national uncertainty, and he made films that were felt responses to this turmoil. As an artist, he was keenly attuned to the signs of historical crisis – the way it was manifest in setting, behavior, action – tangible signs from which he could make images and tell stories. (The ghetto in *Drunken Angel*, the stolen gun in *Stray Dog*, the drainage reclamation project in *Ikiru* – these narrative devices and the imagery he created from them enabled Kurosawa to give his viewers panoramas of social collapse and heroic responses of rectification.) For Kurosawa, periods of historical crisis held moral significance because from them the outline of a better future might emerge. As an artist of the apocalypse, Kurosawa was drawn in his art to periods and settings that resonated with the wrenching era of Japan in its post-war years, and he found the most significant of these in the Sengoku Jidai, the hundred year period of civil war in Japan's sixteenth century, from which he made his great samurai films. *Seven Samurai*, *The Hidden Fortress* (1958), *Throne of Blood* (1957), and *Ran* (1985) are set in this period, while *Kagemusha* studies the transition from this relative anarchy to the prolonged political stability of the Tokugawa Era (1600–1868).

Kurosawa was well aware that most of Japan's samurai films were set in later periods, typically the Tokugawa period when the *ronin*, or unemployed samurai, might serve as figures of movie legend. He noted:

> I think there's a misunderstanding not only on the part of Westerners, but on the part of younger-generation Japanese as to what a Samurai is. In fact, the profession of the warrior began around the eleventh or twelfth century and most of the films that you and I see are set in the seventeenth or eighteenth century, a period of peace when the professional warrior had an entirely different code of ethics and way of behaving . . . I think I'm the only one who has ever made films about the sixteenth-century civil wars.[7]

During the Sengoku Jidai, Japan lacked a strong central authority, and rival armies commanded by regional warlords attempted to seize power and land from each other. The era is rife with epic tales of greed, bloodshed and treachery, and Kurosawa drew from this dark legacy to make *Ran* and *Throne of Blood*, which portray human affairs in terms of endlessly recurring cycles of ambition and violent destruction. The samurai in those films embody the thirst for power, treachery and overweening pride that much of the historical record points to in these wars. (In this respect, Kurosawa made significant alterations in the films' Shakespearean sources, *Macbeth* and *King Lear*, removing the moral dialectic of good and evil from the plays. In *Ran*, for example, the Lear character, Hidetora, is not a tragic figure of undeserved suffering. He is a ruthless warlord who has spilled rivers of blood.)

Significantly, these samurai do not represent the tenets of bushido, the ideals of samurai life (temperance, loyalty, austere disinterest in wealth and power) that were formulated in the Tokugawa era as a way of rationalizing the new, bureaucratic status which warriors had assumed in a time of peace.

At the same time, the Sengoku period had positive qualities that attracted Kurosawa and that enabled him to use the samurai genre to explore one of the profound issues that organizes his filmmaking, namely, the emergence of an individualism that transcends group and class. The turbulence of that era served to generate a peculiar kind of freedom – it made the class lines more permeable than they would be in the Tokugawa period, when they were explicitly codified and fairly rigid. The Sengoku period has been termed a time of change, when the world turned 'upside down', as class dissolved and 'persons in inferior positions challenged those in authority and often took mastery over them'.[8] The chaos and anarchy of the period contained its dialectical opposite, the seeds of progressive social development. As a prominent historian has noted:

> The troubled times of Japan's civil wars provided the lower classes with both the occasion for independence and the opportunities for self-advancement. While the feudal wars brought destruction and turmoil, they served also to encourage social mobility and widespread economic growth.[9]

Kurosawa observed, 'The warrior class had much more freedom at that time; a peasant could still become a warrior then',[10] a process that he dramatized in *Seven Samurai* and *The Hidden Fortress*. Kurosawa's work addresses the cultural contradictions that adhere to an ethic of individualism, superimposed on Japan by the Occupation authorities, within a group-oriented culture, and in his samurai films, the Sengoku period offered him an ideal historical framework for portraying these contradictions, as well as a parallel with the social disruptions of his own era.

Kurosawa felt the resonance between his period and the Sengoku period in the dialectical combination of chaos and destruction against the potential for freedom and social development. The physical action of his samurai films is an index of these processes, of a world shaken to bits and where the harbingers of change are everywhere apparent, most especially in the specter of firearms, which herald: a) contact with the West (firearms were introduced by the Portuguese in 1543 and replicated by Japanese technicians) and the incipient threat of cultural change which such contact carried; b) the obsolescence of the samurai and his traditional weaponry of sword and lance; and c) the mechanization of violence and war and the wholesale slaughter of the twentieth century which the new technologies of violence would make possible. In *Seven Samurai*, all of the heroes who perish do so by gunshot (no one can touch them with a sword). In *Yojimbo*, the villain wields a pistol, and his clan has allied itself with the future (a merchant economy and the incipient forces of capitalism that it represents). *Kagemusha* climaxes with the Battle of Nagashino in 1575 in which a powerful samurai clan was wiped out by volleys of musket fire in a harbinger of the future. The epic massacre in *Ran*, and the fratricidal treachery it instigates, is waged with musket fire. The epic massacres portrayed in

*Kagemusha* and *Ran* are clearly intended by Kurosawa as commentaries on contemporary violence and warfare, and it is significant that both films derive from a period of great darkness and pessimism in his social outlook, when the dialectic of positive and negative that he found in the Sengoku period had resolved to starker perceptions of negativity and loss. It was only in the final period of his filmmaking, comprised of *Dreams* (1990), *Rhapsody in August* (1991), and *Madadayo* (1993), that he transcended this thoroughgoing pessimism.

As did Kurosawa, Peckinpah reached his career zenith during a period of protracted historical turbulence. This included the savagery of the Vietnam War and the wrenching domestic unrest that it caused, the assassinations of the Kennedys and Martin Luther King, the Tate-LaBianca killings, civil rights protests, and the anti-establishment youth movement.[11] The upheavals of the late 1960s, in particular the various forms of political violence and social unrest, confirmed his sense of the centrality of violence and aggression in human affairs and a conviction that American society would founder, and democracy be lost, unless a way could be found to constructively channel these darker impulses. More specifically, Peckinpah was keenly attuned to the zeitgeist and was a passionate critic of contemporary American politics. He bitterly opposed the Vietnam War, supported black Americans in their quest for civil rights, and considered Nixon, Haldeman, and the rest of that administration to represent a kind of contemporary fascism that was subverting American democracy.

His disenchantment with contemporary America helps to fuel his love for the Western and his ability to use it as a critique of the present day. Like Kurosawa's samurai films, his Westerns portray heroes caught in times of historical transition that are eroding the conditions of their life, and the only choices open to these characters lie in how they will lose, on their terms or on the terms of the suits and politicians who are taking over the country. As Peckinpah's vision of American history darkened, the bumbling and relatively benign bankers of *Ride the High Country* (1962) give way to the murderous railroad baron Harrigan who incites the opening massacre in *The Wild Bunch* and the assassination-sponsoring Sante Fe Ring of business and political leaders in *Pat Garrett and Billy the Kid* (1973). In his contemporary life films, these character types become even more corrupted and ruthless, killer apes in suits that populate *Bring Me the Head of Alfredo Garcia* (1974), *The Killer Elite* (1975) and *The Osterman Weekend* (1983).

In Peckinpah's Westerns, the signs of historical eclipse are manifest, forces that are undermining the lives of the heroes, outlaws and renegades whose primitive codes of honor he set against the barbarism of Vietnam-era America. As signposts of urbanization and the modern era, automobiles kill, nearly kill, or are used to torture the heroes of *The Ballad of Cable Hogue* (1970), *Ride the High Country* and *The Wild Bunch*. As outlaws, the Wild Bunch is running out of space and time in a modernizing West. Significantly, the Bunch must leave the US for Mexico in order to find some of the old frontier freedoms. In 1913, the Bunch is poised on the very threshold of a modern world that will institutionalize violence and mechanize it so that it can be practiced on a much wider scale than a renegade band of outlaws can muster. Thus, when the Bunch makes its last stand, the outlaws find themselves fighting with a machine gun and hand grenades, as Peckinpah amplifies the scale of violence and includes technologies that threaten to burst the boundaries of the Western and transmogrify it into the war film. Unlike the Bunch, Pat Garrett aims to grow old with the country, but that film's narrative structure forecloses on his efforts. The film begins and ends with his murder by the Santa Fe Ring, which had hired him years before to kill the Kid, and this narrative structure ensures that all of Garrett's efforts to adjust to a changing West are tempered by the viewer's awareness of his ultimate failure. Moreover, Peckinpah considered Garrett's killing a prototype for the killings of JFK and Martin Luther King, and in an early version of the film he included a title card certifying this conviction.

Both Peckinpah and Kurosawa developed particular and complex relationships with genres centred on an evocation of the past. Peckinpah's pessimism and bitterness were more thoroughgoing than Kurosawa's, at least until *Kagemusha* and *Ran*, but in the Western he had found an ideal form, as Kurosawa did in his sixteenth century period films, for exploring conditions of historical trauma and crisis, and cultural contradiction (the individual and the group in Kurosawa, renegade honor and institutional corruption in Peckinpah) such that the symbolic strategies of art offered felt resonance with the conditions of his own life. This is one of the reasons that the genre films by Kurosawa and Peckinpah are so extraordinary. The samurai film and the Western were not just a set of story conventions and movie situations for these filmmakers. They believed deeply in these genres, regarded them as holding the truth of myth, and identified closely and in exquisitely personal terms with the historical periods of sixteenth century Japan and the American frontier. Their intense personal conviction charges the material of their films with the urgency of that which, for the filmmaker, is very real.

Kurosawa was keenly aware of the warrior tradition in his culture and closely identified with it. His father was a military instructor, and Kurosawa recalled that his childhood home had a samurai atmosphere. Young Akira trained in the art of kendo (swordfighting) and recalls a summer in the country where he fished, swam, and hiked, as a time when he lived 'a kind of mountain samurai's existence'.[12] He was delighted to learn that his family had an ancestor who was a famous warrior. He compared his brother to a 'masterless samurai'.[13] Years later, when he was an apprentice director on location in the Hakone Mountains, the sight of extras in costume fired his imagination with the imagery of medieval Japan:

> In the morning as we rode along in our car in the wan light of pre-dawn, we could see the old farmhouses on both sides of the road. Farmers dressed as extras, wearing their hair in topknots, clad in armor and carrying swords, would emerge from these houses, throw open the huge doors and lead out their horses. It was as if we had really been transported back into the sixteenth century. They would mount and ride along behind our car. Rolling along past massive cryptomeria and pine trees, I felt that these, too, were part of that ancient era.
>
> When we arrived at the location, the extras led their horses off into the forest and tethered them to trees while they built a huge bonfire. The

farmers gathered around the fire, and in the dim forest their armor caught
gleams of light from the roaring red fire. It made me feel that I had stumbled
on a band of mountain samurai in the woods.[14]

This is the imaginative response of a filmmaker for whom the past is not a remote
part of history but a living and sensuous reality coterminous with the present. The
samurai genre permitted Kurosawa to live inside this mythic cultural space and to
make it as palpably real as his filmmaking powers permitted.

The same process of deep personal identification with a genre underlay
Peckinpah's work and is one source of its greatness. Peckinpah was born in 1925
into a family of prominent California lawyers, and he spent his summers at his
grandfather's ranch in the Sierra Nevada mountains. The rugged hills still contained
pockets of frontier personality, with towns named Coarsegold and Finegold (a
naming tradition he carried over into his films) and with old-time cowboys and
prospectors still hanging around with tales about the old days that fired young Sam's
imagination. At his grandfather's ranch, he learned to hunt, ride, and herd cattle,
and he imbibed a spiritual outlook on the wilderness in which the 'high country'
was a form of divine bounty and furnished the terms for measuring a person's
integrity and morality. Those youthful summers connected Peckinpah, in his own
mind, with the old frontier as a still-living presence.

But just as the American frontier would close and the Wild West pass out of
existence, so, too, did Peckinpah's portion of it. He assumed that his grandfather's
ranch would always remain in the family, but, upon the death of Denver Church,
Sam's mother sold the property, and Peckinpah did not learn about this until it was
too late. The loss of the ranch carried tremendous emotional consequence for him
because it symbolized the loss of his boyhood and his ties to the old West. It
strengthened his sense that he was out of time, that he did not belong to the modern
age, and that the world he identified with was gone. Thus, his emotional and artistic
gaze would, in significant respects, be a backward looking one. 'I grew up on a
ranch. But that world is gone . . . I feel rootless, completely. It's disturbing, very
much so. But there's nothing you can do about it, nothing.'[15] This sense of loss
intensified his identification with the Western genre because that form was about
a world that no longer existed. Indeed, when the Western emerged in literature,
painting and theater toward the end of the nineteenth century, the wilderness was
already disappearing. Fredric Remington understood this, and it drove him to paint
the people and places that were then vanishing. When the movies appeared in 1895,
the frontier had been declared closed by the Bureau of the Census for a full
five years. The Western is, at its heart, a nostalgic genre because it is about a
world that was eclipsed. Peckinpah understood this, and he understood how it
approximated the conditions of his own life:

> I am a child of the old West. I knew at first hand the life of cowboys, I
> participated in some of their adventures and I actually witnessed the dis-
> integration of a world. It was then inevitable that I should speak of it one
> day through a genre which is itself slowly dying: the Western.[16]

The artistic relationship that Kurosawa and Peckinpah shared with their respective genres carries these significant cultural, conceptual, and emotional components, and these are given form in the material of their films by a shared visual style, a similar deployment of the techniques of filmmaking. To a large extent, it was their attraction to the physicality of violence and its visual rendering that shaped the emergence of a shared visual strategy for capturing it. Indeed, the formal structure of their work provides one of the clearest examples of Kurosawa's informal mentoring of Peckinpah. The Japanese director was famous for shooting with telephoto lenses and multiple cameras (covering a scene with three and four cameras running simultaneously). Because telephoto lenses capture a narrow angle of view (i.e. less of the area before the camera), they facilitate the use of multiple cameras since they make it easier to prevent the cameras from seeing each other. Peckinpah, too, came to rely on multi-camera shooting, especially as it facilitated montage editing by furnishing a larger variety of optical perspectives. To this extent, he also employed telephoto lenses, though he combined them with zooms and wide angle lenses in ways that Kurosawa never did. Furthermore, his camera set-ups were more unpredictable than those of Kurosawa, who tended to favor cameras set up at right angles to one another. As a result, the optical changes from shot to shot in Peckinpah's films are more audacious, harder to anticipate, and keep the viewer visually off-balance, qualities that are at their most accentuated in *Straw Dogs*. Nevertheless, the multi-camera approach, facilitated by telephoto lenses, was an invaluable way of filming action and of creating montages from the resulting footage, and it was the method of choice for both filmmakers.

This continuity of formal design has its greatest relevance for Kurosawa and Peckinpah's choreography of violence. Once again, as mentor, Kurosawa furnished the inspiration. Of greater significance, he wrote the textbook for modern movie violence, and in this regard, he altered the face of contemporary film. That textbook is contained in a brief scene in *Seven Samurai*, where the hero, Kambei (Takashi Shimura), kills a thief who has kidnapped a child. Kurosawa shot the scene with multiple cameras running at different speeds. He then intercut the footage – five slow motion shots of the dying thief crashing through a door, rising up on tiptoes, and falling to the ground – with normal speed shots of horrified onlookers.

So many of the essential discoveries have been made here by Kurosawa about how to use slow motion to accentuate moments of violence. The slow motion inserts must be brief; otherwise the more natural tendency for slow motion – to impede the flow of movement and bog it down – comes to the fore. By keeping the slow motion shots brief, Kurosawa can easily slip into and out of the decelerated moments and – here is the really crucial point – he can give them a kinetic charge – can energize them – with reference to the surrounding, normal speed material. In this regard, Kurosawa's initial use of slow motion in his first film, *Sanshiro Sugata*, is instructive because there Kurosawa merely dropped one slow motion shot into the body of a normal speed scene. The slow motion insert is interesting, effectively unexpected, and vivid, but, because he is using only one shot, Kurosawa does not create a dynamic contrast of different frames of time and space by extending them across the length of an edited sequence, as he does in *Seven*

*Samurai*. In *Sugata* the slow motion shot has a minimal relationship to the surrounding material. In *Seven Samurai* the slow motion is an integral part of the structure. The editing weaves it into an extended relation of counterpoint across the sequence and its dramatic action. Watching the two scenes, you feel the difference. In *Sanshiro Sugata*, the effect is surprising and interesting. In *Seven Samurai*, it is *exciting* and *dynamic*. Kurosawa showed filmmakers how to reference slow motion with normal speed action – by using multiple cameras and montage editing – and how this technique could extend and intensify moments of violence – extend them because it prolonged them, intensify them because of the perceptual shocks caused by the misaligned frames of time and space.

The consequences for world cinema have been enormous. Although Kurosawa would show only an occasional interest in this kind of editing, subsequent filmmakers found this brief scene a fascinating visualization of movie violence. They studied it, copied it, and, in the years since, have endlessly elaborated it in ever-grander terms. And, although it was director Arthur Penn in *Bonnie and Clyde* (1967) who first brought this stylistic template to American film, it would be Peckinpah who would elaborate it at longer and greater lengths and who would become the filmmaker whose name was synonymous with slow motion violence. Searching for a memorable way to launch his gangsters into movie history, Penn turned to Kurosawa's work in designing the slaughter scene that climaxes *Bonnie and Clyde* (1967), as automatic weapons cut down the gangster couple. Penn shot the scene with four cameras running simultaneously and at different speeds to produce a montage in which he could intercut various degrees of slow motion to make the depicted violence look both spastic and balletic. Penn said that this approach to filming the climax of the movie came to him as a kind of epiphany, all at once, that he knew instantly how to film it and that this realization derived from having seen Kurosawa's work.[17]

Released in 1967 and hugely popular with audiences, *Bonnie and Clyde* offered the most elaborately stylized cinema violence yet seen, and it brought Kurosawa's technique into the mainstream, setting off a race among subsequent filmmakers to outdo each other in elaborating and exaggerating this technique. The following year, in *The Wild Bunch*, Peckinpah determined to surpass Penn. To make sure of this, he had a print of *Bonnie and Clyde* shipped to his Mexican location for screening a few days prior to the start of principal cinematography on *The Wild Bunch*, and, indeed, he filmed two slaughter scenes opening and closing the film that used slow motion in a multi-camera montage to extend the ferocity of the action to a then-unprecedented degree. Peckinpah's elaboration of Kurosawa's design was to amplify its scale, taking Kurosawa's brief shot series and Penn's brief montage and extending these into an edited sequence of much greater duration and complexity. Under Peckinpah's instructions, editor Lou Lombardo intercut multiple lines of action to create a fractured and kaleidoscopic presentation of the elaborate gun battles that open and close the film. The results for cinema were epochal.

From the elaboration given to it by Peckinpah and Penn and because of the visibility and popularity of their work, Kurosawa's technique – of multi-camera montage incorporating slow motion – has now passed to virtually every contemporary filmmaker seeking to make screen violence vivid and poetic. It is not an exaggeration to say that the device has now become a canonic structure of contemporary cinema, widely dispersed across a range of films and filmmakers on an international scale. The device has become an enduring rhetorical form, the essential rhetoric of contemporary movie violence.

Moreover, it has trapped many filmmakers drawn to it to the extent that the rhetoric has become its own end, a fetish of technique. It did not trap Kurosawa, however. He maintained only an occasional interest in slow-motion montage, and while he continued to study the phenomenon of human violence, in films like *Ran*, he refused to present it so as to glorify it or to pump it up with a false grandiloquence. Instead, he saw where violence has taken humanity and where graphic violence would take cinema and its filmmakers. He refused to go there, and so his work transcends its own flamboyant violence because Kurosawa retained a moral control and perspective over his material and style.

Peckinpah, too, became disillusioned with the rhetoric of movie violence that he had done so much to popularize. When he made *The Wild Bunch*, he believed in the idea of catharsis, that viewers might purge socially destructive impulses in the safe realm of art to the benefit of society as a whole. This idea had a compelling force for him at a time of great national turmoil – the Vietnam War, the race riots, and the political assassinations of the late 1960s. Thus, as a filmmaker bringing graphic violence to cinema in a way that was changing the medium – Hollywood films until then had been sanitized by the Production Code – he could believe that the terrifying visions of violence and aggression that he brought to life with his cameras could benefit society as a whole by showing the truth of violence – its capacity to destroy all of the finer things in life – a truth that had been suppressed by the sanitized quality of prior decades of American film.

However, many viewers reacted to the violence in *The Wild Bunch* and *Straw Dogs* with exhilaration and manifest aggression, responses that were contrary to Peckinpah's intended meanings in those films. Reflecting upon this, toward the end of his career Peckinpah retracted his previous belief in the cathartic value of violent art. In his last film, *The Osterman Weekend*, he suggested that the effects of violent media content lay in inducing aggression rather than mitigating it.

Action films tend to be violent films, and with their status as seminal figures in the history of screen violence, Kurosawa and Peckinpah are, therefore, a set of parent figures for action cinema. They have conceived and choreographed some of the most extraordinary action sequences in the history of cinema. These include the battles between samurai and bandits in *Seven Samurai*, the frenzied horseback riding through the demonic forest in *Throne of Blood*, the massacre of Hidetora's retainers and the burning of his castle in *Ran*, the prolonged assault on David and Amy Sumner's house in *Straw Dogs*, and the extended train robbery and bridge blowing sequence in *The Wild Bunch*. The latter sequence is a model of elegance in its construction and design. Like these other scenes, its editing does not impose a particularly fast pace upon the action, and this point in reference to the work of Kurosawa and Peckinpah is worth stressing in light of the furious pacing typical of contemporary action films, which has tended to strip action of the organic significance it has in the work of Kurosawa and Peckinpah. The acceleration of pace in contemporary filmmaking is as much a result of the industry's use of nonlinear editing systems as it is of audience taste. Nonlinear editing systems, like the Avid, enable editors to access and manipulate complex arrays of shots more easily than is possible using a traditional linear approach, and one result of this change in the technology of film editing has been a general movement toward faster pacing.[18]

Because of the shift toward electronic, nonlinear editing, action films today have become synonymous with fast-paced storytelling, and a detrimental consequence, alluded to earlier, has been the substitution of action or violence for narrative logic, with explosions and gun battles helping to finesse gaps in story or character motivation. By contrast with this present state of affairs, Kurosawa and Peckinpah, who both were renowned for being extraordinary editors, were not typically directors of fast-paced movies. In fact, they tended to favor a slow pace. *Throne of Blood*, *Ran*, *Yojimbo*, *The Wild Bunch*, and *Straw Dogs* all feature a deliberate, measured, unhurried pacing, which enables Kurosawa and Peckinpah to carefully construct a moral and thematic framework within which the extraordinary violence of their films can occur. The violent episodes in each grow organically from the story situations and help to thematize the narrative issues. In *Ran* and *Throne of Blood*, for example, the violence of the sixteenth century samurai wars symbolizes the cruelty and aggression of humanity within a cosmic frame, with the worlds in those films viewed as if by a Buddha in tears. The slaughter of the merchants and gangsters in *Yojimbo* is a neo-Confucian wish-fulfilling fantasy about the end of a corrupt, money-driven economy. The alliance in battle between the farmers and samurai in *Seven Samurai*, across a gulf of class hatred and animosity, holds out the utopian possibility of an organic community in a world rent by predation and exploitation. The aggression in *Straw Dogs* is Peckinpah's cautionary fable about the negatively transforming consequences of rage and hostility. The trend-setting violence in *The Wild Bunch* accorded with Peckinpah's sense of the historic brutality of the frontier and the expansion of the American empire over the bodies of weak or minority peoples, and with his sense of the twentieth century as a century of mechanized, wholesale slaughter. The setting of the film in 1913 gestures toward the outbreak of the First World War: Pike Bishop's outlaw gang uses a machine gun – the weapon of the First World War – to mow down its enemies. Peckinpah had inflected his West so that it became a prelude to the massive warfare of the new century.

Peckinpah and Kurosawa, then, did not simply innovate in the filmic means used to visually present scenes of physical violence. Certainly, they were masterful at showing violence in memorable and haunting ways. The human porcupine at the end of *Throne of Blood*, the thug strangled and nearly decapitated by an animal trap in *Straw Dogs* are flamboyantly imaginative images that stay in a viewer's mind. But it was their *attitude* toward violence that gave them the power and skill to show it in horrific and haunting ways. This is to say that they were modernist filmmakers, not postmodernist ones for whom movie violence is so much artifice and special effect. Kurosawa and Peckinpah shared an abiding sense of the realities of human violence. They might turn their cameras upon it, make visual poetry of it, but for them violence was not simply an effect or a movie image. Their images derived from this world, which is to say that they were socially engaged filmmakers whose art was a response to qualities in life that they found intolerable. As a result, the violence in their films is embedded in a coherent moral and philosophical framework that gives it meaning and that makes of it a commentary on this world. The slow pacing they imposed upon their work through its editing is an essential means of relating action and violence to context and commentary. The violent episodes in Kurosawa or Peckinpah do not rush viewers past problematic narrative areas in ways too fast to invite contemplation. Quite the opposite in fact – their violence typically functions as parable and commentary.

To accomplish this contextualization of action and violence, they were drawn to the athletic genres of the samurai film and the Western, and each perceived in his respective genre a configuration of artistic and historical elements that resonated with the filmmaker's existential situation in the lived present. By inflecting the elements of genre, Kurosawa and Peckinpah imaginatively redrew the boundaries of the present age by making a strategic incursion into an aesthetically rendered past. Because they identified in deep personal terms with the materials of their genre, the work they created has uncommon power and urgency. Their methods and their results redefined the samurai film and the Western and furnish exemplary models of the finest achievements of which action cinema is capable.

## Notes

1  See my book-length studies of these directors: *The Warrior's Camera: The Cinema of Akira Kurosawa*, revised and expanded edition, Princeton, NJ: Princeton University Press, 1999, and *Savage Cinema: Sam Peckinpah and the Rise of Ultraviolent Movies*, Austin: University of Texas Press, 1998.
2  Sam Peckinpah Collection, Margaret Herrick Library, Los Angeles – correspondence folder no. 35, letter of April 4, 1968.
3  Sam Peckinpah Collection, general-miscellaneous folder no. 127, letters of December 30, 1968 and June 23, 1969.
4  Sam Peckinpah Collection, general-miscellaneous folder no. 175, letters of February 28, 1980 and March 25, 1980.
5  Sam Peckinpah Collection, *Cross of Iron* script notes, folder no. 26, letter of February 5, 1976.
6  Stephen Prince 'The Legacy of Kurosawa Outside Japan', lecture, Simon Fraser University, British Columbia, October 2000; Stephen Prince *The Warrior's Camera*, pp. 13–18.
7  Dan Yakir 'The Warrior Returns', *Film Comment*, 16, November–December 1980, p. 56.
8  Neil McMullin *Buddhism and the State in Sixteenth-Century Japan*, Princeton, NJ: Princeton University Press, 1984, p. 63.
9  John Whitney Hall 'The Castle Town and Japan's Modern Urbanization', in John W. Hall and Marius B. Jansen (eds) *Studies in the Institutional History of Early Modern Japan*, Princeton, NJ: Princeton University Press, 1968, p. 172.
10  Yakir 'The Warrior Returns', p. 56.
11  I explore the significance of the late 1960s for Peckinpah's work in *Savage Cinema*, pp. 27–45.
12  Akira Kurosawa *Something Like an Autobiography*, trans. Audie Bock, New York: Alfred A. Knopf, 1982, pp. 64–8.
13  Ibid., p. 81.

14  Ibid., p. 114.
15  Dan Yergin 'Peckinpah's Progress', *The New York Times Magazine*, October 31, 1971, p. 92.
16  Sam Peckinpah Collection, folder no. 96, *Le Devoir* interview, October 10, 1974.
17  Gary Crowdus and Richard Porton 'The Importance of a Singular, Guiding Vision: An Interview with Arthur Penn', *Cineaste*, 20: 2, Spring 1993, p. 9.
18  http://www.nonlinear3.com/brandt.htm. This article compares traditional film editing and electronic, nonlinear editing by comparing six feature films (three films per method) on a shot-by-shot basis in order to explore each method's impact on the visual structure of a feature film. Among the differences uncovered are those of pacing, with digital editing tending toward the imposition of a faster pace (as measured by shot length).

## Chapter 21

## TONY WILLIAMS

## *THE DIRTY DOZEN*
## The contradictory nature of screen violence

R OBERT ALDRICH'S *THE DIRTY DOZEN* is a film many worlds removed from Steven Spielberg's *Saving Private Ryan* (1998) in terms of questioning the supposed nobility of the Second World War as 'the good war'. Both during its time of release and up to the present day, the film has suffered from critical disclaim as being little better than a cynical, nasty production, playing upon gratuitous feelings of male violence. Forced to witness the hanging of a frightened young serviceman by his military superiors, Major John Reisman (Lee Marvin) finds himself 'volunteering' for a mission behind enemy lines commanding soldiers either facing execution or life imprisonment. He has to whip these reluctant men into shape so that they will merge into a fighting unit who will delay the German High Command immediately before D-Day. Reisman's anti-authoritarian attitudes eventually strike a responsive chord so that the Dozen see the American brass as their real enemies as well as the Germans. Reisman's men include a diverse number of dangerous elements such as former gangster Victor Franko (John Cassavetes), violent religious fanatic Maggot (Telly Savalas), angry black soldier Jefferson (Jim Brown), who has defended himself against racism, as well as briefly commissioned officer Wladislaw (Charles Bronson), who has 'fragged' his superior when he attempted to run away from battle with medical supplies, and gentle accidental killer Samson Posey (Clint Walker). After successfully forming this group into a fighting unit, Reisman leads a night assault on a French chateau, which is temporarily disrupted by Maggot's assault on a German female. The remnants of the Dozen finally succeed in incinerating as many of the German High Command and their ladies as possible by trapping them in a cellar. Only Reisman, military policeman Sergeant Bowren (Richard Jaeckel) and Wladislaw survive the mission. They return to a cynically manipulative military command they feel the utmost disdain towards. The film ends with Wladislaw's remark that 'killing generals could get to be a habit'.

Strongly reliant on the male testosterone imagery represented by actors such as Lee Marvin, Ernest Borgnine, Charles Bronson, Jim Brown, Telly Savalas,

Ralph Meeker, and Richard Jaeckel, the film superficially appears to be little better than a macho action movie. However, *The Dirty Dozen* rewards any study of screen violence especially in studies of contradictory responses on the part of different spectators. It also represents a particular product of screen authorship on the part of its director which bears a particular relationship to his other films and to the cultural and historical era in which it emerged.

On its initial release in 1967, Robert Aldrich's *The Dirty Dozen* provoked conflicting reactions. While establishment critics such as Bosley Crowther condemned the film for its supposed glorification of violence, audiences responded entirely differently. The film was a box-office success, enabling director Robert Aldrich to fulfill his long-cherished dream of purchasing his own studio. As Stephen Prince notes, *The Dirty Dozen* was the box-office success of 1967,[1] appearing in the same *annus mirabilis* year of screen violence that saw the release of Arthur Penn's taboo-breaking *Bonnie and Clyde*.[2] Soon to reach his final days as *New York Times* film critic, Bosley Crowther reacted to the film by expressing unease with both changing times and new depictions of screen violence. Describing *The Dirty Dozen* as 'a blatant and obvious appeal to the latent aggressiveness and sadism in undiscriminating viewers', Crowther believed it was little better than a 'glorification of killing by hardened criminals who are willfully trained by a hard-bitten major (Lee Marvin) with an evident sadistic streak'.[3] He ended his original article by lamenting the presence of Sergio Leone's *For A Few Dollars More* (1965) and the Italian Western which he described as 'socially decadent and dangerous as LSD'.[4]

However, a week later the eminent critic learned that he was out of touch with several of his readers, who related both *The Dirty Dozen* and *For A Few Dollars More* to the changed historical conditions of the Vietnam era. Although reflecting subjective generational reactions, Crowther's respondents expressed dissatisfaction with a venerable critic clearly out of touch with changing values. A wife, teacher, and mother complained about Crowther's callousness in criticizing 'a picture that shows the "inner sensitivities" of criminals who are given a chance to redeem themselves by performing a "productive" mission'. For them, Crowther's attitudes would not be shared by 'people whose families may be involved in Vietnam'.[5] Another reader criticized Crowther's squeamishness towards a Leone film which appeared in a society 'which reads panegyrics to the Vietcong-killing power of the M-16 rifle'.[6] Such responses are not necessarily accurate. Nor do they demolish Crowther's original arguments. Other than their initial meeting and dance with the 'tarts' supplied for their entertainment, it is doubtful whether the dozen, as represented by John Cassavetes, Charles Bronson, Jim Brown, and Donald Sutherland, exhibit any 'inner sensitivity' during the film. Clint Walker's Samson Posey is perhaps an exception, as is lost cause Maggot (Telly Savalas). Furthermore the Vietnam associations of *For A Few Dollars More* are extremely arbitrary and difficult to assign to a film made in a different cultural environment.

While *Bonnie and Clyde* is now firmly established within the critical canon, *The Dirty Dozen* is usually regarded as beneath any form of serious critical consideration. Aldrich's film is still ignored or disdained both by feminists and male critics such as Jonathan Rosenbaum in *Movies as Politics*. But Penn's movie gains from the director's prestigious position in the auteur canon, something Aldrich never exactly achieved – at least in America. In contrast to Aldrich's film, *Bonnie and Clyde* represents that lost Camelot world of a 'once and future Hollywood' when European New Wave artistry and American technology reached its highest, if temporary, collaboration. Aldrich's film, by contrast, utilizes a particular Hollywood generic framework without inserting the self-conscious sophistication of the European New Wave into its framework.

*The Dirty Dozen* is also an extremely ambivalent film. It never delivers any explicitly educational position but instead represents the supposed good war as an ugly arena of violence in which everyone, including fictional characters and audiences, ends up tarnished and corrupted by participating (voyeuristically or not) in the spectacular bloodshed of a supposedly 'good cause'. This may be less due to the deliberate use of gratuitous violence but more to the director intuitively recognizing the complex nature of violent representation in real life and fiction. Furthermore, the film's cynical approach to its subject matter may also owe much to an implicit ideological critique of the 'good war' philosophy dominating most classical Hollywood war movies prior to the Vietnam era. We must also remember that Aldrich himself belonged to a 1930s cultural generation that faced the post-war onslaughts of Cold War and McCarthyist attempts to roll back New Deal philosophies and practices. During this period, cultural New Deal movements became demonized by conservative Republicans in a manner foreshadowing the condemnation of the 1960s by Ronald Reagan and Margaret Thatcher. Aldrich had previously worked with talents such as John Berry, Charles Chaplin, John Garfield, and Joseph Losey, whose involvement in wartime patriotic left-wing movements resulted in blacklisting.

The public may have been ready for a film such as *The Dirty Dozen* at this particular time. As well as growing dissatisfaction with American military involvement in the Vietnam War, a previous 'forgotten war' of the earlier decade may have also haunted public consciousness. The American losses suffered during the Korean War actually exceeded what would be the final tally of the Vietnam War. Although Cold War witch hunts effectively silenced any criticism of President Truman's self-styled 'police action', a growing wave of discontent slowly developed in America which would come to question the ideologically affirmative images of Hollywood's traditional war film – despite the success of John Wayne's *The Green Berets* (1968).

European audiences and critics apparently viewed a different film from their American counterparts. As Aldrich himself stated:

> The whole nature of war is dehumanizing. There's no such thing as a nice war. Now American critics completely missed that, so they attacked the picture because of its violence, and for indulgence in violent heroics. Now fascinatingly, European critics all picked up on the parallel between burning people alive and the use of napalm, whether they liked the picture or not. They all got the significance of what was being said.[7]

*The Dirty Dozen* echoes the anti-authoritarian attitudes common to many of Aldrich's films.[8] It also develops the iconoclastic spirit of his earlier anti-Second

World War 'good war' film *Attack!* (1957), which criticized the American military bureaucracy during the Battle of the Bulge and questioned the very nature of heroism. *Attack!* also contained a striking performance by *The Dirty Dozen*'s future star Lee Marvin in the role of a corrupt colonel manipulating the conflicting forces under his command for his future civilian political career. *The Dirty Dozen* not only subverts traditional elements within the Hollywood war movie but also contains traces of a *film noir* mood Aldrich had experimented with in *World for Ransom* (1954), *Kiss Me Deadly* (1955), *Attack!* (1956), and *The Garment Jungle* (1957).

Apart from two major book length studies, Aldrich remains either a generally neglected figure in contemporary criticism or superficially dismissed in popular discourse as a macho purveyor of violence in very much the same manner as Sam Peckinpah and John Woo are generally treated.[9] Aldrich shares the same set of problems as these two directors in terms of his responsibility and complicity involving the representation of screen violence. *The Dirty Dozen* appears, on the surface, to be a film which legitimizes the use of violence. But the very nature of its legitimization remains questionable during several scenes which are by no means as celebratory of the mayhem and murder occurring on the screen as certain critics believe. However, Aldrich faces similar problems affecting other directors employing the spectacular techniques of screen violence.

As Stephen Prince points out, Scorsese and Peckinpah often found it difficult to disengage themselves:

> from the sensuous gratifications of assembling spectacularized violence. While one should not doubt the sincerity of their belief in their own stated intentions, one may still be amazed at their blindness to their own artistic complicity in stimulating the aggressive reactions of their viewers.[10]

However, one may ask whether the problem really lies in 'artistic complicity'. Features endemic to the spectacular representation of violence, especially in the war genre, may also be responsible in subverting the best intentions of directors to result in misunderstood readings.

Many critics tend to condemn the spectacular representation of violence on screen, blaming directors and audiences for gratuitous indulgence. But the actual situation is more ambivalent. In an interesting essay Claudia Springer argues that:

> to feel excitement while viewing a representation of violence is not necessarily to desire to participate in brutality. To blame viewers for responding with a rush of adrenaline to a film's combat sequence is to lose sight of the difference between actuality and representation.[11]

Indeed, combat sequences 'have to be understood contextually in relation to how the narrative surrounding them mediates the sheer spectacle of combat'.[12] Although Springer argues that 'any effective anti-war film must counteract the ambiguous signifying system of the combat sequence with an unequivocal and decisive narrative',[13] the very spectacular nature of violent representation may frequently undermine and contradict the narrative's intentions. Such a situation affects any war film, especially those having an anti-war message. Commenting on *Platoon* (1986) which certainly does not *intend* to glorify war, Springer notes that not only 'might different spectators respond in widely disparate ways, but an individual spectator could experience conflicting yet simultaneous responses that include both pleasure and displeasure and complicate a coherent reading'.[14] Writing at the time of *The Dirty Dozen*'s release, Joseph Morgenstern noted a specific cultural and historical context determining screen violence whereby the Second World War 'brought back primitivism which had been on the skids since 1918, and its popularity today has not discernibly declined'. Morgenstern characterizes *The Dirty Dozen* as an 'ingeniously primitive film' which 'spends more than two hours on an outlandishly detailed setup for a half-hour payoff in which the GI demolition squad really demolishes, the charges explode, the Kraut machine guns chatter, and the victims (including lots of screaming females) cry themselves a river of blood'. Morgenstern then concludes by defining these features as 'trash' which has 'the bad grace to give itself away'.[15] Although noting an interesting historical framework conditioning both the genre and the film, Morgenstern never explores this context of cultural primitivism but instead falls back on the problematic 'gratuitous violence' discourse that Charles Barr found in British contemporary reviews of Peckinpah's *Straw Dogs*.[16]

The attack on the mansion is certainly the spectacular climactic moment that *The Dirty Dozen* builds up to. But it is not as gratuitous as Morgenstern believes. Although Aldrich has often been associated with violent films, the cultural nature of his apocalyptic violence has never received appropriate treatment in most studies of his work. Despite the prevailing tendency to associate apocalyptic violence with the end of the millennium,[17] this feature occurs in earlier decades.

The apocalyptic violence contained in the climactic scenes of *The Dirty Dozen* has its origins both in Aldrich's *Kiss Me Deadly* as well as contemporary American fears concerning the nuclear age. As many critics have noted, *Kiss Me Deadly*'s baroque visual style parallels its content. Arnold and Miller aptly point out that the film finally:

> becomes *film noir* at its most paranoid. The camera shifts, cranes, hides, and scurries – a creature of the night, peering into and out of the shadows in a world which, the film suggests, perhaps *deserves* the cleansing purgation of the Bomb.[18]

The film also contains several metaphors from a classical world which are not only redundant in a post-war anti-intellectual context but have also become corrupted by the dangerous world of the Atomic Age. Among these are Pandora's box, Lot's Wife, and the head of the Medusa. The Medusa reference initially appears superfluous. But it also occurs in a striking stream of consciousness passage in William Styron's bleak modernist novel *Lie Down in Darkness* (1951) which appeared four years before Aldrich's film. Although the director may not have been familiar with this work, it contains striking parallels to the world of *Kiss Me Deadly*, namely in its critique of a now-redundant code of Southern gentility and the decline of formerly dominant classical and humanist values in a world heading towards the destruction represented by the atomic bomb. As the doomed Peyton rushes head-long towards suicide, her stream of consciousness monologue uncannily reproduces both the individual and social dilemmas of a new apocalyptic age. Peyton reacts at a young scientist's description of the atomic bomb as 'Man's triumph' with the following comment:

> the science is getting so cluttered with offshoots that it begins to look like Medusa's hair – unwilling to accept the historical determinism, tragic as it is to the spirits of neo-humanists, the historical determinism – may I not need even say propriety, to use your word? – they are unable to accept the pure *fact* in all its beauty.[19]

Peyton's final thoughts echo the violently apocalyptic climax of *Kiss Me Deadly*: 'Perhaps, I shall rise at another time, *though I lie down in darkness and have my light in ashes*' (italics mine).[20] The post-war world presented by William Styron rapidly moves towards an apocalyptic individual and universal destruction symbol-ized by the image of the atomic bomb. It is the ruthless creation of a scientific establishment which is now devoid of any supposed humanitarian claims.

The American political establishment which dropped the bomb on two cities at a time when the Japanese were seeking peace terms was as ruthless as the mili-tary bureaucracy depicted in *The Dirty Dozen*. These latter figures cynically practice manipulative 'use and abuse' principles rather than following the 'good war' philos-ophy of traditional Hollywood movies. Indeed, they represent the dehumanizing nature of the Korean War military and political establishment which could have used the bomb at any time despite the hazards facing their own men, to say nothing of the millions of civilians who would have died in the process. Far from being a macho war film, *The Dirty Dozen* actually employs significant cultural resonances as well as the fear of the atomic bomb (which *could* have been used in Korea) to engage in deconstructing the premises of the traditional war movie.

Aldrich began his deconstruction of the traditional Hollywood war film in *Attack!* by using the dominant visual motifs of *film noir*. In *The Dirty Dozen*, he relies less on this visual style but more upon the doomsday imagery of apocalyptic violence signified by the atomic bomb in the closing scenes of *Kiss Me Deadly*. The bomb is a man-made scientific invention in the earlier film; the Dozen represent its human counterpart. They are the product of a special form of military operation sanctioned by the American High Command who are responsible for a destructive scenario in which every member of the team may not survive. General Worden's (Ernest Borgnine's) cynical use of his men foreshadows the manipulative tactics of General McKenzie (Richard Widmark) in *Twilight's Last Gleaming* (1977), who not only has no concerns for his military team placing the nuclear bomb outside the silo but will also place responsibility for the murder of the President on his team of trained assas-sins. As Raymond Durgnat points out, both the Korean War and the atomic bomb were important influences on both 1950s *film noir* as well as the later decade's obses-sion with violence and death. Among the various influences he sees involving 1960s cinema entering into its 'Jacobean period' is 'a post-Hiroshima sense of man as his own executioner, rather than nature, God or fate'.[21]

Several films dealing with the Korean War appeared both during and after the conflict. But none, with the exception of Samuel Fuller's *The Steel Helmet* (1950) and Lewis Milestone's *Pork Chop Hill* (1959), approached the complex and varied number of cinematic representations evoked by the Vietnam War. Durgnat's comments concerning cinematic sublimation of the Korean War in 1950s *film noir* foreshadow the different generic representations such as the western, urban gangster, and science fiction which also indirectly treated Vietnam themes during the actual time of the conflict.[22] Furthermore, at the time, the Korean War nearly resulted in a nuclear holocaust on the part of the competing world powers involved in the actual conflict.[23] Since Aldrich had already critiqued the military bureaucracy in *Attack!* for its cynical attitude towards servicemen and presented a society heading towards nuclear destruction in *Kiss Me Deadly*, the infernoesque violence characterizing the latter third of *The Dirty Dozen* may be regarded as the work of a director warning his audiences about the consequences of post-war apocalyptic violence. By using the 'good war' period of traditional Hollywood war movies, the director actually delivers a message applicable to both Korean and Vietnam eras.

Scholar and Korean War veteran Paul Edwards has also noted the Korean War's alternative imagery to traditional Hollywood Second World War depictions. Despite ideological attempts to revive this legacy as in Steven Spielberg's *Saving Private Ryan* (1998), Edwards points out that because the lesson of the Korean War:

> was so contrary to what we want to remember, Americans have repressed it. They have decided that it has nothing to tell us. But, as many veterans will tell us, until America faces the Korean War and provides for it a place in the American myth, the awesome experience will have been primarily in vain.[24]

If Aldrich reworked classical *film noir* to reflect the apocalyptic culture of the postwar Korea era in *Kiss Me Deadly*, he does the same thing to the traditional Hollywood war film in *The Dirty Dozen*. The original script by Nunnally Johnson reflected the type of traditional war movie Aldrich wished to distance himself from. He employed Lukas Heller as an additional scenarist to bring the movie more in line with his creative concerns. The result is a more violent film containing an anti-authoritarian discourse also present in his other works.[25] The Allied and German establishments are condemned as equally corrupt. But they both ironically exist in environments of enlightenment and culture which are now as contaminated as the declining classical imagery facing an apocalyptic doomsday scenario in *Kiss Me Deadly*. Mike Hammer begins a mission which eventually results in his death in the post-Atomic Age.[26] If Reisman is more streetwise than Mike Hammer, the Dozen represents twelve extensions of the original thuggish persona represented by Ralph Meeker in the original film. It may not be entirely coincidental that Meeker plays a supporting role in *The Dirty Dozen* as a reluctant Army psychologist who is silently skeptical about the military establishment's fascination with the entire mission. Both Reisman and his men are condemned to a macabre duty. The High Command hopes the Dozen will not only perform their mission successfully; they also expect the team to become their own executioners in a no-win situation, thus saving the establish- ment from performing the type of grotesque capital punishment witnessed in the film's prologue. Although the theme of prisoners sent on dangerous wartime missions had already appeared in films such as Roger Corman's Second World War drama *The Secret Invasion* (1964) and the forgotten Korean war film *The Nun and the Sergeant* (1962), what makes *The Dirty Dozen* distinctive is a creatively hybrid mixture of elements. For example, many commentators have noted that the Dozen place the German High Command and their ladies in a position similar to Jews in gas chambers. Reisman not only orders his men to pour gasoline down the air vents but also grenades. His methods evoke the napalm used in Vietnam. Yet, although napalm is popularly associated with the Vietnam War, it was first used extensively in the Korean conflict.[27] The violent conflagration in the latter part of *The Dirty Dozen* may not be due to deliberately manipulative gratuitous violence but more to a director seeing ironic connections between conflicts American ideology wished to keep apart: the Second World War, Korea, and Vietnam. Although ex-Marine Lee Marvin recognized the dark side of the Second World War imagery employed in the film, they are also inherent within Korean and Vietnam War contexts.[28] *The Dirty Dozen* is thus a highly complex film using neither the didactic premises of pro- war or anti-war film formats. It contains an inherent complexity in many scenes, raising it far above the level of a formula production.

The pre-credits scene contains several ominous images, opening with the mili- tary execution of a scared young soldier. Unlike the original novel we are given no clue as to the nature of his crime. The only feeling conveyed by Aldrich is the mechanical nature of an institutional operation and the question as to what actual purpose this display serves. Since Reisman appears at the ceremony with feelings of unease and disdain on his face, it is evident that the spectacle is as much a lesson for him as the audience who watches. When the condemned man goes through the trapdoor Aldrich abruptly cuts to a low-angle shot of his feet plunging towards both the screen (and the audience). Reisman then leaves as the chaplain begins a useless funeral oration. Before he attends his next appointment with the American High Command, Major Armbruster (George Kennedy) warns him about the meeting, 'John. This time it's serious. You've got to co-operate.' Aldrich depicts the High Command in the positions of judges at a military court martial, inhabiting a room whose classical architecture and busts parallel not only the castle prison containing American condemned prisoners but also the German chateau he will attack later in the film. We never learn why Reisman faces the position of his forced mission, only that he 'is very short on discipline'. It is evident that his superiors see the mission as a convenient excuse to dispose of twelve condemned men as well as a subordinate officer who has become a nuisance to them.

Reisman takes on the mission as a military Christ figure whipping his twelve disciples into a cohesive team. Aldrich displays subversive religious imagery not only in the 'Last Supper' sequence prior to the actual mission but in paralleling Reisman with his earlier 'hero' Mike Hammer whose knightly quest to rescue the

Great Whatzit's Holy Grail and free Velda ends in not only his own destruction but that of the rest of the world. The world of *The Dirty Dozen* is not only as cynical and violent as those depicted in *Kiss Me Deadly* and *Attack!* but one where Western values of culture and humanitarian enlightenment have become entirely corrupted. When Reisman and Wladislaw enter the French chateau they encounter a civilized world of manners and Palm Court orchestra. But it is one inhabited by the ruthless representatives of a military machine also responsible for the holocaust. If the poems of Christina Rossetti are now the last echoes of a 'world for ransom' heading towards destruction, the chateau and its inhabitants represent the twentieth century perversion of an earlier Enlightenment era whose rationality now results in genocide. Aldrich subtly links connections between these two eras in one significant scene. When the Judas figure of Maggot enacts his perverted form of romantic sadism upon the helpless German female (Dora Reisser), Aldrich discreetly reveals an eighteenth century miniature in the same room. It depicts a cultured gentleman dancing with a female in a seductive pose. By killing her, Maggot begins an apocalyptic 'Judgement Day' which ushers in the film's climactic mayhem.

After the German High Command and their ladies have fled into the wine cellars like Jews trapped in gas chambers, Reisman tells one of his men guarding the French servants and captured Germans to 'Feed the French and kill the Germans'. Although this scene appears humorous, it has macabre overtones. In a sequence edited from the film, the French obviously witnessed Reisman's men performing the very same functions as the S.S. and Wehrmacht in murdering captured prisoners. They would see no difference between their 'liberators' and their captors. One other ironic scene which remains in the film reveals the servants running outside the chateau and then retreating inside to immediately experience the same holocaust as the trapped Germans.

Later, when Reisman orders gasoline to be poured down the air vents into the cellars, the previously compliant Sergeant Bowren (Richard Jaeckel) cannot believe this order. He pauses and questions it until he sees that his superior officer is deadly serious. This scene not only represents a significant questioning of the implications of the entire mission on the part of a subordinate character but also parallels those atrocities, both past and present, committed by 'our side'. The My Lai massacre committed by American soldiers on helpless Vietnamese civilians was only a year or so away. Finally, when the remnants of the Dozen act like football spectators and cheer on Jefferson (played by football professional Jim Brown in his prime) as he runs and drops the grenades down the air vents, most contemporary audiences participated. However, on hindsight, what Jefferson is really doing is participating in an atrocity. This image not only parallels Aldrich's later visions of the corruption of sport in American society in films such as *Ulzana's Raid* (1972) and *The Longest Yard* (1974) but also implicates audiences in the action. By cheering Jefferson, spectators are guilty of condoning actions usually committed by the so-called 'enemy' but now performed by representatives of 'our side'. The Dozen perform their particular version of a holocaust condoned by the American high command. Only three survivors remain at this apocalyptic Judgement Day scenario: 'savior' Reisman and two other disciples who may represent Aldrich's cynical view of the

Holy Trinity – Father, Son (Wladislaw) and Holy Ghost/Voice or voice of the Father (Sergeant Bowren). 'Trinity' was also a code name of the Manhattan Project. The holocaust reference is by no means accidental. When Reisman earlier spoke to Wladislaw in his prison cell, the latter read an issue of *Stars and Stripes* with the feature article titled, 'What it means to be a Jewish Girl'. The Dozen's violent mission not only represents an Allied version of the holocaust but also implicitly evokes apocalyptic imagery associated with both the Korean and Vietnam conflicts.

Although many other arguments could be made against reading the film in the usual manner of a macho-orientated violent movie, certain problems do exist which prevent an 'against the grain' interpretation from gaining acceptance. Both then, and now, audiences usually enjoy the spectacular violence appearing in the film rather than interrogating the reasons as to why it is used, evoking an endemic problem involving the representation of violence on screen. This particularly affects films which attempt to take alternative positions but end up by becoming over-whelmed by the very feelings they attempt to oppose. Prince notes that fiction may not be an appropriate arena for those directors who attempt to condemn violence.[29] Aldrich makes the attempt by utilizing a cultural and historical framework which situates his use of violence in a particular critical perspective. But Springer aptly notes:

> combat sequences have to be analyzed in relation to their narrative frame-works, especially in a film that was intended to make an antiwar statement, for only a strong narrative can articulate an antiwar position. When a film attempts to turn the spectator against war by presenting a bloodbath, it paradoxically can evoke unconscious drives and desires that take pleasure in vicarious danger. Films that rely on combat sequences for their antiwar message are in effect attempting to be anti-combat, and that strategy is as riddled with contradictions as would be an anti-musical film comprised exclusively of song and dance.[30]

This observation may explain the difference between what Aldrich attempted and the usual audience response to *The Dirty Dozen*.

The film attempts to provide a very different perspective on the very subject of war, conditioned by Aldrich's radical 1930s sympathies as well as the changing times of the Vietnam era. But it remains trapped within certain conventions affecting the representation of screen violence as well as the tendencies exhibited by several audiences who prefer to view it within a certain context of pleasurable masculine (and non-interrogative) entertainment. *The Dirty Dozen* attempts to challenge these conventions but not entirely successfully. Like the reduction of the original Dozen to one survivor Wladislaw and the military's incomprehension of what they have actually done, the mission is only partially successful. Like those unfeeling British officers who gleefully told their enlisted men who had served on the European Front, 'Now for a crack at the Japs', Robert Webber's General Denton looks forward to Wladislaw's return to active duty. After Wladislaw's remark, 'Boy! Oh Boy! Killing officers could get to be a habit round here' (affirmed silently by

Reisman), the camera changes to Aldrich's well-known climactically ambivalent overhead shot suggesting future uncertainty. Three revealing colors of red (hospital blanket), white (sheets), and blue (Sgt Bowren's dressing gown) remain in the screen. They depict not only Aldrich's ironical perspective concerning a bureaucracy responsible for the savage nature of violent destruction but may also involve a critique of those audiences preferring gratuitous indulgence in violence rather than exploring the real implications. While certain audiences may prefer the color red, Aldrich also displays those two other colors of the US national flag, giving viewers the opportunity to draw their own conclusions.

## Notes

1 Stephen Prince *Screening Violence*, New Brunswick, NJ: Rutgers University Press, 2000, p. 12.
2 For critical responses to this film both past and present see John G. Cawelti (ed.) *Focus on Bonnie and Clyde*, Englewood Cliffs, NJ: Prentice-Hall, 1973, and Lester Friedman (ed.) *Arthur Penn's Bonnie and Clyde*, New York: Cambridge University Press, 2000.
3 Bosley Crowther 'Movies to Kill People By', *Screening Violence*, pp. 51–2. This article originally appeared in *The New York Times*, July 9, 1967.
4 Ibid., p. 53.
5 Bosley Crowther 'Another Smash at Violence,' *Screening Violence*, p. 54. The article originally appeared in *The New York Times*, July 30, 1967.
6 Ibid.
7 Pierre Sauvage 'Aldrich Interview', *Movie*, 23, 1976–7, p. 59.
8 See, for example, Edwin T. Arnold and Eugene L. Miller *The Films and Career of Robert Aldrich*, Knoxville, TN: University of Tennessee Press, 1986; Alain Silver and James Ursini *What Ever happened to Robert Aldrich? His Life and His Films*, New York: Limelight Editions, 1995.
9 For an interesting analysis of the very complex nature of screen violence both past and present see Stephen Prince *Savage Cinema: Sam Peckinpah and the Rise of UltraViolent Movies*, Austin: University of Texas Press, 1998.
10 Prince *Screening Violence*, p. 199.
11 Claudia Springer 'Antiwar Film as Spectacle: Contradictions of the Combat Sequence', *Genre*, 21, 1988, p. 479.
12 Ibid., p. 480.
13 Ibid., p. 480.
14 Ibid., p. 485.
15 Joseph Morgenstern 'The Thin Red Line', *Screening Violence*, p. 48. The article first appeared in *Newsweek*, August 28, 1967.
16 Charles Barr '*Straw Dogs, A Clockwork Orange* and the Critics', *Screen*, 13: 2, 1972, pp. 17–32.
17 Christopher Sharrett (ed.) *Crisis Cinema: The Apocalyptic Idea in Postmodern Narrative Film*, Washington, DC: Maisonneuve Press, 1993.
18 Arnold and Miller *Films and Career of Robert Aldrich*, p. 43.
19 William Styron *Lie Down in Darkness*, New York: Random House, 1951, pp. 366–7.
20 Ibid., p. 386.
21 Raymond Durgnat 'Paint It Black: The Family Tree of the Film Noir', in Alain Silver and James Ursini (eds) *Film Noir Reader*, New York: Limelight Editions, 1996, p. 51. The essay first appeared in *Cinema* (UK), 1970. Durgnat also points out that one of *film noir*'s cycles 'climaxes soon after the Korean War with the shock to Americans, of peacetime conscripts in action' (p. 50). Although the Korean War resulted in relatively few distinctive literary and cinematic representations in contrast to the Vietnam War, there are many parallels

between both conflicts. As W. D. Ehrhart and Philip K. Jason succinctly observe, 'while those who fought the Korean War were closer in age and temperament to the veterans of World War II, the Vietnam War seems to have been a catalyst for many of these poets, releasing pent-up feelings that had perhaps been held in check by the personal and cultural stoicism bequeathed to them by their generational older brothers and by the restraints forced on public utterance by the atmosphere created in the 1950s by Senator Joseph McCarthy and the House of Un-American Activities'. See W. D. Ehrhart and Philip K. Jason (eds) *Retrieving Bones: Stories and Poems of the Korean War*, New Brunswick, NJ: Rutgers University Press, 1999, p. xxxvi. Certain veterans of the Korean conflict compare contemporary attitudes to the conflict as a 'structured absence'. 'The Korean War has not just been forgotten, it has been repressed. During the watershed years of the 1950s and 1960s the Korean War was the counterpoint to the patriotic memories of World War II. It challenged the easy existence of the immediate post-war years, and the death of the dream of "peace in our time"'. See Paul M. Edwards *A Guide to Films on the Korean War*, Westport, CT: Greenwood Press, 1997, pp. 44–5. For parallels between both conflicts see Philip K. Jason 'Vietnam War Themes in Korean War Fiction', *South Atlantic Review*, 61: 1, 1996, pp. 109–21.

22  For the diverse number of generic references used in cinematic treatments of Vietnam see Jean Jacques Malo and Tony Williams (eds) *Vietnam War Films*, Jefferson, NC: McFarland & Co., 1994.

23  For the dangerous escalation involving the use of nuclear weapons in the Korean War see Jon Halliday and Bruce Cumings *Korea: The Unknown War*, New York: Pantheon Books, 1988, pp. 88, 90, 121–8, 152–4; William Steuck *The Korean War: An International History*, Princeton, NJ: Princeton University Press, 1995, pp. 131–2, 145–6, 239–40; Bruce Cumings *Korea's Place in the Sun: A Modern History*, New York: W.W. Norton & Company, 1997, p. 272.

24  Edwards *Guide to Films on the Korean War*, p. 45.

25  See, for example, Ian Jarvie 'Hysteria and Authoritarianism in the Films of Robert Aldrich', *Film Culture*, 22, 1961, pp. 95–111.

26  For a highly perceptive review of *Kiss Me Deadly* and its deliberately hybrid style see G. Cabrera Infante 'Spillana Macabra' in Infante's *A Twentieth Century Job*, London: Faber & Faber, 1991, pp. 59–60. Infante only significantly refers to Aldrich's use of the camera as 'an aesthetic cyclotron' in which he has 'bombarded the absurd truculences of Spillane with inner action protons, megatons of baroque photography and electrons of movement and mobile actors: he has achieved – as the French magazine *Cahiers du Cinema* so well said – the first film of the Age of the Atom' (p. 60). In the opening paragraph Infante comments that he found *Kiss Me Deadly* on a double-bill with a documentary *Hiroshima*, 'as if the latter were a presage of what would happen if the criminals in the former film had won'. The American military in *The Dirty Dozen* are not only *alter egos* to the German High Command in the French chateau but are also more criminal than those they send on a deadly mission. I am grateful to Infante's translator Kenneth Hall for bringing this reference to my attention.

27  See Jason 'Vietnam War Themes in Korean War Fiction', pp. 117–18; Cumings *Korea's Place in the Sun*, pp. 289–90, 293–5; Ehrhart and Jason *Retrieving Bones*, p. xxvii. 'Short of atomic weapons, America rained a fiery destruction from the air with another new weapon, napalm, and later broke massive dams to flood Korea's northern valleys. This is the most disturbing aspect of the Korean War, difficult to write and read about; it is what accounted for the remarkable civilian death toll of more than two million.' (Cumings *Korea's Place in the Sun*, p. 290).

28  'It's not just the men in the chalet who were Nazis; the women were part of it too. I liked the idea of the final scene because it was their job to destroy the *whole* group and maybe in some way speed up the demise of the Third Reich. We glorify the 8th Air Force for bombing cities when they killed 100,000 people in one night, but remember there were a lot of women and children burned up in those raids.' Arnold and Miller *Films and Career*

*of Robert Aldrich*, p. 127. Marvin had earlier defined his character as being in essence one of the Dozen 'without having committed the crime, but I think he ends up being a tremendously sympathetic character even though it's done under the auspices of being brutal and rough and all of those values'. See Allan Eyles 'The Private War of Robert Aldrich', *Films and Filming*, 13: 13, 1967, p. 6. However, the reaction of Richard Jaeckel's Sergeant Bowren at Reisman's orders to drop the napalm down the vents articulates quite a different reaction.

29 'Filmmakers who wish to use graphic violence to offer a counterviolence message – that is, to use violence in a way that undercuts its potential for arousing excitatory responses in viewers – may be working in the wrong medium. The medium subverts the goal.' Prince *Screening Violence*, p. 29.

30 Claudia Springer 'Antiwar Film as Spectacle: Contradictions of the Combat Sequence', *Genre*, 21, 1988, pp. 486–7.

## Chapter 22

## PETER KRÄMER

## 'IT'S AIMED AT KIDS – THE KID IN EVERYBODY'

### George Lucas, *Star Wars* and children's entertainment[*]

WHEN *STAR WARS* WAS RELEASED in May 1977, *Time* magazine hailed it as 'The Year's Best Movie' and characterized the special quality of the film with the statement: 'It's aimed at kids – the kid in everybody.'[1] Many film scholars, highly critical of the aesthetic and ideological preoccupations of *Star Wars* and of contemporary Hollywood cinema in general, have elaborated on the second part in *Time* magazine's formula. They have argued that *Star Wars* is indeed aimed at 'the kid in everybody', that is, it invites adult spectators to regress to an earlier phase in their social and psychic development and to indulge in infantile fantasies of omnipotence and oedipal strife as well as nostalgically returning to an earlier period in history (the 1950s) when they were kids and the world around them could be imagined as a better place. For these scholars, much of post-1977 Hollywood cinema is characterized by such infantilization, regression and nostalgia.[2] I will return to this ideological critique at the end of this essay. For now, however, I want to address a different set of questions about production and marketing strategies as well as actual audiences: What about the first part of *Time* magazine's formula? Was *Star Wars* aimed at children? If it was, how did it try to appeal to them, and did it succeed? I am going to approach these questions first of all by looking forward from 1977 to the status *Star Wars* has achieved in the popular culture of the late 1990s. I will then look backward from 1977 to the long period of gestation of the *Star Wars* project and its gradual transformation into a children's film, that is a film primarily, but not necessarily exclusively, addressed to children. Finally, I am going to return to the year 1977 and examine the initial reception of *Star Wars* as an adventure for the whole family and as a model for Hollywood's future.

### 'Let the wookiee win': living in the late 1990s *Star Wars* universe

When the *Star Wars* prequel *Stars Wars: Episode 1 – The Phantom Menace* was released in May 1999, *Variety* declared it to be 'the most widely anticipated and heavily hyped film of modern times' and argued that 'those most looking forward (to it) . . . are mostly people – now in their 30s – who were kids when episodes four through six were released'.[3] While thus acknowledging that the original trilogy had most powerfully affected children, the *Variety* reviewer expressed considerable disappointment that the new instalment was not aimed primarily at the adult fans those children had become, but 'directly at a new crop of children, who are familiar with the originals via video or the recent "Special Edition" hardtop reissues'. This focus on children accounted for the weakness in story construction and characterization the reviewer detected in *The Phantom Menace* for its excessive cast of extraterrestrial creatures and its 'pretty standard-issue tyke hero', the 9-year-old Anakin Skywalker. Highly critical of the film, the reviewer nevertheless predicted that it would become 'one of the biggest' hits of all time and also acknowledged the genius of the man behind the saga: 'Lucas may again assert his status as the shrewdest marketer among filmmakers, if he can capture the new generation while still taking the old-time fans along for the ride.'

Indeed, in September, *Variety* predicted that *The Phantom Menace* might gross about $500 million in foreign markets, thus becoming the fourth highest grossing film in foreign markets in history, after the romantic action epic *Titanic* (1997, $1,233 million) and the science fiction adventures *Jurassic Park* (1992, $563 million) and *Independence Day* (1995, $503 million).[4] That same month, the film's domestic box office take was reported to be $422 million, making it the third highest domestic grosser in history (after *Titanic*, $600 million, and the original *Star Wars*, $461 million in various releases), and its broadcast fee was projected to be $80 million.[5] Eventually, *The Phantom Menace* grossed $920 million worldwide ($430 million domestically and $490 million abroad), which was twice as much as the box office take of its nearest competitors in 1999, the sci-fi actioner *The Matrix* and the supernatural thriller *The Sixth Sense*.[6] Together with the several billion dollars generated through promotional tie-ins and merchandising as well as TV, video and DVD sales, the box office returns would seem to vindicate Lucas's decision again to make what is first and foremost a children's film. In fact, in response to early criticism from fans and reviewers who had seen test screenings, Lucas right from the start had been upfront about the nature of *The Phantom Menace* and of the *Star Wars* saga as a whole. In the week before the film's release, for example, the *New York Post* reported:

> Lucas . . . shot down complaints that [*The Phantom Menace*] . . . is too much of a kiddie flick, with goofy, computer-generated characters and prolonged, video-game-like battles. 'I don't think it's any more kid-friendly than any of the other *Star Wars* films,' he said. '*Star Wars* is basically a serial for children – that's what it's always been.'[7]

A few months after the release of *The Phantom Menace*, I began an undergraduate course on Spielberg and Lucas with the question: What role has the *Star Wars* phenomenon played in your life? The response of my (mainly British) students, most of whom had not even been born when the first *Star Wars* film was released, astonished me. Whether they had spent their childhood in Britain, South Africa, Arab countries or the States, they had all been aware of *Star Wars*. They had seen the films, often in the wrong order, on video (regular or pirate) or TV or at the cinema during one of numerous re-releases; and, more importantly, they had listened to the soundtrack, read the books, played with the toys, dressed up as the characters, acted out scenarios from the films and invented new ones. Even the few students who did not like *Star Wars* said that their childhood had been completely overshadowed by it, that the saga's characters, stories and catch phrases had been a primary reference point for their peer group and also within their families. For better or for worse, my students reported that in effect they had all been inhabiting the *Star Wars* universe when they were kids, and to a large extent they were still living in it today.[8] Somewhat paradoxically, having grown up, many now felt, much like *Variety*, that *The Phantom Menace* was too childish, yet this did not take anything away from the overall impact of the saga.

This anecdotal evidence about the centrality of *Star Wars* for childhood in the 1970s and 1980s, is supported by all kinds of statistical evidence of the presence of *Star Wars* products in the contemporary cultural marketplace – the continued success of the films on TV and in various video, DVD and cinema re-releases, the dozens of *Star Wars* novels and related books which have been published since the 1970s,[9] and the sale of many billions of dollars worth of products based on, or tied in with, the films. For example, by the late 1980s *Star Wars*-related toys had grossed an estimated $2 billion, and helped to reshape the toy industry by moving fantasy action figures to its very centre.[10] *Star Wars* has also been ranked very high in polls of all-time favourite films. As early as 1978, for example, *Star Wars* came second after *Gone With the Wind* in a Minneapolis student poll, and in June 2001 it was at number seven in the Internet Moviedatabase's 'Top 250 movies as voted by our users'.[11]

All of this evidence points towards the conclusion that, at least in the Western world, since the 1970s several generations of children have grown up with *Star Wars*, and they have maintained their attachment to the *Star Wars* universe into adulthood, passing their fascination on to their own children. Surveys taken during the highly successful theatrical release of the special edition of *Star Wars* in February 1997 indicated that a third of the audience were families, many of them no doubt parents revisiting their own childhood experiences and sharing them with their children.[12] Indeed, my students had moving stories to tell about the ways in which the experience of *Star Wars* was complexly interwoven with familial relationships – from the girls who unsuccessfully fought with their older brothers for the choice parts in *Star Wars* playacting (everyone wanted to be Han or Darth Vader, no one wanted to be the wookiee) to the boys who established a secret code with their fathers, commenting on their mothers' interference with a resigned 'Let the wookiee win' (because they get very angry and dangerous when you don't). So how did *Star Wars* achieve such a dominant position in children's lives? And was this George Lucas's original intention?

## From action-adventure to children's film: the evolution of *Star Wars*

When in 1974/5 George Lucas first began to publicize the production of *Star Wars* in the trade and general press, the film was variously described as an 'outer space action adventure', a 'sci-fi pic', a 'space fantasy', 'a space opera in the tradition of Flash Gordon and Buck Rogers', or '*2001* meets James Bond'.[13] That this was not exactly going to be a film suitable for children is indicated by comments such as the following: '[The film] deals with sci-fi on a sociological level, how technology affects humans.'[14] In an interview with the *Los Angeles Times* in June 1976, Lucas stated that the soon-to-be-completed film was 'aimed primarily at 14- and 15-year-olds', and interviewer Charles Champlin added that it would be 'a high-energy, Boy's Own adventure'.[15] Reinforcing this emphasis on male teenagers, the production notes for *Star Wars* quoted the preface Arthur Conan Doyle wrote for his novel *The Lost World* (1912):

> I have wrought my simple plan
> If I give one hour of joy
> To the boy who's half a man,
> Or the man who's half a boy.[16]

The market research programme which was initiated in the summer of 1976 soon confirmed that, judging by people's responses to its title and a brief description of the film, *Star Wars* was most likely to appeal 'primarily (to) young male moviegoers, ages 25 and under', while its emphasis on technology and battle provoked a negative reaction from females and older people. So as to counteract such resistance, the advertising campaign which was developed from this research aimed to highlight the film's human characters and its mythical dimension in addition to its action and special effects. The advertising was to be placed in media (such as newspapers, magazines, radio and television) which would 'impact primarily against 12 to 24 year old moviegoers and, secondarily, against moviegoers ages 25 to 35'.[17] Thus, in 1976, market researchers failed to consider *Star Wars*' potential appeal to the sub-teen audience, and Lucas himself, who was later to declare that he saw *Star Wars* as a children's movie, was reluctant to foreground this fact in the initial publicity for the film. Where did the market researchers' blindspot and Lucas's reluctance stem from?

Until the 1960s, Hollywood had considered its audience to be potentially everyone, although it was well known that the most regular moviegoers were teenagers and young adults under 30 (who bought up to three-quarters of all tickets). Rather than concentrating exclusively on this core audience, Hollywood studios focused most of their energies on producing inclusive films, which aimed to offer something for everybody without offending anyone. The industry's self-regulation through the Production Code tried to ensure that every film was suitable for even the youngest members of the audience. Indeed, audience surveys for the film industry's trade organization, the Motion Picture Association of America (MPAA), in the 1950s showed that 31 per cent of all tickets were bought by children aged 14 and younger; the market share of children under 10 was an astonishing 16 per cent (thus almost every sixth ticket was bought for a young child).[18]

However, throughout the 1960s, and in particular after 1967, Hollywood increasingly focused on the teenage and young adult audience, especially males. In 1966 the Production Code was effectively suspended, and in 1968 it was replaced altogether by a ratings system designed to warn parents about films which were unsuitable for their children, thus, in effect, removing children from the audience of a significant part of Hollywood's output.[19] In the wake of the critical and commercial impact of films such as *Bonnie and Clyde* in 1967 and 1968, the industry's output began to include a large number of aesthetically innovative and thematically challenging films which often included graphic depictions of sexual and violent acts.[20] Taking their cue from exploitation specialists AIP, the Hollywood studios increasingly based their operations on the so-called 'Peter Pan Syndrome', which a 1968 article outlined as follows:

a) a younger child will watch anything an older child will watch; b) an older child will not watch anything a younger child will watch; c) a girl will watch anything a boy will watch; d) a boy will not watch anything a girl will watch; therefore e) to catch your greatest audience you zero in on the 19-year old male.[21]

Obviously, this doctrine worked against the production of children's films, by assuming that films addressed to children were putting off the movies' core audience and were unnecessary anyway (because younger children would want to see the films of their older siblings), and also by prioritizing the assumed taste of teenage males for sex and violence (which did, of course, work to exclude younger siblings from many films, which received an R or an X rating for sex, violence or bad language).

Hollywood's focus on the young male audience did not go unchallenged. Articles in the trade and general press of the early 1970s demanded that Hollywood pay more attention to the female audience.[22] A similar campaign focused on the importance of the child audience. In January 1972, for example, Jerry Lewis stated in a *Variety* article entitled 'Children, Too Have Film Rights' that '(o)ne of the largest segments of the motion picture audience is ignored', if it was not actively prevented from moviegoing through frequent X and R ratings. Lewis pointed out that today's children were also important as tomorrow's teenage and adult audience, and that their movie-going habit had to be developed early so as to be carried over into later life. He called for more G rated films to be specifically addressed to children.[23] In a 1974 poll, over half of the respondents said that filmic sex and violence kept them away from movie theatres, and 76 per cent said that not enough family pictures were being produced.[24]

In 1975, *Variety* pointed out that in recent years 'the entertainment industry has relied more and more on bud and sis to talk dad into a few bucks extra', and that the present generation of children had 'more to spend on its own amusement' than any previous generation. With other sectors of the entertainment industry, especially the music business, addressing ever younger customers, *Variety* asked:

'can the PG pic be far behind?'[25] The latest cinema audience research conducted in the same year confirmed the importance of the interaction between children and adults by concluding that '(p)arents with children under 13 attend more often than parents with children aged 13–17'.[26] Similarly a survey of female heads of households found that women living with children were more likely to go to the cinema at least once a month than those without children. Only 22 per cent of women in households without children went at least once a month; for women whose youngest child was between 6 and 17 the proportion was 41 per cent, and if the youngest child was under 6, the proportion was still as high as 30 per cent. According to this research, then, a large proportion of regular moviegoers were family groups rather than singles or couples.[27]

It is in the context of such research and debates concerning Hollywood's relationship with the child audience that George Lucas developed *Star Wars*. Following the commercial failure of his first feature film in 1971, the bleak, detached and highly stylised science fiction film *THX 1138* (which also contained a fair amount of nudity and violence), Lucas decided that he would next try a more optimistic and emotionally engaging project, either a nostalgic autobiographical picture about his youth in small-town America or a new version of *Flash Gordon*, a sci-fi adventure serial which he had liked as a child.[28] The autobiographical project was realized first as *American Graffiti*, a film for teenagers and for adults looking back on their teenage years, which upon its release in August 1973 would become one of the most profitable films of all time. Before *American Graffiti* was released, however, Lucas returned to his sci-fi adventure, which in the meantime had lost its connection with *Flash Gordon* (the rights of which he had considered to be too expensive) and turned into an original story, based on Lucas's extensive research into myth, fairytales and classic adventure stories. Lucas's story treatment was rejected by Universal, yet he was able to make a deal with Fox in 1973.

From the earliest outlines, Lucas's story combined the depiction of space battles and galactic civil war with strong religious and metaphysical elements, and it heavily featured teenage characters as well as father figures.[29] While Lucas had always seen his story as fantasy and fairytale rather than straightforward science fiction, the famous tagline 'A long time ago in a galaxy far, far away . . .', which so evocatively echoed the classic fairytale opening 'Once upon a time . . .', did not appear until the fourth draft of the screenplay in January 1976. Other important elements which clearly signalled *Star Wars*' status as a children's story were the two robots that first appeared in a draft outline of 1974, and then gradually moved to the very centre of the story. Inspired by Akira Kurosawa's *The Hidden Fortress* (1958), Lucas wanted to tell his epic story from the point of view of two marginal and lowly characters: 'I was looking for the lowest person on the pecking order.'[30] This description fits the social status of children as much as it fits that of robot servants, and tiny R2D2 clearly serves as a stand-in for a young child, albeit a very precocious one, while C3PO may be seen either as a bickering older sibling or even as a fussy, yet caring mother figure. Friends and colleagues advised Lucas not to focus the first fifteen minutes of the film so exclusively on the robots, and instead to open with his male protagonist Luke Skywalker. Lucas did in fact rewrite the script along these lines, but in the end he felt that the robots provided the best entry point for the audience into the world of the film.[31] This would appear to be a crucial decision; in the final film, the space battles and galactic intrigues are mediated by the robot duo, who act much like a team of slapstick clowns or cartoon characters, thus inviting especially very young viewers to enter into the film's adventure.

Another important storytelling device, which Lucas developed gradually, was the foregrounding of Princess Leia. A comparatively minor character in the early outlines and drafts, she becomes quite central in later screenplay versions and serves as an important point of identification especially for young female viewers. She is the only character mentioned in the film's opening scroll and is thus introduced as a central figure in the war against the Evil Empire: 'Pursued by the Empire's sinister agents, Princess Leia races home aboard her starship, custodian of the stolen plans that can save her people and restore freedom to the galaxy.' Apart from the robots, Leia is also the first central character to appear on the screen. Lucas commented later:

> I felt that I needed to have a woman in the script. The interesting thing is she does get in jeopardy, but she is very capable of taking care of herself; . . . I wanted a woman to be at the center of the story . . . She is a leader.[32]

As to the male protagonists of his story, Lucas's early outlines and drafts were focused on Jedi knights and their sons. In later scripts, the central male character, Luke Skywalker, became progressively younger and also turned into an orphaned boy living and working on a farm with his aunt and uncle, wishing to escape from this dreary life and to embark on space adventures like his dead father. This transformation brought Luke much closer to the children in the audience, and also to many poor orphaned fairytale heroes. Lucas's notes indicate that he saw him 'as an ugly duckling, sort of like Cinderella; he is made fun of and wants to become a star pilot, but when he is confronted with reality, he still thinks like a farm boy. He is honest, simple, and good-hearted'.[33]

From this account of the development of the *Star Wars* project it is clear that Lucas gradually reshaped his space adventure into a fairytale about youthful and childlike characters, making sure that the opening sequence helped to ease children, girls as well as boys, into the strange and violent world of the film. This focus on the child audience eventually became so obvious that Lucas was asked by the studio not to use subtitles for some of the alien languages spoken in the film:

> [T]he studio said to me, 'What about the children who can't read the subtitles?' I said, 'It will encourage them to learn how to read or it will bond them with their parents as they are reading the subtitles to them.'[34]

Here, Lucas acknowledged the importance of the interaction between parents and children in the audience, putting the parents in the role of the storyteller of old. And he did so right from the start with the long opening scroll which contained important information that young children would certainly want to know about.

Thus, by 1976, Lucas clearly saw *Star Wars* as a children's film, yet he did not say so in public. It was only in the spring of 1977, shortly before the film's release, that Lucas finally admitted publicly that his main target audiences were in fact children, both young teenagers and pre-teens. In the cover story of the April 1977 issue of *American Film*, for example, Lucas is quoted as saying: 'I decided I wanted to make a children's movie, to go the Disney route', because he had realized that 'a whole generation was growing up without fairytales'.[35] While Disney's animated features had a special status as commercially successful quality products, on the whole the field of children's films was considered to be neither respectable nor economically viable. *American Film* commented: 'George Lucas has gone out on a limb. . . . He has spent $8 million in a genre where movies are usually done as cheaply as possible, resulting in shoddiness.'[36] This kind of comment helps to explain why Lucas and distributor Twentieth Century Fox were so reluctant to label *Star Wars* as a children's film – the label was feared to disqualify the film in the minds of most cinemagoers. Nevertheless, after the film's release, *Time* magazine and much of the rest of the press immediately, and unapologetically, emphasized its tremendous appeal to children as well as its nostalgic address of adults.

## 'I believe, I believe': the initial reception of *Star Wars*

*Variety*'s summary statement in its review of *Star Wars* read: 'Outstanding adventure-fantasy. All-age appeal.'[37] This emphatically included children, yet the reviewer felt it necessary to counteract established prejudices: 'Make no mistake – this is by no means a "children's film" with all the derogatory overtones that go with that description.' Instead, *Star Wars* was 'a superior example' of Hollywood's unique 'movie magic', which had previously been best exemplified by 'the genius of Walt Disney', who had, of course, made films for children. Vincent Canby in the *New York Times* was more willing directly to address the film's special appeal to children: '*Star Wars* is good enough to convince the most skeptical 8-year-old sci-fi buff, who is the toughest critic.'[38] And the *Los Angeles Herald-Examiner* emphatically embraced the film's intimate links to classic children's fiction:

> 'I believe, I believe' may be the only proper response to *Star Wars*. 'I believe in Tinkerbell and flying nuns, prissy robots and talking lions, munchkins and King Arthur's Court.' George Lucas is Peter Pan and we're wide-eyed children he sweeps off into Never-Never Land.[39]

The film's few detractors also acknowledged its powerful hold on children. Molly Haskell, for example, wrote in *Village Voice* that *Star Wars* catered:

> to a 'family market' defined by its pre-pubescent age level, somewhere between 10 and 14. Adults who have been complaining . . . that there are no movies to which they can take their children now are having their prayers answered. Why movies should be required to perform this cultural babysitting service I don't know, but far be it from me to ban the magical formula that can keep the American family together and young forever!ate[40]

However, the most important recognition of the film's powerful hold on children was the merchandising craze which developed a few weeks into the film's release, when its huge success had been assured. In June 1977, the *Hollywood Reporter* announced deals being made between Lucas and various manufacturers, including toy companies such as Kenner, to launch *Star Wars* product lines which would generate 'possibly the largest (merchandising income) ever for any motion picture', thus beating the previous market leader in this field, Disney.[41] Of course, the film also broke all existing box office records, earning $165 million in rentals (and close to twice that amount at the box office) during its 1977 release and its first re-release in 1978, leaving the previous record holder *Jaws* (with rentals of $121 million) far behind.[42]

For the *Chicago Sun-Times* it was immediately clear that *Star Wars* heralded a new era; it was '[t]he first movie of the 1980s', a decade which, the writer expected, would see Hollywood's return to the production of family fare.[43] Indeed, in an October 1977 article highlighting the importance of films for child development, a psychologist held up *Star Wars* to the entertainment industry as 'an example of entertainment with a high absorption value for children', especially for those under the age of 12.[44] And at the beginning of the following year, a headline in the *New York Times* proclaimed: 'Family Movies Making a Comeback.' Movie theatres both on Broadway and in the suburbs were switching from sex and violence to family fare. A film executive was reported to have said that 'he foresaw "more and more" general and family films, mainly because of the stunning box-office success of such films as *Star Wars*'.[45]

Arguably, this is precisely what has happened.[46] In retrospect, we can see that the positive reception of the film by the press and its unprecedented success with audiences, including many present and future filmmakers such as Steven Spielberg and James Cameron, made *Star Wars* a turning point in American film history by moving family films, addressed to children and their parents as well as to the core cinema audience of teenagers and young adults, back to the centre of the American and global entertainment industry. From the *Superman* series (starting in 1978) and the *Star Wars* sequels (1980 and 1983) to the *Indiana Jones* films (starting in 1981) and *E.T.* (1982), from the *Ghostbusters* movies (1984 and 1989) and the *Back to the Future* series (starting in 1985) to *Who Framed Roger Rabbit?* (1988) and the *Batman* series (starting in 1989), from the *Home Alone* films (1989, 1992, and, much less successfully, 1997) to the *Jurassic Park* films (1993, 1997 and 2001) and *The Lion King* (1994), from *How the Grinch Stole Christmas* (2000) to *Harry Potter and the Philosopher's Stone* (2001), from the *Toy Story* films (1995 and 1999), with their extensive *Star Wars* references, and the blatant *Star Wars* pastiche *Independence Day* (1996) to the 'special edition' re-releases of the original *Stars Wars* films (1997) and the prequels *The Phantom Menace* (1999) and *Attack of the Clones* (2002) – most of Hollywood's superhits since 1977 are basically, like *Star Wars*, children's films; more precisely, they are children's films for the whole family and for teenagers, too. These box office hits also tend to be the films that sell best on video, draw the biggest television audiences and have the most successful merchandise. In other words, these films are the cornerstones of today's media empires (including, most notably, TimeWarner, Disney, News Corp./Fox,

Vivendi-Universal, Viacom/Paramount and Sony/Columbia) and touchstones for today's consumers of popular culture.[47]

Obviously, the success of *Star Wars* did not create this state of affairs, but it definitely helped it along. Ironically, in its original conception *Star Wars* was far removed from the then disreputable category of the children's film, and it was only by following the logic of his own material, and by being open to the surrounding debate about the need for family entertainment in Hollywood, that Lucas was finally able to create his most influential movie. To return to *Time* magazine's formula, we can say that *Star Wars* and much of subsequent popular entertainment is indeed aimed at the kid in everybody *and* at actual kids, targeting children as an important, even primary audience segment. Does this mean that adult audiences are being 'infantilized' by being made to regress to a childish frame of mind?

Elsewhere I have engaged with this critique of contemporary Hollywood by suggesting that most of Hollywood's biggest hits since the 1970s are best understood as 'family-adventure movies', that is films which are addressed at children and their parents as well as teenagers and young adults, revolve around the spectacular adventures of familial groups (very few of which are traditional families), and portray both childhood and family life in far from idealized terms – loss, loneliness and longing, lies, betrayal and misunderstanding, latent aggression, guilt and a crushing sense of responsibility.[48] We can easily see how this last point applies to the *Star Wars* saga: Teenage hero Luke Skywalker has lost (or so it seems) both his parents, and then loses his aunt and uncle, who have taken care of him, but have also severely restricted his life. Their death does in fact free him to become who he wants to be, and since it follows a fight Luke has had with his uncle, it could be seen as a form of wish-fulfilment. Luke's aunt and uncle have lied to him about his father as do his mentors, and father-substitutes, Obi-Wan Kenobi and Yoda; Luke initially mistakes his strong feelings for Leia for romantic love, not knowing that she is his sister. When he eventually learns the truth about his family, he is warned that he might be as morally weak and corruptible as his father, the evil Darth Vader, while at the same time feeling responsible for Vader's redemption as well as for the fate of the known universe, certainly not an easy burden to carry. Luke's father fights and injures him seriously on two occasions, and, what is perhaps worse, he does his best to corrupt him. In the end, of course, Vader is redeemed, yet he dies in the process as did Obi-Wan and Yoda, adding to the long list of people Luke has lost in his life (although some of them continue to be present to him as spirits). Anakin Skywalker's childhood and youth in the prequels are similarly fraught with loss, guilt and responsibility.

If it is argued that the *Star Wars* saga addresses 'the kid' in adult spectators and takes them back to their childhood, then it also has to be acknowledged that, much like the fairytales Bruno Bettelheim analyses in his classic 1975 study *The Uses of Enchantment*,[49] the films confront spectators with a very challenging vision of childhood, family life and the difficult process of growing up, which is, however, in the end always completed successfully (as it also is in fairytales). Playing on the paradoxical title of another archetypal contemporary Hollywood blockbuster, one might therefore say that *Star Wars* and many of the big hits made in its wake invite spectators to regress to maturity.

## Notes

\* This essay was first published, in a slightly different form, in *Scope: An Online Journal of Film Studies*, December 2001, http://www.nottingham.ac.uk/film/journal/articles/its-aimed-at-kids.htm Research for this essay in American archives was made possible by a Small Research Grant from the Arts and Humanities Research Board.

1 'Star Wars: The Year's Best Movie', *Time*, May 30, 1977, unpaginated clipping on *Star Wars* microfiche in the British Film Institute.

2 See, for example, Robin Wood ''80s Hollywood: Dominant Tendencies', *CineAction!*, 1, Spring 1985, pp. 2–5.

3 Todd McCarthy 'Mighty Effects, But Mini Magic', *Variety*, May 17, 1999, pp. 53–4.

4 Don Groves '*Phantom* Phenomenal As Summer Wanes', *Variety*, September 6, 1999, p. 12.

5 John Dempsey 'Theatricals Rate Second Look', *Variety*, September 20, 1999, pp. 33–4.

6 'The Top 125 Worldwide', *Variety*, January 24, 2000, p. 22.

7 Bill Hoffmann 'N.Y. is Taken by "Force"', *New York Post*, May 10, 1999, p. 7.

8 For an in-depth discussion of the complex ways in which dedicated *Star Wars* fans engage with the saga, see Will Brooker *Using the Force: Creativity, Community and Star Wars Fans*, New York: Continuum, 2002.

9 For an overview of *Star Wars* fictions, see Ted Edwards *The Unauthorized Star Wars Compendium: The Complete Guide to the Movies, Comic Books, Novels, and More*, Boston: Little, Brown, 1999.

10 Gary Cross *Kids' Stuff: Toys and the Changing World of American Childhood*, Cambridge, MA: Harvard University Press, 1997, Chapter 7.

11 'Films Top Minneapolis Student Poll', *Daily Variety*, December 15, 1978; unpaginated clipping in 'Surveys (1970–1979)' file, Academy Center for Motion Picture Study, Academy of Motion Picture Arts and Sciences (AMPAS), Beverly Hills; Internet Moviedatabase, http://www.us.imdb.com/top_250_films, accessed June 29, 2001.

12 Surveys quoted in Claudia Puig '*Star Wars* Makes A New Killing At The Box Office', *The Guardian*, February 4, 1997, p. 13.

13 See, for example, '*Star Wars* Prod'n Begins In January', *Daily Variety*, June 30, 1975, and 'Alec Guinness Lands Top Role in *Wars*', *Daily Variety*, March 24, 1976; unpaginated clippings on *Star Wars* microfiche No. 3, AMPAS. Also Larry Sturhahn 'The Filming of *American Graffiti*', *Filmmakers Newsletter*, March 1974, pp. 19–27, reprinted in Sally Kline (ed.) *George Lucas: Interviews*, Jackson: University of Mississippi Press, 1999, pp. 14–32; Stephen Farber 'George Lucas: The Stinky Kid Hits the Big Time', *Film Quarterly*, 27: 3, Spring 1974, pp. 2–9, reprinted in Kline *George Lucas: Interviews*, pp. 33–44.

14 'Young Directors, New Films', *American Film Institute Report*, Winter 1973, pp. 45–6.

15 Charles Champlin 'Futurist Film's Tricks to Treat the Eye', *Los Angeles Times*, June 20, 1976, calendar, pp. 1, 42.

16 Quoted in ibid.

17 Olen J. Earnest '*Star Wars*: A Case Study of Motion Picture Marketing', *Current Research in Film*, 1, 1985, pp. 7–13.

18 Opinion Research Corporation *The Public Appraises Movies*, booklet contained in file MFL x n.c.2607 no. 11, Billy Rose Theatre Collection (BRTC), New York Public Library. Survey of 5,021 people conducted in June and July 1957.

19 The original ratings were: 'G for general audiences, all ages admitted; M for mature audiences – parental guidance suggested, but all ages admitted; R for restricted – children under sixteen (later raised to under seventeen years of age . . .) would not be admitted without an accompanying parent or adult guardian; X for no one under seventeen admitted.' The M category was soon renamed PG. Jack Valenti 'The Voluntary Movie Rating System' in Jason E. Squire (ed.) *The Movie Business Book*, 2nd revised edition, New York: Fireside, 1992, p. 399. From the 1960s onwards, Hollywood's neglect of the child audience went so far that children under 12 were not even counted in audience surveys any more.

20  Cf. my discussion of production trends in the late 1960s and early 1970s in 'A Powerful Cinema-going Force? Hollywood and Female Audiences since the 1960s', in Melvyn Stokes and Richard Maltby (eds) *Identifying Hollywood's Audiences: Cultural Identity and the Movies*, London: BFI, 1999, pp. 96–7.

21  Robin Bean and David Austen 'U.S.A. Confidential', *Films and Filming*, 215, November 1968, pp. 21–2, quoted in Thomas Doherty *Teenagers and Teenpics: The Juvenilization of American Movies in the 1950s*, Boston: Unwin Hyman, 1988, p. 157.

22  Krämer 'A Powerful Cinema-going Force?', pp. 96–7.

23  Jerry Lewis 'Children, Too Have Film Rights', *Variety*, January 5, 1972, p. 32. In fact, a similar call for more children's films had previously been issued in the early 1960s. See John C. Waugh 'Trail Blurred in Film Capital', *Christian Science Monitor*, November 21, 1962, and Rose Pelswick 'Needed: Family Films', *New York Journal-American*, July 12, 1964, unpaginated clippings in 'Children as Audiences – Cinema' clippings file, BRTC. See also 'A Family Movie', *Christian Science Monitor*, September 19, 1962, unpaginated clipping, 'Cinema – Audiences' clippings file, BRTC.

24  'Anybody surprised?', *Variety*, August 28, 1974, unpaginated clipping, 'Cinema – Audiences' clippings file, BRTC. For a more extensive discussion of this topic, see Peter Krämer, '"The best Disney film Disney never made": Children's Films and the Family Audience in American Cinema Since the 1960s', in Steve Neale (ed.) *Genre and Contemporary Hollywood*, London: BFI, 2002, pp. 183–98.

25  Jim Harwood 'Advertisers Sensitive to Change in Kiddies' Purchasing Power', *Daily Variety*, February 20, 1975, unpaginated clipping in 'Audiences (1974–1976)', clippings file, AMPAS.

26  A. D. Murphy 'Demographics Favoring Films Future', *Variety*, October 8, 1975, p. 3.

27  Newspaper Advertising Bureau *Shoppers on the Move: Movie-going and Movie-goers*, November 1975; research conducted during 1974; file MWEZ x n.c.26,510, BRTC.

28  See John Baxter *George Lucas: A Biography*, New York: HarperCollins, 1999; Garry Jenkins *Empire Building: The Remarkable Real Life Story of Star Wars*, New York: Simon & Schuster, 1997; Dale Pollock *Skywalking: The Life and Times of George Lucas*, Hollywood: Samuel French, 1990.

29  See Laurent Bouzereau (ed.) *Star Wars: The Annotated Screenplays*, New York: Del Rey, 1997.

30  Ibid., p. 9.

31  Ibid., p. 24.

32  Ibid., p. 14.

33  Ibid., p. 23.

34  Ibid., p. 49.

35  Stephen Zito 'George Lucas Goes Far Out', *American Film*, April 1977, p. 9, reprinted in Kline *George Lucas: Interviews*, pp. 45–54.

36  Ibid., p. 13.

37  *Variety*, May 25, 1977, reprinted in Chris Salewicz *George Lucas: The Making of His Movies*, London: Orion Media, 1998, pp. 123–5.

38  Vincent Canby 'Comic-Book Sci-Fi', *New York Times*, May 26, 1977, p. C18: 1.

39  Richard Cuskelly '*Star Wars*: "I Believe, I Believe"', *Los Angeles Herald-Examiner*, May 25, 1977, pp. B1, 4.

40  Molly Haskell 'Galactic Graffiti', *Village Voice*, June 13, 1977, pp. 40–1.

41  Frank Barrow '*Star Wars* Product Bonanza', *Hollywood Reporter*, June 8, 1977, pp. 1, 9.

42  Cobbett Steinberg *Film Facts*, New York: Facts on File, 1980, p. 4.

43  Roger Simon '*Star Wars*: The First Movie of the 1980s', *Chicago Sun-Times*, June 5, 1977; unpaginated clipping, *Star Wars* microfiche, No. 4, AMPAS.

44  Joe Gallick 'Choosing a Healthy Show for Children', *New York Sunday News*, October 9, 1977, p. L10.

45  Judy Klemesrud 'Family Movies Making a Comeback', *New York Times*, February 17, 1978, p. C10.

46  See Peter Krämer, 'Would You Take Your Child To See This Film? The Cultural and Social Work of the Family-Adventure Movie', in Steve Neale and Murray Smith (eds) *Contemporary Hollywood Cinema*, London: Routledge, 1998, pp. 294–311.

47  For a discussion of a particularly striking example of this intimate connection between individual films, media empires and consumers see Peter Krämer 'Entering the Magic Kingdom: The Walt Disney Company, *The Lion King* and the Limitations of Criticism', *Film Studies*, No. 2, Spring 2000, pp. 44–50.

48  Krämer 'Would You Take Your Child To See This Film?'.

49  Bruno Bettelheim *The Uses of Enchantment: The Meaning and Importance of Fairy Tales*, New York: Penguin, 1975.

## Chapter 23

# BARRY KEITH GRANT

## MAN'S FAVOURITE SPORT?
## The action films of Kathryn Bigelow

## Introduction

**W**ITH ONLY A FEW FEATURES TO HER CREDIT – *The Loveless* (1983, co-directed with Monty Montgomery), *Near Dark* (1987), *Blue Steel* (1990), *Point Break* (1991), and *Strange Days* (1995)[1] – writer/director Kathryn Bigelow succeeded in establishing herself as the only female filmmaker specializing in action films who, at least to this point, can claim the status of auteur. Bigelow's films employ, in the words of Anna Powell, 'stunning and expressionistic visuals, rapid narrative pacing, thrilling and visceral scenes of eroticised violence and physical action',[2] providing all the expected pleasures of action films. Yet at the same time they also work within the various genres that fall within the category of action cinema – cop films, buddy and road movies, westerns and horror films – to question their traditional and shared ideological assumptions about gender and violence.

Some critics have hesitated to call Bigelow an auteur because of her personal and professional association with James Cameron, the creator of such muscular action movies as *Terminator* (1984) and *Terminator 2: Judgment Day* (1991) who also produced *Point Break* and wrote and produced *Strange Days*. Certainly her biological status as a woman has entered into the discourse surrounding Bigelow, with critics and reviewers often referring not only to her gender but also to her physical attractiveness – hardly the kind of discourse that generally surrounds male directors.[3] Yet close analysis of her films reveal a remarkable consistency of style and theme that, as with most canonical male auteurs, works in relation to the parameters of genre.

The action film is perfectly suited to Bigelow's themes. The representation of violence is of course central to the genre, and as Steve Neale notes, the ideology of masculinity which it traditionally has worked so hard to inscribe centres on 'notions and attitudes to do with aggression, power, and control'.[4] Bigelow's first film, the short *Set-Up* (1978), which shows two men fighting in an alley while on the soundtrack two theorists interpret the violence, is in a sense a paradigm for her features to follow. All explore the nature of masculinity and its relation to violence, especially within the context of spectatorship, largely by playing on the look of the viewer as conditioned by the generic expectations and conventions of traditional action films. The 'false' beginnings of both *Blue Steel* and *Near Dark*, which are tests of perception for Bigelow's protagonists as well as for the viewer, are only the most obvious instances of the importance of looking and the look in her films.

Critics have duly noted the thematic and stylistic importance of vision in Bigelow's films – her 'cinema is essentially a discourse on vision', writes one[5] – a theme that likely has its roots in her days as a film studies student at Columbia University in New York City, at a time when the influence of feminist gaze theory was at its height. Much as Sirk and Fassbinder had approached the genre of melodrama or 'the woman's film', providing their pleasures while critiquing the ideology that underpinned them ('bending', in Sirk's phrase), so Bigelow works within the action film. Her music video for the pop band New Order's 'Touched by the Hand of God' is indicative of her approach: just as in the video she incongruously films the new wave band with the iconography of costume and the conventions of performance associated with heavy metal, thus foregrounding and questioning their masculine coding, so Bigelow's films mobilize a range of the genres traditionally regarded as 'male' precisely to interrogate that term specifically, as well as the politics and pleasures of gendered representations in genre films more generally. Gavin Smith is thus absolutely correct in describing her work as 'metacinema of the first rank'.[6]

## Men with guns

While action in film has been popular ever since the Lumières' train entered the Ciotat Station, the action film as a recognizable genre for the definition and display of male power and prowess was clearly established with the rousing swashbucklers of Douglas Fairbanks (*The Mark of Zorro*, 1920; *The Black Pirate*, 1922) and Errol Flynn (*Captain Blood*, 1935; *The Adventures of Robin Hood*, 1940). The depth of the genre's masculine perspective is painfully clear in a movie like *True Lies* (1994, written and directed, ironically, by Bigelow's former husband, James Cameron). At one point in the narrative Jamie Lee Curtis is forced to succumb to the humiliating process of visual objectification in a scene that exceeds any narrative requirement (thinking she must do so to save her husband's life, she is made to enter a hotel room and strip for the pleasure of an unknown male spectator sitting in the shadows). The apparent joke is on her, since she does not realize (but we do) that the mysterious man is in fact her husband, whom she does not know is a spy. The husband is played by Arnold Schwarzenegger – 'an anthropomorphised phallus, a phallus with muscles', in the apt words of Barbara Creed[7] – the actor who more than any other embodies the action film in the 1980s and 1990s and who, in this scene, explicitly functions as the ego ideal of the male viewer.

It is stating the obvious to say that successful action stars often rely on anatomy rather than acting. Male action stars such as Schwarzenegger, Sylvester Stallone,

Jean-Claude Van Damme, Steven Seagal, Chuck Norris, and Bruce Willis offer impressively muscular bodies for visual display and as the site of ordeals they must undergo in order to triumph at narrative's end. Critics such as Yvonne Tasker and Susan Jeffords have discussed the contemporary action film's exaggerated masculinity as an expression of patriarchal ideology, the reassertion of male power and privilege during and after the Reagan administration and in an era of eroding hegemony.[8] It is no accident that the hyperbolically masculine action film gained popularity roughly at the same time that other genres, traditionally regarded as 'male', were beginning to be opened up to revisionist readings.

Into the 1980s, genres and genre movies remained almost exclusively the cultural property of a white male consciousness, the centre from which any difference regarding race, gender, and sexuality was defined and marginalized. In all the action genres, it was white men who had to get the job done, whether driving the cattle, solving the crime, capturing the spies, or defeating the aliens. Movies such as *Westward the Women* (1951), in which a wagon train of women successfully make the cross-country trek to California, were only the exceptions that proved the rule. In every type of action film, women and visible minorities assumed subsidiary and stereotyped roles, serving as hindrances, helpers, or rewards for the white male's doing. With the ghettoized exceptions of musicals and melodramas – at one time referred to in the industry as 'woman's films' – most genre movies addressed an assumed viewer who was, like almost all of the filmmakers who made them, white, male, and heterosexual. But by the next decade many contemporary genre movies sought to grapple with and redress the implications of traditional generic representations of race and gender, often deliberately acknowledging and giving voice to those previously marginalized by mainstream cinema, including women, blacks and gays.

The film that more than any other provided the impetus for this new generic transformation was, undoubtedly, *Thelma and Louise*. One of the most popular movies in North America in 1991, *Thelma and Louise* is a generic hybrid of the western, the buddy film, and the road movie – three of those genres traditionally regarded as male – and the outlaw couple movie, the protagonists of which had always romantically involved heterosexual couples. *Thelma and Louise* reversed Hollywood's conventional definition of woman's place as the domestic sphere and reimagined the buddy movie as female adventure. The acts of rebellion on the part of the two women, like blowing up the tanker truck of a driver who makes obscene gestures at them, come to seem nothing less than imaginative acts of retribution for all women, transcending their personal plight. As Peter Chumo observes, 'what Bonnie and Clyde do for Depression evils, Thelma and Louise do for the evil of sexual violence . . .'.[9]

In the film's controversial ending, Thelma and Louise drive over the edge of the Grand Canyon rather than capitulate to the police. The last image is a freeze frame of the car in midair, just beyond the apogee of its arching flight, followed by a fade to white. This ending is, of course, a direct reference to one of the most famous of buddy movies, *Butch Cassidy and the Sundance Kid* (1969), and it sparked considerable debate regarding *Thelma and Louise*'s political value. Did it signify suicidal defeatism or triumphant transcendence? This debate in itself was significant for, as Rebecca Bell-Metereau noted:

> Critics did not concern themselves with the outcome of *Butch Cassidy and the Sundance Kid* [or] *Easy Rider,* because a male death in the conclusion is sacrificial, symbolic, and Christ-like. A female death at the end of the story rarely receives such a heroic interpretation, from feminists or non-feminists.[10]

The contentious but popular reception of *Thelma and Louise*'s ending suggests how novel the film was at the time.

Regardless of how one reads the film's ending, the fact that it was the subject of such heated debate suggests both the complexities of gendered representations in popular cinema generally and the difficulty of finding a place for women in the action film specifically. Many recent genre films are content merely to borrow *Thelma and Louise*'s gender 'gimmick', simply plugging others into roles traditionally reserved for white men. But in reversing conventional representations, they are prone to fall into the trap of repeating the same objectionable values. The question of whether female action heroes such as Sigourney Weaver's Ripley in *Alien* (1979) and its sequels or Linda Hamilton's Sarah Connor in *Terminator 2: Judgment Day* are progressive representations of women or merely contain them within a masculine sensibility has been a matter of considerable debate. It is just here that Bigelow's films constitute a site of generic intervention, for while they often reverse generic expectation (the female cop in *Blue Steel*, for example, or the black female bodyguard and feminized male protagonist in *Strange Days*), they also employ a variety of stylistic means to question the gendered values that animate action film genres.

## The children of Eisenhower and Coca-Cola

*The Loveless*, Bigelow's first feature film, remains her most avant-garde or experimental. Set in the 1950s, the film is a generic amalgam of mainstream biker movies of the period, particularly *The Wild One* (1954), and the celebration of gay iconography in Kenneth Anger's experimental film *Scorpio Rising* (1963). As such, *The Loveless* might more accurately be described as an anti-action film because of its stylized compositions and deliberately slow pace – especially curious given the kinetic potential of a movie about guys on motorcycles. The main character, Vance (Willem Dafoe), accurately describes the film's style when he tells the other bikers: 'We're going nowhere . . . fast.'

The minimal plot involves a group of bikers (all men, with the notable exception of the bleach-blonde Debbie Sportster) who converge on a small Southern town on their way to the drag races at Daytona, waiting while one of them does some necessary repairs to his motorcycle. Their presence catalyses the townspeople, who respond to them either with desire or fear, these extreme and polar reactions coming together in a violent climax featuring a shoot-out in a roadside bar and the suicide of a local girl. The bikers function like the monstrous other of the horror film (in fact, there are a number of correspondences between them and the vampire clan in the later *Near Dark*), a graphic representation of the return of the repressed. And like the more sympathetic monsters of some progressive horror films, they are less evil then merely different in their bohemian lifestyle.

*The Loveless* works toward its violent climax not so much as a necessary dramatic resolution, but more because, like Michel and Patricia in Jean-Luc Godard's *A bout de souffle* (1959), the characters are trapped within the constraints of genre. A tragic outcome seems inevitable, a given, the kind of ending we expect when free-spirited bikers confront rednecks in movies like *Easy Rider* (1969). But the specific form this violent climax takes in *The Loveless*, turning in on the town and making the townspeople the victims, is a more subtle political critique. Appropriately, *The Loveless* contains many references to Godard's work – most obviously in the shots of Vance driving in the open convertible with Telena (Marin Kanter), the local jail-bait. The sense of buoyant freedom as they drive, the way Kanter turns her head away from the camera, and her short, boyish haircut, all deliberately echo Jean Seberg in *A bout de souffle*. *The Loveless*'s bold colour palette, use of deliberately choreographed tracking shots (a central element of what Brian Henderson calls Godard's 'non-bourgeois camera style'),[11] and vivid deployment of consumer iconography (the brilliant red Coke machine in the filling station) all invoke Godard's distinctive style of political filmmaking.

The actors are often filmed doing nothing, even being completely motionless, in Brechtian tableaux. Vance tellingly says in the opening scene, when the woman with the flat tyre asks him what he does for a living, 'not a whole lot'. These shots are frequently held longer than the time required for narrative comprehension, encouraging us to examine their studied composition. As a result, the characters – male and female – become objects of aesthetic contemplation for the spectator. The images are often composed so that the actors are decentred in the frame, emphasizing the iconographical import of gesture (smoking a cigarette, drinking a Coke) or costume (motorcycle jacket, boots). In the roadside diner – Bigelow's equivalent to the Parisian cafe for Godard – when they wonder where one of their group is, Debbie comments that he must be outside 'fine-tuning his sideburns'. The film's first image is of Vance laconically combing his hair before heading out on the highway. Bigelow thus subverts the traditionally masculine gaze of the camera, fetishizing, as in Anger's more experimental work, the accoutrements of the biker subculture. The languorous shots of the bikers ultimately reveal them as poised, posed, performing, so that any sense of a monolithic or essential masculinity is called into question. This subversion is literalized in the climax, and the violence precipitated, when Telena's abusive and belligerent father discovers one of the bikers wearing women's undergarments beneath his leather in, significantly, the bar's men's room.

### Terror in a Texas town

Bigelow's second feature, *Near Dark*, is a generic hybrid of the western and the vampire film in the venerable tradition of such unassuming genre fare as *Curse of the Undead* (1959), *Billy the Kid vs Dracula* (1965) and *Jesse James Meets Frankenstein's Daughter* (1966), but with considerably more serious ambitions. As Christina Lane points out, both genres 'have traditionally been used to work through ambivalent feelings toward nature and civilization, and both usually tell stories in which threatening natural forces are purged for the sake of society'.[12] Both genres are structured by binary oppositions that at root reflect the ongoing tension between individual desire and social responsibility – civilization and its discontents, in Freud's terms – in the western, as a topographical mapping onto the frontier and in the horror film, as a psycho-social projection.[13] *Near Dark* mixes elements of both genres, revealing their common conventional gendered assumptions.

A midwestern farm boy, Caleb (Adrian Pasdar), seemingly falls in love at first sight with an attractive female vampire named Mae (Jenny Wright) after a romantic evening together. Mae bites Caleb, who turns almost immediately into a vampire and is snatched away by the vampire clan, a terrible family reminiscent of those in horror movies like *The Texas Chainsaw Massacre* (1974) or *The Hills Have Eyes* (1977) or westerns like *My Darling Clementine* (1946) or *Wagon Master* (1950). But Caleb, like the classic western hero, refuses to kill except in self-defence, allowing Mae to do it instead and then drinking her blood. In a final showdown at high midnight on main street, Caleb, now cured by a blood transfusion performed by his father, destroys the vampire clan, literally earning his spurs.

In the denouement, Caleb administers the same cure to Mae, who in the film's final shot, can now step into the sunlit promise of domesticity, the place typically reserved for women in the western – see, for example, *High Noon* (1952) or *Shane* (1953) – and a gaping absence in Caleb's family, given the unexplained absence of a mother. (This absence, unmentioned by the characters, is addressed by the film in the scene of the three family members having dinner, the fourth chair at the table noticeably empty.) This ending recalls that of numerous horror films, particularly Tod Browning's *Dracula* (1931), which concludes with the romantic couple ascending a long flight of stairs in the vampire's dark crypt to the security of sunny daylight and church bells on the soundtrack.

*Near Dark*'s narrative closure thus seems emphatically to restore patriarchal gender politics, as do both the classic horror film, when the monster is destroyed and civilization made safe, and the western, when the bad men or Indians are defeated and the frontier tamed for settler families. But given the rest of the film, this ending rings hollow, like the apparently happy ending of Sirk's *All that Heaven Allows* (1955) in which the heroine, seeking to define herself as a desiring subject, can be reunited with her lover only when she is summarily forced into the position of nurturer after he is seriously injured while hunting. In both cases the apparent happy ending fulfils generic convention but lacks thematic conviction.

Bigelow suggests that the happy ending of *Near Dark* is intended to be read as similarly perfunctory and ironic, given the sexual meanings of vampirism both within generic tradition and in *Near Dark* specifically. The sexual basis of the vampires' allure is shown when, during a typical night of feeding, we see Severen (Bill Paxton) use his charm as a hitchhiker to attract two women who pick him up in their truck hoping for a good time. The attractive Mae, a seemingly archetypal bluejean baby, arouses such strong desire in Caleb that it threatens to destroy his traditional family by luring him away from home and the daytime world. Further, this desire threatens to erupt and destroy bourgeois stability at any moment, as we see when Mae comes back, a literal return of the repressed, after Caleb is cured of his vampirism. Unhesitatingly, Caleb rushes to hug Mae, noticeably exposing his neck to her as they embrace. Like the popular song, the film asks, 'How are you gonna keep 'em down on the farm after they've seen Paree?' – a question that directly acknowledges the necessity of repression for maintaining traditional social values. Like Bohemian Paris, Mae represents the siren song of desire, so in the course of the narrative she must be literally defanged and thrust into the glaring sunlight of normalcy. Now saved by her man, no longer feminized, she will likely take her place in that empty chair, adopting the kind of maternal role Caleb had tried to impose on her when they were vampires and he fed from her blood like a helpless, hungry infant suckling at its mother's breast.

The film consistently contrasts Caleb's normal, good family with the undead, evil family of the vampires. The vampires are capable of terrible violence, as we see several times in the film and especially in its memorable set piece, their decimation of a roadhouse and its occupants. This violence is tinged with eroticism throughout, and it intoxicates even as it repels, a perfect expression of Susan Sontag's description of the appeal of monster movies as 'the aesthetics of destruction, with the peculiar beauties to be found in wreaking havoc, making a mess'.[14] During the massacre, Caleb, like the spectator, watches mesmerized, even finding himself participating against his will when he sends a tough-looking biker flying through the air with one punch ('Did I do that?' he asks with bemusement). Christopher Sharrett complains that the vampire clan is 'wholly repugnant and destructive', so that, in contrast to the kinds of horror films Robin Wood calls progressive, there is no sympathy generated toward them.[15] He views the vampires as unproblematically other, but I would suggest that *Near Dark* does indeed problematize the relation of the normal and monstrous once we accept the seductive and violent pleasures the film offers. Their inherent appeal is underscored by the fact that the monstrous patriarch Jesse (Lance Henrickson) is associated with American history (he claims to have fought for the Confederacy), and that the clan travel across middle America, the centre of what poet Allen Ginsberg called the 'heart of the Vortex' out of which American violence emanates.[16] Despite the film's apparent rigid contrast between the daytime world of the farm family and the night-time world of the vampire clan, we are implicated in the latter, all of us near dark.

## Sleeping with the enemy

*Blue Steel* is a stylish police thriller that exploits to the fullest the action film's conventional association of the gun with the phallus, exploring the representation of the gun as a totem of masculine power. From the opening credit sequence in which the camera penetrates the interior of a Smith and Wesson handgun, *Blue Steel* (according to one critic, the term is American slang for an erection)[17] explores the genre's iconographical fetishization of the pistol. By making possession and control of the gun a contest between a police*woman* and a male criminal, the film fore-grounds the metaphorical and gendered implications of one of the primary icons of the action film.

The plot involves a rookie female cop, Megan Turner (Jamie Lee Curtis), whose gender troubles all the men in the film once she dons her uniform. Intervening in a supermarket robbery, Turner shoots and kills the hold-up man, while one of the cowering bystanders in the store, Eugene Hunt (Ron Silver), secretly pockets the thief's handgun. As the film progresses, Eugene becomes increasingly psychotic, obsessed with the image of Turner wielding her weapon and usurping phallic power. In the final violent confrontation, Turner manages to kill the seemingly unstoppable Eugene.

Some have read the film as empowering for women. Megan is like the hero of a rape revenge film, an example of Carol Clover's 'final girl'. In this sense, the cast-ing of Curtis, protagonist of the prototypical slasher film *Halloween* (1978), is particularly resonant.[18] After all, it is Megan who defeats Eugene in battle, not her superior, the suitably named Detective Nick Mann (Clancy Brown), who is 'disarmed' when Megan handcuffs him to their car door during her penultimate confrontation with Eugene. Nevertheless, *Blue Steel* suggests that the triumph of Megan and the femininity she represents can only be limited because of the entrenched power of patriarchy since the film contextualizes the male world of Eugene as a monstrous extension of normative masculinity.

Employing a standard motif of the horror film, Eugene is doubled with Megan's abusive father (Philip Bosco), emphasizing a continuity between apparently mascu-line norms and the horribly psychotic. Also, like Patrick Bateman in Brett Easton Ellis's controversial novel *American Psycho* (1991), published the year after the release of the film, Eugene is a stockbroker, his position of economic privilege apparently allowing him the power to commit horrible criminal acts, including murder, with impunity. Both works link their central male character's craziness to capitalism, competition, masculine identity, and violence. Eugene hears voices in his head and so expresses a desire for quietude – an understandable wish given his profession: on two occasions we see him screaming and wildly gesticulating in a sea of commodity traders, all male, on the floor of the stock exchange. (It is in this same space that Eugene first fantasizes shooting the gun he has picked up at the super-market.) When Mann asks Megan why she became a cop, she ambiguously replies, 'Him', which, as Tasker notes, may refer to her abusive father specifically or more generally to 'the man', to men, to the many potential Eugenes.[19]

The film employs other conventions of the horror film, particularly the were-wolf film. Eugene is hirsute, with a dark beard, and associated with the night; at one point we see him digging for his gun like an animal under the full moon in New York's Central Park (Eugene's last name, remember, is 'Hunt'). These asso-ciations of masculinity with violence and animality appear throughout Bigelow's films: hothead biker Davis (Robert Gordon) in *The Loveless* literally barks at his friends and yelps wildly as he fires his gun in the violent climax in the bar, while in *Near Dark*, when Caleb thinks he has killed Severen by running over him with a diesel truck, another icon of phallic power, he similarly howls with satisfaction.

Violence is associated with male animality in Bigelow's films because violence is seen as an inherently masculine quality. *Blue Steel* demonstrates this idea visually, in its painterly images combined with careful foley work that emphasize the physical and sensual qualities of the gun. Frequently the film emphasizes the texture and tactility of guns – the way hands caressingly grip them, how they slide across a table or are provocatively unbuttoned from a holster – as well as the sounds they make. Viewers are seduced, within the context of the action film, by the power of the phallus, like the men in the film in their more extreme ways.

Megan's desire to be a cop thus becomes a desire to enter into the phallic domain, literalized in her struggle with Eugene over possession of the gun. Her uniform is a sign of transgression as Megan encroaches on a traditionally male world, an idea made clear at the beginning of the film in the montage of Megan suiting up for graduation. Individual shots fetishize parts of her uniform reminiscent of the shots of the bikers' costumes in *The Loveless*. The character's gender is initially indeterminate, but then, as she buttons her shirt, we glimpse her lace bra underneath. Viewers are likely taken aback for a moment, 'disarmed' like the several men in the film when they see her in uniform the first time or learn what her job is. Megan's wearing of a traditionally male uniform also suggests the extent to which, apart from the masculine propensity toward violence, gender is a constructed performance, dependent upon the semiotics of style for meaning.

## Imitation of life

If *The Loveless* deconstructs the action, *Point Break* is a thoroughly successful reconstruction. As the story unfolds, viewers are treated to some terrific action sequences, the most memorable of which is an extended chase, effectively photographed through alleys, houses, and backyards with a modified Steadicam that adeptly places us squarely within the action. (Bigelow would use the same strategy more trenchantly in the opening of *Strange Days*.) A combination of buddy and caper movie, it nevertheless has the same objective of subverting the power of masculinist generic myth by challenging our sense of the conventions of 'realism' characteristic of classic Hollywood cinema. In Sirkian fashion, Bigelow treats the action excessively in *Point Break*, pushing the macho mysticism into overblown spectacle. As Tyler (Lori Petty) – the lone woman in the film's hypermasculine world of skydiving, surfing, and bankrobbing – disgustedly opines at one point while the men are busy bonding on a beach, 'There's too much testosterone here for me'.

The film's plot concerns a band of bank robbers who commit heists because they are devoted surfers who need to maintain their cash flow as they travel around the world in search of the perfect wave. The gang is known as the Ex-Presidents because they wear masks of former US presidents while committing their robberies. The case is being investigated by a pair of FBI agents, seasoned Angelo Pappas (Gary Busey) and hotshot rookie Johnny Utah (Keanu Reeves). Undercover, Utah infiltrates the gang and experiences a conflict between his duty as agent of the law and the spiritual bond he has developed with the gang's leader Bodhi (Patrick Swayze).

The film, it is true, offers some direct (and humorous) social criticism with its band of presidential bank robbers – particularly when 'Nixon' jumps up on a counter to declare 'I am not a crook!' and when Bodhi, wearing his Reagan mask, waves a gas pump in the air and ignites a filling station into a flaming fireball.[20] But for the most part *Point Break* is more sly in its subversion of the masculine myths of action cinema, frequently reminding us that it is only a movie, a generic construction. The male characters are clearly types rather than rounded individuals. Keanu Reeves' typically flat performance style ironically works well here, emphasizing Johnny Utah's lack of psychological depth. His name is itself something of a mythic amalgam, at once evoking the American West and the western, as well as legendary athleticism in the masculine world of football (Utah was a college football star; his name recalls that of both Johnny Unitas and Joe Montana, two legendary quarter-backs), and the fact that he is a fictional character in the tradition of *Johnny Guitar* (1954) and *Johnny Handsome* (1989).[21]

If action movies exhibit a masculine homosocial hysteria mapped onto the excessive display of the male body,[22] then *Point Break* is a paradigmatic action movie. The male characters are on constant display, even to the point that the gang are identified by the tan lines on their buttocks when they 'moon' for the security cameras at one of the banks they rob. The film emphasizes Swayze's body and long blonde tresses, and pushes its representation of the surfer gang's macho comraderie to the point of parody. This excessive treatment comes to a head, as it were, in the climax when Utah jumps out of an airplane without a parachute in a determined attempt to catch Bodhi, who had jumped moments before with the last one. The sequence of Utah's windy free-fall toward Bodhi and clasping of him in midair becomes a hysterical visualization of the repressed homoerotic subtext of the buddy movie. The two men embrace as they grapple, their windswept faces together in intimate close-up as they tussle for either the gun or the pullcord ('Pull it, pull it,' Bodhi cries). And as we see in the subjective zoom shot of the ground rapidly coming nearer, for both men it is an experience in which the earth has moved. The sequence ends with them rolling on the ground, the parachute flapping gently to the ground in post-coital calm.

## Back to the future

*Strange Days* is set just slightly in the future of the film's release, in Los Angeles on the day before New Year's Eve, 1999. Lenny (Ralph Fiennes), a black market dealer in 'clips', an outlawed form of total cinema produced by a new technology that taps directly into the cerebral cortex for both recording and playback, must learn to abandon the simulated memories of his former girlfriend (Juliette Lewis), however realistic, and embrace a new life in the real world with Mace (Angela Bassett). Through this metacinematic metaphor, violent action and eroticism are critiqued as voyeuristic, sadistic, and decidedly masculine. It is not surprising that Bigelow has called *Strange Days* her most personal film.[23]

The film begins by positioning us as viewers of one of these clips, although it is only in retrospect that we realize this, since no exposition precedes it. On the soundtrack we hear someone say 'Boot it', and the image seems to form as pixels, but the meaning of this is unclear. Once the clip boots, there is no apparent difference, such as a frame within a frame or disparity in image resolution, to mark these images as a film within the film rather than as images within the world of the film. For all intents and purposes, what we are seeing *is* the film – and by extension, any action film. We are thrust immediately into the viewing dynamic, our identification fully mobilized, despite the fact that as yet we do not know who 'we' are. Like clip users within the world of the film, we are fooled by the reality status of the sequence.

As in *Point Break*, we are immersed in the action, a part of it, featuring Bigelow's tour-de-force use of the subjective camera. In what seems like one lengthy, technically breathtaking shot (there are actually a couple of disguised cuts) on a par with the opening shot of Welles's *Touch of Evil* (1958) or Altman's *The Player* (1992), the viewer is put into the perspective of one of the participants. 'We' drive up to an Asian restaurant with a group of robbers, sitting in the back seat; commit robbery, intimidating staff and patrons in the process; frantically flee from the arriving police in a confusing shootout; attempt to escape across a series of rooftops, police in hot pursuit; and finally, plunge to 'our' death in the street below when we fail to make the leap from one rooftop to another. In this opening sequence we know only that we are male, as indicated by the dialogue, and by the hands we see from 'our' physical point of view, à la *Lady in the Lake* (1946). But the individual man here is in fact irrelevant – we are, the film immediately suggests, *masculinity itself*. The apparent long take maintains a consistent point of view and thus heightens our sense of presence throughout the action, the appeal of which is marked as racist and sexist since the victims of our abuse are 'fucking chinks' and 'bitches', as our invisible surrogate calls them.

This astonishing opening sequence exposes the subjective camera common to such genres as action and slasher movies as nothing less than a tool of naked male aggression. Many of the violent action sequences that follow in *Strange Days* involve the victimization of women with the SQUID apparatus, in the infamous manner of Mark Lewis (Karl Bohm) in Michael Powell's *Peeping Tom* (1960). It is no coincidence that (with the exception of Mace's one reluctant SQUID trip for Lenny's sake) the only users we see in the film are male. (The extent to which women are involved in the production or consumption of SQUID clips may be read as an indication of their moral corruption, as in the case of Faith.) Thus the subsequent scenes of violent action in the film cannot be viewed with the same kind of 'innocent' pleasure we may have brought to the opening sequence, for we have been made aware of the gendered dynamics involved in such pleasure.

But strangely – or perhaps not strangely, since this is, after all, a Hollywood movie – *Strange Days* builds to a climax that denies what has come previously, that seems to recuperate its own ideological critique. In the climax, Lenny, along with his friend, a female bodyguard (Angela Bassett), try to give to the police commissioner a clip that has recorded the truth about the killing of a popular militant black rock star by two racist white cops. The two policemen confront the woman during the wild celebration on the eve of the millennium and begin to assault her with their nightsticks. The scene obviously invokes the infamous tape of the Rodney King beating, which also occurred in Los Angeles; but in the movie, unlike the real world, the crowd of onlookers responds by actively banding together to fight this act of racial oppression. Finally, the honest white male commissioner, brandishing the evidence in his raised hand, parts the suddenly compliant crowd like the archetypal patriarch Moses parting the Red Sea and calls for the arrest of the two rogue cops. Power, ultimately, is retained in the (literal) hands of the white male, who now supersedes the once-capable and independent black woman.

## Conclusion

Robin Wood has angrily dismissed *Strange Days* as 'a tease and a cheat' because of the emphatic way it compromises its own premises.[24] But this response may be somewhat ungenerous, for it is no more an ideological cheat than the majority of mainstream American movies are. Perhaps it seems more disappointing because of how radical its initial premise is. Wood more accurately might have called *Strange Days*, in his own terms, 'an incoherent text'. Such texts, for Wood, are fractured or fragmentary, but have a 'consciously motivated incoherence [that] becomes a structuring principle, resulting in works that reveal themselves as perfectly coherent once one has mastered their rules'.[25] Bigelow herself has described *Strange Days* as 'at war with itself'.[26] From this perspective, the film's ideological contradictions speak quite eloquently of the tensions inherent in the situation of a woman making action movies about the traditionally male genre of action movies. Indeed, this position seems as fraught with difficulties as Megan Turner seeking phallic power in the male world of the police force, only with the penetrating, affective power of the motion picture camera instead of a gun. *Strange Days* does collapse at the end – an ending, significantly, that Bigelow stretches out for almost twenty minutes rather than elides – but this collapse serves to emphasize the limited place and power of women in mainstream cinema, whether in front of the camera or behind it.

In a sense, Bigelow's embrace of the action genre's pleasures while simultaneously critiquing them demonstrates a mastery of the master's own language. Although excess is more often associated with melodrama and the musical, it is certainly an important quality of the action film as well. The excess in Bigelow's action films serves as self-reflexive commentary on the genre and the masculine culture it celebrates, much as the excess in Douglas Sirk's melodramas commented on the ideology of the genre in which he was working and the cultural contexts of Eisenhower America. Although Sirk was working within the constraints of the studio system while Bigelow has made her films in the postclassical context of the new Hollywood, the analogy is apt, for both directors exist within the contexts of popular cinema, which is so thoroughly structured at every level by generic principles.

In the introduction to their pioneering anthology, *Screening the Male,* Steven Cohan and Ina Rae Hark note that:

> film theory has for the most part confidently equated the masculinity of the
> male subject with activity, voyeurism, sadism, fetishism, and story, and the

femininity of the female subject with passivity, exhibitionism, masochism, narcissism, and spectacle. In this scheme of homologous differences the power, stability, and wholeness of masculine subjectivity at the expense of femininity seem all too axiomatic and thus, universal and uncontestable.[27]

Kathryn Bigelow uses the action film to address fundamental issues of genre, gender and spectatorship, and to negotiate a place for women both in front of and behind the camera within traditionally masculine discourses. While many recent action movies have tended to reinscribe traditional patriarchal values,[28] Bigelow's work includes a remarkable series of films that have resisted the genre's conservative thrust. Like the new genre films of the 1970s that John Cawelti described as 'set[ting] the elements of a conventional popular genre in an altered context, thereby making us perceive these traditional forms and images in a new way',[29] Bigelow's action films are generic interventions that invite and encourage speculation about the nature of popular cinema.

## Notes

1   *The Weight of Water* (2000), a melodrama featuring Sean Penn and Elizabeth Hurley weaving together two narratives a century apart, has received rather limited release. Le Studio Canal+, the French company that produced the film, has not yet released it on video. *K19: The Widowmaker* (2002), a Cold War thriller, has Bigelow returning to the masculine terrain of the action genre as it is often emphatically depicted in submarine films.

2   Anna Powell 'Blood on the Borders – *Near Dark* and *Blue Steel*', *Screen*, 35: 2, Summer 1994, p. 136.

3   Christina Lane discusses some of these comments in *Feminist Hollywood: From Born in Flames to Point Break*, Detroit: Wayne State University Press, 2000, pp. 103–4.

4   Steve Neale 'Masculinity as Spectacle', *Screen*, 24: 6, November/December 1983, p. 5.

5   Laura Rascaroli 'Steel in the Gaze: On POV and the Discourse of Vision in Kathryn Bigelow's Cinema', *Screen*, 38: 3, Autumn 1997, p. 232.

6   'Momentum and Design: Kathryn Bigelow Interviewed by Gavin Smith', *Film Comment*, 31: 5, September/October 1995, p. 46.

7   Barbara Creed 'From Here to Modernity: Feminism and Postmodernism', *Screen*, 28: 2, Spring 1987, p. 65.

8   Yvonne Tasker *Spectacular Bodies: Gender, Genre and the Action Cinema*, London and New York: Routledge, 1993; Susan Jeffords *Hardbodies: Hollywood Masculinity in the Reagan Era*, New Brunswick, NJ: Rutgers University Press, 1994.

9   Peter N. Chumo II, 'At the Generic Crossroads with *Thelma and Louise*', *Post Script*, 13: 2, Winter/Spring 1994, p. 5.

10   Rebecca Bell-Metereau *Hollywood Androgyny*, 2nd edition, New York: Columbia University Press, 1993, p. 248.

11   Brian Henderson 'Towards a Non-Bourgeois Camera Style', *Film Quarterly*, 24: 2, Winter 1970–1, pp. 2–14.

12   Lane *Feminist Hollywood*, p. 110.

13   See, for example, Jim Kitses *Horizons West*, London: British Film Institute, 1969/ Bloomington: Indiana University Press, 1970, chapter 1; and Robin Wood 'An Introduction to the American Horror Film' in Robin Wood and Richard Lippe (eds) *American Nightmare: Essays on the Horror Film*, Toronto: Festival of Festivals, 1979, especially pp. 8–11.

14   Susan Sontag 'The Imagination of Disaster', in *Against Interpretation and Other Essays*, New York: Delta, 1966, p. 213.

15    Christopher Sharrett 'The Horror Film in Neoconservative Culture', in Barry Keith Grant (ed.) *The Dread of Difference: Gender and the Horror Film*, Austin: University of Texas Press, 1996, pp. 259–61. For Robin Wood's distinction between 'progressive' and 'reactionary' horror films, see Wood 'Introduction to the American Horror Film'.

16    Allen Ginsberg 'Wichita Vortex Sutra', *Planet News*, San Francisco: City Lights, 1968.

17    Powell 'Blood on the Borders', p. 145.

18    Powell 'Blood on the Borders', p. 147. See also Carol Clover *Men, Women and Chainsaws: Gender in the Modern Horror Film*, Princeton, NJ: Princeton University Press, 1992.

19    Tasker *Spectacular Bodies*, p. 147.

20    Kathleen Murphy describes the scene as 'berserker campaign iconography promising good times, a tiger in every tank'. 'Black Arts', *Film Comment*, 31: 5, September/October 1995, p. 53.

21    Interestingly, Reeves would later star in an even more apt role as *Johnny Mnemonic* (1995).

22    See Cynthia J. Fuchs 'The Buddy Politic', in Steven Cohan and Ina Rae Hark (eds) *Screening the Male: Exploring Masculinities in Hollywood Cinema*, London and New York: Routledge, 1993, pp. 194–210.

23    'Momentum and Design', p. 48.

24    Robin Wood 'The Spectres Emerge in Daylight', *CineAction*, 43, 1997, p. 7.

25    Robin Wood *Hollywood from Vietnam to Reagan*, New York: Columbia University Press, 1986, p. 46.

26    'Momentum and Design', p. 49.

27    Cohan and Hark *Screening the Male*, p. 2.

28    Karen Schneider 'With Violence if Necessary: Rearticulating the Family in the Contemporary Action-Thriller', *Journal of Popular Film and Television*, 27: 1, Spring 1999, pp. 2–11.

29    John Cawelti '*Chinatown* and Generic Transformation in Recent American Films' in Barry Keith Grant (ed.) *Film Genre Reader II*, Austin: University of Texas Press, 1995, p. 191.

## Chapter 24

## RACHEL WILLIAMS

## 'THEY CALL ME "ACTION WOMAN"'[1]
## The marketing of Mimi Leder as a new concept in the high concept 'action' film*

THE BIG-BUDGET HOLLYWOOD action movie has been viewed by critics as the fiercely guarded preserve of the white male. For example, Richard Dyer argues that the genre is primarily concerned with legitimising the 'thrills' of 'straight white men'.[2] Such a claim is certainly not without foundation given that female characters (and indeed non-white and non-heterosexual characters) have been under-represented in these films and, more importantly for this article, few women have directed them. Despite this there is, as Dyer himself acknowledges, evidence that the Hollywood action movie is beginning to admit 'others'. This cinematic enclave is no longer exclusively inhabited by, to borrow Susan Jeffords' phrase, the 1980s 'hard bodies' of John McClane (Bruce Willis in the *Die Hard* series) and John Rambo (Sylvester Stallone in the *Rambo* series). They have been joined by the protagonists of *Thelma and Louise* (1991), Sarah Connor (*Terminator 2* (1991)), Clarice Starling (*The Silence of the Lambs* (1991) and *Hannibal* (2001)) and Evelyn Carnahan (*The Mummy* (1999) and *The Mummy Returns* (2001)) to name but a few. However as directors of Hollywood action movies, women remain suspiciously absent.

Given the rarity of the female action-director in Hollywood it is reasonable to expect that when she does step into the cinematic arena her 'alien' presence in a 'male' sphere will cause a degree of anxiety. Some of those who run the industry, as well as some of those (such as film critics and journalists) who surround it may be compelled to inquire how she is to be normalised in such an unusual role? How is her 'transgression' into the 'macho' territory that is the action film to be understood? The fact that media interest surrounds women directors like Mimi Leder and Kathryn Bigelow who step into this territory suggests that, for many observers, their presence does require explanation. For example, many of the media texts surrounding Bigelow deal obsessively with the details of her femininity (her clothes, face, hair and so on), leading one to infer that her femaleness is overemphasised in order to balance her status as a director of 'male' films. In this way commentators are able to find a space for Bigelow within traditionally male-dominated Hollywood filmmaking.[3] Similarly, some of the marketing strategies employed in selling Mimi Leder's *The Peacemaker* (1997) and *Deep Impact* (1998) reveal that those in charge of marketing and publicising the films also made a 'space' for Leder within the big-budget action arena by exploiting her femininity: although in Leder's case it was not her appearance that was singled out, but rather the way in which her 'femi-nine' style of directing offered a new perspective on the traditional action film. In other words, Leder functions as a new female concept ('Action Woman') in the high concept action film.

My analysis uses the press kits issued by DreamWorks/Paramount for *The Peacemaker* (1997) and *Deep Impact* (1998), two variations on the high concept 'action' film directed by Leder, to illustrate the gendered strategies employed in the selling of a 'mainstream' woman director's films. I am not trying to argue that the way in which these films were marketed is somehow emblematic of the way all female-directed films are positioned in the marketplace, or indeed to suggest that every film made by a woman filmmaker is automatically sold to the public with reference to her gender, although this remains a strong tendency in the marketing of women director's films. In the press kit for Martha Coolidge's *Angie* (1994), for instance, a female member of the cast (Aida Turturro) is quoted as saying that with Coolidge 'at the helm there is an automatic understanding of some of the intricate details that are unique to women'. The production notes for Allison Ander's *Grace Of My Heart* (1996) inform us that 'the filmmaker who . . . has given us very real stories of uncompromising women in the nineties, now turns the clock back for a bright, honest look at a woman struggling to find her own voice in the male-dominated world of music', quoting Anders saying that the idea of a woman searching for her voice 'resonates for me on a very personal level'. In Leder's case her status as a woman director at the helm of *The Peacemaker* and *Deep Impact* was used to provide meaning differentiation in what has typically been classified as a generically 'male' commodity: the big-budget action movie.

Before embarking on a discussion of gender-based differentiation in the marketing of *The Peacemaker* and *Deep Impact*, it is worth mapping the ways in which these films simultaneously and paradoxically position themselves as conforming to the type of films from which they also seek to distinguish themselves. The marketing does not completely reject all recognisable aspects of the big budget 'action' film, but rather seeks to demonstrate that these have been used in a different way.

Although the action movie is not a clearly defined or definable genre, since it is a form which cuts across a wide variety of generic boundaries, it is possible to point to some production elements identified by José Arroyo as indicative of 'action/spectacle' which are, to a greater or lesser extent, shared by Leder's films.[4] These elements include 'high production values', a 'pattern of structuring the narrative around spectacular action set pieces' and a 'reliance on CGI and special effects'.[5] Both films had budgets of $50 million and upwards.[6] *The Peacemaker* includes four lengthy set pieces involving chases, gunfire and explosions. There is a train crash in Russia which ends with the detonation of a nuclear weapon; a car chase through the streets of Vienna which ends with the heroes' car blowing up; a helicopter pursuit to get back some stolen nuclear weapons; and a race through the streets of Manhattan to catch a terrorist who plans to set off a nuclear weapon. Similarly *Deep Impact* contains two notable sequences: one in which a group of astronauts land on a comet and plant nuclear devices which they hope will destroy it; and one where a massive tidal wave flattens the east coast of America while the film's teenage lovers race to get out of its path. Not surprisingly all these set pieces are dependent on extravagant special effects. However, since it is the marketing of Leder's films that concerns me here I want to move away from any attempt to pin them down as clear-cut examples of the 'action' film and concentrate on illustrating the ways in which they demonstrate a marketing strategy which is conventional for the big-budget Hollywood film.

Justin Wyatt argues that high concept is 'perhaps *the* central development . . . within post-classical cinema, a style of filmmaking molded by economic and institutional forces'.[7] He defines the high concept film as one which has a very strong sense of style, which is generic and which relies on recognisable character types. Most importantly, it is also one which possesses strongly marketable elements or 'marketing hooks'. In short, it is a film whose central narrative idea can be encapsulated in a 'one-line concept', and a simple but striking visual image and/or logo which finds its way onto the film's posters and other publicity material. Although Wyatt argues that high concept theory only applies to those Hollywood films which possess a very specific set of stylistic and production traits, much of what he says can be applied to post-classical film in general.[8] Here then, I do not intend to establish whether or not all these traits are present in Leder's films; rather, I intend to use Wyatt's work to give a sense of the typical marketing tactics employed to sell many big budget Hollywood films and to illustrate how *The Peacemaker* and *Deep Impact* both use and depart from them.

In several ways both *The Peacemaker* and *Deep Impact* fit Wyatt's model of a high concept film. They are generically based, although arguably *The Peacemaker* can be best defined as a straight action-thriller (a 'high-tech action thriller' according to the production notes) whereas *Deep Impact* is a more complex generic hybrid, incorporating elements of the disaster film, space film, love story, family melodrama, action film and so on. To some extent both films make use of stock characters. For example, *The Peacemaker* presents us with Thomas Devoe (George Clooney), a wisecracking, gung-ho hero who is reluctant to follow orders, and Aleksandr Kodoroff (Alexander Baluev), a dastardly Russian General who taunts our hero and kills without mercy. Similarly in *Deep Impact* there is an old hero (here an astronaut named Spurgeon Tanner played by Robert Duvall) brought back from retirement for one last battle, and an ambitious young reporter called Jenny Lerner (Téa Leoni) trying to make a name for herself. In addition both films have, and duly exploit, marketing hooks. *The Peacemaker* uses its big name stars as a selling point: Clooney (extremely well known for his role in *ER*) and Nicole Kidman. *Deep Impact*, on the other hand, chooses not to sell itself on its handful of fairly famous cast members (Duvall, Vanessa Redgrave, Morgan Freeman, Maximilian Schell), perhaps because it was thought that they would fail to provide the same degree of audience recognition as Clooney and Kidman. Instead, thanks to its plot which revolves around a comet which is on a collision course with the Earth, it capitalises on a topical subject (pre-millennial angst) and, as I go on to discuss, also a topical reinvention of the action-disaster mode as 'woman's film' made fashionable thanks to the success of *Titanic*. Finally, both *The Peacemaker* and *Deep Impact* are pre-sold on the reputation of Steven Spielberg as a director of countless blockbusters since he is one of the three men behind the studio, DreamWorks, which put the film into production.

If we turn to the film's marketing campaign, the press advertisements used to sell both films also fit aspects of Wyatt's argument. The fact that *Deep Impact* was far more successful than *The Peacemaker*, which performed relatively poorly at the box office, need not prevent us from recognising its marketing strategy as high-concept in nature since, as Wyatt points out, such a strategy is not an absolute guarantee of success.[9] The name of each film is written in bold, graphic type and serves as an 'identifiable logo' that acts to 'identify the film visually'. In the case of *Deep Impact* two of the range of press ads simply consist of the film's logo, and the logos of the three studios involved in its production, on a dark background, effectively cutting out any unnecessary and distracting visual clutter, and turning the film's title into a kind of brand name. The images chosen to represent each film are also visually striking, 'instantly recognizable' and able to 'define the film's theme' in a way that might identify them as high concept in nature.[10] *The Peacemaker* stresses the action one can expect from the film by choosing a shot of Clooney and Kidman running side by side, he with a gun in his hand. Above their heads their surnames are written in the same type as the film's logo, emphasising their 'star quality'. That the film is an 'action-thriller' is further suggested by the tag line: 'Every nuclear device in the world has been accounted for . . . Except one'. *Deep Impact* superimposes a shot of a couple embracing over a scene of a huge comet-induced tidal wave about to engulf New York. This image, along with a tag line summing up the narrative in six words ('Oceans Rise. Cities Fall. Hope Survives') distils the film's content into a neatly packaged cinematic commodity which provides the audience with knowledge of what to expect before they even enter the cinema: a disaster movie, human drama, special effects, action, excitement, and so on.

*Deep Impact*'s poster features imagery reminiscent of that used to sell *Titanic* (1997). Both posters depict a young couple embracing in the top half of the frame, while below them a disastrous scene (*Deep Impact*'s tidal wave) or the signifier of an impending disaster (*Titanic*'s illustration of the bow of the ship) is depicted. This is not surprising when we consider that Paramount was involved in the making of both films, and perhaps inevitably seized on the phenomenal success of *Titanic* as a means of improving *Deep Impact*'s chances at the box office. In order to achieve this the studio chose an aspect of *Deep Impact* (the love between a teenage couple set against a background of impending disaster) which is only one part of the narrative to function as the film's key selling point, and forge a connection with another film, *Titanic*, in which the love affair between two teenagers is at the centre of the narrative. The studio further tied the films together by using the same musician (James Horner) to write both soundtracks, and including a trailer for *Deep Impact* during screenings of *Titanic*.[11] In addition the executive who presided over Paramount's marketing campaign for *Titanic* (Arthur Cohen) was Paramount's advertising chief during the marketing of *Deep Impact*.[12] Cohen's previous work for the cosmetics company Revlon suggests that he came to the film industry with extensive experience of marketing to women, an experience exploited in the campaigns for films like *Titanic* and *Deep Impact*.

Peter Krämer has argued that *Titanic* was sold primarily as a 'woman's film', emphasising as it did a strong female protagonist, as well as the tragic love story at its centre. He argues that it was by appealing to a female audience, which Hollywood is usually guilty of neglecting, that the makers of the film ensured its financial success. Krämer's assumption that women have 'preferred genres' such as the 'Love Story' is potentially dangerous in its essentialism (not every woman who saw the film necessarily saw it because the romance of the story appealed to her), but it is fair to assume that elements such as romance, emotion, human relationships and so on are *perceived* as being attractive to woman by those in Hollywood (usually men) who set out to establish a female audience for their films.[13]

As indicated above, one way of achieving this is by using a semi-romantic image on the film's poster in order to create certain audience expectations. The makers of *Titanic* also ensured that the film's advertising 'clearly indicated that there would be more to *Titanic* than the spectacle of disaster', that it was a 'different kind of blockbuster': one which would appeal to women.[14] Similarly, all the publicity material surrounding *Deep Impact* stressed that this was not just another action/disaster film, but one which cared about the characters depicted, and which wanted the audience to care about them too. The press kit for the film tells us that, '[A]n audience will be very surprised by this picture . . . They may go in thinking it's a big spectacular kind of picture. And while it's epic in size, they'll be surprised to find themselves carried away by the personal stories.' A lobby card depicted Leoni's female journalist superimposed over a picture of the comet hitting earth. In this way the marketing indicated that a woman was central to the film's narrative: a factor which has been identified as one of the key features of women's genres in general, and the 'woman's film' in particular.[15]

The selling of *Deep Impact* as, in part at least, a 'woman's picture' in the mould of *Titanic* is not the only route through which gender creeps into the marketing of Leder's films. The publicity for *The Peacemaker* and *Deep Impact* also use the figure of the woman director as a useful tool in selling the films as something different (implicitly more 'feminine') than their generic markers might lead audiences to expect.

The creators of *The Peacemaker* are eager to point out that their film is not just another 'traditional action movie', but one which approaches its material 'in a fresh way that . . . set[s] it apart from the genre'. The production notes attempt to establish the serious nature of the project, informing us that it evolved from an article by a pair of veteran investigative journalists about nuclear weapons smuggling in the former Soviet Union, an idea subsequently developed by the screenwriter (Michael Schiffer) into a well-researched and plausible narrative scenario. Added to this, they explain, the plot is different from that of the 'traditional action movie' because it provides a complex motivation for its terrorist villain rather than relying on racial/national stereotyping, and it also takes into account the human events which drive the larger narrative. Leder herself is quoted as saying: 'I didn't approach this as an action movie, but instead as a dramatic human story. It does encompass a vast, large scope, but at the core is one man's personal tragedy which drives the action.'

The suggestion that such a novel approach comes courtesy of a *woman* director is made explicit: 'Also setting *The Peacemaker* apart was the choice of a woman to direct the film. Making her feature film directorial debut, Mimi Leder became one of only a handful of woman directors to break into the action arena.' The women director becomes the one who can breathe new life into an old genre, who can utilise her supposed 'femininity' in order to cut through the traditionally 'masculine' stereotypes of the action film. Her gender, and the different slant on things that this is seen to provide, are used to differentiate the film in a competitive marketplace.

This strategy of painting woman as the genre's 'saviour' is lent additional weight through the presentation of Kidman's role. The production notes inform us that 'saving the world from nuclear attack rests equally on the shoulders of Devoe [Clooney] and his partner, Dr Julia Kelly, played by . . . Nicole Kidman'. Kidman herself is quoted as saying that the chance to play the role of 'a strong, intelligent woman' drew her to the film. Thus the female presence in *The Peacemaker*, both on-screen and behind the scenes, is brought to the fore in the film's publicity. Nevertheless it is significant that despite the fact that Clooney and Kidman appear jointly and receive equal billing in the film's key marketing image, Clooney is featured more heavily in the publicity stills which come with *The Peacemaker*'s press kit. He appears in four out of the five images, sharing only two with Kidman. She, on the other hand, features in only three shots, two shared with Clooney. One of the shots, featuring Clooney standing alongside a wall and pointing a gun in standard action-man mode, has been cropped to remove Kidman from the scene (another version in which Kidman *is* standing behind Clooney appears with a review of the film in *Empire*).[16] Such a discrepancy perhaps suggests a tension at the heart of the film's marketing strategy between the desire to use conventional tactics and exploit the recognisable figure of the male action-hero, and an equally strong determination to show that *The Peacemaker* is more than the sum of its 'macho' generic parts.

The press kit for *Deep Impact* does not contain any statements quite as obvious in their intent. Such direct references to Leder's gender are bypassed in favour of a more subtle approach which builds on the *Titanic*-esque approach outlined above, drawing attention to the content and feel of the film as a marker of gendered difference. Unlike the almost identically themed 'earth-in-peril' movie *Armageddon* (1998), released two months later, the press kit for *Deep Impact* concentrates on the humanity of the situation over and above its potential for staggering special effects. The fact that these two films utilised very different marketing strategies is hardly surprising given that they had to differentiate themselves in the competitive context of the summer blockbuster season. Their marketing strategies could be described as diametrically gendered.

Whereas *Deep Impact* depicts itself as a gentler, more woman-friendly blockbuster, *Armageddon* revels in its sheer excess and the macho nature of its narrative and protagonists. As befits a film produced by Jerry Bruckheimer and financed by one of the most aggressive proponents of movie marketing, Disney, *Armageddon* opted for a more traditional action blockbuster marketing strategy, selling itself primarily on the sheer size of the spectacle on offer: whereas *Deep Impact*'s comet was the size of New York, *Armageddon*'s asteroid was the size of Texas. As Bruckheimer commented on the official *Armageddon* web site, 'I love stories that are bigger than life'. This web site also tells us that the film's hero, Harry Stamper (Bruce Willis), is 'a hard-nosed guy . . . [who] comes from a long line of independent men'; just in case we have missed the point, Bruckheimer throws in a handy comparison by telling us the film is like 'the Dirty Dozen in outer space'.[17] Yet despite their eagerness to emphasise the film's testosterone level, the makers of *Armageddon* apparently also wanted to make sure there was something for the women in the audience. According to Rod Dreher, they sought to repeat *Deep Impact*'s success with women filmgoers and make their film known to a female audience by recutting the film's trailer to be less 'hardware-oriented' and more 'people-oriented'.[18] In addition they ran trailers which emphasised the romance between the Ben Affleck and Liv Tyler characters during the popular television series *Ally McBeal*.[19]

*Deep Impact*'s production notes play down the elements one might expect from the conventional blockbuster. For instance, we are told that, 'For all its epic sweep and stunning images, it is above all a human story, as each individual struggles in the face of extinction to find what matters most to him or her'. Or, 'Inevitably special effects are going to come into play, because you can't tell a story of this scope without them. Here they'll enhance the human drama and provide a background for the whole story to come alive.' The film is pitched as character-driven, emotional, and concerned with the philosophical questions raised by confrontation with an apocalyptic event ('How would you live today, tomorrow, next week, if you knew the world might end in a year?'). In fact it could be argued that *Deep Impact* was on one level marketed as an issue-based drama, drawing on Leder's association with the television series *ER*. The press kit for *The Peacemaker* tells us that Leder:

> had originally come to the attention of the producers for her award-winning work on the series *ER* . . . The producers recognized that her ability to blend fast-paced action and human emotion – which are the hallmarks of the series – made her the perfect choice to direct this film.

*Deep Impact*'s press kit similarly informs us of this connection, telling us that the 'threads of this immense human drama are brought together by director Mimi Leder. A two-time Emmy winner for her work on television's *ER*'. In this way *ER* becomes a point of reference generating audience expectations of character-driven yet action-packed drama, which treats the issues it raises in a serious, intelligent way.

Such expectations are further underlined when we are reassured that *Deep Impact* is not just there to entertain, but also to get audiences thinking and asking themselves questions. Leder herself says:

> This movie is not just about special effects and disasters . . . It is about the people – about us – about what we would do were a comet to hit the

earth. There's a multitude of choices in the characters' lives . . . and hope-
fully one [sic] will walk out of this movie re-evaluating their lives and the
choices they've made.

Leder comes close here to implying that her film has a message, that we should
think about what we have done with our lives, and what we still have left to do.
Linda Seger has argued that many women filmmakers are careful to avoid espousing
anything close to a message in their work for fear of being typecast as 'feminine'
or 'feminist'. She writes:

> Issues make good drama . . . [But] these topics are not easily sold. Putting
> the positive into one's work is not always seen as dramatic, high concept,
> or commercial . . . Most mainstream women filmmakers shy away from
> any desire to do message drama . . . In fact, most understand the dangers
> of dealing with issue-oriented material.[20]

If we want to see evidence of such marginalisation at work we can point to a review
in *Empire* magazine of *Deep Impact* on its video release. Ian Nathan comments that
'Mimi Leder elects to play soap with a bunch of really dumb characters', and that
the film is 'so laughably a TV movie, it makes *Armageddon* look like rocket science'.[21]
By comparing *Deep Impact* with both a TV movie and a soap opera, Nathan picks
out two genres which are frequently associated with both issue-based drama and a
'feminine' sensibility. Designating the film a TV movie he refers in derogatory
fashion to an area of filmmaking where many women directors have had considerable success, often using it as a career stepping stone to greater things. His comment
could also be interpreted as a veiled criticism of Leder, who began her directing
career with television series like *LA Law*, *China Beach* and *ER*, as well as several
TV films.[22]

   Words like 'personal', 'poetic', 'emotions', 'emotional', and 'intimate' – all
used in the publicity for *Deep Impact* – could be said to have feminine connotations:
all evoke passive and interior (popularly stereotyped as feminine) rather than active
and exterior (popularly stereotyped as masculine) qualities. Through the reiteration of such terms, the filmmakers seem to want to render the epic as everyday,
and thus catch an audience who might be put off by a more typical action-disaster
film. In the minds of Hollywood executives at least, such people are usually thought
to be women.

   Whereas *Armageddon*'s marketing strategy can be seen to trade primarily on its
adherence to the norms of the big-budget action film, *Deep Impact* sells itself as a
film which, while it uses these norms as a framework, seeks to go beyond them.
This extension of the generic framework occurs primarily through the positioning
of the film as both a *female* (in terms of its director) and a *feminine* (in terms of
narrative content) text. I am aware here of the risk of implying that *Deep Impact*'s
marketing strategy was narrower than it actually was. Peter Bart notes that
Paramount felt that it could not afford to be too subtle in its marketing campaign
and, despite the objections of some of its creative team, ran television ads and

trailers which concentrated on the destructive power of the comet.[23] If the positioning of *Deep Impact* as 'female' and 'feminine' was not the only strategy used to sell the film, it was certainly one of the key strategies. In the wake of *Titanic*'s success with female moviegoers (*Newsweek* estimated the film's female audience at 60 per cent) the makers of *Deep Impact* obviously felt that they too could capitalise on the industry's latest rediscovery of the female audience, including elements in the marketing (romance, relationships, emotions) which they perceived would appeal to that demographic.[24] Yet, as with the marketing of *Titanic*, which played on acclaimed action director James Cameron's reputation, this did not preclude *Deep Impact* from reaching out to a wider demographic.

It is not surprising that the makers of *The Peacemaker* and *Deep Impact* used Leder as one way of differentiating their films in the marketplace, since choosing a woman to direct them was the kind of unique event that helps to create interest and publicity. In fact it would have been more unusual if they had not done so. With a woman director at the helm of a 'different' kind of action cinema these films had something to make them stand out. Judging by the articles and reviews which mention Leder's name in this context the tactic served both films well. To take three examples, at the time of *The Peacemaker*'s American release Amy Wallace wrote an article about Leder proposing that 'women action directors might bring something different to the screen' (that is, in Leder's terms, a '"smart" action movie'), and stating that Leder, on the evidence of comments she had made about directing *The Peacemaker* (that it was 'like childbirth') and the 'family' themes of her next project *Deep Impact*, was 'not afraid to be a woman at work'. Similarly film critic Michael Wilmington commented that *The Peacemaker* illustrated that DreamWorks was 'trying to give us a progressive variation on the usual high-tech clichés. The director and one of the good guys are both women'.[25] Leila Segal wrote a piece on Leder in *The Guardian* prior to *Deep Impact*'s British release in which she argued that the director had managed to breathe new life into a traditionally masculine genre, reliant on 'special effect, hi-tech hardware and violence'.[26] By stressing the 'femininity' of *The Peacemaker* and *Deep Impact* (and Leder's role in developing that femininity) the filmmakers were seemingly intent on detracting from the more conventional elements of each film in order to make them appear novel, and as a result potentially more attractive, to audiences who either have little interest in such movies or have become jaded with them.

Using a woman director to sell a film problematically equates a director's gender (female) with certain (feminine) thematic concerns, thus reinforcing rather than overturning traditional stereotypes about the kind of generic material female directors are best suited to. For instance, some critics of *Deep Impact* saw a direct correlation between the film's focus on people rather than explosions and the fact that it was directed by a woman. For Janet Maslin, Leder 'directs with a distinct womanly touch. Within the end-of-the-world action genre, it's rare to find attention paid to rescuing art, antiques, elephants and flamingos'[27]; in Leah Rozen's eyes she:

> brings – how to say this without sounding patronising? – a woman's touch
> to the disaster genre. Although she includes several obligatory, let's blow

stuff-up special effects sequences, *Impact*'s midsection is devoted to touchy-feely scenes of characters who . . . strive to get their relationships in order before the comet hits.[28]

The female director's gender may serve as an interesting topic for media discussion, potentially bringing her recognition, but it can also quickly become the primary topic for debate, leaving other questions about, say, the director's cinematic style and influences unaddressed. For this reason many women directors (especially those working in Hollywood) demand to be referred to simply as directors since, as they point out, male directors are never, or rarely so explicitly, gendered.

The fact that female directors often refuse to wear the tag of 'woman director' suggests that there are a number of underlying tensions within those cinematic marketing strategies which choose the director's femaleness as one of their marketing hooks. For example, in an article about *Little Women* in which Winona Ryder talks about the film as a female-bonding experience, the film's director Gillian Armstrong denies that her gender had any bearing on the way the film was made. Armstrong insists that she is merely a 'film director and an artist', stressing the film's entertainment factor rather than any feminist message.[29] However, on the evidence of its central advertising image (the March Sisters and their 'Marmee' rather than any of the male characters) the film was primarily sold as a 'chick flick', with Armstrong promoted as one of the 'chicks' who made it. In an interview with *Empire* designed to publicise the release of the film Winona Ryder comments that there is 'an unspoken understanding' when you are working with a female director rather than a man, and that female directors are more able to 'talk about sexuality and sensuality'.[30] This discrepancy points to the existence of tensions between the way a film is marketed and the way the film's director might wish it had been marketed (that is, without such stereotypical references to gender). In Mimi Leder's case such tensions are perhaps evident in her willingness to talk about her desire to bring changes to the action movie, but her refusal to state definitively that such changes are directly motivated by her gender, even though the press kits for her own films strongly imply it. Thus Wallace cites her as saying, 'What differentiates this movie from others in this genre is that we put a human face on the terrorist. Is that because of my femaleness? I don't know'.[31] She also tells the *Director's Guild of America Magazine* of her hope that 'one day [. . .] I'm just called "Mimi Leder, director" instead of "Mimi Leder, the action director" or "Mimi Leder, the female director"'.[32] Clearly Leder is unwilling to say that her artistic choices are determined by biology. Nor should one necessarily expect her to. Such an explanation not only has the potential to be both simplistic and patronising, but may also bring with it an attendant pressure to stand as some kind of female role model, one who is heralded (thanks to her 'feminine' approach to generic film), as rescuing a 'masculine' mode (action) for women, and indeed for more artistically discerning filmgoers in general. Indeed Mimi Leder has expressed concern about the way in which several female journalists held her up as a 'poster child' for female directors when she made *The Peacemaker*. Both male and female directors are subject to the same career finishing box office flops (Elaine May's *Ishtar* (1987) and Michael Cimino's

*Heaven's Gate* (1980) for example), but it is only for women that personal failure can be extrapolated into a representation of women's tendency to fail as a whole.

The phenomenal box office success of *Titanic* turned many traditional ideas about blockbusters, their marketing, and the nature of their audiences upside down. Warren Buckland suggests that the blockbuster is 'aimed at an undifferentiated popular audience rather than at any particular sector of the viewing population'.[33] However, *Titanic* and *Deep Impact* arguably sought to target a female audience within the structure of a wider campaign addressed to a mass audience. In other words, the female demographic was viewed as a niche market who could be lured into the cinema on the promise of seeing a new, more female-friendly blockbuster (one with less emphasis on special effects and more on characters). The danger of such a strategy is that it is still predicated on the assumption that there are 'men's' and 'women's' movies which have an almost exclusive appeal to the corresponding gender. To argue, as Krämer has done, that *Titanic* was able to secure a mixed audience because it had enough action to interest 'Hollywood's main target audience of young males' is an inadequate explanation for either that film, *Deep Impact*, or any other since it makes stereotypical assumptions about what attracts women or men to see a film (love and romance for the women, high-tech action for the men), without taking into account that the many different women who viewed these films would not all have had the same reasons for seeing them.[34] When a female director is factored into the equation (as Leder was in the marketing of *The Peacemaker* and *Deep Impact*) the temptation is to suggest that her gender is inextricably tied to the elements of the film which are gendered as female. Conversely, her contribution to the action side of the equation is downplayed, and the possibility of naturalising a woman in the role of action director is only partially fulfilled.

This examination of the marketing of Leder's films has highlighted some of the many ambiguities inherent in being a woman director working in Hollywood. Revealing that one's gender can be packaged and exploited (often without one's agreement) as a marketing tool demonstrates how difficult it is for female filmmakers to escape the 'woman' part of the phrase 'woman director'. Equally, Leder's case shows that women can be taken seriously as the directors of highly commercial, mass-marketed and mass-distributed films, which is extremely important in an industry like Hollywood which prefers to off-set financial risks by using filmmakers with a track record of financial success. Mimi Leder may have had experience of directing for television only when she was given the job of helming *The Peacemaker*, but this was unimportant since Spielberg's involvement as one of the owners of DreamWorks was enough of a guarantee in itself. After all, only by tackling the widest possible variety of films will women directors ever break out of that Catch 22 situation which dictates that a woman director cannot be trusted with genre X because she has no experience of working in it. It remains to be seen whether other women directors will be able to capitalise on Leder's entrance into action blockbuster territory, or if they will remain simply a marketable novelty in that generic arena. Leder says, that while she has been called 'Action Woman', she can 'direct anything'. Perhaps she is all too aware that this tag is at heart an empty concept in a film industry always searching for new marketing hooks (a fresh concept in the high concept film) rather than something which honestly functions to allow women greater directorial freedom.

## Notes

  \*  A version of this essay originally appeared in *Scope: an On-line Journal of Film Studies*, December 2000.

  1  Amy Wallace 'Shooting for a Role in a Male Film Genre', *Los Angeles Times*, September 25, 1997, p. A1; *Los Angeles Times Online*, November 10, 1999, http://pqasb.pqarchiver.com/latimes.

  2  Richard Dyer 'Action', in José Arroyo (ed.) *Action/Spectacle Cinema: A Sight and Sound Reader*, London: BFI, 2000, p. 18.

  3  For further discussion of Kathryn Bigelow and her films see, for example, Christina Lane *Feminist Hollywood. From Born in Flames to Point Break*, Detroit: Wayne State University Press, 2000; Yvonne Tasker *Spectacular Bodies: Genre, Gender and the Action Cinema*, London: Routledge, 1993, pp. 153–66; Yvonne Tasker 'Bigger Than Life', *Sight and Sound*, May 1999, pp. 12–15; and Needeya Islam '"I Wanted To Shoot People." Genre, Gender and Action in the Films of Kathryn Bigelow', in Laleen Jayaman (ed.) *Kiss Me Deadly: Feminism and Cinema for the Moment*, Sydney: Power, 1995, pp. 91–125.

  4  As proof that the action form is not constrained by genre one only has to consider the wide variety of films written about in José Arroyo (ed.) *Action/Spectacle Cinema: A Sight and Sound Reader*, and in Marshall Julius *Action! The Action Movie A-Z*, London: Batsford, 1996. These books cover martial arts films, sword and sorcery and science fiction movies, policiers, westerns, comic book and television adaptations and virtually everything else in between.

  5  Arroyo *Action/Spectacle Cinema*, p. 218.

  6  According to the *Internet Movie Database*, *The Peacemaker* had a budget of $50 million, and *Deep Impact* had a budget of $75 million.

  7  Justin Wyatt *High Concept Movies and Marketing in Hollywood*, Austin: The University of Texas Press, 1994, p. 8.

  8  Wyatt *High Concept Movies*, p. 60. The fact that Wyatt's model is more inclusive than he acknowledges is one of the central weaknesses of his theory.

  9  Wyatt *High Concept Movies*, p. 78.

10  Wyatt *High Concept Movies*, pp. 4, 122.

11  Rod Dreher 'For "Impact" Studios, the Earth Moved', *New York Post*, May 12, 1998; *New York Post Online*, January 10, 2001 http://promotions.nypost.com/051298/ 1731.htm.

12  Peter Bart *The Gross: The Hits, The Flops – The Summer That Ate Hollywood*, New York: St Martin's Griffin, 2000, p. 171.

13  Peter Krämer 'Women First: "Titanic" (1997), Action-adventure Films and Hollywood's Female Audience', *The Historical Journal of Film, Radio and Television*, 18: 4, 1998, pp. 599–619.

14  Krämer 'Women First', pp. 606, 610.

15  In 'Pedagogies of the Feminine' Charlotte Brunsdon identifies the 'representation of and identification with female protagonists' as one of the issues which concerns those who study women's genres (*Screen Tastes. Soap Opera to Satellite Dishes*, London: Routledge, 1997, p. 173). For further discussion of women's genres and the 'woman's film' see, for example, Mary Ann Doane *The Desire To Desire. The Women's Film of the 1940s*, Bloomington: Indiana University Press, 1987; Jeanine Basinger *A Woman's View: How Hollywood Spoke to Women, 1930–1960*, New York: Knopf, 1993; and Annette Kuhn 'Women's Genres: Melodrama, Soap Opera, and Theory', in Charlotte Brunsdon, Julie D'Acci and Lynn Spigel (eds) *Feminist Television Criticism: A Reader*, Oxford: Oxford University Press, 1997, pp. 145–54.

16  Ian Nathan 'Review of *The Peacemaker*', *Empire*, November 1997, pp. 44–5.

17  Originally available via a link on *The Internet Movie Database*, March 6, 1999, http://www. uk.imdb.com. No longer available on the web.
18  Rod Dreher 'The Hitch On Trailers', *New York Post*, June 28, 1998, *New York Post Online*, March 28, 2000, http://www.nypost.com.
19  Richard Corliss 'Aieee! It's Summer!!', *Time*, May 11, 1998, 151: 18, *Time Online Archives* September 2, 2001, http://www.time.com/time/magazine/archives.
20  Linda Seger *When Women Call The Shots. The Developing Power and Influence of Women in Television and Film*, New York: Henry Holt, 1996, pp. 240–2.
21  Ian Nathan 'Review of *Deep Impact*', *Empire*, December 1998, p. 138.
22  For example Randa Haines, who went on to direct the Academy Award winning film *Children Of A Lesser God* (1986), began her career in this way. Moreover, many women film directors have worked in television before making feature films, including Martha Coolidge, Penny Marshall and Betty Thomas.
23  Bart *Gross*, pp. 171–2.
24  David Ansen 'Our Titanic Love Affair', *Newsweek*, International edition, February 23, 1998, p. 47.
25  Wallace; Michael Wilmington 'Peace Offering', *Chicago Tribune*, September 26, 1997, p. A, *Chicago Tribune Online*, May 26, 2001, http://pqasb.pqarchiver.com/chicagotribune.
26  Leila Segal 'A Piece of the Action', *Guardian*, May 19, 1998, p. 7.
27  Janet Maslin review of *Deep Impact*, *New York Times*, May 8, 1998, *New York Times Online Archives*, September 2, 2001, http://search.nytimes.com/search.
28  Leah Rozen review of *Deep Impact*, *People*, May 25, 1998, *People Online Database*, July 10, 1998, http://www.people.aol.com/people/movie_reviews/98/deep.html.
29  Larissa MacFarquhar 'Sweet 'N' Jo', *Premiere*, January 1995, pp. 76–7.
30  Jeff Dawson 'Little Miss Perfect', *Empire*, March 1995, p. 79.
31  Wallace 'Shooting for a Role in a Male Film Genre'.
32  Patricia Troy 'Mimi Leder Helms DreamWorks First Feature', *DGA Magazine*, September/October 1997, *DGA Magazine Online*, October 26, 1998, http://www.dga.org/index2. php3.
33  Warren Buckland 'A Close Encounter With *Raiders of the Lost Ark*: Notes on Narrative Aspects of the New Hollywood Blockbuster', in Steve Neale and Murray Smith (eds) *Contemporary Hollywood Cinema*, London: Routledge, 1998, pp. 166–7.
34  Krämer 'Women First', p. 600.

# Index

Note: page numbers in italic denote references to figures.

*48 Hours* 10

Abbas, Ackbar 270, 278
Abel, Richard 2, 18, 53
*A bout de souffle* 375
Academy of Science Fiction, Horror and
    Fantasy Films 153
action-adventure films: authorship 11–12;
    chronotope 104, 110–16; early 19–20,
    25, 115; outside Hollywood 10–11
action-adventure genre/genres 1, 3–6, 11,
    71, 74–8, 371
action babe cinema 9, 201–16
action genre/genres 1–12, 17, 116, 188,
    226, 261, 386; and male power 372,
    385; as vehicle for ideas 331–2
action heroes 109–10, 110–13, 148, 203,
    261; sensitive roles 169; spaghetti
    westerns 314, 318–20, 321–4
action heroines 5, 169–71, 187–8; action
    babe cinema 201–16; female combat
    films 172–5, 202; Latinas 4, 9–10,
    186–98
adventure: early films 75–6; European
    films in 1950s and 1960s 325; ideology
    76–7; narratives 1, 7–8, 187–8; *see also*
    Greek adventure narrative
*Adventures of Kathlyn, The* 42–4, *45*, 60, 63

*Adventures of Robin Hood, The* 6, 77–8, 372
African American heroines 188, 196–7
Aldrich, Robert 346, 347, 348, 350–5
*Alien* films 9, 73, 170, 189, 195, 203,
    215, 264
Allied Artists 140–1
*All that Heaven Allows* 376
*Alone in the Jungle* 38
Alonso, Maria Conchita 189
Altman, Rick 239–40
Ambrose, Stephen T. 158, 159
*American Film* 365
*American Graffiti* 363
American International Pictures (AIP)
    140–1, 362
*Anaconda* 8, 186, 187, 190–2, *191*
Ander, Allison 190, 386
Anderson, G.M. ('Bullets') 35
Anger, Kenneth 374, 375
*Angie* 386
animation 156, 202, 365
*Anne of the Indies* 5, 76, 78
Appadurai, Arjun 219
*Armageddon* 390–1, 392
Armbruster, Carol 33
Armstrong, Gillian 394
Arnold, Edwin T. 349
*Arrival of a Train* (Lumières) 156, 372

Arroyo, José 1–2, 3–5, 190, 207, 260, 264, 386
*Arsene Lupin* 39
Asia/Asians 10, 274–5
Asiaphilia and Asiaphobia 270, 279
*Attack!* 348, 351, 353
audiences 104, 158–9; blockbusters 103, 395; early action films 34–5, 40; Hollywood's policy 361–3, 367, 395; Macdonald's view of mass culture 92; serial melodramas 44, 58–60, 67; *Star Wars* 360
auteurs/authorship 11–12, 346, 371
*Auto Bandits of Paris, The* 40
automobile: and youth culture 131, 139–42; *see also* car chase sequences
aviation films 75, 76

Babbington, Bruce 89
*Bad Man, The* 53
Bakhtin, Mikhail: chronotope 104–7, 108, 110, 116; dialogism 103–4, 105–7; Greek adventure narrative 104, 107–10, 111, 112, 114
Bancroft, Anne 172, 180
Banderas, Antonio 284, 285, 287
Barr, Charles 349
Barrymore, Drew 201, 210
Bart, Peter 392–3
Barzini, Luigi 310
Bassett, Angela 169–70, 189
*Battle, The* 35
*Battlecreek Brawl* 272, 273, 275
*Battle of Gettysburg, The* 37–8
*Battle of San Pietro* 162
*Battle of the Somme* 156
Baym, Nina 241
Bazin, André 103, 313–14, 317
Bean, Jennifer 3
Bell-Metereau, Rebecca 374
Bellour, Raymond 24, 27
Beltrán, Mary 9–10
*Ben-Hur* 7, 75, 86–9, 91, 96
Benjamin, Walter 17, 28, 157, 158
Berenstein, Rhona 76–7
Berg, Charles Ramírez 187, 189
Bergfelder, Tim 324, 324–5
Berry, Halle 201, 206, 209
Berry, John 347

Berumen, Frank Javier Garcia 188
Bettelheim, Bruno 367
*Beverly Hills Cop* 10, 274
Biblical epics: Macdonald's critique 85, 86–8, 89, 90, 90–2, 96
Bigelow, Kathryn 11, 170, 371–83, 385–6
biker movies 374
Billson, Anne 153–4
Biograph 23, 24, 33, 35, 54–5, 63
*Biograph Bulletins* 54
Bison films 34, 37
Blaché, Herbert 31, 39–40
*Blackjack* 287
black performers 10, 196–7
*Black Viper* 54
*Blade Runner* 287, 288
Blaxploitation films 197
*Blazing the Trail* 37
*Blind Fury* 287, 288
blockbusters 2, 3, 84–5; appealing to women 389, 390–1, 395; high concept action 5, 6–7, 190, 386; post-1977 103, 104, 108, 110, 115, 155, 202–3
*Bloodsport* 292–3
*Blue Steel* 169–70, 371, 372, 374, 377–9
Blumenberg, Hans 163
Bly, Robert 236
bodies 17, 71–4, 75, 170–1, 187–8; action babe heroines 205–6, 207, 216; action heroes 111–13, 203; Demi Moore's stardom 171–83; Macdonald's anxieties 94, 94–6; and masochistic spectacle 239; physicality of Latina heroines 187–9, 193–4, 198; Russell Crowe's stardom 243–4, 245–6; women in Greek war films 304
Bond films 4, 108, 109–10, 112, 116, 207
*Bonnie and Clyde* 132, *133*, 340, 346–7, 362
Bonnot gang 39
Bont, Jan de 11
Bordwell, David 134, 146, 155, 216, 269, 271, 272, 279
Bourdieu, Pierre 85, 97, 223
Bowser, Eileen 19, 31, 44
Brandt, Joe 60
Branigan, Edward 134

*Breakdown* 221–33
Breuer, Josef 23
Britain: audiences for serial melodramas 58–9; co-productions with Hong Kong 270; westerns 312
Brokaw, Tom 154
*Broncho Billy's Christmas Dinner* 35
Bronson, Charles 112
Bronston, Samuel 90–1
Brown, J.A. 73
Bruckheimer, Jerry 390–1
Brunet, Paul 61
*Buccaneers Girl* 78
Buckland, Warren 160, 395
buddy films 10, 263–4, 272, 373, 380
*Buffy the Vampire Slayer* 202, 288
Bukatman, Scott 119, 120
*Bullitt* 131–42, *135–7*
Bullock, Sandra 170
Burch, Nöel 114
Bush, George 71–2, 73
Bush, W. Stephen 36, 39
*Butch Cassidy and the Sundance Kid* 373–4

Cage, Nicolas 113, 242
Callenbach, Ernest 332
camera techniques: Bigelow's films 375, 379, 381; car chases 132–4, 137–9, 142, 146–8; *Django the Bastard* 320, *322–3*; Kurosawa's films 339–41; *Ringo and His Golden Pistol* 314–17, *315–16*, *318–19*; *Saving Private Ryan* 161–2; war epics 153
Cameron, James 11, 264, 366, 371, 393
Campbell, Colin 38
Canby, Vincent 365
*Cannonball Run* films 131, 139, 142, 272–3
Capa, Robert 161–2
capitalism: and cars in *Breakdown* 226–7; global 219, 221, 231, 270; Macdonald's concerns 92, 93
Carroll, Nöel: on *The Seven-Ups* car chase 143–6
cars: chase sequences 130, 131–48; *see also* automobile
Carter, Lincoln J. 32
*Cast Away* 242, 243
Castle, Irene 64

catharsis: Peckinpah's idea of 341; *Saving Private Ryan* 154, 156–9
Cawelti, J. 74
censorship 33, 157; *see also* National Board of Censorship
CGI (computer graphic interface) 269, 276–7, 278, 281, 386
Champlin, Charles 361
Chang, Terence 271
Chan, Jackie 207, 269, 270, 271, 272–7, 280
Chaplin, Charles 347
*Charlie's Angels* 9, 170, 201, 206, 207, 208, 209–11; Hong Kong influence 269, 277, 280
*Charlie's Angels: Full Throttle* 9, 171, 215
Charney, Leo 28
chase films 23–4, 130
*Chicago Tribune* 44, *45*, 63
children: in recent action-adventure films 252, 254–6, 292
children's entertainment: *Star Wars* 358–67
*China O'Brien* films 271, 272
Chow Yun Fat 211, 271, 272, 275, 278, 280
*Christmas Eve Tragedy* 33, 34, *34*
chronotope 104–13, 115–16, 116
Chrysler Corporation 226, 227
Chumo, Peter 373
Cinecittá 311
cinema of attractions 18, 23–4, 115, 142, 156
cinema of effects 7
CinemaScope 77
cinematography 126, 136
circus films 75
civil rights movement 236, 336
Civil War films 35, 37–8, 39, 55–6
Clark, Mike 222
class: appeal of early westerns 37; appeal of sensational melodramas 32, 44, 58–60, 66, 67; and changing US demographics 220; issues in *Breakdown* 221–33
*Cleopatra*: Macdonald's critique 86, 88, 93–4
*Cleveland Leader* 35, 36, 38, 39, 42
Clooney, George 193, 387, 388, 390
Clouse, Robert 269, 271

Clover, Carol 204, 378
Coham, Steve 243, 245–6, 254, 382–3
Cohen, Arthur 388–9
Cohen, Mary 141
Colbert, Claudette 93
Cold War 229–30, 347
colonialism: and adventure films 76, 77, 78
Colors 189
comedy: chase films 130, 148; family themes 254; gender-exchange roles 169, 170; in Hollywood action-adventure 73; in women's action roles 209–10
comic strips: action babe heroines 202, 208–9, 215; heroes 291
Commando 112, 153, 260
computer-generated images 201, 207
computer graphic interface see CGI
Connery, Sean 112, 243
consumer culture: issues in Breakdown 221, 225–6, 228, 232–3; patriarchal 202–3
Coolidge, Martha 386
Corbucci, Sergio 325
Cord of Life, The 54
Corrupter, The 272
Cortés, Carlos E. 187, 188
Costa, Mario 313
Courage Under Fire 169, 171, 172, 173, 180
Cousins, Mark 156
Creed, Barbara 372
crime thrillers: chase sequences 130, 131, 143; early French 32, 39, 40–2
crime and urban action 4, 7, 189
Cross of Iron 333
Crouching Tiger, Hidden Dragon 11, 201, 202, 207, 208, 210–11, 215, 277, 278, 280–1
Crowe, Russell 235, 242, 243–4, 245–6, 247
Crowther, Bosley 346
Cruise, Tom 174, 242, 277
Cunard, Grace 65
Curtis, Jamie Lee 169–70, 260, 372, 378
Curtiz, Michael 6

Daily Telegraph 153, 158
D'Antoni, Philip 143
Dargis, Manohla 277

Darnell, Linda 188
I Daskala me ta Chryssa Mallis/The Teacher with the Golden Hair 300–1, 302
Davis, Geena 170, 174, 261
Death Wish 112
De Bont, Jan 104, 114
Deep Impact 386–96
De Havilland, Olivia 6
Delaney, Samuel R. 120
De Laurentiis, Martha 231
Deliverance 222, 223, 227, 232; compared with Breakdown 228–9
Del Toro, Benicio 190
demography: and ethnicity in USA 190, 197–8, 219–20
De Niro, Robert 181
Dern, Laura 169
Desperado 11
Desser, David 271
detective films 42, 46
dialogism 103–4, 105–7
Diaz, Cameron 201, 206, 207, 210, 277
Die Another Day 9
Die Hard 72, 104, 106–14, 116, 261
Die Hard With a Vengeance 112
digital effects 269; action babe films 201, 207; Hong Kong action films 276–7, 277–80
dime novels 33, 54, 56–7, 76
Ding-Tzann Lii 270, 272, 275
Director's Guild of America Magazine 394
Dirty Dozen, The 345–55
Dirty Harry 112, 136
Dirty Mary, Crazy Larry 131, 141
disaster films 74, 76, 241–2, 389, 393–4
Disclosure 171, 176, 178, 180, 182
Disney 180, 365, 366, 391
Django the Bastard 310, 313, 318–20, 322–3, 324, 325
Doane, Mary Ann 25
Doherty, T. 140
Dole, Carol M. 189, 192
Double Team 272, 292, 293
Douglas, Michael 182, 242
Doyle, Arthur Conan 361
DreamWorks 386, 388, 393, 395
Dreher, Rod 391
drive-ins 140–1
Drunken Angel 334

*Drunken Master* 273
*Duel* 139, 147–8
Duncan, Robert 95–6
Durgnat, Richard 350–1
DVD extras: action babe films 206, 207, 211–14
Dyer, Richard 2, 174, 176, 188, 198, 203, 284, 294, 385

Eastwood, Clint 112, 242, 311
*Eat My Dust* 131, 148
Ebert, Roger 194, 222, 223, 228, 231
Éclair (company) 36, 40, 44
Edison 66
Edwards, Paul 351
Ehrenreich, Barbara 93
Eisenstein, Sergei 27, 64, 65
Eitzen, Dirk 142–3
Eleftheriotis, Dimitris 11
Ellis, Brett Easton 378
Ellis, John 177–8
Elsaesser, Thomas 159
Emmerich, Roland 11
*Empire* (journal) 158, 178–9, 243
*Enough* 186, 198
*Enter the Dragon* 270, 271
Esparza, Moctesuma 190
ethnicity *see* race/ethnicity
Europe: and American film industry 44–6; market for melodramas 32; popular cinema in 1950s and 1960s 324, 324–5; Second World War 77
European actors 284–95
*Europe by Night* documentaries 325
Evans, Peter 89
*eXistenZ* 120
*Exploits of Elaine, The* 56, 61, 64

Fairbanks, Douglas 6, 8, 74, 75, 77, 372
fairytale: *Star Wars* 363, 364–5, 367
*Falling Down* 228, 236
Faludi, Susan 236–8, 245
family: audience of *Star Wars* 360, 365, 366, 367; issues in Spielberg's films 164; themes in early action films 4–5, 24; themes in recent action-adventure films 244–5, 252–3, 254, 263–5, 367
Famous Players 37

fantasy 4, 8, 201, 202, 216; and family themes 156, 254, 255, 265; *Star Wars* 363, 365
*Fantomas* series 40–2, 44
fascism: threat of 77, 85
Fassbinder, Rainer Werner 372
*Faster Pussycat, Kill! Kill!* 188
*Fast and the Furious, The* 186, 195
*Fatal Beauty* 73–4
*Fatal Hour, The* 54
*Fatal Ring* 59, 64
fatherhood 252, 253
female combat films 172–5
female directors 385, 392, 393–5
*Female Spy, The* 53
femininity 203, 204, 378, 392; and 'death of the Great White Male' 237, 239; in female combat movies 73, 173, 178, 179–80; Latina heroine as distanced from 187, 188, 192, 198; marketing of female directors 385–6, 390, 392–3
feminism 178–9, 252, 372, 392; film criticism 8–9, 198
*FHM* magazine 206
*Fifth Element, The* 11
*Fight Club* 236, 237–8
*Film Daily* 74, 76
*film noir* 348, 349, 350–1
*Film Quarterly* 332
*Film Review* 256–7
film studies 12, 84–5, 103
*Final Fantasy: The Spirits Within* 201, 206, 208, 212, 215
Final Girl 202, 204, 378
Fine, Michelle 231
First World War 64, 156, 342
Fishburne, Laurence 10
*Fist of Legend* 279, 280
*Flaming Barriers* 75
Flynn, Errol 6, 75, 372
*For a Few Dollars More* 346
Ford, Francis 65
Ford, Harrison 169, 229, 242
Ford, John 221, 228, 309
Ford Motor Company 226–7
foreign films: and the American market 3, 31, 33–4, 39
Fore, Steve 272, 273, 280
*Fortress, The* 290

Fox, William 60
Fox (company) 72, 75, 363, 365
Fradley, Martin 5, 9
Franchi, Franco 325
Frank, Thomas 139
*Frantic* 222, 229
Frayling, Christopher 310, 319, 321
Fregoso, Rosa Linda 187, 188
*French Connection, The* 131, 132, 134–6,
    137, 146, 147, *148*
*Frenchman's Creek* 77, 78
French melodramas 31–44
Freud, Sigmund 23, 24–5, 157–8
Frey, William 219–20
Friedkin, William 134–6, 146
*Fugitive, The* 289
Fuller, Mary 63
Fuller, Sam 12
*Full Metal Jacket* 172–3

Galiani, Abbé 163
Gallagher, Mark 9, 252
*Game of Death* 272
Gamson, Joshua 198
Garfield, John 347
Garrone, Sergio 325
Gaumont Company 31, 33, 38, 39,
    40–2
Gemma, Giuliano 313
gender 4, 5, 8–10, 75, 109; in action
    babe spectacle 202–5, 207–10, 216;
    Bigelow's approach 371, 372, 374,
    376, 383; in boot camp films 172,
    179, 181; challenging of types in
    *Girlfight* 194–5; dynamic in
    melodramas 64, 67; dynamics of
    *Breakdown* 224; and family themes
    252, 257; feminine heroes and
    masculine heroines 169–70, 175; in
    historical adventure films 78; and ideas
    of mass culture 93–4; transgressions
    72–3; *see also* femininity; masculinity;
    sexuality
genre: Bakhtin's view 116; Bigelow's
    approach 371–2, 373, 376, 383;
    hybrids and conventions 3, 71, 190,
    309, 310, 326, 373, 375–6; and
    national identity 320; and subgenres of
    serial melodramas 56; *see also* action

genre/genres; action-adventure
    genre/genres
Gere, Richard 173, 174
Germany: westerns 312, 321
*Ghost* 176
*Giant Robot* magazine 281
Gibson, Helen 66
Gibson, Mel 108–9, 169, 242
*G.I. Jane* 9, 171–5, 178–9, 180–1, 182,
    203
Gilbey, Ryan 179
Ginsburg, Allen 95, 377
*Girlfight* 186, 187, 190, 193–5, *194*, 197,
    215
*Girl and the Motor Boat, The* 53
*Girl Reporter's Big Scoop, The* 56
Girl Spy series 55–6
Gish, Lillian 64
*Gladiator* 5, 9, 235, 237, 242–50
Glickenhaus, James 269, 274, 280
globalization: issues in *Breakdown* 219,
    221, 231, 232–3
Godard, Jean-Luc 375
*Goddess, The* 66
*Godzilla* 1
Goldberg, Whoopi 73, 289
*Goldeneye* 110
Golden Harvest 271–2
Goldstein, Jenette 189, 215
Goldstein, Richard 154, 159
Golem, Menahim 291
*Gone in 60 Seconds* 131, 141
Gonzalez, Deena J. 197
Gordon, Don 134
*Gospel According to St Matthew, The* 88,
    91–2, 92
*Grace Of My Heart* 386
Graham, John 236
*Grand Canyon* 228
*Grand Prix* 138
*Greatest Story Ever Told, The*: Macdonald's
    critique 86, 87–8, 91, 93
*Great Train Robbery, The* 7, 130, 324
Greek adventure narrative: Bakhtin's
    analysis 104, 107–10, 111, 114
Greek war films 5, 11, 297–306
Greenburg, Clement 92
*Greystoke: The Legend of Tarzan, Lord of the
    Apes* 289–90

Griffith, D.W. 23, 24, 25, 53–5
Grossberg, Larry 220
Gross, Larry 1, 103, 104
Grossman, Harry 60
*Grotto of Torture, The* 38–9
*Guardian* 158, 393
Guerrero, Ed 10, 189
Guinan, Texas 75
*Gumball Rally, The* 131, 141–2
*Gun Crazy* 134
*Gunga Din* 77
Gunning, Tom 7, 23, 25, 142, 143
*Gynaika stin Andistasi, Mia/A Woman at Resistance* 300–1, 304–5

Halberstam, Judith 197, 210
Hale's Tours 115
Hamilton, Linda 71, 170, 171, 189, 203, 374
Hammond, Michael 9
Hancock, John 158
Hanks, Tom 161, 242, 243
Hansen, Miriam 19
Harareet, Haya 88
*Hard-Boiled* 11
*Hard Target* 291, 292
Hark, Ina Rae 382–3
Harlin, Renny 11
Harrison, Louis Reeves 40
Haskell, Molly 365
Hatfield, Hurd 88
Hauer, Rutger 284, 285, 287–8, 293
Hawks, Howard 12
Haworth, Ted 333
Hayles, N. Katherine 126
*Hazards of Helen, The* series 18, 19, 20–3, 24, 25–8, 55, 65, 66
Hearst, William Randolph 61, 64, 65
Heidegger, Martin 28
Heller, Lukas 351
Heller, Zoe 177
Henderson, Brian 375
heroes *see* action heroes
heroines *see* action babe heroines; action heroines; women warrior films
Heston, Charlton 87, 88, 94
heterosexuality: action babe heroines 204–5, 206; affirmation of in early action films 25; Latina heroines 193,
195, 198; *see also* white, heterosexual masculinity
Hickman, Bill 137
*Hidden Fortress, The* 334, 335, 363
high concept cinema 2, 5, 201, 204, 386, 387, 396
*Highlander* 290
historical adventure films 8, 77–8
historical epics 7, 84–5, 242; Macdonald's condemnation 85, 86–97
*Hitcher, The* 287, 288
Hollywood: audiences targeted 39, 361–3, 367; classic gender roles 203; and crisis of white masculinity 235–6, 239, 242, 249–50; genres and generic hybridity 3, 71, 190, 309, 310; high concept films 387; and Italian film market 310, 312; and Latina action heroines 186–7, 195; pervasiveness of car chase 131, 139; significance of 'Big Loud Action Movies' 103, 104; *Star Wars* as model 358; and westerns 313–14; and youth market 139; *see also* New Hollywood cinema
*Hollywood Reporter* 366
Holmes, Helen 64, 65
Holmlund, Christine 11, 73, 187, 209–10
Holstan, James 219
Hong Kong film industry 11
Hong Kong/Hollywood action films 269–81
*Hook* 253
Hopper, Dennis 109, 112
Horner, James 388
horror films 11, 254, 325, 378; *see also* slasher horror; vampires
Horton, Andrew 131
hot rod films 140
*Hunted, The* 290
Hunt, Leon 6, 11, 96–7
Hynes, Samuel 154, 155

Ice Cube 191, *191*
ideology: of adventure 76–7; and articulation of gender 8–9, 67; bodies in action-adventure 71–4; preoccupations of *Star Wars* 358; referent of Latina action heroines 198
*Ikiru* 334

illusion: in *The Matrix* 119–28
imperialism 76–7, 270
Ince, Thomas 37
*Indecent Proposal* 171, 175, 176
*Independence Day* 10, 359, 366
*Independent* (newspaper) 157, 179
*Indiana Jones* films 71, 108, 160, 254
Ingrassia, Ciccio 325
*In the Grip of Alcohol* 35–6
*In the Land of the Lion* 38
International Film Service 61, 65
Irons, Jeremy 112
Italian westerns *see* spaghetti westerns
Italy: film market in 1960s 310,
    311–13
Iyer, Pico 232

Jackson, Alan 227
Jackson, Reverend Jesse 196
Jameson, Frederic 154
Jancovich, Mark 7
Janssen, Famke 201, 204, 209
Japan 331, 350; Kurosawa's background
    333–4, 337–8
Jarvie, Ian 294
*Jason and the Argonauts* 6
*Jaws* 7, 103, 160, 366
Jeffords, Susan 71–2, 73, 187, 253, 263,
    373, 385
Jet Li 189, 270, 275, 277–80
*Jingle All the Way* 255
*Johnny Mnemonic* 286
Johnson, Nunally 351
Jolie, Angelina 170, 204, 206, 207; in
    *Tomb Raider* 201, 212–15, *213*
Jovovich, Milla 206; in *Resident Evil* 195,
    201, 212–15
Julius, Marshall 115
*Jumpin' Jack Flash* 289
jungle films 35, 37, 38–9, 46, 75, 76–7
*Junior* 169, 255
Jurado, Katy 188
*Jurassic Park* 8, 169, 227, 254, 359

*Kagemusha* 333, 334, 335–6, 337
Kalem company 18, 35, 42, 55–6, 65,
    66–7
Kaminksi, Janusz 161
Kant, Immanuel 106

Kaplan, E. Ann 241
*Karate Kid, The* 272
Karezi, Jenny 299, 300, 304
Kay-Bee westerns 37
Keegan, John 153, 154
Kennedy, John F. and Robert F. 336
Kennedy, Liam 238
Keystone films 130
*Kickboxer* 292–3
Kidman, Nicole 387, 388, 390
*Kill Bill* 215
*Killer, The* 11
Kim Tai-chung 272
*Kindergarten Cop* 169, 253, 255
King Hu 281
King, Martin Luther 336, 337
*King of Kings*: Macdonald's critique 88,
    90–1, 91, 93
*Kings of the Forest* 38
Kirby, Lynn 19, 23, 25, 157
*Kiss Me Deadly* 348, 349–50, 351, 353
kitsch: Macdonald on historical epics 88,
    89, 92, 93
Klein, Naomi 209, 238
*Konserto gia Polyvola / Concert for Weapons*
    300–1, 304
Korean War 350, 350–1, 352
Koszarski, R. 75
Kozloff, Sarah 285
Krabbé, Jeroen 284, 285, 288–9, 293
Kracauer, Siegfried 157
Krämer, Peter 164, 257, 260, 389,
    395
Krutnik, Frank 239
kung fu 206, 271
*Kung Fu* TV series 270
Kurosawa, Akira 12, 331–43, 363
Kusama, Karen 194–5

*Ladies World, The* magazine 63
Laemmle, Carl 57, 60
Lahue, Kalton 65
Lambert, Christophe 284, 285, 289–90,
    291
Lancaster, Burt 75
Lane, Christina 376
*Lara Croft: Tomb Raider* 9, 201, 205,
    212–15, *213*, 252
*A Lass of the Lumberlands* 62

*Last Action Hero* 1, 254, 254–6, 284, 294;
   compared with *Lost in Space* 257–9
Latina action heroines 4, 9–10, 186–98
Lavery, David 119–20
Lazenby, George 269, 271
Le Blanc, Maurice 39
Leder, Mimi 385–96
Lee, Ang 11, 211
Lee, Bruce 269, 271, 272, 274, 276,
   278, 280
Leone, Sergio 310, 325
*Lethal Weapon* films 72, 109, 110, 261,
   263–4, 278, 294
Leung, William 211
Levine, Joe 86, 88–9
Lewis, Jerry 362
*Life of an American Fireman* 52
Lincoln, Elmo 75
*Lionheart* 291, 292, 293
*Lion's Revenge, The* 38
*Little Women* 394
Liu, Lucy 189, 201, 210
*Lives of a Bengal Lancer, The* 77
*Living Daylights, The* 289
locations 7–8, 108, 294; *The French
   Connection* 136; historical epics 91–2;
   spaghetti westerns 324
*Lock Up* 73
Loftin, Carey 137, 138–9
Loken, Kristanna 9
Lombardo, Lou 340
*Lonedale Operator, The* 24, 25, 27
*Lonely Villa, The* 25, 55
*Longest Yard, The* 353
*Long Kiss Goodnight, The* 153, 170, 261–2,
   264
Lopez, Jennifer 9–10, 195, 198; in
   *Anaconda* 186, 187, 190–2, *191*, 197;
   in *Out of Sight* 187, 190, 192–3
*Los Angeles Herald-Examiner* 365
*Los Angeles Times* 361
Losey, Joseph 347
*Lost in the Jungle* 35
*Lost in Space* 254, 256–9
*Lost World, The* 6, 7–8
*Loveless, The* 371, 374–5, 379
Lucas, George 103, 108, 359, 361,
   363–5
*Lucille Love: Girl of Mystery* 57, 65

Lumière brothers 156, 372
Lundgrun, Dolph 71, 284, 285, 285–6,
   291, 293

McCarthyism 347
Macdonald, Dwight 85–97
McGowan, J.P. 65
McQueen, Steve 133, 134, *136*, 137, 141
McTiernan, John 104
*Magnificent Seven, The* 333
Maltby, Richard 142, 143
*Man from Hong Kong, The* 271
Mankiewicz, Joseph 94
Marchetti, G. 74
*Margrave's Daughter, The* 39
*Mariarchi, El* 11
marketing: Leder's films 385–96; *see also*
   merchandising
*Mark of Zorro, The* 77–8, 372
martial arts: action heroines 202; Hong
   Kong action 211, 269–81
*Martial Law* TV series 275
Marvin, Lee 348, 352
masculinity: action genre perspective 9,
   372; action heroes 112, 148, 261; and
   adventure 76; Bigelow's exploration
   371–2, 377–9, 380, 381, 382–3; in
   *Breakdown* 223–4; challenging of
   stereotypes in *Girlfight* 194; crisis of
   235, 237–9, 240, 254, 271; gender
   exchanges 203, 204; in *Gladiator*
   243–4, 245–6, 247, 248; in historical
   epic 94–6; shifts in films with family
   themes 253–4, 257; *see also*
   'musculinity'; white, heterosexual
   masculinity
Maslin, Janet 393
masochism: narratives 235–6, 239–41,
   243, 249–50, 292
mass culture: blockbusters 103;
   Macdonald's anxieties 85, 92, 93–4;
   sensational melodramas 32, 40, 44, 59,
   67
*Master, The* 275
*Matrix, The* 10, 119–28, 170, 206, 215,
   242, 359; Hong Kong influence 269,
   274, 277, 279–80, 280
Mature, Victor 75
*Maximum Potential* 287

*Maximum Risk* 291, 292
Mechanic, Bill 190
media empires 366–7
Meeker, Ralph 346, 351
Melley, Timothy 239
melodrama 44; dramaturgy of *Saving
   Private Ryan* 159–61; early films 4,
   52–67; as film genre 3, 56, 61–2;
   gendered action spectacles 241;
   *Gladiator* 245; Greek war films 297,
   298, 299–301, 303; sensational thrillers
   4, 31–46; serials 2, 18–19, 42–4, 55,
   56–67
memory: in *Saving Private Ryan* 159–61
men's style magazines 205, 206, 210
merchandising 114–15; *Star Wars* 359,
   360, 366; *see also* marketing
Metz, Christian 104–5, 111
middlebrow culture: Macdonald's critique
   85–6, 88, 89, 96–7
middle class: depiction of in *Breakdown*
   221–2, 228
Mifune, Toshiro 332
Miller, Eugene L. 349
*Million Dollar Mystery, The* 60, 63
Miserocchi, Anna 313
*Mission Impossible* films 2, 4, 277
*Mi Vida Loca / My Crazy Life* 190
Miyoshi, Masao 225
modernity 17
Modleski, Tania 253, 262
*Monaco Forever* 291
*Mondo Cane* 325
Moore, Demi 9, 171–83, 203
morality: America and the western 314;
   concerns about melodrama films 31–2,
   34, 44–6; Greek war films 299; and
   violence in Kurosawa and Peckinpah
   342–3
Moreno, Rita 188–9
Morgenstern, Joseph 349
Moricone, Ennio 311
Morris, Meaghan 269, 272
*Mortal Kombat* 290
*Mortal Thoughts* 176
Moss, Carrie-Anne 170, 277
Mostow, Jonathan 221, 231
Motion Picture Association of America
   (MPAA) 361–2

*Motion Picture Herald* 74
*Motion Picture Magazine* 64
*Motion Picture News, The* 67
Motion Picture Patents Company (MPPC)
   33, 54
*Moving Picture News* 34, 35, 42
*Moving Picture World* 22–3, 32, 33, 36, 39,
   40, 42, 44
MTV 202
Mulvey, Laura 8, 155, 203, 204, 205
*Mummy, The* and *The Mummy Returns* 9, 385
Murphy, Eddie 10
'musculinity' (feminine) 174–5, 181, 189,
   203
music: Greek war films 299, 300; *see also*
   soundtrack
musicals 4, 5, 85, 265
Musser, Charles 115, 324
Musto, Michael 286–7
Mutual 62, 64, 65–6
*My Family / Mi Familia* 189
*Mysteries of New York, The* 64
*Mysterious Fingerprint, The* 41

narcissism: and paranoia 238–9, 250
narrative: car chase techniques 134;
   chronotope of action films 104, 106,
   108, 111; *Girlfight* 194–5; Greek war
   films 298–9; *The Hazards of Helen* series
   20–3, 26–7; historical epic 96;
   Hollywood action-adventure 71; *The
   Matrix* 123, 126; *Saving Private Ryan*
   159–61, 162; and spectacle 2–3, 5–6,
   6–8, 84–5, 142–8, 203–4; structure
   and themes of melodrama 3, 52, 61–2,
   64; war films 155
Nathan, Ian 392
National Board of Censorship 31, 33–4,
   54–5
*National Enquirer* 181
national identity: America and the mythic
   West 230, 314; and generic
   conventions 309; spaghetti westerns
   320–6
nationalism: Greek war films 11, 298–9,
   301; and manhood in *Breakdown* 223,
   224, 226
Neale, Steve 3, 85, 242, 371
*Near Dark* 371, 372, 375, 375–7

Needham, Hal 139
Neel, Susan Rhoades 230
Neill, Alex 161
*Neil of the Navy* 64
Nerlich, M. 76
Nero, Franco 318, 319
*New Centurions, The* 136, 138
New Deal 347
New Hollywood cinema 1, 190
Newman, Kathleen 189
New Order: video 372
*New Statesman, The* 58–9, 154
New Wave/Nouvelle Vague 105, 347
New Woman 19, 67, 75
*New York Dramatic Mirror* 31, 31–2, 34, 35, 37, 39, 42, 44; on serial melodramas 18, 57, 63
New York Motion Picture Company (NYMPC) 34, 35, 37
*New York Post* 359
*New York Sunday Tribune* 39
*New York Times* 136, 288, 346, 365, 366
*New York World* 34
*Nickelodeon* 34
Nicolas Power company 46
Nielson, Brigitte 71, 73, 179
*Nighthawks* 287, 288
*No Mercy* 289
*No Retreat, No Surrender* films 272, 291
Norris, Chuck 271, 274, 291, 373
*El Norte* 189
Nouvelle Vague/New Wave 105, 347
novel: Bakhtin's dialogism 104, 105–7, 107; *see also* dime novels
*Nowhere to Run* 291, 292
*Nun and the Sergeant, The* 352

Oberholtzer, Ellis 56, 57, 58, 59
*Observer* 243
*Ocean's Eleven* 11
O'Day, Marc 4, 9
O'Donnell, Patrick 238, 239
*Officer and a Gentleman, An* 172, 173, 174
O'Hehir, Andrew 2
*Once upon a Time in China* series 269, 275, 276, 277, 278
*Open Switch, The* 55
*Osterman Weekend, The* 287, 288, 336, 341

*Ouchard the Merchant* 33–4
*Our Mutual Girl* 65
*Out of Sight* 11, 186, 187, 190, 192–3

Papadimitriou, Lydia 5, 11
Paramount 66, 222, 386, 388–9, 392–3
paranoia: definition 235; in Hollywood action films 235–42, 249–50
paraspaces: in *The Matrix* 120–8
Pasolini, Pier 88, 91–2, 92
*Pat Garrett and Billy the Kid* 336, 337
Pathé (American branch) 59, 64–5
Pathé Frères 31, 33, 35, 57; sensational thrillers 33–4, 35–6, 38–9, 53, 61, 62
*Patria* 64–5
patriarchy: in *Breakdown* 223–4; in consumer culture 202–3, 215–16; and gender politics 373, 376; *Gladiator* 245; Greek war films 304, 305; villains in action babe films 208
patriotism 224, 232
*Peacemaker, The* 386–96
*Pearl of the Army* 64
Peckinpah, Sam 12, 331–43, 348
*Peeping Tom* 381
Penn, Arthur 105, 340
*Pentathlon* 286
Pérez, Richie 196
*Perils of Pauline, The* 56, 60, 64
Pfeil, F. 72, 253, 255, 261, 294
Phillips, Norma (later Carolyn Wells) 65
*Photoplay* 56–7, 59, 63
physical action: chronotope of action films 106–7; fitness of action babes 206–7; Greek adventure heroes 111; Hollywood action-adventure 71, 75, 203; samurai and western genres 331–2
physicality *see* bodies
*Pictures and Picturegoers* 25
pirate films 77, 78
place: relationship with space in US 219–20, 228, 232–3
*Platoon* 153, 349
*Player's Club, The* 180
*Point Break* 71, 153, 371, 379–80
Polan, Dana 238
*Police Story* 273, 274
police thrillers 131, 134–6, 143
Political Film Society 153

*Politics* (periodical) 95
popular culture 97, 201–2; and *Star Wars* 358, 367
population *see* demography
Porter, Edwin S. 52, 53
POV shots: car chases 132, 137, 146–8, *148*; *Out of Sight* 193
Powell, Anna 371
Power, Tyrone 75
*Premiere* magazine 175
Prince, Stephen 346, 348
*Prison on the Cliff, The* 39
prison films 74, 75, 76
*Private Benjamin* 172, 173
Production Code 341, 361, 362
*Protea* 44
*Protector, The* 273, 274–5
*Punisher, The* 286, 287, 289

Quinlan, Kathleen 221

race/ethnicity 4, 9–10, 73–4, 77, 78; challenging of stereotypes 10, 72, 189, 196; demographic shifts in US 190, 197–8, 219–20; in *Gladiator* 247; and locations 294
racism: links with adventure films 76, 77; Macdonald's critique of Biblical epics 89, 90; Reagan and Bush 73; responses in Blaxploitation films 197
*Raiders of the Lost Ark* 7, 189
*Raiders of the Seven Seas* 78
railroad thrillers 55, 56, 65–6, 75, 115, 157
*Rambo* films 71, 110, 112
Ramsaye, Terry 63
*Ran* 334, 334–5, 335–6, 337, 341, 342
*Rashomon* 332
Ratner, Brett 274
*Raw Deal* 112
Ray, Nicholas 88, 91
Rayns, Tony 275
Reagan, Ronald 71–2, 73, 373
realism: car chase films 131, 134, 136–8; police thrillers 134–6; *Saving Private Ryan* 153–6, 161; and war 156–7
*Red Ace, The* 65
*Red Scorpion* 286, 287
*Red Sonja* 73

Reeves, Keanu 109, 189, 242, 277, 286, 380
Reeves, Steve 88, 94
*Regarding Henry* 169, 253
Remington, Frederic 338
*Replacement Killers, The* 272
Republic 75
*Resident Evil* 186, 187, 195–6, 208, 212–15
Reynolds, Sidney 60
*Rhinestone* 169
Riblet, Douglas 130
Rickman, Alan 112
*Ride the High Country* 332, 336
*Ringo and His Golden Pistol* 310, 313, 314–18, *315–16*, *318–19*, 320, 324
*River Wild, A* 169
road movies 131, 373
*Robin Hood* 6, 75, 77
Robinson, Sally 240–1
*Robocop* 112, 189
*Rock, The* 110
*Rocky* films 286
Rodat, Robert 155, 254
Rodriguez, Michelle 9–10, 186, 189, 197, 198; in *Girlfight* and *Resident Evil* 186, 187, 190, 193–6, *194*, 201, 215
Rodriguez, Robert 11
Rogers, Mimi 256–7, 259
Roizman, Owen 136
romance quest: in action babe films 208
*Romeo Must Die* 269, 277–8, 279
Romijn-Stamos, Rebecca 201, 206, 209
Rosenbaum, Jonathan 346
Rosza, Miklos 91
Rothrock, Cynthia 269, 271, 272
Rourke, Mickey 272
Rozen, Leah 393–4
*Rumble in the Bronx* 272, 273–4, 275, 276
rural spaces *see* urban and rural spaces
*Rush Hour* 273, 274, 275
Russell, Kurt 221, 229, 231, 242
Russo, Mary 19
Ryan, Meg 169, 171, 174
Ryder, Winona 394

Sabatini, Rafael 77
safari films 76
Sammo Hung 269, 271, 275

*Samson and Delilah* 75
samurai films 331–2, 333, 334, 343
*Sanshiro Sugata* 332, 339–40
*Saving Private Ryan* 9, 153–64, 238, 345, 351
Savran, David 240
Schatz, Thomas 1, 196
Scheider, Karen 244, 252
Schiffer, Michael 389
*Schindler's List* 159, 161
Schivelbusch, Wolfgang 23
Schnapp, Jeffrey 17
Schneider, Karen 244
Schneider, Tassilo 321
Schwarzbaum, Lisa 222, 223, 230
Schwarzenegger, Arnold: in *Last Action Hero* 254, 255, 284, 294; masculinity 10, 71, 73, 75, 112, 148, 372–3; sensitive roles 169, 171, 203, 253, 255; in *True Lies* 259
science-fiction 119, 120, 188, 254, 363; melding with action genres 189; writers 120
*Scorpio Rising* 374
Scorsese, Martin 348
Scott, Ridley 11, 178–9, 180–1, 287
Seagal, Steven 290, 373
Seberg, Jean 375
Second World War 77, 237, 298; films 238, 345, 348, 349, 352; Japan in aftermath 333–4
*Secret Invasion, The* 352
*Secret Kingdom, The* 59–60, 66
Segal, Leila 393
Seger, Linda 392
Seitz, George B. 57–8
Selig Polyscope Co. 35, 38, 42–4, 63, 66
Sennett, Mack 130
sensational melodramas 3, 18–19, 31–46, 52–3, 157; in feature-film era 53–5, 56; serials 2, 18–19, 42–4, 55, 56–67
September 11 attacks 295
*Set It Off* 8, 10, 197
*Set-Up* 371–2
*Seven Pearls, The* 62
*Seven Samurai* 331, 332, 333, 335, 339–40, 341, 342
*Seven-Ups, The* 131, 132, 143–6, *144*, *145*

sexism: depiction of in *Breakdown* 223–4; responses in Blaxploitation films 197
sexuality: in action babe cinema 203, 204–5, 206; Demi Moore's stardom 175; and family themes 252; Latina heroines 187, 188, 189, 198; Macdonald's anxieties 94, 95–6; *see also* femininity; gender; masculinity
*SFX* magazine 206
*Shanghai Noon* 273, 274, 275, 275–6
Sharrett, Christopher 377
shell shock: Freud on 157–8; in war films 157, 158, 162
Shephard, Ben 154, 155
*Sheridan's Ride* 37
Shklovsky, Viktor 28
shock: and early cinema 17–18, 23, 27, 156, 157; *see also* shell shock
*Showdown in Little Tokyo* 286, 287
Sierra Nevada: Peckinpah's upbringing 338
*Sight and Sound* 2, 172, 243, 281
silent cinema: action-adventure traditions 6, 7; melodramas 4, 52–67; war films 153
Silver, Joel 72, 279
Silverman, Kaja 239, 240
Simmel, Georg 157
Singer, Ben 2, 5, 18–19, 32, 157, 158
Sirk, Douglas 309, 372, 376, 382
slasher horror 204, 378, 381
slow motion techniques: Kurosawa 339–41
Smith, Gavin 372
Smith, Greg 142–3
Smith, Julian 131
Smith, Murray 134
Smith, Neil 233
Smith, Paul 239
Smith, Will 10
*Smokey and the Bandit* films 131, 132, 139, 146, *147*
*Snake in the Eagle's Shadow* 273, 278
Snipes, Wesley 10, 189
Sobchack, Thomas 74–5, 208
Soderbergh, Steven 11, 192, 193
soundtrack: action babe films 201; *Saving Private Ryan* 155, 162; spaghetti westerns 315, 317; war epic 153
Soviet avant-garde cinema 27–8

spaces: and place in US 219–20, 228, 232–3

space and time: in *The Matrix* 124–5; *see also* chronotope

spaghetti westerns 11, 309–26

special affect: *Saving Private Ryan* 156–9, 163, 164

special effects 71, 386; *Saving Private Ryan* 154–5; spectacle 5–6; *The Matrix* 121, 126

spectacle: action babe films 201–2, 202–5, 207–15; action cinema 17, 142; disaster films 389; films with family themes 257; gender-bender action films 179; Greek war films 299–300; historical epic 84–5, 87–8; male masochism 239–40; and middlebrow culture 89; and narrative 2–3, 5–6, 6–8, 84–5, 142–8, 203–4; war epics 153, 154–5

'Spectaculars' 84

spectatorship: Biblical epics 92; Bigelow's approach 372, 383; cinematic identification 204; melodrama films 59; *Saving Private Ryan* 163

*Speed* 2, 104, 106–14, 115–16, 153, 170

Spielberg, Steven 103, 366, 395; and *Saving Private Ryan* 153–5, 156–7, 158–9, 161–2, 163–4

Springer, Claudia 348–9, 354

Springer, Kimberly 196–7

spy fictions 254

spy films 325; *see also* Girl Spy series

*Spy Kids* films 11, 186, 254

Stables, Kate 205

Stack, Peter 222, 223

stage melodramas 32; emulation of by early film melodramas 52–3, 56, 61

Staiger, Janet 134

Stalinism: Macdonald's concerns 85, 92, 93

Stallone, Sylvester: masculinity 10, 71, 73, 75, 112, 148, 372–3, 385; sensitive roles 169, 203

Stamp, Shelley 19, 42

stars: action babe heroines 206, 207; Crowe and his body 243–4, 245–6; Demi Moore and her body 171–83; in Hollywood action-adventure cinema 6;

Hong Kong action 270, 272; paranoid roles 242; polysemic identities 176–8; in serial melodramas 64

*Star Wars* 2, 7, 103, 108, 254, 358, 360–7

*Star Wars: Episode I – The Phantom Menace* 2, 358–60, 366

Steffen, Anthony 318, 319

Stevens, George 88, 90, 91–2

Stone, Sharon 170

storytelling 8; *see also* narrative

*Strange Days* 169–70, 371, 374, 380–2, 382

*Straw Dogs* 332, 339, 342, 349

*Stray Dog* 332, 334

Streep, Meryl 169

Stringer, Julian 275

*Striptease* 171, 175, 176, 178, 180, 183

stunts: car chase films 133, 138–9, 143–4, 144–6; Hollywood action-adventure 71; Hong Kong action films 273; melodramas 19

Styron, William 349–50

*Subway* 290

*Sugarland Express, The* 131, 138

survivalist films 74, 76

suspense: car chase sequence in *The Seven-Ups* 143–6

swashbuckler films 74–5, 77–8

Swayze, Patrick 176, 380

swordplay films 12, 281

*Tango and Cash* 73

Tarantino, Quentin 11

Tarzan films 75

Tasker, Yvonne: on action genre 72–3, 75, 187, 189; on Latina heroines 193; on 'musculinity' 174–5, 179, 182, 203; on 'spectacular bodies' 71, 94, 112, 187, 191, 285, 373, 378

taste: Bourdieu's theory 223; concerns about melodrama films 31–2, 34, 58

Taubin, Amy 155, 155–6, 179, 180

Taves, Brian 8, 9, 76, 77–8

Taylor, Elizabeth: Macdonald's critique of *Cleopatra* 93–4, 94, 95

technology: colour film 77; and early cinema 23, 25, 52, 156; filmic time and space 105; filming car chases

138–9; and marketing of action films 115; relationship with humans in *The Matrix* 119, 126–7; *Saving Private Ryan* 154; *see also* camera techniques; CGI; wirework
television: action babe TV series 202, 215; Leder's career 392
*Terminator* films 71, 203, 215; *Terminator 2: Judgement Day* 9, 112, 171, 253, 254, 255, 371, 374, 385; *Terminator 3: Rise of the Machines* 9; *The Terminator* 9, 253, 371
text: Bakhtin's dialogism 104, 105–7, 111
Thanhouser (company) 63–4
theater *see* stage melodramas
theaters/picture houses: showing melodrama films 58–9, 60
*Thelma and Louise* 180, 373–4, 385
*Thief of Bagdad, The* 6, 8, 75
Thompson, David 155
*Three Men and a Baby* 253, 262
*Three Musketeers, The* 75, 77, 77–8
Thring, Frank 88
*Throne of Blood* 334, 341, 342
Thurman, Uma 215
Ticotín, Rachel 189
Tidyman, Ernest 136
*Timecop* 291, 292
*Time* magazine 358, 365, 367
*Times Literary Supplement* 154
time and space: in *The Matrix* 124–5; *see also* chronotope
*Tingler, The* 115
Tirelli, Jaime *194*
*Titanic* 359, 388, 388–9, 393, 395
*Tomb Raider see Lara Croft: Tomb Raider*
*Tomorrow Never Dies* 108, 207
*Top Gun* 174
*Total Recall* 71, 72, 120, 170, 187, 189
tourism: issues in *Breakdown* 221, 224–5, 226, 227, 228, 230, 232–3
*Traffic in Souls* 42, *43*
*Trainer's Daughter, The; Or, A Race for Love* 52–3
trauma: special affect of war films 156–9, 164; theory 23, 24–5, 157–8, 241; and thrills 17–18, 28
travel genre: and spaghetti westerns 324–5

*True Lies* 170, 259–61, 262–3, 263, 264, 372
Tsivian, Yuri 27–8
Tsui Hark 275, 276–7
Tucker, Chris 272
Tunney, Tom 287, 291–2, 293
Turturro, Aida 386
*Twilight's Last Gleaming* 350
*2001: A Space Odyssey* 116

*Ulzana's Raid* 353
*Unbreakable* 242
*Under the Shadow of the Guillotine* 40–1
United States of America (USA): atomic bomb attacks on Japan 350; changing ethnic demographies 190, 197–8, 219–20; and 'death of the Great White Male' 236–8; and Italian film industry 311–13; and patriotism 224, 232, 245; Peckinpah's disenchantment with 336; represented in *Gladiator* 242–3, 245; significance of westerns 314
*Universal Soldier* 112, 286, 287, 291, 292, 293
Universal studios 37, 42, 57, 64, 65, 75, 363
urban and rural spaces 219–20
*USA Today* 222, 236

vampires 202; in *Near Dark* 375–7
Van Damme, Jean-Claude 269, 272, 284, 285, 373; Europeanness 290, 291–3, 293–4, 294
*Vanishing Point* 131, 138, 139, 141
*Vanity Fair* magazine 1796
*Variety* 33, 33–4, 53, 58, 131, 133, 359, 362–3, 365
Vaughn, Robert 141
Vega, Alexa 186
Verhoeven, Paul 11
Vice, Sue 106, 108
video games: and action babes 201, 202, 215
Vietnam war 271, 336, 341, 346, 351, 352, 353
*Village Voice* 154, 365
violence: Bigelow's approach 371, 371–2, 377, 379, 380; in *Breakdown* 221, 224, 230–1; and depiction of black

characters 196, 197; *The Dirty Dozen* 346; early film melodramas 52–3, 54, 55, 56; French crime thrillers 39, 40–1; gender exchange films 170; historical epics 96; images in *Saving Private Ryan* 155; in Kurosawa and Peckinpah 336, 341, 341–3, 348, 354–5; spectacularized 348–9; war epics 153

Vitagraph 59–60, 64, 66

Voight, Jon 191, 208

Volcano, Del LaGrace 210

Voltaire 163

Vougiouklaki, Aliki 299, 300, 301, 302, 303–4

Wachowski Brothers 127–8, 206, 274, 279, 280

Wade, Lillian 38

Walker, Alexander 179

Wallace, Amy 393, 394

Wallace, Bill 274

Walsh, John 157

Wang Du-Lu 211

Wang Yu 271

*Wanted: Dead or Alive* 287–8

war: Aldrich's views 347–8, 351, 354–5

war films 74, 153, 265; boot camp narrative 172–5; early melodrama 46, 64; *see also* Civil War films; Greek war films; *Saving Private Ryan*

Warner brothers 36, 72, 75, 133, 270

*War Neuroses: Netley 1917, Seale Military Hospital 1918* 157

*War on the Plains* 37, 38

*War's Havoc* 55–6

Washington, Denzel 113, 173

Watkins, Evan 223

*Way of the Dragon* 271

Wayne, John 112

Weaver, Sigourney 170, 189, 203, 374

Weintraub, Fred 269, 271

Weissmuller, Johnny 75

Weitz, William 158

Wells, Carolyn *see* Phillips, Norma

Welsh, James M. 2, 3–4, 5–6, 7, 11

West, the: changing American perceptions of 230–1, 233; Peckinpah's nostalgia 338; spaghetti westerns 314, 324, 325

westerns: action heroes and heroines 187–8, 261; early melodramas 34–5, 37, 38, 55; hybrids 309, 310, 373, 375–6; Peckinpah's vision 336, 338; and samurai films 331–2, 333, 343; women's roles 75–6; *see also* spaghetti westerns

*West Side Story* 188–9

*Westward the Women* 373

*What Happened to Mary* 62–3

white, heterosexual masculinity 72–3, 238, 240–1, 245, 294, 373, 385

White, Pearl 59, 61, 64

whiteness 284; American family in recent action-adventure 244–5; and class conflict in *Breakdown* 221, 227–9, 230–1; and racism in 1930s jungle films 76–7

*Wid's Year Book* 60–1

Wiedemann, Julius 215

Wiegman, Robyn 236

*Wild Bunch, The* 331, 332, 336–7, 340, 341, 342

*Wild One, The* 374

Wilinsky, Barbara 44

Williams, John 155, 159

Williams, Kathlyn 35, 44, 63

Willis, Bruce 71, 112–13, 169, 175, 242, 373, 385

Willis, S. 73

Wilmington, Michael 393

Wilson, Owen 272

Wilson, President Woodrow 65

wirework 269, 277, 278, 279, 281

Wolf, Naomi 215–16

'woman's film' 372, 373–4, 388, 389

women: in action films of 1970s and 1980s 209; in early westerns 75–6; and mass culture 93–4; in patriarchal settings 203–4; in pirate adventures 77–8; stories in Greek war films 297, 299, 300–1, 302–6; *see also* action heroines; female directors

women warrior films 73–4

Wong Fei-hung 280

Woo, John 11, 269, 271, 272, 279, 348

Wood, Aylish 6

Wood, Robin 377, 382

Woods, Frank 41

Woodward, Kathleen 19
Woolsey, Ralph 136
working class: appeal of melodramas 32–3, 35, 40, 58–9, 67; depiction of gang in *Breakdown* 222–3, 230–1
World Trade Center bombings 295
Wreszin, Michael 95
Wright, Will 310
Wyatt, Justin 387, 388
Wyler, William 87, 89
Wylie, Philip 93
Wynn, Ed 87

*Xena Warrior Princess* 202
Xiong Xin-xin 272
*X-Men* 201, 208, 209, 215
*XXX* 6

Yates, Peter 134
Yeh, Sally 275
*Yellow Menace, The* 58
Yen, Donnie 278

Yeoh, Michelle 201, 206, 207, 211, 271, 277, 280
*Yojimbo* 332, 333, 335, 342
Yordan, Philip 91
youth culture: and the automobile 131, 139–42
*Ypolochagos Natasha/Lieutenant Natasha* 300–1, 303–4
Yuen Cheung-yan 206, 210, 277
Yuen Kwai 272, 279
Yuen Siu-tin 273
Yuen Wo-Ping 206, 210, 270, 274, 277–80, 281

Zhang Che 281
Zhang Ziyi 201, 206, 211, 278
*Zigomar* 36, 39, 44
*Zigomar II* 40
*Zoot Suit* 189
*Zudora (The Twenty Million Dollar Mystery)* 63–4
*Zu: Warriors of the Magic Mountain* 276